THE MEDICAL MALPRACTICE SURVIVAL HANDBOOK

THE MEDICAL MALPRACTICE SURVIVAL HANDBOOK

American College of Legal Medicine

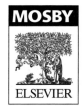

MOSBY
ELSEVIER

1600 John F. Kennedy Blvd.
Ste 1800
Philadelphia, PA 19103-2899

THE MEDICAL MALPRACTICE SURVIVAL HANDBOOK   ISBN-13: 978-0-323-04438-7
ISBN-10: 0-323-04438-7

Library of Congress Cataloging-in-Publication Data
The medical malpractice survival handbook / American College of
  Legal Medicine. – 1st ed.
    p. ; cm.
  ISBN-13: 978-0-323-04438-7
  ISBN-10: 0-323-04438-7
    1. Medical personnel–Malpractice–United States.   I. American
College of Legal Medicine.
    [DNLM: 1. Malpractice–legislation & jurisprudence–United States.
2. Liability, Legal–United States.   W 44 AA1 M4895 2007]
  RA1056.5.M417 2007
  344.7304′11–dc22   2006029578

Acquisitions Editor: Rolla Couchman
Editorial Assistant: Sarah Yusavitz
Project Manager: Bryan Hayward
Cover Designer: Gene Harris
Text Designer: Gene Harris

Printed in China

Working together to grow
libraries in developing countries

www.elsevier.com | www.bookaid.org | www.sabre.org

ELSEVIER   BOOK AID International   Sabre Foundation

Last digit is the print number: 9   8   7   6   5   4   3   2   1

The *Medical Malpractice Survival Handbook* of the American College of Legal Medicine is written specifically for physicians and other health care providers. While physicians are the primary focus of this Handbook, the term "physician" in this Handbook includes all allied health care professionals as well.

The ACLM proudly publishes its first *Medical Malpractice Survival Handbook*, which focuses specifically on the accused physician in medical malpractice litigation. It is designed for physicians, whether or not they have been accused of medical malpractice. It is authored primarily by medical doctors, who have practiced their medical or surgical specialties all of their lives, and who are sufficiently qualified to deal with this difficult, highly charged, and sensitive subject, by virtue of being attorneys at law, as well as having been involved directly with medical malpractice litigation.

The ACLM is the foremost established organization in the United States concerned with medical jurisprudence and forensic medicine. The ACLM, founded in 1955, has devoted itself to addressing problems that exist at the interface of law and medicine. The ACLM serves as a natural focal point for those professionals interested in the study and advancement of legal medicine. The ACLM is composed of health care and legal professionals whose diverse education, training, and experience enable the College to promote interdisciplinary cooperation and an understanding of issues where law and medicine converge. Indeed, the ACLM is a professional community of physicians, attorneys, dentists, allied health professionals, administrators, scientists, and others with a sustained interest in medical-legal affairs. The central mission of the ACLM is education in legal medicine. Through its medicolegal resources, the ACLM educates and assists health care and legal professionals, advances the administration of justice, influences health policy and improves health care, promotes research and scholarship, and facilitates peer group interaction.

The *Medical Malpractice Survival Handbook* is structured in a way that describes what a physician goes through and what he or she needs to know to assist them during the period of malpractice litigation. The Handbook depicts in essence "a medical malpractice lawsuit in the life of a physician." The Handbook is divided into four sections: Physicians and Malpractice (ten chapters); Etiology of Malpractice (nine chapters); Malpractice Lawsuits Resolution (eight chapters); and Liability of Specialties (sixteen chapters). A glossary of terms is included.

The format of the *Medical Malpractice Survival Handbook* is uniform. Almost every chapter begins with an introduction and "Case Presentation," followed by a comprehensive discussion of the topic in that chapter. Almost every chapter contains certain "Golden Rules" that highlight the message that is being imparted to the reader. Finally, "Further Reading" is provided at the end of most chapters. This Handbook may be considered as an overview type publication, which is selectively referenced, and not a detailed, exhaustive, scholarly, and extensively referenced book. For more details and references, the reader is referred to the American College of Legal Medicine textbook, *Legal Medicine*, 7th edition, Mosby, 2007.

The *Medical Malpractice Survival Handbook* is comprehensive, timely, necessary, and helpful to all medical professionals. During the past three decades, there have been three medical malpractice crises in the United States, one in the early 1970s, the second in the mid-1980s, and the third in the early 2000s. In 1956, the number of medical malpractice claims was reportedly 1.5 per hundred covered physicians. During the first and second medical malpractice crises, the number of medical malpractice claims per 100 physicians rose sharply. By 1990, the number of medical malpractice claims had increased to 15 per hundred covered physicians, a tenfold increase from 1956. Since 2000, the average trends of medical malpractice appear relatively flat nationally, although some states reported a decline in frequency, while other states have experienced a rise in the frequency of medical malpractice claims. The percentage of patients injured by medical negligence who actually bring suit is very small. The estimates range from one in eight to one in ten, and of those who file lawsuits, only one in three receives any compensation.

Despite tort reform, increases in the number of medical malpractice lawsuits, higher awards, rising malpractice premiums, and a decreasing number of insurance companies that insure physicians for medical malpractice have resulted in crises of both affordability and availability. This is particularly evident in high-risk surgical specialties, including obstetrics, neurosurgery, and orthopedics. Some doctors may pay the higher premiums, while others may practice defensively and drop high-risk patients and procedures, some move to other states where insurance rates are more affordable, and some retire early from medical practice altogether.

There is enough blame to go all around to everyone involved in medical malpractice. It is alleged that physicians are disregarding patient safety and have exorbitant rates of medical errors. Patients have become very litigious. Trial attorneys file too many frivolous medical malpractice lawsuits. Jury awards are out of control, and judges are not helping either. Malpractice insurances companies are accused of price gouging, and their premiums have skyrocketed. It is no wonder that distrust is rampant among all those who are concerned with the medical malpractice crisis.

Presently, there are continuing efforts, both at the state and federal levels, aimed at remedying some of the inequities of the medical malpractice crisis of the 21st century. The goal of such legislation is twofold: to make medical care and hospital services accessible and safe to patients, and to make medical liability insurance available and affordable for all health care providers.

Time-hardened experience has proven that to be forewarned is to be forearmed. This dictum is applicable to medical malpractice prevention. Prophylaxis indeed beats malpractice. Medical malpractice is preventable. Prophylactic awareness by physicians of malpractice liability, coupled with the adoption of preventive programs, should minimize allegations of malpractice. Victory is achievable when preventative alertness diminishes the need for aggressive legal defense.

Competently trained, experienced physicians and surgeons are mindful of legal liability. They follow a course of medical and surgical care that is commensurate and consistent with their skill, knowledge, ability, and experience. Such physicians and surgeons, when accused of medical malpractice, rarely lose in a court of law. On the other hand, medical and surgical errors, mistakes, major judgmental miscalculations, and obvious negligence are difficult to defend. The quintessential physician and surgeon must pursue professional actions that are in the best interests of the patient. This prevails even if it demands personal inconvenience.

One of the most potent and proven methods of prevention of medical malpractice is to educate physicians about the medical and legal ramifications of medical malpractice lawsuits. Physicians should be educated about malpractice litigation stress, how to react when confronted with a medical malpractice lawsuit, how to communicate with the defense attorney, and they should have a good grasp of the legal process. Active physician participation in the defense of a medical malpractice lawsuit is the key to a successful outcome.

On behalf of the ACLM and its membership, it is my honor and privilege to extend our deep appreciation, thanks, and gratitude to all the authors and contributors of the textbook chapters, the deputy editor, and the members of the Textbook Editorial Committee. Their contributions represent true labors of love to the ACLM and its educational endeavors in the field of legal medicine.

Finally, special thanks are expressed to all the staff of Elsevier, especially Rolla Couchman and his co-workers, for their tremendous help and contribution toward the development and publication of the *Medical Malpractice Survival Handbook*.

S. Sandy Sanbar, M.D., Ph.D., J.D., F.C.L.M.
Editor
Chairman, ACLM Medical Malpractice
Survival Handbook Editorial Committee

Gary Birnbaum, M.D., J.D., F.C.L.M., Director of Family Practice, Hillcrest Hospital, Cleveland, and Clinic Health Systems, Mayfield Heights, Ohio

Robert A. Bitonte, M.D., J.D., M.A., LL.M., F.C.L.M., Clinical Professor, Department of Physical Medicine and Rehabilitation, University of California (Irvine), Orange, California

Denise Brigham, B.S.N., R.N., C.I.P., C.C.R.P., Interim Director, University and Medical Center Institutional Review Board, East Carolina University, Brody School of Medicine and Pitt County Memorial Hospital, Greenville, North Carolina

James T. Brown, M.D., F.A.C.E.P., Clinical Assistant Professor of Surgery, Department of Surgery, Section of Emergency Medicine, University of Illinois College of Medicine at Peoria, Peoria, Illinois

Fillmore Buckner, M.D., J.D., F.A.C.O.G., F.C.L.M., Obstetrics and Gynecology (ret.); Lecturer, Legal Medicine; Past President, American College of Legal Medicine, Mercer Island, Washington

Melvin L. Butler, M.D., J.D., F.C.L.M., Internal Medicine, Gastroenterology, and Geriatric Medicine; Medical Director, Tennessee Correctional Medical Services, Franklin, Tennessee

Scott D. Cohen, M.D., J.D., F.C.L.M., Chief, Section of Urology, Department of Surgery, McLeod Regional Medical Center, Florence, South Carolina

John P. Conomy, M.D., J.D., F.C.L.M., Neurology; Health Systems Designs; Administrative and Professional Liability Law, Chagrin Falls, Ohio

Kenneth A. DeVille, Ph.D., J.D., Professor of Health Law, Brody School of Medicine; Private Practice of Health Law, Greenville, North Carolina

David R. Donnersberger, Jr., M.D., J.D., M.A., F.C.L.M., Department of Medicine, Evanston Northwestern Healthcare, Northwestern University Feinberg School of Medicine, Evanston, Illinois

Charles R. Ellington, Jr., M.D., J.D., F.C.L.M., Family Practice, Legal Medicine; Assistant Professor, Southern Illinois University School of Medicine, Decatur Family Medicine Residency Program, Decatur, Illinois

Jonathan Fanaroff, M.D., J.D., F.C.L.M., Assistant Professor of Pediatrics, Case School of Medicine; Associate Director, Rainbow Center for Pediatric Ethics, Rainbow Babies and Children's Hospital, Cleveland, Ohio

Marvin H. Firestone, M.D., J.D., F.C.L.M., Psychiatry and Forensic Psychiatry; Former Hirsch Professor of Healthcare Law and Ethics, George Washington University; Past President, American College of Legal Medicine; Deputy Editor, ACLM Textbook, *Legal Medicine,* 7th edition; Lecturer in Legal Medicine; Private Practice, San Mateo, California

Judith A. Gic, R.N. (ret.), C.R.N.A. (ret.), J.D., F.C.L.M., Private Practice, Medical-Legal Litigation, Louisiana, Eastern and Central South; Private Practice, Health Provider Licensure, Louisiana; Medical-Legal Consultant; Editor, Medical-Legal Q & A, American College of Legal Medicine, Schaumburg, Illinois; Sustaining Member, American Association for Justice, Washington, D.C.; Former President, Academy of New Orleans Trial Lawyers, New Orleans, Louisiana

Victoria L. Green, M.D., M.H.S.A., M.B.A., J.D., F.C.L.M., Emery Department of Gynecology and Obstetrics; Associate Professor, Medical Director, Ob Gyn Satellite Clinics, Grady Health System; Director, Gynecology Comprehensive Breast Center, Atlanta, Georgia

Curtis E. Harris, M.S., M.D., J.D., F.C.L.M., Chief of Endocrinology, Chickasaw Nation, Ada, Oklahoma; Assistant Clinical Professor, Oklahoma University Health Sciences Center; Adjunct Professor of Law, Oklahoma City University School of Law, Oklahoma City, Oklahoma

Katherine A. Hawkins, M.D., J.D., F.A.C.P., F.C.L.M., Internal Medicine–Hematology; Associate Clinical Professor of Medicine, Albert Einstein College of Medicine, Bronx, New York

Hugh F. Hill, M.D., J.D., F.A.C.E.P., F.C.L.M., Assistant Professor, Johns Hopkins University; Director, Fast Track, Johns Hopkins Bayview Medical Center, Baltimore, Maryland

Alan C. Hoffman, J.D., F.C.L.M., Attorney at Law; Legal Education; General Civil and Health Law; Alan C. Hoffman & Associates, Chicago, Illinois

Matthew L. Howard, M.D., J.D., F.A.C.S., F.C.L.M., Staff Otolaryngologist, Department of Head and Neck Surgery, Kaiser Permanente Medical Center, Santa Rosa, California

James R. Hubler, M.D., J.D., F.A.C.E.P., F.A.A.E.M., F.C.L.M., Clinical Assistant Professor of Surgery, Department of Surgery, Section of Emergency Medicine, University of Illinois College of Medicine at Peoria, Peoria, Illinois

James C. Johnston, M.D., J.D., F.C.L.M., F.A.C.L.M., Consultant Neurologist and Attorney at Law, Private Practice, San Antonio, Texas, USA; Barrister and Solicitor, High Court of New Zealand, Auckland, New Zealand

Michael S. Lehv, M.D., J.D., F.C.L.M., Plastic and Reconstructive Surgery; Adjunct Professor of Law, Capital University Law School, Columbus, Ohio

Thomas R. McLean, M.D., M.S., J.D., F.A.C.S., F.C.L.M., Clinical Assistant Professor of Surgery, University of Kansas; Staff Surgeon, Eastern Kansas VA Health Care System; CEO, Third Millennium Consultants, LLC, Shawnee, Kansas

Daniel L. Orr II, D.D.S., Ph.D., J.D., M.D., F.C.L.M., Clinical Professor of Oral and Maxillofacial Surgery and Dental Anesthesiology, University of Nevada School of Medicine; Legal Medicine Education, Las Vegas, Nevada

Michael M. Raskin, M.D., J.D., M.S., M.P.H., M.A., F.C.L.M., Voluntary Associate Professor of Radiology, University of Miami School of Medicine, Miami, Florida; Neuroradiologist, University Medical Center, Fort Lauderdale, Florida

Ben A. Rich, J.D., Ph.D., Professor of Bioethics, University of California, Davis, School of Medicine, Sacramento, California

S. Sandy Sanbar, M.D., Ph.D., J.D., F.C.L.M., Past President, American College of Legal Medicine; Editor, ACLM Textbook, *Legal Medicine*, 7th edition; Medical Consultant, Department of Disability Services, Social Security Administration, Oklahoma City, Oklahoma; Cardiologist, Royal Oaks Cardiovascular Clinic; Attorney at Law, Law of Medicine; Clinical Sub-investigator, The Oklahoma Hypertension and Cardiovascular Center, Oklahoma City, Oklahoma

Philip A. Shelton, M.D., J.D., F.C.L.M., Ophthalmology; Past President, American College of Legal Medicine; Medical Director, St. Luke's Cataract and Laser Institute, Tarpon Springs, Florida

Robert Turbow, M.D., J.D., F.C.L.M., Pediatrics–Neonatology, Attending Neonatologist, Phoenix Children's Hospital; Adjunct Professor of Biology, California Polytechnic State University, San Luis Obispo, California; Chief Executive Officer, PatientPatents, Inc., San Luis Obispo, California

Terrence J. Webber, M.D., J.D., F.C.L.M., Anesthesia–Pain Management; Legal Medicine; Private Practice, Lakewood, Colorado; Attending Staff Anesthesiologist, University of Southern California, Keck School of Medicine, Department of Anesthesiology, Los Angeles, California

Cyril H. Wecht, M.D., J.D., F.C.L.M., Anatomic, Clinical, and Forensic Pathology; Adjunct Professor, University of Pittsburgh School of Medicine; Adjunct Professor, Duquesne University School of Law; Past President, American College of Legal Medicine; Past President, American Academy of Forensic Sciences, Pittsburgh, Pennsylvania

Augustine S. Weekley, Jr., M.D., J.D., F.C.L.M., Board of Directors, American Association of Nurse Attorneys, Tampa Bay Chapter, 2006; National Health Lawyers Association, American Society of Law and Medicine; Florida Certified Healthcare Risk Manager, President, Bay Area Healthcare Risk Management Society, 1995; Hillsborough County Bar Association; Diplomate, American Board of Surgery; Fellow, American College of Surgeons; Fellow, International College of Surgeons, American Society of Abdominal Surgeons, American Medical Association, Florida Medical Association, Hillsborough County Medical Association

CONTENTS

SECTION 3: MALPRACTICE LAWSUIT RESOLUTION

SECTION 4: LIABILITY OF SPECIALTIES

PHYSICIANS AND MALPRACTICE

American Medical Malpractice

Fillmore Buckner, M.D., J.D., F.A.C.O.G., F.C.L.M.

COMMON LAW

To comprehend American medical malpractice law, it is necessary to understand something of the history of the Common Law. British North America inherited our law, as we did our language, from England. As Judge Story once wrote, "Our ancestors brought with them the common law's principles and claimed it as their birthright." Most of the European countries originally occupied by the Romans adopted a form of law based on the Roman law codes. That law is called Civil Law. England's law, on the other hand, was based mainly on Scandinavian (Danish) law with a dose of folk law of undetermined origin thrown in.

Even after the Norman invasion, little was done to change the basic concepts of English law. The principal difference after the invasion was that the Norman kings considered themselves to be the head of the court and to bear the responsibility for the justice rendered by the courts. They also introduced the idea of legal policy reflecting political policy and in particular royal political policy. In other words, these kings viewed the justice system as a political power tool to increase their wealth and control. The courts would forever after be viewed as servants of some economic or social interest.

The system was consolidated by Henry II. By 1240 the baronial/manorial courts were strictly social meetings and held no real legal status. In the shire courts and royal courts, the key features of the common law, the jury and courts of record were in place. These developments were probably the result of multiple compatible factors working in unison even though the reassertion of royal control and power was instrumental.[1] There is no doubt that the royal judges saw a need for a national system of law that was rational and uniform in its application and the feudal court was incompatible with that system. Finally, the idea must have had wide support in the secondary and tertiary layers of aristocracy. It was certainly in their interest to have an objective royal court hear their case rather than the self-interested baron. Though more interested in the bottom line than the strength of the court system, Henry II, one of England's most competent and professional kings, left England with a strong, enduring system of courts and law that, through accumulated decisions, could build upon itself and adjust to changing times and circumstances.

It was called the Common Law. One should not be deceived by its name. It was not law designed to protect the common man. It takes its name from the fact that it was the law that Henry II made common to all of England. The two forms of law differ significantly.

CIVIL LAW

Civil law is a codified system of law. That is, the law is spelled out in a series of written laws adopted by the jurisdiction. Common Law is largely judge-made law. It may incorporate some statutory elements on specific issues, but even statutes are subject to judicial interpretation. Judges in the Civil Law are academics specially trained for their positions and act as prosecutor, judge, and jury. Civil law is, therefore, inquisitorial in nature and heavily dependent on the written word.

ADVERSARIAL SYSTEM

In contrast, Common Law is an adversarial system in which the oral argument between the parties plays a much larger role. Judges are chosen from the practicing bar and are not usually academics. The judge is essentially a referee and instructs the jury who make the ultimate decision on the merits of the case. In common law the law is made by judges who hear a disputed case on appeal. Those decisions become precedent for future cases. However, higher appellate courts or future appellate courts of the same level can overturn or overrule a prior decision if circumstances change or new information develops. Therefore, change, albeit slow and irregular, is a constant element of the common law.

Under the early common law, cases were more or less confined to one of three categories: Property Law, Contract Law, and Criminal Law. There was little attention paid to compensating the individual for personal wrongs (tort law) for a little over a century. Doctors were therefore immune to suit for what we would call malpractice today.

BEGINNING OF MEDICAL MALPRACTICE IN ENGLAND

Between 1346 and 1381, during the Black (Bubonic) Plague, 50% of the population of Europe and two-thirds of the English population was wiped out by the epidemic.[2] The loss of manpower was a major blow to the English economy. The people who survived the plague became as important as real property (land) and personal property (including livestock) in the English economy. Therefore, a physician's mistake that deprived the economy of a worker became important enough to be brought before the courts. Physicians suddenly lost their immunity for practice errors. Actually, it was an even worse scenario, the physician became *strictly liable* for an unfavorable outcome, and, because there was no tort law (law governing injury to a personal interest), the physician was prosecuted under the criminal law for mayhem. By 1364 it had become obvious that this was too draconian a remedy and two property terms that had been previously used occasionally in livestock cases were introduced to permit civil cases. "Trespass" (trespass by force and arms) was charged for direct injury and "trespass on the case" for indirect injury. New writs were permitted, and cases were brought in royal courts and London's city courts with alarming frequency fully commensurate with the litigious present.

INITIAL CAUSES OF MALPRACTICE

A search of contemporary documents reveals that in the 14th century cases were brought against physicians with remarkable frequency for charging excessive fees, for keeping the fee despite a failure to cure, for exacerbating the original complaint, medical neglect, mayhem, maiming, and death. The courts dealt with these charges with a combination of fines to redress the financial losses of the patient and to punish the physician as well as imprisonment and forbidding future practice.[3] It has been suggested that many of the physicians' problems stemmed from the practice of physicians to undertake the cure of the patient and not to merely treat the patient.[4] The medieval patient equated cure with fee, "No cure, No fee!" In the absence of any really effective treatment modalities, this was a natural recipe for disaster.

By 1375 the concepts of fault and standards of care had been introduced, but the malpractice actions went on at an accelerated rate. By 1415 the London guilds had established rules for mandatory consultation and a series of fines for not doing so. In 1417 the Surgeons' Guild introduced a compulsory malpractice insurance pool.

The high rate of suits continued well into the 17th century. Indigent migrants and criminals were being shipped to North America as indentured servants as early as 1650, and the rate of voluntary migration to North America increased steadily thereafter.

MEDICAL MALPRACTICE DURING THE COLONIAL PERIOD

Claims are made that there were no malpractice cases during the colonial period, but that claim does not seem to be verified by the records.[5] First, there were few physicians practicing until the 18th century. Second, the colonial courts were not courts of record and although physicians were frequent defendants during the 18th century, it is impossible to determine what they were sued for. Third, it is easy to underestimate the frequency with which the inhabitants sued each other in the British North American Colonies. It appears obvious to any person looking at the local records of the time that the settlers in the new land were every bit as litigious as their countrymen in England. For example, between 1672 and 1684, in Essex County, Massachusetts, alone, the residents filed some 3000 actions. A survey of the court actions in New York and Maryland reveals comparable numbers. These numbers are even more startling when one realizes that the entire population of British North America is estimated to have been only about 300,000 by the end of the century.

In 1753 an Oxford law professor wrote up his lectures and published them as *Blackstone's Commentaries on the Laws of England*. Although the first American editions of this book were not published until 1771, by the time of the revolution it is estimated that there were as many copies in America as in England. The only volume found in greater numbers in Colonial America was the Bible. The drafters of the American Constitution were well versed in Blackstone. *Blackstone's Commentaries* became the basis of American law until the second half of the 19th century and perpetuated the malpractice law of England.[6]

AMERICAN MEDICAL MALPRACTICE

After the revolution, the American courts became courts of record, but, in spite of this advantage, there is no reliable count of actions against physicians prior to the Civil War. We know there were disciplinary actions, fee disputes, medical society disputes, and malpractice actions in the trial courts, but exactly how many has never been determined. Although some 27 malpractice cases were brought as appeals to state supreme courts from 1794 to 1861, from 1794 to 1835 malpractice cases unrelated to death were extremely uncommon and marked by a preponderance of defense verdicts. However, beginning in 1835 the courts were inundated with medical malpractice cases. The vast majority of these suits were related to orthopedic treatments, fractures, dislocations, and amputations. Over time, improved immobilization, bandaging, and draining techniques combined with the introduction of anesthesia had resulted in advances in the treatment of compound fractures, fracture-dislocations, and badly comminuted fractures. The result was fewer amputations but an increase in deformed and frozen limbs and an increased number of deaths. The situation was aggravated by three factors: (1) physicians' reluctance to report objectively or failure to note their results in fracture therapy; (2) the use of texts that did not adequately discuss sepsis, angulation, shortening, and other deformities resultant from the new treatments; and (3) unrealistic expectations of the public generated by the reports of the new technology. It was estimated that nine out of ten physicians in western New York had been charged with malpractice. The *Boston Medical and Surgical Journal* reported 48 cases and contained numerous editorials and comments on the situation.

FIRST AMERICAN MALPRACTICE CRISIS

The first American medical malpractice crisis occurred in the 19th century. Much like their modern counterparts, attorneys placed ads in newspapers soliciting potential clients who felt they might have been injured by medical care. The response of the physicians to the malpractice situation was also much like that of their modern counterparts. Lawyers were decried, but fellow physicians were equally chastened. Patients were accused of ruining caring physicians for economic gain. There were frequent claims from all levels of the profession that the malpractice crisis was driving physicians from practice, deterring the best students from entering the field, and spelled the rapid downfall of the profession.

This malpractice increase never completely abated. It was slowed by Frank Hasting Hamilton's work on the results of fracture therapy that culminated in his book, *Deformities in Fractures*, and by the ensuing Civil War, but continued to test the limits of defendant-favoring courts to break out overtly again after World War II.

The end of the Civil War signaled a boom in industrialization never seen before. Suddenly, all of America was a country of engines, machines, locomotives, and a web of ever growing miles of steel track. The broad-shouldered farm worker along with a steady influx of immigrants became broad-shouldered industrial workers. These inexperienced workers and the newly introduced engines, machines, and locomotives formed a catalytic mixture for the production of injuries.[7] Nothing in the existing common law prepared the American courts for this sort of injury or this sort of situation. It was a new industrial revolution and a social upheaval of mammoth proportions leaving an army of dead, injured, and maimed in its wake. New law was needed to handle this industrial onslaught and its resultant injuries.

LAW OF NEGLIGENCE

American courts responded by adopting the *law of negligence* from the English courts which had developed it some 30 years earlier. The orthodox view is that the law was designed specifically to shift losses to the victim of an accident rather than leaving them with the injurer unless the injurer was blameworthy (negligent) and the victim blameless. The purpose of this shift was a combination of economic policy, poorly disguised class distinction, and a judicial and legal tradition of noncompensation. The courts were attempting to encourage the growth of the new industrial base by providing an industrial subsidy, protection from injured victim compensation. From organized medicine's point of view, courts were trying to protect industry and physicians from attacks by an "irresponsible working class." Medical society writers decried what they interpreted as their attack by the poor and working class.

Soon defenses to claims of negligence developed. Even though the English case precedents in general played a minor role in American jurisprudence at that time, three English cases were almost immediately invoked by the courts. *Butterfield v. Forrester*, an 1809 riding accident case, established the doctrine of *"contributory negligence."* Contributory negligence made it impossible for the injury victim to recover against the injurer if the victim was negligent in any degree at all. In 1837, *Priestly v. Fowler* introduced the doctrines of *"assumption of the risk"* and *"the fellow servant rule."*[8] The third case, *Feofees of Heriot's Hospital v. Ross* (1846), introduced the doctrine of *"charitable immunity."*[9] Charitable immunity provided general immunity in charity cases.

However, there was one negligence doctrine that was remotely favorable to the plaintiff, *res ipsa loquitur* (the thing speaks for itself), which was also imported from England.

The courts also developed a series of laws limiting the death benefits in cases resulting in fatalities. *Statutes of limitation*, which in general favor defendants, were vigorously enforced without regard to fairness by courts committed to noncompensation.

The *locality rule*, which was unknown in the common law and unknown in English negligence law, was adopted as a further measure to ensure noncompensation. The locality rule gave rise to the *conspiracy of silence*, whereby one physician in a community would not testify against another in the community. Medical societies fostered the conspiracy of silence. As the medical societies gained in strength from 1865 to the early 20th century, they put increasing pressure on their members to refrain from supporting any suit. The net result was that from 1871 to 1950, despite the fact that the number of malpractice suits brought continued to rise at a rate that exceeded the rate of population growth, plaintiffs routinely lost or were grossly undercompensated by the courts.

AMERICAN MEDICAL MALPRACTICE AFTER THE 20TH CENTURY

World War II on the heels of the New Deal brought social changes of unheard-of proportions. The GI bill opened up college and professional schools to the masses where before the war only one in twenty Americans could afford a college education. The aging American judiciary began to be replaced by judges no longer dominated by a noncompensation mentality. Liberal juries were allowed more freedom to compensate adequately. The war had also brought an age of specialization and great medical technical innovation. These changes, coupled with the loss of the locality rule and charitable immunity, a change from contributory negligence to *comparative negligence*, the negation of assumption of the risk by the concept of *informed consent*, relaxation of the statute of limitations, the adoption of effective discovery rules, fewer long-term physician–patient relationships, unrealistic patient expectations, and several large medical malpractice awards in areas as geographically diverse as New Jersey, California, and Florida, all combined to recreate the situation physicians faced prior to the adoption of negligence.

NOTES

1. It is estimated that about 5% of the royal income came from the justice system—most from the writ and recording fees but also from the crown's claim on the personal property of those executed for crimes.
2. Because there was no accurate census at the time, such figures are estimates based on church records, burial records, tax rolls, and contemporary accounts.
3. In London, through the guilds and city government, there was a licensing regulation that could take civil action against the serious malefactor.
4. Although the administration of certain medication was also the basis of certain physician charges unrelated to whether a cure was obtained or not.
5. The infamous Potts Hogmeat case is recorded as early as 1621.
6. *Blackstone's Commentaries* remained the principal text in American Law Schools for an even longer period. It was reprinted through the entire 19th century.
7. By 1890 train accidents alone had produced an estimated 42,000 killed and injured.
8. Actually, assumption of the risk was adopted in England as early as 1799 in the lesser known case of *Cruden v. Fentham,* but American courts adopted it from *Priestly v. Fowler.*
9. The English case was overturned in England some 20 years later, but was invoked in *McDonald v. Massachusetts General Hospital*, 120 Mass. 432 (1876) and *Perry v. House of Refuge*, 63 Md. 20 (1885) and became a continued doctrine in American courts.

Medical Malpractice Stress Syndrome

S. Sandy Sanbar, M.D., Ph.D., J.D., F.C.L.M.
Marvin H. Firestone, M.D., J.D., F.C.L.M.

GOLDEN RULES

1. Medical malpractice lawsuits are extremely stressful.
2. The allegation of medical malpractice may be extremely traumatic to the accused physician.
3. The primary manifestations of medical malpractice stress syndrome are psychological symptoms (e.g., acute or chronic anxiety and depression), and the secondary manifestations are physical symptoms.
4. The accused physician must acknowledge that he or she may be suffering from a medical malpractice stress syndrome.
5. The distressed physician should seek support, understanding, and comfort from immediate family members, close friends, defense counsel, and professional colleagues.
6. The physician needs help to acknowledge and address the fears of medical malpractice stress.
7. The accused physician must continually be reminded that being sued for medical negligence is a predictable hazard of medical practice in our times.
8. Education of the sued physician about medical malpractice stress is the key to dealing with the fear of litigation.

The purpose of this chapter is to provide an overview of the medical malpractice stress syndrome (MMSS), its symptoms, diagnosis, and management in hopes of providing physicians who are suffering from, or who are caring for other litigation-stressed physicians, with the necessary tools to effectively manage this disorder.

CASE PRESENTATION

Dr. Ray Sunshine is a 43-year-old second-generation family physician. While in medical school, Dr. Ray met and fell in love with his classmate, Angela. They got married the same month they graduated from medical school. He and his wife have three children, two daughters and a son. After Dr. Ray and his wife graduated from medical school at the University of Florida, Dr. Ray completed a residency training program in Family Medicine; Angela also trained at the University of Florida as an Emergency Physician. He has been practicing medicine for 12 years, working with his wife, Angela, and his father, Christopher, at the Family Medical Clinic, in Sun City, Florida.

On January 13, 2001, at approximately 1:00 P.M., Dr. Ray returned from lunch to resume his work at the Clinic. His nurse approached Dr. Ray and informed him that the Sheriff (a patient treated by his father) was here to see him. The Sheriff was ushered into Dr. Ray's office. The two of them exchanged greetings. Apologetically, but in a businesslike manner, the Sheriff served Dr. Ray with a summons and complaint, alleging medical malpractice. The Sheriff told Dr. Ray that he was being sued by one of his patients. The Sheriff said goodbye and walked out of the office.

Dr. Ray was stunned, shocked, and dismayed. He could not believe that he was being sued by one of his patients. He had never been sued before. He could not think of having done wrong to his patients. He thought to himself: "All my patients love me. Who would do such a horrible thing?" He had flashbacks of many patients that he had treated in the last few years. He gently placed the petition on his desk without opening it, and he stepped away from his desk, all the time staring at the petition.

His forehead became sweaty, as did the palms of his hands. His hands were shaking and his body felt like it was trembling all over. His chest felt tight and he could not breathe deeply enough. He had goose bumps all over. He became weak and nauseated. His lunch-filled stomach felt heavy, and he was afraid he might vomit any time. He felt momentarily unstable on his feet and dizzy. Dr. Ray could not believe what was happening to him.

Nurse Susan knocked at his door and entered the office to inform Dr. Ray that his first afternoon patient has been waiting to see him. The doctor, now visibly pale and diaphoretic, did not look back to acknowledge the nurse's presence. Instead, he walked two steps and sat in a nearby chair, with his head bent forward. He felt ashamed and did not want to tell his nurse what had happened. He took his handkerchief out of his back pocket and wiped his forehead.

The nurse, realizing that there was something wrong, asked the doctor if he felt all right. The doctor did not answer at first, but then he told the nurse to cancel all his patients for the rest of the day because he was not feeling well. The nurse then informed Angela, Dr. Ray's wife, that Dr. Ray was not feeling well.

Angela excused herself and ran to her husband's office. He was still sitting in the chair, staring at his desk. "Honey," she said, "What is the matter? What is bothering you? Are you hurting anywhere?"

Dr. Ray could not talk. He felt lonely even in his wife's presence. Guilt feelings were running through his mind. Angela asked him what the Sheriff was doing here. Dr. Ray stared at the petition on his desk and nodded ever so slightly. Angela walked toward the desk, picked up the envelope, opened it, and slowly read allegations of negligence and gross negligent acts by her husband. She was shocked herself, but she quickly realized that her husband was suffering from an acute stress disorder.

Angela called her father-in-law, Dr. Christopher, who was in his office, and informed him about Dr. Ray. He rushed to Dr. Ray's office and expressed concern and when he was informed of the lawsuit, he told his son that when he was sued by one of his patients for medical malpractice, he likewise suffered symptoms of distress throughout the five years of litigation, until the lawsuit ended in his favor.

Dr. Ray's malpractice litigation lasted three years, during which time both his wife and father were extremely sympathetic and supportive. Nevertheless, Dr. Ray suffered distress symptoms throughout the course of the litigation. The trial ended with a defense verdict. Dr. Ray was relieved, but continued to suffer from symptoms similar to those who have post-traumatic stress disorder.[1]

STRESS OF MEDICAL MALPRACTICE LITIGATION

Medical malpractice lawsuits are extremely stressful. They are predictable hazards of medical practice. Some medical professionals view malpractice lawsuits as an inherent part of providing medical care. Indeed, no individual physician is immune from medical malpractice, and the majority of physicians are affected, directly or indirectly, by patients alleging negligent professional care as the cause of their injuries.

It is known that litigation distress may affect any individual who is involved in litigation. There are predictable effects of medical malpractice lawsuits on the defendant physicians characterized by the medical malpractice stress syndrome, a unique variation of the well-accepted litigation stress syndrome.

Even though medical malpractice lawsuits are common, most physicians are ill-prepared to deal with the devastating psychological effects of medical malpractice litigation on the physicians, their families, and their medical practices.

The stress of medical malpractice litigation may directly contribute to physical illness of the physician, as well as dissatisfaction with medical practice leading to burnout and early retirement. Tragically, if the reaction of the physician is extreme, depression may lead to suicide.

MANIFESTATIONS OF MMSS

An allegation of medical malpractice (or charges of unprofessional or unethical conduct by a physician's peers) may be extremely traumatic to the accused physician, regardless of whether or not the allegation has merit. The emotional turmoil that results can be debilitating.

The primary manifestations of medical malpractice stress syndrome are psychological symptoms (e.g., acute or chronic anxiety and depression), and the secondary manifestations are physical symptoms. The physical symptoms may be manifestations of a new disorder or may represent an aggravation of a preexisting disorder.

ANXIETY SYMPTOMS

The accused physician may develop excessive worry, which would occupy over 50% of waking hours. The physician may have difficulty controlling the worry. When such worry symptoms last over six months, it is characterized as persistent or chronic.

The physician may complain of restlessness, tiredness, difficulty concentrating, irritability, tense muscles, and/or insomnia. Such anxiety symptoms interfere with the physician's daily life both at work and at home.

Some physicians develop feelings of anger, bitterness, shock, dismay, guilt, shame, irritability, frustration, distrust, loneliness, and diminished self-esteem; and the physician may manifest hyperactivity.

The accused physician may react by emotionally distancing himself/herself from family members, friends, and professional colleagues. Interest in work, food, recreation, and sex may be diminished. The accused physician may become insecure, may develop concerns about ability and competency to make decisions, may compulsively order unnecessary tests on patients, and may have thoughts of changing careers.

The physician may resort to alcohol, or self-medication, in an attempt to self-medicate many of the uncomfortable symptoms. The accused physician who is already suffering from a preexisting medical illness, such as coronary artery disease, diabetes, hypertension, or gastrointestinal disease, may exacerbate or aggravate those disorders, thereby causing more physical symptoms and signs related to those disorders.

CONSULTATION WITH TREATING PHYSICIAN

The accused physician must acknowledge that he or she may be suffering from a medical malpractice stress syndrome. It is sometimes difficult for the physician to formally seek medical or psychiatric attention from a colleague. Especially when the symptoms of anxiety and depression are severe, or where there are thoughts of suicide, the distressed physician should seek prompt psychiatric assistance.

Management and control of the symptoms of MMSS under the supervision of a treating physician should never be underestimated. The amelioration of the stress symptoms will lead to a feeling of wellbeing, confidence, and behavioral control, thereby reversing the agonizing mental turmoil. Reduction of stress symptoms will also allow the physician to think and act with greater objectivity, to remain focused, and to maintain a healthier perspective on the litigation process.

DISCUSSIONS WITH FAMILY, CLOSE FRIENDS, AND COLLEAGUES

A friend in need is without question a friend indeed. The distressed physician should seek support, understanding, and comfort from immediate family members, close friends, and professional colleagues. In particular, open and candid discussions with one's spouse, and maybe even the children, may reassure all the family members. This can lead to greater support and understanding of any unusual behavior.

Discussions with physician colleagues, particularly those who have been through malpractice litigation, can be helpful. Reaching out to family, friends, and professional colleagues for emotional support should not be construed as a sign of weakness. Just the opposite, it is the imprimatur of a wise and strong person, one who is not afraid to confront reality, no matter how harsh it may seem.

MEETING WITH DEFENSE COUNSEL

This topic is discussed in detail in Chapter 8. The meeting(s) between the accused physician and the defense counsel can be extremely helpful in educating the physician about the legal system and addressing fears and concerns about the litigation. The physician who develops rapport and trust with the attorney, who gains a thorough understanding of the legal process, and who assists the legal counsel to understand the factual issues related to the alleged negligence claim, will benefit immensely by gaining confidence, thereby reducing the stress of litigation.

MANAGEMENT OF MMSS

In March 2005, at the 45th Annual Conference of the American College of Legal Medicine, in Las Vegas, Dr. Louise B. Andrew, who is an expert in this area, presented the S. Sandy Sanbar Lecture, which dealt with this personal, sensitive, and difficult subject of malpractice litigation stress, and the following discussion is derived in part from that excellent lecture, as well as from the selected references at the end of this chapter.

Dr. Andrew noted the following four essentials of management of MMSS:

1. Replace mystery with knowledge.
2. Replace shame with confidence.
3. Provide insight into the players and drama while being enacted.
4. Provide tools and strategies for combating the emotional and physical stress of litigation.

Dr. Andrew pointed out that charging the physician with malpractice is perceived as a "wound to the heart." In every known bad medical treatment outcome, the physician blames self long before the patient begins to blame. Hence, the physician already has a wound to self-esteem by the time the legal claim is made. Every step in the legal process, while ostensibly designed to reveal the truth and serve justice, is perceived by the physician as an attempt to prove intentional wrongdoing by the physician. This is related to the psychological vulnerabilities of the accused physician and the lack of understanding of the legal process.

The physician needs help to acknowledge and address the fears of medical malpractice stress, all of which are appropriate to the situation. These include:

1. Loss of control.
2. Loss of livelihood.
3. Loss of reputation.
4. Loss of assets.
5. Loss of significant supporters.
6. Lack of knowledge about the process and potential outcomes.

Education is the key to dealing with fear. The physician should be encouraged to:

1. Attend supportive educational meetings.
2. Read available materials on litigation stress support.
3. Seek advice from experienced colleagues, malpractice and estates lawyers, counselors, or consultants.
4. Ask questions, and acknowledge that this is not the physician's sphere of expertise.

The physician can do a number of things, including:

1. Begin to transform one's personal definitions.
2. Pay more attention to one's own needs.
3. Assemble a personal survival kit.
4. Pay more attention to the needs of one's principal supporters.
5. Reframe the case as a "Passion Play," and hone one's acting skills for the court drama. According to Dr. Andrew, the physician should recognize that he or she is an actor involved in a malpractice lawsuit "drama" which is not of the physician's own making nor under his/her control. The arcane script is written by people who have long been dead, by morbid "poets," and by modern-day pirates. Indeed, only part of the physician's professional persona is involuntarily involved in the "Passion Play."

It is important, according to Dr. Andrew, to arm the physician with psychological armor. The physician should be taught that, to the extent that he or she forgets the actual goal of the plaintiff (money), and accepts the stated goal (justice), he or she can and will be disempowered. Therefore, to the extent possible, the physician should ignore what the other side says or does and focus on the fact that the plaintiff is only entitled to money.

The physician must remember that knowledge is power and must be acquired. The physician should be encouraged to access resources, including counselors and consultants in litigation stress and witness preparation, talk to close colleagues, and attend support groups. Physicians who have been involved in malpractice litigation should share their experiences and their successes with their colleagues.

The accused physician must continually be reminded that being sued for medical negligence is a predictable hazard of medical practice in our times.

Medical malpractice litigation is one of the most stressful events of the life of any physician. But it is survivable and surmountable. It can be an experience from which the physician can actually become a better doctor. Nietzsche said, "What does not destroy me, makes me stronger."

The physician can derive therapeutic benefit from the following:

1. Being actively involved with the defense attorney team.
2. Participating in official discovery requests.
3. Assisting in identifying qualified experts.
4. Performing medical literature research to determine nuances of medical care.
5. Attending as many depositions and as much of the trial as feasible.
6. Preparing diligently for appearances by thoroughly knowing the medical records and the medical literature.
7. Becoming educated and comfortable in dealing with the tactics of the plaintiff's attorney and the time and scheduling difficulties required by legal proceedings.
8. Becoming educated about medical malpractice stress and its effects on the physician.
9. Recognizing that there are inherent conflicts of interest between the insurer and the physician.
10. Being prepared to seek counsel by a private attorney if conflicts are perceived with being represented by an insurance company appointed attorney or if claims are not covered or if an excess judgment beyond coverage is possible.

FURTHER READING

Andrew L, Managing Medical Malpractice Stress, 2003, last accessed February 26, 2006; http://www.magmutual.com/risk/malpractice-stress1.html

Charles SC, Wilbert JR, Franke KJ, *Sued and Nonsued Physicians' Self-Reported Reactions to Malpractice Litigation.* Am. J. Psychiatry 142(4):437–440 (1985).

Charles SC, *How to Handle the Stress of Litigation.* Clin. Plast. Surg. 26(1): 69–77 (1999).

Charles SC, *Coping with a Medical Malpractice Suit.* West. J. Med. 174(1): 55–58 (2001).

Reading EG, *Malpractice Stress Syndrome: A New Diagnosis?* Md. Med. J. 36(3): 256–257 (1987).

Reading EG, *The Malpractice Stress Syndrome.* N.J. Med. 83(5):289–290 (1986).

REFERENCE

1. Diagnostic criteria from the *Diagnostic and Statistical Manual of Mental Disorders*, 4th Edition, with text revision (APA 2000) (DSM-IV-TR) for Acute Stress Disorder (DSM-IV-TR 308.3) and Post-Traumatic Stress Disorder (DSM-IV-TR 309.81) other than Criterion A (the stressor), describe the signs and symptoms suffered by physicians who suffer MMSS.

Malpractice Lawsuits: Prevention, Initial Handling, and Physician Concerns

S. Sandy Sanbar, M.D., Ph.D., J.D., F.C.L.M.

GOLDEN RULES

1. Build malpractice-proof shelters to survive the most predictable, yet least anticipated events in the life of any physician.
2. Shelter and protect personal assets.
3. Practice immaculate risk management and quality assurance.
4. Avoid the element of surprise by preparing for possible malpractice litigation before it occurs.
5. Physicians should have faith in themselves, their families, and all others who help them.

Shelters are built to prevent destruction from natural and unnatural catastrophic events, such as hurricanes, tornados, earthquakes, and wars. By the same token, a medical malpractice lawsuit could potentially be very damaging. Just as we build shelters for sundry disasters, every practicing physician should build a malpractice-proof shelter that can withstand the highest category of malpractice lawsuits. Coupled with the shelter, a detailed proactive plan of action must be in place to deal with the onslaught of a malpractice lawsuit. This chapter attempts to provide the potential defendant doctor with the materials needed to build a malpractice-proof shelter, and some recommendations for a plan of action.

CASE PRESENTATION

For the purposes of this chapter, the facts and circumstances surrounding the case in the preceding chapter on medical malpractice stress syndrome are applicable.

MALPRACTICE CLAIMS PREVENTION

Practicing good medicine, in and of itself, is not a guarantee that a physician will avoid being hit with a medical malpractice lawsuit. "To err is human," and physicians do make mistakes. The multidisciplinary medical practice poses a compounding effect on medical errors, particularly because of the tough choices that are made by a number of physicians involved in the care of the patient. And bad outcomes may result even with the best of medical care, which may lead to frustrated, dissatisfied, and disgruntled patients.

The physician should therefore build a variety of "shelters" aimed at minimizing the risk of malpractice, handling dissatisfied patients, protecting one's assets, and dealing with being hit by a medical malpractice claim.

MALPRACTICE SHELTER CONSTRUCTION

One of the building materials used for the construction of the malpractice-proof shelter is made of a special kind of "steel and concrete" commonly known as product "RM-QA," short for the durable mix of *Risk Management and Quality Assurance*.

Risk management centers on patient injury prevention. Risk management can be seen to be a response by the medical and health care professions to the medical malpractice crisis. It is aimed at reducing and preventing injuries from medical malpractice, and other errors or deficiencies in clinic and facility operations, and minimizing the legal consequences of those injuries.

Risk management can be defined as "the process of attempting to identify and reduce or manage incipient risk of injury to patients in the clinic, hospital or any medical care setting." Risk management is prospective in outlook. Problems in the delivery of health care are often multifaceted in nature, and the solutions to the problems must correspondingly be interdisciplinary. That is why several "columns of RM" are used to build a shelter to withstand malpractice.

Quality assurance is distinct from risk management, although quality assurance activities may supplement risk management techniques. Quality assurance is retrospective in its approach to medical problems. It emphasizes review after patient injury, and evaluation of trends in patient injury, and focuses on a cumulative, rather than an individual, standard to measure health care.

For example, consider the hospital setting. After the *Darling* case (*Darling v. Charleston Community Hospital*, 312 N.E. 2d 614 (Ill., 1965), hospital liability for professional acts of its employees, in addition to its traditional liability, has continued to increase in scope. An examination of subsequent landmark court decisions establishes a number of duties or standards that a modern hospital owes to its patients: exercising reasonable care in providing proper medical equipment, supplies, food, and other support to its patients; providing safe physical premises; establishing effective procedures to provide prompt and accurate diagnosis and treatment of patient injury and illness; adopting internal policies to protect the safety and interest of patients; exercising reasonable care and guaranteeing adequate care; exercising reasonable care in the selection and retention of hospital employees, and the granting, continuance, and renewal of staff privileges for staff physicians; establishing correct procedures for record keeping and review of incidents; and providing for effective organization of department procedures.

RISK MANAGEMENT BY NONPHYSICIAN STAFF

Allied health care professionals share the responsibility of ensuring that the duty owed to patients is appropriately carried out by the clinic or facility department. As the primary health care provider of patient care, nursing personnel are often the most capable of establishing, continuing, and evaluating systems for risk management and quality assurance. Nurses are also the primary source of data from which programs are developed. Cooperation of nursing personnel in clinics or hospitals therefore is essential in the developing and maintenance of a risk management or quality assurance program.

Nursing personnel are aware of the need to notify risk management of an injury, incident, or an unusual occurrence. Such reporting normally takes the form of an "incident report." Comments on the incident report provide a description of the incident, and corrective measures taken, and note the result or effect on the individual patient. The fact of an incident report is not generally noted in the patient's records. An incident report is classified as a legal document. By use of good observation and prompt documentation of observations, necessary information to aid in improving patient care and protecting the physician's interests is maintained.

Risk management and quality assurance activities may urge clinic and hospital personnel to be careful to follow standard rules for record keeping. This would require personnel to: record promptly observations and actions on paper or computer; write legibly; record when a report is made of medical problems; never erase a section of a patient's records to correct mistakes; document all therapy orders or specific instructions; and record performance of assigned tasks.

INCIDENT REPORT

Incident reports, and other clinic and hospital data, such as audit and pathology committee reports, can lead to better understanding of patient mishaps. Plans for prevention or reduction of further occurrences can be created, and future inservice needs on the part of the clinic or hospital staff can be identified.

Risk management programs in the nursing setting recognize that the majority of successful suits against nurses involve a pattern of risk situations: administration of medication, assisting in surgical suite, falls, burns, electric shocks, faulty equipment, nosocomial infection, mistaken identity, or misinterpretation of signs or symptoms. The largest percentage of patient incidents occurs between the hours of 8:00 A.M. and 11:00 A.M., the busiest time of the hospital. Special problems of particular clinics and institutions are also to be considered and identified, and action taken to reduce those inherent risks. For example, a geriatric orthopedic facility will have more risk associated with patient injury due to falling than would a typical medical-surgical floor.

RISK MANAGER

The risk manager plays an essential role in cementing the "RM columns." The risk manager assists the physician in developing plans to deal with a variety of risks, including, for example, methods for classifying medication errors by type by computer data management, and recording of error rates by individuals. These plans are useful tools for improving performance of health care providers, and reducing the risk to patients within the medical or hospital setting.

FEAR NOT AUTOPSIES

One of the most important but underused methods of quality assurance is the autopsy. An apprehensive health care provider might expect an increase in the number of autopsies performed to result in a higher level of liability of the physician and hospital. This has not proved to be the case. Rather, pathologists recognize that findings at autopsy in the majority of cases reduce the risk of loss, rather than result in a greater exposure to liability. Pathologists have estimated that over 40% of death certificates would be inaccurate when compared with autopsy findings. Moreover, the information obtained by autopsy can assist the family by alleviating possible doubts, guilt, or grief resulting from misunderstanding about the cause of death. Autopsy is not only useful in providing diagnostic or therapeutic feedback, explanation, detection of safety and occupational hazard, and contributing to continuing education of clinical physicians, but also in clarifying the cause of death in a wrongful death action.

INJURY CONTROL

Essential to the concepts of risk management and quality assurance is problem identification, followed by measures to ensure that risk to patients or staff will not recur. The most important component of risk management program is staff education. Such a program involves: identifying patterns of incidents, patient injuries, or undesired results; determining specific errors that may contribute to those injuries; evaluating potential problem areas to determine alternatives to decrease the risk or hazard to the patient; evaluating changes in procedures or techniques that might decrease patient risk; and implementing such new procedures or techniques.

Supervision of injury control is usually done through safety officers. The risk manager and quality assurance individual, or respective committees in a hospital setting, supervise all aspects of quality assurance and risk management and can fully integrate the data obtained and implement effective inservice continuing education for health care practitioners. Such education focuses not only on the lines of communication and responsibility concerning risk management or quality assurance, but also emphasizes the need to modify the behavior of the health care practitioner, particularly techniques and conduct during patient contact.

Most malpractice claims involve cases where a poor relationship between the health care practitioner and the patient exists, and a poor outcome results from treatment. A number of potential sources of professional and hospital liability can be eliminated or reduced by careful attention to the health care practitioner–patient relationship, and heightened attention to controllable patient risk.

With physicians and hospitals treating increasing numbers of patients, caring for higher risk patients, and employing more complicated procedures and innovative techniques, the possibilities for human error are compounded. Risk management and quality assurance are directed to delivering the highest possible level of health care to the individual patient, and also to reducing the potential of occurrences that result in liability of the health care provider for improper or negligent treatment.

ASSET PROTECTION

There are a variety of methods used to protect the physician's physical assets, including the purchase of malpractice insurance, creation of trusts or limited liability companies to shelter assets, and the distribution of assets to family members, among other techniques. The physician should seek counsel and develop plans early on to structure such important shelters along with sound estate, and even retirement, planning. Frequently, physicians act too late to prevent personal asset losses, to the detriment of the entire family. A detailed discussion of asset protection techniques is beyond the scope of this Handbook.

An integral part of sheltering is the process of dealing with the hauling winds of a "*malpractice storm.*" The physician should have a plan of action to confront the onslaught of an undesirable, unwelcome, and stressful medical malpractice lawsuit. The following are practical suggestions aimed at assisting the physician to navigate the best possible course to deal with the process of malpractice litigation, from the personal, professional, financial, and legal standpoint.

AVOID THE ELEMENT OF SURPRISE

The great majority of physicians are aware of the fact that an integral part of practicing medicine is professional medical liability, the price of doing business. The medical student learns early on about medical negligence. Upon graduation, before seeing the first patient and before acquiring hospital privileges, the physician must obtain professional liability insurance. Nevertheless, the physician can never prepare fully to confront a malpractice lawsuit, and hence the element of surprise.

Occasionally, the physician knows that negligence did occur, and he or she may be encouraged to be the first person to inform and perhaps apologize to the patient, as noted in a subsequent chapter.

In some instances, the patient, or a related family member, may provide the first clue to the physician, or to a member of the physician's staff, that a malpractice lawsuit is being contemplated.

However, the physician may receive some notice from a plaintiff attorney, which is often in writing, though occasionally by a telephone call. That can be a "shocking" surprise.

THE INITIAL REQUESTS

The plaintiff attorney may forward a letter requesting to either meet with the physician or for medical information and medical records. At this stage, it is critical that the physician be apprised personally of such a request, before the request is processed by the staff. The physician should be careful to review the medical records, to avoid expressing opinions that are not already contained in the medical record, and to be cautious about expressing opinions about other physicians involved in the care and treatment of the patient.

If the physician is concerned about potential negligence, it behooves the physician to check first with the risk manager, insurance company, or defense attorney, *before* responding to the *potential* plaintiff attorney's request.

The physician may receive correspondence from an attorney stating that the patient intends to file a medical malpractice lawsuit. Such letters are "legal notice of intent to sue" and may be sent to the physician in order to extend the statute of limitations by a certain statutory period. The intent to sue notice is generally forwarded by certified mail and clearly indicates that the patient is considering a suit against the physician. In this situation, the physician must review in details the patient's medical information and immediately discuss the same with the risk manager, liability insurance company, and possibly the defense attorney.

Finally, the first notice by the physician may be the actual receipt of the medical malpractice lawsuit, formally referred to as a *complaint*, which states the name of the plaintiff patient and the name(s) of the defendant(s), doctor(s), and hospital(s).

The complaint is accompanied by the *summons*, which is a legal document issued by a court announcing to the defendant that a legal proceeding has been started against him or her, that a file has been started in the court records, and announcing a date by which the defendant(s) must either appear in court, or respond in writing to the court or the opposing party or parties.

THE "SHOCKING" COMPLAINT

No physician can ever be prepared enough to read the strong and "shocking" language that is used in the complaint to describe the physician's negligent conduct, the horrible injuries sustained by the patient, and the consequent phenomenal damages. In a medical malpractice lawsuit, the plaintiff patient, or estate, retains, or hires, a private attorney to file a civil complaint. The complaint is a short and plain statement of the "facts" that form the basis of the claim against the physician. The facts are embellished, blown way out of proportion, and deliberately intended to "shock" the defendant in a public manner. Everything that the physician has worked for and dedicated his or her life to is suddenly shattered by the harsh language in the complaint.

The exact theory of the plaintiff's case may not be spelled out in the complaint, and may not be figured out until the defense attorney is able to formally question the plaintiff and the plaintiff's medical expert. States may require that, *prior* to filing a complaint, the plaintiff attorney must obtain proof of negligence by the defendant from an appropriate expert medical witness.

The complaint should state, however, the four elements of medical negligence:

1. That the physician owed a duty to provide the patient with a standard medical treatment.
2. How the physician fell below the standard of medical care when providing the patient with medical treatment.
3. How the failure of medical treatment caused injury to the patient.
4. What damages directly resulted from the breach of the alleged standard of medical care.

Many states limit the amount of the award for damages. However, in most complaints the damage claim demand will be potentially unlimited. One cannot depend upon the damages stated in the complaint as the limit of the amount requested.

As with the notice of intent to sue, the physician should very promptly forward the complaint to the insurance agent and/or insurance company. In fact, notification of the insurer should occur as soon as the physician receives any indication of a possible or pending claim. Where the physician has a claims made liability policy, the notice of the existence of any type of claim can be critically important in determining whether or not the physician is covered by the liability insurance policy. The physician should also mark his or her calendar to follow up and make sure that the legal papers are being promptly handled by the insurance agent, insurance company, or risk manager. The physician should keep a copy of the complaint and send the original to the agent, insurance company, or risk manager.

It is important for the physician to secure proof that the insurer has been notified and that the notice has been received, for example by hand delivery, by certified letter, or return receipt requested. The liability insurance company generally selects the defense attorney. The insured physician may also hire a private attorney. The uninsured physician hires his or her own defense attorney.

The physician should not depend on the office staff to properly handle the legal papers. These papers should be placed in a stack separate from other reports.

The physician must formally respond to a claim within a certain time limit as specified by law. This is usually a formality, accomplished by defense counsel, denying the allegations, thereby placing the lawsuit at issue. The failure of the plaintiff to do so in a timely manner may result in a default judgment against the physician.

LITIGATION PROCESS

The whole process of civil litigation will be discussed in detail in Section 3. The trial is preceded by a period of discovery where demands for documents are made, interrogatories are submitted, depositions of the parties

and witnesses are taken, including expert witnesses, and attempts are made
to dismiss or settle the case, otherwise a trial is inevitable.

The trial will be attended by all the parties and their attorneys. The
physician will need to be there during the entire trial. Medical malpractice
trials typically run from one to three weeks. They are usually scheduled by
courts in most states within a year after the filing of suit, but the range can
run from less than a year to as much as four years or longer. In general, the
average malpractice lawsuit is not resolved for up to four years. Suits tend
to progress in stages, with quiet intervals and repeated starts as deadlines
are missed, events rescheduled, and new information is revealed. Each time
the defendant physician revisits the case after a period of quiescence can act
as a re-trauma, bringing back symptoms of the initial shock and anger, or
adding salt to a nonhealing malpractice wound.

ALTERNATIVE DISPUTE RESOLUTION

Chapter 22 is devoted to this important method of resolving malpractice
disputes without formal litigation. Favored by the courts, alternative dispute resolution (ADR) includes nonbinding arbitration or mediation. Some
courts may force ADR, but the court cannot force the parties to settle. In
some circumstances, the court may appoint the arbitrator and/or mediator.
In other cases, the parties may get together to jointly hire a mediator to
assist the parties to an ultimate resolution.

The fact that a case is arbitrated or mediated does not necessarily mean
that a successful settlement will be achieved or that the case should necessarily be settled. Many arbitrations/mediations do not result in settlement
and the case will then proceed to trial.

DISPOSITION AND OUTCOME OF MALPRACTICE LAWSUITS

Many malpractice lawsuits are voluntarily dismissed by the plaintiff's attorney. The court may also dismiss the case with prejudice for lack of prosecution by the plaintiff. Some cases may be dismissed by the court on summary
judgment if the plaintiff fails to produce a competent expert who will
testify that the standard of care was breached by the defendant physician in
the care and treatment of the patient. The parties may settle the case. Based
on the insurance policy, the defendant physician generally has a right to
consent or refuse to consent to settlement.

Relatively few malpractice cases go to trial where the jury makes a
decision as to whether or not the defendant physician met the standards of
care or fell below standards of care, caused the injury, and the amount of
the money damages that will be paid as a result of the injury.

A default judgment may result from failure to properly respond to a civil
complaint. This in turn may cause the insurance company to refuse to
defend the physician and refuse to pay for any judgment. In addition, a
default judgment means that the physician cannot even defend himself or
herself on the issue of whether or not they did something wrong.

THE DEFENSE COUNSEL

Normally, the physician has little or no input in the assignment of the defense attorney. The insurance carrier will make this assignment. But the physician may know the more experienced defense attorneys in the area, and they may agree to work with the insurance company.

The defense attorney will normally contact the physician by letter or telephone. It is important for the physician to get to know the attorney's personality and ability to defend. Concerns with the attorney's representation should be expressed promptly by the physician. If the personality conflict or dissatisfaction with representation persists, the physician should contact the insurance carrier who appointed the attorney and strongly express the concern. Usually, the insurance company will appoint new counsel if the physician's dissatisfaction is justified. The hiring of a private defense attorney is the subject of Chapter 8.

The physician should tell the defense attorney everything he or she knows about the case. Discussions with the defense attorney are privileged and cannot be disclosed to any third party by the attorney. This is known as the "attorney–client privilege." The physician should also tell the defense attorney about problems that may exist regarding the care and treatment, including problems that may exist regarding other caregivers.

In addition to defense counsel, the physician may discuss the case with their spouse or a counselor, but no one else. The physician may discuss their feelings about getting sued, but not the details of the case. Discussions with anyone, other than the attorney, spouse, or counselor, can be discovered by the plaintiff's lawyer.

The defense attorney will advise the physician not to directly call the plaintiff or the plaintiff's attorney and explain what happened.

The defense attorney may involve the physician in the selection of the defense expert, who cannot be a friend, relative, or someone with whom the defendant physician has regular contact. The defense expert must be truly independent. The physician may know a leader in the field that is the subject of litigation, with quality credentials and medical/legal experience. The physician defendant may volunteer the names of such leaders, thereby participating with the attorney in the defense of the case.

The defense attorney will advise the physician whether or not peer review documents are protected by statute. This protection is necessary since open and honest discussion is required in peer review. Occasionally, the other side will seek to obtain peer review documents. On rare occasions, the court will order that the peer review documents be examined "*in camera.*" This means that the court will look at the peer review documents without the attorneys or parties. Peer review documents are almost always protected as long as they have not previously been voluntarily disclosed to third parties.

Finally, the defense attorney will advise the physician not to deliberately alter the patient's medical record. This is referred to as spoliation and is illegal. Spoliation is the subject of Chapter 5.

However, the physician can make a careful note of what was left out or incorrect, and add it as an addendum that is **clearly** labeled as such and dated as of the writing (not the clinical interaction). The physician should check with their attorney to see if an addendum would be advisable at this late date, or could be misinterpreted.

PERSONAL ATTORNEY

The subject of hiring a private or personal attorney by the physician is discussed fully in Chapter 8.

LITIGATION COSTS

Based on the language of the liability insurance contract, the insurance company typically pays the defense costs, any settlement or judgment payments, and sometimes compensation for the physician's time spent during trial, but not for full replacement of the physician's income lost during the litigation process.

Malpractice insurance companies generally do not reimburse the expenses of the physician's own personal attorney, do not pay for monetary awards that exceed the policy limits, and do not pay for punitive damages.

Judgments that exceed the policy limits are exceedingly rare. Whether the physician is responsible for the excess award depends on the circumstances and conduct of the insurance company. If the physician asks the insurance company to settle the case within the policy limits before judgment and the company refuses, the physician would probably have a bad faith action against the insurance company for failing to settle within the policy limits. In the absence of bad faith by the insurance company, the defense attorney may attempt to negotiate a settlement with the other side, recognizing that any money paid in settlement above the policy limits will be paid out of the physician's pocket. Bankruptcy is not a desirable option.

Most insurance companies do not pay for any judgment relating to alleged illegal behavior. However, in some instances the insurance company may defend the physician, but will seek reimbursement if the physician is found guilty of such misconduct. Similarly, some licensure actions may be defended by the insurance company if the case relates to an alleged malpractice claim.

CONSEQUENCES OF SETTLING OR LOSING
A MALPRACTICE LAWSUIT

Every physician defendant has to be concerned about the unpleasant consequences of settling or losing the malpractice lawsuit. These consequences include the following:

First, from the financial standpoint, once the settlement amount has been negotiated and agreed upon or the damage verdict has been rendered by the jury, the insurance company will pay the settlement in exchange for a dismissal of the lawsuit and a release of all claims against the physician. Where the case proceeds to trial and the jury renders a money damage verdict that is within the policy limits, the defense attorney and the insurance company will decide whether to appeal or pay the verdict. If the verdict exceeds the policy limits, the physician may be personally responsible for payment above and beyond the policy limits, as discussed earlier.

Second, in the event of settlement, regardless of the amount, the National Practitioner Data Bank (NPDB) is notified of the nature of the case and the amount of the settlement or loss. Under normal circumstances, the insurance carrier will report the physician to the NPDB or State Medical Board. If the physician is practicing within a self-insured group, the representative of risk management of that group will have the responsibility of reporting. By law, they will receive a copy of the report forwarded to the NPDB. The physician will be allowed to supplement that report or argue that the report is incorrect.

Third, in many states, if the settlement or loss is over a certain amount, the State Medical Board is also notified. In the event of a number of settlements or losses within a designated period, the State Medical Board may decide to investigate the physician's medical practice. The physician may be subject to an investigation by the State Medical Board in the event of a number of settlements or losses within a designated period of time or in the event that a patient makes a complaint against the physician.

Fourth, the insurance companies profit from collecting premiums. They do not like to pay settlements or judgments! However, the physician has certain contractual rights with the insurance company; it must comply with the insurance contract while the physician is insured. The insurance company will review internally whether or not they wish to keep the physician as an insured after expiration of the policy. The physician's premium rates will in all likelihood increase, which will be dependent upon the amount of the settlement, the current economic strength of the insurance company, as well as other economic factors.

LITIGATION RECORDS

The physician defendant should personally keep in a safe place his or her own "litigation records," including the complaint, settlement documents, release, and, if the case goes to trial and is lost, the verdict and judgment entry. When applying for hospital privileges, licensing, medical, managed care, and sundry other organizations, the physician will be asked questions regarding all past lawsuits. The physician will need to disclose these lawsuits and how they ended, i.e., dismissal, settlement, or verdict.

Medical Brief (or Medical Memorandum)

S. Sandy Sanbar, M.D., Ph.D., J.D., F.C.L.M.
Marvin H. Firestone, M.D., J.D., F.C.L.M.

GOLDEN RULES

1. The medical brief can be an extraordinary tool when preparing a medical negligence case.
2. A medical brief, or medical memorandum, should be prepared in complex malpractice lawsuits.
3. The medical brief should be meticulous, comprehensive, and inclusive of all the medical and nursing care rendered to the patient.
4. The medical brief can be extremely helpful to both the defendant physician and the defense counsel.
5. The objective evidence in the medical brief may prove absence of medical negligence, thereby bringing peace of mind to the physician.
6. On the other hand, if the evidence indicates that there may be negligence, the medical brief will serve to focus attention on the issues at hand and may promote settlement.

The *medical brief*, also called the medical memorandum, is a comprehensive compilation of legally relevant medical facts of the case in litigation, with supportive data and conclusions from the medical literature, textbooks, and treatises, as well as opinions of medical experts. The medical brief is the attorney's work product. It is therefore not subject to discovery by the opposing side during the pretrial process or during the trial proceedings. However, it may be submitted to the judge, as a part of a pretrial brief or court memorandum, in order to inform the judge about the medical issues of the case that are being litigated.

The medical brief is distinct from the medical report. The medical brief is usually prepared, at the request of the attorney, by a medical individual (e.g., a physician or nurse) and is generally kept confidential from opposing parties.

The medical report, on the other hand, is prepared either by a physician who attended the patient and who has personal knowledge of the medical facts, or by an expert medical witness whose source of information is review of pertinent medical records. Medical reports that are written by an expert witness who intends to testify in court are generally discoverable. The attorney who is in possession of the written medical reports may be required to show those reports to the other side either before or during the trial. In contrast, medical reports of expert witnesses who do not intend to testify in court may not be discoverable.

The requirement for a comprehensive medical brief by most practicing attorneys is infrequent; it is demanding in time, effort, and expense. Therefore, a medical brief is warranted only in special cases where the medical facts are very complicated and where the alleged damages are substantial. In contrast, medical reports are relatively brief, less time-consuming, and are similar to comprehensive discharge summaries. Most physicians are well familiar with the preparation of medical reports.

The following are two sample medical briefs of actual cases, but the names have been altered. The medical evidence is presented, and it may be followed by brief comments, supported by peer-reviewed medical literature. The medical literature that supports the facts of the case is not included in this chapter. Physicians are very familiar with searching the medical literature for any medical disorder. Some attorneys prefer not to have the medical literature listed in the medical brief. The medical literature is readily accessible on the internet for both the plaintiff and defense counsel.

I. MEDICAL BRIEF: FIRST SAMPLE

Mr. John Senior, who was then 80 years old, was involved in a motor vehicular accident (MVA), which will be described shortly. (This represents an actual case; the names are fictitious.)

Medical History Prior to MVA

Prior to the MVA, John had the following diagnoses:

1. Coronary arteriosclerosis, and secondary ischemic cardiomyopathy.
2. Status post-coronary angioplasty, with stent placement in the left anterior descending coronary artery.
3. Sick sinus syndrome.
4. Permanent, pervenous, dual-chamber pacemaker, implanted in 1998, for #3.
5. Aortic stenosis, moderate in severity.
6. Hypertensive cardiovascular disease.
7. Left ventricular hypertrophy.
8. Transient cerebral ischemic attack in 1996, due to carotid arteriosclerosis.
9. Status post-bilateral carotid endarterectomy, for #8.
10. Chronic renal insufficiency.

Last Exam by Family Physician Prior to MVA

The patient visited his family physician due to onset of sore throat and cough (no sputum). The patient had no chest pain. His weight was 195.4 lbs.,

B.P. 130/82 mm Hg, and temperature 98.6°F. No laboratory tests were performed. The family physician diagnosed an upper respiratory infection, and he prescribed an antibiotic and a cough medication.

MVA and EMS Care at Scene of Accident

About three hours after visiting his family physician, the patient was a front-seat passenger in a car driven by his wife, when the car was struck by another car on its front end. The airbag deployed. The patient remained in his seat trapped by the deployed airbag until the arrival of the EMS. He was promptly removed from his seat, evaluated, and attended to appropriately. He had lacerations of the nose, and a reddened area across the chest. He complained of chest pain under the left breast and into the sternum. The chest pain did not radiate to the jaw or arms. He had wheezing on inspiration, but his respirations were nonlabored. His B.P. was 160–170/84, pulse 68–71, and respirations 20. His EKG rhythm strip revealed pacemaker rhythm, with premature ventricular contractions every third heart beat (trigeminy). He was treated with oxygen at 3 L/min per nasal canula, and an IV was started with normal saline solution. The diagnosis was MVA with left chest pain.

Hospital Emergency Department

The patient was transported via ambulance to the Emergency Department of a Medical Center. Upon arrival, the severity of the left chest pain was 5, on a scale of 1 to 10. The emergency physician noted that the patient had facial abrasions and wheezing bilaterally. The hematology was normal; the white blood count was 6900, Hgb 14.1 g, and hematocrit 40.9%. The BUN was 27 mg/dl, creatinine 1.5 mg/dl, and glucose 148 mg/dl. The EKG revealed a pacemaker rhythm with ventricular capture, rate 72 bpm. The chest x-ray report by the first radiologist (#1) stated: "A vague interstitial prominence is present in the left perihilar region suspicious for early pneumonia. The right lung is clear and the heart is enlarged." The impression by the radiologist was: "Probable early left-sided pneumonia." The impressions by the ER physician were: left chest contusion, left pneumonia, and bronchospasm.

Hospitalization

The patient was hospitalized at a City Medical Center. The attending was his family physician; he had seen the patient earlier that day at his office prior to the MVA. On admission, the pain in the left side of the chest was described as 6 on a scale of 1 to 10. The patient had shortness of breath, congestion, and dry cough. He had bruises over the left chest and face, secondary to the MVA. At 23:30, the nurse, R.N., noted that the patient's skin was flushed, with bruises over the face and the left chest, secondary to the MVA, and his respirations were labored, on 3 L/min oxygen. His weight was 194 lbs., temperature 98.6°F, pulse 63, respirations 22, and B.P. 168/77 mm Hg.

The electrocardiogram monitor revealed pacemaker rhythm, rate 71, and premature ventricular contractions. *At 18:40 hours, the heart rate dropped to 55 beats per minute; the pacemaker did not sense the bradycardia* (emphasis added). At 19:40 hours, the heart rate was 63 beats per minute. At 20:25 hours, the pacemaker rate was 71 beats per minute. Hematology showed a white blood count of 9200. The BUN was 24, creatinine 1.4, and glucose 127. At 12:30 hours, the total CPK was 219, MB fraction <5.0, and the troponin-I was 0.8 ng/ml, indicating possible minimal or early myocardial injury. At 18:40 hours, the total CPK was 200, the CK-MB was <5.0, and the troponin-I was 0.5.

Transfer to Intensive Care Unit

The attending physician saw the patient for the first time at the hospital, examined him, and stated that the patient had chest pain and shortness of breath, following the MVA, and he suspected secondary congestive heart failure. That same day, the patient developed respiratory distress at 7:45 A.M. Three nurses assessed the patient and noted that the patient desaturated and became cyanotic despite the oxygen per nasal canula. The pulse oxymetry dropped to 82%. The patient complained of chest pain. A non-rebreathing mask was placed by the respiratory therapist, and more oxygen was administered. Morphine, 2 mg, and Lasix, 40 mg, were administered intravenously at 7:50 A.M. The patient was transferred from his regular hospital bed to the intensive care unit at 9 A.M. His son was at his bedside, and the attending physician was notified about the patient's transfer at 9:15 A.M. At 11:52 hours, an AP portable chest x-ray was obtained and interpreted by a second radiologist (#2) as follows: "This is a poor inspiratory effort, which accentuates the heart size and the vascular pattern of the lungs. There does not appear to have been significant change from the previous study."

Cardiology Consultant and Echocardiogram

A cardiologist was consulted and examined the patient. His impression and recommendations were: "Patient presents with probable pneumonia on the left side and now also has decompensated congestive heart failure in the setting of noncardiac disease and aortic stenosis. The patient is on appropriate antibiotic therapy and will start him on intravenous diuretics for control of his blood pressure. Will check Echocardiogram to assess his cardiac status and will follow with you."

The echocardiogram was performed. The impression on the echocardiogram request was acute pulmonary edema and valvular heart disease.

"INTERPRETATION:
1. Dilated left atrium. Other cardiac chamber sizes are normal.
2. Dense aortic sclerosis.
3. Dense mitral sclerosis.
4. Aortic stenosis with restricted cusp separation.
5. Concentric left ventricular hypertrophy.

6. Overall right ventricular and left ventricular systolic function is normal. There is inferior left ventricular hypokinesia.
7. Left ventricular ejection fraction is 55%.
8. No pleural or pericardial effusion noted.
9. Mild TR. Mild MR.
10. Critical aortic stenosis. Mean pressure gradient 28, peak pressure gradient 46. Calculated aortic valve area is 0.7 cm^2."

Course in the Hospital

The patient's temperature rose to 101.4°F on the second day of admission, pulse 62–64, respirations 22–26, and B.P. 146/70 mm Hg. On the third day of admission, the maximum temperature was 100.2°F and subsequently the temperature was mostly in the normal range. The WBC was 10,600, Hgb 12.8 g, hematocrit 36.5%, BUN 34 mg/dl, creatinine 1.7 mg/dl, total CPK 173–179 IU/L, and MB fraction <5.0 ng/ml. The troponin-I was 0.8 ng/ml at 02:50, and 0.6 ng/ml at 10:12 hours. The EKG revealed pacemaker rhythm with ventricular capture at a rate of 72 beats per minute. The chest x-ray was reported by the third radiologist (#3) as follows: "The dual lead right subclavian pacemaker is seen overlying the right ventricle. The heart size is enlarged. Pulmonary vascular congestion is seen along with some interstitial edema. Overall, I do not see any significant change from the previous day's x-ray. IMPRESSION: 1. Findings most consistent with congestive failure." A second portable AP upright chest x-ray was obtained at 18:10 hours. The radiologist's (#3) report stated: "The heart size continues to be enlarged with pulmonary vascular congestion and edema. No pleural effusions are seen. There is a suspicion of a left anterolateral 5th rib fracture. IMPRESSION: 1. Congestive changes with suspicions of a left 5th rib fracture."

During the hospital course, the EKG monitor revealed pacemaker rhythm, with variable rates from 60 to 75 beats per minute, and premature ventricular contractions. Atrial fibrillation was noted on the sixth day of hospitalization, at 15:43, with a ventricular heart rate of 83 bpm.

On the fourth day of hospitalization, the EKG revealed a pacemaker rhythm with ventricular capture at a rate of 59 bpm. The chest x-ray, interpreted by the radiologist (#2), showed significant clearing of the pulmonary vascular congestion. The heart remained enlarged. There was elevation of the right diaphragm with atelectasis in the right lower lobe. On the fifth day of hospitalization, the chest x-ray, interpreted by the radiologist (#3), showed the heart size enlarged, and there was a proven left lung infiltrate. On the sixth day of hospitalization, the chest x-ray, interpreted by the radiologist (#3), showed no significant change from the fifth day of hospitalization. The heart was enlarged, and there continued to be some left basilar infiltrate. The last chest x-ray (#4) revealed interval clearing of the left lower lung infiltrate, normal pulmonary vasculature, cardiomegaly, and stable position of the dual lead cardiac pacemaker.

During his hospitalization, the patient was treated with diuretics, ace inhibitors, digoxin, Hytrin, antibiotics, pain medications, and nitroglycerin. During his entire hospitalization, the patient received respiratory therapy

5–6 times daily, with Albuterol 2.5 mg and Atrovent 0.5 mg. The kidney function tests gradually became more abnormal. On the eleventh day of hospitalization, the BUN had risen to 52 and the creatinine was 1.9. On the thirteenth day of hospitalization, the discharge date, the BUN was at its highest level, 70, and the creatinine was 2.5. The patient was not complaining of chest pain. His vital signs were stable. The patient was discharged after two weeks to be followed as an outpatient.

Discharge Medications and Discharge Diagnosis

The patient was discharged on Levoquin, Lanoxin, Demadex, Monopril, K-Dur, Hytrin, Nitropaste, Nitrostat, Ecotrin, Celebrex, and Celexa. The discharge summary was dictated by the cardiologist. The discharge diagnoses were:

1. Acute decompensated congestive heart failure.
2. Pneumonia, left lower lobe.
3. Renal insufficiency, chronic.
4. Known coronary artery disease with ischemic cardiomyopathy.
5. Mild aortic stenosis.
6. Subendocardial myocardial infarction.

Emergency Medical Services and Nursing Care

As a consequence of the injuries caused by the MVA, the patient received prompt service by EMS and at the Emergency Department. He was hospitalized, successfully treated by the attending physician and the consulting cardiologist, and received excellent nursing care. As of three months post hospitalization, the patient was alive.

Review by Another Cardiologist

One month after hospitalization, at the request of the car insurance defense counsel, another cardiologist reviewed the above case, and rendered the following opinion:

> I have carefully reviewed the medical record and laboratory information you provided concerning Mr. John Senior. As you know, Mr. Senior was involved in an automobile accident on April 2, 2001, and was hospitalized at the Medical Center for evaluation of shortness of breath. During his hospitalization, he was noted to have cardiac isoenzyme evidence of a minimal, non-Q-wave myocardial infarction with maximum troponin of 0.8 recorded two days later.
>
> Although this level of troponin would suggest a minimal myocardial infarction, the timing of the troponin elevation would suggest that the minimal myocardial infarction occurred shortly after admission, and would not be related to the automobile accident. The cardiac isoenzymes pinpoint the time of myocardial infarction as occurring after admission

to the hospital. In my opinion, there is no causal relationship between the myocardial infarction and the motor vehicle accident.

Mr. Senior has a well-documented history of serious vascular disease including coronary artery disease with previous stent placement, hypertensive cardiovascular disease with a known hypertensive and ischemic cardiomyopathy, and significant left ventricular dysfunction.

He presented to the Medical Center with a pneumonia and acute exacerbation of his congestive heart failure. Mr. Senior's minimal myocardial infarction was related to his known underlying ischemic heart disease and his decompensated congestive heart failure. The motor vehicle accident was not a contributing factor to the minimal myocardial infarction noted during his hospital admission. The medical bills from the second day of hospitalization and onward would likewise not be related to the auto accident.

If I can be of any further assistance or provide any additional information, please do not hesitate to contact me.

Review of Chest X-Rays in 2003

Three months post hospitalization, the second radiologist (#2), who interpreted the chest x-rays during the hospitalization, provided the following report:

80 YO male, passenger in MVA 4/2/01. Airbag deployed.

Finding 1
Initial CXR 15:10 showed left perihilar infiltration.

Repeat CXR next morning showed little change in the left lung infiltrate. By second or third day of hospitalization, there had been significant clearing. This is typical for pulmonary contusion.

Contusion may rapidly clear in 24–48 hours but usually resolves over 72 hours. If persist or increase over time think of complications such as infection, Pulmonary Edema, Adult Respiratory Distress Syndrome [ARDS], etc.

Finding 2
Right diaphragm was elevated but this was present before the MVA so felt to be eventration and not diaphragm laceration. There were linear increased markings in right base c/w (compatible with) atelectasis.

Finding 3
The patient had cardiomegaly initially but this was not significantly changed from the exam prior to the hospitalization following the MVA.

On day 2 the pulmonary vascularity was mildly increased. On day 3 the patient had developed frank pulmonary vascular congestion with pulmonary edema c/w the myocardial contusion.

By day 11 the pulmonary contusion had cleared. The pulmonary vascular congestion had cleared and the heart had returned to its pre-injury size.

Retrospective Case Review Diagnoses

In retrospect, the hospital discharge diagnoses of the above case should have been as follows:

1. Motor vehicular accident and airbag deployment, causing the following injuries to front-seat passenger:
    (a) Nonpenetrating blunt chest wall trauma.
    (b) Pulmonary contusion of the left lung.
    (c) Myocardial contusion.
    (d) Premature ventricular contractions, atrial fibrillation.
    (e) Transient pacemaker malfunction.
    (f) Congestive heart failure, pulmonary edema, and hypoxemia, treated.
    (g) Skin bruises of the face and anterior chest wall.
    (h) Probable fracture of the 5th left rib.
    (i) Aggravation of chronic renal failure, in part secondary to ace inhibitors.
2. Known coronary artery disease, ischemic cardiomyopathy, post-coronary angioplasty of LAD with stent placements twice in left anterior descending coronary artery.
3. Aortic stenosis, mean pressure gradient 28 mm Hg, peak pressure gradient 46 mm Hg, calculated aortic valve area 0.7 cm^2.
4. Mild mitral and tricuspid regurgitation by echocardiography.
5. Permanent, pervenous, dual-chamber pacemaker.
6. Hypertensive cardiovascular disease, with left atrial enlargement.
7. Known carotid artery disease, post-bilateral carotid endarterectomy.

Discussion of the Medical Evidence

The case reported here is typical for pulmonary contusion and myocardial contusion, and attendant complications, resulting from a nonpenetrating blunt chest trauma, caused by a MVA and airbag deployment.

The initial chest x-ray taken at the ER was interpreted as "probable early left-sided pneumonia." The ER physician, attending physician, and cardiologist accepted the radiological diagnosis of pneumonia. Furthermore, the attending physician treated the patient with intravenous antibiotics for a presumed *bacterial pneumonia*. However, the patient had been in a MVA, had evidence of blunt trauma to the anterior chest, complained of left-sided chest pain after the MVA, had on admission a normal temperature (98.6°F) and a normal WBC (6900), had a nonproductive cough, and had no sputum exam or culture to suggest a bacterial infection.

The consulting cardiologist concurred with the diagnosis of pneumonia and the antibiotic treatment. Even the cardiologist who reviewed the case in March 2002, on behalf of the car insurance defense counsel, accepted the diagnosis of pneumonia. None of the physicians even considered the differential diagnosis of pulmonary or myocardial contusion, at a time when a high level of suspicion should have been maintained based on the history and clinical findings.

Several chest x-rays were obtained during the patient's hospitalization (13 days), and were interpreted by four different radiologists. The chest x-ray requisitions noted MVA and contusion as the reasons for obtaining the x-rays. None of the radiologists included pulmonary contusion or cardiac contusion as differential diagnoses. One of the radiologists noted probable fracture of the left fifth rib. However, review of all the chest x-rays two years later by one of the four radiologists provided a different interpretation: pulmonary and cardiac contusion and heart failure, and not pneumonia.

Chest Trauma: Pulmonary and Myocardial Contusion

Pulmonary contusion is the most common lung parenchymal injury in blunt chest trauma, and 70% are caused by MVA. Other chest trauma includes myocardial contusion, cardiac tamponade, aortic rupture, rib fractures, pneumothorax, flail chest, hemothorax, tracheobronchial injuries, and post-traumatic pulmonary pseudocyst. In pulmonary contusion, the injury causes alveolar hemorrhage and parenchymal destruction and manifests as alveolar collapse and lung consolidation, which are maximal during the first 24 hours after injury and generally resolve within 7 days. The diagnosis of pulmonary contusion is often made clinically and confirmed by chest x-ray. When there is doubt about the diagnosis of pulmonary contusion, computerized tomography scanning can easily distinguish chest wall from parenchymal or mediastinal injury. Early diagnosis and therapeutic intervention aimed at minimizing the pulmonary injury progression provides the greatest chance for survival. The development of acute respiratory distress syndrome and pneumonia in the setting of pulmonary contusion, especially in the elderly, is ominous and carries a high mortality rate (50%). The management of patients with pulmonary contusion is supportive.

Myocardial contusion, bruising of the cardiac muscle, or concussion may also result from blunt chest trauma. The patient with myocardial contusion is prone to all the complications possible with acute myocardial infarction, including a variety of dysrrhythmias, electrocardiographic and cardiac enzyme abnormalities indicating myocardial injury, and heart failure, pulmonary edema, and in rare instances cardiogenic shock and death. Pacemaker malfunction may sometimes develop as a result of blunt chest trauma as occurred transiently in this case.

Failure to Diagnose

All the physicians involved in this case failed to diagnose the patient's problem. However, the patient was treated superbly at the Medical Center. The question arises as to whether the patient has a sustainable medical malpractice case against the physicians.

From the medical standpoint, the patient cannot prevail in a medical malpractice lawsuit, because no medical damages could be attributable directly to the failure to diagnose. In fact, Mr. Senior received optimal medical treatment and recovered successfully.

However, the improper diagnosis could have prevented the patient from recovering from the car insurance company for injuries caused by the MVA. The medical expenses alone exceeded $50,000. And the patient's medical records at the Medical Center, and the opinion of the cardiologist expert witness for the insurance company, indicated that the patient's hospital illness was unrelated to the accident. Under the circumstances, the judge would rule against the patient, in favor of the insurance company. Had this been the outcome, the patient could justifiably file a medical malpractice lawsuit against the physicians for failure to diagnose, and the damages that directly resulted from the failure to diagnose were the proceeds that should have been paid to the patient from the insurance company.

By retrospectively acknowledging the incorrect diagnosis by the radiologist, the car insurance company had to settle the claim, and the physicians could no longer be sued for malpractice.

II. MEDICAL BRIEF: SECOND SAMPLE

A 39-year-old male was initially treated medically for gallbladder disease, and subsequently underwent cholecystectomy. Postoperatively, he developed symptoms, signs, laboratory, chest x-ray, and EKG findings that were compatible with pulmonary embolism. The latter diagnosis was missed until it was demonstrated at autopsy.

Plaintiff's Contentions

1. The clinical, laboratory, electrocardiographic, and chest x-ray findings documented in the decedent's medical records indicate that he could and should have been suspected of having pulmonary embolism following the abdominal surgery and prior to his death.
2. The failure by the physicians who attended and cared for the decedent to consider the diagnosis of pulmonary embolism fell below the standards of the medical community.
3. The failure to diagnose and treat the pulmonary embolism was in all probability the legal cause of death in this case.

Medical Facts

This is a case of a 39-year-old white male who died following abdominal surgery. His height was 6 ft 1 in. and his weight was approximately 270 lbs. His medical records reveal the following past history:

1. Thyroidectomy for hyperthyroidism with goiter.
2. Hypertension, with recorded blood pressures of 162/118 and 170/120.
3. Obesity with weight varying from 251 to 300 lbs.

Five years prior to surgery, his electrocardiogram was within normal limits. Six months prior to surgery, his weight was recorded as 251 lbs. and his blood pressure was within the normal range.

First Hospitalization

The patient had gallbladder symptoms and was admitted to a local community hospital. His diagnosis was acute cholecystitis, nonfunctioning and presumably containing stones. The diagnosis was substantiated both clinically and by laboratory tests. He had fever, rapid pulse, elevated white blood count, and nonvisualization of the gallbladder by x-ray. He was treated with medication including antibiotics and discharged three days later; cholecystectomy was deferred.

Second Hospitalization

Seven months later, the patient was readmitted to the same local hospital due to "apparently an attack of gallstones colic." Surgery to remove the gallbladder was recommended. However, his physician noted that because the decedent had a respiratory condition with coughing, it was advised to wait until the respiratory infection cleared. During that hospitalization, the decedent had an elevation in his white blood count to 14,300 (with 79% polys, 10% stabs, and 11% lymphs) indicative of infection. His gallbladder did not visualize after injection of 2 doses of gallbladder dye on two successive days, confirming the previously diagnosed nonfunctioning gallbladder. He was treated with an antibiotic while he was hospitalized and discharged two days later from the hospital; cholecystectomy was deferred again.

Third Hospitalization

The patient was readmitted two months later for the third time to the same local hospital. His physician noted that he "had blacked out and fell on the job and was brought in an ambulance complaining severely of chest pain, shortness of breath and seemed to be in acute emergency situation." "He was wet with sweat, he was apprehensive, very tense and nervous," noted his physician. He was diagnosed as having an acute coronary attack. His electrocardiograms were abnormal but not diagnostic of an "acute coronary attack." The decedent was treated with anticoagulants (heparin followed by coumadin) as well as other medications. Pulmonary embolism was not considered in the differential diagnosis.

During this third hospitalization, the patient had initially a normal white cell count (8000). Certain serum enzymes were elevated (alkaline phosphatase 155, LDH 345, and SGOT 258; these enzymes are derived from tissue cells, e.g., liver, lung, and muscle). His heart rate was slow at 39 times per minute (normal being 60–100). Three weeks later, his chest x-ray was reported as negative (normal). But his white blood count rose to 13,500 (normal below 10,000), and the serum enzymes showed only slight elevations in CPK and SGOT. The following day, the LDH was 415 and SGOT 465, being substantially elevated, indicative of some tissue cell damage.

The admission nurse's report noted that the "patient was admitted to the service of Dr. X complaining of shortness of breath, nausea and pain in the chest. Stated he has been nauseated for two or three days." He was given for pain morphine sulfate 1/6 grain and Vistaril 25 mg. Four hours later on the same day, the nurse noted that "the patient reports pain more severe and more in epigastric area than in chest. Dr. X here." The patient was given Norflex and Valium.

The next day, the Doctor's Progress Notes stated "less tenderness over gallbladder—surgery deferred." However, later that day the doctor performed a cholecystectomy. The physician described the gallbladder as "little" in the operative note. *There was no pathology report* of the gall-bladder removed by the surgeon.

The patient was given Demerol 100 mg and atropine 0.4 mg for preoperative medication. However, the same note then added that surgery was postponed and the patient was given orange juice and Jello. The dosages of Demerol and atropine were repeated four hours later and sometime thereafter the patient was taken to the operating room for cholecystectomy. He was returned to his room in good condition.

During the next three days the decedent was treated with an antibiotic (Polycillin). For pain, he received Demerol and then was switched to Levo-Dromoran. Vistaril was given for nervousness. The decedent had a large amount of drainage from a Penrose drain in his abdominal wound. Four days postoperatively, biliary drainage from the drain site was described as "moderate amount."

Over the next several days the patient continued to complain of not feeling well, and he had abdominal pain with intermittent nausea and large amounts of biliary drainage from his drain site. He was described as restless and unable to sleep. Nine days postoperatively, Dr. X visited the patient and shortened his drainage tube. Additionally, the patient was given an enema which was productive of a large amount of soft formed stool. The nasogastric tube was removed, diet was progressively increased, antibiotics and narcotics were continued, and the wound sutures were removed. On the tenth day postoperatively, he complained of feeling depressed, "terrible," and "intermittently nauseated."

Summary of Nurses' Reports

Admission day: Patient complained of shortness of breath, nausea, and pain in chest.

Day 2: States he feels good. No voiced complaints. Cholecystectomy was performed.

Day 3 (Post-op day 1): Restless; coughing and spitting small amounts of blood clots and mucus. Complains of being depressed; nervous and jumpy; temperature up to 101 degrees; not perspiring.

Day 4 (Post-op day 2): Coughing; restless; very nervous; temperature 104 degrees.

Day 5 (Post-op day 3): Very restless and nervous; very depressed; coughing (and) spitting mucus.

Day 6 (Post-op day 4): Very restless 8 hours; unable to void; amber-colored urine; appears concentrated.

Day 7 (Post-op day 5): Nervousness; states doesn't feel very well; complains of pain.

Day 8 (Post-op day 6): Complains of pain; states he has hurt all night; not feeling well.

Day 9 (Post-op day 7): Complains of pain.

Day 10 (Post-op day 8): Restless.

Day 11 (Post-op day 9): Patient very depressed today; all day and tonight (11:30 P.M.); very weak; temperature 99.4 degrees; pulse 80 times per minute and respirations 20 to 28 times per minute.

Day 12 (Post-op day 10): Tired; very depressed; temperature 98.4 to 102 degrees; pulse 86 to 106 times per minute; respirations 20 to 32 times per minute.

Day 13 (Post-op day 11):

1. 7:00 A.M.—complains of severe pain under left breast. Given Talwin 60 mg for pain with Vistaril 25 mg for restlessness at 7:05 A.M.
2. 7:30 A.M.—complains of severe pain in left chest; temperature 100.6 degrees; pulse 96; respirations 44 times per minute (which is rapid); blood pressure 92/80 mm of mercury. He was given Demerol 50 mg intramuscular for pain.
3. 9:25 to 9:45 A.M.—complains of severe pain in the left chest. He was given Sinequan (tranquilizer), Demerol 100 mg with Vistaril 50 mg intramuscular for pain.
4. 2:00 P.M.—complains of severe chest pain; again states it feels like muscle cramp; states pain is more severe. He was given Levsin with phenobarbital (an antispasmodic and anticholinergic drug) and Norflex (muscle relaxant), and Demerol 100 mg with Vistaril 50 mg for pain.
5. 4:00 P.M.—patient complains with chest pain. 5:45 P.M.—patient given Demerol 100 mg and Vistaril 25 mg for chest pain; patient says he can't stand the pain.
6. 8:00 P.M.—given 15 mg (1/4 grain) morphine for pain and a barbiturate, sodium amytol 3 grains (200 mg).
7. 10:30 P.M.—patient expelled large amount of flatus; complains of severe chest pain; patient's color pale; skin clammy; blood pressure 130/80. Given morphine 15 mg (1/4 grain) for pain.
8. 11:30 P.M.—restless, nervous.

Day 14 (Post-op day 12):

1. 1:45 A.M.—blood pressure 140/90; complains of pain under right breast. (This is the first notation that the right chest is now involved.) Morphine 15 mg (1/4 grain) given at 1:50 A.M.
2. 6:00 A.M.—severe pain under breast. Given morphine 15 mg again for pain. Temperature 100.2 degrees; pulse 96; respirations 24 times per minute.
3. 4:00 P.M.—complains of pain in right side of chest; given injection, for pain again. Temperature 101.6 degrees; pulse 116; respirations 22 times per minute.
4. 7:00 P.M.—more morphine 15 mg (1/4 grain) given for pain in the right side of chest.

Day 15 (Post-op day 13):

1. 1:45 A.M.—morphine 15 mg (1/4 grain) for pain in chest.
2. 4:00 A.M.—short of breath; nauseated; vomited moderate amount of mucus with bright blood, small amount; skin clammy; perspiring; temperature 99 degrees; pulse 100; respirations 24 times per minute.
3. 4:30 A.M.—morphine 15 mg (1/4 grain) with 50 mg Vistaril given for left-sided chest pain; very tense and upset; shortness of breath; pulse 132 times per minute; respirations 30 times per minute; blood pressure 140/110.
4. 7:30 A.M.—restless; slightly cyanotic (blue in color).
5. 12:00 P.M.—restless; temperature 100.4 degrees; pulse 100; respirations 28 times per minute.

Electrocardiograms were abnormal. They suggested a strain on the right side of the heart and/or ischemia, but there was no evidence of an acute heart attack, i.e., myocardial infarction.

Chest x-rays were abnormal on post-op day 14. The findings were compatible with bilateral pneumonitis and/or pulmonary embolism.

Discharge Summary

This was dictated and signed by Dr. X, who stated that the patient was admitted with nervous tension, gallbladder disease, and gallstone colic on day of admission. He underwent cholecystectomy on the second day of hospitalization due to chronic infected gallbladder. He described his postoperative course as "fairly normal" for the first few days, but "on the 7th day he developed pain in the abdomen and became nauseated. The next day he began to have a little fever and his Penrose surgical drain began to drain bile fluid. This became a massive drainage and he developed an inflammation of the abdominal cavity, peritonitis and bilious. It was considered that the most likely diagnosis was a biliary fistula from the common bile duct or possibly the cystic duct tie had come undone thus allowing the bile to spill out in the abdominal peritoneal cavity. He was running a fever, was very ill and was transferred to the second hospital by ambulance where Dr. Y could check him and possibly reopen him."

Fourth Hospitalization

After discharge from the local hospital, the patient was transferred in the afternoon to another hospital to be attended to by Dr. Y. He was admitted to the Intensive Care Unit of that hospital at 9:30 P.M. A brief admitting note on the Doctor's Progress Notes recorded the history of cholecystectomy two weeks previously, followed by persistent biliary drainage, fever, and probable biliary cutaneous fistula. The decedent had abdominal distention. Laboratory tests on admission revealed abnormal liver function tests; there was a decrease in serum albumin, increased total bilirubin, alkaline phosphatase, LDH, and SGOT.

A chest x-ray was taken on this hospital admission, which revealed patchy areas of atelectasis, pneumonitis in the left hilum, right lateral lung field, and left lung base. Prominent markings were seen at the base of the left lung and the possibility of atelectasis or poor aeration was also considered. The radiologist's impression was that both lungs had areas of atelectasis and/or pneumonitis in the left hilum, left lower lobe, and right lateral lung field. Abdominal x-rays were interpreted as showing distended loops of small bowel without gas seen in the distal colon, suggesting the possibility of colonic obstruction or postoperative ileus. The hospital radiologist stated, "If symptoms persist, a barium enema may be feasible to definitely exclude any obstruction in the lower colon."

On the evening of admission to the hospital, the patient was taken to the operating room by Drs. Y and Z for exploration. There was an area of bile peritonitis, which was localized to the site of the previous operation. The small bowel was distended but there did not appear to be generalized bile peritonitis, and therefore the entire abdomen was not explored. Drains were placed down to the foramen of Winslow and brought out through a separate stab wound in the right flank; the abdomen was closed with through and through retention sutures. The patient tolerated the procedure moderately well and was sent to the recovery room in fair condition.

The patient returned to the Intensive Care Unit on the second day of this hospital admission. His color was reported as better. His hemoglobin was 13 and his urine output was good. On the third day of admission, his blood pressure was good; his temperature was 101 degrees. On the morning of the fourth day, he became extremely apprehensive, and later that evening he suddenly became dyspneic and his blood pressure dropped to 0; he sustained a cardiac arrest and he could not be resuscitated.

Autopsy Findings

The most pertinent finding and immediate cause of death was a massive large saddle embolus starting within the right ventricle of the heart and passing through the pulmonary tract to the pulmonary arteries. The embolus was approximately 1/2 inch in diameter and was kinked and curled upon itself as it entered the lung, at the hilum, distributing throughout the upper and lower branches of the pulmonary arteries in the lung with massive infarction of both lower lobes in the posterior dependent surfaces of the lungs. Microscopic examination of the lungs showed considerable dilatation of the arterial blood vessel channels filled with emboli, both in large and smaller caliber vessels. On external and internal examinations, the lungs revealed anthracosis, marked acute congestion, edema, and multiple nodular focal areas of pulmonary infarction from embolization. It was stated that the source of the embolus was not identified but the caliber suggested the lower extremities. Since the decedent was a very large and obese man, it was extremely difficult to detect the source. The remainder of the autopsy was not remarkable. The preliminary pathologist's comment was, "The sudden and immediate cause of death in this individual was massive pulmonary emboli probably from the lower extremities." The decedent died at the age of 39 years from pulmonary embolism proven by autopsy.

CHAPTER 5

Spoliation: Record Retention, Destruction, and Alteration

Alan C. Hoffman, J.D., F.C.L.M.
S. Sandy Sanbar, M.D., Ph.D., J.D., F.C.L.M.

GOLDEN RULES

1. "In God we trust. All others must document." (JCAHO)
2. Thou shalt not tamper with medical records.
3. Practice to deceive and a tangled web thou shalt weave.
4. Errors should be corrected promptly once detected.
5. After a record is made, errors should be corrected or edited only by using the proper methodology.
6. Establish and implement policies for retention and destruction of medical records, including electronic or computerized medical records.

MEDICAL RECORDS

Medical records are legal documents and health care providers should be careful when creating and maintaining them. The medical record consists of more than just a patient's chart in that it can include bills, reports of laboratory tests, sundry procedures, and various radiological and other techniques, as well as old tests and/or results. Spoliation, i.e., alteration of medical records, is becoming a significant problem. Written, typed, or computer-generated words about a patient's medical history, chief complaints, physical examinations, nurses' notes, treatment, discharge instructions, and follow-up encounters frequently determine the outcome of a medical malpractice lawsuit. Some physicians or other health care providers may resort to written entries, even if they were changed, in order to "explain" or otherwise deflect liability for their medical negligence.

Malpractice attorneys know that evidence of spoliation of records in medical negligence actions can strengthen the client's case. Consequently, plaintiff attorneys are becoming more sophisticated in reviewing medical charts. They apply the mantra *"Assume nothing,"* and believe that record tampering is far too common to think that it does not happen in a malpractice case.

Jurors tend to believe physicians and what they see in black and white. Proof of altered records is a sure way to anger and alienate jurors.

45

CASE PRESENTATIONS

Case 1: Cut and Paste Entries. Anna Ware, a medical doctor, was hired to see and treat patients at the Bedside Clinic, which was owned by Charleton Hospital. There was a regular referral pattern between Bedside Clinic and Charleton Hospital, but there was no open disclosure that Bedside Clinic was owned by Charleton Hospital, and that Dr. Ware was in fact an employee of Charleton Hospital. Dr. Ware had a custom and practice of writing her notes when seeing a patient and putting those in the patient file.

At some point in time, while Bedside Clinic was still owned by Charleton Hospital, Dr. Ware as well as other doctors in Bedside Clinic changed their practice behavior and went to a dictation system. The doctors took notes in the office but in addition dictated after the patient left. When the notes came back, doctors cut and pasted the notes over the original handwritten note. This practice amounted to spoliation of evidence. The Bedside Clinic was owned and controlled by Charleton Hospital, and as such, JCAHO applied. Hospital records cannot be altered, changed, or amended except by drawing a line if there is an error, writing the word "error" next to the error, and signing and dating the changed entry. By pasting over handwritten records, a handwriting expert was unable to view the inks in the original records and the fibers to verify whether or not they were written by different pens at different times, and therefore the records were deemed altered.

The appropriate way to supplement the original handwritten entry was to cut and paste the typewritten entry underneath and initial the date on the entry as to when the cut and pasted entry was attached to the record.

Case 2: Destruction of Documents. Hospital Systems, Inc. controls a number of hospitals in its system including Cornucopia Hospital. Each hospital was required to have various hospital policies and procedures including departmental policies and procedures for the Department of Radiology, Laboratory Department, and others. One of the departments was known as a Transitional Care Unit or skilled nursing facility within the hospital. The skilled nursing facility had a Medical Director and the policies and procedures set forth criteria as to what doctors could admit to the Unit and what doctors were required to write on patients. The doctors had a general policy and procedure for record retention and destruction. Cornucopia Hospital did not follow its policies and procedures but destroyed thousands of pages of policies and procedures without any destruction log whatsoever. During the same period, Hospitals, Inc. had developed a series of systemwide policies including a systemwide policy and procedure for record retention and destruction, which was very specific and which by its terms covered all of its operating units and subsidiaries.

Cornucopia Hospital was a subsidiary hospital completely owned by Hospitals, LLC, which was owned and controlled by Hospitals, Inc. The latter also had other ventures including nursing homes and other community facilities and practices. Cornucopia Hospital failed to follow the systemwide policy of the hospital and failed to follow its own policy, albeit a policy that was different with regard to record retention and destruction.

Hospital policies may in some situations have a bearing on a physician's care. Because Cornucopia Hospital destroyed prior applicable policies, a defendant physician was not able to turn to the policy in a malpractice case relative to who was responsible for a patient in the Transitional Care Unit at a given point in time, based upon the hospital's policies and procedures.

DISCUSSION OF ISSUES

Errors should be corrected promptly once detected. After a record is made, errors should be corrected or edited only by using the proper methodology. The proper method is for the physician to draw a single line through the incorrect information without obliterating it. Then the correct information is recorded above, below, or beside the original incorrect data, and is initialed and dated. It is important to be able to read what has been edited or changed in the clinic or hospital records.

It is inappropriate to delete recorded information with correction fluid. Erasing, blotting out, or adding information at a different time than the original note was made are not appropriate ways to correct a record.

Definition of Spoliation

Spoliation is defined as the "intentional or negligent destruction, mutilation, alteration or concealment of evidence." An act of spoliation increases the likelihood that one party gains an unfair advantage in litigation. Spoliation of evidence may be committed by a party to a lawsuit, a party's agent or attorney, or even a nonparty. Spoliation arose in an effort to equalize the playing field in the judicial system as against an individual for not being able to present credible evidence to the fact finder.

Spoliation can include medical records, financial records, telephone records, billing records, pharmacy prescriptions, policies, and procedures as well as physical evidence, namely medical records, or mundane physical objects, such as hospital beds or medical equipment.

Common types of spoliation include adding to an existing record at some later date, the intentional placement of inaccurate medical information in the records, lack of information regarding the exact time of patient treatment by nurses, the recording of the same or constant vital signs (so-called "perfect vital signs syndrome"), the recording of treatment provided at a date *after* the patient has been discharged or transferred to another hospital or extended care facility, the omission of significant medical information or "fraudulent concealment," dating a record as if it were written at a previous date, the complete rewriting or retyping of part of the medical record (e.g., discharge summary), and hiding or destroying the medical record.

The Tort of Negligent Spoliation

A civil cause of action for negligent spoliation of evidence is available in at least four jurisdictions, including Florida, Montana, Illinois, and New Jersey. The elements of this tort are as follows: the existence of a potential civil claim; a legal and contractual duty to preserve evidence relative to that action; destruction of the evidence; significant impairment of the ability to prove the potential civil action; causation between the destruction of evidence and the impairment; and damages.

In most states that recognize negligent spoliation, the duty to preserve records arises only when the spoliator voluntarily undertakes to preserve the evidence, the spoliator enters an agreement to preserve, the other party has specifically requested that the evidence be preserved, or that a duty exists by virtue of statute, especially a relationship between the spoliator and the victim.

In order to protect and successfully perfect a prima facie case under a negligent spoliation theory, one must create a record from the moment the injury occurred. A simple request for evidence to be preserved is not enough. If one obtains a commitment from a defendant, it must be backed up in writing. The writing must state pursuant to the conversations of such and such date that the other party has agreed to preserve the instrumentality or the evidence. If an agreement cannot be fulfilled, then the alternative is to seek court protection through an order of protection to preserve evidence. If there is likelihood that evidence will be destroyed upon commencement of the lawsuit, an ex parte order of protection may be sought; however, one would have to demonstrate a probability of irreparable harm in order to succeed.

Spoliation of evidence may be committed by a party to a lawsuit, a party's agent or attorney, or even a nonparty. Most often, spoliation issues arise in the context of civil cases. However, spoliation of evidence may also arise in the context of a criminal case.

Intentional Spoliation of Evidence

Arizona, Indiana, Kansas, Michigan, and Minnesota have refused to recognize the tort of intentional spoliation of evidence. However, the plaintiff could pursue a claim under the tort of "fraudulent concealment."

A tort of intentional spoliation has been recognized in Alaska, California, Kansas, Montana, New Jersey, New Mexico, and Ohio. The elements of the tort of intentional spoliation of evidence include: the existence of pending or probable litigation involving the plaintiff; defendant's knowledge of the pending or probable litigation; intentional destruction or significant alteration of the evidence; intent to disrupt plaintiff's pending or probable lawsuit; destruction of the lawsuit caused by destruction or alteration; and damages.

Spoliation Detection Methods

A number of techniques have been used by forensic chemists, document examiners, ink-dating specialists, fingerprint specialists, computer experts, and DNA specialists to determine whether a document has been altered. Proof by such experts and specialists that medical records have been altered will not only increase the value of the case but also attack the general credibility of the witness who may have been involved in the spoliation.

The ink-dating specialist may prove that a certain entry in the medical record was made at a different time than the physician, hospital, or nurse claimed at deposition. The ink-dating technique can detect an alteration made with a different pen, determine the age of the document, or determine the age of the particular ink. The specialist can date ink in about 75% of lawsuits to within six months of use with reasonable scientific probability.

The methods of dating ink include the identification of a chemical date tag that is found in inks made before 1994, the utilization of chromatography to separate and identify the components of the ink, and comparison with known dated standards of the questioned ink. Infrared image converters or special lasers can detect ink of the same color used at different times. Inks luminesce differently and emit light, which can be photographed to make effective court exhibits.

Some reports of test results can be used on thermal paper, e.g., electrocardiograms, echocardiograms, fetal monitor strips, and others. These medical records can be examined using scientific techniques that make legible otherwise disappearing provider notes. Where notes are made directly in the medical record, they may produce an imprint on paper underneath, which is easily detected.

Other sophisticated methods utilized by both the plaintiff and defense attorneys include the recovery from the hard drive of computer-generated records and deleted entries with the use of highly sophisticated computer retrieval systems.

Implications of Spoliation

Defense attorneys dislike altered medical records, because they immensely complicate the defense. The statute of limitations may be tolled or extended. The trial may be bifurcated to try the allegations of spoliation separately from the rest of the trial. The value of the lawsuit is increased. The despoiler or wrongdoer is presumed at fault, unless the defense proves otherwise. There is a risk of punitive damages in certain states. The jury may become angry and unforgiving.

Types of Spoliation Remedies

"*Spoliation inference*" is the oldest and most common remedy, which is available in almost all jurisdictions. If a party to a lawsuit destroys, conceals, or fails to produce evidence under his control, the jury may infer that the evidence would have been unfavorable to that party. It is difficult to predict how a jury instruction on spoliation inference might affect the outcome of a case. The jury is not instructed to infer any specific fact, but only to infer that the evidence would have been "'unfavorable" to the party who destroyed it.

"Shifting the burden of proof" is employed in a number of courts to create a rebuttable presumption against the spoliator on those issues to which the destroyed evidence was relevant.

Other civil sanctions the court may impose upon the spoliator include the *exclusion of some of the spoliation's own evidence, monetary fines, and default judgment* (where the spoliator is the defendant on the underlying claim) or *dismissal of claims* (where the spoliator is the plaintiff).

Criminal statutes of a number of states prohibit the alteration, concealment, or destruction of evidence for the purpose of preventing availability and inhibiting judicial proceeding. The spoliation of evidence can carry with it a number of sanctions against the offending party or their attorneys.

Record Retention

The health care industry not only keeps medical records, it also keeps business records. Sometimes health and business information is combined. According to Section 1(c) of the Uniform Preservation and Business Act, business records include: books of accounts; vouchers; cancelled checks; payroll; correspondence records of sale; personnel; and equipment and production reports. While federal law does not define hospital business records, the federal adaptation of the Uniform Photographic Copies of Business and Public Records Act 28 U.S.C. 1732 defines business records as "any memorandum, writing, entry, print, representation or combination thereof, or any act, transaction; occurrence or event . . . in the regular course of business. . . ." Regardless of whether a particular health care record is called a business record, personnel record, financial record, or some other kind of record, keeping proper business records is crucial to the successful operation of a health care facility.

Under the Department of Labor, as an employer, health care providers must keep comprehensive payroll records for all employees.

Under the Equal Employment Opportunity Commission, entities subject to the Civil Rights Act must keep personnel, employment, and other records having to do with hiring, promotion, demotion, transfer, layoff, termination, pay, and selection of individuals.

Under the Equal Pay Act, employers are required to keep payroll records for at least two years in cases involving age discrimination. The Health and Administration Act requires that employee exposure and medical records be kept by the employers for 30 years.

The Food and Drug Administration does not specify a length of time for keeping of records of blood transfusions. The Department of Health and Human Services requires retention of many records and is responsible for specifying retention periods, including Medicare contracts and reimbursement records; providers of services must maintain sufficient financial records and statistical data to determine costs payable under Medicare.

Many federal and state statutes and regulations provide for a specific retention period. A statute of limitations does not itself discuss how long a hospital or medical entity should retain records.

It is important to know that while a medical practitioner or provider may be working in a facility such as a hospital, that provider is at the will of the facility or the hospital. Hospitals may fail to follow their own policies and procedures or fail to follow other guidelines with regard to record retention. In doing so, a medical provider is unable to rely on existing policies and procedures that existed at the time relative to certain things that went on in the hospital. When the records, policies, procedures, films, or other items are destroyed, a presumption is raised with regard to an inference that the records, policies, procedures, and other items contain something unfavorable to the party that lost them. While the medical practitioner may not be the one who has lost them, the medical practitioner for all intents and purposes may have been the one who could have relied upon them to exculpate him or her from a situation of malpractice but cannot do so because of the missing items.

From a practical standpoint, a medical practitioner will normally not criticize a co-defendant or another medical provider; however, when a plaintiff raises the issue of nursing records, it can be smeared against everyone. It is therefore important that a medical provider who is rendering care and treatment in a facility such as a hospital, long-term care facility, or a similar facility should seek a modification to the contractual agreement whereby the facility agrees to be responsible if *it* fails to maintain the records, policies, procedures, reports, scans, radiographic studies, and others in accordance with the existing policies and procedures either in the facility at the time, or in accordance with federal, state, or accrediting agencies.

Hospital records, especially in the medical-legal area, are among the most important types of evidence in lawsuits. Therefore, various records should be retained for at least a period equal to the statute of limitations even if other laws require a shorter period or there is no retention stated.

One of the areas in which spoliation can occur is the saving of body specimens, tissue samples, or radiographs. Most private pathology facilities and hospitals do not have the storage facilities to maintain an inventory of all materials, and many times they are not even considered.

Statutes of Limitations for Preservation of Evidence

Hospital, medical, and dental records should be retained for at least ten years, or as required by law. For example, in Illinois the statute of limitations for causes of action for breach of alleged duty to preserve evidence is five years.

Instruction to the Jury about Spoliation

It is difficult to predict how a jury instruction on spoliation may affect the outcome of a case. The jury is not instructed to infer any specific fact, only that the evidence would have been "unfavorable" to the party that has destroyed the evidence. A number of courts, perhaps in an effort to impose a more effective sanction, implore rebuttal presumption against the spoliator, shifting the burden of proof to the party to whose issues the destroyed evidence was relevant.[1]

Survival Strategy

Individuals responsible for health care business records, including hospitals and medical offices or other facilities, must regularly develop and monitor a records retention program in the regular course of business, evaluate the records, document the development of the retention program, and obtain the various and sundry approvals.

A health care entity must systematically develop a business records retention program that deals with all types of records and all types of media; creates retention and destruction schedules; obtains approvals for the program; performs day-to-day management of the program; and documents the programs.

In setting up a records retention program, the entity that establishes it must address all types of records including reproductions. Reproductions often have the same legal effect as the originals, so destroying only the originals does not accomplish anything. The retention program must also address "information copies" and similar copies.

Because all media have the same legal effect as a paper original, one must address all media, including microfilm and computer records. If the records manager can properly destroy an original, the entity does not need to keep copies in any media. If, however, the entity needs to keep a record, the records manager should consider whether good business practice dictates copying the original into an optical storage disk or otherwise preserving information more efficiently. The retention program should provide for the destruction of computer and other media as it does for paper records. If the original paper records are destroyed, then one must have a log as to how and in what course of business the records have been destroyed. It would seem very strange if one set of medical records in a hospital or clinic was destroyed out of sequence as compared to a normal aging, or when hospital records are recorded on an optical disk or microfilm and then destroyed. This could of course give rise to the presumption that there was something in terms of inks, paper, overwrites, or other things contained in the original that would not be preserved and could not be viewed on microfilm or digital copies. It must be remembered that a microfilm or digital copy once made will not allow a handwriting expert to analyze inks or look for pressure marks on a piece of paper or writing.

The records manager must determine how long to keep the records, based on federal and state statutes and regulations that provide for a specific retention. Once a record retention and destruction program is established, it is imperative that one obtains written approvals for the record retention schedule and procedure from the entity's chief executive officer, chief financial officer, compliance officer, legal counselor, and tax counsel.

Destruction of Records Including Medical Records

Keep a list of destroyed records that includes the patient's name and birthday, the date of the last visit, and the date the records were destroyed. The method of destruction must protect the confidentiality of this information, such as shredding or burning. Disposing of records in the trash does not provide adequate protection, and could lead to allegations of breach of confidentiality.

The time frame for the destruction of patient medical records begins from the date of discharge or from the date of outpatient/ancillary services rendered or the last date of treatment if there was an agency treatment.

FURTHER READING

Bell DA, *et al.*, *An Update on Spoliation of Evidence in Illinois.* 85 Ill. B.J. 530 (1997).

Claypoole RL, Ramey GQ, *Guide to Records Retention in the Code of Federal Regulations* (Diane Pub. Co., 2004).

Casamassima AC, *Comment: Spoliation of Evidence and Medical Malpractice.* 14 Pace L. Rev. 235 (1994).

Cotton CV, *Document Retention Programs for Electronic Records: Applying a Reasonableness Standard to the Electronic Era.* 24 Iowa J. Corp. L. 417 (1999).

Hancock WA, *Guide to Records Retention* (Business Laws, Inc., 1993).

Medical Records and the Law: An Illinois Guide to Medico-Legal Principles and Release of Information (Illinois Medical Record Association, 1994).

Palmer RG, *Altered and "Lost" Medical Records.* Trial (May 1999).

Record Retention Reference (Illinois Hospital and Health Systems Association, 1999).

The Sedona Conference, *The Sedona Guidelines: Best Practice Guidelines and Commentary for Managing Information and Records in the Electronic Age* (Sept. 2004).

REFERENCE

1. *Nichols v. State Farm Fire and Casualty Co.*, 6 P. 3d 300 (Alaska, 2000).

Medical Error Disclosure and Apology

S. Sandy Sanbar, M.D., Ph.D., J.D., F.C.L.M.

GOLDEN RULES

1. The medical concepts of mistake, error, and bad result require *medical* judgments, whereas the legal concepts of fault, negligence, and culpability are defined by *legal* standards.
2. Injured patients are willing to forgive, if the physician is upfront with them.
3. Medical mistakes do not trigger most malpractice suits, but rather "anger" over being spurned by caregivers after something goes wrong.
4. The great majority of malpractice claims arise from communication breakdowns.
5. Full disclosure not only improves the litigation climate but also encourages better safety practices.
6. In some states, apology laws shield doctors from legal liability for apologies. State law, however, does not protect a doctor's admission of error, a stumbling block to full disclosure.
7. The acceptance of full disclosure rests primarily with doctors, and to a lesser degree with lawyers and legislators.

Medical errors do happen and could be harmful indeed, and full disclosure of such errors is increasingly encouraged and favored. Indeed, patients have a right to full disclosure of adverse events caused by medical management. To do otherwise would constitute culpable deception.

Ethically, religiously, psychologically, and practically, the recognition of a wrong requires acknowledgment, acceptance of responsibility, and restitution. Culturally, apology may be a norm in some societies, e.g., Japan. The apology serves to restore harmony, heal some wounds, and promote equitable solutions.

Against this backdrop is a continuing struggle to find balance between two powerfully competing impulses—namely, the compelling urge to say "I'm sorry" on one hand and the unavoidable peril of legal liability.

The purpose of this chapter is to present the current state of affairs when confronting the complex task of walking a fine line between medical disclosure and apology on the one side and fear of admitting liability on the other.

Physicians are increasingly reaching out to patients and families to explain and apologize for medical errors. The physicians' responses to medical errors, including blunders, have generally been to duck and deny, which represents a longstanding and deeply entrenched policy of admitting no wrong. But the question arises as to whether it is in the best interest of physicians to never have to say "I'm sorry" to the patients who are adversely injured.

In general, the physician who is aware of having made a medical error should communicate that information to the patient. When it actually comes to disclosing the error, a number of questions arise such as: What is the state law regarding apology? What ought the physician do? How to do it? What to say? What not to say?

PURPOSE AND BENEFIT OF APOLOGY

When medical errors result from diagnostic procedures or treatment, an apology from the attending physician can be beneficial to both the patient/family and the health care provider(s). The purpose of the apology is to convey a human, compassionate, and empathetic response to the patient's misfortune. Such conduct by the physician is reasonable and ought to be supported within limits because it may be conducive to the patient's healing. Indeed, apology in the setting of medical errors is becoming increasingly acknowledged by states and codified in law.

Apology by a compassionate physician benefits the patient by easing the worry, decreasing anxiety, and alleviating confusion, thereby causing immediate and significant positive effects. Patients feel that some of their questions have been answered and are reassured by their doctor's continuing support.

An apology that is warm, sympathetic, and genuinely caring can be enormously comforting to a patient beset with both pain and uncertainties. It may result in some peace of mind and may decrease the recovery period.

The immediate benefit to the physician is a sense of relief that things are in the open. The physician who is sincerely able to say to an injured patient "I'm sorry" would feel ethically uplifted and gratified to salvage what may have been a friendly, longstanding, and respectful physician–patient relationship. Tangible and positive things begin to occur for the physician and the patient, spiritually, psychologically, and perhaps even legally. Some patients would not sue their physician if they receive full disclosure and an apology. On the other hand, the uninformed patient is more likely to seek litigation, and once the litigious process has been set, abandonment of the malpractice lawsuit by the plaintiff is less likely.

Of course, the apology may be extremely unpleasant, humbling, humiliating, and may be regarded as a stain on the physician personally and professionally. The apology may be misconstrued by the patient as legal weakness on the physician's part. It could be in conflict with the liability insurance contract. And it might be introduced as evidence of wrongdoing in court in a subsequent proceeding.

LAW OF APOLOGY
Voluntary Mutual Agreements

The physician and the patient may voluntarily enter into a mutual agreement to keep an apology confidential, thereby excluding its discovery and admissibility as evidence in a subsequent court action. Such confidentiality agreements are often limited by statutory provisions and, if the agreement serves to preclude a court from hearing evidence, it is often disregarded as contrary to public policy.

Common Law

At common law, an apology that admits fault is ordinarily admissible to prove liability. All statements made in the course of settlement negotiations, including an apology, can be admitted into evidence. Therefore, an apology can be admissible as evidence at trial, and an apology that is entered into evidence is considered to be an admission. There are two exceptions to the common law rule: first, apologies framed as a hypothetical are not admissible; second, apologies that are preceded by exclusionary words such as "Without prejudice to any of his legal rights, the defendant admits…" are also inadmissible.

Depending on the wording, an apology may be viewed by the court as an innocent expression of sympathy versus an overt, highly probative admission of wrongdoing. The choice of words becomes critical in distinguishing a mere apology from a clear admission of liability, as depicted in the following cases.

In *Greenwood v. Harris*,[1] the defendant doctor operated mistakenly on an "intra-abdominal tumor," which was an enlarged, gravid uterus. Postoperatively, the defendant physician reportedly said "… this is a terrible thing I have done. I wasn't satisfied with the lab report. She did have signs of being pregnant. I should have had tests run again. I should have made some other tests … I'm sorry." The Oklahoma Supreme Court held that it was not possible to interpret the defendant's statements other than an admission that the defendant failed to use and apply the customary and usual degree of skill exercised by physicians in the community. But in *Sutton v. Calhoun*,[2] the Oklahoma Supreme Court held that the defendant doctor's statement that he had made a "mistake" in cutting the patient's common bile duct at surgery could not be considered an equivalent of an admission of negligence.

In *Phinney v. Vinson*, the Supreme Court of Vermont concluded that an apology is *not* the automatic equivalent of legal liability for wrongdoing.[3] In *Phinney*, the plaintiff argued unsuccessfully that the apology alone was sufficient evidence of liability. In *Senesac v. Associates in Obstetrics & Gynecology*,[4] the Vermont Supreme Court held that an alleged statement by the defendant doctor to the effect that she had "made a mistake and she was sorry, and that it had never happened before" was not sufficient to establish breach of the standard of care.

Rules of Evidence

The rules of evidence, both federal and state, make it difficult for physicians to apologize to upset, disappointed, angry, or hurt patients, even though apologizing could be positively beneficial.

Under the Federal Rules of Evidence, which have been adopted by most states, overt admissions by the parties are admissible in court. Furthermore, an apology need not be an overt admission but merely a statement. In a malpractice lawsuit against a physician, what would conventionally be considered "hearsay" testimony by the family alleging that a nurse told them that the doctor was overheard to say, "I'm sorry that I chose that particular treatment," may be considered by the judge as an admission by a party-opponent. The judge has final discretion in matters of admissibility of hearsay evidence.

But an apology may be *inadmissible* as evidence if it falls under the definition of a subsequent remedial measure or under the rule on compromise and offer to compromise. To be inadmissible in court, the apology must be an integral part of the settlement negotiation, i.e., the apology as an admission of fault must occur during the course of settlement negotiations, and not merely during the business discussion.

Federal Rules of Evidence provide that evidence of furnishing, offering, or promising, to pay medical, hospital, or similar expenses occasioned by an injury, is *not* admissible to prove liability for the injury.

Finally, the Federal Rules of Evidence defer to applicable state law, in considering apology as admissible evidence or admission. The claim or defense shall be determined in accordance with state law. For example, mediation, which is an alternative dispute resolution method, is a well-established and effective method of barring apologies from admissibility, because state law provides that no evidence of anything said or admission made for the purpose of mediation is admissible in any civil action, and that all communications, negotiations, or settlement discussions between participants in the course of mediation remain confidential.

State Law Governing Apology

The physician, in some states, may express genuine remorse in apologizing to a patient without being exposed to legal reprisal. Apology laws have been enacted by some states to confer immunity on doctors and health care providers when they state apologies and offer expressions of grief. The statements and expressions will not be used against the physician in court. Some statutes specifically state that statements of concern, regret, and even acknowledgment of fault are not admissible as evidence in court against a physician in a subsequent lawsuit. The goal of the apology laws is to encourage a frank, comfortable, and open dialogue between physicians and their patients, without fear of recrimination. However, no state has enacted a statute that excludes from evidence an apology that admits fault.

The following states have passed apology, or so-called "I'm sorry" statutes, as of the date of writing this chapter: Arizona, California, Colorado, Florida, Georgia, Hawaii, Idaho, Illinois, Maryland, Massachusetts, Montana,

North Carolina, Ohio, Oklahoma, Oregon, Texas, Virginia, Washington, and West Virginia. Pennsylvania, Florida, and Nevada have passed laws mandating written disclosure to adverse events or bad outcomes to patients and families. Vermont has not passed an apology statute, but it has case law that provides immunity for doctors' apologies.

A typical example of an apology statute is the California Evidence Code 1160, which limits the exculpatory provision to sympathy and benevolence. It states that the portion of statements, writing, or benevolent gestures expressing sympathy or a general sense of benevolence relating to the pain, suffering, or death of a person involved in an accident shall be inadmissible as evidence of liability in an action.

In states without an "I'm sorry" statute, when a physician harms a patient, it would be considered prudent to apologize, with the approval of all parties concerned, including the hospital, risk manager, and liability insurance carrier.

SURVIVAL STRATEGY
Develop a Disclosure Policy

In 2001, the University of Michigan Hospitals and Health Centers (UMHHC) began acknowledging harmful mistakes and offering compensation to injured patients, and as a result the new policy saved the Health Centers $2.2 million a year in litigation costs. The Veterans Health Administration has adopted a disclosure policy as well.

The UMHHC (www.med.umich.edu/patientsafetytoolkit/disclosure/howto.doc) has developed guidelines pertaining to the disclosure of medical errors. The guidelines provide extensive suggestions for physicians and health care providers as to what to do before, during, and after disclosing errors, along with ABCDE reminders and techniques for delivering bad news in a good way. The ABCDE reminders are: Advance preparation; Build a therapeutic environment; Communicate well; Deal with the patient/family reactions; and Encourage and validate emotions.

Physicians ought to develop a written medical practice error disclosure policy that is adopted and added to the clinic policy and procedure manual. The disclosure policy should be provided for review by the liability insurance company and should be given to all employees to read. The policy ought to specify which errors are disclosed, who should be disclosing, and who to disclose to besides the patient. The UMHHC guidelines are briefly summarized. The reader is encouraged to read the complete guidelines.

1. *Before disclosing*, the guidelines provide that physicians acknowledge any self-deprecating emotions; approach the process of error disclosure with the attitude that it is the right thing to do; presume goodwill; and notify risk management personnel. The physician ought to preserve the confidentiality of patient information; inform fully the leaders of the clinical team; gather all the facts in the case; assemble documentation and be prepared to review the chart with the patient/family member; and determine who from the

medical team should have the conversation with the patient/family. Be prepared to have a conversation and prepare a script and role-play; be sensitive to the patient's ethnic culture; determine who should be present with the patient; be prepared ahead of time with answers; and consider thoughtfully the potential harm of disclosure to the patient/family. If the event is serious, a meeting should be arranged as soon as possible in order to brief the patient/family about what happened, the course of action, treatment, and follow-up.

2. *During* the disclosure, the UMHHC guidelines suggest that the conversation takes place in a private setting and that the physician be seated during the conversation. Everyone present in the room should be introduced. *The physician should avoid making a direct admission of fault at this stage.* The physician ought to ascertain what information the patient may already have; inquire how much detail the patient wants to know; and convey the information in simple terms and slowly, thereby minimizing distress to the patient, describing what happened and how it happened. In addition, the physician ought to identify and offer any support that is available to the patient and his/her family; inform the patient/family about patient follow-up and measures that will be utilized to prevent this error from happening again; and express appropriate regrets and concern about the patient/family. Periodically pause silently to allow the patient/family time to absorb the information and to ask questions.

3. Finally, *after* the disclosure, the UMHHC guidelines indicate that it is paramount how the physician responds after the bad news. The physician ought to acknowledge the patient's/family's emotions; avoid any appearance of insensitivity, and be empathetic and compassionate; and should not respond to anger with anger. The physician ought to be a good listener, welcome and value input from the family, help and assist the family get the information they seek, inform the patient/family who to contact for further questions or concerns and how they can be reached, and inform the patient/family that the matter will be followed up by the manager/supervisor/supervising physician, and that the institution will handle "systems" problems by referral to the Quality Program for review. The physician ought to arrange follow-up meetings to provide updates about the event to the patient/family. The physician need not panic if a lawsuit is threatened.

The Colorado Physicians Liability Insurance Company (COPIC) has developed the 3Rs Program Regarding Patient-Injury Situations:

1. Recognize.
2. Respond to.
3. Resolve.

COPIC (http://callcopic.com/cic/index.htm) offers to reimburse patients for out-of-pocket expenses (up to $25,000) that are not covered by their health insurance, and loss of income, $100/day (up to $5000). In addition, COPIC provides points toward premium discounts for physicians who are enrolled in the 3Rs Program.

PITFALLS OF APOLOGIZING

Some injured patients may want the truth to be told, and take some remedial action, including the filing of a malpractice lawsuit. Therefore, when apologizing, the physician should avoid admission of fault. Based on the apology, the patient may file a complaint with the state board of medical licensure and supervision, which may be investigated and brought for review by the administrative board. The apology may tempt a trial attorney to find fault by the physician and encourage the plaintiff to sue the physician.

The apology may also trigger a review by the liability insurance carrier, which may in some cases result in a higher premium.

The physician's error and apology might be brought to the attention of the Committee of Hospital Review of Adverse Outcome, and in very rare instances results in a summary suspension of hospital privileges. Medicare or Quality Reviews may be triggered.

A final decision that is adverse to the physician may be reported to the National Practitioner Data Bank.

CONCLUSION

The disclosure of medical error and apology is encouraged. The apology may be protected by state statutes. The physician ought to develop a disclosure policy and adopt it for the clinic, based on established models and guidelines.

The disclosure of errors is best in a private setting, considerate, honest, uninterrupted, and should avoid sweeping statements, written statements, and promises that cannot be kept. The disclosure ought to be documented in the patient's chart.

The patient ought to have some control during the disclosure. And the disclosure is not a one-shot deal; it usually involves multiple meetings, telephone calls, discussion of injury care, follow-up visits and consultation, and discussion of cost of care.

FURTHER READING

Rabow M, McPhee S, *Beyond Breaking Bad News: How to Help Patients Who Suffer*. West. J. Med. 171:260–263 (1999).

Moore S, *The Toughest Task: How to Break Bad News*. Excellence Clin. Pract. 3(2):1–3 (2002).

Liang B, *A System of Medical Error Disclosure*. Quality and Safety in Health Care 11:64–68 (2002).

University of Michigan Hospitals and Health Centers: www.med.umich.edu/
   patientsafetytoolkit/disclosure/howto.doc
The Sorry Works! Coalition (Legislation Initiatives & How to Set Up a Policy):
   www.sorryworks.net

REFERENCES

1. *Greenwood v. Harris* (1961, Okla.) 362 P. 2d 85.
2. *Sutton v. Calhoun* (1979, C.A. 10 Okla.) 593 F. 2d 127.
3. *Phinney v. Vinson*, 606 A. 2d 849 (Vt. 1992).
4. *Senesac v. Associates in Obstetrics & Gynecology* (1982) 141 Vt. 310, 449
A. 2d 900.

CHAPTER 7

Professional Liability Insurance

Michael S. Lehv, M.D., J.D., F.C.L.M.

GOLDEN RULES

1. Read thy policy.
2. Policy language shall be your guide.
3. Ambiguities shall be settled in favor of the insured.
4. Understand the definition of a claim.
5. Tail coverage shall turn a claims made policy into an occurrence policy.
6. Fraud and alterations may be punished by cancellation or noncoverage.
7. Nonpayment of premiums shall be punished by cancellation.
8. Gaps in coverage shall be punished by infinite financial jeopardy.
9. A time may come to pass when you must question your assigned attorney.

Almost all physicians maintain some form of medical professional liability insurance, commonly known as "malpractice insurance."[1] Unfortunately, the reality of current medical practice is that most physicians, over the course of their professional lifetimes, will need to use it. Because of the wide variety of policies and coverages, physicians and even lawyers often have difficulty in understanding the complexities. This chapter will present a detailed analysis of a typical medical malpractice policy that should assist the reader both in selecting a policy and using it in the event of a claim. At the outset, several common situations involving medical professional liability insurance will be presented, each posing several questions. The answers will be provided as the chapter progresses.

CASE PRESENTATIONS

Situation A. Dr. Thrifty carries a medical malpractice policy with $300,000/$600,000 coverage limits. During one policy year she settles three malpractice claims for $150,000, $400,000, and $200,000. Will Dr. Thrifty have any personal responsibility for these settlements? If she is sued a fourth time, what personal outlays might she have to make?

Situation B. Dr. Olde carries an occurrence medical malpractice policy and has paid the premiums yearly over the course of thirty years in practice. When he retires, he simply stops paying the premiums. If he is later sued for an incident that occurred while he was in practice, will he be covered?

Situation C. Dr. Modern carries a claims made medical malpractice policy with Company A and has paid the yearly premiums over the course of thirty years in practice. When she retires, she simply stops paying the premiums. If she is later sued for an incident that occurred while in practice, will she be covered? What if Modern doesn't retire but purchases insurance from Company B, will she have coverage for an incident while she was insured with Company A?

ELEMENTS OF A MEDICAL PROFESSIONAL LIABILITY INSURANCE POLICY

The Policy as a Contract

A medical malpractice policy is a form of legal agreement (a contract) between the physician (the insured) and the insurance company (the insurer). The contract (the policy) specifies that the insured will pay the insurer a premium in exchange for the insurer's agreement, in the event of a claim, to pay (1) the costs of any resulting verdicts or settlements and (2) the costs of investigating the claim and defending the insured. The policy is a special type of contract where there is usually little opportunity for one party (the insured) to bargain with the other (the insurer) over the terms of the contract.[2] Courts recognize this inequality in bargaining power and the fact that the insurer is totally responsible for the wording of the policy. When disputes arise over terminology that is considered ambiguous, the advantage is usually given to the insured.

Sections of the Policy

Most modern malpractice policies are written in language that is comprehensible to the average physician and always includes a section providing definitions of legal terms. Thus, doctors can and should read their policies, not just when they are notified of a claim, but also soon after they receive the policy. This is the only way to ensure that any misunderstandings are resolved before a claim is made, rather than at the time a claim is filed when the stakes are much higher.

Binder or Certificate of Insurance

Prior to the receipt of the actual policy, the physician will usually receive a "binder" or "certificate of insurance" that functions as a guarantee that the policy has been issued and that coverage is in place. It is not a substitute for a policy and only provides a portion of the information included on the "declarations page."

Declarations Page

The first or second page of a policy usually contains a Summary of Coverage, or as commonly known, the Declarations Page. This lists the name of the policyholder, the insured individuals and entities, dates of coverage including the retroactive date,[3] the limits of coverage, any deductibles, the type of policy, e.g., claims made, the insureds' medical specialty, and the premiums charged. Also included is a list of "endorsements," "riders," or "amendments" that function as modifications or addenda to the main policy. These may include additional benefits of coverage, additional exclusions of coverage, or changes in policy terminology required by law. If the policy includes an additional certificate of insurance, it is best to use that rather than the declarations page when providing proof of insurance to a hospital, managed care organization (MCO), or state medical board. The certificate typically does not contain personal information such as mailing addresses and premium charges.

The Insureds

Coverage is strictly limited to those physicians or entities listed on the declarations page. Most insurers automatically include the physician's corporate or business entity as a named insured for no additional premium. This is generally "shared" coverage with the physician when considering the maximum amount the policy will pay in the event of a claim. The same holds true for any nursing or administrative employees who are covered automatically along with the physician. Other professionals who are working with or employed by the physician, such as psychologists optometrists, chiropractors, or anesthetists, are not covered unless specifically listed as additional insureds on the declarations page. These individuals commonly carry their own liability insurance. Nurse practitioners and other paramedical personnel generally require specific policy coverage as named insureds. "Slot coverage" is coverage available to additional named insured physicians or paramedicals on an interchangeable basis.

When a solo practitioner purchases malpractice insurance, he or she is not only the physician being insured but is also the policyholder. When a medical group or other entity provides insurance to its employees or partners, the policyholder and insured may not coincide, although the policyholder is generally required to be a named insured.

Restrictions on Specialty

Medical liability policies are issued for a particular medical or surgical specialty. The physician's specialty determines, in good measure, the risk that the insurer is undertaking and is a principal factor in setting the premium rate. If a physician officially changes his or her specialty or materially alters his or her practice by performing procedures ordinarily considered to be within a different specialty, the company must be notified. Failure to do so may result in cancellation of the policy or noncoverage of the added procedures.

Restrictions on Territory

Another factor determining the insurer's risk is the physician's geographic location. There are often significant differences in both the frequency of claims and the size of jury award between various venues (cities, counties) within a state and between states. Premiums are based on a specific practice location and changes must be reported to the insurer.

Limits of Coverage

The declarations page traditionally specifies the policy limits as two numbers separated by a slash, e.g., $100,000/$300,000. The first number refers to the maximum amount the insurer will pay for any one claim and the second to the aggregate limit for all claims during the policy period, typically one year. Some policy summaries specify the policy limits separately as "per claim" and "aggregate," rather than using the traditional format. In determining the maximum amount the insurer will pay for "indemnification" (verdicts and settlements), the insurer's cost of defending the insured is usually in addition to the per claim limit. However, some policies will specify that defense costs are included in the yearly aggregate limit of coverage, meaning that they are subtracted from the aggregate limit when calculating the amount available for indemnification.

Turning to the questions posed in sample Situation A: Dr. Thrifty's first claim for $150,000 is less than her per claim limit of $300,000, so she would have no personal obligation. Unfortunately, her second settlement of $400,000 exceeds her per claim limit by $100,000, leaving her with that amount as a personal obligation. Her last claim of $200,000, although less than the per claim limit, brings her aggregate total to $650,000, which exceeds her policy limit for the year by $50,000. Thus, Dr. Thrifty would be personally liable for another $50,000 and perhaps for an additional sum if her insurer subtracts its defense costs from the aggregate limit it will pay for indemnification.

If there is a fourth claim against Dr. Thrifty, clearly she will be personally obligated for any verdicts or settlements because she has already reached the $600,000 policy period aggregate limit. Furthermore, once that limit is met, most insurers will not cover any new defense costs, leaving her completely on her own. Anticipating the plight of a physician in this situation, some insurers will mercifully provide a specified amount of coverage, for example, $25,000, in excess of the aggregate limit for defense costs associated with disciplinary actions instituted by a state medical board. For this or any other exceptions to apply, they must be stated in the policy.

POLICY TYPE

Occurrence Insurance

There are two broad categories of professional liability insurance, "claims made" and "occurrence." It is vital to thoroughly understand their differences. Until the first malpractice insurance crisis in the 1970s, virtually all policies were written as occurrence insurance. This means that once the policy is in force (i.e., premiums paid and the policy issued), any "occurrence" or "incident" during the policy period will be covered regardless of when the claim is made against the insured, even if the policy is no longer in force. Looking at Situation B, Dr. Olde would have coverage after retirement even though he is no longer paying any premiums. While on the surface this seems advantageous for the physician, there are some serious shortcomings inherent in occurrence insurance.

First, because the premiums paid in any particular year are paying for the defense and indemnification costs of a claim that might be made ten or twenty years in the future, it is difficult for the insurer to estimate both the future "frequency" and "severity" of the risks. Every physician is aware that as society in general, and patients in particular, become more litigious, the frequency of malpractice claims increases. Quantifying that increasing risk is difficult and so insurers must hedge their bets by charging seemingly disproportionately high premiums.

In addition to increasing claims frequency, with time, the costs of indemnification (size of verdicts and settlements) increase, as do defense costs. This is due to inflation, the tendencies of judges and juries to make larger awards, and the increasing complexity and duration of the litigation process. Again, estimating the severity (size) of future awards and settlements is difficult, leaving insurers with little choice other than to charge sufficiently high premiums. Finally, because occurrence insurance coverage continues even after the policy is no longer in force, any incident in any one year that develops into a claim, regardless of how far in the future, must be paid for by that single year's premium plus any investment returns the insurer earns on that premium.

When combined, these factors result in the second major problem with occurrence insurance: insurers may be forced out of business if their premiums are inadequate or their investments falter. When this happens, the insured is theoretically left without any coverage for incidents that occurred while the policy was in force but have not yet developed into claims. In reality, because insurance is regulated by the states, when a company fails, every state provides some protection to their insured physicians in the form of State Guaranty Association coverage discussed below. Furthermore, as we shall see, coverage for this period of time may also be available from other insurance, when and if the physician purchases another policy.

Another quirk of occurrence insurance is the possibility of legal arguments arising as to what constitutes the actual occurrence. If, for example, a surgeon insured under an occurrence policy leaves a sponge in the abdomen, is the date of occurrence the date when the surgery was performed, or when the patient developed symptoms and required treatment? If two different insurers provided coverage for each of the two possible occurrence dates, each may attempt to deny coverage by invoking the definition most favorable to its position. The eventual resolution of such disputes may require the physician to seek a "declaratory judgment" by a court. Such judgments only result in a determination of which insurer is responsible for covering the claim, not a resolution of the claim.

Claims Made Insurance

The second major category of professional liability insurance is the claims made form, which accounts for the vast majority of malpractice policies offered today. Under a claims made policy, coverage is available only for claims first made against the insured while the policy was in force and for which the original incident occurred while the insured was covered by that company and occurred no earlier than the retroactive date. Thus, there are two major conditions for a covered claim, the first being that the malpractice incident must occur either while the insured was a policyholder with that company or at some time after the retroactive date but before being insured with that company. The second condition is that the claim against the insured must be made while the policy is in force.

The retroactive date is one of the few policy provisions that can be negotiated with an insurer. Retroactive coverage, occasionally referred to as "nose coverage," means that the insured can acquire coverage for the period of time while they were insured by a different company or, for any reason, they carried no insurance. Although insurers may make a one-time charge for retroactive coverage, most frequently it is offered gratis as an inducement to purchase the policy when physicians are switching insurers.

Before granting retroactive coverage, some insurers will request a list of any incidents of which the physician is aware that might eventually lead to a claim. Moreover, most policies also include provisions that exclude from coverage incidents occurring during the retroactive period that the physician knew, or should have known, would result in a claim. Thus, it is in the physician's interest to disclose such incidents rather than risk a situation in which the insurer denies coverage. Physicians whose policies have been terminated by one company for reasons of high claims frequency, egregious instances of negligence, criminal activity, fraud, etc., may be unable to obtain retroactive coverage from a subsequent company.

The second major condition for a covered claim under a claims made form is that the policy must be in force when the claim is first made against the insured. Ordinarily, this is not an issue, but what happens when the physician wishes to switch insurers or retire? One option, discussed above, is for the physician to obtain retroactive coverage from the subsequent insurer. The other possibility, and the only one available when a physician retires, is to obtain "tail coverage," or as it is formally known, an "Extended Reporting Period Endorsement." Tail coverage is most commonly offered for an infinite time period but may only be available for a fixed period, such as three years. The company's terms for purchasing tail coverage are included within the policy and typically require the insured to apply for the coverage within a set period of time, e.g., 30 or 60 days. Tail coverage does not change the policy limits, the retroactive date (if any), or the basic rule that the incident that led to the claim must have occurred while the policy was in force or subsequent to the retroactive date.

Most insurers impose a significant charge for tail coverage, usually one or two times the cost of the current renewal premium. The reason for this is that purchasing infinite tail coverage essentially converts a claims made policy into an occurrence policy with all the attendant difficulties the insurer encounters in predicting future risks and costs. In some cases, insurers will offer a tail coverage deductible that is applied to any defense and/or indemnity costs once a claim is made. As a courtesy, most insurers will not charge a retiring physician who has been insured with the company for a sufficient period of time, usually three or five years. Likewise, commonly no charge is made to physicians who become disabled or to the estates of physicians who die. If a physician who is disabled or retired resumes practice, they must purchase a new policy.

Many, if not most, claims made policies currently specify that coverage is afforded only when the claim is first made against the insured *and first reported* to the company while the policy is in force. The word "claim" is always defined within the policy and usually includes the actual notification of a lawsuit, a letter from a patient's attorney to the physician, the voluntary reporting of an incident by the physician to the insurer, or the filing of a claim with the insurer by the patient. "Reporting" a claim means notification of the insurer by the insured that a claim against the insured has been made. A standard requirement for coverage is that the physician promptly report any claims or significant incidents to the insurer. Failure to do so may compromise the insurer's ability to investigate the incident or to later defend a claim. Some policies place a particular time limit on reporting after which the insurer will no longer provide coverage, but usually the word "promptly" suffices, implying "as soon as possible."

A legal issue can arise if the claim is made against the insured very late in the policy period and the insured is unable to notify the company before the expiration of the policy period. This could occur, for example, at the end of the calendar year over a long New Year holiday weekend or if the physician is on vacation and does not see the notification of a lawsuit until after the policy is no longer in force. If the claims made policy is being renewed or tail coverage has commenced, there is no issue because the report can still be made in compliance with the policy provisions. However, if the physician is switching to a new insurer with retroactive coverage, or for some reason is not purchasing any insurance, the questions respectively become: (1) which insurer is responsible and (2) is there any coverage? Some courts have ruled that the policy language controls and that the report must be made within the policy period even if doing so is a practical impossibility. The majority of courts considering the issue, however, have ruled that regardless of the policy language, the insured has a "reasonable" period of time after the claim is made to report it to the insurer, even if the policy is no longer in force.

Examining now Situation C, if Dr. Modern simply fails to renew her policy without obtaining tail coverage and she is then sued during retirement, she will be personally responsible for the claim, as the policy would not be in force when the claim was made. If she purchases insurance with Company B, to maintain coverage for incidents that occurred while she was covered by Company A, she must either have purchased tail coverage from Company A or have purchased retroactive coverage from Company B.

OTHER POLICY PROVISIONS

Deductibles

Insurance deductibles are imposed or offered for a variety of reasons. Deductibles have a strong deterrent effect on the filing of claims, particularly in the case of property or automobile insurance where insureds may methodically calculate their potential losses or savings, factoring in the cost of the deductible. In the context of health insurance the deterrence effect is subtler. Obviously, deterrence is not a factor in the case of medical malpractice insurance because a claim must almost always be filed with the insurer. In this context, deductibles serve primarily to reduce the insured's premium costs or to defray the insurer's defense and indemnity costs.

Voluntary Deductibles

These are deductibles that the insured elects to pay in exchange for a lower premium. They may be structured as fixed amounts, for example, $5000, or as a percentage ("quota share") of the total costs to be defrayed. The amount of the deductible may be applied only to any indemnity payments or as a first dollar offset to defense costs and indemnification. When applied only to indemnity payments (verdicts and settlements), there is no cost to the physician unless a payment is made. When applied to defense costs, the physician's obligation begins immediately upon the insurer's commencement of an investigation and defense of the case. The insured may be billed periodically and must pay promptly to avoid cancellation of the policy. If any unsatisfied deductible amount remains after payment of defense costs, it is then applied to any indemnity payments that must be made.

Deductibles are usually applied on a per claim basis during any one policy period, although some policies may thoughtfully provide a limit on how many times the deductible must be paid (e.g., three). Because physicians with high voluntary deductibles may be reluctant to settle a case, some policies that otherwise do not impose compulsory settlements on the insured may do so when there is a specific deductible amount.

Involuntary Deductibles

Insurers may impose deductibles on a physician as a condition of issuing the policy. This may occur when the physician has a history of incurring multiple small nuisance claims or where the procedures being performed tend to generate such claims. Usually these deductibles will apply on a first dollar basis to defense costs. If there are both voluntary and involuntary deductibles, both must be paid. In addition to involuntary deductibles, premium surcharges may be imposed on a temporary basis as a result of individual risk factors such as an unfavorable claims history or the performance of high-risk procedures.

Definitions of Terms

All policies provide a section that defines a set of legal terms as they are specifically used within that policy. The definitions are not necessarily dictionary definitions but are legally binding when used elsewhere in the policy.

Insuring Agreement

Another policy section sets out the actual "Insuring Agreement" that specifies the conditions under which the insurer will provide coverage and the items it will cover. This section also explains what the insurer considers to be a valid claim against the insured, the extent of its obligations to defend the insured, and a detailed explanation of when a claim is covered. These definitions vary considerably depending on the insurer and physicians are strongly encouraged to thoroughly read this section of their policy to appreciate the precise instances when they must notify the insurer of a claim.

Exclusions

There are two basic classes of exclusions: (1) those that are listed in a section that appears in every policy and which may be termed "standard exclusions" and (2) those that are specific to a particular individual or practice specialty and are appended as endorsements.

Standard Exclusions

Malpractice policies typically have a section devoted to a listing of the standard exclusions. The general rule is that defense and indemnification coverage is available only for acts rendered in the course of a professional service. Thus, if a physician provides nonprofessional spa services in the same location as his office, any incidents arising out of that enterprise would not be covered. Almost all policies exclude indemnification for intentional or criminal acts including sexual misconduct, drug trafficking, defamation, fraud, unlawful discrimination, antitrust violations, and false imprisonment. Many policies, however, will cover the defense costs associated with such claims, in some instances up to a specified limit. However, these provisions usually do not include the defense of any related criminal charges. Whether there is indemnification for punitive damages depends upon the policy provisions and the laws of the state where the policy was issued. In some policies, psychiatrists accused of false imprisonment by patients who believe they have been wrongfully committed to an institution may be granted coverage.

An important exclusion in most policies is that made for any contractual agreements a physician undertakes in agreeing to MCO "hold harmless" or indemnification clauses. These clauses may create an obligation for a physician to indemnify the MCO not only for the physician's acts but for the MCO's acts as well. As liability insurers are unlikely to include a MCO as a covered insured via the physician's policy, the physician's only options are to negotiate with the MCO for removal or modification of the offending clause, or to simply not sign the contract. Less clear is whether a physician's gatekeeper duties in a MCO are covered by his policy absent a written exclusion. When there is any doubt, the physician should discuss the issue with his insurer and obtain a policy endorsement authorizing such activity.

Some insurers include practice restriction in their list of exclusions. These may be quite detailed, voiding coverage for the use of non-FDA-approved drugs, liquid silicone, chelation therapy, or even amphetamines for weight reduction. There may be restrictions on specific procedures such as bariatric surgery, suction lipectomy, or obstetrical services rendered by general practitioners. Other restrictions may be more general, such as limiting office surgery to procedures that the physician had been credentialed to perform in a hospital. These specific restrictions are in addition to the implied restrictions inherent in the policy being issued for a physician's practice in a particular specialty, for example, neurosurgery or internal medicine.

Specific Exclusions

These are exclusions appended to the policy in the form of endorsements and usually limiting a physician's scope of practice. For example, an ortho-pedist with a history of back surgery claims may be excluded from perform-ing back surgery. Endorsements may prohibit the performance of a newly developed procedure, e.g., robotic surgery, until the surgeon obtains certi-fied training in the procedure. Other restrictions may void coverage for extensive office surgery unless the surgeon's facility is accredited.

Additional Benefits

Policies usually include a section listing other benefits the insurer automat-ically provides beyond defense and settlement costs. These may include the insurer's administrative expenses or expenses the insured may incur in the course of their defense, for example, travel, lodging, and lost time from practice to attend legal proceedings. The insurer is also usually responsible for the payment of any bonds for the release of attachments secured by the claimant and for any court-imposed interest on judgments.

DUTIES UNDER A MEDICAL PROFESSIONAL LIABILITY INSURANCE CONTRACT

Duties and Rights of the Insured

The insured's most basic contractual obligation is the payment of premiums when due. If payment is delayed, the insurer may consider it equivalent to a notice to cancel. The insurer, or its agent, will typically send a ten-day notice as commonly required by state law, indicating that the policy does not have a grace period and that payment must be received by a specific date to avoid cancellation. If the policy is claims made, the notice may include an offer to provide tail coverage for a specified premium. Ignoring notices of premiums due or cancellation without the insured obtaining tail coverage may lead to gaps in coverage and eventually place the physician in financial jeopardy.

Malpractice policies also contain a section outlining the insured's obliga-tions. The insured always has a duty to inform the company of any changes in their practices, e.g., part-time to full-time, change in specialty, addition of an office operatory, addition of new partners, or changes in the practice's business model. It is essential that the insurer be informed of any new office locations, and in particular of any changes in practice territory. Any of these changes may require a different premium and/or an endorsement to the policy. The policy may also require the physician to notify the company of any disciplinary actions by a state medical board or health care facility.

There also may be an exclusion of coverage for any incidents that occur while the physician's license has been revoked or restricted.

In the event of an actual or potential claim, the physician is obligated to provide the insurer with all pertinent information as defined in the policy. The policy will describe what incidents constitute a claim. It is essential that the insured provide this information as promptly as possible before any relevant evidence is lost or destroyed. It is also vital under a claims made policy that every effort be made to notify the company during the policy period in order to be in technical compliance with the contract provisions. The insured has a continuing obligation to cooperate in the company's investigation, discussions with attorneys, and attendance at depositions and other legal proceedings. The company will generally require the insured to assert their rights against any individual or entity who may be liable to the insured for any damages related to the claim, for example, another physician involved in the underlying incident. Any damages collected must be returned to the company when the company asserts this "right of subrogation."

Under no circumstance should the insured contact the patient, plaintiff, or opposing attorney, nor should the insured make or volunteer any payments or incur any expenses without the advice and consent of the insurer. The insured is generally considered to be the primary client of the attorney assigned by the insurance company. However, the attorney has a secondary relationship with the insurer and if a conflict arises, it may be advisable for the physician to secure the services of his own attorney. This is particularly true of situations in which the potential damages may exceed the insured's coverage limits, where there are questions about whether a claim is within the policy's scope of coverage, or where the company is also providing coverage to co-defendants.

Consent to Settle

At some point in the policy, the insurer will state its rule on settlements. These are legally binding agreements between a claimant (an actual plaintiff or a patient who has not yet filed a suit) and the physician, where the claimant accepts a monetary payment in exchange for agreeing to pursue no further legal action. Most physician-owned insurance companies will not settle a claim without the physician's consent. Commercial carriers, on the other hand, may include a clause that compels the physician to agree to settle when "deemed expedient." The problem with such clauses is that a settlement must be reported to the National Practitioners Data Bank (NPDB). Insurers generally have a right or even a legal duty to negotiate a settlement even though the physician may not accept it. They also have the right, but not the duty, to file an appeal in response to any adverse outcome in court.

Duties and Rights of the Insurer

The primary duty of the company is to provide the insured with an investigation and defense of the claim, and to provide indemnification in the event of a verdict or settlement. Generally these duties remain even if the insured becomes insolvent or declares bankruptcy. Although insurers are usually free not to renew a policy due to adverse experience with an insured or for any other reason, the circumstances under which they may cancel a policy typically are listed in the policy. Chief among these reasons are fraud or misrepresentation in obtaining the policy, the insured's commission of a criminal act that increases his risk as an insured, e.g., patient abuse or molestation, and egregious or intentional acts of negligence.

Insurers usually reserve the right to inspect a physician's practice including the physical premises, books, and records. These inspections are performed in the context of determining the suitability for offering or renewing insurance. They are not official safety, health, or accreditation inspections.

Under federal law, insurers are required to report all judgments and settlements made on behalf of the insured to the NPDB. Depending on the state, there may also be an obligation to report payments (usually those exceeding a prescribed amount) to state licensing authorities.

OTHER FORMS OF PROFESSIONAL LIABILITY INSURANCE

Self-Insurance

The concept of not carrying medical malpractice insurance and instead "self-insuring," is commonly termed "going bare." This requires that the physician post a bond or letter of credit as required by applicable state statute, restructure finances to shield assets, and inform all patients that he carries no professional liability insurance. The advantages of this arrangement are that the physician avoids paying insurance premiums and also becomes a less inviting target for malpractice litigation.

The shortcomings, however, are generally overwhelming. Many states require liability insurance as a condition of licensure, most hospitals require it as a condition of staff membership, and most MCOs require it for participation. Furthermore, few states provide the necessary homestead exemptions and other protections necessary for securing assets, courts generally take a dim view of protection schemes, and transfer of assets to a spouse carries the obvious risk of divorce. The physician also becomes an undesirable professional partner as his insured colleagues and hospitals automatically become veritable "deep pockets." Finally, self-insurance is viewed by many as being unethical, in that seriously injured patients may be deprived of any real means of compensation.

Despite these negatives, going bare has become commonplace in southern Florida, spurred by a confluence of unique factors including extraordinarily high malpractice premiums, favorable homestead and asset protection laws, licensure statutes facilitating self-insurance, and a critical mass of physicians willing and able to practice without third-party reimbursement. Many hospitals have amended their by-laws to accommodate these physicians and both the public and organized medicine have seemingly acquiesced to the trend. Nonetheless, there is little reason to recommend self-insurance to the vast majority of physicians practicing elsewhere in the country, and it remains to be seen what the long-term outcome will be in southern Florida. So far, physicians facing malpractice judgments and unable to pay them have either lost their licenses or been forced to agree to long-term payment plans.

State Guaranty Associations

Every state has a State Guaranty Association that protects the interests of the insured clients of defunct insurance companies. The funding comes from compulsory fees paid by insurers. When a company fails, the association "stands in the shoes" of the insurer. Any insured physician who has been sued may submit a proof of claim form to the association. The association then attempts to settle the claim or defend it in court. The major issue for physicians is that there is a statutory limit on the amount the association will contribute toward settlement or adjudication of the claim, e.g., $300,000. This potentially leaves the physician with personal exposure for any amount above the association's maximum. Fortunately, in the vast majority of cases, plaintiffs' attorneys recognize the difficulty of securing a judgment against a physician in this situation and most cases are closed without any payment by the physician.

SURVIVAL STRATEGIES

1. Without reading the actual malpractice policy, the physician cannot comply with its provisions. Carefully read through the policy and any accompanying documents as soon as they are received. Likewise, read any subsequent correspondence, particularly any endorsements, riders, or amendments. Leaving this to a time of high emotional stress after a claim is received places you at a major disadvantage.
2. Keep a copy of the policy readily available for reference.
3. Pay premiums immediately upon receipt of an invoice. Payments should be mailed using a trackable service such as FedEx so that receipt can be verified and proven.
4. Be sure that your policy limits comply with any hospital or state licensing authority regulations. Provide a certificate of insurance, if available and acceptable, rather than a copy of the declarations page.
5. Give careful consideration to whether your policy limits, including the yearly aggregate limit, are realistically in line with your previous record of claims and the risks inherent in your specialty. If you have a clean history of claims, consider the use of a voluntary deductible to lower premium costs.
6. In the event of a claim, precisely follow the procedures for notification as prescribed by the policy, including immediate reporting.
7. Preserve all physical evidence, records, and photographs that are in any way related to the claim and in accordance with the insurer's instructions.
8. Do not destroy any evidence despite it being adverse to your case. Do not alter any records in even the most innocent fashion,

including the addition of signatures. If there is any question, consult with the insurer. Evidence of record alteration makes any case difficult, if not impossible, to defend and may lead to cancellation of the policy.

9. If you are switching insurance companies, be sure that there is no coverage gap. This means that for a claims made policy you must either have tail coverage from your current insurer or retroactive coverage from your new company. Verify that you have received either an extended reporting endorsement for tail coverage or that your new policy specifies the correct retroactive date.

10. If you are contemplating retirement, investigate any potential insurers' rules for automatic tail coverage. A low number of required renewals at a slightly higher premium may outweigh slightly lower premiums with expensive tail coverage.

FURTHER READING

AMA, *Medical Professional Liability Insurance: The Informed Physician's Guide to Coverage Decisions* (1998), available to AMA members at http://www.ama-assn.org/ama/pub/category/4583.html (as of Jan. 30, 2006).

Johnson LJ, *Go Bankrupt? Go Bare?* Med. Econ., June 6, 2003, available at http://www.memag.com/memag/content/printContentPopup.jsp?id=111419 (as of Jan. 30, 2006).

Borfitz D, *Malpractice: Is Going Bare the Only Option?* Med. Econ., Mar. 21, 2003, available at http://www.memag.com/memag/content/printContentPopup.jsp?id=111314 (as of Jan. 30, 2006).

Langley v. Mut. Fire, Marine and Inland Ins. Co., 512 So. 2d 752 (Ala. 1987). This case is illustrative of the complexities in medical malpractice insurance litigation.

NOTES

1. Although this term is viewed by some as having a pejorative connotation, we will use it here as an acceptable alternative.

2. The legal term for this type of contract is an "adhesion contract" as one party is forced to adhere to its terms.

3. The retroactive date is discussed later in the chapter under claims made insurance.

The Role of Personal Counsel in Malpractice Litigation

Augustine S. Weekley, Jr., M.D., J.D., F.C.L.M.

GOLDEN RULES

1. Malpractice lawsuits happen.
2. Malpractice insurance does not automatically protect your personal assets.
3. Almost always, the insurance company retains the decision regarding settlement or trial.
4. The health care practitioner can lose protection by failing to follow the terms in the insurance contract.
5. The guidance of a knowledgeable personal attorney may be helpful in dealing with a medical malpractice lawsuit and protecting personal assets.
6. Not every interaction with patients is covered by your professional liability policy.
7. **Read your policy**.

The malpractice insurance company appoints and remunerates its own defense counsel, without physician approval. What is the role of the personal or private defense counsel, hired by the physician?

CASE PRESENTATION

Dr. Goodson was pleasantly tired, not exhausted. It had been a long day at the hospital and his office where he practiced obstetrics and gynecology with his one partner. His wife was tidying up after one of those rare dinners where all the family was present: his wife, his two pre-teens and the baby. They were happy, and getting ready to enjoy the holidays, in their own ways. After reading for a few minutes, it was time for the doctor to wish all goodnight and retire early.

Shortly after midnight, Dr. Goodson received a call from his answering service, asking him to call one of his patients, Mary L., and giving him her number. The answering service person said that Mary was reporting vaginal bleeding. He remembered the patient well, as he had delivered her other two children, now about 2 and 4 years old. This would be her third, and she had advised that it would be her last. Dr. Goodson called his patient, and after a brief discussion, advised her to go immediately to the emergency room at the town's only medical facility. He dressed quickly, and arrived at the hospital about the same time as his patient. They spoke briefly and he ordered her taken immediately to the delivery suite, where he examined her and thought that he could hear faint fetal heart tones. He had earlier asked the nursing supervisor to summon the surgical crew and the obstetrical resident in anticipation of an emergency cesarean section, but they had not yet arrived.

Dr. Goodson connected the fetal monitor and quickly recognized severe fetal distress. An emergency room nurse had inserted a Foley catheter, and he again called for the obstetrical resident to come to the delivery suite stat to assist in the surgical procedure. The anesthesiologist slept in the hospital, and he was immediately available, arriving shortly after the patient. Dr. Goodson again spoke briefly with the patient, advising her that in an attempt to save the baby, he would have to perform an emergency cesarean section, and she readily agreed. He then took a moment to advise her husband who was in a nearby waiting room and began to change into his scrubs. Meanwhile, the OB resident was scrubbing and would shave, prepare, and drape the patient as soon as she was asleep.

During the induction of anesthesia, the delivery team arrived, and quickly began setting up appropriate instruments. As soon as Dr. Goodson was scrubbed, gowned, and gloved, surgery began. At the time of the initial incision, there was no fetal activity or cardiac activity noted on the monitor. Dr. Goodson delivered the baby quickly, who was limp. The doctor attempted to resuscitate the baby.

The doctor also summoned the pediatrician on call, and the in-house hospitalist to assist. Despite prolonged efforts, and all reasonable measures, resuscitation failed. Death of the baby occurred at approximately 3:30 A.M.

Meanwhile, Dr. Goodson had ordered blood after delivery of the baby in an effort to deliver the placenta, which proved to be the source of bleeding secondary to placenta accreta. He also elected to perform an emergency transperitoneal supracervical hysterectomy, which he rapidly performed, after packing off some distended bowel. The patient received two units of blood during surgery. However, the doctor believed that the patient had lost four or five units of blood, so he started additional blood during the rapid closure of the abdominal wound. After completion of surgery, the patient's blood pressure was in the lower limits of normal in the recovery room.

When Dr. Goodson spoke with the patient's husband, Mr. L. was obviously distressed, but seemed to understand the circumstances.

The patient did well for three days. Prior to her discharge on the fourth day, the patient spiked a temperature of 102.6°F. Dr. Goodson cancelled the prospective discharge and saw the patient about four hours later on his regular hospital rounds. There was no evidence of thrombophlebitis, but she had a few rales in both bases, so Dr. Goodson ordered a chest x-ray, throat and sputum culture, deep breathing exercises, frequent coughing, and intermittent positive pressure breathing with a mucolytic aerosol.

Later that night, Mary L. again spiked a temperature, this time to 104.2°F. The nurse notified Dr. Goodson, who ordered a blood culture, and antibiotics added to Mary L.'s IV, and said that he would see her in about two hours, before his 7:30 A.M. case.

Dr. Goodson was surprised when he examined Mary L. that morning. Her abdomen was distended, tympanatic, and quite tender diffusely. He changed her abdominal dressing, and the wound appeared clean and dry. Goodson ordered a nasogastric tube placed on low suction, a blood count, blood culture, urine culture, and a surgical consultation.

After his morning cases, Dr. Goodson saw Mrs. L. again at about 11:00 A.M. She was more comfortable, had received some pain medication, and she was less distended. There was still diffuse abdominal tenderness, however, and her white blood count was just over 25,000, with a shift to the left. The other blood studies were normal, including the electrolytes ordered the day before. There was moderate basilar infiltrate reported on the chest x-ray.

The surgeon ordered another chest film and a flat and upright film of the abdomen, both stat. The radiologist's telephone report again showed some basilar infiltration and free air under both diaphragms, with some intestinal air fluid levels and the possibility of extraluminal loculations. Dr. Goodson did not think this was unusual as a secondary consequence following the laparotomy and hysterectomy.

The surgeon's note was not so reassuring, however. He raised the possibility of some type of septic intra-abdominal process. Dr. Goodson could not understand how this could happen, as the hysterectomy, though somewhat difficult because of the uterine size, went smoothly.

Mary L.'s course over the next 36 hours was "stormy." She underwent an exploratory laparotomy. One of the closing sutures had penetrated the distal ileum, and there was widespread peritoneal contamination. Dr. Goodson treated the peritonitis with peritoneal toilet and intensive antibiotic therapy. The patient continued to have a stormy course, which included multi-organ dysfunction. Dr. Goodson discharged the patient 11 days after her second surgery.

Six days after her discharge, Mary L. re-presented to the emergency room with abdominal pain and distention, nausea, and vomiting. X-rays showed multiple areas of loculated fluid within the abdominal cavity and bilateral basilar atelectasis. Her temperature was 103.4°F, and she was severely dehydrated. The patient received supportive treatment in order to improve and get her in satisfactory condition for surgery, but over the next 12 hours Mary L. developed multi-organ failure and in spite of heroic resuscitative measures, expired on the evening of the third post-admission day.

Despite Dr. Goodson's efforts to console Mr. L. and the family, they were not as understanding as they had been after the fetal death.

Approximately 90 days later, Dr. Goodson received a notice from a plaintiff's attorney, and a request from a plaintiff's attorney to forward a copy of his office records concerning the deceased Mary L. Dr. Goodson immediately notified his medical malpractice insurance carrier with whom he maintained a $250,000/$750,000 policy. The insurance carrier advised Dr. Goodson to send the records, and to open a separate file for correspondence regarding the case. He sent the office records within the week.

Approximately one month later, Dr. Goodson received another letter from the plaintiff's attorney advising that he would be filing a medical malpractice case against Dr. Goodson for the benefit of the husband and the two minor children. The presuit amount demanded was $5,000,000, with the $1,000,000 for the emotional pain and suffering, and loss of consortium of the husband, and the other $4,000,000 to be divided equally among the children for their damages, welfare, and loss of their mother. The attorney also warned that should this matter go to trial, the amount demanded would be far greater.

Dr. Goodson forwarded the letter to his insurance carrier. What else should he do now?

RELATIONSHIP BETWEEN PHYSICIAN AND LIABILITY INSURANCE COMPANY

State statutory and common law (decisional) govern the relationship between insurance companies and their insured. Therefore, the wisdom and the economic feasibility of hiring personal counsel by a health care professional who is a defendant in a malpractice action will vary from state to state.

General Principles

Certain general principles, however, can be set out for guidance. Certain rules can be developed as guidelines for the majority of states, even though other principles are followed in minority states. The focus here will not be to provide the reader with the rules for a specific case or to follow the laws or cases applicable in any jurisdiction, but to raise awareness of the issues to be considered and thereby to assist in making an informed decision.

Insurance policies are actually contracts between the insurance company and the health care provider. As a contract, there are terms that set out the duties and responsibilities as well as the rights and benefits gained by each party to the contract. Once the insurance contract is in force, each party is presumed to know the contents of the policy; therefore, it is advisable to read the policy and learn the duties and responsibilities that you have assumed on purchase of the policy. The various provisions commonly found within these contracts are briefly discussed below.

(a) Many insurance policies contain a clause that permits *settlement* when the company deems it expedient to do so. Such a clause generally protects the insurance carrier from bad faith settlements occurring within the policy limits. This concept is based on common law, but some jurisdictions may have statutory provisions supporting this principle. Such settlements within the policy limits are generally protected, even if the claim has little merit, because most courts believe that such a conclusion to the lawsuit is what the parties really expected on entering into the insurance contract.[1] Some states have legislation that the insurance contract must contain an authorization for the insurer to settle for any amount within the policy claims, regardless of the wishes of the insured, but such a statute may also

additionally require that the settlement must be made with the best interest of the insured in mind.[2]

(b) *Cooperation* with the company, and its representatives, including the
claims adjuster and the assigned defense attorney, is universally required.
Such cooperation extends to the availability of the insured to participate in
discovery, conferences, or trial at any reasonable time.

Generally, the terms of the policy prohibit the insured from admitting
any liability, or attempting the settlement of any claims, even with the
insured's own funds. Some physicians feel that such a settlement is a useful
option when small amounts can settle "nuisance" claims. When one is considering such an option, consultation with private counsel can be helpful,
but generally this benefit is more useful if the insured has reviewed the
policy in advance. Some policies permit such settlements, but generally
only with the consent of the insurance company.

(c) *Coverage* is governed by the terms of the policy, but there may be
certain required minimums mandated by statute. While there may be state
law variations, not every interaction between a health care provider and a
patient or client is necessarily covered by the malpractice policy. The terms
of the insurance contract, in addition to the required cooperation discussed
above, may contain other *coverage exclusions*.

The most common basis for refusal of coverage for some event is generally based upon the term (duration) of the policy. By skipping from carrier
to carrier in an attempt to reduce premium costs, some physicians have
eliminated coverage by avoiding buying tail coverage for the old policy or
retroactive coverage for the new policy. This is particularly dangerous when
dealing with coverage under an "occurrence" policy.[3] It is important for the
provider to know which type of policy is in force, or which type of policy is
being offered.

While state law varies, if the event occurs within the policy period, most
insurers are required to defend all suits, even though the suit may be
groundless, false, or even fictitious. In most states, the insurer's duty to
defend is greater than its duty to indemnify. Thus, an insurer could defend
its insured against a fictitious suit, but refuse to pay a plaintiff the amount
awarded in the judgment. The plaintiff or defendant would then be left to
sue the insurance company. The carrier may issue a *reservation of rights*
letter in circumstances similar to the above, or when some measure of
defense is necessary to protect the insured, but more investigation is necessary to be certain that the alleged event is covered by the terms of the policy.
One who receives a reservation of rights letter should consult personal counsel who may wish to discuss the issue with a carrier representative.

Remember that the insurance policy is for medical negligence. Negligence
generally means that the caregiver has failed to meet the prevailing appropriate standard of care, and as a result the patient has sustained an injury. Some
policies exclude nonnegligent patient injury, that is, injury to the patient
that occurs as a result of some *intentional act* by the physician. Sexual
impropriety, intentional acts that damage a patient, and criminal acts
frequently are excluded by the terms of the insurance contract.

Except where the occurrence clearly falls beyond the term of the policy,
insurers are hesitant to refuse to defend an action against one of its insured,

because if the refusal is later found to be unjustified, the insurer is likely to be found to have acted in bad faith. An unjustified refusal to defend may leave the insurance company (1) liable for the judgment or settlement amount suffered by the insured; (2) liable for defense costs; and (3) liable for any additional damages that can be attributed to the unjustified refusal to defend. Such obligations have been found to exist in a number of states, and it is probable that where the issue arises in other states, the same carrier liabilities will be found to exist.[4]

Settlement

Public policy generally dictates that settlement is to be preferred over litigation.[5] In most jurisdictions, the terms of an insurance policy permit the insurance carrier wide discretion in determining when, or if, a claim should be settled. If, by the terms of the policy, the insured relinquishes virtually all settlement decisions to the insurance carrier, the law then charges the carrier with a duty of "good faith" in protecting the personal assets of the insured. Some jurisdictions prefer terminology that requires the insurer to exercise "due care" in exercising its protective function.[6] However, the "due care" requirement can amount to a mere different interpretation, the lack of which results in "negligence," and the two ideas of good faith or due care tended to coalesce.[7]

The basic *role of personal counsel*, an attorney employed and paid by the defendant practitioner, is to protect the provider's personal assets in the event that a jury renders a verdict which exceeds the limits of the physician's medical malpractice policy (an "excess verdict"). In the broadest possible terms, this is usually accomplished by making a demand on the insurance carrier to settle the claim within the policy limits in order to protect the insured's personal assets.[8] In addressing this matter with the insurer, usually through the company's claims adjuster, it is best if there is a plaintiff's written demand for settlement at a figure that is at or less than the policy limits; however, that is not always necessary, and there are many variables that enter the settlement equation. The more common issues are discussed here.

It is axiomatic that if an insurer has an opportunity to settle a case at a reasonable figure within the policy limits, and does not do so, the insurer is likely to be responsible for the excess verdict on the basis of having failed to exercise, in good faith, the obligation and opportunity to protect the insured.[9] It is the obligation of the insurer to protect the best interests of its insured under all reasonable circumstances. Not to do so demonstrates bad faith on the part of the insurer, and subjects the insurer to liability for the excess verdict.

In fulfilling the function of personal counsel, the attorney will point out to the insurer that there is an opportunity to settle the insured's lawsuit within policy limits, and that the insurer should do so to protect the personal assets of the practitioner. The degree to which the personal counsel must justify that demand by a reasoned letter setting out the rationale behind the demand is a matter of debate, and is again a function of state law. In any jurisdiction, however, the settlement demand letter furnished to the carrier by personal counsel would be Exhibit A in any subsequent lawsuit charging the insurer with bad faith, and attempting to enforce payment of an excess judgment. Therefore, the personal counsel is likely to feel obligated, both to the client and to himself or herself, to present a reasoned argument for settlement. This may appear to the practitioner as though the personal counsel is taking the side of the plaintiff; however, this is not accurate. To perform the function of personal counsel effectively, the attorney must point out to the carrier that there are factors in the case that may sway a jury to find liability on the part of his client. That done, the jury may then award, even proportion, the dollar figure set for damages in such a way that the physician's personal liability insurance limit is exceeded.

Because state law controls and there are so many variations among cases, a physician may be well advised to secure some legal research in his or her specific jurisdiction before making a final decision regarding the making of a settlement demand. Personal counsel can assist in this aspect of making the settlement demand. In some jurisdictions the court decisions are so widely divergent that legislative clarification may even be required, although such amplification could seldom occur in a sufficiently timely fashion to be helpful in any case already in progress.

It will not be a difficult chore for an experienced trial or health care lawyer to cite a few examples of local cases in which huge jury verdicts have been secured by the plaintiff, thus adding some spice to the settlement demand to the insurance carrier. Sending a settlement demand or "bad faith" letter to an insurance carrier that is later found to be inadequate to give the insurance carrier notice of a demand for settlement, might well result in damages being sought against the attorney for legal malpractice by exposing the client's personal assets to an excess verdict, a consequence that the lawyer will find undesirable. Therefore, in most cases, one can expect to pay several hundred dollars for the research and preparation of such a settlement demand letter to the insurance carrier, rather than an inconsequential fee. The total fees for personal counsel will vary widely, depending on the degree of involvement authorized by the client.

When to Engage Personal Counsel

When to engage personal counsel becomes the next question, once that employment decision is made. Generally, earlier is better, but the physician should not expect that the attorney will necessarily address these issues with the insurance carrier immediately. In order to deliver a reasoned demand, the attorney will need to develop a rationale for the settlement demand. This may require that personal counsel delay the demand until after the depositions or other reports of the plaintiff's experts have been secured. Meanwhile, to fulfill the role of personal counsel, the attorney will have contacted both defense and plaintiff's attorneys, asking for copies of significant documents. The receipt of one or more of the summaries by defense counsel of the plaintiff's experts may provide sufficient information for the personal counsel to make a reasoned argument for settlement, setting forth the rationale that will very much parallel the opinions of the plaintiff's experts. The practitioner should not view this as an affront, or as personal counsel siding with the plaintiff, but merely fulfilling the personal counsel's job to point out to the insurance company the weaknesses in the case that justify the settlement demand.

The position stated by personal counsel may be difficult for the physician to accept, because most doctors who are sued feel that they have done nothing wrong. They feel hurt and angry that a person whom they were doing their best to help is now accusing them of malpractice. It all seems unfair, and just wrong. Frequently, it is just that, but the realities of the legal system present concepts that the practitioner must understand and strive to help the appointed defense attorney in planning and executing the defense.

Some practitioners have expressed concern that if they permit a personal counsel to write a settlement demand letter to their insurer, some adverse action may be taken by the carrier, such as a refusal to renew or an increase in premium. When such a decision is made by the carrier, it is generally made on other grounds. Although there could be regional variation, in general insurers are neither surprised nor concerned on receiving such letters. In fact, some carriers routinely write to those of their insured who have become defendants and advise that the provider may wish to seek personal counsel.

Aside from the personal affront, there are cogent reasons why a physician might want a carrier *not to settle*. Many or all of those concerns will follow the doctor through many years of medical practice, and will resurface at the time of each application for new or renewal of hospital privileges, managed care participation, or professional liability insurance coverage.

There is always some apprehension that one's reputation and referral pattern will be negatively affected; a concern may be raised that the carrier will increase premiums, or that the doctor will be uninsurable; medical staff privileges and hospital peer review proceedings are an added cause for alarm; participation in various managed care organization panels may be threatened; there is the inevitable report to the state licensing authorities, with the anxieties of the attendant investigation; and finally, the unpleasant fact that one will now be listed in the National Practitioners Data Bank (NPDB), discussed briefly later. The one element in this discussion that can be said to be uniform throughout the country is the NPDB reporting, because it is a *federal* law, applicable in all states.

While the physician might have many and good reasons not to encourage the insurer to settle, a request or direction to the insurer not to settle, particularly if in writing or otherwise authenticated, as by witnesses, could be dangerous to the financial welfare of the doctor. In such an instance, in the event of an excess judgment, the insurance company will certainly use the direction not to settle as a defense against any attempt to collect the excess judgment from the insurer on a bad faith claim. However, in most jurisdictions, the insurance carrier would still have an obligation of a fiduciary duty of the insurer to the insured, and the duty of good faith in dealing with its settlement obligations. Even when the insured has requested the insurer not to settle, the carrier must fully inform the insured of settlement opportunities, give a good faith estimate as to the probable outcome of the litigation, warn of the possibility of just such an excess judgment, and advise the insured of any steps that he might take to avoid such an occurrence.[10]

If an insured finds that there is reason to believe that the insurer has acted in any way other than the best of good faith, putting the insured's interests ahead of all others, and if the insured has suffered damages as a result, this could be the basis for a bad faith action against the insurer. Just because the provider's personal counsel has written a settlement demand letter, the insurer may not voluntarily pay a large excess verdict, although that is the usual practice. Should the carrier refuse to compensate the insured for damages, such as an excess verdict, it may be necessary to sue the carrier. If it falls to the insured to bring such a lawsuit, it is wise to employ the services of an attorney who is fully familiar with the cases and statutes governing insurance practices in the jurisdiction in which the insured resides. An alternative to a suit by the insured, and the more common practice, is to assign the insured's interest in the bad faith claim to the plaintiff. The plaintiff can then pursue that claim without the direct involvement of the insured as a party; however, the insured and the personal council will likely be involved as witnesses.

Having extensively discussed the duty of the insurer to settle to protect the insured, we now look at the opposite: the duty *not* to settle. Such a situation may arise when there are multiple competing claims facing the insurance company. If an insurer prematurely, and without adequate investigation and consideration of the consequences of its action, settles some claims and exhausts the limits of policy coverage, the carrier can be liable for exposing the insured to the other unsettled, but yet outstanding, claims. This is simply another aspect of the insurer's duty to use all reasonable means to protect its insured: its fiduciary duty of acting in good faith. The example in the fictitious case presentation at the beginning of this chapter was intentionally crafted to illustrate these competing interests.

One court has discussed and nicely illustrated this duty not to settle.[11] The case involved the negligent operation of an automobile resulting in the death of five young people and the injury of six others in which the driver was insured with limits of $100,000 per claim and $300,000 per accident. These amounts were clearly inadequate to cover the damages. The court found that the insurer had three specific duties: to investigate fully and determine how best to limit the liability of its insured; to settle as many of the claims as is possible within the policy limits; and to use wise settlement practices and avoid indiscriminately settling selected claims, thereby increasing the insured's exposure to excess judgments. Attempting a global settlement is one way to achieve the public policy goal of settlement rather than litigation and exercising the carrier's obligation of good faith. In spite of these countervailing interests and duties, an insurer may still have broad discretion in settlement decisions, but in doing so must exercise good faith and due care within the general parameters set out by the courts.

Nonparty Liability

Nonparty liability is an issue that may arise in many malpractice cases. In some states, a part of the liability for medical malpractice may rest on entities not named as parties in the lawsuit. For this reason, plaintiff's attorneys tend to name everyone whom they suspect might have any degree of liability at all; otherwise, the plaintiff may hold the attorney responsible for the proportion of damages attributed to someone whom the plaintiff's attorney failed to sue. A defendant health care provider might want to discuss with private counsel the possibility that the lawsuit does not include people or entities who might have a share in the liability. This "empty chair defense" might shift the burden of damages from the named defendants in the malpractice suit. The circumstances under which one may apportion liability to unnamed defendants will vary by state, if it is permitted at all, but it is worth discussing with personal counsel to see if it is applicable.[12]

Going Bare

Going bare or semi-nude may be permissible in some situations. Various states may have a financial responsibility requirement associated with licensure or re-licensure. Such statutory provisions are directed at the protection of the health care consuming public. Some states provide mechanisms, other than insurance, by which this financial responsibility requirement may be met. Since state law requirements vary considerably, no effort to particularize will be made here; however, this is an area in which the personal counsel of the health care provider can help in understanding the practitioner's duties and responsibilities, which may generally fall into the areas described below.

Many states will require that the health care practitioner maintain medical malpractice insurance coverage at a certain level, but that level may vary depending upon whether or not the provider has hospital privileges. This is apparently an attempt to tie higher policy limits to what is perceived to be more dangerous settings. States may also provide such alternative means of financial responsibility as an escrow account in the amount of insurance coverage otherwise required. Letters of credit from approved financial institutions could also serve a similar purpose.

Under certain conditions, the physician may be totally uninsured, but there may be a requirement that the provider notify patients of this situation by specified mechanisms. There is also a sort of limited coverage that can be purchased in some states. This provides the physician with *defense only* coverage, that is, a policy will pay a defense attorney, but not any settlement or judgment.

The financial responsibility requirements can vary widely from state to state, and some are convoluted. Assistance from personal counsel may be helpful here.

For those with hospital privileges, the hospital by-laws will govern whether or not an individual practitioner is permitted to admit or treat patients in the hospital without specified limits of malpractice coverage, sometimes with a carrier approved by the hospital. This, of course, is a precautionary requirement by some hospitals who distrust certain offshore entities claiming to provide insurance coverage. Not only may hospitals be concerned regarding the welfare of their patients, but also they have a vested interest in not being the sole source of funds to satisfy malpractice judgments or settlements. In addition, there are cases in which the hospital has been held liable for damages done by a malpracticing physician.

This can be based upon vicarious liability, even when the physician is not an employee; on negligent credentialing; on apparent agency, when the physician appears to be acting in the capacity of an employee; or on other agency theories. However, these bases for liability are beyond the scope of this chapter.

State reporting requirements will vary with the jurisdiction, and may be complicated. No generalization can be made regarding state law requirements of reporting malpractice suits, settlements, or judgments. Many states require reporting denial or termination of hospital privileges or insurance coverage by the insurance carrier, the hospital, or the individual physician. Some states require insurance companies to report settlements, and judgments paid, and others require that payments made personally by the practitioner must also be reported.

There may also be a state licensure requirement which prohibits issuance or renewal of a license while there is an unpaid judgment by an uninsured physician. Sometimes the amount of payment is specified, but this would not limit the practitioner's financial responsibility to the prevailing plaintiff.

Another form of "reporting" may exist in those states where a practitioner profile is required to be available on a public website.[13] The practitioner may have varying degrees of responsibility for maintaining the accuracy and completeness of these practitioner profiles. States requiring such practitioner profiles on the web may set varying thresholds for reporting.

Reporting Requirement

The one *consistent reporting requirement* mentioned above arose as a result of Congressional findings of perceived increasing medical malpractice, the need to improve the quality of medical care, and concern that there was increasing medical malpractice in the mid-1980s, and a national problem that exceeded the ability of the individual states to control. There was concern that incompetent physicians could move from state to state and continue damaging the public, and Congress felt that there was an overriding national need to remedy this concern through professional peer review, and to provide immunity to those physicians conducting these reviews. The result was the Health Care Quality Improvement Act of 1986 ("HCQIA or Act"), which created the NPDB.

The legislation setting up the NPDB set out specific reporting requirements, and also established the responsibility of certain entities to query the NPDB. The full range of reporting requirements and the ability to query the NPDB can be found in the *National Practitioner Data Bank Guidebook*, which can be downloaded from the website, www.npdb-hipdb.com.

Originally, the National Practitioner Data Bank required reporting by individual physicians; however, this is no longer necessary if the payment was made by the individual physician from the individual physician's personal funds. Payment by any other entity, including the physician's corporation or professional association, hospital, or employer, carries a responsibility for NPDB reporting. Today personal counsel can help sort out these statutory or hospital reporting requirements.

Because the requirements of the NPDB are universally applicable, and since these reports are of significance to the practitioner, a nonexhaustive review of some of its provisions is appropriate here. Those requiring further details are referred to the above website. The text of the enabling legislation and substantial additional information will be found there.

While the HCQIA substantially deals with peer review activity, and protection of the reviewers, the Act also requires reports of medical malpractice payments; sanctions by medical boards; and of specified professional review actions taken by health care entities, which includes licensed hospitals, health maintenance organizations, and similar managed care organizations, along with professional societies, if they perform formal peer review.[14] The Act provides immunity to those entities that perform peer review in accordance with the criteria set out in the Act, and also sets out the responsibility of certain entities to query the NPDB. There are sanctions available to the Secretary for noncompliance.

If a peer review entity is sued and has fulfilled the good faith requirements set forth in the Act, the defendant is to be awarded reasonable attorney's fees and costs ". . . if the claim, or the claimant's conduct during the litigation of the claim, was frivolous, unreasonable, without foundation, or in bad faith."[15] This provision is another effort to protect those who participate in the peer review process.

Because a number of other entities are required to report occurrences to the NPDB, insurance settlements are not the sole source of NPDB data; however, the activities of these other reporters is not the subject of this chapter. Additional information on reporting may be obtained at the NPDB website.

When a report concerning a practitioner is received by the NPDB, the practitioner will receive an explanatory letter from the NPDB concerning confidentiality, the source of additional information, and the options available to the practitioner. Aside from identifying information, the practitioner may find a reference to the monetary penalty assessed, if any, the status of his position after the adverse action is completed, and a brief description of the reason for the action taken. Once a report has been made, usually only the reporting entity can modify or correct information in the report.

No response from the practitioner is required; however, even if the report is accurate, the practitioner will generally be benefited by outlining mitigating facts related to the reported incident. The practitioner may also correct any addresses, or if the report is completely in error, in that either the event never occurred, or the practitioner was not involved in the event reported, the practitioner may utilize the dispute mechanism; however, the practitioner may not dispute "the reported action itself or the appropriateness of any findings or judgment." The practitioner may submit a clarifying statement, and this is the usual action elected, or one may submit both the statement and dispute the report.

The practitioner is provided with a password, and instructions for logging into the NPDB data bank for the purpose of responding. Only the subject of the report is permitted to submit a statement, dispute, or both. An address is provided for a paper response.

A portion of the report form is reserved for the subject's statement, but one must refer either to the website or to the *NPDB Guidebook* to learn that the subject's responsive statement is limited to 2000 characters, including spaces and punctuation. All characters beyond that limit are truncated. Practitioners also learn from the *Guidebook* that statements may not include any names, addresses, or phone numbers, or reference to the patient by name. If the subject has prepared and submitted a properly completed statement, that information will be made available to all subsequent inquirers.

When Congress learned of an estimate of annual health care fraud losses ranging from 3% to 10% of all health care expenditures, which subsequently has proved to be even larger, it enacted the Health Insurance Portability and Accountability Act (HIPAA).[16] There was then established a program designed to control national health care fraud and abuse. Among these efforts and a myriad of other health-related provisions was the formation of the Healthcare Integrity and Protection Data Bank (HIPDB). For the purposes of this chapter, it is important for the reader to know of the existence of this collected information, but no further discussion is appropriate here.

A later, but still uniform, reporting requirement was established in 1996 when the HIPDB was established. This collection of information was established to control the national health care fraud and abuse crisis, which Congress perceived to be a mounting financial burden. Hopefully, this data bank is of less concern to the reader, but details of the obligation to report and query can be found at the website noted above.

REFERENCES

1. *Shuster v. South Broward Hospital District Physicians' Professional Liability Insurance Trust*, 591 So. 2d 174 (Fla. 1992); *Sharpe v. Physicians Protective Trust Fund*, 578 So. 2d 806 (Fla. 1st D.C.A. 1991).

2. Section 627.4147, Florida Statutes.

3. To provide coverage, an occurrence policy must be in force when the alleged malpractice event occurred; a "claims made" policy covers claims that are made during the term of the policy. Either may have other provisions modifying this general description.

4. District of Columbia, Tennessee, California, Pennsylvania. 44 Am. Jur. 2d, §1417.

5. 70 A.L.R. 2d 416, §5.

6. 44 Am. Jur. 2d, §1399.

7. Id.

8. Note that there are numerous other mechanisms to protect personal assets, but they are not the subject of this chapter.

9. 44 Am. Jur. 2d, §1399.

10. In Florida, the controlling cases would be *Boston Old Colony Insurance Co. v. Gutierrez*, 386 So. 2d 783, 785 (Fla. 1980) and *Odom v. Canal Insurance Co.*, 582 So. 2d 1203, 1205 (Fla. 1st D.C.A. 1991).

11. *Farinas v. Florida Farm Bureau Gen. Ins. Co.*, 850 So. 2d 555 (Fla. 4th D.C.A. 2003), *rev. denied* (Fla. Mar. 17, 2004).

12. See *Fabre v. Marin*, 623 So. 2d 1182 (Fla. 1993) and its progeny.
13. See §456.041, Florida Statutes (2005).
14. 42 U.S.C. §11131–33; 42 U.S.C. §11151(A).
15. 42 U.S.C. §11113.
16. Public Law 104-191, enacted on August 24, 1996.

Liability in Clinical Trials Research

Kenneth A. DeVille, Ph.D., J.D.
Denise Brigham, B.S.N., R.N., C.I.P., C.C.R.P.

GOLDEN RULES

1. Accept only studies for which you and your practice have sufficient expertise and resources to understand and conduct.
2. Do not accept studies in which the risk to participants outweighs the potential benefits and scientific value of the study.
3. Adhere scrupulously to the inclusion/exclusion criteria.
4. Know and follow applicable aspects of the Common Rule and FDA regulations, ICH-GCP standards and institutional or group practice policies, the research contract, and FDA Form 1572.
5. Ensure that the study has been approved by an appropriate IRB.
6. Consult attorney or insurance carrier to determine whether current insurance policy covers claims related to clinical trials.
7. Employ qualified and certified clinical trial coordinators to help administer the trials.
8. Ensure that potential participants are fully and properly informed.
9. Ensure that "alternative treatments" section of the informed consent document is clear and complete.
10. Disclose conflict of interests to participants during the consent process.
11. Follow approved protocol scrupulously.
12. Monitor medical literature related to the trial, study drug, or participant's medical condition for significant new findings that might impact the study.
13. Ensure that participants have 24-hour access to someone knowledgeable about the study.
14. Withdraw participants from a clinical trial according to the protocol, or when the participant's continuation in the study represents a greater likelihood or degree of harm than anticipated at the outset of the study.

A series of highly publicized lawsuits have shaken the world of research on human subjects. In 1999, Jessie Gelsinger died as a result of gene therapy provided in a study at University of Pennsylvania Children's Hospital.[1] The case quickly settled. The next year, University of South Florida and Tampa General Hospital paid $3.8 million to settle a class action suit filed by patients who claimed that they had received insufficient informed consent for various research protocols in which they had enrolled. In *Robertson v. McGee* (2001),[2] 13 patients at Oklahoma University Health Science Center sued in federal court for damages they claim to have received as a result of participation in a clinical trial. The case later settled. The same year, five patients sued researchers at Fred Hutchinson Cancer Center in Seattle, Washington. While a jury cleared investigators in the death of four study participants, it awarded damages in the death of a fifth.[3] A related class action suit on behalf of 82 additional research subjects against investigators is pending.[4] In 2001, *Kernke v. The Menninger Clinic Inc.*[5] involved the inpatient trial of a new medication for schizophrenia. During the trial a participant wandered off from a clinic-sponsored outing and died from exposure. Finally, in 2003, a North Carolina psoriasis patient sued his dermatologist for injuries he believed he received as a result of participation in a clinical trial.[6] The parties settled the suit for an undisclosed amount of money.

Lawsuits involving human research are not new, but they are on the rise. And while there is currently no demonstrable trend, many observers believe that plaintiffs' attorneys have discovered a new and potentially profitable ground for litigation. A research participant who believes that he or she has been injured or wronged as a result of participation in a research study has several different targets. Research participants may sue the study sponsor, study investigator, medical school, hospital, research center, group practice, or other institution connected with the study, as well as the institutional review board (IRB) that reviewed and approved the study. Although multiple defendants will undoubtedly be named in any research-related suit, the primary and ever-present target of such litigation will likely be the physician-investigators who actually conduct the research study. This chapter will outline and discuss the legal elements and viability of lawsuits brought by participants against physician-investigators who conduct clinical trials.

CASE PRESENTATION

Mr. Jones had been a longstanding patient at the dermatology clinic where he was followed for psoriasis complicated by psoriatic arthritis. Dr. Smith, the dermatologist, successfully treated the patient for both conditions with approved medications, specifically methotrexate. Although severe psoriatic arthritis can be debilitating, at 55 years old, Mr. Jones had few manifestations of this disease, allowing him to maintain an active lifestyle in addition to full-time employment in his business. After approximately 10 years on a stable regimen, Mr. Jones was approached by his physician to consider participating in a clinical trial aimed at testing the safety and efficacy of a new investigational drug for the treatment of moderate to severe psoriasis.

Dr. Smith conducted the consent process with Mr. Jones using a document that had received approval by all the necessary bodies, such as the sponsor, research organization, and the IRB. Mr. Jones felt that he understood the consent document and was even able to have language in the compensation for injury section modified to language that was agreeable. Even as an educated lay person, however, Mr. Jones did not have the medical background to specifically request all the additional information necessary to make an informed decision about participating in the research study. He did not understand that he would have the possibility of receiving no treatment for his currently controlled psoriatic arthritis and that, more importantly, without treatment this disease can progress causing damage to his joints. In fact, the protocol sought to prevent this from happening by excluding patients with psoriatic arthritis from being involved in the study. The exclusion criteria were not outlined in the materials provided to Mr. Jones.

Dr. Smith outlined that the protocol required research visits to administer the study drug injections and to perform the physical exams. The regular visits would allow Dr. Smith to monitor Mr. Jones response to the "study drug" and ensure that adverse effects were captured as outlined by the protocol, sponsor, and FDA. Mr. Jones complied with visit requirements. However, despite his progressively worsening condition, nothing changed. Mr. Jones continued to receive a placebo in the first phase, while his skin condition became severely affected by his untreated psoriasis. He became symptomatic from his psoriatic arthritis, again as a result of receiving no treatment. In the second phase of the study, Mr. Jones did receive a reduced dosage of the actual study drug. While his skin condition improved slightly, the study drug was not designed to impact his arthritis, which continued to worsen. Mr. Jones remained active in the research study through the end of the second phase upon the reassurance of his long-time physician that the symptoms he experienced would be temporary and reversible in nature. The arthritis symptoms were not. Mr. Jones sustained probable permanent joint damage that leaves him with a significant negative impact to his quality of life.[*]

ISSUES

Legal Bases of Research Liability

Attorneys will frequently name every potential cause of action they can reasonably identify in order to increase the chance of winning. Thus far, plaintiffs in suits against physician-researchers have asserted claims under a parade of legal theories, including: intentional infliction of emotional distress; outrage; battery; intentional misrepresentation; fraud; the violation of federal research regulations; breach of the right to be treated with "dignity"; medical malpractice; and professional negligence. The relative novelty of human subjects research litigation increases the likelihood that multiple and creative causes of action will be alleged in every case for some time. This practice will undoubtedly continue until a critical mass of suits, successful and unsuccessful, has been litigated sufficiently to uncover the most appropriate and viable causes of action. Until that time, much of the commentary and prognostication regarding lawsuits against researchers must remain guarded.

[*]This scenario is based on the claims made in *Hamlet v. Genentech et al.* (2003). *Hamlet* was settled without resolving any of the allegations.

Potential Actions Against Physician-Researchers

Many potential causes of action claimed against investigators, while theoretically viable, might reasonably be disregarded as highly speculative or easily dismissed on other grounds in most instances.

Intentional Infliction of Emotional Distress

"Intentional infliction of emotional distress" requires: (1) extreme and outrageous conduct that exceeds the bounds of decency; (2) intent to inflict emotional distress or reckless action when it was certain that emotional distress would result; (3) emotional distress so severe that no reasonable person could be expected to endure it; and (4) a causal connection between the defendant's actions and the emotional distress. Although these elements may be present in some isolated research cases, they are not likely to match the facts of a claim against a typical physician-investigator even if a case can be made that he or she acted in a cursory, careless, or negligent manner. Thus, it seems unlikely that suits based on "intentional infliction of emotional distress" will be either broadly successful, or very common.

Outrage

The tort of "outrage" also requires the plaintiff to prove four elements: (1) that the defendant's conduct was atrocious, intolerable, and so extreme and outrageous as to exceed the bounds of decency; (2) that the defendants acted with the intent to inflict emotional distress or acted recklessly when it was certain or substantially certain that emotional distress would result from the conduct; (3) that the defendant's actions caused the plaintiff to suffer emotional distress; and (4) that the emotional distress was so severe that no reasonable person could be expected to endure it. "Outrage" is a cause of action that is rarely sustained, very difficult to prove in those jurisdictions where it is accepted, and would ordinarily not fit the facts of the typical clinical trials lawsuit.

Violations of the DHHS Regulations Governing Research—the So-Called "Common Rule"

Some suits appear to base their claims directly on violations of the DHHS regulations governing research—the so-called "Common Rule" [7]—and similar FDA regulations.[8] But the Common Rule, FDA guidelines, and other federal research guidelines do not explicitly create causes of action as plaintiffs sometimes assert. Therefore, it will probably not be possible for plaintiffs to rely on violation of the Common Rule or the FDA regulations, in and of themselves, as a cause of action. Federal regulations, however, may be legally relevant in other ways that will be discussed below.

Misrepresentation and Fraud

"Misrepresentation and fraud" requires an intentional misrepresentation of a material fact by the defendant on which the plaintiff justifiably relies to make his or her decision. The case against the researchers at the University of Oklahoma was based in part on fraud. The plaintiffs claimed that the investigator convinced participants that the study vaccine was a treatment rather than an unapproved drug that was being tested solely for toxicity. The Gelsinger case as well contained a fraud claim based on the allegation that physician-investigators withheld information regarding their financial interests and the fact that previous subjects had died. At first glance, the elements of fraud seem to fit the relationship between the research subject and investigator relatively well. A research subject consents to participate in a study after the investigator informs him or her of the conditions of participation. It is reasonable for subjects to rely on the investigators' representations made during the informed consent process when making the decision whether or not to participate. But on closer examination, and when litigated, misrepresentation and fraud claims may be harder to maintain. For example, to support the claim, the research subject must demonstrate that the investigator made a false representation "knowing it to be false" or in "reckless disregard" for its falsity. While this may of course be true in some claims, the far more likely situation will probably involve carelessly inadequate information or explanations in the informed consent process. Such failures of consent are potentially actionable (most notably through negligence, discussed below), but they do not fit easily under the rubric of fraud.

Battery

Several research suits have included claims of "battery" against investigators. To prove the legal claim of "battery," a plaintiff must show that the defendant was responsible for an intentional, unwanted, unconsented touching that was either harmful or offensive. There are clear benefits to the research subject plaintiffs in pursuing a battery cause of action. Typically, experts are not required to prove battery as they are in negligence cases. In addition, a plaintiff need not prove actual or tangible damages at all, in order to collect a monetary award. He or she must only demonstrate the unconsented, offensive touching. Finally, juries are allowed to award punitive damages in battery cases. Punitive damages are not available in ordinary negligence cases. The elimination of these evidentiary hurdles and the potential for punitive damages make battery an attractive suit in research litigation in which damages may be hard to demonstrate and the standard of care hard to prove. But ordinarily, battery actions in medical and quasi-medical contexts are successful only where there has been a complete absence of consent, rather than inadequate consent, and thus are quite rare and difficult to maintain. In research litigation, an inadequate informed consent document or process, rather than the absolute absence of consent, is far more likely to characterize the typical research suit scenario.

Violation of Right to be Treated with Dignity — "Dignity Tort" Claims

Some suits have also included a claim that the physician-investigator had violated the research subjects' "right to be treated with dignity." At present, there is no recognized tort encompassing the "right to be treated with dignity." Instead, these series of suits represent plaintiffs' attorneys' attempt to pioneer a new cause of action. According to the suits, the "right to be treated with dignity" in clinical trials is predicated on the Nuremberg Code, the World Health Organization's Declaration of Helsinki, the Belmont Report, federal research guidelines, the common law, and federal and state constitutions.

"Dignity tort" claims that appear in current litigation contend that harms resulting from violations of autonomy and dignity should be compensated, even in the absence of actual injury. Like battery, plaintiffs' attorneys are understandably drawn to the "dignity" tort because it absolves them of the duty of demonstrating that the physician-researcher's actions caused the research participant injury, a key hurdle in many research suits. But despite the hopes of the litigants and their attorneys, the proposed "dignity tort" will undoubtedly fail. The supposed dignity tort is only vaguely articulated in the pleadings and justified only broadly and generally on a range of highly indistinct and questionable grounds. Such a claim would almost certainly have to be created out of whole cloth by the courts. In such rare cases where the law recognizes a technical invasion of an individual's rights or a breach of duty on the part of the defendant in the face of no demonstrable injury, courts sometimes, yet rarely, award only "nominal" damages, e.g., one dollar. Therefore, despite the enthusiasm of plaintiff subjects and the concerns of defendant investigators, breach of dignity will probably play relatively little role in future research litigation.

None of the foregoing discussion should be read to imply that suits based on any one of these legal theories will invariably fail. Any theory, under certain conditions, *could* be successful. However, the most appropriate and most viable claim will ordinarily be a variant of professional negligence, i.e., *research malpractice*. Thus, when evaluating research investigators' legal risk and the future path of litigation, attention should be focused predominantly on how suits will unfold as professional negligence actions.

Suits Based on Negligence

Most research subject claimants will find viable claims only under some theory of negligence—specifically professional negligence. In order to construct a successful negligence action, a plaintiff must demonstrate, by a "preponderance of the evidence" (more likely than not), that the defendant had a duty toward the plaintiff; the duty was breached; the plaintiff suffered harm or damage; and that the breach was the proximate cause of the harm the plaintiff suffered.

Duty

The first element of the negligence claim—duty—will be relatively easy to demonstrate in the vast majority of research cases. After all, even strangers interacting in society have some "duty" to other individuals, even if the content of that duty is relatively modest. It is inescapable that investigators have *some* manner of duty toward their subjects; it is the content of the duty that will be in dispute. The content of a defendant's duty depends on the source of the duty and the nature of the relationship between the physician and plaintiff. Part of the physician-researcher's duty has its origin in the physician–patient relationship and the fact that, in clinical trials, medical care is provided for subjects. In addition, it should be fairly easy to demonstrate that the creation of the researcher–participant relationship creates a duty specific to that relationship. A special duty may attach because the research participant relies on and trusts the physician-investigator's superior knowledge before agreeing to participate in a research project. Participants depend on the physician-investigator to choose and recommend an appropriate study, to properly explain the study, to inform them of the relevant and material issues, and to appropriately conduct the study. Researchers' distinct duty to study participants might also emanate from the protocol and the clinical trial contract that the investigator agreed to follow, and the informed consent document and process conducted with the participant.[9] Whatever the ultimate justification, physician-investigators who recruit patients to enter research trials will invariably be found to have a duty to research participants intrinsically related to their status as researchers. The nature and precise content of this duty, and its breach, will be harder to articulate.

Breach of Duty (Standard of Care)

Demonstrating the second element of the negligence claim—breach of duty—will probably be conceptually and practically difficult, as well as initially unpredictable. There is little relevant case law, or substantial trial court experience available, regarding the construction of a "standard of care" for physician-researchers. Strangers in society, absent any special relationship, have only the duty to act "reasonably" toward one another—i.e., to act as a reasonable person would in the same or similar circumstances. But special relationships between individuals in society create special or additional duties depending on the nature of that relationship. Employers have a duty to provide a safe workplace for their employees. Shopkeepers have a duty to maintain a safe environment for their customers. Professionals of any ilk, physicians, attorneys, architects, engineers, have the duty to act according to the "standard of care" of their calling—as a reasonably prudent professional in the field would act under the same or similar circumstances. Ordinarily, experts in the relevant profession are required to offer evidence of the "standard of care" in the particular enterprise and whether it has been breached. Consequently, expert testimony will play the central role in determining the content of the duty to which physician-researchers will be held—i.e., the "standard of care" against which the physician-researcher's performance will be measured.

Because research suits against physician-researchers are a form of professional negligence—i.e., research malpractice—the use of expert witnesses will ordinarily be required. Expert witnesses secured by plaintiffs and defendants will be likely expected to describe and explain the complicated dual character of the relationship between the physician-researcher and the research participant. After all, physician-researchers cannot be held strictly and merely to the traditional medical malpractice "standard of care" and the duty to act in the best interests of their patients. On the one hand, much of clinical research does not conform to medical standard of care, nor is it always in the absolute best interest of the participants (e.g., placebo-controlled trial designs pairing an experimental drug against a placebo may be offering a choice between two ineffective treatments). On the other hand, a physician-researcher inescapably assumes additional duties beyond those of a mere practicing physician. As one commentator has explained, "we need to cultivate a conception of the moral identity of the physician-investigator that integrates the roles of the clinician and the scientist without giving predominance to the one or the other." According to this view, physician-researchers "should be prepared to sacrifice scientific rigor when necessary to protect patients from exposure to severe suffering or disproportionate risks of harm," but they "should also be permitted to ask subjects to tolerate 'minor risks and mild-to-moderate discomfort … to conform to scientific protocols.' "[10]

In order to describe the content of the standard of care required of physician-researchers, courts will undoubtedly rely on expert testimony to construct a legal expectation that merges the duties of a researcher with those of a practicing physician. Because the case will typically involve medical issues, a physician expert will probably be required. An additional requirement will be knowledge and understanding of the customary practice/standard of care of physician-researchers. An expert may claim this knowledge by virtue of private study, education, or formal training. Knowledge and understanding of physician-researchers' standard of care might derive also from the prospective expert's own experience in conducting, designing, and monitoring trials, or from other administrative or regulatory experience in the running of clinical trials.

The most useful and credible expert witness, of course, will be a physician-researcher who has conducted clinical trials and can claim first-hand knowledge of prevailing practices. In the *Hamlet* (2003) case, for example, the plaintiff claimed that the defendant physician-researcher was negligent by failing, in conducting the experiment, to perform proper and careful practices and procedures in accordance with the standards prevailing in the community in which defendants practiced and pursued pharmaceutical studies at the time. In short, the defendant has been sued for failing to act in accordance with the customary practice of physicians who conduct research. The description and content of the standard will undoubtedly vary somewhat from expert to expert and case to case, especially in the absence of widespread litigation and clarifying case law. But some insight is possible.

The physician-researcher's legal duty to a research participant (standard of care) will be based on a constellation of interlocking considerations defined, articulated, and explained by the testimony of expert witnesses; these include: (1) prevailing medical practice; (2) adherence to the study protocol; (3) applicable policies, codes, and guidelines; (4) relevant statutes and regulations; (5) physician-researcher duties outside the protocol, applicable codes, and guidelines and policies.

Prevailing Medical Practice

As a baseline, physician-researchers will be expected to possess and exercise the degree of skill, learning, and care appropriate for the medical care and procedures involved in the study they have undertaken. If a physician-researcher injures a research participant while performing a standard medical practice that happens to be part of the study (e.g., a lumbar puncture, bronchoscopy, endoscopy, angiography, carotid catheterization, cardiac bypass surgery, etc.), a medical expert will testify that the physician-researcher should be held to the same standard of care as a practicing physician in a typical malpractice claim. Suits based solely on this species of breach of duty will be no more complicated in the formulation and determination of the standard of care and its breach than any other medical malpractice suit. But most research suits will be based on the breach of duty specifically required *of physician-researchers*—not merely the standard of care expected of physicians.

Adherence to the Study Protocol

Expert witness testimony will almost certainly assert that standard of care practice in research requires that the physician-researcher scrupulously follow the protocol for the study that he or she is conducting. Research protocols outline precise, detailed, and specific study duties that frequently exceed the standard of care ordinarily required for a particular patient. Study protocols contain detailed inclusion and exclusion criteria. If a participant who does not meet the defined criteria is enrolled in a study, the investigator has breached the standard of care.

Protocols typically mandate the application of the study drug according to a predetermined and precise schedule. If the investigator varies from the proscribed program, he or she has breached the standard of care. Protocols usually require numerous and repeated tests and procedures intended to collect information for the study, monitor the side effects of the study drug or device, and evaluate the progress of the participant's underlying illness or injury. These tests and procedures could include the histories and physicals; patient-participant surveys; blood drawings; lab tests; x-ray, CT, MRI, and PET scans; bronchoscopies; lumbar punctures; biopsies; EKGs; etc. If an investigator does not perform a required test or procedure at the time indicated by the protocol, the standard of care has been breached. Finally, the protocol usually contains a detailed description of when individual participants should be withdrawn from the study.

Some protocol requirements are related primarily to the collection of data, but many are related to the safety and wellbeing of the enrolled research participants. If it can be demonstrated that a failure to comply with a protocol requirement caused the damage suffered by the research participant, then the investigator can be held liable for damages. A 2003 suit involving Fox Chase Cancer Center claimed that physician-researchers failed to provide protocol-mandated colonoscopies, CT scans, and blood tests designed to detect the recurrence of cancer. The study participant was randomized to a control arm in which he received no study drug and later died of an inoperable abdominal tumor. The 2003 *Hamlet* case, as well, was based in part on the failure of defendants to follow the proscribed protocol. The original pleading claims that the physician-researcher was charged with the "professional responsibility of properly and carefully administering the experiment's protocol in a careful and prudent fashion." Instead, according to the pleading, the defendant failed to appropriately screen and monitor the study participant according to the provisions of the protocol.

These examples underscore the key role of study protocols. Adherence to the study protocol will be an essential feature of the articulation of a physician-researcher standard of care. Experts recruited to explain the standard of care for physician researchers will invariably assert that researchers have a duty to adhere to the protocol. The existence of this duty can be buttressed further by the fact that investigators agree to follow protocol requirements in their clinical trial contracts, in the FDA Form 1572 they sign, in their agreements with the relevant institutional review board, and as part of the requirements of the institutions in which they practice.

It is likely, in many or most suits, that the relevant breach of duty will be based predominantly or solely upon the physician-researcher's failure to adhere to the procedures described in the protocol. Whether a defendant will be able to collect a monetary award will depend on whether the failure to follow the protocol was the cause of the plaintiff's damage (see discussion below).

Policies, Codes, and Guidelines

Expert witnesses will confirm that the requirements contained in the study protocol are an essential component in the construction of the relevant standard of care in a clinical trial. But experts might also extract mandates from ethics codes, policy statements, and guidance documents generated by professional organizations and public interest groups. While these materials ordinarily have no legal force in and of themselves, courts may grant them legal relevance in individual cases if a qualified expert witness convincingly testifies that a code, policy, or guidance document establishes customary practice and represents the relevant standard of care.[11] An expert witness, for example, *might* testify that the Belmont Report, the Declaration of Helsinki, the Nuremberg Code, or the Council for International Organizations of Medical Sciences Guidelines (CIOMS) represent part of the accepted professional standard for physician-researchers. Expert witnesses might be especially likely to draw on the International Conference on Harmonization Good Clinical Practice (ICH-GCP) guidelines as a required source of direction for physician-investigators. The ICH-GCP guidelines were designed to represent an ethical and scientific quality standard for designing, conducting, recording, and reporting trials that involve the participation of human subjects. They have been given additional credibility by their inclusion into the *Federal Register* as a representation of research practices that the FDA considers good clinical practice.[12] In addition, most protocols, clinical trials contracts, and research agreements bind physician-investigators to ICH-GCP directives. The high-profile and widespread reliance on ICH-GCP guidelines suggests that expert witnesses may be very likely to rely on them in the construction of a standard of care for human research activity. Also, some institutions may have incorporated these codes and guidelines into their institutional policies, which further substantiate their relevance in setting practice standards.

Although less likely, selected guidance from professional organizations regarding research behavior might also be grafted onto the standard of care through the testimony of an expert witness. A testifying expert might base an element of the standard of care, in part, from sources such as the codes and statements on the conduct of research promulgated by the American Medical Association, the American College of Physicians, the American Academy of Pediatrics, the American College of Obstetrics and Gynecology, the American College of Surgeons, and the American College of Emergency Medicine. Courts have already accepted the introduction of practice guidelines by expert witnesses as evidence of the standard of care in traditional medical malpractice cases. If courts accept the introduction of similar evidence by experts in research suits, the relevant guidance documents will essentially be given the weight of law by their inclusion into the standard of care in that particular case. And physician-researchers' conduct in clinical trials will be measured against the requirements of the codes accepted by courts as valid articulations of researcher responsibility.

Relevant Statutes and Regulations

In addition to performing according to the foregoing standards of care, in some instances physician-investigators may be required as well to incorporate the guidance contained in federal regulations into the duties they must fulfill when conducting clinical trials. There are two major mechanisms by which federal regulations related to research may become, as well, part of a physician-researcher's required standard of care. Institutions or medical practices that receive any federal monies for conducting human subject research must execute an agreement, called a Federal Wide Assurance (FWA) agreement, with the Office of Human Research Protections (OHRP). This agreement outlines the ethical principles to be observed, but more importantly contains the requirement for researchers to adhere to the "Common Rule." Through the FWA or other processes, many universities, hospitals, academic medical centers, research institutes, and group practices have, in effect, incorporated the "Common Rule" into their institutional policy. The incorporation of Common Rule standards into institutional policy is compelling evidence that individual investigators conducting research within those institutions may be held to Common Rule standards as well as in research liability suits. While the Common Rule merely duplicates and memorializes many accepted research standards and practices, it provides an additional, fairly elaborate, and well-defined set of standards for which physician-investigators *could* be held accountable.

A second mechanism by which federal regulations become relevant to the applicable standard of care is through the item being tested by the research. The FDA has jurisdiction over biologics, such as drugs and devices, used in the provision of health care. A drug or device in a clinical trial is also controlled and regulated by the FDA. For example, a physician-investigator in a private medical practice that does not receive federal funds might not be subject to the Common Rule, but would be subject to the FDA regulations because of the nature of the research. The FDA holds investigators directly accountable for violating the regulations and has the authority to place sanctions against an investigator for severe infractions. The physician-investigator is inevitably accountable for following all relevant regulations governing the research site or test item, a responsibility acknowledged by signed contracts with sponsors, FDA Form 1572 documents, investigator agreements, employment agreements, and investigator certifications from an institutional review board. While neither the FDA regulations nor the Common Rule create a cause of action for injuries to research subjects, either or both could effectively become part of the investigator's required standard of care under certain conditions.

There is one other scenario under which FDA and/or Common Rule regulations could play a role in demonstrating physician-researcher negligence in a liability suit. If the regulations are found to apply for any of the above reasons (a study involving a biologic, a federally funded study, or an institutional agreement that states that the Common Rule will be followed), the negligence *per se* rule might apply. In some situations a judge, rather than an expert and a jury, can declare that a defendant's acts were negligent. Courts will find negligence *per se* when the statute that has been violated was designed to prevent the kind of harm that in fact occurred and when the injured party was a member of the class that the statute intended to protect. Given this analysis, the negligence *per se* rule could make the federal regulations very relevant in clinical trial lawsuits even though the Common Rule and FDA regulations do not create causes of actions for personal injury. Significantly as well, expert witnesses are typically not required in negligence *per se* cases.

Physician-Researcher Duties Outside the Protocol, and Applicable Codes, Guidelines, and Policies

The researcher–participant relationship undoubtedly creates additional duties as well—duties that derive specifically from the fiduciary/trust relationship between the physician-researcher and patient-participant. This portion of the standard of care can only be articulated by expert witnesses at trial who will describe for juries how a reasonably prudent physician-investigator would act in the same or similar circumstances—what researchers view as prevailing responsible practice in clinical trials. Understandably, conjecture regarding this standard is likely to be more unpredictable than any other aspect or component of the physician-researcher's required standard of care, in part because clinical trials litigation is in its infancy, and in part because standard of care can only be annunciated in relation to the particular factual scenario being litigated.

As stated above, some of the physician-researcher's duty exists because the relationship remains, on one level, that of physician and patient. Further duties attach because the research participant trusts and relies upon the investigator's superior knowledge and expertise. Recall the explanation from above that suggests that the roles of clinician and scientist should be "integrated" without giving "predominance" to either and that physician-researchers can legitimately allow subjects to tolerate some additional risks and discomforts for the sake of research. That analysis, however, stipulates as well that physician-researchers "should be prepared to sacrifice scientific rigor when necessary to protect patients from exposure to severe suffering or disproportionate risks of harm."

What kind of duties will experts articulate when explaining the "integrated" duties of physicians and researchers? Issues discussed earlier such as competent procedural performance, adherence to the research protocols, and IRB review are necessary, but not sufficient, components of the investigator's duty to research participants. The investigator has a personal and independent duty to each individual research participant and expert witnesses' opinion in various cases will reflect this responsibility. For example, if an investigator believes that a protocol represents excessive risk, or insufficient benefit in relation to study risks, he or she should undoubtedly refuse to participate and refuse to enroll participants in the study, even though there is an otherwise legitimate protocol that has been approved by an appropriate IRB. Similarly, expert witnesses will likely confirm that a physician-researcher is required to exclude a patient from a study if the physician believes that this individual patient (e.g., because of clinical, psychological, or physical anomalies) is likely to suffer risks beyond those that are anticipated by the protocol. This duty undoubtedly exists even if the excluded participant meets designated inclusion and exclusion criteria in every other way. Expert witnesses will probably assert as well that a physician-researcher has a duty to refuse to participate in a particular research project if he or she does not have the sufficient intellectual, staff, and clinical resources to properly conduct the study. Expert witnesses will probably agree as well that riskier Phase 1 and Phase 2 studies, for example, typically require especially scrupulous attention, exceedingly well-trained staff, and sometimes special clinical provisions and arrangements in order to ensure the safety of the participants. Likewise, if an individual patient is eligible for one of a number of competing studies for the same illness—e.g., cancer, diabetes, asthma, HIV, etc.—the investigator will likely be found to have the duty to explain the competing studies to the patient *and* to recommend the study that is in the best interests of the patient. This conclusion will probably be based on the physician's default and recognized duty to act in the best interests of the patient, even though enrollment in any one individual study might not, strictly speaking, be in the patient's best interest.

In some clinical trials suits, the plaintiff's claim will be based on the physician-researcher's conduct during the trial. Again, expert witnesses will be asked to explain the customary standard of care required of physician-researchers once the study has begun and participants have been enrolled. Again, following the protocol and skillfully performing study procedures are important, but not enough. Investigators obviously have a duty to withdraw patients from studies if that withdrawal is stipulated by the protocol. But physician-researchers almost certainly have an additional duty—one that is likely to be confirmed by expert testimony—to remove patients from research studies even when the protocol does not call for such removal. Patient risk and patient harm, in and of themselves, are insufficient tests of when to remove a patient from a research protocol. After all, risk and sometimes harm are frequently expected consequences of participation in a study or treatment related to the study. Expert witnesses will likely offer testimony, for example, that investigators have a duty to withdraw individual participants enrolled in the study if it becomes clear that the participant (because of individual characteristics or other factors) is being subjected to greater harm or risk of harm than anticipated at the time of enrollment. Both the investigator and the participant based enrollment on a specific set of expectations regarding harm. If those expectations are exceeded, then the original risk–benefit ratio is no longer valid. On a larger scale, if unacceptable increased risk and/or harm become evident to an investigator for all enrolled subjects, he or she may have a duty to suspend research activity on that study, even if the sponsor, IRB, and other investigators are willing to allow the study to proceed. The message remains that IRB and sponsor approval of a study does not necessarily immunize a physician-researcher from claims that a participant should not have been enrolled in a study or should have been withdrawn.

Expert witnesses will clearly confirm that investigators should consider the interim data, adverse event reports, if any, provided by the sponsor during the study to ensure that enrollment of participants in the study is still justifiable. One might also expect an expert witness to claim that investigators have the duty to monitor the clinical and scientific literature related to their study and the safety of their participants. Consider, for example, the physician-researcher who discovers through *JAMA* or the *New England Journal of Medicine* that the study drug on one of his or her clinical trials is associated with a heretofore unknown increased risk of cardiac deaths. Depending on the expert witness's evaluation of the degree of risk, the physician-researcher might have the duty to suspend research activity, even if the sponsor does not. At minimum, the physician-researcher would have a duty to counsel existing participants regarding the significant new information about the study drug as well as revising the consent process and document to reflect the findings and significance. In some instances, again depending on the expert witness's evaluation, additional safeguards or monitoring plans may be deemed part of the physician-investigator's required standard of care.

In sum, expert witnesses are likely to outline a series of professional responsibilities as part of the standard of care that extend beyond written regulations and guidelines and that transcend the investigator's responsibility to follow the protocol.

Damages and Causation

The final element of negligence—the requirement that the physician-researcher's breach of duty *caused* the plaintiff's injury—will likely be the most contested aspect of research injury litigation. Recall that the plaintiff must demonstrate that "but for" the defendant's negligence, the injury would not have occurred. The harm suffered by the plaintiff must also be a "foreseeable" consequence of the defendant's acts or omissions. While this is a clear test in theory, it may sometimes be difficult to prove in cases of research negligence.[13] Plaintiffs will have to demonstrate that their physical harms were proximately caused by the physician-researcher's negligent conduct—that the defendant physician's breach of duty caused the damage. Causation will, of course, be easier to demonstrate if an investigator negligently conducts a particular study procedure and directly injures a participant. But while it might be relatively easy to demonstrate that a researcher strayed from the standard of care defined by the expert, the protocol, or applicable guidelines and regulations, it may frequently be difficult to connect that breach with the harm suffered by the research participant. If the study participant is already ill or injured, and the harm suffered is one that may be associated with the natural course of the illness or with a nonexperimental treatment received concurrently by the participant, the proof of causation could be more challenging. It may be difficult to distinguish participants' research harms from the physical suffering and effects of their preexisting conditions, their underlying illness, and non-study-related, standard of care treatment that they may also be receiving. In some instances, this ambiguity might play a role in discouraging injured participants from even seeking remuneration for their injuries. Because participants expect some side effects, they may be hesitant to seek compensation for injuries suffered during a study.

Many testing and monitoring requirements exist in protocols merely to provide data points for the sponsor of the research. Unless the breach of duty caused the injury suffered by the plaintiff, there will be no award for damages. Some federal guidelines are intended to protect the safety of research participants; some exist primarily to protect the validity of the data collected. In an injury suit, if the violation of an FDA or Common Rule regulation is related solely to the collection of data and is unrelated to safety, then its contravention cannot be the cause of the research participant's injury and he or she cannot collect damages. It is important to note, however, that the investigator might still face serious sanctions by the relevant federal body for failing to abide by application regulations even in the absence of a viable personal injury action.

Informed Consent

Negligently defective informed consent claims occur with some regularity in ordinary medical malpractice actions and they are likely to play an important role in research litigation.[14] For example, in *Berman*, the suit included a claim that the plaintiff would not have consented to participation in the research trial if she had known that the drug in question was available only in tablet form. The *Gelsinger* case involved claims that the participant had not been informed that previous participants had died in the testing of the study drug, and the plaintiff in the *Hamlet* case claimed that he had not been warned of the dangers of participating in a placebo-controlled trial and the risk of developing debilitating arthritis.

Informed consent duties of physician-researchers resemble those of a treating physician in many ways; in other instances those duties will be quite different. Because insufficient informed consent cases are still a species of negligence action, a plaintiff will have to demonstrate the four elements of negligence: (1) duty; (2) breach of duty; (3) causation; and (4) damages.

The existence of a duty, as discussed above, is fairly easy to demonstrate. However, establishing the standard of care required in informed consent for a research study will involve additions that far exceed those required for consent to standard medical treatment. In the absence of specific case law relating to research suits, physician-researchers will have to satisfy the state law requirements for medical informed consent. Ordinarily, the legal doctrine of informed consent for medical treatment requires that patients are informed of the risks and whatever other information that a "reasonable person" would consider material to his or her decision. Therefore, a valid informed consent for a clinical trial involving treatment would include all the information that a potential participant would consider "material" to his or her decision, just as it would for any medical treatment. Presumably, a "reasonable" patient-participant would need to know information such as: his or her diagnosis; the prognosis; the purpose of the study; the study procedures; the benefits and burdens of the treatment options; the benefits and burdens of study participation, etc. Note that the required information is not codified, but rather is gauged by that information that a reasonable person would consider "material." A reasonable person might consider the reimbursement received by the physician-researcher from a drug sponsor "material" to his or her decision to participate in a clinical trial, as might be a fact such as the availability of a study drug "off-study." The type and amount of required information in any particular case would be one of the matters that would be litigated and decided upon by the jury or other finder of fact.

But physician-researchers will also have informed consent responsibilities that exceed the "material information/reasonable person" test frequently applied to ordinary clinical care. As noted above, physician-researchers will almost certainly be held to accepted national standards for investigators, including the above-mentioned Common Rule, FDA regulations, and ICH-GCP standards. These regulations and the guidance documents that accompany them will likely provide additional evidence of the type of duty that physician-researchers have in regard to informed consent. For example, the Common Rule explicitly requires that participants be informed of: research purpose and procedures; risks and discomforts; potential benefits; alternative procedures or treatment; provisions for confidentiality; the existence of compensation for research-related injuries; contacts for additional information regarding participant rights; and the right to discontinue participation without penalty.[15] Similarly, ICH-GCP guidelines, to which the investigator may be held as a consequence of expert testimony, the protocol, and the clinical trials contract, stipulate that potential subjects be informed of "the anticipated expenses, if any, to the subject for participating in the trial." ICH-GCP guidelines also provide the precise procedures that should be followed under a variety of conditions— when the participant is illiterate, for example. As a result, the information included in the informed consent process must include not only information that a reasonable person would consider material, but also those elements and information stipulated by any relevant research regulations or guidance documents that have been grafted onto the standard of care via expert witness testimony.

In standard medical malpractice cases, the written consent document provides evidence that consent was properly obtained. If the document itself is somehow limited or even nonexistent, the physician will still have an opportunity to make his or her case that the consent was properly obtained orally as the document is only part of the entire process. Admittedly, proof of proper consent under these conditions is more difficult. However, in a suit for insufficient informed consent in a research case the consenting process remains important, but the informed consent document itself takes on much greater importance than in ordinary medical malpractice cases. If conformance to the Common Rule and the FDA regulations regarding research are deemed part of the physician-researcher's professional duty—which is likely—then the informed consent document is a required part of the consenting process. In addition, it must match the federally delineated requirements and the investigator could be held to have breached his duty even if the oral consent was full and robust. Indeed, recently in *Lenahan v. University of Chicago* (2004),[16] an Illinois court of appeals found that a plaintiff had a viable cause of action based on the failure to provide a consent document that complied with FDA and Common Rule standards.

If the required information was not included in the informed consent process or document, the plaintiff will still need to demonstrate that a reasonable person, if provided appropriate information, would *not* have agreed to participate in the study. If a reasonable person would have consented even in the absence of full or clear information, then the defective consent form did not "cause" the patient injury, and the plaintiff has no action under the doctrine of negligent informed consent. In many cases such questions will be clear, but in others there will be sufficient ambiguity, real and manufactured, to make the resolution of such cases far from predictable.

It is important to remember as well that in litigated claims related to inadequate informed consent, claims may be interwoven with other assertions of negligent behavior. Consider the case of a research participant placed on a Phase 1 study. Because the essential goal of Phase 1 toxicity studies is the administration of increasingly high doses of a drug until adverse events occur, protocols invariably require tests and evaluations at regular and strict intervals to monitor the anticipated toxicity of the test item. When toxicity levels reach a predetermined level, the protocol requires removal from the study drug. In addition, participants often require access to qualified study staff and facilities, even on nights and weekends, in the event they begin to suffer from the expected toxicity of the study drug. Indeed, it is clearly mandated in the Common Rule that physician-investigator contact information be explicitly included in the informed consent document. If an investigator fails to conduct a test required by the protocol, fails to notice that toxic levels have exceeded alarm values indicted in the protocol, or fails to remove the participant from the study at the required point, the investigator has breached the required standard of care and would likely be liable for any damages caused by that breach. Failure to obtain or monitor test results that identify toxicities and/or subsequent failure to respond appropriately constitutes both deficient medical and research practice. Suppose further, though, that the contact phone numbers contained in the informed consent document were incorrect, or that the staff available through the provided number could not provide assistance for the participant. If the participant began to feel the effects of increased and missed toxicity, he or she would have no way to contact the investigator and secure relief. Any resulting injury might be linked to the inadequate informed consent (the incorrect contact information) or the negligent failure to have resources sufficient to conduct a study of this level of risk, or the failure to provide monitoring tests or to act on them in the event of results that fall outside of acceptable parameters.

In sum, the most viable and likely cause of action against research investigators is some form of professional negligence. Claims based on negligently obtained informed consent are also probable. The basic legal elements of these actions are well established. As courts and attorneys process more of such claims, it will become increasingly easy to describe the nature of the physician-researcher's standard of care and to apply basic professional negligence law fairly directly to the acts and omissions of research investigators. Unless appellate courts accept the creation of a new cause of action, such as a "dignity tort," plaintiffs will still have to prove to a jury that they have suffered injury or damage. The recognition, demonstration, and calculation of damages will be relatively straightforward and will not vary substantially from ordinary personal injury or medical malpractice suits. Damages, in short, will either exist, or they will not. The biggest challenge to plaintiffs attempting to collect damages against physician-researchers will likely involve the demonstration of the causal relationship between the negligent acts and omissions of the investigator (breach of standard of care) and the damages sustained by the subject. Similarly, in informed consent cases, juries will have to be convinced that the plaintiff would not have consented to participation if the omitted information had been included or presented in a way that was understandable. This causation requirement may sometimes prove a formidable barrier to the plaintiff. However, the real-life ultimate resolution of such cases may also depend on how egregious and offensive the physician-researcher's omission appears to the jury.

SURVIVAL STRATEGIES

If potential targets of litigation respond to legal threats in an irrational way, they risk overcorrecting for existing abuses and problems, thus harming rather than benefiting their patients and the public overall. Excessive legal defensiveness, for example, may encourage physicians to abandon research altogether. Usually, however, a rational appraisal of the risks will allow physician-investigators to conduct useful research, avoid lawsuits, and protect the rights and interests of research subjects. Individuals who have been harmed by the negligence or wrongdoing of another should retain their traditional prerogatives to use the courts to pursue compensation and damages. For their part, physician-investigators should respond to current and future research litigation not only with compliance plans, but with a genuine commitment to rigorously evaluate research in terms of its scientific validity, ethics, and threat to patient rights and health. In order to recruit potential subjects for future projects, physician-researchers will need to maintain and, in some cases, regain the trust of potential research participants so that they will feel comfortable serving as research subjects.

Finally, as physicians are already aware, patient injuries can occur even in the presence of utmost care. Therefore, it is essential that physician-researchers are sufficiently insured against potential clinical trial claims. Physicians should not assume that their current medical malpractice policy will cover injuries incurred during a clinical trial. Medical malpractice carriers may be disinclined to defend and pay claims on research procedures when the terms of the insurance contract limit coverage to suits for damages based on medical care. Physician-researchers should consult with an attorney and their insurance carrier to determine the extent of their coverage. If necessary, they should investigate the possibility of appending a rider to the policy to ensure that research injuries are fully covered in the policy. In addition, physicians should scrutinize the contracts they sign with clinical trial sponsors. These agreements should include "indemnification" clauses that stipulate that the sponsor will be liable for claims based on the clinical trial as long as the trial was conducted according to the protocol and there was no negligence on the part of the physician-investigator. It should be noted that indemnification clauses do not mean that a physician-researcher cannot be sued, but only that the sponsor will have to reimburse for any damages ascribed to the physician and covered under the agreement. Conversely, researchers should also be wary of indemnification agreements that require the researcher to compensate the sponsor for losses related to the clinical trial. Indemnification clauses take many forms and should be examined by an attorney so that the physician-investigator understands the nature of his or her exposure under the contract.

FURTHER READING

"Clinical Trials Litigation," http://www.sskrplaw.com/gene/index.html. [Best single source for information regarding ongoing clinical trial lawsuits. The site contains the original pleadings/complaints for many recent research suits.]

DeVille KA, *The Role of Litigation in Human Research Accountability.* Accountability in Research 9:17–43 (2002).

Hawkins K, *Hospital Wins Lawsuit over Death of Clinical Study Patient.* The Legal Intelligencer 229(100):1 (Nov 19, 2003).

Miller FH, *The Hidden Hazards of Clinical Trials.* Trial 39(10): 50 (2002).

Miller FG, et al., *Professional Integrity in Clinical Research.* JAMA 280:1449–1454 (1998).

Morreim EH, *Medical Research Litigation and Standard Tort Doctrines: Courts on a Learning Curve.* Houston J. Health Law & Policy 4:1–86 (2003).

REFERENCES

1. *Gelsinger v. University of Pennsylvania* (C.P. Phil. Co., 2000).
2. *Robertson v. McGee* (4:01 CV60 D. Okla. 2001).
3. *Berman v. Fred Hutchinson Cancer Center* (No. C 01-0727R, 2001).

4. *Dagosto v. Fred Hutchinson Cancer Center* (No. 02-2-0603-9SEA, King County, Washington Superior Court, 2004).

5. *Kernke v. The Menninger Clinic Inc.*, 173 F. Supp. 2d 117 (D. Kan. 2001).

6. *Hamlet v. Genentech et al.* (03 CVS 1161 Superior Court, Wake County, N.C., 2003).

7. 45 C.F.R. Part 46 (2002) [DHHS regulations on conduct of human subjects research, "The Common Rule"].

8. 21 C.F.R. Parts 50, 54, 56 (2004) [FDA regulations on conduct of clinical trials].

9. *Grimes v. Kennedy Krieger Institute*, 782 A. 2d 807 (Md. Ct. App. 2001).

10. Coleman CH, *Duties to Subjects in Clinical Research*. Vanderbilt Law Review 58:387–449 (2005).

11. Campbell A, Glass KC, *The Legal Status of Clinical and Ethics Policies, Codes, and Guidelines in Medical Practice and Research*. McGill Law Journal 46:473–489 (2001).

12. *Guidance for Industry E6 Good Clinical Practice: Consolidated Guidance*, International Conference on Harmonization Good Clinical Practice (ICH-GCP), 1996 [Published in the *Federal Register* May 9, 1997 (62 F.R. 25692).

13. Mastroianni AC, Faden R, Federman D, "Legal Considerations." In Mastroianni, Faden, and Federman, eds., *Women and Health Research: Ethical and Legal Issues of Including Women in Clinical Studies*, Vol. 1, pp. 129–174. Washington, D.C.: National Academy Press, 1994.

14. Mello MM, Studdert DM, Brennan TA, *The Rise of Litigation in Human Subjects Research*. Annals of Internal Medicine 139(1):40–45 (2003).

15. 45 C.F.R. §46.116.

16. *Lenahan v. University of Chicago* (Nos. 1-02-25-2513 and 1-02-2867, Ill. App. Ct., March 31, 2004).

Criminalization of Malpractice

Judith A. Gic, R.N. (ret.), C.R.N.A. (ret.), J.D., F.C.L.M.

GOLDEN RULES

1. Prosecutions are publicity nightmares where even winning can be a form of losing; avoidance is the most important thing.
2. If you fear a prosecution is imminent:
   (a) Hire a criminal-law lawyer.
   (b) Hire a public relations consultant with experience in representing criminal defendants.

Criminal prosecutions for medical malpractice grab headlines, partly because they are so rare. *Successful* prosecutions resulting in conviction are rarer still. But a conviction is not necessary for the notoriety flung up by a prosecution to ruin a reputation and a practice. Worse, police may seek arrest warrants on probable cause at the instigation of prosecutors, and prosecutors possess a tremendous degree of discretion in deciding whether to seek an indictment against a person.

That discretion lies at the root of the policy debate on criminalizing malpractice.[1] Whether a bad outcome was the result of simple negligence (to be remedied through civil litigation) or was the result of some greater degree of negligence (to be punished through prosecution) may be a very difficult call to make, but still it remains entrusted to prosecutors and grand jurors (and ultimately to trial jurors) who are likely not to have any medical knowledge.[2] If an awful lot seems to ride on the battle of hired-gun expert witnesses in malpractice litigation, imagine staking your freedom on it in a criminal trial.[3]

At the outset, we want to emphasize that this chapter is about negligence-based prosecutions, not those heinous cases where a physician or other caregiver intentionally injures a patient. Of the negligence-based cases, we see two basic types: those that involve pain management and those that do not. Our reason for categorizing the cases in this fashion rests on a couple of factors. First, the pain management cases are sometimes surrounded (perhaps opportunistically by defendants seeking a public relations advantage) by policy debates that do not bedevil the other kind of cases. These debates go to whether doctors adequately treat chronic pain or are being unfairly targeted in the national effort to control drug abuse. Cases of the other kind are simply about spectacularly bad treatment decisions, about which the only possible policy debate is whether civil litigation should be the sole remedy.

A closely related factor that separates the pain management cases from the rest is the appearance that the former sometimes—not always, but sometimes—involve high-volume practices that focus not on patient care but on writing prescriptions just because patients want them. For these two reasons, these cases are usually not just about a medical mistake and may be presented (or at least spun) as the prosecution of drug dealers willing to trade away their patients' welfare for their patients' money. While comprehensive information about prosecutions of doctors is not available—no single resource counts all the cases from all of the criminal jurisdictions within the United States—it appears that prosecutions are somewhat more common in the pain management area. Our case study does not involve a pain management fact pattern, but we will comment on it below.

CASE PRESENTATION

John Biskind, M.D., performed a late-term abortion on LouAnne Herron at his medical clinic. During the procedure, he tore a 2¾-inch gash in Herron's uterus with a medical instrument. He did not realize this during the procedure and completed it as he normally would. Herron was moved to the recovery room. The recovery room was ordinarily staffed with an R.N., but not that day. The only staff (besides Dr. Biskind) included an undegreed medical assistant and the clinic administrator.

Approximately three hours later, Biskind knew that Herron was still in the recovery room, which was longer than usual. He also knew that she had some external bleeding through the vagina, but he thought that her bleeding was not more than usual. According to the medical assistant, Biskind came into the recovery room and checked the IV bag (which contained a clotting agent), and then told Herron that everything would be all right. But the assistant also testified that Herron appeared to her to be bleeding much more than any other patient she had seen in the recovery room.

With Herron still in the recovery room, Biskind left the clinic a little after 4 P.M. to run a personal errand. While he was gone, the clinic administrator phoned to tell him that Herron had no detectable pulse and was having difficulty breathing. Biskind did not return immediately from his errand. At 4:24 P.M., the clinic administrator called paramedics. Shortly after they arrived, Herron died of blood loss from the uterine puncture.

A jury convicted Biskind of manslaughter and he was sentenced to five years in prison.[4] Arizona law defines manslaughter in part as "[r]ecklessly causing the death of another person," and it defines "recklessly" as follows:

"Recklessly" means, with respect to a result or to a circumstance described by a statute defining an offense [such as the death of another person], that a person is aware of and consciously disregards a substantial and unjustifiable risk that the result will occur or that the circumstance exists. The risk must be of such nature and degree that disregard of such risk constitutes a gross deviation from the standard of conduct that a reasonable person would observe in the situation.

A jury also convicted the clinic administrator, but on the lesser charge of negligent homicide for her failure to schedule an R.N. for the recovery room on the day of Herron's abortion and for failing to call paramedics sooner. Arizona law states that negligent homicide occurs "if with criminal negligence … [the defendant] causes the death of another person." It defines "criminal negligence" as follows:

> "Criminal negligence" means, with respect to a result or to a circumstance described by a statute defining an offense, that a person fails to perceive a substantial and unjustifiable risk that the result will occur or that the circumstance exists. The risk must be of such nature and degree that the failure to perceive it constitutes a gross deviation from the standard of care that a reasonable person would observe in the situation.

ISSUES

Criminal prosecution of medical malpractice is not new. Among the earliest reported and affirmed American convictions is *Commonwealth v. Pierce*, an 1884 case from Massachusetts. The defendant (an unlicensed person holding himself out as a physician, which was typical of the era; the absence of a license was irrelevant to the legal analysis) treated his patient by wrapping her with kerosene-soaked rags. He left the patient's house, but a couple of hours later the patient's husband sent for Pierce to return because the treatment was so painful. The defendant returned and succeeded in urging the patient to allow the treatment to continue. The rags stayed on for about three days. The result was tragic; the patient died about seven days later.

The chief issue at trial was whether the defendant knew or should have known that kerosene would hurt, not help. The prosecution offered a witness who testified that the defendant had treated her with kerosene and the result was burning and blistering of the skin where the kerosene was applied. The defendant testified that he had used kerosene before with only minor and temporary skin injuries.

Massachusetts's high court held that medical practitioners are no different from others who work with dangerous materials:

> If persons who are engaged in operating steam-engines are guilty of gross carelessness or foolhardy presumption, and injuries result, they are criminally liable. So, with apothecaries, if a person without knowledge and skill deals with deadly drugs, he may be guilty of gross carelessness amounting to presumption, and be criminally liable. Whenever men are called upon to act with dangerous agencies, the law holds them to some degree of criminal responsibility. If they are grossly careless, or reckless and presumptuous, they are guilty. *The same general principle applies to medical treatment*. The government must show, not merely the absence of ordinary care, but gross carelessness amounting to recklessness. [Emphasis added.]

The court further held that the jury was entitled to decide that the defendant should have realized the dangers of kerosene and that his failure to do so was gross carelessness.

In the years since *Commonwealth v. Pierce*, criminal law terminology has changed somewhat, but the principles that *Pierce* relied upon are easily traceable in the *Biskind* case and in other instances of medical malpractice prosecutions. The most important issue is whether the government will be able to present evidence of something more than the lack of ordinary care. Here, the Arizona statutes operative in the *Biskind* case, which are derived from the Model Penal Code, are typical of the possibilities. There may be evidence that the defendant was aware of a risk but chose to disregard it (the recklessness possibility), or failed to grasp a risk that was so blindingly obvious that any reasonable physician in that position would have grasped it (the criminal negligence possibility). An ordinary malpractice claim certainly encompasses these possibilities—any case of recklessness or criminal negligence falls within the circle of malpractice. Any practitioner charged with a malpractice-rooted crime could also be sued in a civil court for the same conduct. But as we have noted, prosecutions are rare; most malpractice is what the *Pierce* court called "merely the absence of ordinary care."

Despite the proof from *Pierce* (and other 19th-century cases) that prosecution of doctors for malpractice is not a new phenomenon, a recent observer might have thought it was, given the vigor of debate lately on the subject. The case that seems to have sparked that debate was California's unsuccessful prosecution of an ER physician at a rural hospital. He was charged with second-degree murder, involuntary manslaughter, and willful injury to an infant. The infant's condition was beyond the capabilities of the rural hospital at which the child was presented, so the physician arranged for treatment at a better-equipped facility. He discharged the infant to the parents for them to make the one-hour drive on their own instead of arranging for transport by ambulance or medical helicopter. The infant stopped breathing while on the way and eventually died. The facts were apparently very unfavorable for the prosecution, as the trial judge threw out all charges on grounds of insufficient evidence of criminal liability. The medical establishment took the prosecutorial overreaching as an opportunity to lambaste the policy choice of using the criminal justice system to hold a doctor accountable for an error that could have been remedied (and perhaps was, eventually) by civil litigation.

Though the American Medical Association still carries a policy statement that expresses its opposition to prosecution of malpractice, there does not appear to be any meaningful effort among state lawmakers to rewrite their laws to eliminate the prosecution of malpractice. Such an effort would be hard to justify. Just as *Pierce* shows that there is nothing new in prosecutions or the theories on which they are based, there is also nothing unusual or aberrant in these prosecutions from a broader legal perspective. Where prosecution is based on a charge of recklessness or criminal negligence, the question for the jury is similar to the familiar civil law question of malpractice as a deviation from the standard of care. The only difference is that the criminal law seeks to prove a deviation of extreme degree. A criminal prosecution relies on nothing more than an extension of the same basic framework that supports civil liability for professional negligence.

This very similarity is one argument that has been used to oppose prosecution—why should doctors be jailed as criminals if they can be sued for millions? The argument holds that the same conduct should not be subject to both civil and criminal penalties, and that civil penalties are enough. But that does not explain why society should abandon criminal penalties when the facts warrant their application and when it would not abandon them in another context—say, a situation where reckless driving results in both a civil lawsuit by an injured victim and prosecution by the state. Who would claim to be satisfied if the private remedy preempted the public remedy? Likewise, prosecution for medical crimes is not based on some special category of criminal laws that apply only to health care professionals, but rather on state manslaughter and homicide statutes that apply to all people in all situations.

We noted at the outset that prosecutors have also trained their sights on physicians with pain management practices, and that these cases may present elements of malpractice in the form of recklessness or criminal negligence, plus some drug-related criminal charge. For example, in one case a grand jury indicted a physician on felony charges of dispensing medicine without a valid reason. The doctor had previously been the object of a state medical board proceeding. The board found a complete lack of medical evidence to support the physician's prescription-writing practices. Concerning one patient, the board found that the physician routinely wrote prescriptions for Xanax, Valium, Vicodin, and later Lorcet, but had performed no objective medical tests to diagnose the origin of the pain, had provided no treatment other than narcotics, had no plan for achieving pain relief, and had never performed any evaluation to determine the effectiveness of treatment. The evidence also showed that the physician knew that the patient was obtaining pain medications from at least one other physician and that he continued writing prescriptions after he learned that the patient had tested positive for marijuana plus two other drugs—codeine and morphine—that the physician had never prescribed. This patient died from an apparent overdose. The board's fact-findings listed four other patients who died of apparent overdoses and concluded that the physician's level of practice was below the accepted standard of care and presented a threat to his patients' health and safety. Press reports indicated that the physician's office did not take appointments but treated patients on a first-come, first-served basis. According to one article, they "typically began lining up before dawn to assure that they got in the door. By the end of a busy day, as many as 150 to 200 patients had passed through his doors." Presumably, the availability of the drug charge made it unnecessary to charge manslaughter or negligent homicide. The case is apparently still pending.

SURVIVAL STRATEGIES

To cite avoidance as a survival strategy may seem trivial. Naturally you should avoid being prosecuted—what else would you do? But avoidance really is key, much more so than in a civil malpractice case. Professional survival is not really at stake in the average civil malpractice lawsuit, even in the event of losing the case. In a criminal malpractice case, on the other hand, losing the verdict might mean losing your freedom, and even winning might be worse (because of the publicity) than losing a civil case. Avoidance as a strategy might be difficult to fill with meaningful content—how should someone go about avoiding a spectacularly bad mistake?—but it is not trivial. On the contrary, it is the most important survival strategy because survival will be difficult once a case gets filed.

And while answering how you would avoid a spectacularly bad mistake might be difficult to answer, it is probably worth pondering from time to time. Everyone has some notion of their strengths and weaknesses, and everyone has some idea of the problematic circumstances in which they do not perform at their peak.

Once avoidance becomes moot, prompt retention of a criminal-law lawyer is the next best step. As in any other type of malpractice litigation, absolute fidelity to the patient chart is crucial, as attempts to alter, remove, or add documentation may unravel and, if so, will point irresistibly toward the defendant's consciousness of guilt.

Finally, to maximize your chances of professional survival, consider hiring a public relations consultant with experience in representing criminal defendants. In the event of acquittal, you will want (and may very well need) to rebuild your practice as quickly as possible. Assistance in helping to blunt negative pre-trial publicity may be crucial in that post-trial endeavor.

FURTHER READING

Filkins JA, "Criminalization of Medical Negligence." In *Legal Medicine/American College of Legal Medicine*, 7th ed., ed. S. Sandy Sanbar *et al*. Philadelphia: Mosby, 2007.
1 Model Penal Code & Commentaries (1985).

REFERENCES

1. American Medical Association, Policy H-160.946, The Criminalization of Health Care Decisionmaking (on file with author), available at http://www.ama-assn.org.

2. Smith AM, *Criminal or Merely Human? The Prosecution of Negligent Doctors*. 12 J. Contemp. Health L. & Policy 131 (1995).

3. Van Grunsven R, *Criminal Prosecution of Health Care Providers for Clinical Mistakes and Fatal Errors: Is "Bad Medicine" a Crime?* 29 J. Health & Hosp. L. 107 (1996).

4. Associated Press, *Abortion Doctor Sentenced to 5 Years in Death of Patient*. Arizona Republic, May 4, 2001.

ETIOLOGY OF
MALPRACTICE

Etiology of Malpractice

S. Sandy Sanbar, M.D., Ph.D., J.D., F.C.L.M.

GOLDEN RULES

1. The cause of medical malpractice is most commonly the result of negligence.
2. The plaintiff generally bases the malpractice lawsuit not only on negligence but also on other allegations.
3. The physician should be cognizant of the various etiologies, or causes of action, of medical malpractice, most of which are listed in this chapter.
4. The physician should obtain from defense counsel case(s) similar to one's lawsuit in order to read and be acquainted with the legal methods and analysis of the case.

The purpose of this chapter is to provide an overview of the legal theories, or causes of action, by which the patient as a plaintiff may bring a lawsuit against a physician. The etiology, or causes of action, of medical malpractice are:

1. Medical negligence.
2. Wrongful death.
3. Loss of a chance of recovery or survival.
4. *Res ipsa loquitur* ("the thing speaks for itself").
5. Battery and assault.
6. Lack of informed consent.
7. Abandonment.
8. Breach of privacy and confidentiality.
9. Breach of contract or warranty to cure.
10. Products or strict liability for drugs and medical devices.
11. Vicarious liability for the actions of other health care providers.
12. Negligent referral.
13. False imprisonment.
14. Defamation.
15. Failure to warn or control.
16. Negligent infliction of emotional distress.
17. Outrage.
18. Failure to report.
19. Fraud and misrepresentation (deceit).
20. Loss of consortium.

The majority of the legal theories presented briefly in this chapter are discussed in detail in other chapters of this Handbook.

CASE PRESENTATION

In 2000, the Supreme Court of Oklahoma, in *Sarah J. Franklin v. Kyle Toal, M.D., and Norman Regional Hospital Authority, a Public Trust* (19 P. 3d 834), vacated the opinion of the Court of Civil Appeals, reversed the judgment of the trial court, and remanded the case with instructions for the trial court to enter partial summary adjudication on the issue of liability in favor of plaintiff and against defendants and for trial on the issue of damages only, and to enter judgment for plaintiff which was to include appeal-related costs. The Supreme Court of Oklahoma held that the trial court erred in denying plaintiff's motion for directed verdict against the defendants.

In the *Franklin* case, the defendant physician performed heart surgery on plaintiff at defendant hospital. After plaintiff's chest cavity was opened, a phrenic nerve pad was placed beneath her heart. However, the pad was not removed from plaintiff's chest cavity before the incision was closed. Defendant physician admitted that he had a duty to remove the pad. Jury rendered verdict in favor of defendants. Trial court denied plaintiff's motion for a judgment notwithstanding the verdict, or, in the alternative, a new trial, and plaintiff appealed. The appellate court affirmed.

The Supreme Court of Oklahoma vacated the appellate court's opinion. Defendant physician's failure to remove the pad was a breach of his duty and was the proximate cause of plaintiff's injury. Based on defendant physician's admission that it was his duty to remove the pad, no judgment was involved in failing to remove the pad. He simply forgot to remove the pad, and there was no excuse for failing to remove it. The only reasonable inference to be drawn from the evidence was that defendant physician was negligent. Defendant hospital also failed under its articulated duty to use ordinary care and it was also negligent.

ISSUES

The term *malpractice* refers to any professional misconduct that encompasses an unreasonable lack of skill or unfaithfulness in carrying out professional or fiduciary duties. The term *medical malpractice* is used in this chapter because of the common and traditional usage in claims alleging medical negligence by health care professionals. The term *physician* is used in this chapter to mean any health care professional.

Negligence is the most common basis for a medical malpractice action imposing liability on a physician. However, physicians may be involved in legal actions based on the other legal theories listed above. The physician must be aware that a medical malpractice lawsuit can be brought simultaneously under several legal theories. If the plaintiff patient wins under any of these theories, recovery of a monetary award from the defendant physician may result.

ETIOLOGY OF CAUSES OF ACTION AGAINST A PHYSICIAN

1. Medical Negligence

Medical negligence is a breach of the physician's duty to behave reasonably and prudently under the circumstances that causes foreseeable harm to another. For a successful suit under a theory of negligence or in legal terms to present a cause of action for negligence, an injured patient (plaintiff) must prove each of the following four essential elements by the preponderance of evidence.

Duty

Duty, the first element of the negligence theory of liability, is created by the physician–patient relationship. The "life" of medical practice, both generically and specifically, is generally a contract, referred to as the physician–patient relationship. Both medically and legally, it is considered a "sacred" or fiduciary relationship. The physician–patient contract may be entered into with the physician by a third party on behalf of the patient, as in the case of a managed care organization.

Duty requires that a physician possess and bring to bear on the patient's behalf that degree of knowledge, skill, and care that would be exercised by a reasonable and prudent physician under similar circumstances. The physician owes the patient a duty to act in accordance with the specific norms or standards established by the profession, commonly referred to as standards of care, to protect the patient against unreasonable risk. The defendant physician may fail to exercise the required skill, care, or diligence by either commission or omission (i.e., by doing something that should not have been done or by failing to do something that should have been done). It may not matter that the physician has performed at his or her full potential and in complete good faith. Instead the physician must have conformed to the standard of a "prudent physician" under similar circumstances.

There is no clear definition of the duty of a particular physician in a particular case. Because most medical malpractice cases are highly technical, witnesses with special medical qualifications must provide the judge or jury with the knowledge necessary to render a fair and just verdict. As a result, in nearly all cases the standard of medical care of a "prudent physician" must be determined based on expert medical testimony. In the case of a specialist the standard of care by which the defendant is judged is the care and skill commonly possessed and exercised by similar specialists under similar circumstances. The specialty standard of care may be higher than that required of general practitioners.

Although courts recognize that medical facts usually are not common knowledge and therefore require expert testimony, professional societies do not necessarily set the standard of care. The standard of care is an objective standard against which the conduct of a physician sued for malpractice may be measured, and it therefore does not depend on any individual physician's knowledge. In attempting to fix a standard by which the jury or the trier of fact may determine whether a physician has properly performed the requisite duty toward the patient, expert medical testimony from witnesses for both the prosecution and the defense is required. The jury or the trier of fact ultimately determines the standard of care, after listening to the testimony of all medical experts.

Breach of Duty

Breach of duty, the second element of medical negligence, must be proved by the plaintiff. The plaintiff alleges that the physician failed to act in accordance with the applicable standard of care and did not comply with, and hence breached, the requisite duty. The applicable standard of care must be proved before the plaintiff can prove that the physician breached that duty. In most cases, expert witnesses for the prosecution and the defense address the question of breach of duty while testifying as to the standard of care owed.

There are exceptions to this rule. Expert testimony may not be required if a plaintiff presents evidence showing that the defendant physician's substandard care is so obvious as to be within the comprehension of a lay person. Another exception is the judicially imposed standard of care. Generally, courts rely on medically established standards of care to determine a health care provider's duty and breach of that duty. Some courts have required a "preferred" rather than the usual, ordinary standard of care. To that end, the courts have rejected the testimony of medical experts as to the accepted medical standard of care when they thought it inappropriate, and decreed their own, i.e., judge-made, standard of medical care.

Causation

Causation, the third element, must also be proved by the plaintiff alleging medical negligence. The plaintiff must show that a reasonably close and "causal connection" exists between the negligent act or omission and the resulting injury. In legal terms this relationship is commonly referred to as *legal cause* or *proximate cause*. The concept of causation differs markedly from that of medical etiology in that it refers to a single causative factor and not necessarily the major cause or even the most immediate cause of the injury, as is the case with medical causation or etiology.

Although causation may seem to be an easy element for plaintiffs to prove, it is frequently the most difficult and elusive concept for the jury to understand because of the many complex issues. Legal causation consists of two factual issues—*causation in fact* and *foreseeability*.

Causation in fact may be stated as follows: An event A is the cause of another event B. If event B would not have occurred but for event A (known as the *"but for"* test), causation exists. The "but for" test is easily passed in some cases but not in others. Consider the following contrasting examples. The patient with an intestinal perforation resulting from a surgeon's failure to remove an instrument from the abdominal cavity may suffer subsequent abdominal abscess, surgery, or death. But for the retained instrument, such a complication would not have occurred. In contrast, a physician's delay in the diagnosis of a highly aggressive malignant neoplasm might not necessarily affect the patient's chance of survival.

Foreseeability is the second causation issue. A patient's injuries and other damages must be the foreseeable result of a defendant physician's substandard practice. Generally the patient must prove only that his or her injuries were of a type that would have been foreseen by a reasonable physician as a likely result of the breach of the medical standard of care.

The law of causation varies widely from jurisdiction to jurisdiction, and its proof is currently in flux. In *Daubert v. Merrell Dow Pharmaceuticals*,[1] the U.S. Supreme Court addressed the admissibility of scientific evidence in a case involving expert testimony concerning causation. This decision, which is followed in most jurisdictions, allows judges great discretion in deciding what scientific evidence is or is not admissible, especially as applied to the causation element.

Damages

Proof of damages, the fourth element of the medical negligence suit, encompasses the actual loss or damage to the interests of the patient caused by the physician's breach of the standard of care.

There can be no recovery of damages if the patient is not harmed. The exception to this rule is "*nominal* damages," where a token sum, economically worthless, is awarded a plaintiff who has had his or her honesty, integrity, or virtue challenged and is vindicated by the satisfaction of having his or her claim honored. Although rare, the significance of an award of nominal damages is that it may serve as a prerequisite to the award of punitive damages.

The purpose of awarding damages in a tort action is to ensure that the person who is harmed is made "whole" again or returned to the position or condition that existed before the tort of negligence. Because it is generally impossible to alleviate the effects of an injury resulting from medical malpractice, public policy demands redress through the award of monetary compensation to the plaintiff. The legal fiction is that money makes the damaged patient whole.

Damages may encompass compensation for a wide range of financial, physical, or emotional injury to the plaintiff patient. The law has recognized certain categories of damages, but categorization is often imprecise and inconsistent because some of these categories overlap and are not strictly adhered to by courts of all jurisdictions.

Compensatory damages are awarded to compensate the patient for losses. There are two types of compensatory damages—*special* and *general*. *General damages* are awarded for noneconomic losses, including pain and suffering, mental anguish, grief, and other related emotional complaints without any reference to the patient's specific physical injuries. *Special damages* are those that are the actual but not necessarily the inevitable result of the injury caused by the defendant and that follow the injury as foreseeable and natural consequences. Typical items of special damages that are compensated by a monetary judgment include past and future medical, surgical, hospital, and other health-care-related costs; past and future loss of income; funeral expenses in a case involving death; and unusual physical or medical consequences of the alleged injury, such as aggravation of a preexisting condition.

If a wrong was aggravated by special circumstances, *punitive or exemplary* damages, in addition to the injured patient's actual losses, may be awarded. *Punitive damages*, which are rarely awarded in medical negligence cases, are intended to make an example of the defendant physician or to punish his or her egregious behavior. Such damages generally are awarded when the defendant's conduct has been intentional, grossly negligent, malicious, violent, fraudulent, or with reckless disregard for the consequences of his or her conduct.

2. Wrongful Death

If negligence results in the death of a patient, recovery may be based on the doctrine of wrongful death. A wrongful death is a death that occurs earlier than it would have ordinarily. If negligence is the legal causation of the patient's death, then his or her statutory survivors or personal estate may bring an action in "wrongful death." The action is considered to be a derivative one; it cannot be brought unless the decedent would have had a cause of action had he or she survived. Its rationale is to benefit the survivors. The action is thus a creature of statute, and allows the decedent's survivors to maintain civil actions. Recovery includes *pecuniary* damages, or that amount that the decedent could reasonably have been expected to contribute if his or her death had not ensued, plus damages for emotional injury.

3. Loss of a Chance of Recovery or Survival

Loss of a chance of recovery or survival caused by the negligence of a physician has been recognized by the majority of states. Courts weigh the diminished prospects for a plaintiff whose statistical future expectations are already severely impaired. Liability is imposed for negligence that merely increased the probability of an already probable negative outcome, as in the case of failure to diagnose a malignancy or acute myocardial infarction.

However, the majority of U.S. jurisdictions retain the "but for" test, i.e., the negligently injured patient must prove that the chance for recovery or survival was probable, was more likely than not, or was better than even. The rationale for this all-or-nothing approach is that less than probable losses are speculative and unfairly impose liability based on unquantified possibilities. The majority position is that what the measure "might have caused" is an insufficient quantum of evidence.

Under the majority theory, a plaintiff with less than a 50/50 chance cannot be harmed to a compensable degree by negligent care.

4. *Res Ipsa Loquitur*

Res ipsa loquitur, which literally means "the thing speaks for itself," is a legal doctrine that relieves the plaintiff from the requirement of proving duty and breach of duty through a physician expert witness. In other words, negligent care may be presumed. *Res ipsa loquitur* requires the plaintiff to show only that the outcome was caused by an instrumentality in the exclusive control of the defendant, that the plaintiff did not voluntarily contribute to the result, and that the injury was the type that normally does not occur in the absence of negligent care. After the plaintiff shows these elements, the burden of proof may shift to the defendant physician to prove otherwise. For example, the patient who discovers that a sponge or an instrument was left within his or her abdomen during surgery may have a *res ipsa loquitur* case. However, causation and damages may need to be proved by expert testimony.

5. Battery and Assault

In medical injury cases battery is not a negligence action but an intentional tort. The law in general recognizes that an individual should be free from unwarranted and unwanted intrusion. In legal terms, touching another person without that person's express or implied consent is a battery. The attempt to touch another person without consent is an assault. Assault can be considered an attempt at battery.

The law in all jurisdictions places considerable importance on this principle of personal autonomy, which traditionally has been reinforced by legislation dealing with patients' rights. In the medical setting, battery most often involves undesired medical treatment or nonconsensual sexual contact. To successfully prove a claim of medical assault or battery, the plaintiff must show that he or she was subjected to an examination or a treatment for which there was no express or implied consent. The treatment provided must be substantially different from that to which the patient agreed. There also must be proof that the departure was intentional on the part of the physician. Unlike claims made under the negligence theory of consent, there is no need to prove actual harm in battery cases, although harm may have occurred. The amount of damages of course relates directly to the amount of harm in most cases. For example, an operation that is not consented to but saves the patient's life likely will not result in damages, except in rare cases. However, if the patient suffers painful, crippling, or lingering effects, significant damages may be awarded.

Specific examples of medical battery include the performance of sexual "therapy" by a psychiatrist or other mental health care professional in the name of treatment, the unauthorized extension of a surgery to nonconsented bodily organs unjustified by the original procedure, and the nonconsensual treatment of Jehovah's Witnesses or others whose religious convictions limit therapeutic alternatives. Expert testimony regarding standard of care and breach of standard of care is not necessary in battery cases.

Although in some jurisdictions recovery still may be based on assault and battery theories, through legislation (sometimes as part of reform measures) most jurisdictions have removed the right to bring such an action because it is subsumed under other medical malpractice causes of action. This change is a result of the now nearly universal acceptance of the doctrine of informed consent. A physician may be negligent if he or she diagnoses or treats a patient without obtaining informed consent or an adequate informed consent for such a diagnostic or treatment procedure.

6. Lack of Informed Consent

Patients must be capable of giving consent, must possess adequate information with which to reach a decision regarding a diagnostic procedure or treatment, and must be given ample opportunity to discuss alternatives with the physician. A failure to meet the requirements for an appropriate and adequate informed consent may be a departure from the recognized standard of care and may result in an action for failure to obtain "informed consent" against a health care provider.

Consent is a process, not a form. Physicians may fail in their duty to patients when they rely on a form or document for achieving "informed consent." Such a form can never replace the exchange of information between a patient and a health care provider, which is necessary to fulfill the requirements of an adequate informed consent.

7. Abandonment

Generally a physician has no duty to provide care to a person who desires treatment. However, a physician who agrees to treat a patient accepts the duty to provide continuity of care. Legal recognition of this duty follows from the reality that a sick or injured person is at risk until cured or stabilized. No physician can be available at all times and in all circumstances. Yet, the physician must provide an adequate surrogate when unavailable. Many physicians meet this obligation by making arrangements with a partner or nearby colleague in the same or similar field of practice. Backup may be provided by directing ambulatory patients to a nearby, physician-staffed hospital emergency department. Brief lapses of coverage are generally reasonable. For example, it is unlikely that a physician would be successfully sued for failure to attend simultaneous cardiac arrests for which no other physician was available. Physicians are sued when the unavailability of coverage for several hours harms a patient.

This duty to provide continuing care is extinguished when the physician dies, when the patient no longer requires treatment for the illness under consideration, or when the physician gives reasonable notice to the patient of his or her intention to withdraw from the case. In the case of withdrawal, the physician must give the patient time to arrange for care from another qualified physician or must arrange for a substitute physician who is acceptable to the patient. The original physician must provide emergency care for the patient's condition and related medical problems until the patient has established a relationship with the new physician. A duty to provide care may generate a duty to third parties under certain circumstances.[2]

With the accelerated growth of managed health care plans, many physicians have become members of various health care networks. In some cases a physician may opt to leave a network to join another. Such an action *per se* does not necessarily end a physician–patient relationship, particularly if the patient opts to continue the relationship outside of the network payment scheme. Any physician who wishes to discontinue caring for patients previously seen in such a system may notify those patients of a change in managed care participation and arrange for appropriate transfer of care to a successor physician.

8. Breach of Privacy and Confidentiality

State and federal (HIPAA) laws impose on physicians a duty to respect the privacy interests and confidentiality of their patients' information. Generally, everything said by a patient or his or her family members to a physician in the context of medical diagnosis and treatment is confidential and may be revealed only under certain circumstances. In many states the physician–patient relationship is recognized by a statute that sets forth exceptions to the general rule of confidentiality, including investigations by medical examiners, and possible cases of infectious diseases. Some states rely on common law in this area. Each practitioner should know the rules that apply in his or her state and establish procedures for his or her employees to act accordingly.

In general, health care providers can safely release medical information to other treating physicians or consultants. In life-threatening emergencies, certain information pertinent to the patient's treatment also may be revealed to other medical personnel, even if the patient is unaware.

9. Breach of Contract or Warranty to Cure

When a physician promises to cure or to achieve a particular result and the patient submits his or herself for treatment, the physician is generally liable if the treatment fails to achieve the promised result. The unhappy patient in such a situation can sue the physician in contract rather than in tort. This form of medical malpractice suit has become less common in recent decades. The major advantage for the plaintiff in a contract suit is that a medical standard of care need not be shown. The plaintiff must prove only that a promise was made and relied on, the promise was not kept, and damages resulted because of the broken promise. The plaintiff in such a suit must prove how he or she was damaged by the physician's breach of promise. A successful plaintiff generally recovers an amount of money that would place him or her in a position comparable to the position he or she would be in had he or she not agreed to treatment. In many cases this amounts to a return of the surgeon's fees, plus a small sum for related expenses. Damages may be exceedingly high in some instances, however, such as when a professional performer is scarred or killed.

Most physicians at one time or another prognosticate for their patients. Courts understand this aspect of medical practice. Breach of contract or warranty actions usually arise when a physician sells a patient on a particular operation. To prevent a plethora of unwarranted suits, many states provide that no legal action may be taken for breach of a contract to cure unless the physician's promise is in writing.

10. Products or Strict Liability for Drugs and Medical Devices

Products or strict liability (i.e., not negligence-based liability) is imposed on manufacturers, sellers, and distributors of unreasonably dangerous and defective products for injuries resulting from their use. Such liability is independent of negligence law and a defendant's degree of care is irrelevant in lawsuits based on the concept of strict liability. However, the law recognizes that every drug and device used in medical practice is potentially hazardous. Therefore manufacturers, sellers, and distributors of such products are not liable for damages if they give adequate warnings about how to avoid the risks and make their products as safe as possible. These warnings must be given clearly, prominently, and in a timely manner, and they must be given to the proper person. Overpromotion of a product can negate the effect of otherwise adequate warnings.

Products liability is mentioned here because many medical malpractice suits also include claims for harm caused by the physician's alleged failure to inform and adequately warn the patient of a dangerous or defective product in his or her role as "learned intermediary."

Products liability reduces the plaintiff's burden of proof. It is much easier to prove that a product warning was not given or was inadequate than it is to show that a physician violated the standard of care. The plaintiff must show only that the product was defective or that the warning of its nondefective hazards was faulty and the deficiency of product or warning was a cause of the injury. Foreseeability is not required to make a case of strict liability against a defendant.

A products liability case can be brought when a defendant physician is uninsured or underinsured, and a solvent pharmaceutical house or device manufacturer may be found liable to pay a share of any judgment. Sometimes a defendant physician brings the drug manufacturer, or device company, into the suit as a "third-party defendant," requiring it to pay part or all of the plaintiff's damages, or the defendant treating physician also may be the seller of the drug or device.

11. Vicarious Liability for the Actions of Other Health Care Providers

Physicians usually employ or supervise other less qualified health care professionals, and consequently owe their patients the duty to supervise nurses, technicians, and other subordinates properly. The duty to supervise may create vicarious liability, whereby one person may be liable for the wrongful acts or omissions of another. Several legal doctrines must be discussed in this context.

Respondeat Superior

Respondeat superior states that an employer is liable for the negligence of his or her employees. For example, if a physician's office nurse injects a drug into a patient's sciatic nerve, causing injury, that patient may sue the physician for the nurse's negligence.

Captain of the Ship Doctrine

Physicians also may be held vicariously liable for the negligence of hospital employees whom they supervise under other legal doctrines. For example, surgeons have been sued for errors and omissions by operating room personnel under the "captain of the ship" doctrine. This doctrine holds a surgeon liable based on the legal action that he or she has absolute control, much like the captain of a ship at sea who is responsible for all the wrongs perpetrated by the crew. This doctrine was intended to offer a remedy to persons injured by negligent employees of charitable hospitals, which were otherwise legally immune from suit under the doctrine of charitable immunity.

Borrowed Servant Doctrine

The "captain of the ship" doctrine has been largely replaced by the "borrowed servant" doctrine in such situations. This latter doctrine holds surgeons responsible for hospital employees' negligent acts that are committed under their direct supervision and control.[3]

12. Negligent Referral

Physicians frequently request consultations from other physicians, especially regarding hospitalized patients. A referring physician usually is not liable for the negligence of the specialist. However, the referring physician may be liable for the specialist's misdeeds if each physician assumes that the other will provide certain care that is omitted by both or if they neglect a common duty (e.g., postoperative care).[4]

Physicians cannot attend or be available to all patients at all times. They have the duty to provide another physician to care for their patients when they cannot. Just as physicians generally are not liable for consultants' malpractice, they need not answer for care provided by other physicians who cover their practice. Exceptions include the use of covering physicians who are also partners and the negligent selection of covering physicians.

13. False Imprisonment

False imprisonment is a tort that protects an individual from restraint of movement. False imprisonment may occur if an individual is restrained against his or her will in any confined space or area. The plaintiff is entitled to compensation for loss of time, for any inconvenience suffered, for physical or emotional harm, and for related expenses. A physician holding a patient against his or her will, in absence of a court order, could be held liable for false imprisonment. Such situations arise in cases involving involuntary commitment of a patient with a mental disorder, where a patient is held without compliance with laws governing civil commitments.

14. Defamation

A statement is defamatory if it impeaches a person's integrity, virtue, human decency, respect for others, or reputation and lowers that person in the esteem of the community or deters third parties from dealing with that person. A defamatory statement can be made either in writing, which is called libel, or in verbal communication, which is called slander. In general, truth is an absolute defense to defamation. Some jurisdictions have a rule that a statement that is substantially true, when published with good motives and justifiable ends, shall be a sufficient defense, even though it may not be literally true. For example, if a physician states publicly that a nursing home has 50 complaints against it and there were only 30, the statement likely would not be held defamatory.

15. Failure to Warn or Control

The failure of a physician to warn the patient or a third party of a foreseeable risk is a separate and distinct negligent act.[5] A physician's duty of care includes the duty to identify reasonably foreseeable harm resulting from treatment and, if possible, to prevent it. It is increasingly recognized that a physician has the responsibility to warn patients of dangers involved in their care. Failure to advise the patient of known, reasonably foreseeable dangers leaves the physician open to liability for harm the patient suffers and injuries that patient may cause to third parties.

The courts have imposed on a physician the duty to warn when medications with potentially dangerous side effects are administered. If an administered drug might affect a patient's functional abilities (such as ambulation), the physician is obliged to explain the hazard to the patient or to someone who can control the patient's movements (e.g., family members or others who can reasonably be expected to have contact with the patient). The same duty is owed to patients engaged in any activity that may be hazardous, such as driving a car or operating machinery.[6] Similarly, when a physician learns that a patient has or may have a medical condition with dangerous propensities that may impair the patient's control of his or her activities, the physician has a duty to warn the proper persons, such as the patient's family members or others in contact with the patient. This duty to warn may apply whether the condition is completely diagnosed or is still under study.

In a number of cases, physicians have been held liable to injured third parties for failure to warn them of the potentially dangerous mental condition of a patient. Similarly, patients' next of kin have successfully sued after the patients committed suicide, which could have been foreseen and potentially prevented by a physician.

The duty of the physician to warn has generally been narrowly construed in non-mental-health cases.[7]

16. Negligent Infliction of Emotional Distress

Some courts have recognized negligent infliction of emotional distress as an independent cause of action in which a patient's harm was caused or aggravated by the patient's reasonable fear for his or her own physical safety. Presently, third parties, such as the next of kin or bystanders to someone else's injury, are also regarded as having a cognizable claim.

An action for wrongful infliction of mental distress may be based on either intentional or negligent misconduct. The action will not lie for mere insults, indignities, threats, or annoyances.

17. Outrage

The courts have been imposing an additional liability for the tort of "outrage." As applied to health care providers, "outrage" is an extension of the doctrine of strict liability, i.e., liability without the proof of negligence. The tort of outrage involves deliberate infliction of mental suffering on another, without physical injury. The aggrieved party may be either the actual victim, or merely a third party affected only indirectly.

There are four elements to outrage:

1. The wrongdoer's conduct was intentional or reckless; that is, the wrongdoer deliberately caused emotional distress in a given individual, or the wrongdoer knew—or should have known—that emotional distress would be a likely result of his action.
2. The conduct was outrageous and intolerable, offending the generally accepted standards of decency and morality. This requirement serves to limit frivolous "outrage" suits and avoids litigation in situations where only bad manners, unpleasantness, or hurt feelings are involved.
3. There was a causal connection between the wrongdoer's action and the emotional distress.
4. The emotional distress was severe.

18. Failure to Report

Every jurisdiction has a list of diseases that must be reported to the authorities. The physician's failure to conform to the statutory requirement may make him or her liable for criminal penalties. Failure to report also has been held to be negligence *per se* (not requiring proof of negligence) in civil suits brought by injured patients or third parties. Statutes in many states require physicians to report battered children and abused elderly patients to the proper authorities. The physician is generally exempt from any civil or criminal liability for making a report pursuant to the terms of the statute. If the physician fails to report such abuse, he or she may be held liable to any individual who is damaged by this failure.

19. Fraud and Misrepresentation (Deceit)

Fraud and misrepresentation are intentional torts that involve deceit. They have sufficiently common features and are treated collectively in this discussion. A showing of deceit requires proof of all of the following:

1. The defendant knowingly made a false representation.
2. The false representation was made in order to benefit the person making the representation or to cause harm to another person.
3. The plaintiff relied on the misrepresentation as true.
4. The plaintiff was injured as a result of his or her reliance.

Fraud and misrepresentation can be applied to the practice of medicine; for example, a physician who left a foreign body in a patient during an earlier procedure but fails to tell the patient the real cause of complications or symptoms. The patient's consent for the second surgical procedure is obtained on a false basis. This constitutes fraud or misrepresentation. In such a case, expert medical testimony is not required. Furthermore, most professional liability insurance carriers will not provide defense counsel or reimbursement for damages to a physician in this situation except under a reservation of right. Punitive damages may be awarded as well.

20. Loss of Consortium

Courts are increasingly recognizing a physician's liability to third parties when the physician negligence results in emotional injuries and damages as an isolated phenomenon or as a consequence of or in conjunction with physical injury. *Consortium* is that conjugal fellowship of husband and wife, and the right of each to the company, cooperation, affection, and aid of the other in every conjugal relation. Because all family members suffer emotional injury when one is injured, damages for loss of consortium are being awarded to husbands, wives, certain unmarried partners, parents, and children.

Loss of consortium includes loss of services, and loss of companionship, security, society, aid, comfort, love, affection, solace, and guidance.

REFERENCES

1. 509 U.S. 579 (1993).
2. *Grimsby v. Samson*, 85 Wash. 2d 52; 530 P. 2d 291 (1975).
3. *Lewis v. Physician's Ins. of Wisconsin*, 627 N.W. 2d 484 (2001).
4. *Craig v. Murphree*, 35 Fed. Appx. 765 (10th Cir., 2002).
5. *Weitz v. Lovelace Health Systems*, 214 F. 3d 1175 (10th Cir. N.M., 2000)
6. *Cram v. Howell*, 680 N.E. 2d 1096 (1997).
7. *Martinez v. Lewis*, 969 P. 2d 213 (Colo., 1999).

Breach of the Physician–Patient Relationship

Ben A. Rich, J.D., Ph.D.

GOLDEN RULES

1. Strive to make your encounters with patients (and their families) transparent.
2. Regardless of your medical specialty, cultivate an inclination and ability to relate to your patients as persons and to treat them with respect. Remember that another word for an angry patient is plaintiff.
3. Remember that the physician–patient relationship is a fiduciary one, in which establishing and maintaining the trust and confidence of the patient, and maintaining fidelity to the patient when confronted with conflicting interests, is absolutely essential.
4. Mindfully practice effective communication strategies in all aspects of medical practice—with patients, family members, and professional colleagues.
5. Treat the medical record as vitally important to good patient care and to the minimization of risk of professional liability.
6. Establish and maintain clear expectations of your patients, particularly where their behaviors may have an important impact on the outcomes of treatment.
7. Be aware of relevant local organizational or institutional policies, procedures, and protocols, as well as national clinical practice guidelines that may have a role in establishing the standard by which your care of patients will be evaluated.

CASE PRESENTATION

Lewis Hand presented to a Humana Hospital facility emergency room (ER) complaining of a headache that had persisted for 3 days. Dr. Boyle, the ER physician, established that Hand had a history of hypertension and that his father had died of a ruptured aneurysm. Dr. Boyle observed Hand over a period of hours, noting that his symptoms varied with blood pressure levels, which Dr. Boyle was able to control to some degree with medication. Following the period of observation, Dr. Boyle made the determination that Hand should be admitted to the hospital. As a Humana Health Care Plan participant, Hand's admission required review and approval by another designated physician. Dr. Boyle was informed that Dr. Tavera was the physician on call that evening for the purpose of

133

authorizing such an admission. Dr. Boyle briefed Dr. Tavera by telephone on Hand's case, but Tavera concluded that Hand could be adequately treated with medication as an outpatient and therefore refused to approve his admission to the hospital. Hand was sent home where he suffered a stroke several hours later.

In the malpractice suit brought by Hand, his claim against Dr. Tavera was dismissed by the trial court on the grounds that no physician–patient relationship between the two had ever been established and thus Dr. Tavera owed no duty to Hand. The review by the court of appeals considered the narrow question of whether a physician–patient relationship existed between Hand and Dr. Tavera, not the broader secondary question (assuming that it did) of whether a duty of care had been breached. The appellate court carefully considered two contractual provisions—one between Hand and the Humana Health Care Plan, and another between the Southwest Medical Group (which employed Hand) and Humana. By virtue of these contracts, the appellate court concluded that Humana owed an obligation to provide Hand with necessary and appropriate medical treatment, and that Humana had contracted with Southwest Medical Group, among others, to meet such a patient care obligation.

The court of appeals therefore reinstated Hand's negligence claim against Dr. Tavera, concluding that "the Humana plan brought Hand and Dr. Tavera together just as surely as though they had met directly and entered the physician–patient relationship … [because] when the health plan's insured shows up at a participating hospital emergency room, and the plan's doctor on call is consulted about treatment or admission, there is a physician–patient relationship between the doctor and the insured."[1] Once the existence of the physician–patient relationship between Hand and Dr. Tavera had been established as a matter of law, the question of fact as to whether or not Dr. Tavera had breached that relationship would be determined in the malpractice trial that followed, and would be based upon expert testimony and other evidence as to whether or not Dr. Tavera's conduct fell below the applicable standard of care.

ISSUES

In one sense, the topic of this chapter—breach of the physician–patient relationship—encompasses many of the other topics to which specific chapters of this Handbook are devoted, e.g., improper disclosure of confidential information (Chapter 13), lack of informed consent and refusal (Chapter 14), and negligence (Chapter 15). Therefore, the reader should consider other chapters as potential sources of additional information on the issues considered in this chapter.

As the case presented above indicates, the complexities of our health care system and modern health care contractual relationships materially implicate the establishment of and potential ways in which a physician–patient relationship may be breached. Traditionally it was true that most physician–patient relationships were not established through formal written contracts, but rather were implied when a patient sought a physician's care and the physician undertook to provide such care. The same was true in both primary and specialty care situations. The extensive penetration of managed care into the U.S. health system, and the increasing frequency with which individual patients move from one health plan, and hence from one primary care physician or specialty care network, to another, has introduced a new third party, the managed care organization (MCO), into the equation, but has not resulted in changes in certain fundamental professional obligations and legal principles governing a physician's duty to a patient and what acts or omissions may constitute a breach of that duty. Indeed, courts have consistently demonstrated an inclination to hold fast to the traditional legal and ethical principles governing the physician–patient relationship, despite the significant changes that have taken place in health care delivery over the last 20 years. Consequently, we will begin our discussion with those core professional values and legal principles.

The Fiduciary Nature of the Physician–Patient Relationship

The physician–patient relationship, like the attorney–client relationship, is a quintessential example of what is known generally as a fiduciary relationship. Such relationships are characterized by expectations of trust and confidence that are reposed by a vulnerable party in the other party who holds him or herself out as possessing specialized knowledge, expertise, and experience. Society, through both laws and codes of professional ethics, imposes upon the party in whom the vulnerable party entrusts this trust and confidence an obligation to act solely in the interests of the vulnerable party, and to use their expertise only so as to promote the other party's interests and wellbeing. Therefore, despite health policy discussions about the appropriateness of individual physicians taking into account the costs of medical procedures and treatments to a health plan or society, such considerations cannot, as a matter of prevailing law, properly influence a physician's decision whether or not to offer or recommend such procedures and treatments to patients when necessary or appropriate to diagnose or treat medical conditions. Moreover, any form of artifice, deception, or lack of diligence in the pursuit of the other's interests, or incompetence, may be the basis for disciplinary action by a professional licensing authority and/or malpractice judgment in the courts.

The exponential growth of managed care organizations (MCOs) in recent decades has created the perception, if not in some instances the reality, of potential conflicts of interest between a physician's professional duty to their patient and their contractual obligation to such MCOs. The role of the primary care physician (PCP) as "gatekeeper" to specialty care within a health plan, the capitation system by which PCPs are compensated by MCOs, and the financial benefits to the PCP that may accrue from the limitation of patient referrals for specialty care create at least the appearance of threats to the most essential feature of the physician's fiduciary duty to the patient, which is to act only so as to further his or her interests, and not those of some larger group of health plan participants, or the physician. The courts have been relatively consistent in their refusal to allow changing modes of funding the provision of health care services to materially alter an individual physician's responsibility toward an individual patient. Indeed, one court noted that "the physician who complies without protest with the limitations imposed by a third party payor, when his medical judgment dictates otherwise, cannot avoid his ultimate responsibility for his patient's care."[2]

One of the ways in which medical jurisprudence has sought to reduce the imbalance of power between physician and patient is the formulation and imposition of the duty to obtain the patient's informed consent to any medical intervention, and to respect the informed refusal of a patient to undergo a recommended medical intervention. The failure of a physician to advise a patient about the nature of the proposed intervention, its risks, benefits, and alternatives, and the prognosis with or without treatment, will constitute a breach of the physician's duty to a patient and a departure from the prevailing standard of acceptable care (see Chapter 14 for a more detailed discussion and analysis of this topic).

When discussing options for diagnosis or treatment of a patient's condition, physicians should strive to be scrupulous in clearly distinguishing between that which they merely *offer*, because it is in the realm of possibility and hence perhaps required by the doctrine of informed consent, and that which the physician genuinely believes to be most appropriate and beneficial to the patient, and therefore actually *recommends*. Keeping this distinction in mind is important because patients generally assume that a physician would not even mention an intervention or course of treatment unless he or she believed the patient should undergo it, even though that might not in fact be the case. This distinction is particularly critical when a physician discusses treatment options of last resort, life-sustaining interventions, or participation in clinical trials for gravely ill or terminal patients (see Chapter 9).

Contractual Issues in the Physician–Patient Relationship

Typically, the nature of the physician–patient relationship, particularly in the primary care setting, is not specifically delineated or circumscribed by written contractual provisions. While the court that considered the case described at the beginning of this chapter did so as the primary basis for concluding that a physician–patient relationship existed between Tavera and Hand, despite the fact that they had never met, historically and in most instances written agreements are not the deciding factor. In the absence of any written contract, generally acceptable expectations will control the extent of the physician's responsibility to the patient and the determination of when there has been a failure on the part of the physician to fulfill those responsibilities. However, in the event there is a written contract specifically setting forth the physician's responsibilities to the patient, as well as, perhaps, the patient's responsibilities within that relationship, then the contract will be controlling so long as the patient knowingly and voluntarily entered into it. Contracts in which one party, in this circumstance the patient, was not at liberty to negotiate the terms of the contract, or otherwise unable to seek comparable care elsewhere, are considered by the law to be "contracts of adhesion" and are highly disfavored. Consequently, any ambiguities in the contractual language will be construed in favor of the patient.

For obvious reasons, physicians rarely execute written contracts with patients that purport to guarantee or otherwise ensure certain results from medical treatment—what are characterized by the law as "express warranties." A circumstance approximating a written assurance of outcome might be drawings or sketches provided to a patient by a plastic surgeon illustrating the anticipated results of cosmetic surgery. Unless there were specific written contractual provisions clearly indicating that the provision of such visual representations did not constitute a warranty of the results, patients might reasonably rely on such sketches and a material departure from the results could give rise to a breach of contract claim by the patient.

It should not be surprising that a physician might make oral representations that minimize the risks or exaggerate the likelihood of benefits confronting the patient in undergoing a recommended medical intervention. When a risk with major adverse consequences arises, or the anticipated benefit of a major intervention fails to be achieved, the patient in such circumstances is likely to believe that there has been a breach of the physician–patient relationship. If there is a significant disparity between the oral representations made by the physician and any written disclaimers in the consent form, some courts might be inclined to permit the patient plaintiff to present evidence to the jury that the physician's representations were so materially different from the consent form as to constitute a material misrepresentation of fact that would allow the case to go to the jury.

There are a surprising number of cases in which physicians have made verbal statements that courts have ultimately determined to be contractual warranties of results. The critical distinction that courts seek to make is between statements that fall within the category of "therapeutic reassurance," and statements that cross the line into a guarantee of certain results or a warranty of "cure." Telling a patient "We will take good care of you" is clearly no more than reassurance, even if the outcome of treatment is not what either the patient or physician hoped for, whereas telling a patient that if she undergoes a coronary artery bypass grafting procedure she "will never have chest pain again" is arguably a warranty of a certain result. There will, inevitably, be many cases that fall within a gray zone somewhere between a statement that is obviously no more than a well-intentioned reassurance of a worried patient, and a clear promise that a certain outcome will not simply be pursued but actually achieved. Avoiding these gray areas is part of the art (as opposed to the science) of medicine that involves effective communication of risk and benefit by the physician to the patient.

One area that has proven to be "fertile" for breach of warranty claims against physicians is sterilization procedures. A statement that the procedure (bilateral tubal ligation) was "permanent and irreversible" might reasonably be interpreted by a patient as a warranty that, if properly performed, the patient will be assured of never becoming pregnant again.[3] Since there is a small but recognized statistical possibility that even a properly performed tubal ligation or vasectomy may not render the patient permanently unable to procreate, physicians must be very careful how they frame their representations to patients, and carefully document in the medical record what they actually do say. From a risk management perspective, physicians would be wise to consider providing the patient with a written explanation about the procedure that clearly disclaims any guarantee or results, and then document in the record that the patient acknowledged having received, reviewed, and understood its contents.

Another area of practice in which breach of contract suits have been successful involves changes in the nature of the procedure or the person who performs it. In some circumstances, patients consent to performance of a particular procedure or performance of a procedure in a particular way. If the physician fails to obtain consent to perform the procedure in another way or to perform an alternative procedure if circumstances at the time justify doing so and the patient is not "available" to agree to the change, e.g., is under general anesthesia or heavily sedated, a breach of contract action might be allowed. Also, courts have consistently held that "ghost surgery," in which unbeknownst to the patient a physician other than the one known to the patient performs the procedure, can be the basis for a breach of contract claim. Therefore, physicians must be careful to allow themselves as much flexibility as they believe may be reasonably necessary in order to appropriately address unanticipated circumstances through their prior consent discussions with patients.

There are several reasons why a patient plaintiff will be inclined to pursue a breach of warranty claim in addition to, or perhaps even instead of, a claim of negligence against a physician. One is that in a number of jurisdictions no expert testimony is necessary in order for the plaintiff's case to go to the jury.[4] That is because the crux of the complaint is not that the physician departed from the prevailing standard of care, which can only be established through expert testimony, but rather that he or she failed to produce the result that they promised. Thus the critical issue in the latter claim is not the applicable standard of care, but rather the precise nature of the promise and whether or not what was promised was in fact provided. Another reason why patients may be inclined to invoke a breach of warranty claim if the facts support it is that in some jurisdictions the statute of limitations is longer for contract actions than for tort actions. If the statute of limitations has run on a malpractice claim, a breach of contract claim may offer the only possibility of recovery to a prospective plaintiff.

One form of contractual provision in the health care setting that has been consistently repudiated by the courts is the "exculpatory clause." Such clauses are an effort by health care institutions or professionals to force patients to waive their right to pursue professional liability claims arising out of the care about to be provided. Even in instances in which the *quid pro quo* has been the provision of free care, courts have ruled such clauses to be invalid because they are considered to be against the public interest.[5] Courts have shown themselves to be amenable to partial limitations on the right of patients to sue under special circumstances. A typical example would be a form signed by the patient releasing the physician and health care institution for liability for the adverse consequences stemming from the patient's refusal of a particular intervention, such as a blood transfusion.[6]

A relatively new form of contract that has received increasing attention, particularly in the pain medicine community, is known as an "opioid contract." With the increased emphasis upon the importance of effective assessment and management of pain to quality patient care, and the growing acceptance of the need that some patients with moderate to severe chronic pain (of both malignant and nonmalignant origins) have for opioid analgesics, the opioid contract has been touted as a means of carefully circumscribing the parameters within which opioid therapy will be provided.[7] Common provisions of such contracts include requirements that the patient do the following:

- Secure opioids only from one physician.
- Fill prescriptions at a single pharmacy.
- Scrupulously follow the dosing schedule of the prescribing physician.
- Consistently keep follow-up appointments.
- Submit to periodic drug screening panels to ensure against drug abuse or diversion.

Failure of the patient to adhere to the provisions of the opioid contract may result not merely in the refusal of the physician to prescribe opioids for the management of the patient's pain, but discontinuation of the physician–patient relationship.

Such contracts have not met with universal acceptance. Some physicians argue that such contracts place an adversarial, or at least accusatory, cast upon the physician–patient relationship, while others maintain that to single out opioid analagesia for such contracts inappropriately places the physician in the role of drug law enforcer.[8]

The Role of the Consulting Physician

The case presented at the beginning of this chapter is a special instance of a consulting physician, in which the consult or review prior to hospital admission is a requirement of a managed care plan. However, clinical consults are very common in contemporary medical practice. When the consulting physician actually examines the physician, regardless of whether it takes place at the request of the patient or the patient's physician or health insurance company, a professional relationship with the patient is established. Not only must the consulting physician meet the applicable standard of care, but he or she must act reasonably to ensure that the patient's interests are protected. Even in situations in which the consulting physician never examines the patient, so long as that physician provides a professional service such as reviewing laboratory or test results, as is common in pathology, radiology, or cardiology, a relationship with the patient will be recognized.

What are sometime referred to in the vernacular as "curbside consults," in which one physician informally asks another physician for their insights into a clinical issue, are unlikely to be sufficient to create a professional relationship, since the "consulting physician" will probably not have any identifying information about the patient. As a matter of public policy, courts want to encourage such professional interactions.

"Good Samaritan" Provisions

Except in a couple of states, no one in the United States, including a physician, is legally obligated to come to the aid of another person. Nevertheless, most physicians believe that their moral and/or professional responsibility does require that they render aid to strangers in an emergency, regardless of when or where they may encounter it. The law of virtually all jurisdictions has sought to encourage physicians to act in this way through what has come to be characterized as "Good Samaritan" statutes. Such provisions do not provide blanket immunity from liability for negligence. However, they do prevent recovery for malpractice for care rendered without compensation and outside of the usual clinical setting, unless the physician can be shown to have acted in a grossly negligent manner.

Patient Abandonment

Once formed, a physician–patient relationship is expected to continue until the reasons for the initiation of the relationship no longer exist or the parties mutually agree that the patient's care should be transferred to another physician. Abandonment occurs when a physician unilaterally, and usually abruptly, ceases to provide care for the patient, and fails to take appropriate measures to secure alternative care for the patient. Cases of patient abandonment typically arise after a period in which the patient has consistently failed or refused to keep appointments, comply with a treatment plan (nonadherence), or regularly engages in abusive or disruptive behavior in the clinical setting in which care is provided. While the physician–patient relationship is not one in which physicians are bound to patients indefinitely regardless of the patient's behavior, the vulnerability of patients is generally viewed as such that physicians are expected to tolerate a certain degree of patient nonadherence to the treatment regimen or conformity with the niceties of interpersonal relationships without resorting to renouncement of their professional obligations. Physicians who practice exclusively or substantially within the ambit of a particular managed care organization may be subject to plan policies or procedures that govern the transfer of care from one primary care physician to another or that address other acceptable means of disengagement from an established physician–patient relationship.

If patients have demonstrated a pattern or practice of behaviors that are incompatible with an effective physician–patient relationship, but fail on their own initiative to seek alternatives for their medical care, then it is within the prerogative of the physician to terminate the relationship. However, the physician should adhere to certain well-recognized steps when disengaging from a professional relationship with a patient:

1. It is advisable for the physician to provide the patient with prior notice that certain behaviors, whether in the form of disruptive or abusive conduct toward the physician or clinic personnel, repeated, last-minute cancellation of or failure to keep appointments, or persistent nonadherence to treatment plans or other physician recommendations, will result in termination of the professional relationship. Such prior notice should be given in clear, unequivocal, but nonthreatening terms, ideally followed up with a letter specifying the problematic behaviors and reiterating the need for them to change if the relationship is to continue.

2. If, after multiple oral and at least one written warning, the problematic behaviors continue and are sufficiently troubling to warrant termination of the professional relationship, then the physician should orally, followed up immediately thereafter with a confirmatory letter, notify the patient that as of a designated date, perhaps 30 days hence, the physician–patient relationship will be formally terminated. In the interim, the patient should be reassured that his or her genuine medical needs will be met.

3. The physician should, at the very least, provide the patient with the contact information for several physicians or clinics in the vicinity where he or she may seek alternative arrangements for their care. While a physician may choose to actually contact other physicians in order to try to arrange for continuity of care, this is not essential in order to successfully defend against a potential charge of patient abandonment. However, such efforts on the part of the physician may dissuade an otherwise unhappy or dissatisfied patient from making such a charge in the first place. If the physician is successful in arranging for another physician in the area to take the patient, then the transferring physician will be in a better position to hold firm to the previously communicated deadline for the discontinuation of the physician–patient relationship, since the patient will have an identified source of competent medical care.

SURVIVAL STRATEGIES

Be Mindful of the Circumstances in Which a Physician–Patient Relationship Exists

This strategy may, on first impression, appear to state the obvious. However, in our increasingly complex, interwoven, rapidly paced, and diverse system (the skeptics say "nonsystem") of health care, it may not always be readily apparent to a busy physician that a brief encounter, either with a medical colleague or a patient, may have been minimally sufficient to give rise to a physician–patient relationship with all of its attendant responsibilities. Ask yourself, might a reasonable person (not necessarily just a reasonable physician) believe that my words or actions engendered a professional relationship with attendant obligations to the patient, even though I am not actively and on a continuing basis involved in the patient's care? If the answer is yes, then the physician should carefully record the nature and extent of their engagement, and determine that he or she is comfortable with what they said or did, as well as with their knowledge of how things will proceed thereafter with regard to that patient.

Be Knowledgeable of and in Compliance with the Applicable Standard of Care

Material departure from the relevant standard of care is both medical malpractice and also a breach of the physician–patient relationship, in that providing competent patient care is the essence of the practice of medicine. Other chapters in this text, particularly those in Section 4, provide detailed discussions of liability-generating acts and omissions in the various medical specialties. It is important to be aware that in an increasing number of jurisdictions the standard of care is not exclusively determined by the usual custom and practice of physicians with similar training and experience caring for similar patients. Nationally promulgated clinical practice guidelines, whether evidence or consensus based, may be utilized by plaintiffs' attorneys to successfully demonstrate that the usual custom and practice is itself substandard in light of the current state of medical science and technology and the views of nationally recognized experts of what constitutes appropriate patient care in any particular situation. Physicians cultivate their ignorance of such widely disseminated guidelines at their own risk. Similarly, hospital or health plan policies, procedures, and protocols can be sufficient to create a standard of care binding upon physicians who practice within those plans or institutions.

Effective Communication with each Patient is Critical

There is an old saying, relevant to both the practice of medicine and law: "Don't say it so that anyone can understand it; say it so that no one can misunderstand it!" This admonition goes far beyond the admonition that informed consent in patient care can only be achieved if the physician eschews medical jargon in discussing risks, benefits, and alternatives with patients. It encompasses the consistent practice of asking your patient to repeat in their own words important information, warnings, advice, or recommendations you have just conveyed to them. The ultimate goal of the informed consent process is not patient consent, but patient understanding of all circumstances pertinent to the decision or decisions that must be made about care and treatment.

There is another well-established fact about medical malpractice claims, i.e., there are two essential conditions precedent to the filing of one. The first is an unanticipated bad outcome. The second is a failure to establish or a breakdown in the trust, confidence, and rapport that is the hallmark of an effective fiduciary relationship. Both of these essential elements are directly linked to good communication. Also, the extended discussion in this chapter concerning physician promises or warranties of results implicates communication strategies, particularly the occasionally fine distinction between "therapeutic reassurance" and a promise to produce a specific therapeutic outcome. Physicians who are particularly careful in their choice of words, and diligent in confirming what the patient actually heard, are much less likely to be found to have crossed the line from appropriate reassurance to inappropriate guarantees of results.

Scrupulous Documentation in the Medical Record

Timely and appropriately detailed documentation in the medical record can often be the bane of the busy clinician. Nevertheless, it continues to be essential to sound medical practice and to the successful defense of physicians who are charged with professional negligence or other breaches of the physician–patient relationship. Most experienced medical malpractice defense attorneys will affirm that the time a physician spends consistently and carefully documenting medical encounters and interventions will be justly rewarded if only one malpractice claim can be successfully defended by means of a detailed and accurate medical record. On the other hand, significant gaps in the medical record may give the appearance of substandard patient care to a jury, whether or not it actually occurred.

FURTHER READING

Atiyah PS, *Medical Malpractice and the Contract/Tort Boundary*. Law & Contemp. Probs. 49:287–303 (1986).

Hall M, *Law, Medicine, and Trust*. Stanford L. Rev. 55:463–527 (2002).

Hickson GB, *et al.*, *Patient Complaints and Malpractice Risk*. JAMA 287:2951–2957 (2002).

Hurwitz B, *Clinical Guidelines and the Law*. BMJ, 311:1517–1518 (1995).

Kraman SS, Hamm G, *Risk Management: Extreme Honesty May Be the Best Policy*. Ann. Int. Med. 131:963–967 (1999).

Levinson W, *et al.*, *Physician–Patient Communication: The Relationship with Malpractice Claims Among Primary Care Physicians and Surgeons*. JAMA 277:553–559 (1997).

Mehlman M, *Fiduciary Contracting: Limitations on Bargaining Between Patients and Health Care Providers*. Univ. Pitt. L. Rev. 51:365–417 (1990).

REFERENCES

1. *Hand v. Tavera*, 864 S.W. 2d 678 (Tex. Ct. App., 1993).
2. *Wickline v. State*, 192 Cal. App. 3d 1330 at 1645 (1986).
3. *Depenbrok v. Kaiser Foundation Health Plan, Inc.*, 79 Cal. App. 3d 167 (1978).
4. *Hasse v. Starnes*. 915 S.W. 2d 675 (Ark. 1996).
5. *Tunkl v. Regents of the University of California*. 383 P. 2d 441 (Cal. 1963).
6. *Shorter v. Drury*, 695 P. 2d 116 (Wash. 1985).
7. Fishman SM, *et al.*, *The Opioid Contract in the Management of Chronic Pain*. 18 Journal of Pain and Symptom Management 27 (1999).
8. Hurwitz W, *The Challenge of Prescription Drug Misuse: A Review and Commentary*. 6 Pain Medicine 152 (2005).

CHAPTER 13

Improper Disclosure of Confidential Information

David R. Donnersberger, Jr., M.D., J.D., M.A., F.C.L.M.

GOLDEN RULES

1. Physicians who transmit health information in electronic form for billing or transferring funds for payment are subject to all of the rules and penalties of HIPAA.
2. Disclosure of Personal Health Information (PHI) is appropriate if:
   (a) given to the patient;
   (b) given to anyone specifically authorized by the patient;
   (c) required by law; or
   (d) used for purposes of treatment, payment, or in usual business operations.
3. Physician disclosures of PHI to hospital quality assurance, risk management, institutional research, and ethics review committees are appropriate.
4. Beware of disclosure of PHI to patients' family members and "representatives":
   (a) Know the recipient of the PHI.
   (b) Ask the patient to specifically authorize who can receive PHI.
   (c) If the patient cannot make decisions, consult advance directives or ask the family to appoint a spokesperson.
   (d) Document the process in the chart.
5. Use caution when sharing PHI with health care entities not in the usual course of your business operations, treatment, or billing.
6. Never "lend" your EHR password to anyone else, especially your family members, secretary, or nurse.
7. Close all EHR accounts before leaving a terminal or PDA!

The physician–patient relationship creates an obligation on the part of the physician to protect certain confidential patient information. Cultural assumptions about the relationship between the physician and the patient create a duty on the part of the physician to keep information private. Improper disclosure of that information, or breach of that duty, should necessitate some punishment of the physician and some compensation to the patient. The concept seems self-evident. This chapter will differentiate between commonly cited assumptions, advisory guidelines, and binding laws that populate the landscape of physician disclosure of confidential information.

145

Case A. On busy medical rounds in the Intensive Care Unit (ICU) an attending physician stops in to see her patient with advanced dementia and aspiration pneumonia on a mechanical ventilator. The physician knows that the patient's dedicated daughter is the power of attorney for health care decision making and assumes that there is a happy family situation. While in the ICU, the physician is notified of a phone call from the patient's son in a distant state. The physician explains the patient's dire situation. The son asks the physician to explain the medical details to the "family" attorney on speakerphone so that the son can begin to "tidy up" his dad's affairs. The physician also faxes the lawyer some medical records. Later that day, the patient's daughter calls the physician in an irate state. She explains that her estranged brother filed papers alleging that she has committed elder abuse. He is seeking the appointment of a guardian to strip her of her status as power of attorney and that she may no longer be able to access her father's sizable estate to pay for his ongoing care at home. She states that her brother is manipulative and has a long history of attempts to access their father's estate for his own use.

Case B. A busy private, multi-specialty medical group has been recruited by a local hospital system to have its paper medical records merged into the hospital's comprehensive electronic health record (EHR) system. The relationship is mutually beneficial to the hospital and the group. The hospital and its many specialty centers gain increased accessibility, uniformity, and continuity of records for thousands of patients from a new referral source. The private multi-specialty group is able to free up space and reduce document expenses by going "paperless," and in doing so convert a chart storage room into a new lab. The cost of computerizing the medical records is paid by the hospital system. Three months after the merger of medical records, a patient of the multi-specialty group learns that her private records (formerly kept in paper form in the group's locked offices) were accessed electronically by a medical student rotating at the hospital. The medical student had no legitimate, professional reason to access the confidential information, but has spread sensitive psychiatric and obstetric information in the community. The patient is outraged and wonders why her confidential medical information was converted into electronic records without her permission and then shared with a hospital system, thousands of hospital employees, and hundreds of caregivers with whom she has no professional relationship. She asserts that her records were shared without her permission and done so for the financial benefit of her former medical group and the hospital system.

ISSUES

Introduction

Physician stewardship of patient confidential information is not as clearly articulated in the law as many think.

First, new federal regulation known as the Health Insurance Portability and Accountability Act of 1996 ("HIPAA")[1] creates federal civil monetary and criminal penalties for improper disclosure of confidential patient information, but does so without giving patients rights to personally sue a doctor for misuse of confidential information. Under HIPAA, patients make complaints of improper disclosure of confidential information to the Office of Civil Rights of the Department of Health and Human Services and proceedings are brought in administrative hearing.

Second, prior to HIPAA, physician responsibilities for protecting confidential patient information were explicitly codified only in the ethical and professional standards of the profession and the language of state licensing acts. A cause of action in court to recover financially for losses caused by an improper disclosure must be grounded on less specific state common law theories of breach of confidence or invasion of privacy. Of course, myriad mandatory reporting laws make it obligatory for physicians to disclose certain confidential patient information to protect public health or prevent crimes. In those cases, there is no violation of professional standards or a breach of confidentiality cause of action.

Third, the legal concept of *doctor–patient privilege* needs to be differentiated from the topic discussed in this chapter. Legal actions are governed by rules of evidence that determine the admissibility or discoverability of certain information. Privilege refers to a class of information that is exempted from use in court. The right to exert privilege to prevent certain information from being used belongs in some instances to the person in possession of the information (physician) and in some instances to the person who is the subject of the information (patient). Specifically, the doctor–patient privilege never historically existed in English and American law. The privilege was created only later by state statutes. Today, however, there are many exceptions to statutory doctor–patient privilege stemming from mandatory reporting of public health information, in all matters pertaining to criminal cases, and in malpractice and workers compensation cases where the patient puts his medical condition into issue. Despite popular cultural assertions to the contrary, the concept of doctor–patient privilege is largely without legal viability.

Foundations of Physician Confidentiality

Thousands of years ago the original version of the Hippocratic Oath enunciated the physician's duty to honor patient confidences, describing a breach of that duty as something shameful. Modern versions of the Hippocratic Oath, recited at medical school commencements everywhere, do not diminish the original oath's emphasis on the duty of the physician to keep private the confidences of patients.[2] If anything, the modern version elevates the importance of patient privacy by situating it in the paragraph that reminds physicians to save life, to be humble witnesses to death, and never "to play at God."

The ancient Greeks no doubt understood that medical care was a societal good. Healing loved ones, prolonging life, and promoting a healthy community serve basic human desires and put to good use the technological and scientific advancements created by society. Both in ancient and modern times, medical care functions most successfully when the patient is assured of complete confidence on the part of the physician.

The inevitable vulnerability one feels when sharing both nakedness and illness is surely the most fundamental source of the need for physician confidence. Within the family relationship the sharing of nakedness and illness is accepted because there exists an automatic assumption of protection, selflessness, and love. Expert medical care, however, is provided to an enormous degree outside of the protections of the family structure. Only if one is guaranteed that their vulnerabilities are protected—body, behavior, and illness—can patients feel secure in divulging their most human conditions. Medical care and the benefits it imparts on society are optimized when patients are honest with their physicians. The guarantee that society holds the physician responsible for confidential stewardship of that private information is an absolute requisite for medicine to function and yield benefits to the community.

Modern Restrictions and Penalties Involving Disclosure

Explicit codification of the physician responsibility to protect the confidentiality of patient information is found in advisory, nonbinding form in the Hippocratic Oath and the AMA Principles of Medical Ethics.[3] Violations of these principles carry no penalties as they are not enacted or judicially endorsed, and therefore do not carry the enforceable power of state or federal law. Each state, however, has enacted legislation defining the scope and licensing requirements for the practice of medicine. Some state laws may explicitly describe the physician responsibility to protect confidential patient information. Others like the Illinois Medical Practice Act of 1987 may specify examples of dishonorable physician conduct that warrant discipline, such as failure to "safeguard patient confidence and records within the constraints of the law."[4]

It is essential to understand that violation of these licensing or disciplinary regulations results in *professional penalties* to the physician who improperly discloses confidential patient information. These penalties range from formal letters of sanction to permanent revocation of medical licenses. Hospitals and health care systems can likewise restrict or revoke physician privileges to practice within their institution for improper disclosure or use of confidential patient information. These penalties can severely impact a physician's reputation and ability to earn a living, but they do not carry criminal or civil penalties that would allow for financial awards for aggrieved patients or jail time for the physician.

In most states, patients who suffer damages as a result of physician disclosure or misuse of confidential information seek redress under the common law theories of breach of confidence and invasion of privacy. Since a universally accepted cultural expectation of confidentiality exists between physician and patient, the law implies a contractual obligation or duty of confidentiality in the physician–patient relationship. The breach of the duty to protect patient confidence results in damage to the patient. The patient can assert the right to have the damage redressed by bringing an action against the physician seeking a monetary reward to make the patient "whole" again. Such civil actions can occur simultaneously with professional disciplinary investigations by state medical licensing bodies.

Since the advent of HIPAA in 1996 there has been new federal attention paid to the issue of privacy of patient records and improper disclosure or misuse of confidential information. HIPAA applies to all health care providers, including physicians, who transmit health information in electronic form for billing or transferring funds for payment. Physicians who electronically transmit health information to Medicare for purposes of reimbursement are subject to the HIPAA rules. Employees of physicians who are subject to HIPAA regulation are themselves subject to the penalties laid out in HIPAA.

HIPAA creates civil monetary fines for improper disclosure of confidential patient information. For the purposes of HIPAA, confidential patient health information is regarded as *individual identifiable* patient health information—what the Act calls patient's *protected health information* or PHI. The civil monetary fines created under HIPAA are imposed by the Office for Civil Rights of the Department of Health and Human Services. Investigation into *covered entities*, such as physicians, for improper disclosure of PHI is conducted by the Office of Civil Rights after a patient or other source makes a complaint. An action against the physician is then brought by the Office of Civil Rights in federal administrative court. The patient does not have an individual right to sue the physician or seek monetary award under HIPAA. Only disclosures of PHI that are not done knowingly are punishable by these civil penalties. The $100 civil penalty may be avoided in some circumstances where the disclosure is reasonable and cured within 30 days or when there was no knowledge that the conduct was a violation.

HIPAA also creates very severe criminal sanctions for *knowing* or purposeful disclosure of individually identifiable patient information.[5] The Department of Justice enforces theses criminal actions. Simple violations of PHI can result in fines up to $5000 and imprisonment in jail for a term of up to one year. Disclosures or misuse of PHI under false pretenses carries a fine of up to $100,000 and up to five years of imprisonment. Disclosure or misuse of PHI that is committed with the intent to sell or use the individually identifiable information for commercial advantage, gain, or malicious harm carries a fine up to $250,000 and up to ten years in prison. The criminal penalties under HIPAA apply to the employees of a physician practice, as well as to doctors and physician corporations. Moreover, the officers of a corporation whose employees improperly disclose PHI are subject to criminal penalties. In other words, the physician who operates a medical practice as a corporation is not protected from criminal penalties if an employee improperly discloses PHI.

Confidential Patient Information, PHI, and the Medical Record

The definition of confidential patient information is fluid and varies under different applications. For the purpose of common law actions of breach of confidentiality and invasion of privacy, a community standard would be applied by state courts to define the information shared within the physician–patient relationship that is expected and historically considered to be private. In other words, state courts would ask "What does the community and what does prior case law accept as information that a physician should keep private?" Although not all states accept the invasion of privacy theory as a viable cause of action to seek recovery for improper physician disclosure of patient information, some invasion of privacy logic probably applies. To that end, no information that is publicly known would likely be considered confidential.

State medical boards and licensing agencies can be broader in the determination of what behavior constitutes improper physician use or disclosure of confidential patient information. Because state law widely empowers these bodies with the regulation of medical practice and physician conduct, there is great latitude afforded them to determine unethical or unprofessional behavior. Sanctions can vary from letters of censure to permanent revocation of license based on the severity of the misuse or disclosure.

Under HIPAA the definition of confidential patient information is laid out explicitly. As introduced earlier, the language of the Act refers to confidential patient information requiring physician protection as protected health information or PHI. The type of patient health information that physicians must protect from improper use or disclosure under HIPAA is information that is *individually identifiable*. In other words, HIPAA strictly protects health information that is particular to a patient and carries with it some identifying feature like name or address. Under HIPAA a physician is prohibited from disclosing PHI unless expressly authorized by the patient, required by law, or used for treatment, payment, or health care operations.

Disclosure of Electronic Health Records (EHR)

In April 2004 President Bush created the Office of the National Coordinator for Healthcare Information Technology (ONCHIT). The Office is responsible for coordinating nationwide implementation of Electronic Health Records (EHR) through various free-market incentive strategies and standardization programs. Long before 2004, physicians became aware of EHR systems as their hospitals, labs, and offices became computerized. One of the goals for the widespread application of these systems was improved data monitoring and sharing among appropriate parties.

The reality of the nationwide implementation of EHRs is the creation of new dilemmas for physicians to navigate, including new risks of improper disclosure of confidential patient information. The most important rule of thumb for avoiding improper disclosures in the world of EHR is to "sign out" of computerized charts when they are not actively being used. Open EHRs on doctors' computers, at nursing stations, and on PDAs become violations of HIPAA as soon as someone other than the physician views them. While it can be argued that walking away from an EHR without closing the account is inadvertent, it might be argued that to do so was somehow a purposeful or knowing action or part of a pattern of willful physician neglect. If that argument is persuasive, the conduct is subject to the most severe criminal penalties under HIPAA. More dangerous still is the risk of malicious behavior perpetrated by someone accessing a physician's unclosed electronic chart for purposes of order entry. While improper viewing of PHI can land a physician in jail, bogus or inexpert order entry can kill a patient. Another pitfall that may justify criminal penalties under HIPAA includes the situation of a physician "lending" his EHR password to someone else to save time or increase productivity. In the rush to implement and incentivize EHR systems, there are many situations where physicians will be faced with difficult decisions about sharing PHI electronically.

SURVIVAL STRATEGIES

HIPAA suggests that protected health information (PHI) can be any kind of individually identifiable information: demographic, insurance, billing, or medical. This broad definition includes any information pertaining to a patient that carries with it an identifier unique to that patient. An EKG tracing that carries the patient's social security number, a computer CD with a patient's radiographic images and billing information, an email about therapies from a doctor to a patient with an email address on it, or a faxed page from a hospital chart with an imprinted date of birth and address all constitute PHI. Of course, the spoken word is not exempt from PHI. Telephone calls, voice mail, text messages, data recordings, conversations with medical students and nurses in the hospital, and face-to-face conversations on the street fall within the ambit of PHI and the protections of HIPAA.

The most difficult set of circumstances for the physician involves interpreting the situations where disclosure is proper or improper. PHI can always be shared with the patient. For many other situations, however, individually identifiable patient information should be shared only after the physician has obtained specific written patient authorization that includes the name of the recipient. Release of PHI to entities that may necessitate this level of specific authorization include those involved primarily in advertising, marketing, or internet business; employers and schools; attorneys seeking information without a subpoena or court order; other patients trying to contact your patient; and insurance companies that have never covered your patient or that are not involved in your efforts to collect a payment.

Sharing PHI with entities that are involved with billing, treatment, and health care operations should not cause a problem under the HIPAA rubric. These recipients of PHI include current insurers and billing clearinghouses; current and former treating physicians providing care or follow-up; hospital and health care businesses involved in continuing or outpatient care; pharmaceutical, medical device, and research companies tracking outcomes; hospital committees or employees involved in ethical or research review issues, disease reporting, quality review, risk management, or credentialing in the normal course of business; and government and police agencies seeking information under court order or for required mandatory purposes.

Areas that are unclear in regard to disclosure of PHI often involve two distinct situations. First, physicians often assume that their patients' spouses and family members have the same selfless dedication and care for the patient's wellbeing that the physician has. This of course is not axiomatic. Dysfunctional family dynamics and financial motivations often place family members, and surrogate decision makers, at odds with one another and the patient's best interest. Disclosure of PHI in these situations can be fraught with peril. It is best to ask the patient to specifically identify who is authorized to receive PHI, and if that is not possible, require the family as a whole to appoint a spokesperson for communication with the physician. Documenting the conversation in the chart and having a nurse or social worker witness the conversation is ideal. Only those family members or representatives whom the patient has identified as involved in their care or involved with their medical bills are automatically authorized to receive PHI.

Secondly, disclosure of PHI to health care organizations can be problematic when the motivation in disclosing the information is primarily economic and disclosure is not done in the usual course of operations, treatment, or billing. This situation often arises when physicians share access to PHI with health care entities interested in marketing or expanding their database of future patient-consumers. Even if a physician determines that disclosure of PHI is authorized because it pertains to some aspect of treatment, billing, or health care operations, HIPAA may still require that the patient receive advance notification of the intended use. As always, advanced and explicit patient authorization is the best plan for guaranteeing compliance with HIPAA requirements.

FURTHER READING

LeBlang TR, Basanta WE, Kane R, *The Law of Medical Practice in Illinois*, 2d ed., 2 vols. Rochester, N.Y.: Lawyers Cooperative Publishing Company, 1996.

Mueller CB, Kirkpatrick LC, *Evidence Under the Rules: Text, Cases, and Problems*, 5th ed. Aspen Publishers, 2004.

Rieger KS, "Federal Health Information Privacy Requirements." In *Legal Medicine/ American College of Legal Medicine*, 7th ed., ed. S. Sandy Sanbar *et al*. Philadelphia: Mosby, 2007.

Schwartz VE, *Prosser, Wade and Schwartz's Torts*, 11th ed. Foundation Press, 2005.

REFERENCES

1. HIPAA, 65 Fed. Reg. 82462 (2000). HIPAA protections, 45 C.F.R. §164.500, 164.501. HIPAA penalties, 42 U.S.C.A. 1320d-6, revised as of October 1, 2004. HIPAA website available at www.hhs.gov/ocr/hipaa/

2. Hippocratic Oath, classical and modern versions. Available at www.pbs.org/ wgbh/nova/doctor/oath_classical.html and www.pbs.org/wgbh/nova/doctor/ oath_modern.html. See also Orr RD, *et al., Use of the Hippocratic Oath: A Review of Twentieth-Century Practice and a Content Analysis of Oaths Administered in Medical Schools in the U.S. and Canada in 1993*. J. Clin. Ethics 8:377–388 (1997).

3. AMA Principles of Medical Ethics, adopted June 17, 2001. Available at www.ama-assn.org/ama/pub/category/2512.html

4. Administrative Standards of the Illinois Medical Practice Act, 68 Ill. Adm. Code 1280–1290.

5. Winn PA, Who is Subject to Criminal Prosecution under HIPAA? Available at www.abanet.org/health/01_interest_groups/01_ehealth.html

Lack of Informed Consent and Refusal

Hugh F. Hill, M.D., J.D., F.A.C.E.P., F.C.L.M.

GOLDEN RULES

1. Patient autonomy outweighs your professional opinion and your good intentions.
2. The patient's consent protects the provider.
3. For consent to serve as a defense, it must be "meaningful," i.e., real.
   (a) The patient has to know what he is consenting to.
   (b) The patient has to have the intellectual capacity to consent.
4. A signed form can be a manifestation of, but not a substitute for, actual consent.
5. Treat refusal of recommended care like informed consent. Make it an "informed refusal."
6. Obviously necessary care can be refused without it being "crazy", but such refusal does raise the question.
7. In a nonemergency situation, get questions of who can consent for the patient clarified first.
8. People in another's custody, be it police or family or nursing home, are not automatically unable to refuse treatment.
9. Where anyone has or might raise capacity questions, document your basis for your assessment.
10. Approach every single informing session, for consent or refusal, the same way you approach patients every day: with ultimate concern for their wellbeing, and respect for them as individuals.

CASE PRESENTATION

Imagine yourself, after a long and distinguished career, now serving as a hospital's Clinical Administrator. Today, the real "suits" are off doing whatever and you are temporarily in charge. Suddenly, an agitated group bursts into your office.

"You've got to do something!," demands a surgeon.

"Right now!," explodes from several throats.

You quickly learn that a patient is on the operating table for a triple A repair, but the charge nurse refuses to let the case proceed because there is no signed consent form in the chart. The patient has been medicated, but is not yet asleep. Everyone in your office has an opinion. Your senior scrub nurse points out that the patient came for the surgery and climbed off the gurney onto the table. The surgeon believes the patient will sign now and, besides, the surgeon already has another form signed at his office. The anesthesiologist doesn't want to agitate what he believes is a high-risk patient.

You check your own pulse, taking a moment to appreciate how nice your day had been—up until now.

ISSUES

Most of what we understand about informed consent we learned by exposure to routine practice in our training, and most of it is correct. Patients who voluntarily seek medical attention have agreed to accept the usual basics of history and physical and even a few common procedures, like vital sign measurements. Patients manifest further acceptance of simple slightly invasive procedures, like blood drawing, by holding out their arm, or rolling up their sleeve on request. So, in the case above, the scrub nurse's comments about the hypothetical patient make some sense.

For surgery involving general anesthetics, we all expect that the patient will have to sign something permitting the procedure. A hospital's rules may require it, or just by experience we know that this paperwork has to be completed before the operation. We speak of "consenting the patient" or of "getting the informed consent signed." The charge nurse above is doing his job by insisting on the proper form. But that situation is unusual. Is a reflexive order to reschedule the surgery the best response?

The majority of health care interactions are straightforward. But marginal situations, questions about details of informed consent, and refusals of recommended care all require some understanding of the applicable law. In this chapter, we will reach that understanding by a quick simple review of background and principles.[1] A few examples will demonstrate application of that understanding and we will try to unravel the knotty situation our imaginary Clinical Administrator confronts. Then, we will put it all together with survival strategies—the questions you want answered.

Background

Our law grew out of real controversies decided by courts. Judges followed the precedent of rules laid out in previous similar cases, and patterns of reasonable expectations appeared. In the dim past, categories may have appeared naturally, and lawyers began to ask courts to rule for their clients by citing these categories. In each category, criteria (and thus defenses) developed into requirements, including both theories and facts. Informed consent law's precedents appear in the category of suits for "battery."

The word is familiar to us in association with acts of violence: a "battery" of artillery, a "battering" ram, a "battered" woman. The English common law came to define "battery" as a harmful or offensive unpermitted touch. Even from our childhood, we recall the line drawn between words and touching. Through cases and decisions, judges made it clear that all injuries resulting from the touch were injuries for which the victim could sue.

This rule about the extent of liability for an unpermitted touching may be clearer with an example from a nonmedical context. A vulnerable plaintiff can recover for even surprising injuries from simple contact: a push or shove of an individual with a bleeding diathesis might cause major problems. Lawyers speak of the "thin-skulled plaintiff" and say the tortfeasor, the person causing the harm, "takes his victims as he finds them." The injured party's vulnerability is not a defense—the accused defendant has to try and show that the contact was in fact permitted, explicitly or implicitly (such as by participation in a sport). Thus, predictably, questions arose about what was "permitted."

In the common law of battery, consent could be given in words, by behavior, or implied in the circumstances. The law of battery applied to medical treatment. (The common law early created an exception for emergencies.) In the medical context, lots of touching is expected, but without consent, liability for battery can follow. The early cases, and even into the first half of the last century, were not concerned with extent of information communicated, but rather whether or not there was any consent and often with procedures that went beyond what the patient had expected.

Remember that this law early developed in a pre-anesthetic era. Particularly in amputations, a surgeon's speed was prized. A 19th-century description captures the essence: The surgeon and his assistants would approach the patient, the instruments concealed behind their backs. The patient would be asked one more time if he would have it (the limb) off. If he agreed, the assistants held the patient down and the surgeon proceeded, regardless of any objections the patient might subsequently raise. But what happened when the patient later claimed he had never consented, or had been duped, or the job was botched?

Patients could sue for compensation. If the procedure—the touching—had been consented to, the patient had to prove negligence, i.e., that the operator failed to meet the standard of care. But if the patient could assert that there was no consent, then the operator could be liable for all injuries, even if the procedure was flawless!

Thus, today, when a patient or family member goes to the lawyer's office to discuss the possibility of a lawsuit against a health care professional or institution, consent can be pivotal. If the patient never consented, it is a very different case. In some states, the lawyer will not have to hire expert witnesses to prove negligence. Think about this in reverse, and you will never forget the importance of being able to prove that your patient consented. If the lawyer cannot find an expert to say there was negligence, he may be left with nothing except attempting to claim that there was no consent!

This brief history lesson should begin to reveal several points. Consent is not just another piece of aggravating paperwork, consent can serve as a critically important defense to a lawsuit, and consent can be manifested in various ways. You may have some hint of why legal battles focus on procedures, even though some of the drugs we prescribe entail hazards as well. And we also begin to beg some of the questions that often arise, such as "Did the patient really consent?" and "What was the extent of the consent, what did he consent to?"

"Informed" Consent

This term that we all now use did not appear in the law until 1957. We know there were earlier cases focused on the extent of the procedure permitted, but the content of the consent got little attention otherwise. Historically, plaintiffs could attack the validity of a consent based on fraud or misinformation. Now, in the last 50 years, lack of information can invalidate the patient's consent.

The public's growing perception of an ethical duty to warn of consequences of procedures was influenced by new research codes. Nazi medical experiment atrocities evoked the Nuremberg Code, which said that research subjects' voluntary consent is valid only if they know what is to be done to them, its hazards, and the effects on their health.[2]

Following 1960, courts throughout the country addressed cases involving claims of a duty to warn and the idea that consent had to be informed. States differ in how they have incorporated the doctrine. Many have moved suits for lack of informed consent out of battery and into medical malpractice. A few states disallow suits for battery based on lack of informed consent; many keep the claims for complete lack of consent in battery and apply medical malpractice procedures to suits based on the adequacy of the information communicated.

Many state legislatures have passed statutes on informed consent. Those statutes articulate meanings developed through case law and precedent. Some statutes address the adequacy of the "informed" part of the definition.

Whether a creature of tradition or statute, the question is: How much information must be communicated and understood to make the patient's consent informed? Our hypothetical aneurysm patient voluntarily got onto the operating table, but does the hospital know how much information and what information he had before he demonstrated his willingness to undergo the procedure?

We all have the general idea that patients have to know basically what is proposed, the expected outcome and the risks of the proposed procedure, what may happen if the procedure is not attempted, and what alternatives exist. For many procedures, we could make a long list for several of those elements. It makes sense to start with the most common ones, but then how far down the list should we go? In addition to not wanting to take unnecessary time discussing a list of maybes, we realize that it is possible to confuse a patient with TMI—too much information.

American law has two approaches to answering the "how much" question. Like many legal decision rules, reviewing courts apply a test.

What would a reasonable physician say? The first test that courts used was the "reasonable physician": What would a reasonable physician tell a patient? This community standard is closer to a standard of care analysis for negligence, requiring expert testimony.

What would a reasonable patient want to know? Many states now apply the "reasonable patient" guidance: "What would a reasonable patient want to know before undergoing the procedure?" Predictably, this shift meant more litigation, and initially left providers guessing or overreacting. The reasonable patient standard can be further modified to make it more idiosyncratic. The standard jury instruction in an informed consent case in the District of Columbia reads: "That _____ was a risk which a reasonable patient, acting under the same or similar circumstances as the plaintiff, would likely think of as something he should know in making a decision as to the treatment he is to receive. . . ."

The Emergency Exception

While generally well known, even this obvious exception has gray areas and questions. In the most extreme situations, for patients obviously unable to express their wishes, where the patient undeniably must have instant attention, and no family or other substitute decision maker is immediately available, we do what we must. The law allows us to presume that the patient would consent, if able. By this point in your reading, you will be able to spot the issues that arise: How desperate is the situation? How much time do you have before you must act, and what will happen if you don't? What exactly, and how much, do you have to do? Recognizing these issues is not an exercise in legal sophistry; under Survival Strategies, we will discuss the practical responses. Our aortic aneurysm patient causes some concern to our anesthesiologist. Is this an emergency exception situation?

What happens when an unforeseen situation arises during a consented procedure? This "extension" problem is related to the emergency exception and is analyzed the same way: Is there time to find the correct family member? Would waking the patient up and performing a second procedure be riskier than proceeding? But this extension doctrine will not work as an exception if it is something that should have been anticipated and covered by informed consent, like intraoperative bleeding.

Therapeutic Privilege

Anyone who has attempted to obtain informed consent from an anxious patient with a history of angina has wondered, "Can we do this without causing chest pain?" Another exception to the requirement for informed consent that appears both in statutes and case law is the therapeutic privilege. If the information and discussion would be dangerous for the patient, they can be limited.

Authors caution against reliance on this privilege and counsel careful documentation of its basis. The physician considering using this exception has to specify the patient's circumstance, reasonably believe the information would cause or risk serious harm, and provide what information can be safely offered.

Waiver

Patients sometimes say, "Whatever you say, doctor. I trust you." If this comes up in a preoperative counseling session, the question begged is one that may be raised later by the patient's or family's lawyer: Was the refusal made knowingly?

Both case law and statute recognize that a patient's rejection of attempts to give information is a defense to a suit. But the problem will be proving that the patient did so. Notes in the chart and patient signed statements can help. Some practitioners simply refuse to proceed with a patient who insists on remaining ignorant.

Capacity to Consent

All these questions can come up in a specific situation, and they can all lead to one of the most troublesome issues of informed consent. To understand and use information and exercise judgment, the patient must have the physical ability to perceive and to respond, and the mental ability to process and prioritize. Mental "competence" is overused; the better concept is "capacity," because the issue is not global mental ability, but the ability to engage in one transaction—consent.

The law sometimes presumes that the individual's status invalidates the capacity to consent. The most common situation of this type involves minors. There are many exceptions, such as "emancipated minors" and minors seeking medical attention to reproductive issues, in states where statutes allow minors, usually above some specific age, to consent for themselves. Other treatment interventions can be court ordered or required by statute and regulation, such as for communicable diseases.

Most patients, and most situations, are straightforward: the patient is an adult and shows no sign of having a problem with understanding and making a medical decision, or the patient is comatose or otherwise obviously so impaired that the lack of capacity is unarguable. The question of capacity can arise from past indications, a family member's question, or simply the circumstances, but most often the health professional perceives a problem, or potential problem, and raises the question. The starting point is an assumption of capacity; anyone who believes otherwise has to prove it. But some situations so strongly suggest incapacity that the provider finds himself documenting proof that the patient really can understand and make decisions.

So we sometimes have to assess—and document—a patient's capacity. A good basic formulation is that the person must have the ability to understand what is proposed and the consequences of accepting or rejecting the intervention. A patient need not be fully functioning constantly in every respect to meet this standard. For example, lucid moments may allow valid consent. The patient clearly does not have to understand the pathophysiology of the problem, or every detail of all the possible outcomes. Listing anoxic brain death or irreversible circulatory collapse are unimportant, to most people; the critical understanding is that death may result.

Capacity is always contextual. Older cases dealt with coercion. Otherwise mentally functional individuals can have their ability to voluntarily consent overwhelmed temporarily by fear. The patient's own values may be strange to the physician, but must be respected. Unusual philosophical or religious beliefs do not necessarily mean that the patient lacks capacity. However, a choice clearly inconsistent with a lifelong value system does raise questions about capacity.

Substituted Consent

When capacity is lacking, the physician has to find someone else to consent.[3] Since the law often restricts who may consent for incapacitated patients, the family member or other person who is most available may not be the right source.

If a court has declared the patient to be under guardianship, *including making medical decisions*, or if a patient prior to his or her infirmity has signed advance directives and authorized a substitute decision maker, the person to ask for consent is obvious.

Without a court order or advance directives, physicians sometimes look to the "next of kin." Many states have statutes prescribing which relative and in what order. These statutes may track the order of inheritance of those who die without a will. They do not identify individuals within a class; for example, two siblings may have equal authority. Lack of consensus among family and others who claim to be empowered to consent or refuse is dangerous for the provider.

Refusal

So, if the patient or substitute decision maker refuses recommended care, or requests a suboptimal alternative, isn't that the end of it? No! And this is one of the most important messages in this chapter. Refusal has to be informed, comparably to consent.

One example will demonstrate the logic used by courts holding providers liable for not informing the refusing patient. Over a six-year period, a generalist took care of a woman and routinely performed pelvic exams. But the patient refused pap smears because of the cost. When she finally saw a gynecologist, she was diagnosed with advanced cervical cancer. She died at age 30. Her family sued and the California Supreme Court said the jury should be told that the physician had a duty to inform his patient of the risks of refusing the pap tests.[4]

In the context of an informed consent counseling session, this will not be difficult. The provider is already discussing the risks and alternatives, including refusing to do anything, and the risks of those alternatives. Sensitivity to the legal issues and extra effort are required when routine procedures are rejected informally.

Applying Background and Issues to the Example

In the hypothetical case with which we began this chapter, we recall that the surgeon had a copy of a signed document in his office. It can be quickly faxed to you, but if it is not identical to the hospital's own form (bypassing for the moment the question of whether you have the authority to authorize proceeding with a substitute form), how do you judge its adequacy?

Here, it turns out that the surgeon planned a two-stage consent process. In his office, he had counseled and explained and had the patient's signature on an adequate form. He had planned to obtain the patient's signature on the hospital form after admission and after another briefer information session.

The anesthesiologist explains that the pre-op meds have not removed the patient's capacity to consent and the surgeon and nurse rush back to the OR with the hospital's own form in hand. You call after them all to remind them to document, breathe a sigh of relief, and return to reading committee reports.

SURVIVAL STRATEGIES

What Do Physicians and Other Health Care Providers Want to Know?

- When is an "informed consent" necessary?
- How do I do it?
- What do I write down?
- What if a patient refuses care?
- Can the patient consent or refuse for himself?

When Is an "Informed Consent" Necessary?

The short answer is whenever you want to protect yourself and your institution from a claim that the patient did not consent. You might consider a formal informed consent process whenever you are proposing a medical intervention with significant risks. Another possible metric is the community standard: situations where others do it, or where hospital rules require it. Another rational way to distinguish circumstances calling for a formal process may be those where consent is not manifested by gesture, such as holding out an arm for blood drawing.

Lumbar punctures serve as an example for discussion. These low-risk, common procedures often carry a clear risk–benefit ratio. But patients may ascribe unrelated problems to an LP, and the idea is frightening to many people. It has become routine in many hospitals to require a formal informed consent prior to proceeding with LP.

We suggest that you use the process for any invasive procedure or one with any more frequent than rare serious risks, and when the patient refuses any care and by doing so incurs serious risks, and any time the patient seems hesitant.

If circumstances do not allow informed consent, do not think that consent is no longer necessary; think that it is not possible. Then, for example, in situations of emergency or waiver, you will know what you have to document— why it was not possible.

How Do I Do It?

Allow sufficient time and focus on the patient. Although this exercise leads to self-protection, initially you will do a better job of giving informed consent if your first thought is for the patient's needs. Including the patient who seems committed to proceeding without information, all need to focus on and attend to what you have to say. "There are some things you need to know" is a better opener than "There are some things I have to tell you."

Start with the proposed treatment or review the problem being treated. *The general nature of the medical intervention should be described.* For example, an orthopedic procedure does not require a list of instruments or description of all involved anatomy, but if hardware will be left inside, the patient might be surprised to find that out later.

Physicians are sometimes advised to tell patients that others will be involved in the procedure. This becomes more important in a teaching situation and where other specialists will perform parts of an operation.

Most providers next go through the risks and benefits of the proposed intervention. In the benefits discussion, it is often important to *make sure the patient understands that no guarantee of any outcome is promised.* The question most often asked by providers about informed consent is "How extensive must be the list of possible complications and adverse outcomes?" There is no one answer to this question applicable across the nation. The standard each state applies, reasonable physician and reasonable patient and variations, will affect the answer, as may the specific patient's own questions and values.

Various authors offer various formulations: reasonably foreseeable risks, material risks, probable complications, known risks, etc. In more scientific terms, these range from common to rare. At the same time, we are told that remote risks do not have to be listed and explained. Given that medical literature includes reports of complications and outcomes that have happened only once, but are thus "known," how much has to be disclosed for a valid informed consent? *We suggest the use of the following rule of thumb: risks of death, permanent limb and organ impairment, all serious and severe possibilities, and temporary minor adverse results that occur more than 5% of the time.*

There are two important limiting factors that make this guideline more useful than it appears at first glance. The precise means of death or organ failure need not be disclosed, rather only the fact that these are possible. Also, lack of causation limits the effect of nondisclosure. The patient who sues claiming lack of informed consent will have to state what he claims he should have been told. If a reasonable patient still would have consented, despite knowing that information, courts have decided that failure to disclose did not cause harm. Some states limit the usefulness of this defense by applying a subjective standard, asking what that particular patient would have done.

If there are other options for treatment, these should be mentioned. Often, the only other option is to do nothing, or to wait. Again, all possibilities need not be discussed, but common alternative and realistic choices can be listed. The physician's own preference and the range of services he can offer are not the only options to raise. Internists should discuss surgical options, even if they do not recommend or even approve, and vice versa.

Effective informed consent is enhanced if the provider treats the discussion of alternatives as an opportunity for dialogue. Choices that the patient may be interested in can be talked about at more length. Here, and throughout the process, patients will be more satisfied if they have the chance to ask questions. To close the session, physicians can ask if there are any other questions or any particular concerns that the patient as an individual has.

What Do I Write Down?

What documentation will protect the physician and hospital from claims that the patient did not consent? This is the question that lawyers who compose or review consent forms ask. Please notice the sequence here; we have addressed how to obtain informed consent before addressing the forms and documentation. The signed form, or the chart note, are not informed consent; they are an indication of that consent and what information was communicated. The note or even the signed form can be strong evidence, but do not mean an automatic win for the defense.

Hospitals have their own forms, with spaces for filling in particulars. The forms state that the patient has been given certain information and, usually, that the patient has had an opportunity to ask questions. What is listed in the blank spaces—and what is not—can become critical in subsequent litigation. The patient's signature can be challenged, but is a powerful indication that the patient was aware of what is on the paper and agreed to it.

The documentation should include the essential characteristics of an informed consent and accurately reflect what was said to obtain consent. *We recommend that the note or form state explicitly that the patient consents to the procedure, that the nature of the procedure was described, that risks and benefits were communicated, that alternatives were listed, and that any questions were answered to the patient's satisfaction.* Caution dictates that documentation include complete lists of risks and alternatives discussed, but this can be impractical. While it can be argued that stating any specific calls for a complete list, we suggest recording at least the most serious of consequences. If the possibilities discussed include death, say "death." This is not an occasion for euphemisms.

Most forms require the signature of a witness. If you want the witness to be able to testify as to what was said in the informed consent session, that person has to be present throughout the conversation. More commonly, the witness is only confirming that the patient signed the document, and has to be present only for the signing.

What If a Patient Refuses Care?

Make the discussion an informed refusal session, to the extent the patient will allow. Patients who do not want to listen or who leave before any discussion are still a potential problem, and their rejection of information should be documented.

Patients who are willing to listen should be warned of the risks they are taking by refusing care or choosing a nonrecommended option. Uncertainty and balancing low chance, severe outcome possibilities make these choices difficult for patients. You can quote numbers from medical literature, but be careful about allowing the patient to grab onto your perception of remoteness. If asked if some serious consequence is unlikely, when the answer is yes, the next words out of your mouth should be, "But it can happen!"

Hospitals and some offices ask patients who refuse recommended care to sign a form. As for informed consent, this form should reflect information communicated. If the patient is risking death, then the documentation should show that the patient was aware of the risk of death. These forms usually have the patient sign a statement that he is accepting responsibility for the consequences of his decision. If the patient refuses to sign, the fact that the information was communicated and the form rejected should be noted in the record.

The formality of this process can be offputting in the physician–patient relationship, but it can also turn some patients around to accepting recommended care. Patients may be impressed with the seriousness of informed refusal. If it is done well, patients can understand that the physician cares intensely about them, and not take it as an attempt by the physician to protect himself.

A patient can withdraw consent at any point in the process. This can be problematic if the patient is already sedated or narcotized. Does he have the capacity to refuse care? Can the process be interrupted safely at that point? Any refusal can beg questions about capacity. The more dangerous the choice, the easier it becomes to imply lack of capacity.

Can the Patient Consent or Refuse for Himself?

First, you have to decide for yourself. Regardless of how you approach the question, most patients will be obviously capable or obviously incapacitated. How you deal with the marginal or unclear situations will depend on how much time the patient has before adverse consequences begin.

In an emergency, patients still have the right to self-determination, but if they lack the capacity to decide, you may proceed if there is no time to find a surrogate or obtain a court order. Remember to include the risks to the patient of force, if they are physically resisting, in your considerations. As soon as you can, write a note explaining why you proceeded without consent.

Often, you can use consultation as you would with any unclear situation. Even a peer colleague, if a psychiatrist is not available, can offer an opinion on the patient's capacity.

Finally, if a family member will not ask a court for a guardianship appointment, you can ask for a court order determining capacity. Even if the patient is already under guardianship for financial affairs, for example, you may still need clarification of the patient's capacity to make medical decisions. For hospitalized patients, this is done by request to the facility's counsel. That lawyer may also be a resource if your patient is not hospitalized.

Regardless of how you reach your conclusion, if the court is not involved, documentation must support it. A conclusory statement is not enough. Whenever the question of capacity comes up, because you are concerned about it, because the patient rejects a needed procedure, when a family member or other member of the health care team brings it up, or whenever the circumstances might raise the issue, the record should reflect the basis of your diagnosis. Some objectivity and prescience are needed here. How will it look, after a bad outcome, to a family member, the press, or the courts? These thoughts should not affect your decision, but must be a factor in your documentation.

Some people do not have the capacity to consent or refuse because of their status. Minors are the most obvious category, and usually a parent is available to consent. Beware the pediatric patient who appears with some other relative or friend—you cannot assume that someone other than a parent has the authority to approve care for the child.

Statutes can create this kind of "status" incapacity as well. Victims of infectious disease, for example, can have treatment forced on them for public health reasons. Police may bring in a suspected drunken driver and demand that blood be drawn for testing. In these situations, avoid establishing a physician–patient relationship. If the person asks about other health issues, make it clear that you are not taking care of him, and those questions should be addressed to his own physician. If the person refuses the treatment apparently required by law, you must decide how comfortable you are proceeding without a specific court order. Arrestees and incarcerated prisoners have not automatically lost the right to refuse medical care.

FURTHER READING

Canterbury v. Spence, 464 F. 2d 772 (D.C. Cir. 1972). Possibly the most frequently cited case in informed consent.

White C, Rosoff A, LeBlang TR, "Informed Consent to Medical and Surgical Treatment," in *Legal Medicine/American College of Legal Medicine*, 7th ed., ed. S. Sandy Sanbar *et al*. Philadelphia: Mosby, 2007.

REFERENCES

1. Rozovsky FA, *Consent to Treatment, a Practical Guide*. Boston: Little Brown, 1984, with supplements.

2. *Making Health Care Decisions*, The President's Commission for the Study of Ethical Problems in Medicine and Biomedical and Behavioral Research, U.S. Government Printing Office, 1982.

3. *Gibbons v Wright*, 91 C.L.R. 423 (1954). "[T]he mental capacity required by the law in respect of any instrument is relative to the particular transaction which is being effected by means of the instrument, and may be described as the capacity to understand the nature of that transaction when it is explained." See also British Medical Association, *Assessment of Mental Capacity*, BMJ Books, 2004.

4. *Truman v. Thomas*, 611 P. 2d 902 (1980). The informed refusal case on pap smears.

Negligence

Curtis E. Harris, M.S., M.D., J.D., F.C.L.M.

GOLDEN RULES

1. Ordinary negligence is common in all human behavior.
2. The best protection against ordinary negligence is error prevention, not legal strategy or risk prevention.
3. Negligence *per se* (statutory negligence) is uncommon in medical malpractice suits, and the effect of such negligence varies from state to state.
4. Gross negligence is commonly alleged but rarely proven. It is the basis of punitive injury claims.
5. Good informed consent is an important defense against any claim of negligence, but is especially important to disprove gross negligence.
6. Criminal negligence is charged for rare, egregious behavior, and is based on reckless and wanton acts, outside normal medical ethics and practice.

The purpose of this chapter is to present an overview of the types of medical negligence, which include: *ordinary* negligence, *per se (statutory) or judicially imposed (case law)* negligence, *gross* negligence, and *criminal* negligence. These represent various degrees of carelessness, divided by the probability of harm and the *imputed* mindset of the person causing that harm.

"Negligence" is carelessness. *Ordinary* human behavior is rife with careless actions, most of which cause no harm, or may do so little harm as to be easily forgiven. We have all received (and dialed) a "wrong number" phone call, and excused the person who dialed it without thinking twice. It is only when the caller dials again that we become upset, or when it becomes obvious the intrusion is somehow intentional that we take action to block the call. Ordinarily, as long as a behavior is not harmful or annoying, and as long as the person who was careless apologizes, negligent acts are forgiven and forgotten as part of our normal social structure, hardly causing a second thought.

To err is human.[1] Medical practice is an error-prone human endeavor.[2] As admirable as the oft-stated goal of eliminating all medical error might be, to avoid all error in medicine would necessarily involve eliminating both the patient and the physician from the encounter. Arguably, medical practice today is safer than at any time in our history, despite the increased risk of harm associated with increased technology and disease intervention.

However, as medical practice has become safer, so has the public expectation that relies on that safety, often racing ahead of what is possible to achieve.

A "bad outcome" is first treated as a possible or probable mistake, subject to proof otherwise, even in the mind of the treating physician. Malpractice case law is formed by the tension between acts that are *possible* causes of medical misadventures and acts that are *probable* causes of medical misadventures. As it becomes more certain that any given act is the actual cause of an injury, liability for that act increases dramatically.

It is important to note that the most extreme form of medical malpractice, *criminal negligence*, does not involve a premeditated intention to harm another person. Premeditation to harm is an essential element of a criminal act that defines attempted or actual murder, not negligence. Rarely, an ordinary part of medical practice can become a charge of homicide (or murder) if a motive toward profit or a desire to harm a patient can be imputed to the physician, but such a motive must be beyond extreme carelessness. Such acts are unusual in medicine, as the following case describes.

CASE PRESENTATION

The case presented is based in part on an actual case, and is in part fictionalized. It raises several important issues concerning negligence, which are discussed in detail after the case presentation.

Dr. Bob was a Board Certified obstetrician/gynecologist, in practice for over 20 years. (His real name is Robert E. Lee; but his many grateful patients, including the more than 1800 adult children he had delivered in those years, just called him "Dr. Bob.") Dr. Bob held an appointment as an Adjunct Professor at the State College of Medicine, where he had trained and was on staff before entering private practice. He has been the Chairman of the Department of Surgery at his local hospital, Valley View General, where he was also the Chief of Staff two years ago. Due to his long service and generous donations, Dr. Bob served on the hospital's Board of Directors.

Several years ago, Dr. Bob grew weary of the late hours involved in obstetrics, never liked gynecology, and wondered what to do. On a whim, he took a two-week hands-on course in breast augmentation procedures, and a new world opened for him. His popularity and reputation paid off well. Until recently, he owned a free-standing surgical office, where he performed breast augmentation, liposuction, and "tummy-tucks" from dawn to dusk.

One problem quickly became evident, however. At least to the Valley View's ER staff, Dr. Bob was less than competent. His patients often presented to the ER within several hours after surgery with severe bleeding and early infectious complications. In addition, at least once a month, hospital admission was necessary, usually to the on-call surgeon, since Dr. Bob practiced alone and was always out of town on the weekends. A recent death in the ER from bleeding after a combined "tummy-tuck" and liposuction done late one Friday afternoon drew the attention of the local newspaper. After the case was reviewed by the hospital's Peer Review Committee, and no negligence found, the local newspaper forgot about the death. The Committee's sole recommendation, made in confidence, was to ask Dr. Bob to stay in town more often to avoid turning over care to a surgeon the patient has never met.

Dr. Bob was a widower, until he married for the second time last year. He did not remarry for several years because he was devastated by the death of his first wife. She died of bleeding complications in his office after one of his first breast augmentation/liposuction attempts failed. An investigation by the State Medical Board found him guilty of an ethical violation of state law because he had operated on his wife, fined him $2500, and told him to take a course in medical ethics. Unfortunately for his current wife, he did not take the course.

The District Attorney has charged Dr. Bob with murder following the death of his second wife, Susan. She died in his office during a procedure identical to that of his first wife. When interviewed by the local television station, the Medical Examiner described the body as "having been filleted from side-to-side across the abdomen and breast. Mrs. Lee died of massive blood loss consistent with her unattended injuries. I have never seen a reputable surgeon make such incisions."

On investigation, three facts stood out to the District Attorney. First, Dr. Bob employed untrained personnel to assist him in surgery and provide general anesthesia. One was a college student, the other a senior in high school. Second, no attempt was made to call 911 before Susan died. Only after the death occurred did anyone notify emergency services. Further, the surgical records documented that Susan was severely hypotensive throughout the last half of a five-hour procedure, without any effort made to correct the problem. Finally, the newly-married couple had fought bitterly over the months before her death. Dr. Bob had discovered that his wife had continued to see an old boyfriend after the marriage, and broke off the relationship only after extensive counseling. Part of the agreement to break off the old relationship had been Dr. Bob's offer to do the surgery that led to his wife's death. Other facts of the investigation confirmed Dr. Bob's gross incompetence, but were not part of the murder charge.

At trial, the defense team successfully convinced the jury that Dr. Bob, as a surgeon, was grossly incompetent, and that he may have violated medical-ethical standards by doing the surgery on his wife, but that Dr. Bob did not intend to kill Susan. The jury found Dr. Bob guilty of involuntary manslaughter, fined him one dollar, and recommended 6 months' probation. After all of his appeals were complete, the Medical Licensure Board revoked his license. Susan's family sued Dr. Bob through her estate for ordinary and gross negligence, obtaining a judgment of $5 million, including punitive damages. His malpractice carrier refused liability based on the criminal conviction. Today, Dr. Bob practices as a volunteer physician in another state.

ISSUES

Practical Definitions of Negligence

The definition of medical negligence most familiar to physicians is the definition of *ordinary negligence*. As commonly phrased, ordinary negligence is the failure to exercise that degree of care that a careful or prudent physician would have exercised under like circumstances. Such definitions involve the exposure of a patient to an "unreasonable" risk of harm, as judged by a jury (or by a judge) after expert testimony has been given to establish the ever-changing standard of care.[3] Negligence can occur due to something we do or do not do, if the act we fail to do was necessary to prevent an injury.

In the United States, common law and statutory law form an interlocking and complementary set of rules and standards that define all the forms of negligence, including medical negligence. Common law is *case law*, or rules and standards determined by previous court decisions in specific cases. *Statutory law* is law made by the legislature of any given state that is intended to "codify" or to "make certain" case law. Most statutory medical malpractice law merely reflects or enforces previous findings by judges and juries, and does not create new liabilities for physicians. However, statutes can also be a reaction to a finding by a court that is contrary to public policy, as defined by the legislature. In a sense, these laws are an attempt to "put to right" a finding by a court that the legislature considers outrageous. Some states have statutes that create "safe havens" for physicians who follow certain protocols in the treatment of selected diseases, but these statutes have not been challenged in court and have had limited impact.

Negligence per se (or "statutory negligence") is behavior that "can be said without hesitation or doubt that no careful person would have committed." Some states have defined certain medical acts or omissions to be negligence as a matter of law (that is, *per se*). Committing an act defined by such statutes effectively eliminates the plaintiff's need to prove negligence. Operating on the wrong part of the body or leaving surgical equipment inside the body are classical examples of negligence *per se*. However, a minority of states define violations of a statute to be evidence of negligence, not negligence itself. Such evidence is still left to the jury or the judge to weigh, to accept or reject.

Ordinary negligence does not include reckless or intentional behavior. It also does not include the legal concept of a "battery," which is defined as an unpermitted touching, with or without an injury. Until the middle of the 20th century, many successful malpractice cases included some aspect of a charge of battery, especially those cases raising what we now know as "informed consent" issues. A battery occurs only in the absence of any consent. Under current law, it is possible for a patient's consent to be so defective as to be nonexistent, but such a finding is very unusual (see discussion below).

Physicians are frequently charged with reckless behavior in the initial complaint or summons in a case that actually involves only ordinary negligence. This is often done to allow the plaintiff's attorney to later argue that the facts support a charge of "*gross negligence*."[4] Gross negligence is a matter of degree, just as is wanton or reckless behavior. For example, it is certainly gross negligence and reckless behavior to perform surgery while intoxicated, but it is not necessarily negligent or reckless to do the same surgery while sleep-deprived. If carelessness of an extreme degree can be shown, *punitive damages* can be sought. Punitive damages are difficult to obtain, since they are both defined (and limited) by statutory law and are given for a type of behavior that is unusual among competent physicians. Since the purpose of punitive damages is to teach the responsible party a lesson they and others will not easily forget, the court reserves such damages for the most culpable physicians.

There is no clear or bright line between ordinary negligence and gross negligence. It is usually possible to characterize "sloppy" medical practice as either ordinary or gross negligence. However, reckless or wanton behavior (essential to a finding of gross negligence) has important characteristics. It is behavior that involves a known or obvious risk of harm that is done with a conscious indifference to the welfare of another, such that it is the *close equivalent of a willingness that the harm will occur*. Such behavior does not require a proof of the actual motivation of the physician, but if a secondary motive (such as profit or personal fame) can be shown, recklessness is far easier to prove. Any motive other than the general welfare of the patient can be enough to turn an inattentive error into a charge of recklessness. Finally, and possibly most important, negligence that is both offensive and of a type that a nonprofessional lay juror would consider reckless, without the help of expert testimony to establish that it is reckless, will often be found to be gross negligence.

Informed consent law is complex, and is not the subject of this discussion. However, if a physician takes the time to tell the patient of his or her risks, and they are the risks that are normal to the actual situation, it is much more difficult to impute an improper motive to any act of negligence. Therefore, good informed consent indirectly protects against a charge of gross negligence by showing deference to the patient's welfare, evidenced by obtaining his or her consent to a (reasonable) risk, even when that risk actually materializes.

Informed consent is not, however, a permission slip to behave irresponsibly. No person, acting on one's behalf or on behalf of a minor, can legally permit another to intentionally cause them harm. That is, if an injury is the certain or logical outcome of a high-risk intervention, and the harm is far more likely than any other intended benefit, no amount of informed consent can legally permit the act.[5] Simply put, a physician cannot avoid criminal or civil liability for a patient's death by obtaining the patient's consent to kill him or her, even if the patient's death has some benefit for the patient. In the same sense, even though death is a *possible* unintended outcome of a surgery, no one consents to actually die when death is made *probable* by recklessness. Reckless or indifferent behavior can completely destroy the liability protection afforded by informed consent, creating instead a battery (an unpermitted touching).[6] Because a battery that causes harm is a criminal act (a felony or misdemeanor), it is a short step from gross negligence to an act that is prosecuted under the criminal law. Prosecution for *criminal negligence* associated with medical care is at the *discretion* of the public prosecutor, who often looks for (1) patterns of behavior or a single behavior that (2) offends all public decency, and is (3) an offense described by the criminal statutes of the state.

CASE ANALYSIS

Most of the issues raised by the case presentation are probably evident after consideration of the various levels of negligence (above), but it is useful to briefly look at the behavior of Dr. Bob in some detail as an example to avoid.

Ordinary Negligence and *Per Se* Negligence

Among the most important issues being addressed at the state and national level by both the medical profession and lawmakers are uniform standards of care for outpatient, office-based procedures. Not only was Dr. Bob poorly qualified as a plastic surgeon, but he also failed to provide minimal safety standards for outpatient surgery. Normal sterility procedures, pre- and post-operative assessment, and skilled provision of anesthesia are essential to any invasive surgery of the degree practiced here. State statutory law mandates elaborate protections for free-standing surgery centers, and federal law expands those protections through Medicare and Medicaid regulations. However, unless a clinic bills Medicare/Medicaid or falls within the state guidelines of the definition of a "surgi-center," remarkably little statutory law applies to the physician's office. Dr. Bob managed to avoid inspection by his local Department of Health by carefully structuring his billing and office organization to avoid falling within the definition of a surgery center in his state. Evidence of the state's standards for outpatient surgery was entered by the defense into the trial, not to assert *per se* liability, but as evidence of how far Dr. Bob had deviated from expected practice. The public often assumes a level of safety in a physician's office that is not present in all situations, clearly not in Dr. Bob's office. The only protection afforded Dr. Bob's patients was the post-event recovery possible under his malpractice policy, and any general restraint on his behavior caused by the threat of a malpractice suit. Ordinary negligence is the subject of most malpractice suits, as it was in the subsequent suit brought by Susan's family. The proof of ordinary negligence is a "fact-intensive" inquiry, subject to various defenses, none of which were raised here.

Gross Negligence

By the time the criminal prosecution was complete, all the discovery for the malpractice suit was part of the public record. One unique aspect of Dr. Bob's case was that his defense in the criminal trial was gross negligence. He pled gross incompetency in order to avoid the charge by the District Attorney that he intended his wife's death, motivated by anger and jealousy. Absent the *mens rea* (mental state) necessary for a conviction of murder, the jury agreed that his surgical practice *in general* was reckless and that this recklessness was the specific cause of Susan's death. It became impossible for Dr. Bob to defend a malpractice claim against gross negligence based on his own testimony and that of his experts at the criminal trial. Dr. Bob attempted to defend himself by claiming he had told Susan that death was a possible complication of the surgery, and even pointed to a signed consent form as proof. However, as mentioned above, informed consent only applies to ordinary negligence, since no one can give legally binding consent to a surgery performed in a reckless, wanton manner. Thus, that defense was not allowed by the judge.

SURVIVAL STRATEGIES

Since ordinary negligence is carelessness, and since all humans are careless, it is impossible to defend against all human error. It is therefore impossible to practice medicine without error, despite our personal sense that we are doing so on nearly all occasions. The illusion that our practice is (nearly) error-free is exactly that—an illusion. Careful studies of human error, and specifically error in medical practice, point out that the source of most medical error is not a lack of personal concern or care, nor of skill or training, but of "systems" failures, largely out of the control of the physician. It is literally true that most medical errors cannot be solved by the personal resolve and concerted effort of an individual physician to do well. As essential as professional integrity and training are, those qualities will not solve the ongoing problem of medical error.

A number of strategies for avoiding error, limiting liability, and surviving a malpractice suit have been proposed. The literature on these issues is voluminous and impossible to summarize easily. Other authors in this volume deal with some of these issues, and the Further Reading section of this chapter contains several of the best articles in this regard.

That said, two thoughts come to mind as more important than others. One concerns avoiding error, the other, surviving a malpractice suit.

First, avoiding error requires objective, thoughtful restructuring of how we practice medicine. Systems analysts advise hospitals, incident reports and peer review attempt to identify problems proactively, and manufacturers of drugs and medical devices build in safety. However, none of these efforts reaches into our office. We need to begin recognizing risks and developing systems that include redundancy to prevent errors in our offices. Defending a malpractice suit normally involves a bad outcome for which there was some medical intervention. Avoiding adverse events, with or without fault, is our best defense, our best survival strategy.

Second, when sued for malpractice, get good legal and personal counseling. Most malpractice carriers retain experienced attorneys that provide good legal defense. If you have a choice, select your malpractice carrier based on their legal panel. However, the most ignored injury of a malpractice suit is the emotional injury caused to the physician.[7] We tend to blame ourselves for bad outcomes that have little to do with what we did. In addition, the isolation and shame that accompanies a malpractice suit can affect both the professional and personal life of any professional. All state medical associations have a committee whose role it is to provide confidential counseling for the emotional devastation of a malpractice suit. Experience has clearly shown the value of such counseling, but has also documented its underutilization by most physicians. Help is available with a phone call, and can dramatically help us survive malpractice.

FURTHER READING

Harris CE, Chapter 13: "Malpractice," 185–202: In *Practice by the Book*, ed. Rudd and Weir. Bristol, Tenn.: Christian Medical and Dental Associations, 2005. Extended discussion of the emotional cost of malpractice on physicians and recommendations for professional and personal survival.

Sanbar SS, Warner J, "Medical Malpractice Overview." In *Legal Medicine/American College of Legal Medicine*, 7th ed., ed. S. Sandy Sanbar *et al*. Philadelphia: Mosby, 2007.

REFERENCES

1. Mello MM, Brennan TA, *Deterrence of Medical Errors: Theory and Evidence for Malpractice Reform*. Texas L. Rev. 80:1595 (2002). An excellent analysis of the Harvard Medical Practice Study by the lead author. (*See* Brennan *et al.*, New Engl. J. Med. 325:245 (1991), the seminal study on the relationship between medical error and adverse events). Leape L, *Error in Medicine*. JAMA 272:1851 (1994). The oft-cited study of the cause of medical error in practice rather than theory.

2. Furrow BR, *et al.*, *Health Law* (4th ed., West Group, 2003) Supplement Sec. III, "Reforming the Tort System," 61–101. Excellent discussion of medical error, liability, and liability reform from the view of the legal profession.

3. Keeton WP, *Prosser and Keeton on Torts* (5th Ed., 10th Printing, West Group, 2004) Chapters 5 and 6. General reference, negligence law.

4. *Benson v. Tkach*, 30 P. 3d 402 (Court of Civil Appeals, Oklahoma, 2001). Successful allegation of gross negligence in a medical malpractice case.

5. *Miller v. HCA, Inc.*, 118 S.W. 3d 758 (Supreme Court of Texas, 2003). Excellent discussion of informed consent and battery involving the care of a minor.

6. *K.A.C. v. Benson*, 527 N.W. 2d 553 (Supreme Court of Minnesota, 1995). Good summary of intentional acts and battery in medical practice.

7. Christensen J, Levinson W, Dunn P, *The Heart of Darkness*. J. Gen. Intern. Med. 7:424 (1992). A classic study of the effect of iatrogenic error in the absence of liability or fault on physicians' emotional health.

CHAPTER 16

Miscellaneous Torts

Melvin L. Butler, M.D., J.D., F.C.L.M.

GOLDEN RULES

1. Before running the mouth, make sure the mind is engaged.
2. Many malpractice suits stem from failure to diagnose in a timely manner. The physician must ensure that his or her practice has processes in place to prevent lab, x-ray, or other results from "falling through the cracks." One way to avoid such errors is to build in redundancy in the systems that are in place in the practitioner's office.
3. Be very careful when speaking with patients regarding the success of any proposed therapy. A good rule is to avoid the use of the words "never" and "always" when describing side effects or the success of medical or surgical therapy.
4. As in so much of medical practice, common sense and basic decency can go a long way in protecting the physician against lawsuits.

The purpose of this chapter is to present sample cases and discuss the following torts: abandonment of patients, sexual exploitation, assault and battery, defamation and libel, invasion of privacy, violation of civil rights, and fraud and misrepresentation.

ABANDONMENT OF PATIENTS

CASE PRESENTATION

Dr. W., a hard-working family physician, has a large practice. He has a few patients who complain of back and leg pain and who seem to require large amounts of narcotic medications. Recently he has been notified by a local pharmacy that one of his patients has presented a prescription for hydrocodone and the pharmacist found that she had filled a similar prescription, written by another physician, for 90 tablets just a week earlier.

Dr. W. is upset and angry with the patient. He tells the pharmacy not to fill the prescription he wrote and to advise the patient to return to see him in his office. The patient comes to the doctor's office the following day wanting another prescription for hydrocodone. Dr. W. confronts her with the information the pharmacist has given him and tells the patient that he will no longer serve as her physician. Despite the patient's requests that she be allowed to continue seeing him, Dr. W. says that he will not allow it and that he will send her a letter stating this. He also told her that he would list some names of clinics or physicians that might be willing to take her as a patient.

Dr. W. does dictate a letter informing the patient that she has been terminated from his practice and gives her the names of some local clinics that she can call to see if they will give her an appointment. He says that the termination is effective immediately. The letter was sent to her by certified mail. The patient develops abdominal pain and fever three days after receiving the letter of termination. She calls Dr. W.'s office for an appointment but is told that she cannot be seen. No one in his office advised the patient to go to the emergency room if her symptoms continue. Despite calling the other clinics Dr. W. provided, none can give her an appointment for two weeks. Another day passes and the patient is taken by ambulance to a local hospital where she is found to have acute pancreatitis. She subsequently dies in the hospital.

Issues

If a doctor decides that he can no longer treat a patient, he is obligated to notify the patient. In addition, he should provide suitable alternatives for the patient to obtain care in the local area. If he should fail to allow enough time for the patient to find another physician, he may be guilty of express abandonment. The length of time to allow for a patient to establish care with another physician is not set in stone. In general, giving the patient at least three to four weeks would probably be considered reasonable.

Survival Strategies

Dr. W. made a significant error in terminating his patient's care "immediately." At the very least he should have given her three to four weeks to establish care with another physician or clinic. Failing that, he should have allowed for any emergent condition that might necessitate prompt care, regardless of his termination letter. Earlier admission to the hospital might have been life-saving in this situation. The law does not require that a subsequent treating physician be in place at the time of termination. "The standard is one of reasonableness, and an action for abandonment will not generally be upheld when sufficient grounds for termination exist, along with reasonable efforts on the part of the physician to find alternative care."

SEXUAL EXPLOITATION

CASE PRESENTATION

Dr. M., a prominent psychiatrist in his mid-fifties, was treating a young woman in her twenties for a bipolar disorder. During the course of treatment, which consisted of drug therapy as well as some psychotherapy, the woman developed a strong dependence and attraction for the physician. In fact, on several occasions she had told him that he reminded her of her father who had died when she was in her teens. The woman said that she had loved her father deeply and still grieved for him at times.

In the fourth month of therapy Dr. M. asked the patient if she would consider having dinner with him one evening. This she did willingly and over the course of another month the physician had sexual intercourse with the patient on several occasions. When she was doing well from a mental health standpoint the psychiatrist advised her that she did not need to continue seeing him so frequently. The patient took this as rejection by the psychiatrist and in time retained an attorney and sued him for malpractice.

Issues

Courts nowadays consistently hold that a physician, particularly a psychiatrist, who has a sexual relationship with a current patient, has performed an unethical, improper act. All states recognize this to be the basis for at least a civil action.

The fact that many patients develop strong feelings toward their therapist makes them very vulnerable to abuse by an unethical therapist. No matter if the patient freely "consents" to sexual intercourse, the cases have clearly indicated that the consent of such a patient is invalid.

Survival Strategies

Dr. M's attorney might invoke the standard defense to sexual exploitation, that is, the patient consented. In *Benavidez v. United States*, the court held that consent in the therapeutic context is essentially irrelevant and such conduct has traditionally been defined in terms of negligence. Of note, most professional liability carriers routinely refuse to cover cases involving sexual exploitation.

ASSAULT AND BATTERY

CASE PRESENTATION

A surgeon, Dr. S., had just finished a difficult cholecystectomy in which several minor complications prolonged the operation. Outside the operating room, in the hospital corridor, a scrub nurse made a comment to another nurse that Dr. S. had "made some errors" that caused the operation to last longer than it should have. The surgeon, overhearing this, walked up to the two women and, shaking his finger in the nurse's face, yelled at the nurse, "You'd better not spread that kind of (expletive deleted) about me or I will personally take care of your loud mouth." He then stormed out of the area. The nurse, after discussing the incident with the director of nursing at the hospital, filed an assault charge against Dr. S.

Issues

To perform an assault there must be an intentional, unlawful offer to touch a person in a rude or angry manner under such circumstances as to create in the person alleging the assault a well-founded fear of imminent harm, along with the apparent present ability to do the assault if not prevented. As opposed to a criminal assault, the tort of assault only requires the victim to have an "apprehension of contact and it is not necessary that the defendant have the actual ability to carry out the threatened contact."

Survival Strategies

In this case the surgeon, tired and probably frustrated, overheard a comment that caused him to lose his temper. The fact that he spoke in a loud voice, shook his finger close to the nurse's face, and made a profane threat against her person may certainly have convinced her that he was capable of carrying out his threat. Given that this incident was witnessed by another employee of the hospital, Dr. S. might do several things to remedy the situation and avoid going to court. First, he could apologize to the nurse whom he assaulted. This should be done in writing and an offer made to repeat the apology in front of the director of nursing and the chief of the medical staff if the plaintiff so desired. Should this attempt fail, Dr. S. might well find himself in court.

DEFAMATION AND LIBEL

CASE PRESENTATION

A patient sees a physician for a skin rash. The doctor considers a variety of possible causes and orders several tests, one of which is a test for syphilis. The preliminary test came back as positive. Considering the possibility that the man might well be contagious, the physician contacted the health department and gave them the man's name and the results of the test. A confirmatory test was done and was negative. The patient did not have syphilis and the patient sued the physician for defamation. The court in this case declined to impose liability on the physician, reasoning that he had a duty to disclose the preliminary information and was therefore protected in doing so.

Issue

Defamation consists of the wrongful injury to a person's reputation that is caused by communicating a false statement either orally (slander) or in writing (libel). There are different types of defamation or slander. One type applies to *loathsome diseases*. Years ago, if one person told other people that he knew that a certain individual had tuberculosis, syphilis, leprosy, or some other contagious disease, that individual would suffer exclusion from society. Nowadays the advance of medical science has developed cures for many of the diseases that were regarded as permanent, lingering, and incurable in former years. Today there would not be the same social avoidance of one who had recovered from these same diseases. The situation with regard to the person who is HIV positive or who has AIDS is not so easily dealt with.

Survival Strategies

Clearly, the best defense to a suit for libel or defamation is that the statement is true, even if it did cause injury to the plaintiff. In this case the defamatory statement the physician made to individuals at the health department, that his patient had a positive test of syphilis, turned out to be false. However, the majority American rule at common law is that a defendant must not only believe his statements to be true but that he must have a reasonable ground for believing it to be true. The plaintiff, the patient in this case, must prove negligence on the part of the defendant, his physician, or a lack of reasonable ground to believe the statements he made to be true. Thus the doctor, after receiving the test results, felt it his duty to notify other individuals of the patient's positive syphilis test. This would likely provide the doctor with a qualified privilege to make the statements he made to other individuals at the health department. In medical conditions in which a "screening" test, if positive, will require another more sophisticated confirmatory test to be done to firmly establish the diagnosis, it behooves the physician to obtain the second test before notifying any person, other than the patient, that he or she *may* have the disease for which the additional test is being done. Examples of just such a problem can arise in a number of disease states, e.g., hepatitis C and HIV testing.

INVASION OF PRIVACY

A married woman was about to give birth to her child in her home. She and her husband employed in a professional capacity a Dr. DeMay, a physician. Against her desire the physician brought with him another man, a young unmarried man, and he was present during the woman's labor and childbirth. This young man was neither a physician nor a nurse. The woman and her husband believed him to be an assistant physician and that it was necessary for him to be present to help the doctor. Afterwards it was revealed that the "assistant" was a stranger to the doctor and had been brought along because the weather was bad and the physician was "tired" from overwork and needed someone to carry his equipment and a lantern. The woman brought suit and the court found for the plaintiff, noting: "The plaintiff had a legal right to the privacy of her apartment at such a time, and the law secures to her this right by requiring others to observe it, and to abstain from its violation."

Issues

This very old case is still relevant to the practice of medicine today, particularly in teaching hospitals where the attending physician may come into the room of one of his patients with an entourage of several young interns or residents. Common courtesy would require the attending to ask the patient if he or she will permit the others to be present during the visit and if the patient declines, his or her wishes must be honored. This type of case is closely allied to the other matters of consent. The same problem arises when a physician performs procedures and allows another person to be present in the room. If the other individual is not required to be present to assist the physician, e.g., a nurse to assist in a pelvic examination or to assist in minor surgical procedures or colonoscopy examination, then the physician must obtain the individual patient's consent to allow such others to be present.

Survival Strategies

As in the DeMay case cited above, the court will not look kindly on such a flagrant invasion of privacy. The defendant in this case pleaded that the physician was tired and overworked, the weather was bad, he needed someone to help with his equipment, etc. However, there was no requirement for the stranger to be present in the room, or the house for that matter, during the woman's labor and childbirth. The best survival strategy in invasion of privacy cases is to never get involved in such a matter. Always seek consent from the patient if others are to be present, and make it clear to the patient what the need or benefit is in allowing others to be present during the physician's visit to the patient.

VIOLATION OF CIVIL RIGHTS

CASE PRESENTATION

Dr. Y. was in internist who provided medical care, on a part-time basis, to the jail located in his small community. Inmate Jones presented on sick call and was seen by Dr. Y. The inmate complained of a nonproductive cough, present for some weeks. After a brief physical examination the physician ordered a chest x-ray, which was to be done the following day. The radiologist's report noted a 2×3 cm nodule in the left base and recommended that a CT scan of the chest be performed.

Dr. Y. was not scheduled to be at the jail until the following week. In his next visit to the jail, he did not remember inmate Jones or the fact that he had ordered an x-ray on him, thus he did not ask for the inmate's chart to review the x-ray report. When Jones again presented on sick call two months later for increasing shortness of breath and fever, Dr. Y found the x-ray report. He promptly ordered a CT scan of the chest, which showed a lesion in the left base, now measuring 4×5 cm. Biopsy of the lesion revealed carcinoma and further workup showed metastatic disease in the brain. Inmate Jones brings a lawsuit in Federal Court under the Eighth Amendment to the Constitution, alleging "deliberate indifference" on the part of Dr. Y.

Issues

In the landmark case, *Estelle v. Gamble*, the U.S. Supreme Court affirmed federal jurisdiction over prison and jail health care systems and ruled that, where constitutional rights are violated, the courts have not only the right but the duty to intervene. In the Estelle case the court said that the Eighth Amendment was violated when there was a subjective showing of "deliberate indifference" to an inmate's serious medical needs.

Violation of the Eighth Amendment requires a "subjective" showing of "deliberate indifference." This means that it is not enough that the defendant should have known or ought to have known the danger to the inmate. The defendant must know of and disregard a substantial risk. In this case the absence of professional medical judgment in the delivery of medical care will usually satisfy the "subjective test" referred to in the Estelle case.

Survival Strategy

In this case, the medical staff at the prison should have already had some sort of system in place, such as a "tickler file," to prevent lab tests or x-ray reports from being placed in the patient's chart prior to the ordering physician seeing the report. But this does not relieve Dr. Y. of his responsibility to follow up and review the result of the x-ray he ordered. His individual responsibility would require him to either insist that the medical staff at the jail have a system in place, or else he must make his own "tickler file" in order to ensure that he has seen lab or any other testing results he may have ordered on the inmates he has treated. Here, the physician and his attorney might investigate the financing and staffing of the local jail. The best efforts of dedicated medical personnel cannot overcome inadequate financing and/or staffing of a jail or prison and the courts will take this into consideration.

In addition, Dr. Y. may be able to refute deliberate indifference by arguing that had he known the results of the x-ray he ordered he would certainly have ordered the recommended CT scan. By obtaining an oncologist's expert evaluation of the case, it may be argued that the two-month delay in obtaining the CT scan and subsequent biopsy did not have any substantive impact on the natural history of the inmate's prognosis.

FRAUD AND MISREPRESENTATION

CASE PRESENTATION

Dr. K decides to take the plunge and spend quite a bit of money in advertising his services. He is not boarded in any specialty but did two years of family practice residency before deciding to enter solo practice. He has just taken a 5-day course from a company that sells laser equipment for dermatologic problems. After purchasing the equipment needed, he now feels ready to begin treating various skin ailments with his laser. He takes out an ad in the local newspaper advertising his practice and makes the statement that he can remove unsightly tattoos from the skin with no pain to the patient. The third patient he sees in his office has a large tattoo on her neck. He uses the equipment on the lesion but she returns in three weeks with a serious skin infection and the tattoo is still visible. Eventually she sues the physician for fraud and misrepresentation. She claims, among other things, that the doctor "guaranteed" that his treatment would be successful in removing her tattoo.

Issue

A misrepresentation, the falsity of which will be the grounds for an action for damages, must be of an existing fact, and *not* the mere expression of an opinion. In the common law, the mere expression of an opinion, however strong and positive the language may be, is not fraud. In this case Dr. K. staunchly denies that he ever offered any "guarantees" as to the success of his work on removing the patient's tattoo, only that the treatment was usually successful.

The fact that his patient developed a skin infection after the procedure may well require Dr. K. obtaining an expert in the field of dermatology or infectious disease to review his technique in removing tattoos and other skin lesions. If necessary the expert may give his opinion as to the safety, or lack thereof, of his treatment.

Survival Strategies

A physician must be extremely cautious as to any media advertising for his or her services. Using words such as "100% satisfaction guaranteed" or "this treatment is completely safe and effective" should not be used regarding any medical treatment. As Justice Holmes once noted, "The rule of law is hardly to be regretted when it is considered how easily and insensibly words of hope or expectation are converted by an interested memory into statements of quality or value when the expectation has been disappointed." Thus, even though Dr. K. may never have said that he guaranteed his treatment to the patient, she may well believe that was what she heard. Given the case presented here, Dr. K. would probably prevail on the fraud and misrepresentation charge against him since he did not advertise that there were no side effects, only that he could remove the tattoos without pain. Still, this sort of case might well go before a jury if a settlement could not be reached.

FURTHER READING

DeMay v. Roberts, 46 Mich. 160, 9 N.W. 146 (1881).

Bruce v. Soule, 69 Me. 562 (1879).

Estelle v. Gamble, 429 U.S. 97, 97 S.Ct. 285 (1976).

Puisis M, *Clinical Practice in Correctional Medicine.* Mosby Publishers, 1998.

Prosser W, Wade J, Schwartz V, *Torts: Cases and Materials.* University Casebook Series, Foundation Press, 1988.

Boumil M, Elias C, Moes D, *Medical Liability: The Professional Relationship.* West Publishing Company, 1995.

Boumil M, Elias C, Moes D, *Medical Liability: Intentional Torts.* West Publishing Company, 1995.

Liability for Acts of Other Providers

Kenneth A. DeVille, Ph.D., J.D.

GOLDEN RULES

1. A physician can be held financially liable for the negligent or wrongful acts of another individual when:
   (a) The physician is the employer of the individual and the individual is acting within the course and scope of employment.
   (b) The physician has the right to control the other health professional's work and the manner in which it is done (the "borrowed servant" doctrine).
   (c) The physician is engaged in a joint enterprise or partnership with another physician and that arrangement has not been legally formalized in such a way to protect the physician from the imputed liability of partners.
2. Employees and borrowed servants may also be sued individually for the negligent harm they cause.
3. Physicians may be sued for their own negligence in failing to appropriately hire, supervise, monitor, and train employees and others with whom they work.
4. Physicians are ordinarily *not* liable for the negligence of independent contractors.
5. Limited liability partnerships, professional associations, and professional corporations are among the organizational arrangements that can substantially limit physician members' liability for the negligent acts of their partners.

Law has insinuated itself into physicians' everyday professional lives in countless ways. It is well known that physicians can be held liable for damages caused by their own professional negligence. Physicians may also find themselves in litigation for breaches or violations involving contracts with patients and others, criminal law, sexual harassment, billing and coding, HIPAA, and a wide range of other legal and regulatory categories. Under some conditions, physicians who are individually blameless may also be held legally responsible for damages resulting from the wrongdoing of their employees and of the nonemployee health providers with whom they work. This chapter summarizes the most important sources of potential physician liability for the acts of various third parties involved in patient care.

CASE PRESENTATION

Dr. Jones, an obstetrician, has as employees physician assistants (PAs), nurses, receptionists, several assistants and technicians, an office manager, a full-time security guard, and several maintenance employees. Dr. Jones ordinarily spends her mornings in the operating room.

On December 15, 2005, the following events occurred. First, Dr. Jones had an open hysterectomy scheduled on a patient. A nurse anesthetist employed by the hospital was assigned the case. During surgery, Dr. Jones' patient arrests and dies as a result of a mistake by the nurse anesthetist.

Back at the office, Dr. Jones' PA is seeing a patient to explain the results of a recent breast biopsy. The PA misinterprets the biopsy report as benign and mistakenly informs the patient that no further follow-up is required until the following year's annual check-up.

Dr. Jones is also having her office waiting room remodeled. A construction worker follows a patient into the parking lot and robs her.

Next, one of the ultrasound technicians, angry over a sports bet, confronts one of the nurses in a vacant examining room. The technician strikes the nurse on the head with a stainless-steel canister and severely lacerates his head. The technician apologizes, helps the nurse up, and quietly and calmly walks to the employee lounge. After hearing of the assault, the security guard rushes to the employee lounge. Although no words are exchanged, the security guard sprays the technician with pepper spray and immobilizes him with a Taser.

Later that afternoon, a receptionist employed by Dr. Jones stops to pick up office supplies on her way back to the office from lunch. As she pulls out of the parking lot, she strikes a pedestrian who is seriously injured.

At the end of the day, Dr. Jones receives a phone call from an attorney who informs her that one of her office PAs had seduced and had sexual intercourse with one of the practice's patients.

ISSUES

Physicians can of course be held liable when they have breached a specific legal responsibility. But under some conditions, a physician can be held responsible for the actions of a third party even when the physician has acted appropriately in every way. This liability is known as "vicarious liability."

Vicarious liability is indirect liability. It makes no requirement that the physician is negligent in any way; it frankly imposes liability without fault. Vicarious liability is conceptually distinct from lawsuits stemming from negligent supervision wherein physicians may be deemed negligent in monitoring the actions of an employee or other health professional. In vicarious liability actions, persons are held financially liable for the negligence or other wrongful acts of third parties, even though they are not themselves at fault and are not aware of the third parties' actions.

In general, an individual may be held vicariously liable for the negligence of another when there is an "agency" relationship between the two. An agency relationship occurs when one individual (the "agent") has authority to act in the name of another individual (the "principal"). Because the agent is acting in the name and on behalf of the principal, the principal may be deemed vicariously liable for the negligence of the agent. Employer/ employee relationships are one form of agency relationships. Therefore, employer/employee relationships create vicarious liability. Agency and the associated vicarious liability can also be created by a range of nonemployment relationships between physicians and others, including the "borrowed servant" doctrine and relationships created by joint ventures and simple partnerships.

Physicians and Their Employees

It is settled law that physicians may be held liable for the negligence and other wrongful acts of their employees under the theory of *respondeat superior* ("let the master answer"). Secretaries and staff, physicians' assistants, nurses, technicians, and other allied health providers who are employed by a physician create automatic liability for their physician-employers. *Respondeat superior* makes no requirement that the physician-employer be negligent in any way. A physician is "vicariously liable" for the acts of his or her employees performed within the scope and course of their employment. Recall that "vicarious liability" is based not upon the physician's own negligence, but on the physician's relationship to the wrongdoer. The key questions in determining whether a physician will be liable for the actions of another under a theory of *respondeat superior* are:

1. Whether the individual was an employee of the physician; and
2. Whether the individual was performing acts within the course and scope of his or her employment.

Definition of "Employee"

Frequently, the question of whether one individual is the employee of another is clear, but often courts must determine if an employment relationship exists. In evaluating whether an individual is an employee, courts will consider factors such as whether the individual has set hours of work; whether they are paid at regular intervals; whether the work hours are set by the employer; whether the relationship is ongoing; whether the employer is the putative employee's only employer; whether the services performed are an integral part of the employer's business and not a one-time assignment; whether the individual is expected to follow specific and detailed work instructions; whether the employer furnishes the assistance, training, equipment, and other materials required by the employee; and whether the employer provides worker's compensation insurance and deducts taxes and social security payments from pay-checks (see Restatements, Agency 2nd, §220). Although no one factor may be essential, where a critical mass of these factors is present, courts will find that an employer–employee relationship exists.

"Course and Scope of Employment"

If an individual is deemed an "employee" and not an independent contractor, then the employer may be held vicariously liable for the actions performed by the employee in the "course and scope" of his or her employment. Some courts use the phrase "furthering a purpose of the employer" when explaining what employee actions will lead to derivative employer liability. Usually it is fairly easy to determine when an individual employed by a physician is acting within the course and scope of his or her employment. But some guidance is useful for unusual cases.

Employees are typically viewed as acting within the course and scope of their employment when they are discharging a duty or responsibility for which they were hired; when the work occurs substantially within the authorized time and space limits of the work assignment; and when it is intended to benefit the employer (Restatements, Agency 2nd, §228). In addition, the conduct in question must: (1) occur in the location and at the time expected for that work; (2) be construed as a negligent or wrongful way of fulfilling work responsibilities; and (3) be intended to benefit the employer. Therefore, in the context of ordinary medical practice, there is usually no vicarious liability assigned for intentional torts such as battery, assault, and false imprisonment committed by employees of physicians. It is important to note, however, that a physician might be liable for the intentional acts of employees under the theory that the physician failed to sufficiently screen or monitor them. But in this instance, the physician is being held liable for his or her own negligence, not directly for the acts of the employee.

Finally, the act for which the employer may be held liable must occur within the time and space limits of the work assignment. For example, a physician assistant who examines and treats patients at a location outside of that typically used by the medical practice (at the PA's home, for instance), and without the employer's permission or direction, is probably not acting within the course and scope of employment. As a result, the PA's physician-employer probably would not be vicariously liable for any resulting negligence. But employees of physicians who perform tasks in furtherance of their employer's interests and do so outside the confines of the ordinary work setting may sometimes subject the physician to liability. If the practice utilizes home visits by PAs as a means of providing care and serving patients, then the physician-employer would be vicariously liable for resulting negligence as surely as if it occurred in a traditional office examining room.

A physician might also be liable for the torts committed by an employee outside the office setting when the employee is acting at the direction of the physician-employer and discharging a duty for which they were hired. For example, a physician is probably vicariously liable for the negligence of an office assistant who has an automobile accident and injures individuals while picking up lab reports for the practice. The key question in such cases is whether the employee was acting in the employer's interest at the time of the incident.

Independent Contractors

If an individual pays another for services, and the employee test is *not* met, then the party performing the work will likely be considered an "independent contractor." Independent contractors typically provide services on a one-time or on an as-needed basis. The independent contract arrangement may be created and defined through a written contract, or it might be created when the independent contractor is engaged to perform a particular service. Independent contract arrangements typically do not involve long-term contracts. Physicians and physician practice groups may hire independent contractors to perform both medical and nonmedical tasks. The technician who is paid to design and install a computer system in a group practice suite of offices is an independent contractor. A physician who is paid to provide consultation advice to a group practice is probably an independent contractor.

The conclusion that a physician or other individual is an "independent contractor" is of transcendent importance. Quite simply, independent contractors are not considered employees or agents. An independent contractor relationship, unlike the employer–employee relationship, does *not* create vicarious liability. Therefore, physicians are ordinarily not legally responsible for the negligent actions of the independent contractors whom they utilize either for medical or nonmedical purposes. Physicians may, however, be liable for negligent selection of an independent contractor if special precautions are required or if the work performed by the independent contractor is not reasonably inspected. But this liability is based on the physician's direct negligence and is not vicarious.

Physicians' Potential Liability for the Acts of Nonemployees

A physician must often work with third parties who are not his or her employees. Some of these individuals are independent contractors; some are employees of others, of a hospital, or of other physicians. Some of the individuals with whom physicians work are trained health care professionals or other physicians who are professionally independent. Although the physician is not the employer, under some conditions he or she may be held liable for the negligent acts and omissions of those third parties, even those who might otherwise be considered independent contractors or the employees of others.

"Captain of the Ship" and Beyond

The so-called "captain of the ship" doctrine extended vicarious liability beyond employees of physicians. Originating in the late 1940s, the "captain of the ship" doctrine held that a surgeon was vicariously liable for *any* negligence that occurred in the operating room. Most states adopted some form of the "captain of the ship" doctrine even if their courts did not refer to it by name. The "captain of the ship" doctrine applied to lead physicians of any specialty but arose most frequently in the operating room setting. Under the doctrine all individuals, regardless of who served as their employee of record, became temporary employees or agents of the attending surgeon or physician. As a result, surgeons could be held liable for the negligence of any operating room personnel, even if they had not anticipated the negligence and were not themselves negligent. Thus, physicians might be held vicariously liable for actions of hospital employees, like nurses, as well as for those of otherwise independent professionals, like fellow physicians. Thus, a surgeon who is blameless herself could be held vicariously liable for the negligent acts of the anesthesiologist. The "captain of the ship" doctrine, while it reigned, reflected the social, professional, and legal expectations that physicians exercised virtually absolute and final authority over all they surveyed. Clearly these assumptions rested on an increasingly flimsy foundation, but for a short period cultural beliefs about the medical profession supported this unique form of vicarious liability.

The reign of the "captain of the ship" rule was not long. By the 1960s, courts in various jurisdictions began to limit application of the doctrine and most jurisdictions moved away from the view that a surgeon or physician is automatically liable for the acts of operating room personnel.

"Borrowed Servants"

In place of the outdated "captain of the ship" doctrine, the law in many jurisdictions now holds that a physician's liability for the actions of individuals employed by others should be evaluated according to traditional agency doctrine known as the "borrowed servant" rule. According to the Restatement of Agency 2nd, §227: "A servant directed or permitted by his master to perform services for another may become the servant of such other in performing the services. He may become the other's servant as to some acts and not to others."

In practice, the borrowed servant rule holds that an individual may be held vicariously liable for the negligence of a second individual if the former person has the "right" to control the latter's work and the "manner of performing it … irrespective of whether he actually exercises that control or not." Applied to the medical context, this doctrine means that a health professional employed by a hospital, for example, may be deemed a "borrowed servant" of a physician, when the attending physician has the right to control the other professional's work and manner of doing it, even if the physician does not exercise that right. To determine whether a borrowed servant relationship exists, courts may consider: (1) the testimony of experts; (2) prevailing standards of care; (3) contractual agreements; (4) statutorily defined supervision requirements; (5) policy and procedure manuals; (6) the selection and payment of the health professional; and (7) the power to discharge, to determine whether the attending physician had the right to control the manner or details of the health professional's work. No one factor is required. The existence of a right to control is derived from the totality of the circumstances.

The borrowed servant rule, applied in the medical context, allows a plaintiff to claim physician liability for the acts of other health professionals, even where the physicians are not themselves negligent and where there is no allegation that the physicians were aware that negligent conduct was occurring.

The borrowed servant doctrine is an improvement over the "captain of the ship" doctrine that it replaced, but it is still problematic. The borrowed servant doctrine does not seem to accurately match a 21st-century medical environment that typically features numerous skilled, specialized, autonomous and semi-autonomous professionals working in concert with physicians. Moreover, there is no bright-line rule designating when an individual, especially a health professional, becomes a "borrowed servant" of an attending physician. The determination of whether the lead physician has the "right" to control the actions of fellow health professionals is fact-based, which means that it may vary from situation to situation. In addition, the law remains unsettled and jurisdictions are currently split on whether one physician can be held liable under the borrowed servant rule for the actions of another independent professional. For example, while some courts have held that a surgeon may be held liable for the negligence of a nurse anesthetist in an operating room, courts in other jurisdictions have refused to do so under nearly identical circumstances.

Physicians' Responsibility for the Acts of Their Partners

Physicians who participate in joint practice enterprises and partnership arrangements with other physicians face special liability risks. A partnership can be the result of formal written agreements to join together to pursue a particular endeavor. Even in the absence of a formal written agreement, however, partnerships and joint ventures may be implied by law when two or more persons carry on business for profit. In determining whether a partnership or joint venture exists, courts will usually look for evidence that the participants intended to be co-owners of an enterprise. The existence of a partnership arrangement can be inferred from the conduct of the parties. Courts will consider several factors, including the presence of joint ownership, relative contributions to the enterprise, equal management rights, and the sharing of profits and losses, to determine whether a partnership relationship exists.

The effect of a finding of a partnership, either implied or through an explicit written agreement, is dramatic. If a partnership exists, then each partner will be deemed "an agent" of all the others and may act in the partnership's name when conducting partnership business. This rule may have devastating effects in medical malpractice cases. Because each partner is deemed an agent of all other partners, any or all partners can be held financially liable for the medically negligent acts of a partner acting within the course and scope of his authority—i.e., practicing medicine. Each partner may be held "jointly and severally" liable for the professional negligence act of another partner. "Jointly and several liability" means that a medical malpractice plaintiff can sue one or all of the partners for the entire amount of the negligence claim against the negligent partner. This option is available even if the other physicians were in no way negligent themselves, or unaware of the actions of their partner. In contract cases, too, one partner has the legal authority to bind contractually all other partners and expose them to liability even though they were not individual parties to the contract. But in contract claims, claimants must typically sue all partners jointly. Given the legal perils of informal and simple partnerships, they are rarely appropriate business forms for medical professionals.

Supervisory Responsibility

The bulk of this discussion is devoted to explaining the conditions under which a physician might be held liable for the acts of another in the absence of any negligence on the part of the physician. Of course, physician-employers, like other employers, may also be held directly liable if their own actions contributed in some way to their employees' negligence or other wrongdoing, which resulted in plaintiffs' damages. In contrast to vicarious liability, however, these legal claims are based on the physician-employer's own negligence or misconduct, as well as that of the employee. For example, physicians may also be held liable for negligent hiring, training, supervision, or monitoring of an employee, or for failing to establish required or appropriate policies to ensure that their employees understand their responsibilities and job requirements. In hospital settings especially, physicians are also responsible for supervising, training, and monitoring a wide range of health professionals who may or may not be deemed employees of the physicians, including nurses, PAs, nurse practitioners, other physicians, therapists, technicians, and emergency medical technicians.

In actual legal practice, a plaintiff would probably sue the individual employee or agent who was immediately and directly responsible for the negligent act, the supervising physician under the theory of vicarious liability, and the supervising physician for negligent hiring, training, or supervision of the employee. The plaintiff's attorney, at the time of filing, may not have a clear notion of the exact legal relationship of all involved defendant parties, or may not know in advance the parties for which an agency relationship can be demonstrated. In typical cases, plaintiffs would have the easiest time demonstrating the negligence of the employee him- or herself.

However, the employee is less likely to have sufficient personal funds or insurance coverage to satisfy a substantial damage award. In order to cover damages fully, a plaintiff could also simultaneously pursue compensation under a theory of vicarious liability, and under a claim of negligent hiring, training, supervision, or monitoring. If a plaintiff presents evidence sufficient to demonstrate to a judge or jury an agency relationship between the physician and his or her employee, there would be no need to demonstrate the direct liability claims of negligent supervision or monitoring. If, however, the vicarious liability claim fails, then the plaintiff would be forced to rely on direct liability claims such as negligent supervision and training in order to collect damages from the physician as well as the person directly responsible for the plaintiff's injuries. When surveying potential risk in a practice setting, a physician should consider all potential sources of liability.

DISCUSSION OF THE HYPOTHETICAL CASE PRESENTATION

Dr. Jones may be subject to a number of liability claims, both vicarious and direct.

Nurse Anesthetist

Dr. Jones may be held vicariously liable for the acts of the nurse anesthetist if she practices in a jurisdiction that has approved the application of the borrowed servant doctrine to the acts of an independent health profession. If the jurisdiction recognized the borrowed servant doctrine under these conditions, the plaintiffs would also have to demonstrate that Dr. Jones had a right to control the manner and details of the work of the nurse anesthetist. Such evidence, if it exists, might be found in hospital policies and procedures, from the hospital anesthesia manual, and the medical staff bylaws. Dr. Jones' assertion over authority during the procedure would also tend to show the right to control, as would the availability of a physician-anesthesiologist to supervise the anesthetist. Finally, expert testimony could be use to determine whether prevailing practice standards regarding the surgeon–anesthetist relationship suggested that the former had a right to control the latter.

Office Physician Assistant

If harm resulted from the PA's negligent reading of the biopsy report and the subsequent negligent advice, then Dr. Jones, as well as the PA, would almost certainly be financially liable for that harm. Dr. Jones' liability is derivative and flows directly from the fact that the PA is an employee. Dr. Jones might also be viewed negligent in her own right for failing to follow up and check the work of the PA and thereby catching the error.

Construction Worker

Dr. Jones would almost certainly *not* be vicariously liable for the criminal acts of the construction worker. The construction worker is an independent contractor or employee of an independent contractor and Dr. Jones would not be liable for injury suffered by the patient. Moreover, the robbery was an intentional, criminal act and vicarious liability rarely attaches under these conditions. Theoretically, Dr. Jones might be liable for the negligent selection of this construction crew if she knew or should have known that the employees had criminal tendencies. This scenario, though, is unlikely and that liability would be based on Dr. Jones' own negligence in failing to act reasonably in hiring the crew when she knew that criminal action was an increased possibility.

Ultrasound Technician

The ultrasound technician who assaulted the nurse over the sports bet is clearly an employee of Dr. Jones. If the technician had committed a negligent act in the course and scope of his employment, Dr. Jones would clearly be vicariously liable. But employers are not ordinarily liable for the intentional tort of battery and criminal acts of employees. Again, if the technician had a history of violent actions toward other employees and Dr. Jones should have discovered that history, then a claim for negligent hiring might be maintained. That liability is direct liability stemming from Dr. Jones' own purported negligence.

Security Guard

Dr. Jones employs the security guard so she would be vicariously liable under *respondeat superior* for the security guard's negligence. However, the security guard's actions likely constitute battery or false imprisonment—intentional torts—not negligence. Employers are not ordinarily liable for the intentional torts of their employees, only their negligence. Moreover, it is legitimate for security guards and other individuals to use a reasonable degree of force to protect third parties who are in danger. Despite these observations, there is still some chance that Dr. Jones could be deemed vicariously liable in this situation. The force exercised in defense of the nurse (pepper spray *and* Taser) seems excessive and unreasonable given that the technician was no longer violent or visibly angry, and the injured nurse was no longer under attack or in danger. Just as importantly, employers are sometimes held vicariously liable for intentional torts when force is implied in the employment (security), where the employment position anticipates friction, and where the employee is furthering the interests of the employer. Therefore, it is conceivable, albeit not certain, that Dr. Jones might be vicariously liable for the actions of the security guard. As above, if the security guard had a history of excessively violent responses and Dr. Jones should have discovered that history, then a claim for negligent hiring might be maintained. This incident also illustrates the wisdom of contracting out the security duties for the office to an independent company. In this event, an overzealous security officer would likely be found the independent contractor of Dr. Jones and not a source of vicarious liability.

Receptionist

If Dr. Jones' receptionist was at fault when she struck the pedestrian, she may be sued for her negligence. Dr. Jones may also be held liable vicariously. The receptionist is an employee and because she was collecting office supplies, which is almost certainly acting within the course and scope of her employment, she was furthering the course of Dr. Jones' business, even though the activity occurred during the lunch hour, with a private car, and away from the office. Although the receptionist was not acting within the course and scope of her employment during her lunch period, when she stopped to pick up office supplies, she returned to the employ of Dr. Jones.

Unprofessional Conduct of PA

Finally, it is highly unlikely that a court would impose vicarious liability for the damages caused by the inappropriate sexual conduct of the PA. Although the PA is clearly an employee, under no analysis could he be deemed to be acting within the course and scope of his employment. If a claim against Dr. Jones is to survive, it must be based on her own negligence in failing to appropriately hire, train, and supervise the PA or if she knew or should have known of his propensities.

SURVIVAL STRATEGIES

A wide range of practice environments and configurations exist today. Given the wide range of health professionals with whom physicians interact, and the variety of financial and institutional settings in which physicians practice, physicians must be wary of hidden "liability traps" endemic to the modern medical practice environment. Physicians are placed in practice settings in which they must work with other physicians and work with and supervise physician assistants, nurse practitioners, nurses, and technicians that they have not employed or selected. Some of these risks can be diminished if they are identified in advance and neutralized by appropriate policies, protocols, practices, contractual arrangements, or other measures. Qualified legal counsel can help a physician evaluate the risks posed by the physician's employees and his or her association with other health professionals and devise the most appropriate arrangement to limit those risks.

Physician Employers

Physicians will be deemed vicariously liable for negligent acts of their employees performed within the course and scope of their employment. There is, in essence, no legal defense for this manner of liability, even if the physician-employer played no part in the negligence and in fact did everything possible to avoid it. Given this reality, physician-employers should first ensure that they are properly and fully insured against the types of liability that their employees may subject them to. Second, while no amount of physician-employer vigilance can absolve the injuries caused by employee negligence once it has occurred, employers should take all reasonable measures to prevent employee negligence and to nurture a risk-averse culture.

Therefore, physicians should have protocols, policies, and operation procedures for hiring, training, evaluation, supervision, monitoring, and dismissal of employees, as well as procedures in place to limit the liability risk posed by employees. These include robust and explicit policies for interviewing, screening, checking references, and hiring. It would also include ongoing training and education for staff members designed to inculcate appropriate behavior. A practice should also have reasonable monitoring and oversight plans in place as well as disciplinary and dismissal policies for discovered infractions. Even with the best policies in place, there are a finite number of health providers that a physician can effectively supervise. Therefore, it is wise to limit the number of nurses, nurse practitioners, and PAs that are deemed the responsibility of any one physician.

Partnership Practice

Given these legal realities of partnership life, the traditional partnership is rarely the appropriate business arrangement for physicians. Physicians should seek legal counsel before committing to or signing a partnership agreement that might expose them to liabilities created by their partners. Similarly, it is essential that physicians not engage in collaborative practice arrangements or behavior that may be construed as an implied partnership or a joint venture, without proper legal counsel and intervention. Otherwise, they may find themselves unwittingly liable for the legal wrongdoings of their partners.

Fortunately, there is much that physicians can do to protect themselves from these dangers. Qualified attorneys can advise physicians regarding the types of arrangements that might be viewed by the courts as joint ventures or implied partnerships. More importantly, alternative practice organization options are available so that physicians can organize their practices in such a way as to substantially limit their liability for the acts of other health care professionals. The available practice arrangements vary moderately from jurisdiction to jurisdiction, but some form of protection is available in all jurisdictions. For example, all states have some form of the registered limited liability partnership (LLP). In such arrangements, an individual partner's personal liability for the medical negligence of another physician can be limited to the assets of the partnership itself, rather than exposing the assets of the nonnegligent partner to attack. In addition, it would be the partnership assets, not the individual physician member, who would be vicariously liable for the negligent acts of the nonphysician employees of the practice. Individual partners, of course, retain liability for their own acts of negligence. Similarly, professional associations (PAs) available in most states allow members of the corporation to avoid tort and malpractice liability for the acts of other members of the organization. Professional corporations, now available in most jurisdictions, not only immunize physician members from liability claims for acts in which they did not participate, they also can provide tax and capital acquisition advantages unavailable in other organization forms. In addition, shareholder/members are liable for corporation debts only to the extent of their investment. While the professional corporation provides perhaps the most protection for individual physicians from vicarious tort liability and increases the ease of capital acquisition, it is also the organizational form that requires the most legal formality and exercises the most control over the individual physician's practice. Physicians in any of the above-named practice arrangements will still be individually liable for the harm done by their own negligence and by allied health providers if the physician negligently hired, trained, supervised, or monitored an employee or borrowed servant. But this liability is based on the attending physician's own negligence, rather than on the physician's relationship with the allied health provider.

These legal arrangements allow physicians to significantly control the extent of their liability for the acts of other health professionals. It is important to remember, however, that the varying business/practice arrangements have varying implications for potentially equally important issues such as capital acquisition, flexibility, professional autonomy, management control, taxes, and organizational formalities.

Practicing with Potential Borrowed Servants

The central problem with borrowed servant liability is that it does not offer a clear prospective test for when a physician may be held vicariously responsible for the actions of the employee of another. It simply states that borrowed servant liability may attach when the physician has the right to control the manner and details of the work of the employee. The determination is fact-based and will vary from case to case and institution to institution. In order to genuinely scrutinize one's potential liability in a borrowed servant scenario, it would be important to scour the pages of policy and procedure manuals, medical staff bylaws, informed consent documents, and contractual agreements, as well as institutional practice patterns, custom, and practice guidelines. Potential evidence of the right to control other health professionals might be difficult to uncover because it may be tucked away in various and disparate institutional documents. Even if such evidence exists, it may be impractical to eliminate from the institution's practice.

Physicians and surgeons, in fact, desire and need some manner of authority and control over the health professionals with whom they work—even if they have not selected them and do not employ them. Because these protective measures in regard to borrowed servants seem impractical and limited, physicians may desire a greater degree of participation in the selection and supervision of the health professionals with whom they work. This remedy, too, is limited. Physician attempts to exercise close supervision may infringe upon the legitimate prerogatives of otherwise independent health professionals. Moreover, this approach may perversely solve the problem of uncertain liability by increasing the likelihood that a physician will be found to have exercised control over the ancillary health professional's work. A final potential prophylactic measure may be practice contracts in which the hospital or other employer of health professionals agrees to indemnify/compensate the treating physician for any liability he or she might incur as the result of derivative negligence of institutional employees.

FURTHER READING

DeVille KA, *"Captain-of-the-Ship" is Dead: Are North Carolina Physicians and Surgeons Still Liable for Acts of Other Health Professionals?* North Carolina Medical Journal 56(4):166–169 (2003).

Firestone MH, "Agency," in *Legal Medicine* 5th ed. Mosby, 2001, pp. 32–36.

Gore CL, *A Physician's Liability for Mistakes of a Physician Assistant*. Journal of Legal Medicine 21:125–142 (2000).

Keeton WP, *et al.*, *Prosser and Keeton on the Law of Torts*. 5th ed. West Publishing, 1984, §§69–72.

Price SH, *The Sinking of Captain of the Ship: Reexamining the Vicarious Liability of an Operating Room Surgeon for Negligence of Assisting Hospital Personnel*. Journal of Legal Medicine 10:323–356 (1989).

Restatement of the Law, Agency, 2nd. American Law Institute, 1957, §220, §227, §228.

Shandell, RE, Smith P, *The Preparation and Trial of Medical Malpractice Cases*. Law Journal Press, 1990, §8.06.

Uniform Partnership Act of 1997.

CHAPTER 18

The Physician and the Nurse

Judith A. Gic, R.N. (ret.), C.R.N.A. (ret.), J.D., F.C.L.M.

GOLDEN RULES

1. Screen, screen, screen: don't stop being picky about whom you hire.
2. Focus on formal training to help make up the loss of one-on-one mentoring.
3. Pay attention: If your staff is relatively inexperienced and stretched,
    (a) you must be able to see immediately when they are stretched too thin;
    (b) you must be prepared to adjust services when staffing levels are inadequate.
4. Charge your HR department to be proactive:
    (a) Focus on wellness programs that will help keep employees physically and mentally fit.
    (b) Focus on team-building programs that will help new employees quickly learn to work together and resolve interpersonal conflicts with a minimum of disruption.
    (c) Be prepared to investigate when necessary and to take decisive action based upon reasonably established facts; don't let employee problems fester.

For physicians and nurses in the next decade, the dominant challenge will be coping with a very large number of newcomers to the R.N. profession *at the same time* that nurses remain in short supply. The federal government projects that registered nursing will be one of ten occupations in the United States with the largest growth in employment in the period 2004–2014.[1] But the Joint Commission on Accreditation of Healthcare Organizations has also documented the present and growing shortage of R.N.s and its result: overcrowding in emergency rooms, diversion of emergency patients, reduction in number of staffed beds, discontinuation of programs and services, and even cancellation of elective surgeries.[2]

These factors presage a turbulent period as new R.N.s pour into workplaces. The normal opportunities for experienced nurses to monitor and to mentor will be reduced; friction and inefficiencies will increase during the cycles of team-building that will be repeated as new sets of professionals adjust to their colleagues and to the rules of their institutions. Employers, meanwhile, will have to focus on efficiency without sacrificing patient care and in preventing as much as possible (and then addressing when prevention fails) the myriad employment disputes that are bound to arise in workplaces experiencing frequent additions to and moving about of staff. They will also have to resist the pressure to hire applicants without properly investigating the person's background: not all qualified applicants are suitable, as our case study (drawn largely from real events) will show.[3]

CASE PRESENTATION

Nurse RN applied to work at a small public hospital ("Public General Hospital") in Nevada. She had recently moved to Nevada from a Midwestern state, where her first job out of nursing school was at a hospital. She was fired, however, after a series of conflicted encounters with co-workers. She then worked a succession of jobs at nursing homes in the same state. Some jobs she quit. From two, however, she was fired after co-workers observed her treating residents roughly. The residents had never complained and had no family members to complain on their behalf, and the nursing home did not care to solicit complaints from the patients, so they simply fired Nurse RN. The second termination prompted her to move to Nevada.

When she applied to work at Public General, the human resources office queried the National Practitioner Data Bank and received a negative response: it had no derogatory information regarding Nurse RN. Nurse RN had been honest in listing all of her previous employers—she even listed the three jobs from which she had been fired. She explained these occurrences as the result of unfortunate personality conflicts. Public General's human resources office didn't call any of these prior employers for references because the NPDB response indicated that Nurse RN did not lack competence. Her employment history suggested a different sort of issue—difficulty getting along with co-workers—but the director of nursing had gotten a favorable impression during the job interview and the human resources hiring manager, who had been trying to fill this position for a couple of months, thought she was worth a shot.

Shortly after she was hired in early November, the following events occurred at Public General:

November 23: Another nurse notices that Mivacron is missing from a crash cart. She notifies her supervisor. The charge nurse obtains a replacement from the hospital pharmacy.

November 28: More Mivacron is noted as missing from a crash cart. Once again, the charge nurse obtains a replacement from the hospital pharmacy.

December 12: Once again, Mivacron is noted as missing from a crash cart and, once again, the charge nurse obtains a replacement from the hospital pharmacy.

December 19: For the fourth time in less than a month, Mivacron is noted as missing from a crash cart and is replaced from the hospital pharmacy.

December 24: Patient BB dies. Later, after Nurse RN becomes a suspect in his death, he is determined to have died from an overdose of Mivacron.

December 31: More Mivacron goes missing from a crash cart and is replaced from the hospital pharmacy.

January 6: Patient JV dies. The cause is later determined to be a Mivacron overdose.

January 7: Patients JRH and AD die. The cause of both deaths is later determined to be a Mivacron overdose. More Mivacron goes missing from a crash cart and is replaced from the hospital pharmacy.

January 8: Still more Mivacron goes missing from a crash cart and is replaced from the hospital pharmacy.

January 11: Patients JTN and JWW die. The cause of both deaths is later determined to be a Mivacron overdose.

January 24: Still more Mivacron goes missing from a crash cart and is replaced from the hospital pharmacy.

January 25: Yet again Mivacron is noted as missing from a crash cart and is replaced from the hospital pharmacy.

January 28: Nurse RN injects patient LDW with Mivacron. The dose, however, turns out to have been nonlethal.

January 30: The hospital pharmacist and other hospital officials commence an internal investigation into the missing Mivacron. Even as they do, more Mivacron is noted as missing from a crash cart and is replaced from the hospital pharmacy.

Early February: The Mivacron investigators notice that all of the preceding deaths, and virtually all of the other deaths at the hospital since late December, were traceable to sudden declines in patient health that first became noticeable during night shifts, and that Nurse RN always seemed to be on duty during those night shifts.

February 4: Patient EJ dies of what is later determined to have been a Mivacron overdose.

February 6: Public General notifies law enforcement about its concern that Nurse RN may be killing patients.

February 8: The hospital pharmacist notifies the state board of pharmacy about the loss or theft of Mivacron.

February 18: Nurse RN injects patient DR with Mivacron, but the dose turns out to have been nonlethal. He eventually is able to tell investigators that Nurse RN injected him. There was no doctor's order for any sort of injection around the time DR described getting the injection, and there was no chart note that documented the injection.

February 19: Patient DC dies of what is later determined to be a Mivacron overdose.

February 20: Public General fires Nurse RN.

Nurse RN is indicted, accused of murdering numerous patients with overdoses of Mivacron that she stole from Public General's crash carts. While the prosecution is pending, representatives of the murdered patients sue the hospital, various hospital officials (including the hospital administrator and the director of nursing), and the allegedly murdered patients' doctors.

ISSUES

This case study is not primarily about the standard of nursing care or causa-tion; Nurse RN's deviation from the standard of care, and its consequences, are both obvious. Most claims against nurses *are* about the standard of care and/or causation. By drawing our case study from an entirely different fact pattern, we do not mean to minimize the importance of these issues to health care litigation involving nurses. But standard of care is such a famil-iar concept in health care litigation, and the standards are so case-specific, that a case study built around a standard of care scenario seemed likely just to repeat what this book has already covered (see Chapter 15) and, in a chap-ter intended to cover the broad topic of nursing, to have little pedagogical value beyond its specific facts.

The issues that this case study *does* raise include, first, the liability of a health care employer (whether a physician-owned practice or a large institution) for negligent hiring, retention, and supervision. This is a well-established tort claim that plaintiffs use to establish direct negligence (as opposed to vicarious negligence, or *respondeat superior* liability) against an employer. The linchpin of a negligent hiring claim is the allegation (and the proof) that the employer failed to conduct a reasonably adequate preem-ployment screening and, as a result, hired someone who was able to cause damage by taking advantage of his or her position as an employee. Other settings where the claim might arise include, for example, employment of persons to provide services in customers' houses and an employee's misuse of access to customers' houses to commit crimes.

The necessity of a reasonable preemployment screening is the point to which readers should be sensitive, and not the precise contours of what level of screening should have been accomplished in our case study or in response to any particular employment application. That is a state-specific inquiry that need not be canvassed here. At a minimum, though, an employer should query the National Practitioner Data Bank and the licens-ing authorities in every state in which the nurse claims to have a license. The applicant's intentional omission of information about prior employment can, of course, be a very real problem, but that is no excuse to forgo the checks that are possible. Job references may have limited utility as many employers release only the dates of employment and the position held. Some, though, will state whether an ex-employee is eligible for rehire. In this scenario, that information (if Public General had obtained it) would only confirm Nurse RN's self-disclosed terminations, the bare fact of which would probably not be enough to alert it to the risk that Nurse RN would kill patients. In sum, the facts here probably would not support a negligent hiring claim.

But a negligent retention and/or supervision claim could fare much better. The dangerousness of Mivacron and the number of times it disappeared from the crash cart in November and December provided compelling reasons for hospital officials to begin investigating much sooner than they did. Particularly in a small hospital, even the first couple of deaths should have been worrisome, especially considering the disappearance of Mivacron. In the real case, the plaintiffs alleged that the death rate was at least double what it had been the previous year, and that the circumstances of the deaths were apparently unconnected with the patients' reasons for being in the hospital and should have raised suspicions. One of the first patients to die was being treated for a fall, but then experienced respiratory failure. Another early decedent was in the hospital for an appendectomy, but died of cardiac arrest. According to the timeline, even after hospital officials suspected Nurse RN, it still employed her and allowed her so little supervision that she was able to inject at least two other patients. In these circumstances, any health care employer's direct negligence is obvious.

Depending on the plaintiffs' desire to involve other defendants besides the deep-pocket employer, they might also establish direct negligence claims against hospital officials who neglected to initiate an earlier investigation or failed to take more decisive action.

The second issue that this case study raises is the vicarious negligence, or *respondeat superior* liability, of Nurse RN's employer. An employer is usually charged with liability for an employee's conduct in the course and scope of employment. In a straightforward case of vicarious liability, the nurse's conduct is nothing worse than negligent and clearly within the course and scope of employment. For example, if a nurse misinterprets a doctor's order and injects a bigger dose than prescribed, causing injury to the patient, then the employer's vicarious liability could not be reasonably contested. At the other extreme, if an employee while on break commits a battery upon another employee concerning a non-workplace, personal dispute, then the employer would likely not bear vicarious liability for the battery upon the co-worker, since intentional torts are not within the course and scope of the employment and the tortfeasor's ability to carry out the battery was not obviously aided by his position as an employee.

Our case study concerning Nurse RN presents a mix of both scenarios. On one hand, she committed intentional acts that lay far beyond the course and scope of her employment; on the other, her position as an employee provided both the access and the tools for committing those acts. Vicarious liability is certainly a possible result, especially for the later deaths that the hospital's inaction came close to facilitating.

The third issue is the possibility of a claim against any of the physicians who, prior to Nurse RN's attacks, treated those patients. A nonemployer physician—one who has privileges at the hospital where Nurse RN worked, and might have had occasion to provide some instruction to her—generally does not assume vicarious liability as an employer unless he or she exercises such a high degree of supervision and control over the nurse that the physician is deemed to stand in the shoes of the employer, at least temporarily during the period of such supervision and control. The principle may apply, for example, when a surgeon provides specific direction to a nurse during a surgery. Here, the facts indicate that Nurse RN was operating beyond any supervision or control, so a vicarious liability claim against a nonemployer physician would seem unlikely to succeed.

The fourth issue is the possibility of a claim in addition to the state law torts discussed above (pursued either as types of medical malpractice or nonmalpractice torts: characterization would depend on the scope of the state law governing malpractice claims). Because Nurse RN's employer was a public hospital, the hospital and its officials might be held liable for federal constitutional torts in much the same way that, for example, governmental actors in law enforcement can be held liable for violating civil rights by effecting an unlawful arrest, or governmental employers can be held liable for violating an employee's due process or equal protection rights. Here, the civil right at issue is the patient's constitutionally protected right to live. For such a claim to succeed against the hospital itself, the plaintiffs must have evidence proving that the hospital had a custom or policy that caused the constitutional violation at issue. On these facts, such a conclusion is certainly possible: on numerous occasions, the hospital failed to investigate the disappearance of Mivacron, which allowed more to be stolen and patients to be killed. Constitutional torts could also be asserted against hospital officials who were deliberately indifferent to the unfolding situation. This possibility of constitutional tort claims is extremely significant in those jurisdictions where the law would characterize the plaintiffs' claims as malpractice and would apply to them any damages caps contained in the jurisdiction's malpractice law. The reason is that federal constitutional tort claims have no cap on compensatory or punitive damages.

SURVIVAL STRATEGIES

Survival strategies for employers of nurses—be they physician-owned medical practices or institutional employers such as hospitals—must, in the coming decade, focus on addressing the implications of the major trends we identified at the beginning of this chapter: the huge increase in the number of nurses and the continued shortage of nurses.

Employers will be under pressure to hire applicants to fill positions. That attitude, untempered by recognition that suitability for a career in nursing requires more than bare qualifications, will lead to disaster. Careful preemployment screening will be essential.

Monitoring and mentoring will suffer in the coming years because it will be impossible for newer nurses to work as closely with more experienced colleagues. As this one-on-one training becomes less available, employers will have to substitute more frequent formal training sessions. Supervision will also become more of a challenge as staffs become thinner. Improvements in efficiency due to the continued adoption of information technology, particularly as it involves patient records and patient medications, may help alleviate this problem. But to the degree that supervisors have little more experience than those they supervise, it will not really help.

The overall theme here is the need for strong, involved management, both on the professional side insofar as it concerns maintaining the standard of care, and on the human resources side insofar as it concerns a proactive stance in using disciplinary tools to address problems. Without a commitment to both, employers of nurses will not fare well during the next decade of instability, and neither will their patients.

FURTHER READING

Gic J, "Nursing and the Law." In *Legal Medicine/American College of Legal Medicine*, 7th ed., ed. S. Sandy Sanbar *et al*. Philadelphia: Mosby, 2007.

Fleming TM, Annotation, *Hospital's Liability for Injury Resulting from Failure to Have Sufficient Number of Nurses on Duty*. 2 A.L.R. 5th 286 (1992 & Supp. 2004).

REFERENCES

1. Press Release, United States Department of Labor Bureau of Labor Statistics, BLS Releases 2004-14 Employment Projections (Dec. 7, 2005) (on file with author), available at http://www.bls.gov/news.release/pdf/ecopro.pdf.

2. Joint Commission on Accreditation of Healthcare Organizations, Health Care at the Crossroads: Strategies for Addressing the Evolving Nursing Crisis 8 (2002) (on file with author), available at http://www.jcaho.org/about+us/public+policy+initiatives/health_care_at_the_crossroads.pdf.

3. *Atteberry v. Nocona General Hosp.*, No. 04-11330 (5th Cir., Nov. 3, 2005).

Medical Product Liability

Thomas R. McLean, M.D., M.S., J.D., F.A.C.S., F.C.L.M.

GOLDEN RULES

1. More than the physician is involved.
2. Not everyone has the same goals.
3. Deep-pocketed co-defendants often invite trouble.
4. Time is not of the essence.
5. FDA approval may or may not matter.
6. The best defense is a good offense:
   (a) Preserve the product and the maintenance records, and establish a paper trail.
   (b) Physician: know thy machines.
   (c) Physician: know thy procedures and regulations.
   (d) Physician: know thy machine makers.

In 1976, responding to an avalanche of litigation arising from events associated with the use of the Dalkon Shield contraceptive device, Congress passed the Medical Device Amendment to the Food, Drug and Cosmetic Act. Henceforth, the Food and Drug Administration (FDA) was to ensure that medical devices placed on the market were used safely.[1] Since 1976, the FDA has approved over 10,000 devices for use in the health care field. Unfortunately, medical devices are often misused by physicians or defectively manufactured. For example, one thoracic surgeon controlled bleeding near a vertebral foramen using gel foam. The surgeon forgot—until the patient awoke from anesthesia paraplegic—that as gel foam soaks up blood it expands. This mistake cost the doctor and his co-defendants $4.9 million. Alternatively, sometimes the physician is entirely innocent and the device itself is negligently made. For example, over time the impregnated silver atoms in St. Jude's Silzone heart valve leached out of the valve and into cardiac tissue. As a result, St. Jude's Silzone heart valve became dislodged causing some patients to sustain heart failure, stroke, or even death.[2] But when a medical device is associated with an adverse patient outcome, how does the law decide if the physician, the device manufacturer, or both, or others need to provide compensation to an injured patient? This chapter is designed to provide insight into the complex lawsuits involving allegations of both malpractice and defective medical devices.

CASE PRESENTATION

On a routine physical examination, 85-year-old Mr. Smith was found by his internist to have a 7 cm abdominal aortic aneurysm. Mr. Smith, who had the good fortune of only needing to see a physician once a year and did not require any prescription medications, underwent all of the appropriate aneurysm imaging studies. He was ultimately referred to Dr. Sure Hands for aneurysm repair. After discussing the risk and benefits of open and endovascular aneurysm repair with Mr. Smith, Dr. Hands recommended that he undergo endovascular repair, primarily because of his age. Mr. Smith agreed and set a date to have his operation performed at Man's Best Hospital (MBH), the premier hospital in the city.

On the date of the aneurysm repair, Mr. Smith is brought into MBH's state-of-the-art fluoroscopy suite where, in addition to the routine hospital staff and Dr. Hands, is Mr. Easy, who works for Endovascular Stenting, Inc. (ESI), the maker of the endovascular grafts. A year earlier, ESI had obtained FDA approval to market its endovascular graft for the treatment of abdominal aortic aneurysms. Mr. Easy's job is to make available an assortment of grafts and graft deployment devices to endovascular surgeons and, where appropriate, to offer technical advice concerning these products.

Mr. Smith is then prepped and draped and vascular access is gained by the femoral artery. After the guide wire is correctly positioned with fluoroscopy, Dr. Hands finds that it is impossible to pass the endovascular graft deployment device because Mr. Smith's iliac artery is too tortuous. Mr. Easy, who is watching the progress of the case on a second fluoroscopy screen, sees the problem. Mr. Easy tells Dr. Hands that a month before he watched another surgeon struggle with a similar tortuous iliac artery. Mr. Easy then relates how the other surgeon cracked the deployment device in two places to get it to negotiate the tortuous vessel.

Thinking about his situation, Dr. Hands sees how Mr. Easy's suggestion to modify the deployment device would work. So the doctor cracks the deployment device as directed and finds that the device is now able to negotiate the iliac artery. After the endovascular graft is deployed, Dr. Hands performs a completion arteriogram, which demonstrates that the graft is in good position without evidence of endovascular leaks. The doctor then finishes the case by removing the deployment device and sends his patient to the recovery room.

About an hour later, Mr. Smith's leg, on the side used to gain vascular access, suddenly became as pale and cold as the bed sheets and Mr. Smith begins to scream in pain. The recovery room staff calls Dr. Hands, who correctly diagnoses that the patient had acutely occluded his iliac artery. Dr. Hands promptly explores Mr. Smith's iliac artery in the operating room and finds an intimal tear in the iliac artery caused by a sharp edge of the cracked deployment catheter. Although Dr. Hands expertly repairs the iatrogenic vascular injury, the patient nonetheless sustains an ipsilateral compartment syndrome during the period of acute occlusion. Ultimately, Mr. Smith is left with a deformed lower leg and foot drop as a sequel to the compartment syndrome.[3]

ISSUES

Introduction

To be found liable for medical malpractice, a physician must deviate from the standard of care, cause harm, and the patient must sustain damages. In the above hypothetical, which is based on actual facts, most physicians would intuitively understand that (1) breaking something to make it work is a deviation of the standard of care; (2) damaging a blood vessel will cause the blood vessel to acutely occlude; and (3) a patient who sustains a deformity of a lower extremity and a foot drop due to acute iatrogenic vascular occlusion has been damaged. Thus, at first glance to the untrained legal mind, this hypothetical may appear as a straightforward case of physician negligence. But from a legal perspective, because a medical device was involved, much more will transpire if Mr. Smith elects to sue either Dr. Hands or the MBH.

The use of a product in this case inextricably complicates the legal calculus. A product is any tangible object that is distributed commercially for use or consumption. Thus, all of the following are examples of products: central lines, surgical instruments (including deployment devices), any prosthetic material (including endovascular grafts), pacemakers, defibrillators, and any telemedical devices. In the above hypothetical case the product of concern is the endovascular graph deployment device. But while it may seem that the definition of a product is broad, not everything is a product. Services (as occurs when a physician performs a physical examination) or a custom-made surgical instrument that cannot be purchased are two commonplace examples of things that cannot be classified as products.

Whether the maker of the product is responsible for a harm that occurs during the product's use is determined by a set of legal rules known as products liability. Completely independent of the rules for medical malpractice, products liability is important in medical malpractice litigation because of the omnipresent use of products in the practice of medicine. In general, a number of factors determine whether the maker of a product is liable in a products liability lawsuit, including whether the product was: (1) sold; (2) designed or manufactured in a defective manner; (3) abused (modified by the user); or whether (4) the harm caused by the product was foreseeable; and (5) the manufacturer failed to warn the user of a nonobvious danger. Of these factors, the most important is whether the harm caused by a product is foreseeable (e.g., it is foreseeable that a car with a rear-mounted gas tank will explode when the car is struck in the rear) and whether the product maker gave a proper warning to the user. The various products liability lawsuits as they related to these factors are summarized in Table 19-1. However, unlike a medical malpractice action where there can be no liability without a physician being at fault, in a products liability action a manufacturer can be held liable even without a demonstration of fault if the product is unreasonably dangerous. This is referred to as strict liability and is rare in a medical setting because of the FDA's regulations.

Products that are used specifically to diagnose or treat a disease are medical devices. A product is classified as a medical device when, in addition to

Table 19-1 Types of products liability lawsuits. Not all products liability suits are alike. The various forms of products liability lawsuits differ in what is specifically alleged and what needs to be proven.

Allegation	Proof needed	Comment
Negligent product design	(1) Expert testimony that the the manufacturer did not meet the standard of care; (2) another cost-effective design was possible	Litigations is similar to a medical malpractice action
Negligent manufacturing of the medical device	The medical device product did not meet the manufacturer's own standards	See above
Failure to warn	Injury was foreseeable	(1) Manufacturer must anticipate that physician may modify device; (2) warning must comply with FDA requirements
Strict liability	Product was unreasonably dangerous during normal use	Rare in the medical setting because of the FDA's pre-market approval process

being a tangible object that is bought or sold, the product's intended use is to alter human anatomy or physiology by some means other than chemical. (By way of contrast, products that alter anatomy or physiology by chemical means are classified as drugs.) Because of the unique nature of medical devices and their potential for causing bodily harm, there are two additional sets of rules that supplement the general products liability rules to determine if a device manufacturer is liable when a patient is injured. First, the manufacturer must comply with all of the relevant FDA regulations. Second, if a learned intermediary (LI) is involved in the selection of a medical device for a patient, the device's manufacturer does not have a duty to warn patients of foreseeable harm. As used in this context, a physician is an LI. Accordingly, when a physician like Dr. Hands selects a medical device like the endovascular graft, the device's manufacturer does not have to give the patient, who is the ultimate user of a device, a warning concerning the risks associated with the graft.

The importance of products liability actions to physicians is that if a product is involved in a medical misadventure, the ensuing litigation will be more complex because: (1) the patient will file both a medical malpractice action against the physician and a products liability action against the device's manufacturer; (2) because the hospital frequently owns or maintains the device, the hospital will often be named as a co-defendant; (3) the malpractice action and the products liability action will be combined into a single large lawsuit; and (4) because neither the hospital nor the device manufacturer is subject to medical malpractice caps, the stakes are higher.

Many states have a "one-action" rule. Under a one-action rule, for a given occurrence or event, a plaintiff must simultaneously bring all possible lawsuits to the attention of the court. There are two policy reasons for such a rule. First, it promotes judicial economy because a single trial leads to the resolution of multiple lawsuits. Second, the one-action rule is viewed as being fairer to defendants because it prevents the plaintiff from recovering two judgments. For example, in the above case, the one-action rule prevents Mr. Smith from going to court and suing Dr. Hands, claiming that he was solely responsible for his injury, and then separately suing EVS, claiming that the deployment device manufacturer was solely responsible for his injuries. So, to a degree, a one-action rule is in a physician's best interest. On the other hand, the one-action rule substantially complicates a medical malpractice action because more than the physician is involved and time is not of the essence because the number of expert witnesses that must be deposed substantially increases.

Review of Concepts

However, before examining a combined medical malpractice/products liability lawsuit in detail, a brief review of the basic concepts of products liability is appropriate. A medical device is any product that a manufacturer intended to be used to treat a patient, either by a physician or the patient on their own. The law of products liability determines whether the manufacturer of a medical device is liable if a patient should be harmed while a physician is using the medical device. However, products liability law does not exist in a vacuum, and other laws and regulations, such as medical malpractice, FDA regulations, and various state safety laws, are important as they are evidence of the standard of care to be provided. For example, the minimal safety performance standards are defined by the FDA when it grants approval for a medical device to be sold to physicians. However, physicians should be aware that interaction of products liability law, medical malpractice, FDA regulations, and other laws (that are beyond the discussion of this chapter) impose obligations on the manufacturer, physician, and institution where a medical device is used. Table 19-2 summarizes the most substantial duties and obligations imposed on medical device users.

A More Detailed Look at the Complex Interactions of Products Liability and Medical Malpractice

As already mentioned, in a products liability action involving a medical device, the FDA regulations serve an evidentiary function. However, the FDA regulations, and the case law that flows from these regulations, concern only what documentation a medical device manufacturer must provide: (1) to get their device on the market; (2) for their advertisement statements to be appropriate; (3) as a warning to be given to physicians; and (4) what post-sale information must be gathered when a medical device is associated with an adverse patient outcome. Importantly, the FDA regulations have nothing to say about how a physician should practice medicine.

Table 19-2 Summary of the most substantial duties and obligations that the law imposes on those who use medical devices

User	Obligations
Manufacturers	(1) Nonnegligent devices design and manufacturing; (2) FDA approval prior to placing any device on the market; (3) honest and timely compliance with the FDA's post-marketing medical device surveillance; (4) proper training and education of physician users
Physicians	(1) Keep accurate records; (2) be cognizant of the scope of FDA approval for a medical device; (3) use a medical device as a reasonably prudent physician would do under the same or similar circumstances; (4) obtain proper training before using any medical device; (5) convey to the patient all relevant manufacturer or FDA warnings; (6) promptly document all medical device misadventures and report misadventures to the manufacturer and where appropriate directly to the FDA
Hospitals	(1) Ensure that physicians are properly trained and credentialed before they use a medical device; (2) ensure that ancillary care providers (e.g., nurses, therapists) are properly trained before a device is used; (3) ensure that ancillary care providers are properly supervised; (4) ensure that medical device is maintained to the manufacturer's and FDA's standards

Medicine is regulated by licensure acts, scope of practice laws, and medical malpractice, not by the FDA. This means that physicians are free to use a medical device that is not FDA-approved if a reasonable physician under the same or similar circumstances would use the same non-FDA-approved device.

Still, the FDA regulations are not totally independent of medical malpractice action for two reasons. First, whether a medical device has received FDA approval may be introduced as evidence against a physician to help show that the physician acted unreasonably, i.e., that the physician did not meet the standard of care. FDA approval status may also be introduced by the device manufacturer to show that the physician used the device for an "off-label" use. Physicians are free to use FDA-approved devices for nonapproved reasons. But in such cases the device manufacturer may not be liable for the harm caused by the device. Occasionally, however, a plaintiff's attorney will attempt to get into evidence the fact that a medical device never received FDA approval for its collateral emotional impact on a jury. To the general public, FDA approval is viewed as being a "Good-Housekeeping Seal of Approval" for medical devices. Because jurors like to hear that good doctors use the best tools available, the lack of FDA approval may carry a negative connotation in the mind of the jury. Alternatively, if the doctor had a choice between two virtually identical devices, but one was FDA approved and the other was not, the doctor's selection of the non-FDA-approved device may carry a negative connotation.

The second reason why the FDA regulations are of importance to the physician involved in medical malpractice litigation is that not all FDA approval is equivalent. Potentially, FDA approval can be obtained by two processes that are named for the section of federal law that describes the method of approval. Under §510(k), all a manufacturer of a medical device has to do to obtain FDA approval is to demonstrate that the new device is "substantially equivalent" to an existing FDA-approved device on the market. FDA approval via the §510(k) process is fairly cheap and easy to obtain.[4] Often the FDA will grant a device §510(k) approval in a matter of weeks. In contrast, securing FDA approval via the §360 process is much more onerous, and may take years to obtain. §360 approval requires that a device manufacturer has a lot of time and money to bring the product to market because the FDA performs its own rigorous engineering risk analysis of a proposed device to determine if the device is safe. Not surprisingly, only about 2% of medical devices gain market access via the §360 mechanism.

Why would a manufacturer of a medical device elect to undergo the rigors of the §360 FDA approval process when the §510(k) route is much more convenient? Occasionally for some truly novel devices the §360 pathway is the only way to get a device to market because there are no substantial equivalent devices available for comparison. Alternatively, the §360 pathway is elected because of the benefits that flow from §360 approval.[5] If a device is granted §360 approval, then the 1976 amendments to the FDA Act preempt the medical device from state tort law. From a practical point of view, preemption of state law in this context means that the manufacturer of a §360-approved medical device cannot be held liable in a products liability action. Thus, §360 approval provides the medical device manufacturer with a competitive edge in the marketplace over similar §510(k)-approved devices because the manufacturer has fewer insurance costs.

Unfortunately for the physicians, even if a device in a combined medical malpractice/products liability action has received §360 approval, some plaintiff's lawyers will fight the §360 "immunity" by various means. For example, the plaintiff may assert that the device manufacturer had committed fraud on the FDA. If the plaintiff's lawyer should succeed in having the §360 approval overturned, the combined medical malpractice/products liability action will degenerate, as we will see momentarily, into a "finger-pointing" case. However, most of the stratagems for overturning §360 approval ultimately fail, and the product manufacturer is dismissed from the case. Still, from the physician's point of view, such legal tactics are important because the medical malpractice litigation will be substantially drawn out by the products liability litigation. The impact of lengthy litigation on the physician should not be underestimated because, as Charles Dickens described in *Bleak House* over a century ago, protracted litigation extracts an emotional toll from all involved in the litigation, except perhaps for the lawyers.

More Than the Physician Is Involved

From this brief introduction of products liability, physicians need to realize that when they are being sued along with a medical device manufacturer, they are not alone. Frequently, these suits will not only include the medical device manufacturer, but they will also involve the hospital where the device was used. Hospitals become involved in medical malpractice/products liability actions because they own the medical device and/or have agreed to be responsible for the maintenance of the device. As the owner of a medical device, the hospital has a duty to see that patients who are treated with a device receive their treatment in a nonnegligent manner. If a patient is harmed by a medical device and it can be shown that the hospital did not properly supervise the device's use or did not properly maintain the device, the hospital may be responsible to the patient for any harm sustained as a result of a medical device's use.

Moreover, even if the hospital is not named in the suit by the plaintiff, the hospital may be brought into the suit as defendant by motion on behalf of the product manufacturer or physician. The reason that a device manufacturer or physician would want to get a hospital involved in such a suit is to shift blame. More specifically, if it can be shown that a hospital abused a medical device—that is, failed to maintain the device as recommended by the manufacturer—conceptually the hospital could be the sole defendant held liable for a patient's injury. By way of illustration, consider the above hypothetical case as an example of how the product abuse defense might work. When Dr. Hands breaks the deployment device, he abuses the product. But if ESI can show that the hospital had a duty to supervise its endovascular lab, such that the endovascular lab technicians should have stopped Dr. Hands from using a broken device, then ESI may be able to shift blame to the hospital and avoid liability.

An even more interesting question raised in this hypothetical is whether Dr. Hands is acting as an LI. The concept of the LI is that the physician is in the best position to determine what treatments and products are in a patient's best interest. But, as noted above, a consequence of this policy is that medical device manufacturers cannot directly warn patients of the risks and benefits of using their product. Rather, the product manufacturer must advise the physician of the risks associated with a product and the physician must then use this information to make a medical decision. Accordingly, during a combined medical malpractice/products liability action, if the device's manufacturer can demonstrate that the physician was properly warned of the limitation of a device (for example, by prior training or advertisement), the manufacturer will face no liability for failing to warn the patient about nonobvious risks. It is because manufacturers wish to be able to demonstrate that a physician is an LI that a device manufacturer wines and dines physicians who are willing to use their devices.

Moreover, part of the reason that a device manufacturer has a product representative, like Mr. Easy, on site during the use of a medical device is to provide technical assistance to the physician. Such technical assistance, in the event of a medical misadventure with the device, serves to enhance the device manufacturer's assertion that the physician was an LI. Still, in the above hypothetical, Mr. Easy's advice to break the deployment device is interesting. A product representative is not permitted to give a physician advice concerning the use of a device that is inconsistent with FDA's approved instructions on safe usage. In this case, it is unlikely that the FDA approved an instruction that stated that the deployment device could be broken, from time to time, to facilitate insertion. Accordingly, because Mr. Easy did make such a recommendation to Dr. Hands, from a legal point of view, it is an open question whether the doctor was truly acting as an LI in this case. If the doctor in this hypothetical is not an LI, EVS may have liability to the patient for failure to warn of the risks of the device. But regardless of whether a doctor is an LI, the intentional dissemination of technical advice at variance with the FDA's requirements leaves the product manufacturer open to being criminally charged with the misbranding of the medical device.

At first it may seem mysterious why a product representative would give a physician a recommendation for use that is not consistent with the FDA's approval. But if the incentives of the product representative are considered, the mystery vanishes. Product representatives want to sell products, which in this case is the endovascular graft itself. If the deployment device cannot be properly positioned by the physician, the product representative will lose the sale of an endovascular graft. Thus the product representative has an incentive to see that a physician does not become frustrated with a medical device and select an alternative therapy. More generally, it is important for physicians wishing to avoid a lawsuit to realize that the product representative or product manufacturer's interests are not necessarily aligned with the physician's. That the physician's and device manufacturer's incentives are different, in turn, reflects that the goals of treating patients are different. The primary goal of the physician is to ameliorate disease and secondarily to earn a living, whereas the primary goal of a product manufacturer is to make a profit.

The consequences of physicians and medical device manufacturers having different incentives and goals have implications for medical malpractice litigations involving medical devices. Superficially, when a physician, a medical device manufacturer, and a hospital are joined as co-defendants in a medical malpractice/products liability action, all three defendants have the same general goal: to vindicate all of their good names. But the real goal of a defendant in any lawsuit is first to save themselves, and then if possible to save their co-defendants. Because of the two-tiered goal structure of a defendant, each co-defendant will use whatever means are necessary to protect their own self-interests. Accordingly, co-defendants often attempt to shift blame to the other co-defendants, that is, each defendant provides damaging testimony against the other defendants. Plaintiffs' attorneys refer to such cases as finger-pointing cases, which plaintiffs' attorneys love because they virtually always settle.

Another important consequence of a joint medical malpractice/products liability case is that these cases involve at least one, and possibly more, deep pockets. In many states, the possible damage awards that can be recovered from a physician are limited by damage caps placed in the medical malpractice statutes. In contrast, nothing limits the damage awards that are payable by a medical device manufacturer or a hospital. If a jury determines that a medical device manufacturer or a hospital caused a patient harm, these two parties are expected to reach into their deep pockets for assets, reserves, and insurance in order to pay the award in full. Not surprisingly, plaintiffs'

attorneys have been known to attempt to drag a medical device manufacturer into a medical malpractice dispute not only to convert the litigation to a
finger-pointing case, but also to have access to a deep-pocketed defendant.
After all, when it is realized that after expenses are deducted, a plaintiff's attorney earns one-third of a settlement or a jury award, it becomes clear why
deep-pocketed defendants are considered prime targets by the plaintiff's bar.

Funding Complex Litigation: Time Is Not of the Essence

From a practical point of view, once a medical device manufacturer
becomes a defendant alongside a physician in a medical malpractice action,
time is no longer of the essence. This is not only because of the complexities associated with the relationships of the defendants, but also because of
the engineering issues associated with the medical device. Expert witnesses
will need to be deposed to determine whether the device was designed
properly and made correctly, and whether the device was abused. Thus, in
the above hypothetical, in addition to taking expert witness testimony concerning the reasonableness of Dr. Hands' conduct, expert testimony will be
required to explain the design of the graft deployment device, alternative
designs, and cost analyses of those alternative designs. For the physician
defendant, gathering all of this expert testimony will ensure that litigation
will be protracted, thereby prolonging the emotional turmoil of litigation.
And as the years go by, physicians involved in a combined medical
malpractice/products liability action will likely be tempted to settle the case
just to get the litigation over with and behind them.

Yet, getting the physician to think settlement in such complex litigation
is part of the plaintiff's attorney's strategy. Compensation for the expert
witnesses needed in the products liability aspect of the case is perhaps
the biggest expense a plaintiff attorney has in a joint medical
malpractice/products liability case. This creates cash flow problems for the
plaintiff's attorney because the expert witnesses are paid long before a settlement or jury award is received. While there are multiple ways to finance such
cash flow situations, perhaps the easiest and least risky source of money to
fund a products liability case is to get the physician to settle the medical
malpractice action. More specifically, after enough testimony is obtained to
demonstrate that the physician is likely to have to pay something, the plaintiff's attorney will offer to settle the case. If the physician accepts the settlement offer, the plaintiff's attorney will use his or her share of the proceeds
to fund the products liability action against the device manufacturer.
Importantly, if the settlement offer is reasonable and within the physician's
policy limits, the physician's insurer is unlikely to challenge the offer.

SURVIVAL STRATEGIES

Preservation of the Evidence and Establishing a Paper Trail

Once a physician becomes aware that they may be involved in a medical
malpractice action that involves a medical device, the physician needs to

understand that the best defense is a good offense if a finger-pointing case is to be avoided. Frequently, such an offense begins at the time of the adverse event with preservation of the evidence.

In the above hypothetical situation, Dr. Hands should instruct the hospital and/or product representative to preserve the broken deployment device. Because co-defendants have different motivations, sometimes defective medical devices "disappear" or are otherwise misplaced. To ensure that such evidence is not entirely lost, Dr. Hands should consider three other methods to preserve relevant evidence. First, in the present day when it seems everyone's cellular telephone doubles as a digital camera, Dr. Hands should photograph the deployment device and transfer the photograph to a more permanent storage medium. Second, Dr. Hands should consider writing a good-faith letter concerning the adverse medical event to the FDA, with a copy being sent to both the hospital and the medical device manufacturer. Third, Dr. Hands should interview (and memorialize the interview) all other professionals involved (including the product representative). Key issues for the doctor to focus on would be how the device was stored and maintained, hospital policies concerning the storage and maintenance of the device, and where and how the device is to be preserved.

While collecting the above information, the physician must realize that somewhere in the future, litigation may pit the physician against the hospital and/or the medical device manufacturer. Accordingly, after an adverse event involving a medical device, physicians should conduct themselves with decorum because the physician's relationships with the hospital and device manufacturer may become adversarial at any point. Remember, in the event of litigation, the hospital and product manufacturer are not necessarily the physician's friends, regardless of past relationships.

Physician: Know Thy Machines

What evidence should be collected and what questions the physician should ask during post-adverse event interviews will depend on the nature of the medical device. For example, if the device is a defective pacemaker or breast implant that comes directly from the manufacturer, there should be few questions for the hospital. On the other hand, if the medical device actually breaks during treatment of the patient, the details of the device's storage and maintenance by the hospital become paramount. But to ask these questions, the physician needs to actually understand the medical device. Ideally, the physician should have an understanding of how the device is manufactured (e.g., solid-state vs. component construction) and what material was used to construct the device (as this will determine storage and maintenance requirements). At the very least, the physician who uses a medical device should have a working knowledge of the relevant FDA regulations.

Physician: Know Thy Machine Makers

For many physicians, asking questions concerning the engineering of a medical device will be difficult at best. Thus, physicians should carefully select the medical device manufacturers with whom they want to do business. Physicians should not select a medical device manufacturer because they are friends with a product representative or because a colleague endorses the use of the device. Rather the physician who uses a device should select the manufacturer based on articulable reasons that are derived from the physician's own research. Frequently, this will require reading more than the medical literature because major medical device manufacturers are known to capture the relevant medical journals. For example, one manufacturer of an implantable medical device received virtually no negative comments in the medical literature because the manufacturer was a major advertiser in the relevant journal and had hired most of the journal's editorial staff as paid consultants on the defective product.

Admittedly, however, such research is often hard to come by, and even if the desired data concerning corporate performance is obtained, the data may be difficult for physicians to comprehend. But one thing a physician who uses a device should be aware of is the culture of a company. When the culture of a company encourages its employees to take short cuts in production or violate federal regulations in order to bring to market a defective medical device, one should expect that such a culture will produce other types of medical devices that will prove to be defective. The Guidant Corporation is a case in point. The hypothetical in this chapter was based on the fact pattern reported in a settlement entered into by Guidant and one of its subsidiaries (EndoVascular Technologies) and the Department of Justice for the way Guidant marketed its Ancure endovascular graft for the treatment of abdominal aortic aneurysms. Not only did Guidant look the other way when product representatives instructed physicians to break the deployment device to facilitate graft insertion, it also failed to properly report adverse events to the FDA as required by law. Given such a culture, is it any wonder that two years later 40,000 Guidant internal cardiac defibrillators and 28,000 Guidant pacemakers were reported to be defective?

But there is one other aspect of the Guidant corporate culture story that is of importance to medical malpractice litigation. Guidant had an exit strategy. After Guidant settled with the Department of Justice, Guidant placed itself on the market and quickly found a tentative buyer in Johnson & Johnson. What physicians often fail to understand about such sales is that all that is sold are the company's assets. The liabilities, on the other hand, remain with the shell of the original company that is left behind to continue the business. Shell corporations are constructed so that they have minimal hard assets and a system to maintain existing insurance coverage for past events. This means that if sometime in the future, after Guidant's sale to Johnson & Johnson or some other buyer is completed, a patient is injured by a Guidant endovascular graft, defibrillator, or pacemaker, that patient can only recover from Guidant until its insurance benefits run out. This of course means that those plaintiffs who file a lawsuit against Guidant relatively late (i.e., after many others have already filed suit) may collect nothing from Guidant after the assets have been assigned and the insurance benefits have run out.

Still, when a corporation makes a quick profit from the sales of a medical device and then vanishes into bankruptcy leaving only a shell corporation to be sued, that does not mean the plaintiffs harmed by a defective medical device disappear too. On the contrary, if anything, when a company engages in such evasive techniques, it is likely that plaintiffs will go after the physician who used the device with more vigor. Such lawsuits often end in settlements because the (shell) corporation that remains after the sale of the company's assets continues to be tried and convicted of wrongdoing in the popular press (just like Guidant is already experiencing). Accordingly, years later, when the lawsuit between the plaintiff and physician finally comes to trial, the jury is aware that the plaintiff has received nothing from the medical device manufacturer, and will receive nothing if the jury does not take action. The legal system does not encourage juries to use sympathy when evaluating whether a physician was negligent. Unfortunately for physicians, sometimes sympathy is a reality; if so, a physician-defendant may be exposed for excessive damages. Hence, in situations like this, the physician's attorney and insurer will often encourage a settlement.

FURTHER READING

Lehv MS, "Medical Product Liability." In *Legal Medicine/American College of Legal Medicine*, 7th ed., ed. S. Sandy Sanbar *et al*. Philadelphia: Mosby, 2007.

McLean TR, *Monetary Lessons from Litigation Involving Laparoscopic Cholecystectomy*. Am. Surg. 71:606–613 (2005).

McLean TR, *Cybersurgery: An Argument for Enterprise Liability*. J. Legal Med. 23:167 (2002).

Medtronic v. Lohr, 56 F 3d 1335 (11th Cir. 1995).

REFERENCES

1. Medical Device Amendments to the Food, Drug and Cosmetic Act, Pub. L. No. 94-295, 90 Stat. 539 (1976).

2. *In re St. Jude Silzone Heart Valve Product Litigation*, MDL Docket No. 1396; available at http://www.mnd.uscourts.gov/Tunheim_Mdl/Reports/joint_status_report_04-03-18.pdf.

3. Department of Justice, *Guidant Settlement*, June 13, 2003; available at http://www.usdoj.gov/usao/can/press/html/2003_06_12_endovascular.html.

4. §510(k) FDA approval, 21 U.S.C. §510(k) (1994).

5. §360 FDA approval, 21 U.S.C. §360 (1994).

MALPRACTICE
LAWSUIT
RESOLUTION

The American Court System

S. Sandy Sanbar, M.D., Ph.D., J.D., F.C.L.M.

SOURCES OF LAW

The legal system in the United States is composed of four basic types of law: constitutional, legislative, judicial, and administrative. These basic types are found in all 50 states, and in the federal and the local systems. The result is a maze of laws, judicial decisions, rules, regulations, ordinances, constitutions, etc. The same factual controversy may be decided in favor of party A in California, but against party A just a few miles away in the state of Nevada. Also, party A could win in California under California state law but lose in the same state under federal law. Generally, the layman need not concern himself or herself with this maze of law, as competent legal counsel should always be obtainable. Just as the attorney should not treat himself for a medical problem, the health care provider should not attempt to manage legal problems alone. Each should consult with the respective specialists.

Constitutional Law

The United States Constitution, and the constitutions of all 50 states, delineate the powers of the federal and state governments and the executive, legislative, and judicial capacities. Additionally, the federal and state constitutions contain guarantees to individuals against governmental or private action, thereby placing limitations upon governmental powers, and creating a basic guarantee of individual rights. Such rights include prohibition of the taking of private property without just compensation, the right to privacy, to travel, and the right to vote. Similarly, certain freedoms are constitutionally protected, such as the freedoms of speech, association, and religion. A major function of the judges and justices is to interpret the language of state and federal constitutions.

Legislative (Statutory) Law

The legislative and the executive branches of government create, or enact, legislative or statutory law. Statutory law supersedes all other types of law except constitutional law. Statutory laws are usually written in broad terms, and subject to judicial interpretation. They may be changed only by repeal, or modification by further legislation.

The ability to create statutory law in the federal system is expressly allocated to Congress by the United States Constitution. Most state constitutions do not specifically create legislative power in the state legislative branch, but serve only to limit specific areas of legislative power, assuming the implicit existence of state legislative power as retained by the Tenth Amendment. It should be remembered that all law is subject to the ultimate authority of the United States Constitution.

Judicial (Common) Law

The American legal system is part of the common law tradition, as is that of most English-speaking countries. Common law may be defined as that body of law that is based on the precedent value of past decisions of the court, decisions of other courts within the judicial system, public policy, and/or legal reasoning. Prior decisions of the court are interpreted as having precedent value, furnishing examples or authority when considering an identical or similar case. If a case occurs subsequently involving the same questions of law, the court would attempt to adhere to its prior decision(s). This is called the doctrine of *stare decisis*.

Judge-made low, or common law, is extremely diverse, as well as complicated to ascertain. The common law is subordinate to controlling constitutions, statutory law, rules, and regulations. Of course, it is the judge who determines whether the Constitution or statute was intended to apply to the particular facts of the case before the judge, and what the exact interpretation of statutory language is. Great latitude is therefore available to the judge.

Executive/Administrative Law

Administrative law is composed of the various rules and regulations promulgated by administrative agencies. Administrative law tends to deal with technical and specialized areas, which are considered to be complicated or procedurally cumbersome for the legislature to deal with on a continuing basis. Administrative law is often the result of the creation of an agency to deal with problems that require more flexibility than can be created through a statutory means alone. Rules and regulations created by an administrative agency must be consistent with the enabling act created by the particular legislature, and are subordinate to other statutory or constitutional law. An example of an administrative agency within the health care field is the Federal Food and Drug Administration. Because supervision of health care is often highly technical, it is often supervised by governmental agencies, through the administrative law process.

THE COURT SYSTEM

State Court Systems

Typically, state courts consist of three tiers: first, the appellate courts (the highest); second, the district, superior, and circuit courts; and third, the municipal, city, and regional courts.

Appellate Courts

These courts are known as the "courts of last resort." They are "paper courts" and a growing number of the appellate courts are becoming "computerized courts," thereby relying less on paper. They do not retry cases. Instead, they review the record of the proceedings from earlier trials to determine whether or not the lower court committed an error of law with its decision. Typically the state supreme appellate courts comprise five to nine members who rule as a panel.

District, Superior, or Circuit Courts

These are trial courts of "general jurisdiction." They are geographically located throughout the state for convenience. More than 10 million cases are filed in these courts annually. The cases that are brought before these courts usually involve more serious civil and criminal claims such as felony prosecutions and major civil trials.

Municipal, City, or Regional Courts

These are also trial courts but of "limited jurisdiction." Approximately 100 million cases go through these courts annually. They are usually confined to civil suits, involving relatively small amounts of money and minor violations of the law, e.g. minor traffic offenses.

The U.S. Federal Court System

As with state courts, federal courts consist of three tiers: first, the U.S. Supreme Court; second, the U.S. Courts of Appeal; and third, the federal district courts.

The U.S. Supreme Court

This is the one and only highest court of the land. The U.S. Supreme Court receives approximately 5000 petitions each year, but accepts and hears about 150 cases appealed to the Court. A party must submit a "petition for a writ of certiorari," requesting the Supreme Court to hear a case. Usually, four or more justices of the U.S. Supreme Court must agree to hear the case to "grant certiorari" to the petitioner. The cases heard usually involve conflicts over legal interpretations, which have a significant importance in federal law. The court can hear appeals of cases from both the U.S. Courts of Appeal and the state supreme appellate courts. If the Supreme Court denies a petition, the lower circuit court decision stands.

The U.S. Courts of Appeal

The federal court system is composed of 13 courts of appeal distributed throughout the Unites States. There are approximately 150 federal appeals court judgeships, with 6 to 28 judges in each circuit. Judges within each circuit court are divided into rotating three-judge panels. Occasionally, albeit rarely, the entire circuit appellate court judges, sitting "en banc," will hear a case. The courts of appeal include:

    1st Circuit Court—Maine, Massachusetts, New Hampshire, Rhode Island, Puerto Rico.
    2nd Circuit Court—Connecticut, New York, Vermont.
    3rd Circuit Court—Delaware, New Jersey, Pennsylvania, Virgin Islands.
    4th Circuit Court—Maryland, North Carolina, South Carolina, Virginia, West Virginia.
    5th Circuit Court—Louisiana, Mississippi, Texas.
    6th Circuit Court—Kentucky, Michigan, Ohio, Tennessee.
    7th Circuit Court—Illinois, Indiana, Wisconsin.
    8th Circuit Court—Arkansas, Iowa, Minnesota, Missouri, Nebraska, North Dakota, South Dakota.
    9th Circuit Court—Alaska, Arizona, California, Hawaii, Idaho, Montana, Nevada, Oregon, Washington, Northern Mariana Islands, Guam.
    10th Circuit Court—Colorado, Kansas, New Mexico, Oklahoma, Utah, Wyoming.
    11th Circuit Court—Alabama, Florida, Georgia.
    D.C. Circuit Court.
    Federal Circuit Court.

Federal District Courts

There are 91 federal judicial districts (excluding the District Courts of the Virgin Islands and Guam) in the United States. Every state has at least one federal district. The federal district courts will typically hear cases in which the United States is a party, or where there is a federal or constitutional issue. One judge presides over each case, and the parties in most federal civil trials are entitled to juries.

Interaction of State and Federal Systems

The state courts have jurisdiction over controversies arising from the state law, as well as most federal statutory, constitutional, and common law issues. Appeals are generally taken through the state appellate court system, and then to the U.S. Supreme Court. Federal courts have jurisdiction over cases involving a diversity of citizenship among the parties, or a substantial federal question. Appeals are taken through the circuit courts of the federal system, then to the U.S. Supreme Court.

A controversy arising under state law is governed by the state's law regardless of whether it is litigated in the state or federal court system. Federal law governs a federal question, regardless of whether the question is litigated in a federal or state court. Where a controversy involves both state and federal questions, both state and federal laws are applicable. There is thus a great deal of interaction between federal and state law. The determination of what law, state or federal, and the particular state whose law should be applied, depends on a multitude of legal questions that must be applied to individual cases. In cases where federal and state law are directly on point, and directly contradict each other, federal law will govern.

The Adversary System

The judicial process within the United States is generally adversary in nature. The plaintiff's and the defendant's interests are adverse, fostering competition, which allows issues to be decided in an appropriate manner. In doing so, judicial decisions resolve actual present problems, rather than fulfilling the predictive role normally assigned to legislative or statutory law. The adversary system ensures that decisions will be well thought out and vigorously challenged, thereby directing the court to the best available resolution of the problem at hand.

The role of participants, plaintiff and defendant, is to vigorously champion their own interests, while exploring through the court various viable alternatives. They argue their cases, seeking a judicial decision that will *ipso facto* favor one of the parties. When the presentation of both the plaintiff's and the defendant's cases has been completed, the judge passes on the law.

The majority of lawsuits are actually settled before trial, by informal bargaining and compromise among the various people who are involved, the attorneys for the defense and the attorneys for the plaintiff. Otherwise the lawsuit is tried in court, in the presence of a jury. The malpractice lawsuit may be brought either in a state or federal court. The attorney has to determine in which court the case can be tried. The attorneys check the statutes to determine where to try the case, and which court has jurisdiction. The next thing is to determine in which county the case should be tried. This is called the venue, the location, the place where the trial court would hear the case.

The legal action commences when the plaintiff, through his or her attorney, files a complaint (sometimes called a petition). The court summons is also filed with the complaint. The sheriff serves the defendant with the summons and complaint. The documents state that the plaintiff sued the defendant, and the defendant is directed to file a written answer to the attached petition. The defendant is required to answer, usually within 20 days. An extension of time can be requested, and is approved by the judge for good cause. The answer may be a mere denial of the charges. On the other hand, it may include a number of defenses or even countercharges. The period between the answer and the trial is the period of discovery. This is discussed in detail in Chapters 3 and 21. Discovery is the means to determine what the parties have and find out relevant and nonprivileged information. This allows the parties on both sides to discover relevant material, and is done with the approval of the judge. The legal tools that are used for discovery include interrogatories, depositions, and requests for admissions.

Newer Developments in the Court System

The basic American court process is the jury trial, which remains a fundamental element of the U.S. justice system. However, juries decide less than 5% of the disputes brought in most U.S. jurisdictions. The judge may hear some cases without a jury. The overwhelming majority of cases are resolved through negotiations between the parties. The term "settlement" is used when disputes between individuals or those involving businesses are resolved. The term "plea-bargaining" is used in cases concerning a crime. Plea-bargaining provides a means for expediting the disposition of criminal cases in which the facts are not in dispute, thereby alleviating the burden on the criminal justice system.

During the past two decades, both the federal and state court systems have developed new approaches to fulfilling the purposes of the court system. These include: specialized "problem-solving" courts or dockets, which address certain types of disputes or litigants (including business disputes, family disputes, and matters involving children); specialized procedures designed to address the problems underlying traditional legal disputes such as substance abuse, domestic violence, and mental illness; and integration of alternative dispute resolution techniques such as mediation and arbitration into the litigation process.

Court-Annexed Dispute Resolution

In an effort to create a better, faster, and cheaper way of bringing a lawsuit to a conclusion, the American court system has established court-annexed, or court-connected, "alternative" or "complementary" dispute resolution procedures. After all, most cases are settled and do not end in a full-blown trial. Court-annexed dispute resolution programs enable the parties to address the problems underlying their dispute, and to do so at an early stage of the proceedings so as to avoid the substantial costs involved in the pre-trial preparation process. Consequently, the time needed to reach an agreement is substantially reduced. Alternative dispute resolution methods are the subject of Chapter 22; they include mediation, arbitration, early neutral evaluation (assessment of the issues and amount of damages by an expert based on a detailed statement by each party), or summary jury trials (an abbreviated presentation of the evidence and arguments to an unofficial jury). *Mediation* utilizes a professionally trained "neutral" mediator to assist the parties to reach an agreement. Either party who is dissatisfied with the results of the mediation may take the case to trial without penalty. Compared to standard litigation, mediation seems to be better in terms of the level of litigant satisfaction and compliance with agreements. *Arbitration* procedures involve one or more "neutral" arbitrators who are selected by the parties on the basis of their technical expertise. Arbitration decisions are generally binding on the parties and nonreviewable. Arbitration cases include contracts for construction, medical services, brokerage services, or employment.

TYPES OF LAW IN MALPRACTICE CASES

For the plaintiff to win a medical malpractice lawsuit, he or she must demonstrate by admissible evidence that each element of their claim is stronger than that of the defendants. This is often called a preponderance of the evidence test. The presumption is that the defendant is not liable, until the plaintiff has proven otherwise. Medical malpractice lawsuits may involve a number of branches of law, including torts, contracts, agency and administrative law, property, constitutional law, evidence, criminal law, damages, and restitution.

Tort Law

A tort is a civil wrong. Medical malpractice torts can be divided into two categories, intentional and unintentional torts. The types of torts in medical malpractice are discussed in detail in Chapter 11. Intentional torts include assault, battery, defamation, false imprisonment, fraud, and invasion of privacy. It is important to remember that intentional torts do not require proof of negligence. Thus the scope for liability can be considerably greater than in a negligence case. Unintentional torts fall primarily within the area of negligence. The subject of negligence is discussed fully in Chapter 15.

Contract Law

The physician–patient relationship is based on a contract. A contract is an agreement to do something, which is legally binding on one or both parties. The object of the contract can be tangible or intangible goods or services, or an agreement to do or refrain from doing any legal act on the part of one of the parties. A contract can either be unilateral, where it promises exchange for an offer to perform a given act, or bilateral, where a promise to perform is exchanged for a promise on the part of the other party.

A health care provider contract, such as the physician–patient relationship, can be *express*, where the patient and the health care practitioner have reached an *oral or written* agreement concerning the services to be rendered to the patient, and the fees that the patient will receive. On the other hand, a contract may be *implied*, for example where the patient presents himself or herself for treatment. Under such circumstances an implied contract in law is created, based on the presumption that the patient anticipates the necessity of providing reasonable compensation for services rendered, and that the physician in turn expects reasonable compensation to be paid.

Under certain circumstances, a breach of contract action may exist as an alternative to, or in combination with, a medical malpractice negligence claim. Abandonment, for example, can be categorized either as a tort or as a breach of contract. Similarly, a statement by the physician promising a specific result from the treatment and failing to achieve that result may be categorized as a breach of warranty. The general area of warranties in products liability cases is discussed fully in Chapter 19. As with other contracts, a warranty may be either express, specifically setting forth the terms of the warranty, or may be implied. An implied warranty usually falls within two primary areas—warranty of fitness, or a warranty of merchantability. A warranty of fitness means that the seller, if he regularly sells such items, warrants that they are fit for their intended use or purpose. An implied warranty of fitness is present in all transfers of goods within the United States, unless such a warranty has been specifically disclaimed at the time that the sales contract is executed. The warranty of merchantability is an implied warranty on the part of the seller that indicates that the goods provided are fit for use, wholesome, unadulterated, and free of any contamination or other defects that would alter or destroy their usefulness for their intended purpose.

One important point to be noted is that, in most states, the statute of limitations for litigation under a contract theory is of considerably longer duration than that for a tort claim. A contract theory may thus present liability on the part of the health care provider, even when the statute of limitations for a normal negligence claim has expired.

Agency and Administrative Law

Agency and administrative law comes in the form of rules and regulations promulgated on the part of a federal state or local agency, bureau, or other section of the administrative law system. It contains facets of both common law and statutory law, in that the decisions by the agency or administration can take place either in the form of administrative rulemaking, or in the form of administrative adjudications, as would take place in a traditional court of law. Examples of administrative agencies include the Federal Food and Drug Administration, and the Departments of Health, both federal and state, Occupational Safety and Health Administration, Workman's Compensation, State Medical Licensing Boards, and all other forms of regulatory activity impacting medical practice and the health care provider.

Property Law

Property law centers on the ownership of tangible and intangible property that is goods or other items of value. While contract law deals with the transfer of such property between two or more persons, property law deals primarily with the concept of entitlements and ownership. Property law encompasses such areas as titles to real estate, ownership of the health care practitioner's office, and even the family jewels. It involves such intangibles as stocks, bonds, and accounts owing, and even the health care practitioner's status as a member of his or her profession.

Constitutional Law

Constitutional law consists primarily of the interpretation of the federal constitution, and secondarily of the states' constitutions, which are pertinent to the case before a court. They involve such areas as guarantees to individuals of certain fundamental rights, including the right of compensation for taking of private property of someone's domain, the right of privacy, the right to travel, and the right to vote. It includes recognition of procedural requirements, which are necessary before an individual's right to liberty or property can be interfered with by a governmental institution. Constitutional law also describes the fabric of the American system, detailing the organization of government at the federal level, the state government at the state level, and establishing the basic framework of the state and federal relationship. Constitutional law has had a significant impact on the practice of medicine, particularly in the areas of reproduction, abortions, the right to privacy, and in end-of-life matters, such as advanced directives and living wills.

Evidence

The study of evidence is the branch of law that details the nature and type of materials or other presentations that can be brought before the court during the course of litigation. It encompasses the permissible scope of information that a party to a lawsuit can present during trial. It also contains a number of exclusions of topics or areas on the basis of public policy, things that would not be admissible in court. In general, when a given piece of information is sufficiently reliable that it can be considered as useful in assisting the judge or jury to make an informed decision, the judge would allow its admissibility as evidence during the trial. Rules of evidence have had a significant impact on the health care practice in terms of requirements for medical record keeping, the nature of documentation required to be kept by the health care profession, the scope of the physician–patient privilege, and the circumstances under which the physician–patient privilege can be waived by a unilateral act, such as the filing of a lawsuit by the patient against the health care provider.

Criminal Law

Criminal law focuses on the behavioral requirements imposed by the state or the federal government upon the particular individual. In most cases the legal involvement of the practicing health care provider will be limited to forms of civil liability, but the potential for criminal involvement does exist. Under criminal law, the standard of proof required of the state is that of beyond a reasonable doubt. This is considerably different from the standard applied in most malpractice cases, which is simply a preponderance of the evidence. The burden of proof on the state in a criminal prosecution, therefore, is considerably greater than that in a simple malpractice suit. The criminalization of medical negligence in a minority of cases has been of concern during the recent past, and this evolving subject is discussed in Chapter 10.

Damages and Restitution

In all malpractice cases in which liability has been established on the part of a plaintiff, the amount of damages must then be established. Such damages may be nominal, for example one dollar, and serve merely to illustrate vindication on the part of the plaintiff. More commonly, damages will be substantial in nature. Elements of damages, for which compensation can result, commonly include loss of earnings, pain and suffering, incurred expenses such as medical treatment, mental anguish, loss of consortium, and wrongful death. Under certain circumstances, attorneys' fees and court costs can also be assessed against the losing party.

Recent trends and the use of structured settlements have somewhat complicated the computation of damages in malpractice lawsuits, but the theory of damages is to compensate the injured plaintiff who has proved his or her case, and to restore insofar as possible that plaintiff to the original position before the injury occurred. Negligence damages therefore take the form of restitution to the plaintiff, rather than serving as a form of punishment. Under circumstances of gross negligence or other forms of outrageous recklessness, including intentional torts, punitive damages may be awarded. Punitive damages are designed to dissuade the defendant, and all other persons, from repeating the particular act in question. Punitive damages are imposed on the basis of public policy, and serve much the same role as that of a criminal fine imposed by the state under criminal prosecution.

CHAPTER 21

Physician Conduct at Deposition and Trial

S. Sandy Sanbar, M.D., Ph.D., J.D., F.C.L.M.
Marvin H. Firestone, M.D, J.D., F.C.L.M.

The trial is composed of three components: the pretrial events, the trial, and the post-trial proceedings. The pretrial events include formal *discovery* and its components, *interrogatories, depositions,* and *pretrial motions.* The purpose of pretrial proceedings is to better define the legal and factual issues, locate evidence, witnesses and parties, and refine the matters in dispute so that trial can be limited to issues that are in dispute. Discovery in medical malpractice lawsuits is no different from that of any other legal action.

PRETRIAL EVENTS

Interrogatories

Interrogatories are written questions and answers exchanged by all parties involved in litigation, the purpose being to specify what, where, who, and how the facts and circumstances occurred that gave rise to the litigation. Some jurisdictions limit the number of written interrogatories, and in others the number is unlimited. The answers to interrogatories must be signed by the party under oath. Interrogatories serve as an expedient and cost-effective method to discover accurate information about both opposing parties, to obtain additional facts about the case that were not spelled out in the petition, to determine who the fact witnesses are, and to find out the names of the expert witnesses who will testify at trial. Identified participants and witnesses are called by opposing counsel to give *depositions,* which are recorded interrogations by counsel of the opposing parties. *Physical examination* of the plaintiff may be performed by both sides' medical experts. Most often, the discovery process is handled through the offices of opposing counsel; the plaintiff(s) and defendant(s) do not communicate directly. The forensic physician may be consulted by the retaining attorney to assist in formulating relevant questions that may aid in this phase of the discovery process.

Requests for Admission

Requests for admission are factual statements made by one party to another party wherein the responding party must either admit or deny the factual statement. It may include facts about any relevant issue. In most jurisdictions, if the party does not admit or deny a request for admission within 30 days, the statement is admitted and may be relied upon by the expert witness as a basis for any opinion.

Requests for Production

One party may request any relevant document or thing from the other party unless the document requested is privileged. Such requests usually include medical records of the plaintiff. Medical records are important to understanding the diagnoses made by other physicians and the past and current care provided to the plaintiff.

Court-Ordered Discovery

Where one side is not cooperative in giving the information in his or her custody and control, counsel may submit a motion asking the court to:

1. Compel discovery of the evidence;
2. Compel production of a particular document; or
3. Order examination of a person.

Based on the motion(s) submitted by the counsel(s) of opposing parties, the judge determines and concludes what is legally required under the discovery rules.

Motions may also attempt to dispose of the lawsuit entirely, if essential documents or facts are not produced by a party. Where a plaintiff alleges medical malpractice and offers no pretrial evidence in support of the allegations, a motion to dismiss the suit can be granted, which is referred to as *summary judgment*.

Deposition

A deposition is a form of oral testimony given by a witness under oath in response to questions, similar to court testimony, but not in court. The oral questions are posed by an attorney to any person who has information about facts, circumstances, or opinions about the issues in dispute. The responses of the deponent are recorded by a court reporter. The deposition is part of the pretrial discovery procedure and is subject to discovery rules. The recorded testimony is reduced to writing to provide a permanent record. The person whose deposition is being taken is called the *deponent*.

The general purposes of the deposition are: discovery of facts, establishing substance of witness testimony, preserving testimony, and gauging the persuasiveness of witnesses. Depositions are generally taken to obtain evidence that may not be obtainable through other discovery procedures.

If collateral interviews of others would be helpful in doing the forensic medical examination and such other individuals are unwilling or unable to be interviewed by the physician, the physician may advise the attorney to take depositions of those individuals. The retained expert physician may provide questions for the attorney to ask during the deposition that the physician would have asked if there were an opportunity to perform a collateral interview. In the alternative, the retained expert physician may accompany the attorney to the deposition as an advisor and provide written questions in real time for the attorney to ask. The physician may also suggest necessary and helpful follow-up questions during the deposition. Such assistance to the attorney in the role of advisory witness is allowed in most jurisdictions.

Where one side is not cooperative in giving the information in its custody and control, counsel may ask the court to compel discovery of the evidence, compel production of a particular document, or order examination of a person, which the court concludes is mandated under the discovery rules.

A witness who, for one reason or another, might not be available at the time of trial, can be deposed and the transcript of the testimony later used at trial. Examining counsel can require the deponent to state the names and identities of other persons who may be witnesses or who may have pertinent information. This information may lead in turn to further depositions or other discovery procedures. With those things in mind, the plaintiff or defendant can more realistically appraise the merits of the lawsuit. In most instances, cases cannot be properly evaluated for settlement until counsel on both sides have completed discovery. Counsel will have an opportunity during the deposition to evaluate the relative strength of his or her position.

Deposition as an Impeachment Tool

A deposition serves the purpose of fixing a witness's story. If the deponent later contradicts his or her deposition while testifying at trial, his or her deposition can be used for the purpose of impeachment by showing prior inconsistent testimony. It is believed that juries are inclined not to believe witnesses who have had their testimony impeached.

Deposition May Encourage Settlement

The deposition is usually intended to benefit the side asking the questions. The deponent is under a general obligation to answer all questions except those seeking privileged information. Questions that are asked by counsel can include both information that is admissible in court, and information that is calculated to lead to other admissible information, such as the identity of other witnesses to an occurrence. This is intended to permit trial preparation and encourage settlement.

Conduct of Deposition

While a deposition may be conducted anywhere, it will probably be in the office of the examining counsel. The setting is normally informal, quite unlike the typical courtroom in which the witness may later testify. After stipulations by counsel the witness will be administered the oath, in the same manner and with the same legal responsibilities as if the witness was actually testifying before a court of law.

Examining counsel may have multiple reasons for taking a deposition. The form of questions usually reveals counsel's major interest. If questions are primarily for discovery reasons, the questions will be broad, to encourage rambling answers that might reveal new facts. On the other hand, if the deposition is conducted primarily to produce admissible evidence, the questions will be precise and sharply focused.

Expert Medical Testimony During Deposition

In medical malpractice and other professional liability litigation, a qualified professional must testify about the "standard of care" applicable to the case facts and must testify that the practice in question fell below the required standard.

During deposition, the defendant health care practitioner may inadvertently become the plaintiff's expert medical witness when answering hypothetical questions at deposition. The plaintiff's attorney asks the defendant physician to agree that it would be contrary to good practice not to hospitalize a patient who had the classical symptoms of appendicitis set forth in the Merck Manual. If the doctor agrees, he or she has then become the plaintiff's expert. The patient will testify that he had the classical symptoms, and expert testimony necessary to get the case to the jury will have been supplied by the defendant.

A traditional question asked during depositions is a "why" question. Plaintiff's attorney will often decline to ask such a question during cross-examination in court, for fear of allowing the witness to make a speech that can damage or destroy the plaintiff's case. This reasoning is invalid in the course of an oral deposition. During deposition, the question "why" may serve to define the validity of a particular course of medical treatment or procedure. "Why" a particular procedure was done, or "why" a particular mode of treatment was instituted, or "why" a particular drug was ordered, may well be crucial to the plaintiff's case.

A list of typical questions that might be asked during the deposition of a physician includes:

1. Did you take a history of the patient's case?
2. What was the history given you?
3. What significant factors did you find on physical examination?
4. What was your diagnosis?
5. Why was that your diagnosis?
6. What other factors were present that could have then led you to a different diagnosis?
7. Did you rule out X?
8. Why did you rule it out (or decide against it)?
9. What course of treatment did you decide upon?
10. Why did you decide upon that course of treatment?
11. What drugs did you prescribe in treatment?
12. Why did you prescribe those drugs?

Independent Medical Examination

The defendant may request that the plaintiff be examined by the defendant's retained physician. The retaining attorney should provide all documents relevant to medical issues for the physician's review before the expert examines the plaintiff. The attorney may have difficulty determining what is relevant to the physician's assessment. Therefore, the physician should request that all discovery material be provided. The physician then can determine which documents are relevant and which are not and review only those documents that are useful in evaluating the medical issues under consideration.

The defendant will have only one opportunity for such an examination unless good cause exists (as determined by the court) for a second such independent examination. During this examination, it is not uncommon for the plaintiff to have his or her own attorney or a family member present or to bring a tape recorder to the session. If such a condition is disruptive to the examination, it may be brought to the court's attention and the judge will rule on the issue. Results of the independent medical examination and the forensic physician's opinions are documented in a report. This report is available to all parties in the litigation. The report of the examination is usually requested in advance of taking the physician's deposition.

The physician should explain clearly to the evaluee at the outset of the clinical interview the purpose of the examination, the fact that no physician–patient relationship is being established to provide care, and to whom the report of the examination will be sent. The physician should elicit a complete and detailed history of the incident causing injury during the plaintiff's clinical interview. He should consider all contributing causes to the medical disorder claimed, including discussion of past medical and psychiatric history. All relevant medical records previously reviewed by the examiner may be discussed with the injured party during the interview. Any laboratory or psychological testing previously performed may also be reviewed with the plaintiff, including the raw data, if pertinent.

Privileges

The deponent's attorney has the right to advise him or her not to answer questions that the attorney believes are *improper or out of the scope of the deposition.* That right is exercised very sparingly, because refusal to answer gives interrogating counsel the right to compel the answer or even adjourn the deposition and to get a court order to require the deponent to answer.

Certain matters are outside the scope of examination. These include legally privileged matters such as communications between a lawyer and a client, and matters that are clearly irrelevant to the suit at hand and an invasion of privacy. A *privilege* is legal protection to keep certain information from disclosure. The scope of discovery is sufficiently broad that it is sometimes difficult to tell when something is irrelevant. The test of relevance at deposition is only whether the inquiry might lead to admissible evidence, not that the evidence be required to be itself directly admissible.

TRIAL EVENTS

Jury Selection

Most trials of medical malpractice are conducted with a jury present. The trial of a medical malpractice suit begins by the selection of jurors from among those called for jury duty. The judge begins the jury examination *voir dire* by identifying the patient and the physician, and their respective attorneys. Next, the judge or the attorneys will acquaint the prospective jurors with the nature of the case and the issues to be presented; then the judge or attorneys may ask questions of the jury panel in order to "weed out" those potential jurors who may have a particular bias.

Some facts about a prospective juror may be at odds with the situation presented in the case. Having a family member who was a victim of malpractice or a relative who is a physician may be some factors that will prevent a prospective juror from being fair and impartial. Such a factor is grounds for challenge of the acceptance of the juror by the court, called "challenge for cause." Counsels are entitled to disqualify any number of jurors by challenge for cause. If a juror is challenged for valid cause, the judge makes such a determination and the prospective juror will not sit on the case. Prospective jurors may be challenged for a number of causes. A juror may have committed a crime that would disqualify him or her from jury service, may have some interest or have participated in the arbitration of the dispute between the plaintiff and the defendant, may have an action pending with one of the parties, or have formerly been a juror in the same case. Similarly, the employer or employee, agent or attorney, or relative of either party, and those who can be shown to be prejudiced or partial to either party or lack competency in the English language, will also be disqualified. Counsels are entitled to disqualify any number of jurors for cause. If a juror is challenged for a valid cause, the judge makes such a determination and the perspective juror will not sit on the case.

Each attorney is also entitled to an equal number of "peremptory challenges," which means that the attorney may refuse a prospective juror without stating any reason. After the jury has been selected, the trial begins.

Opening Statements by Counsels

The trial starts with the plaintiff's opening statement. Opening statements are summaries of the case that set out the allegations of fact upon which the plaintiff and defense cases rest. The openings may itemize the evidence in each side's case, but are composed by counsel and are not the evidence on which the jury must base its decision. The opening statements set the stage for the presentation of the cases by the plaintiff and defendant. The attorneys inform the jury what they intend to prove. The jury next has the opportunity to hear all the relevant testimony, to examine tangible evidence, and to observe the witnesses as they testify.

Presentation of Plaintiff's Case

The plaintiff has the burden to prove the main facts that establish the claim of malpractice. This must include the four essential elements of negligence: duty, departure from duty, direct cause, and damages (the "4D's"). All essential elements must be proven by a preponderance of evidence (i.e., more likely than not or more than 50%).

The plaintiff is the first to present evidence (the case in chief), generally by direct examination of witnesses. Evidence may include not only testimony by witnesses with personal knowledge of facts in the case, but also documents or other tangible items or material that is relevant to prove a fact or circumstance in the case.

The defense attorney is entitled to cross-examine the witnesses. Cross-examination will attempt to point out to the jury any weaknesses, gaps, or inaccuracies in the testimony. To challenge the witness's credibility, depositions may be used to show that a witness has testified differently at trial than at deposition. The cross-examining attorney is permitted to confront the witness with previous inconsistent testimony and then may ask the witness to resolve the discrepancy.

Motion for Directed Verdict

After completion of the plaintiff's case, the defendant's lawyer may submit a motion to the judge and argue that even if all of the plaintiff's evidence is taken as true, no case cognizable in law has been proven by the preponderance of evidence against the defendant physician. If the judge agrees, then the plaintiff would have failed to make the minimal showing required by law to support the malpractice cause of action, and the case is dismissed. This motion by defense counsel is called a *motion for directed verdict*; briefly stated, it says "so what?" If the motion is denied, the defense will then proceed with the defendant's case.

Presentation of Defendant's Case

The defense attorney presents evidence to establish that some essential element of the plaintiff's claim is lacking. What is required by defense counsel is to demonstrate that the plaintiff's counsel indeed failed to prove an essential element of negligence, which can prove fatal to the plaintiff's case. Since the plaintiff has the burden of proving all of the elements of the claim, a defense is effective if it can convince the jury that the plaintiff has failed to satisfy the burden of proof of even one element. The defendant's attorney may also present direct evidence that shows that some element of the plaintiff's claim is not true, thereby convincing the jury of the defendant's point of view.

The defense counsel may also succeed in resisting the plaintiff's proof by presenting a variety of affirmative defenses. These are not contradictions of what the plaintiff has offered as facts, but include immunity for negligent treatment conferred by Good Samaritan laws, violations of the statutes of limitations, or some other defense allowed by law.

At the conclusion of the presentation of the defendant's case, the defense counsel may again present a motion for a directed verdict based on the evidence presented in defense of the malpractice lawsuit.

Closing Arguments

To conclude the case presentation, the attorneys on both sides deliver their closing arguments. They briefly restate their cases and summarize the evidence for the jury that each believes dictates a verdict for its side. The counsel for the plaintiff is allowed to go first, followed by defense counsel. Next, the counsel for the plaintiff is allowed a rebuttal after the defense counsel gives his or her closing argument. The defense counsel will also be permitted to present the final rebuttal.

Jury Instructions

After the closing arguments, the judge has the duty to instruct the jury with respect to the applicable law. The instructions define legal concepts that the jury will be asked to apply, such as the burden of proof, negligence, proximate cause, and other principles. The judge will also advise the jury what legal conclusions are expected to be drawn from the evidence. Through the judge's instructions, the jury applies those legal standards to the facts that they believe have been proven by evidence presented during the trial.

The attorneys for both sides will have ordinarily submitted requested jury instructions to the judge. The judge decides whether or not to give the instructions requested by either party, to give some portion of those instructions, or to give only his or her own instructions. If either attorney objects to an instruction given or refused to be given by the judge, the objection is registered with the judge and counsel may submit an alternative instruction for the record.

The jury adjourns following the judge's instructions to consider the evidence. The jury reaches a verdict, finding either for the plaintiff and awarding damages (compensation) that it deems appropriate, or it may find for the defendant.

POST-TRIAL PROCEEDINGS
Post-Verdict Motions

The party against whom the verdict is rendered may ask the judge to enter a *judgment notwithstanding the verdict* ("NOV" or "JNOV"), which means that, based upon all of the evidence, no reasonable person would have concluded as the jury did. The judge is usually unwilling to overrule a jury's verdict, but where a jury has given a verdict that is clearly a product of passion or prejudice or not supported by evidence, judgment "NOV" will be awarded.

The losing side may move for a *new trial*. A new trial may be granted at the discretion of the judge when, without fault of the losing party, a fair trial was prevented through irregularity in the proceedings, misconduct of the jury or the prevailing party, accidental or unfair surprise, or excessive damages have been given. A new trial may be granted if the verdict is not sustained by sufficient evidence or is contrary to law. Also, where newly discovered evidence is available that could not, with reasonable diligence, have been discovered and produced at trial, a new trial may be granted.

Final Judgment on the Verdict

The judge enters a final judgment on the verdict and written notice of the verdict provided to the parties. If the judgment is in favor of the defendant, it will forever preclude the plaintiff from bringing suit against the defendant for all matters that were raised at trial or related to the facts underlying the medical malpractice suit. On the other hand, if the judgment is for the plaintiff, that money judgment becomes an enforceable debt against the defendant and/or the defendant's insurance carrier

Alternative Dispute Resolution of Claims

S. Sandy Sanbar, M.D., Ph.D., J.D., F.C.L.M.

Alternative dispute resolution (ADR) represents a variety of methods aimed at resolving lawsuits, including medical malpractice, without formal adjudication or a full-blown adversarial trial. The goal of ADR is to effectuate the resolution of lawsuits in a manner that is expeditious, less formal, less adversarial, less expensive, and acceptable to all parties concerned.

The interest in and the utility of ADR methods in medical malpractice litigation have been developing in the past few decades, fueled by the increase in medical malpractice claims, the sky-rocketing damages awarded for those claims, and the resulting increase in medical malpractice insurance costs. States have legislated different solutions aimed at processing and resolving medical malpractice disputes outside traditional litigation, including screening panels, voluntary arbitration, and mediation of disputes. Other efforts within the traditional civil law setting have included mandatory settlement conferences, court-ordered arbitration, mini-trials, and summary jury trials.

The purpose of this chapter is to provide an overview of some of the ADR methods (Table 22-1) that may be employed in resolving medical malpractice lawsuits.

TRADITIONAL OR "INTEREST-BASED" MEDIATION

Traditional mediation, also known as interest-based mediation, is a process by which a neutral third party assists disputing parties in negotiating a resolution. The mediator merely assists the parties; he or she has no formal power to impose any outcome on the parties. The mediator acts as a facilitator for communication between the parties. Mediation is a voluntary process entered into by the parties in an effort to resolve their dispute. The major advantages of mediation include the private nature of the process and the confidentiality of its results.

"RIGHTS-BASED" MEDIATION

This differs from traditional mediation in that there is a focus on the legal rights of the parties. Thus, the process is more akin to evaluative processes, described below.

Table 22-1 Alternative dispute resolution methods
Traditional or "interest-based" mediation
"Rights-based" mediation
Early neutral evaluation
Private judging
Pretrial screening panels
Arbitration
Med-Arb
Mini-trial
Summary jury trial

EARLY NEUTRAL EVALUATION

This is usually a courts-annexed process that requires the parties to have their dispute assessed by an experienced third-party neutral evaluator on the basis of short presentations by both parties. It is a rights-based procedure, and in that regard similar to arbitration and formal adjudication. Usually, the third-party neutral is a volunteer attorney chosen by the court.

PRIVATE JUDGING

This is also known as "rent-a-judge," usually selected from a group of retired judges who are interested in being active on a part-time basis. Private judges are paid by the parties involved and may be empowered by state statute to enter final judgments that have precedential value and are appealable to appellate courts.

PRETRIAL SCREENING PANELS

Screening panels usually are involved in state-mandated pretrial assessments of medical malpractice cases. Plaintiffs, before submitting their medical malpractice claim for trial, are required to have their case assessed by a special panel; this panel usually is composed of physicians or other medical professionals, attorneys, and laypersons. The panel hears the plaintiff's case and may issue a nonbinding opinion. Usually, either party can bring the case to court, regardless of the panel's assessment. Some states allow the panel's findings to be introduced as evidence in the court adjudication. Difficulties center around the administrative burdens these panels represent and the associated delays; furthermore, assessments may be made too early in the process, before discovery has been accomplished.

ARBITRATION

Arbitration is a formalized system of dispute resolution in which parties provide proofs and arguments to a neutral third party who has the power to impose a binding decision on the parties. Multiple arbitrators may be utilized. Arbitration is similar to formal adjudication except that the parties are allowed only limited or no pretrial discovery and the hearing is less formal. The rules of evidence are not as rigidly applied in arbitration proceedings.

Arbitration has been mandated by law for certain conflicts, such as labor disputes. It may be binding or nonbinding. Unlike formal adjudication, once an arbitration decision has been made, there is no default mechanism through which the decision is enforced. Both the Federal Arbitration Act and the Uniform Arbitration Act give courts jurisdiction to confirm, or refuse to confirm, an arbitration decision.

Arbitration may be simply defined as a method by which the parties to a dispute submit their differences to the judgment of an impartial party. The impartial party may be an individual or a panel, and may occur either by mutual consent of the parties or by statutory provision. There are four general categories of arbitration:

1. *Compulsory*. Each malpractice dispute would be submitted to arbitration.
2. *Voluntary*. Each malpractice dispute could be submitted to arbitration, but in contrast with compulsory arbitration, under this category the right to a jury trial is not lost; this applies to both the plaintiff and the defendant.
3. *Binding*. The arbitration award would be final and binding, with respect to both liability and damage determination.
4. *Nonbinding*. The arbitration award would not be final, and either the plaintiff or defendant may elect to litigate a claim from the beginning, a situation that is costly both in time and money.

Submission to arbitration may be accomplished either by a clause in an initial contract stipulating that future disputes will be arbitrated, or by a subsequent agreement to submit an existing dispute to arbitration. Arbitration has several advantages over litigation, including rapid deposition of cases, selection of arbitrators who are knowledgeable in the medical and legal field, and relaxation of certain exclusionary rules of evidence. Such advantages also include diminution of the likelihood of exorbitant and unreasonable awards, minimization of publicity, and the speedier resolution than is possible due to the overall case load in the congested court system. Support for the use of arbitration is a means of resolving medical malpractice disputes, which has come from such diverse sources as the St. Paul Fire and Marine Insurance Company, the Secretary's Commission on Medical Malpractice of the Department of Health, Education and Welfare, and the American Medical Association.

The disadvantages of arbitration include difficulty under some state laws of obtaining binding arbitration, problems of arbitration contracts that are imposed, not negotiated, minors' rights and third-party rights, adverse attitudes of judges and attorneys toward arbitration, and the risk of further expense due to preparation for two separate hearings, where a trial after arbitration is available. Additionally, the constitutionality of arbitration under some state laws may be subject to question.

MED-ARB

Med-Arb is a combination of mediation and arbitration. Its primary advantage is its potential efficiency. Here, the parties agree to mediate their disputes first, using a neutral third party as a mediator. If mediation does not result in an agreement or settlement, then the mediator changes roles and becomes an arbitrator with the power to issue a final and binding decision with regard to the dispute.

MINI-TRIAL

This method is utilized most often for evaluating business and commercial disputes. The process is voluntary and confidential. Attorneys representing each party make some representations to a panel composed of a neutral advisor and high-level executives from each party who have the power to accept a settlement.

SUMMARY JURY TRIAL

Here, a judge and an advisory jury drawn from the jury pool are used. The jurors are not told that their role is advisory until after they give their verdict. Following the verdict, the jurors are interrogated about their decision. Subsequently, the attorneys and their respective executive representatives attend a mandatory conference to discuss settlement. If no settlement occurs, the advisory jury verdict is not admissible in future final adjudication procedures. Summary jury trials are time-consuming.

CHAPTER 23

Medical Expert Testimony

John P. Conomy, M.D., J.D., F.C.L.M.

GOLDEN RULES

1. Expert medical witnesses are virtually essential to the litigation of medical malpractice actions. They are not parties, but are party witnesses.
2. Expert witnesses, unlike other witnesses in litigation, offer opinions to the court. In the end, courts determine the relevant standard of care.
3. Whether plaintiff or defendant, learn to work with and learn from your attorney.
4. In all phases of a lawsuit, the physician should remember to act professionally.
5. Admit valid points raised by "the other side." They are virtually always there. They have some substance to them.
6. Be particularly attentive to expert testimony in medical malpractice cases.
7. Do not attempt to have personal contact with an expert witness outside of your attorney's direction.
8. Having survived a medical malpractice case, you may want to petition your alma mater, local medical school, medical society, and national medical organization to assume an educational role about basic law as it pertains to doctors of medicine.

GENESIS OF EXPERT WITNESSES

Who needs an expert witness? For much of the historical time of the common law, that is, since about 1150 in the time of King Henry II of England until quite recently, no one needed an expert witness in medical malpractice actions or much of any other action in litigation. After all, a presiding judge, sergeant, or magistrate could take judicial notice of the fact that the earth was flat or spherical (depending on the time and jurisdiction) or that the unfortunate victim's leg was broken, badly set, and painful. A common law jury, petit or grand, could decide the same thing without superfluous help. For much of the history of law, witnesses were presented to the court to attest to facts of a matter in dispute and their opinions, well founded or not, were inconsequential. Opinions regarding facts, once those facts were verified, were a matter for the judge and jury.

All of this began to change in common law jurisdictions in the late 19th century when the fields of science, medicine, and engineering became complex and their understanding, much less their explication, exceeded the life experience, grasp, and reach of lawyers, judges, and gentlemen (and much later, ladies) of the jury. Experts became a useful and ultimately a necessary addition to the resolution of disputes and the leveling of justice in criminal and civil matters. Expert witnesses came to the courtroom to express their opinions based upon specialized, factual knowledge of some sort, in order to assist the judge and jury in the application of those facts to the litigated matter at hand. Experts of all sorts came to abound. Joining doctors of medicine were "expert" bridge builders, nautical navigators, safe-crackers, money changers, educators, economists, physicists, bartenders, alienists, economists, and pickpockets among the plethora of otherwise common men and women who came to play a special, opinionate role in systems of common law justice.

By the end of the second decade of the 20th century in American courtrooms, the presence of expert witnesses in medical malpractice actions became common. This steep increase in the utilization of medical expert witnesses coincided with the increasing growth of medical knowledge, medical specialization, and medical technology in the United States and around the world. At the current time, it is nearly impossible to imagine a medical malpractice action spun out without the heavy participation reaching to a dominant role of medical expert witnesses (although such rarities still exist).

ROLE OF THE EXPERT WITNESS

The legal role of expert witnesses, including medical experts, is to assist the trier of fact (that is, the judge in "bench trials" and/or the jury in jury trials) in moving some fact in evidence in one direction or another, either toward the position of a plaintiff or the position of a defendant, in the matter at hand. The expert witness role is itself a difficult and tense role in any legal action and particularly so in matters of medical malpractice. Its difficulty and tension are magnified by the fact that our system of justice is based upon adversary principles and presentation. Trials are frequently brutal events. At the end of them a winner and a loser are declared. At the conclusion of these contests, each of these major participants may be about equally bloodied in the senses of emotional drain, physical exhaustion, and economic costs.

Expert witnesses, an anomalous legal breed because they articulate intentionally persuasive opinions in a litigation proceeding, are obligate participants in this system of legal battle, having been invited to the courtroom, with rare exceptions, by parties to the dispute and only rarely by the presiding judge. Expert witnesses are paid for their services to clients by the party who called them. They are party witnesses, and their testimony resides in "mere opinion," a matter long suspect in the common law.

CASE PRESENTATION

A Professor of Surgery waited in a line of traffic for a signal light to change. While waiting there, another automobile, speeding and out of control, hurdled five cars behind him, landing on the roof of the Professor's car and killing him. The driver of the offending vehicle had experienced an epileptic seizure. He had been told by his treating physician that "he could drive a car when his blood levels of anticonvulsants came up." The offending driver was known to be noncompliant with treatment and to suffer complex partial seizures, or psychomotor epileptic attacks, every three or four weeks. The surgeon's family brought suit against the treating physician. Through expert testimony the plaintiffs (in this case, the surgeon's surviving wife and children) established that the treating physician was required to be familiar with impaired drivers' reporting requirements in his state, and that he had a positive duty to warn the epileptic driver not to drive a car, given that his seizures were temporarily disabling and were occurring on a frequent basis. These measures were offered as the relevant standard of care under the fact pattern of this case. The failure to warn, an act of omission on the part of the defendant treating doctor, was considered negligent and the cause of death of the surgeon. The defendant doctor attempted, through personal and expert testimony, to shift responsibility to the epileptic driver entirely. The settlement of the case resulted in a plaintiff's award.

REGULATION OF EXPERT WITNESSES

Legal definitions of expert witnesses (of which medical experts are a subspecies) are defined by the Federal Rules of Evidence (and these are Acts of Congress) formulated to safeguard and make reliable the opinion testimony of experts. Expert witnesses are persons who, by virtue of knowledge, skill, experience, training, or education, may assist a trier of fact. The "or" is important. An expert witness need not fill all the defining criteria in a perfected manner, or at all. Many medical experts will measure splendidly against all of these experiential yardsticks, however. Expert witnesses may rely and call upon knowledge from the facts of the case, their own knowledge, or the facts known by others relied upon by other experts in the pertinent field of endeavor. An expert witness may rely upon hypothetical facts presented to her or him in the course of litigation in the process of forming an opinion. In a carve-out not accorded other witnesses, medical experts express opinions regarding "ultimate issues" in a civil case, such as addressing the liability of a plaintiff in being negligent or whether or not some aspect of care or treatment was the cause of a person's damage.

The Federal Rules of Evidence guide the participation of medical expert witnesses in the federal courts. Most medical malpractice actions, however, are tried in state courts, so called "courts of local jurisdiction." The Common Pleas Courts of most counties in the United States are examples of such courts, and to the Federal Rules of Evidence these courts add Rules of Locality. Federal courts, as a matter of comity, will generally recognize these state or local rules. Generally, such state rules add to the federal rules criteria of valid medical licensure, standards for percentages of time spent in the active practice of medicine (generally including teaching, research, or other relevant activity), and, less commonly, some evidence of connection with the jurisdiction in which the case was originated or the venue in which the matter in litigation is being heard. Federal courts and most state courts permit and can require review of an expert witness's litigation history. Such lists, along with professional résumés, medical licensure history, and lists of publications, are available to the parties for their review.

Case law, that is, the determined or settled common law of the local state or federal court system in which litigation is being played out, will specifically tailor the limits of choice and testimony of the medical expert witness with respect to finely drawn issues. These include not only qualifications but also fees, the limits of exploration of potential biases, the production of legal records, history of litigation testimony, personal past history, and much, much more. This immense set of case-derived standards and qualifications is weighty, complex, and is the province of trained and experienced medical malpractice lawyers. Case law parameters are most frequently set in the appellate holdings of affected courts. It must be firmly recognized that it is the court, and not the plaintiff, defendant, lawyers, or jury, who determines who is a medical expert. That is the duty, albeit an assailable one, of the trial judge.

If this brief description generally sets out what an expert medical witness is, it becomes important to say what a medical expert witness is not, or need not be. That witness need not be famous or have attracted professional acclaim or notable academic recognition. A medical expert witness need not be a practiced teacher, an author, or a decorated professor. The medical expert, while likely to practice in a field of medical practice shared by a medical defendant, may neither be obliged to do that. The medical expert witness is not required to be credentialed by a medical or surgical specialty examining board. It is true that many if not most medical expert witnesses are "credentialed" by virtue of a glossy professional patina and will fill all the expectations of a "real pro" in the ordinary and medical sense, but it is not what the law requires. In practice, the medical expert will most often embrace criteria expected of an accomplished medical doctor as well as filling the necessities demanded by common law criteria, local court rules, and the federal law.

INHERENT TENSIONS INVOLVING THE EXPERT MEDICAL WITNESS

The tensions inherent in the expert witness role, whether it is in reviewing records, providing reports where and when required, appearing for interrogation in depositions, or in courtroom testimony, are multiple and frequently distressing. The medical expert witness, like it or not (and usually not), is bound up in the play of an adversary system pitting one party, nearly always

a brother or sister in medicine, against another in a courtroom. The expert
is not part of the adversary arrangement, but his or her presence has been
arranged by the court, under the aegis of attorneys, to explicate a series of
facts and opinions generally deemed favorable to the party those attorneys
represent. The medical expert witness (outside of those uncommon situations
in which an expert appears at the invitation of the court) is a party witness,
speaking to the interest of a single party, ostensibly without bias, with perfect honesty and without the taint of advocacy. This is a very, very tough role
indeed, and some would opine an impossible one. Yet it is the way of our
legal system, and the role can be honestly served given constant moral vigilance to certain safeguards and principles requiring constant awareness of
the expert's role. This process of focus, restraint, fairness, and perspicacity,
representing the process of law and its administration, is spoken to in Karl
Llewellyn's excellent little work, *The Bramble Bush.*

PARTIES TO LITIGATION AND THE EXPERT WITNESS ROLE

For the party to a medical malpractice suit (and please be mindful of the
fact that doctors of medicine, sharing the propensity to negligent injury as
do all other human beings, appear as plaintiffs as well as defendants in these
exercises) the recognition of legitimate diversions of opinion, given the
same set of medical facts and knowledge of the art and science of medicine,
are the standard for tort litigation and not exceptions to some general rule.
While truth is at the font of justice, truth may assume more than one guise
and, when placed against a set of unique facts, be explicated in more than
one way. Medical malpractice cases are virtually never exercises in distinguishing black from white, but are invariably based in discerning shades of
gray in both the presentation of evidence and the application of law. The
"doctor in the courtroom" must be rigorously self-disciplined and set aside
personal interest, opinion, and inevitable emotional upset to listen atten-
tively and analytically to, think about, and evaluate what "the other side" has
to say, and to grant those points that are valid. This admonition pertains to
plaintiffs, defendants, attorneys, expert witnesses, judges, and literally to
everyone in the courtroom.

The pressures, both self-generated and externally driven, upon expert
witnesses in the courtroom setting particularly can be immense. On one
hand, there is the sense of professional loyalty and historic bonding to be
acknowledged among physicians. Testifying to wrongfulness or its consequences on the part of another physician by an expert medical witness is a
burdensome and anxious situation. On the other hand, not to address trans-
gressions in the standards of care or to identify the consequences of negligent medical actions or to acknowledge them when they occur, however
intimidating the experience may be, is a form of "professional courtesy" to
be condemned. The medical expert witness also resides beneath the
Damoclean sword of professional sanctions, ranging from informal but bitter
shunning to loss of professional society membership and state medical society sanctions. These retributions, deserved or not, are virtually exclusively
reserved for medical expert witnesses who testify on behalf of plaintiffs.

Miscreant medical experts who represent the defense are treated with greater acceptance and leniency and may virtually lie through their teeth with impunity, meeting with no more than expressions of surprise, disappointment, and regret on the part of plaintiff and plaintiff's counsel. This unjust tendency, hopefully soon to be corrected, has its roots in political attitudes and reflects the usually unjustified public notions that tort litigation is generally brought by money seekers with little harm ever done to them (think of hot coffee at McDonalds Restaurants), and that doctors of medicine are good men and women who need protection even in the face of some degree of wrongdoing, including that emanating from judges and juries, regardless of issues of fact or matters of law.

Before leaving this section, it is necessary to state an additional admonition. Expert witnesses are not parties, and they are not legal advocates for a party, for a singular position, or for a certain outcome. That is the attorney's job. To become such is to become the "spit and image" (as Peter Huber has stated it in *Galileo's Revenge: Junk Science in the Courtoom*) of the lawyer who employs them. If advocates for anything, expert witnesses are advocates for their own independent analysis of the facts before them, and the tailored address of specific issues in the case before them. In the case of the medical tort process these elements consist of duty of care, breach of that duty (negligence), causation (the linking of negligence to injury), and resultant damages, physical, emotional, and monetary.

Lastly, there is the matter of money. It is despicable that a medical expert witness has an interest, conveyed by contingency or some other form of future promise ("We will pay you when we win" says the party or attorney via a letter of protection or some other instrument). Arrangements such as these not only encourage dishonesty; they virtually guarantee it. Expert medical witnesses should be paid for their time and their professional effort. They should not be compensated for rendering specific or client-favorable opinions, nor should their payment reflect the outcome of the case at hand. Be mindful also of the fact that expert witnesses of all kinds are paid by the party contracting for their services. Their likely costs should be calculated and understood ahead of time.

WORKING WITH ATTORNEYS

If a physician finds him or herself sued by a patient claiming a negligent injury resulting in compensable damage, that physician will generally be requested by legal counsel to identify potential experts and perhaps to gather relevant medical literature. The doctor's usual choices involve experts known to them locally or nationally whose reputations are based in medical practice and publication. What the doctor involved tends not to know are such a designee's particular opinion, and whether or not that person can be an effective witness. The courtroom is no place for an expert witness, no matter how professionally illustrious, who does not understand the legal process and who is not blessed with excellent communication skills, including the skill of listening. "Trial learning" should not occur at your trial. It is a decided advantage to deal with experts who are not only knowledgeable, but rigorously honest, available to the consulting attorney, and effective and affable in front of a jury.

Attorneys can discover the novice medical expert witness and may well know the more seasoned one. They are generally well equipped to seek out either variety. Some attorneys actually prefer unseasoned expert witnesses, claiming that relative courtroom virginity is an advantage at trial. What the plaintiff or defendant physician cannot do is to become engaged in focused or sustained personal contact with an expert witness, either an actual or a potential one, even when the witness may be an acquaintance of the "doctor in the courtroom." Such activity violates the general rule against separation of witnesses (and both the expert and the "doctor in the courtroom" are witnesses) and allows for the assumption of contamination of testimony by bias, undue influence, coercion, and the like. Such *ex parte* contacts may be grounds for mistrial, sanctions, or both. The affected physician, working through his attorney, will have opportunity to know the expert witnesses' qualifications, to review their reports and depositions, and to study learned treatises that may have been used to support that expert's opinions. Working with the doctor's attorney, these pieces of evidence in any case will form the basis of factual matters to be addressed at settlement, or in the alternative, at trial.

The role of expert medical witnesses relative to attorneys and their clients is correlative. The expert witness should never contact the plaintiff, defendant, or other witnesses in the matter, or seek personal, outside help unless it is done with the employing attorney's knowledge or request and approval. Such contacts are neither routine nor common. If carried out for any reason, the participation of employing counsel should be obtained before the fact.

For both the expert witness and the party physicians in the matter, the review of materials and opinionate positions is a matter of ongoing and mutual education. Frank and focused discussion (with at least 50% of the sessions devoted to listening) are required of everyone. No matter the training and experience of the lawyers involved, they are generally not doctors of medicine, and even for the few who are, they are unlikely to be truly expert in the matter at hand. Involved physicians, plaintiff or defendant, are admonished not to become their own lawyer. The deposition conference and the courtroom are the lawyer's emergency room and operating suite. Physicians cannot practice there, any more than a lawyer, no matter how renowned, is likely to walk in from the street and fix an intracranial aneurysm, manage psychotic rage, replace a hip, or treat mycoplasma pneumonia. Once depositions and trials commence, the physician's role, as party or party witness, is a more passive one than usual medical behavior and physician mindset would dictate. It consists of quiet equipoise, attentiveness, candid responsiveness, and answering questions and behaving in both a normal human and predictably professional fashion, no matter how compelling the inclination to do otherwise may be. Here is the rule: Doctor, stay cool, be honest, be candid, and be yourself, particularly if yourself can be a little bit humble. And expect an emotionally draining situation in the courtroom.

Be mindful of the fact that expert witnesses make their appearance in medical malpractice actions long before the dawn of trial. They are frequently asked to review medical records for the issues of merit prior to the time a case is filed. They often author reports—under some circumstances, a multitude of them. Once a case is filed, they may be deposed, and deposed on more than one occasion. All of this material, done on the part of plaintiff or defendant, can be made available to all parties. This trial of opinion and testimony may see the light of day in court, or be part of the substance of pretrial, court-approved settlement. This latter ending marks the termination of more litigated cases than do actual trials.

COURTROOMS

Courtrooms are not happy places. While tales and jokes involving courtroom jocularity abound, and while at times courtrooms can be theaters of the absurd, they are infrequent sites of laughter, felicity, and levity. They exist as fora to serve the effects of trouble, generally of a variety that human beings, in all their ingenuity, make endlessly and repeatedly for themselves. They are there as platforms for the peaceful settlement of disputes and exist as alternatives to rape, pillage, blood revenge, barn burning, crop destruction, cattle slaughter, impressment, slavery, and other traditional and less peaceful means of resolving disputes, all of which preceded the King's Bench and other progenitors of our modern trial courts. Medical malpractice actions are torts. They are civil actions, and with great rarity, criminal ones. Losers at a civil trial are not "guilty" of anything. They are merely liable. Winners in a civil court contest are not "innocent." They merely prevail. If they prevail, they are awarded money in historic lieu of the less peaceful actions cited above.

For all their traditional sanctuary-like appearance, courtrooms are not houses of worship. The Deity generally loses visibility after oaths are leveled. And courtrooms, much more for the liable than those who prevail, are not happy places. It is attributed to John Barrymore in reference to divorce courts, but applicable to all courts, to say that "love comes back from the courtroom the way paper napkins come back from the laundry." The same may be said of happiness in general relative to all courtroom actions.

EVIDENCE INTRODUCTION BY THE EXPERT
MEDICAL WITNESS

The admission of evidence in medical malpractice cases is guided by State and Federal Rules of Evidence in a manner analogous to the rules guiding witnesses. There is no particular "carve-out" for medical evidence in the Federal Rules. A good deal (too much, actually) is made of the "Frye Rule" and the "Daubert Rules," and a bit will be said about them later.

The common evidence available in medical malpractice cases is embodied in the medical record and its derivatives: imaging studies, laboratory tests of all kinds, pathology and autopsy reports, medical bills, consultative records, certain video and audio recordings, and at least for purposes of collateral issues of witness credibility, consistency, and rebuttal, a range of depositions, the elucidation of prior criminal convictions, and for the expert witness, the presentation of records that outline participation in prior litigation. These things are "hard evidence" and they are available to all parties. In addition, the use of demonstrative evidence is common. This includes anatomic models, artist's renderings, and the like. Whatever the evidence, its presentation in the courtroom is decided by the presiding judge. There is no automaticity or free pass to the presentation of any evidence by any witness. It is not common, but neither is it rare, to medically examine or demonstrate an injured person in court, in front of a jury.

Medical records are routinely obtained from party physicians, from hospitals, and from other treating sources. There is omnipresent temptation to "perfect" such records by redacting them in some way. These include "correcting" dates, adding clarifying or "late" notes, and the like. The party physician must resist the temptation to do this, even when such modifications seem necessary and justified. Rewriting history in this sense is wrongful, generally easily discovered, and potentially very damaging. In its most egregious forms, rewriting the medical record brings judicial sanctions.

THE *FRYE* AND *DAUBERT* RULES

The *Frye* and *Daubert* Rules pertain to scientific evidence in general. *Frye* was a case decided six decades ago, which included the presentation of lie-detector materials to a jury. That was allowed in *Frye*, whose general rule still breathes as viable law. It states that if a sizable and reputable minority claims a scientifically based theory, then data derived by such persons shall be admitted into evidence. It is not simply the "majority view" that will be heard by the court. One can imagine the correctness of this view, say in the matter of Ignaz Semmelweis, presenting the notion that "clean hands may carry the disease" in reference to puerperal fever in 19th-century Vienna. One can also imagine the distortion of scientific evidence based on *Frye* should a legal contest arise as to whether or not the moon is made of green cheese (and there is at least one scientific paper on this subject) simply because a minority of lunar investigators hold this opinion.

The *Daubert* Rules arose in litigation involving the drug thalidomide (*Daubert v. Merrill Dow*), which reached the U.S. Supreme Court. That court set out a series of criteria evaluating scientific studies for evidentiary use. *Daubert* requires peer review, the demonstration of scientific methodology, and the explication of error rates for scientific studies among its key essentials. It does not exclude the *Frye* Rule and does not incorporate it. Important progeny of the *Daubert* Rules excludes the invocation of personal experience alone as a basis for the submission of scientific evidence. Evidentiary materials subject to *Frye* and *Daubert* analysis is most frequently presented by expert witnesses.

In practice, while most jurisdictions have adopted the *Daubert* Rules wholly or with some modification, they have retained the *Frye* Rule and, in practice, call upon either with a low frequency. Their invocation is generally done to challenge (i.e., prevent) the presentation of scientific evidence or its presenter from court proceedings. Hearings and motions regarding these rules, and the admissibility of scientific evidence under them, can be held by the presiding judge and attorneys out of the presence of the jury. The medical expert presenting scientific evidence meeting with a *Frye* or *Daubert* may be subject to a *voir dire*, or exploratory and qualifying examination regarding it, prior to the presentation of the debated evidence in open court.

THE SCOPE OF EXPERT WITNESS TESTIMONY

Medical expert witnesses appear in malpractice trials at the request of both plaintiff and defendant. The witnesses generally are members of the same medical specialty as the defendant, but, as stated, this is not an invariable strategy. It is frequently necessary to obtain expert opinion from experts in more than one medical specialty if the facts of the case demand it. Testimony relative to duty of care does not arise frequently, but, like the other elements of tort, must be addressed by expert witnesses when it arises. In general, medical experts testifying to issues of standards of care are of the same specialty as the defendant, but most jurisdictions will accept standard of care testimony from disparate specialists if the testifying expert witness is able to show credible knowledge and experience with the issues at hand. Hence, an orthopedist or radiologist may testify in an action involving a neurosurgeon regarding a protruded intervertebral disk, and a neurologist in an action involving a phlebotomist relative to a peripheral nerve injury. Cases involving non-standard-of-care issues, that is, tort issue other than negligence (those being causation and damages), often require the testimony of disparate experts.

Having stated this, it is critical to point out that medical experts, no matter at whose calling they appear, do not create standards of care. They articulate them. The "standard" itself is determined by the court in the process of litigation, and in the end is a matter for judge and jury. Medically trained persons boggle at this revelation and cannot understand how a nonmedical judge and layperson jury can arrive at such a determination. The fact of the matter is that they do, and they do it routinely. That is our system of justice. The feats of medical discernment are certainly no more difficult, say, than the determination of standards of behavior for the likes of business executives at Enron or corporations like AT&T. Ordinary men and women take on the civil wrongs of such entities, the understanding of which is beyond most medical people, and fix the wrongs, whether correctly or not, routinely.

For plaintiffs and defendants in a medical malpractice action, it is critical that what an expert is testifying to is clearly understood. It is not usual that a single medical expert witness will testify to all aspects of a malpractice claim. Knowing how to discern these elements and to be of some useful participation in their own litigation, the doctor involved needs to spend considerable time with their attorney and to learn the rudiments of evidentiary and civil trial procedure rules.

FURTHER READING

Federal Rules of Evidence 2005–2006. West Group, 2005.

Federal Rules of Civil Prodcedure. West Group, abridged, 2005.

Huber P, *Galileo's Revenge.* HarperCollins, New York, 1991.

Conomy JP, *The Neurologist in Courtroom: Expert Witnesses.* The Neurologist No. 4:250–252 (1996).

Gomez JCB, *Silencing the Hired Guns: Ensuring Honesty in Medical Expert Testimony Through State Legislation.* Journal of Legal Medicine 26:385–399 (2005).

Matson JV, Suha FD, Soper JG, *Effective Expert Witnessing,* 4th ed. CRC Press, New York, 2004.

Speilman BJ, Rich BA, *Expert Testimony: Bridging Bioethics and Evidence Law (Symposium).* Journal of Medical Ethics 33:2 (2005).

Klawans H, *Trials of an Expert Witness.* Demos Publishing Co., 2006.

Llewellyn K, *The Bramble Bush.* Oceana Publications, 1981.

Medical Malpractice Defenses

S. Sandy Sanbar, M.D., Ph.D., J.D., F.C.L.M.

GOLDEN RULES

1. The physician should be knowledgeable of the general defense theories available in medical malpractice lawsuits, most of which are discussed in this chapter.
2. The physician, assisted by the defense attorney, should identify the specific defense(s) applicable to one's lawsuit.
3. The physician should ask the defense attorney to provide examples of appellate cases that have utilized the specific defense(s).
4. A successful defense of a medical malpractice lawsuit is based, not merely on errors by the plaintiff, but on sound defense legal theories, which are critical for a verdict in favor of the physician.

The physician defendant has a number of defense theories that may be applicable against the plaintiff's claims alleging medical malpractice. These include the following:

1. Absence of one of the four essential elements of negligence.
2. Good Samaritan laws.
3. Agreement with patient to exempt health care provider from liability.
4. Statutes of limitations: failure to file a malpractice claim in a timely manner.
5. Arbitration agreement.
6. Federal and state institutional immunity.
7. Charitable immunity.
8. Assumption of the risk.
9. Contributory and comparative negligence.
10. Last clear chance and avoidable consequences.
11. Prior and subsequent negligent physicians.
12. Satisfaction and release.
13. Exculpatory agreements and indemnification contracts.
14. Settlement of malpractice claim.

CASE PRESENTATION

In 2002, the Supreme Court of Mississippi affirmed a summary judgment in favor of the defendant in the case of *Martha K. Ekornes-Duncan v. Rankin Medical Center and Steven L. Chouteau* (808 So. 2d 955, 2002).

The Rankin County Circuit Court, Mississippi, granted judgment in favor of defendants, physician and medical center, in plaintiff mother's wrongful death action alleging medical negligence in the treatment of her son. The mother appealed. The mother alleged that the trial court erred in granting summary judgment to the medical center and also found error with the trial court's decisions to deny her motions for continuance, prohibit introduction of demonstrative evidence, allow the introduction of undisclosed business records, limit cross-examination of a medical expert, and permit improper closing arguments.

The appellate court found that the mother failed to show any negligence on the part of the medical center by appropriate expert medical testimony. Even if the affidavits were allowed, the negligence assigned had already been provisionally diagnosed. There was nothing to substantiate the mother's claim that she suffered injustice or prejudice from the denial of her motions for continuance. The mother's claims that she was prejudiced by the trial court's allowing the physician to use a log book were not properly before the appellate court. Defendants' closing argument was not improper as an objection was made and sustained, the statement was rephrased, and counsel took the opportunity to further address the statement during his closing. Short jury deliberations did not automatically evidence bias or prejudice.

The judgment was affirmed by the Supreme Court of Mississippi.

ISSUES

1. Absence of One of the Four Essential Elements of Negligence

As shown in the case presented above, a defendant physician or hospital can defeat a negligence claim by showing the absence of one or more of the following requisite elements of medical negligence.

Absence of Duty

Where there is no duty owed to the patient by the physician, a negligence claim generally fails. If a physician can show that no physician–patient relationship exists, this "no duty" defense may suffice to defeat the plaintiff's action.

Physicians generally have no duty to treat new patients or patients of years past, with some exceptions. This may be true even where the physician is "on call." In some cases, even though a physician treats or diagnoses a condition, a duty exists only between the physician and the patient's employer (e.g., in certain occupational settings in which a physician, such as a plant physician, is employed).

Courts rarely hold that the "no duty" defense applies and have even held that a simple telephone consultation between a physician and emergency department personnel may be sufficient to create a professional relationship between the physician and patient, with the attendant requirements to comply with such duty. Pre-certification review of a case may also create the potential for liability.

A physician who wishes to withdraw from the care of certain patients, plans to relocate his or her practice, or simply retires must notify affected patients in a manner in which an ordinary and reasonably prudent physician would do so in the same circumstances. Such notice is best made in writing and mailed postage paid to the patient's last known address. All patients receiving ongoing care for potentially serious ailments should be notified by certified mail, return receipt requested, at the last known address. Such patients should be informed that their physician will continue to see them for emergencies during a certain fixed and reasonable period of time. The physician may recommend a successor physician, provide a list of suitable physicians, or offer to forward records or copies of records (at reasonable or no cost) to another physician chosen by the patient.

In practice, when a physician retires or moves and sells his or her practice to a succeeding health care provider, patients' records are often sold as part of the transaction. However, physicians should be warned that many states have medical record retention acts, and these acts usually do not provide an exception for record-keeping requirements even in such a transfer.

No Breach of Duty (Compliance with the Standard of Care)

The defendant physician must controvert the second element of the plaintiff's proof of negligence—breach of the standard of care. Because the plaintiff has the burden of proof, if all expert testimony and other evidence are equally balanced, the defendant physician will prevail. Because the rules of evidence generally prevent nonphysicians from testifying about the medical standard of care, the physician should attempt to prove compliance with the standard of care through the testimony of a credible medical expert. Because the jury or the trier of fact usually considers treating physicians (other than the defendant) credible, both the plaintiff patient and the defendant physician may seek to recruit one of the treating physicians to give supportive testimony. In practice, especially in past years, nondefendant treating physicians were often reluctant to appear, particularly if they received referrals from the defendant physician or were otherwise socially or professionally connected with him or her. For this reason, physicians engaged to testify for the plaintiff often are nontreating physicians who have no personal connection with the parties.

Other sources of evidence, in addition to expert testimony, include medical textbooks and other published medical data. The admissibility of such evidence as proof of the standard of care varies among jurisdictions. Medical texts or treatises may be effectively used to cross-examine the adverse medical expert; such cross-examination is accomplished by framing a proposition in the exact language used by the author of the medical text and asking if the witness agrees or disagrees. In such a situation, of course, the text must first be endorsed as being authoritative and relevant to the issue under consideration. Medical negligence cases tried in federal court, under the Federal Rules of Evidence, allow statements from authoritative texts or medical journals to be read directly into evidence.

The defendant physician is not necessarily held to a standard of care advocated by the patient's medical experts. If there are alternative methods of diagnosis or treatment, and if the substantial minority of physicians agree with such alternatives, the physician may not be found negligent for using such alternatives, even though the majority of physicians do not adhere to such an alternative. In other words, employing a different method of diagnosis or treatment from that commonly used is not by itself evidence of a violation of the standard of care, especially if a "substantial minority" of "respected" physicians would have acted similarly under similar circumstances.

Lack of Causation

The plaintiff cannot recover damages from a defendant physician unless the physician's malpractice caused the plaintiff's injuries. Under most theories of recovery, a plaintiff is required to prove that such malpractice was the actual cause-in-fact of injuries and that those damages were reasonably foreseeable. This element frequently affords an adequate defense for the physician, particularly in cases involving the misdiagnosis of cancer.

Traditionally the patient cannot be compensated for a delay in diagnosis and treatment if the delay did not materially affect the outcome of the disease. For example, a minimal delay in the diagnosis of a fatal high-grade malignancy may not have made a difference in the patient's outcome and therefore would not be compensable. In other words, death would have ensued despite earlier diagnosis and treatment. Jurisdictions following this traditional approach hold that in such a situation a plaintiff cannot recover any damages unless he or she can prove that there was a greater than 50% chance of survival if the diagnosis had been made earlier and treatment had been timely.

Recently a growing trend has been to allow recovery for *"loss of a chance"* of a cure or improved outcome, which was described above. Thus, some jurisdictions allow a plaintiff's case to reach the jury even if the patient did not have a greater than 50% chance of survival or improved outcome in the absence of the physician's negligence. This "loss of a chance" doctrine, when applied by these courts using a "relaxed causation" or "substantial reduction" standard, focuses on the degree to which the defendant physician "cost" the plaintiff access to an improved chance of survival or recovery. The measure of damages is based on the portion of harm suffered by the patient as a result of the delay. The physician's defense is to controvert or minimize, through expert testimony, the percentage allocated to his or her delayed diagnosis.

Some jurisdictions no longer require plaintiffs to show that they have already suffered an actual loss because of a delay in diagnosis and treatment but require only some potential loss. In these jurisdictions the lost chance is viewed as a separate form of compensable injury. The focus is not on the ultimate physical harm but rather on the increased risk of harm because of the lost opportunity. In such "separate injury" jurisdictions the lower burden of proof allows the plaintiff recovery even if the plaintiff has been treated and is apparently healthy at the time of trial.

No Damages

The prevention or reduction of awarded damages is the defendant's primary goal in a lawsuit. To recover a monetary award, a plaintiff must introduce testimony and other evidence of damages, which often is difficult. In some cases the patient receives insurance or government benefits to cover expenses. In states that have eliminated the "collateral source" rule, evidence of such payment may reduce or obviate monetary damages.

2. Good Samaritan Laws

Under certain circumstances, where a physician who happens to be present, or is readily available, renders emergency service where he or she has no legal obligation to do so, the Good Samaritan laws of most jurisdictions protect the physician even if negligent. For example, Good Samaritan laws protect the physician who renders medical care in emergencies that take place in areas outside the health care setting, such as in an airplane, at the scene of a car accident, in a restaurant, and other public places. Sometimes, the rendering of medical care to emergencies inside a health care facility by a physician who is not responsible for the individual may also be covered under the Good Samaritan laws. Presently, many Good Samaritan laws specify guidelines where malpractice claims of ordinary, but not gross, negligence may be dismissed before reaching the jury.

3. Agreement with Patient to Exempt Health Care Provider from Liability

A physician or an institution may attempt to enter into an agreement with a patient whereby medical services will be offered at a reduced price to the patient in consideration of exempting the health care provider from liability for ordinary negligence. The limitation of liability for negligence by contract is referred to as an exculpatory clause, and it has been utilized, for example, in a charitable research hospital. Such an agreement has uniformly been held *unenforceable in medical malpractice cases*, being contrary to public policy.

4. Statute of Limitations: Failure to File a Malpractice Claim in a Timely Manner

Standard Rules

The statute of limitations (or repose) is that period of time during which a plaintiff can bring a malpractice action against a physician, which varies depending upon the circumstances of the case. In general, that period of time is governed by state statutes and may be limited to two years. However, the statutes of limitations may be extended for patients who cannot discover the misdiagnosis in time, for those with legal disability, and for children. For example, in Wisconsin, a five-year statute of limitations (repose) was held unconstitutional where the patient (child) did not discover the misdiagnosis until four years following the expiration of the limitations period.

The statutory period of limitation commences when the malpractice cause of action accrues, that is, when the allegedly negligent act occurs, or when the allegedly negligent act results in injury or damage, depending on the jurisdiction. In some jurisdictions a mere misdiagnosis, without injury or damage, may not trigger the statute of limitations; the latter is triggered by the injurious result of the misdiagnosis.

In the case of minors and the disabled, courts have interpreted conflicting state statutes of limitations by considering the constitutional issues that the malpractice case may raise.

The statutory period of limitation may be modified by other state statutes, for example, to allow for administrative reviews of malpractice claims by a State Department of Insurance prior to commencement of the malpractice lawsuit.

Discovery Rules

A major exception to seemingly rigid statutes of limitation is the so-called "discovery rule." Some medical injuries may not be discoverable by the patient during the period applicable to the statute of limitations, because an injured patient may be unaware of the injury or may not be able to reasonably associate injury with an act or omission of the physician. Additionally, in some jurisdictions, a plaintiff must first obtain favorable expert medical testimony that negligence has occurred before filing a malpractice lawsuit.

Simply stated, the "discovery rule" allows the injured patient to file a malpractice action within a specified period of time from the date that the injury is actually discovered, or should have been discovered, if the injured has exercised reasonable diligence. Virtually all jurisdictions recognize the "discovery rule" as an exception to the statutes of limitation. Many jurisdictions apply the discovery rule only to situations where the injury is inherently unknowable, or to malpractice actions where a foreign body is left in the patient postoperatively, such as sponge-in cases.

The "discovery rule" is further subdivided into pure and hybrid. Pure discovery rules permit a malpractice claim to be brought in some states for an indefinite period of time, so long as the injury has not been discovered, or reasonably should not have been discovered. Some states follow the hybrid discovery rule, which states that the discovery of the injury triggers the running of the statute of limitation, although an ultimate cap or limit is placed upon the time within which discovery must occur.

Fraudulent Concealment Rule

There are other situations that toll the statute of limitations, thereby extending the time for bringing a malpractice action. If a physician is found to have "knowingly concealed" a negligent act or omission, i.e., fraudulent concealment, the statute of limitations may be tolled. The statutory period of time to file a complaint begins when the plaintiff "should have known" about the negligent act or omission.

Continuing Treatment Rule

Another situation arises where patient treatment continues for a period of time, during which it is difficult to ascertain when the negligence occurred. Some jurisdictions have adopted a "continuing treatment" rule to determine the time of injury for purposes of the statute of limitations. The continuing treatment rule provides another exception to the statute of limitations by extending the time allowed for the filing of a complaint. The malpractice action would only accrue, thus activating the statute of limitations, when treatment of the medical condition ceases.

    The tolling of the statute of limitations has been the subject of legislative reform in a number of jurisdictions, and several reform measures have been initiated to provide clarification of the discovery rule.

5. Arbitration Agreement

A physician or an institution may privately, or pursuant to legislation, enter into an agreement with a patient to arbitrate a medical malpractice claim. The purpose of the agreement is to avoid litigation, and *not* to avoid liability. Arbitration is merely an alternative to a full-blown litigation. An agreement to arbitrate a medical malpractice claim, particularly one that follows statutory procedure, is generally enforceable because it does not violate due process and is constitutional. If an agreement to arbitrate is accepted by the parties, basic requirements of due process must be met, and there must be a fair composition of the tribunal or arbiters.

6. Federal and State Institutional Immunity

The Eleventh Amendment of the U.S. Constitution prohibits an individual from bringing a private claim against the state. Hence medical care facilities, which are providing health care by state or federal government, were historically immune from liability, based on governmental immunity. More recently, federal and state governmental immunity has been substantially eroded.

    In 1946 the federal government enacted the Federal Torts Claim Act, which permits an individual to sue the federal government for most torts, including medical malpractice. The limits of liability are $100,000.

    Similarly, state government immunity has seen erosion in modern times. A state hospital may not be sued for negligent acts by its employees, which are considered discretionary tasks, as opposed to ministerial tasks. A discretionary task involves a decision about what medical care is needed. In contrast, a ministerial task by a state hospital employee is the act of actually carrying out the discretionary decision. If a jury finds that the task performed by the state hospital employee is a discretionary decision, then the hospital would be protected by the state governmental immunity. On the other hand, if the act performed by the state hospital employee is ministerial, the hospital would not be protected by the state government immunity.

The military and other federal employees may not be permitted to sue the government for service-related injuries. Military physicians are granted immunity from prosecution for medical malpractice under the Military Medical Malpractice Statute. The Federal Employee Compensation Act does not allow relief under the Federal Torts Claim Act. Instead, most military and federal employees are entitled to various administrative benefits for personal injuries.

7. Charitable Immunity

Historically, charitable institutions were afforded either absolute or qualified immunity from liability for acts of negligence. The doctrine of charitable immunity was applicable to nonprofit charitable institutions, whose financial resources were limited, and because such institutions provided medical care for all regardless of the ability to pay.

More recently, the doctrine of charitable immunity has been abrogated in a number of states, because of the recognition that injured patients should be compensated for breach of standards of due care. In 27 states, charitable immunity has been totally abrogated. Some states have placed limits on liability of hospitals and other charitable organizations to $20,000 or less per occurrence, thereby retaining charitable community beyond those limits.

Some states have abrogated charitable immunity in medical malpractice cases that involve reckless disregard of the patient's rights, wanton or willful misconduct, or gross negligence.

8. Assumption of the Risk

Before a physician subjects the patient to a diagnostic or therapeutic procedure, the patient is informed about the risks of the procedure. If the informed patient chooses to proceed with knowledge of the risks, that patient may assume the responsibility for a resultant adverse outcome. Emphasis is placed on what the patient actually knew. If the patient knew that a certain risk was associated with a medical procedure, and he or she willingly submitted to that procedure, the patient will not be permitted to file a malpractice lawsuit for any injury that resulted from the known risk.

The patient may *expressly* assume the risk of a medical procedure or treatment, for example, by signing a consent form, which clearly indicates that the patient had knowledge of the risk, understood and appreciated the nature of the risk, and voluntarily elected to incur that risk. Under certain circumstances, assumption of the risk may be *implied*.

Nontraditional experimental therapies may constitute an inherent risk, unless the treatment was negligently selected. An informed patient who chooses nonconventional experimental treatment, in lieu of traditional medical treatment, might be assuming the risk of aggravating his or her medical condition.

9. Contributory and Comparative Negligence

The patient who contributes to his or her own injury may either be precluded from recovery of damages, or may not recover fully, for the injuries from an alleged negligent physician. Some states follow the traditional doctrine of *contributory* negligence, which requires the plaintiff to be free of any fault or negligence, in order to recover damages.

Other states follow the doctrine of *comparative* negligence, where the fault or negligence by the plaintiff operates to decrease the plaintiff's damages, based on the percentage of fault by the parties. The defendant physician may also prove comparative negligence against other physician(s) who may have subsequently treated the patient in a negligent manner.

10. Last Clear Chance and Avoidable Consequences

A patient, who is not responsible for his or her injury, may have some opportunity to either avoid or mitigate the damages resulting from the injury, based on the doctrine of avoidable consequences or the doctrine of last clear chance. These two doctrines are applied after the negligent act has caused the harm. Thus the plaintiff may not recover the damages that he or she could have avoided or mitigated.

11. Prior and Subsequent Negligent Physicians

There are situations where one physician causes an injury to the patient, who then goes to another physician and sustains an aggravation of the same injury. An alleged negligent physician may also be liable for aggravating injuries caused by a subsequent negligent physician. However, the court may choose to apportion the percentage of fault and damages by the defendants.

12. Satisfaction and Release

Satisfaction simply means that the injured person has received full compensation by someone for the injury that he or she sustained. *Release*, on the other hand, is the surrender of the cause of action, which is the basis of a lawsuit, regardless of whether the injured has received *satisfaction* or not.

Traditionally at common law, where there are multiple defendants, for example, an individual who was injured in a motor vehicle accident and who sues the auto insurance company, the hospital, and the treating physicians, a *release* of one of the joint defendants releases all of them. Thus, an express settlement with the auto insurance company for all injuries sustained constitutes a *release*. Consequently, to avoid unjust enrichment by the plaintiff, a malpractice action against the hospital or doctors is no longer permitted.

Many states have modified by statutes the common law interpretation of *release*. Under the Uniform Contribution Among Tortfeasors Act, the release of one defendant does not automatically release all. Instead, the defendant would only be released from liability *if the release so provides*. Thus a general release may not be adequate to relieve all defendants. The release should be more specific and preferably inclusive of all parties concerned.

In the absence of a release, subsequent claims against other defendants would, under applicable statutes, be set off by the amount of damages that had been received by the plaintiff.

13. Exculpatory Agreements and Indemnification Contracts

Exculpatory agreements between physicians and patients appear to relieve the physician of liability for negligence. Although such contracts occasionally are upheld in other theories of liability, they are consistently struck down in the medical malpractice context. The rationale for not acknowledging such agreements is simply that they are contracts of adhesion. The fact that an ill patient is not in a position to negotiate terms or to reach a fair meeting of the minds, which is essential for binding contract equity, dictates such an approach.

Contracts of indemnification usually arise between physicians and other individuals or institutions. For example, a hospital may agree to pay (indemnify) any damages incurred by the president of its medical staff for any liability resulting from carrying out the duties of that office.

Conversely, the chief of anesthesiology may agree to indemnify the hospital for any malpractice damages arising from the operation of the department, if no hospital employee is found to be negligent. Both types of contract are generally upheld and effectively transfer enormous financial burdens from one party to another. Although such agreements often are represented as standard terms in an employment contract, they must be considered carefully.

14. Settlement of Malpractice Claim

Practical aspects of defending any particular malpractice claim dictate the need for consultation with counsel and the malpractice insurer. In most cases a malpractice insurer provides counsel under the policy to defend the claim. Although a physician may believe that the best time to settle a malpractice claim (from his or her point of view) is at the time such a claim occurs, procedural matters and substantive matters must be considered, and the physician's personal legal counsel may be able to give the best advice on this point.

The physician should contact his or her professional liability carrier as soon as there is even a suggestion of a potential claim and ask for a representative to handle the matter. The physician should always insist that an attorney rather than a claims adjuster handle the matter, even if the physician is willing to admit fault. Private legal counsel should be retained to handle potential liability not covered by the policy or to advise the physician regarding negotiating a settlement in the course of the litigation. This advice is particularly important because the Health Care Quality Improvement Act of 1986 (42 U.S.C. §§11101 *et seq.*) requires that the settlement of any medical malpractice claim for any amount in excess of $1 be reported. In practice, negotiation and settlement of a medical malpractice claim rarely occur before the phase of formal discovery procedures, which occur during the months between the filing of the suit and the scheduled trial.

CHAPTER 25

Damages in Medical Malpractice

Robert A. Bitonte, M.D., J.D., M.A., LL.M., F.C.L.M.

GOLDEN RULES

1. Do not try to make a fool of the jury.
2. It is essential to know the status of the plaintiff, before the incident, extremely well.
3. Hire an expert to assess damages and prepare a Life Care Plan if necessary.
4. Be familiar with new and existing statutes that may limit damages recoverable.
5. Know your policy limits and any limitations.
6. Know the amount of damages that have been awarded in similar cases.
7. Never alter medical records.

The reader of this Handbook by now has learned the basic tenets of medical malpractice. To be found liable for medical malpractice, a physician must deviate from the standard of care, cause harm, and the patient must sustain damages.

It is this last element that this chapter addresses. Damages are not to be equated to physical harm alone in the context of medical negligence litigation. In fact, damages can be alleged and found in instances where there is no actual physical harm done or found. Damages are best thought of as the quantification in dollar terms of the total value the plaintiff seeks to obtain from his or her litigation. This includes economic losses and noneconomic losses, from the time of his alleged harm to the end of his life expectancy.

Most physicians and some attorneys become preoccupied with the issue of whether the accused physician breached the appropriate standard of care. Some defense attorneys do not appreciate that an often subtle physical harm can cause enormous money damages, and do not devote enough time and resources to the evaluation of this component of a medical negligence claim. This can be a disastrous oversight. For example, any injury to any person requiring daily attendant care for just a few hours per day for the rest of the plaintiff's life can easily justify a claim of seven figures.

Savvy plaintiffs' counsels, as well as defense counsels, are well aware of the costs of medical negligence litigation. Professor Frank McClellan,[1] in his book on medical malpractice, states that assessing the merits of any case costs at least $2000, and most cases require an expenditure of $5000 to $10,000. If the case goes to trial, costs may exceed $50,000, and expenditures of $75,000 or more are not extraordinary. Average defense costs are equally expensive. In a 1991 article, the author cites $34,500 as the average defense cost of 45 cases that went to trial in North Carolina. It can be no wonder then that an experienced attorney who proceeds with a medical negligence case feels that the potential reward outweighs the cost and potential loss, by a lot. If damages are viewed as the score of the litigation contest, the plaintiff's goal is to run up the score. As a defendant, limiting damages to only reasonable is the goal.

To evaluate damages properly, one must know what they are, and how to affix a dollar amount to each.

CASE PRESENTATION

Mrs. Smith is a 55-year-old, non-insulin-dependent diabetic of ten years' duration. Her attention to her diabetes was less than optimal, and she developed skin ulcers on her left foot previously that had healed with some extensive treatment. She had developed chronic skin changes over both feet, indicating compromised circulatory status of both feet. Prior to her alleged injury, secondary to medical negligence, there was no medical evidence of fallen arches in either foot. There was credible evidence of osteopenia of both feet.

During a physical examination by a physician, Mrs. Smith states that her right ankle, after a range of motion examination, "popped," and she could not walk on the foot/ankle because of pain.

Mrs. Smith went to an emergency room the same day. She was examined. No swelling was noted, and no x-rays were taken. She was given crutches. An Ace wrap was applied, and she was given some nonopiate pain relievers. She was to follow up with a local physician.

After failing to return to the follow-up examination, Mrs. Smith returned to the emergency room two weeks later complaining of increased pain and swelling of her right foot and ankle. Swelling was apparent and x-rays revealed a trimalleolar fracture that was operated upon, and repaired with hardware. Several months after her original surgery she dislodged some of the hardware, which had to be eventually surgically removed. Approximately one year after her injury, she developed a fallen arch on the injured right foot and now walks placing weight on her midfoot covered only by thin skin and no fat pad.

The medical record revealed that Mrs. Smith was not working at the time of the alleged injury and that the only job she had in the prior ten years was of a part-time salesperson in a retail budget store.

For purposes of this chapter and analysis, we will assume that the examining physician did in fact fall below the standard of care in the evaluation of Mrs. Smith and also that this fall below the standard of care caused the right ankle and foot fracture, as well as the fallen arch.

The ultimate question is, "So what? What are the damages that can be proved with some credibility?"

ISSUES

Introduction

It is fundamental in tort law that the plaintiff is entitled to be made whole, to be compensated fully for all loss sustained by the tortfeasor's negligence.[2] To the extent possible, the injured party is to be restored to the position he or she would have occupied had no wrong occurred. It is also fundamental law, however, that an aggrieved party cannot recover remote, contingent, or speculative damages.

There are generally two classifications of damages in medical negligence, as well as in other negligence actions. These classifications can be extremely important, as some states have enacted statutes that limit the recovery available in one or both of these categories. In other states there are no limitations.

One classification of damages is called *general damages*, which cannot be fixed with any degree of money exactitude. General damages (Table 25-1) include physical and mental pain and suffering, loss of enjoyment of life, and impairment of future earning capacity. See Table 25-1 for a more complete listing of legally cognizable losses. One should also keep in mind

---

Table 25-1 A list of specific elements of damage

Physical injuries:
  Past loss of earnings capacity
  Future loss of earnings capacity
  Medical care expenses—past and future:
    Physicians
    Hospitals
    Therapists
    Attendant care
    Nursing care
    Supportive equipment
    Diagnostics
    Pharmaceuticals
    Transportation
    Supplies
  Physical pain and suffering
  Mental pain and suffering
  Disfigurement
  Loss of ability to enjoy life
  Curtailment of life expectancy
  Increased risk of future harm

Mental distress:
  Past loss of earning capacity
  Future loss of earning capacity

(continued)

Table 25-1 A list of specific elements of damage (cont'd.)

Medical care expenses—past and future:
  Psychiatrists
  Psychologists
  Hospitals
  Diagnostics
  Transportation
  Pharmaceuticals
  Attendant care
Harm to relationships
Loss of ability to enjoy life
Fear of future injury

Loss of consortium:
  Spouse's loss of affection and sexual relationship
  Children's or sibling's loss of affection

Death cases:
  Decedent losses
  Future earning capacity (less personal and family maintenance expenses)
  Funeral expenses
  Medical expenses
  Pain and suffering

Family members' losses:
  Financial contributions of decedent to family
  Services
  Society
  Sorrow

Wrongful birth (patient's damages):
  Birth expenses
  Medical care and expenses
  Education expenses
  Mental distress
  Diminution of earning capacity

Wrongful life (child's damages):
  Education expenses
  Medical care expenses
  Mental distress
  Pain and suffering

that some jurisdictions have a more restricted or permissive view of available categories of losses. These hard to exact damages are also referred to as *noneconomic damages*.

The second category, *special damages*, compensates the injured person for specific out-of-pocket financial expenses and losses and includes such items as actual loss of earnings, hospital, medical, and nursing expenses, the cost of drugs, and the future medical care of the injured person. These special damages are also referred to as *economic damages*. Again, these categories can be critical.

A third category of damage compensation is also available to a plaintiff who prevails in showing certain circumstances. These are called *punitive or exemplary damages*. These types of damages are available upon a showing of the malicious, wanton, and willful act of the defendant. This type of damage award is not compensatory in nature, but instead is to punish and deter certain types of behavior. Behavior that has been found to warrant this type of damage award has been gross negligence on a finding of indifference to a patient's obvious deteriorating condition. Altering, falsifying, or withholding medical records to avoid medical malpractice claims have also supported the request for punitive damages. Obviously, this behavior is to be completely avoided.

Damages Cannot Be Remote, Contingent, or Speculative, and Must Be Proved by the Plaintiff

It is necessary for the plaintiff to establish that the damages sought arose from the injuries and were caused by the malpractice. If the damages sought in a medical malpractice case involve the aggravation or activation of a preexisting condition or disease, it is generally recognized that the physician-tortfeasor is liable only for damages for the aggravation, and not for the preexisting condition itself.

In any analysis of damages, the issue of time is crucial. Where a loss into the future is anticipated, any measure of loss, multiplied by a modifier of time, can have an enormous impact on an eventual damage claim and award.[3] See Table 25-2 for an example of some claimed damages in Mrs. Smith's claim.

It should be appreciated at the outset that the level of proof required to prove damages is a lesser degree than that required to prove the physician breached his duty of care and caused injury or harm.

The essential starting point for any damage evaluation is to establish a portrait of the plaintiff prior to the alleged medical malpractice.

Assessment of Damages

Evaluating the plaintiff prior to the alleged injury is the crucial first step in any damage analysis. Lifelong prior medical records will give an excellent picture of the health of the individual prior to the alleged injury. The medical record will provide a good idea as to a person's lifestyle, as well as occupations and family status. This is a crucial and critical step in a damages analysis and cannot be neglected.

Table 25-2 Selected items from Mrs. Smith's Life Care Plan presented at trial

1. Medical Services, Physicians

Item No.	Nature of need	Frequency	Estimated cost
1	Podiatrist	Q 1 mos	
2	Orthopedist	Q 6 mos	$7,000
3	Internist	Q 2 mos	$21,000
4	Dermatologist	Q 6 mos	$5,600
5	Psychiatrist	8×	$1,600

2. Diagnostic Tests

Item No.	Nature of need	Frequency	Estimated cost
6	Nerve conduction velocities	Q 2 years	$4,480
7	X-ray, right foot	Q year	$3,682
8	X-ray, right ankle	Q year	$3,682
9	Chest x-ray	Q 5 years	$907
10	EKG	Q 5 years	$277
11	Blood panel	Q 6 mos	$2,100
12	Glycohemoglobin	Q 3 mos	$1,848

3. Services and Supplies

Item No.	Nature of need	Frequency	Estimated cost
13	Physical therapy evaluations	Q 3 years	$2,587
14	Custom orthotic shoes	Q year	$12,600
15	Occupational therapy evaluations	Q 3 years	$2,587
16	Reclining wheelchair	Q 7 years	$1,019
17	Shower wheelchair	Q 4 years	$525
18	Personal assistance, medical assistant level	2.5 hours/day	$229,950
19	Environmental changes	Once	$25,000
20	Community-based exercise, pool	Q month	$5,040
21	Homemaker services	2 hrs/day	$163,520
22	Case manager	1.5 hrs/week	$152,880
23	Hospitalizations for illness and falls	7 days/Q 4 years	$33,440
24	Vicodin		$8,400
25	Glucophage		$8,400

Note: All cost calculations based on life expectancy of 81 years stated in Commissioners' 2001 Standard Ordinary Mortality Table and recent information from the Center for Disease Control and Prevention.

In Mrs. Smith's case, it can certainly be argued that some of the claimed diagnoses for future care are a result of her diabetes, which indeed she had prior to the alleged malpractice.

Life expectancy is also a crucial component of a damages claim. Invariably, any future loss found would be multiplied by the time the loss will be incurred.

Life expectancy should try to be evaluated by some credible sources. Work life expectancy should try to be established through some credible testimony or tables. But a precaution is warranted. Where a curtailment of life expectancy is a recognized loss, a defendant may inadvertently prove this for the plaintiff.

In a plaintiff's objective to prove damages, he or she will try to show an alteration of the life of the plaintiff after the alleged injury. The plaintiff's case will lose much credibility if they try to show a preinjury to the plaintiff that never existed. A plaintiff who had a poor work record, abilities, or education will have a difficult time showing that he or she has had a spectacular career curtailed. Without testimony or evidence of frequent human activities regularly undertaken prior to the alleged injury, it will be difficult to show that these activities will be curtailed.

Where less dramatic or obvious injuries have occurred, but yet the injuries will require extensive, specialized care or prolonged care is anticipated, the services of a life-care planner may be used. These usually are rehabilitation physicians or specialized nurses. These individuals have expertise in relying on good medical foundation to propose a long-term care plan. Defendants would be wise to insist that a part of their evaluation of the ongoing needs of the plaintiff will be evaluated by their own life-care planner. Just saying "It ain't so" is a precarious defense.

Accuracy and precision, within realistic limitations of damage assessment, is the goal. We have acknowledged that the plaintiff's case will lose much credibility if they attempt to portray a preinjured plaintiff that never existed. Well-documented and equally devastating results have occurred when defendants have tried to trivialize, diminish, or deny injuries that could not be talked away. One only needs to read a juror's perspective in the referenced case *Melis v. Kutin, Harper, and St. Vincent's Medical Center*[4] to understand what a hazardous approach this is in trying to diminish damage exposure. In short, nobody likes to be made a fool of, especially, and including, juries.

A difficult aspect of damages for plaintiffs, defendants, and juries alike to quantify with precision are the noneconomic damages that have been discussed above. Again, these are often referred to as *pain and suffering* and have many subcomponent parts (Table 25-1). Plaintiffs' counsel has a myriad of ways and arrangements to try to establish pain and suffering damages. Certain testimony and the medical record will be used in part. Testimony is difficult to control and predict.

On the other hand, the medical record speaks for itself. An allegation of pain should be supported in the medical record to some extent, by a complaint of pain, a prescription for pain medication, a tender examination, therapeutic modalities, self-treatment, something to help bolster the allegation of pain. An absence of something in the record to substantiate pain should be noted and pointed out to the jury.

Also, always remember that it is the preinjured plaintiff that must be compared to the postinjured plaintiff. If a painful condition was found prior to the alleged incident of malpractice, then it is difficult to claim damages in total for this condition. If a quantity of analgesics was taken before the alleged incidence, and if the same quantity is taken after the incident, it will again be difficult to claim damages in total for any pain caused after the incident.

Suffering is very difficult to express, quantify, or deny because of the extremely subjective nature of the concept. Regardless, the medical record can provide insight into this aspect of the claim by looking for complaints to the physician or treating personnel; and help sought to alleviate any suffering by the plaintiff, such as referral and treatment by a psychiatrist, psychologist, religious personnel, or family counselors, would indicate the existence of such a claim. The lack of such a finding is a valid line of reasoning to defend against the quality and quantity of such a claim.

In the hypothetical of Mrs. Smith, the medical records could support the claim of Mrs. Smith requiring psychiatric care and pain medication. In addition, neither of these was used prior to the alleged incident.

Applicability of Statutes and Laws

Without question, some laws and statutes have been the best defense for establishing damages, as well as setting legal limits for some types of damages in medical malpractice actions. Few defense or plaintiff attorneys have to be reminded of their existence. Their pure existence limits not only the upside value of the case, but also whether the case is ever filed. Each state either has laws in this matter or not. It is wise to review these in your jurisdiction.

In addition to statutes and laws that place limitations on the amount of an award that plaintiffs may obtain, there are other statutes that permit a reduction of the award when the plaintiffs may be getting other economic benefits. This is quite different from the usual tort scenario, where this is not permitted. If the plaintiff is covered by a government-sponsored health insurance that will pay future medical bills, or has paid medical bills, the damage claim can be reduced by this amount. Here again, the medical record provides valuable information and insight into the possible existence of such payors.

Still other statutes in some states allow for periodic payment of a medical malpractice money damage judgment. These statutes are familiar to both plaintiff and defense attorneys who specialize in medical malpractice.

Different jurisdictions have laws relating to the kind of arguments that plaintiffs' counsel may make in an attempt to establish the elusive value of noneconomic damages. Counsel on either side of the debate will generally know these laws.

"Diminishing Policies"

Physicians should be well aware of the type of malpractice insurance they have purchased. A *diminishing policy* has a feature that reduces the amount of coverage to pay a claim by the amount of money that has been spent defending and investigating a claim. If liability is likely, and damages appear high, physicians might be encouraged to settle early while the majority of the insurance coverage is available.

SURVIVAL STRATEGIES

Obtain All Medical and Employment Records as Soon as Possible

In most medical malpractice cases, an inordinate amount of time at the outset of a malpractice case will be spent analyzing the claimed incident itself. While this is being accomplished, available medical records and employment records should be sought immediately. If these are left to be obtained toward the end of case preparation, valuable information may not be obtained. In the hypothetical case presented above, review of medical records that went back many years before the incident revealed that Mrs. Smith had longstanding diabetes, and had developed serious conditions of her feet prior to the alleged incident. Although it was credibly shown that the ongoing care of her injured foot would be considerable, there was no doubt that some of these costs would have been incurred even without the incident.

There is no substitute for being able to paint a portrait of the plaintiff prior to the alleged incident. The earlier the process is started, and the more information that is obtained, the better the portrait will be, instead of a sketch.

Employ a Specialist in the Evaluation of Damages

It would be unheard of in medical malpractice litigation to proceed without an expert to speak and testify about the standard of care provided, and whether it caused the harm.

More and more plaintiffs' attorneys are utilizing specialized physicians and nurses to testify regarding their clients' resulting injuries, impairments, and future disabilities. Along with this testimony, a Life Care Plan is also produced to quantify future care. It is money well spent that the defense hire such a specialist to ensure that the plaintiff's expert has made a presentation based on a verifiable foundation, as well as to prepare an opposing opinion as to damages and costs.

Review Applicable Statutes

Although some legislation capping damages in medical malpractice actions is 30 years old now, such as in California,[5] legislation in some states is of very recent vintage. Be sure to review these with defense counsel to get an idea of what possible exposure might be limited by statute.

The physician should be aware of any statutes that permit the reduction of damages by payments to the plaintiff by third parties.

Know Your Policy Limits, and Limitations

It is essential for the physician to know the policy limits and any limitations in their policy, such as a diminishing benefit clause. A frank discussion with defense counsel and an insurance representative should make this information readily available.

Be Aware of Damages Awarded in Similar Cases

Although the jury is given great deference in its findings of damages, it is not necessarily the final word.

Through some legal prerogatives, in some jurisdictions, the judge has the ability to increase or decrease the jury award of damages. This is often done by comparisons of damages awarded in similar cases. All medical malpractice cases are different to some degree and a close similarity is as good as one can do.

FURTHER READING

Fiscina S, Boumil M, Sharp D, Head M, *Medical Liability.* St. Paul: West Publishing, 1991.
Pegalis SE, *American Law of Medical Malpractice,* 3rd ed. Thomson/West, 2005.
Vidmar N, *Medical Malpractice and the American Jury.* Ann Arbor: University of Michigan Press, 1995.

REFERENCES

1. McClellan FM, *Medical Malpractice: Law, Tactics, and Ethics.* Philadelphia: Temple University Press, 1994.

2. Louisell DW, Williams H, *Medical Malpractice,* 2nd ed. Matthew Bender, 2005.

3. Weed RO (Ed.), *Life Care Planning and Case Management Handbook,* 2nd ed. CRC Press, 2004.

4. *Melis v. Kutin,* No. 20105-80, 88LO3317 (N.Y. Superior Court, Trial Division, October 1990).

5. California Civil Code, §§ 3333.2, 3333.1; California Civil Procedure Code, § 667.7.

CHAPTER 26

Countersuits by Physicians

Charles R. Ellington, Jr., M.D., J.D., F.C.L.M.

GOLDEN RULES

1. Courts generally disfavor physician countersuits.
2. The strict legal criteria must be met to win a countersuit.
3. To win a malicious prosecution case, there must be a lawsuit filed against the physician without probable cause, with malice, and the suit must be terminated in favor of the physician. This termination cannot be on technical grounds but must reflect on the merits of the case.
4. Settling a case eliminates your chances of successfully suing for malicious prosecution.
5. In some states, the physician must show special damages to win a malicious prosecution claim. Special damages are those beyond what a physician would normally incur in a lawsuit.
6. To win an abuse of process case, the physician must show that the other side made improper use of the legal process for an ulterior purpose.
7. An ulterior motive alone is not enough to win an abuse of process claim.

In the current medical malpractice system, physicians face many medico-legal challenges. Evidence suggests that some physicians, especially those in high-risk specialties such as obstetrics/gynecology and neurosurgery, are retiring early, limiting their practice, or leaving medicine altogether, due in no small part to escalating malpractice insurance costs and runaway jury verdicts. The American Medical Association states that, as of 2006, 20 states are currently in a medical malpractice crisis and 23 others are showing signs of a crisis. At the center of this problem is the frivolous lawsuit. Evidence shows that only 20% of malpractice suits are based on adverse events related to negligence, but 50% of all malpractice suits result in a verdict for the plaintiff. Further, the cost of defending a malpractice suit at trial, even where the physician wins, is about $91,800. Although various reforms have been proposed or enacted, the problem of unfounded medical malpractice litigation remains. One potential defense is the physician countersuit.[1] This chapter will provide insight into this legal remedy and explain when and where it may be appropriately used.

CASE PRESENTATION

Mrs. I. Sue Yoo, a 55-year-old female, went to see her family physician, Dr. I. M. Brilliant, for her routine annual exam. During the visit Mrs. Yoo stated that she had been having chest pain off and on for several weeks. She described the pain as a substernal burning and heaviness lasting up to an hour. It occurred about two times per week and was not associated with any activity. It radiated to her back but not her arm. She also complained of acid reflux symptoms, especially after eating two large burritos at the local Mexican restaurant. She could not remember if the chest pain was associated with food. After reviewing her risk factors, including smoking, obesity, and a family history of coronary artery disease, Dr. Brilliant ordered an EKG, which showed normal sinus rhythm with no obvious abnormalities. No prior EKGs were available.

Ever conscientious, Dr. Brilliant referred Mrs. Yoo to a cardiologist, Dr. Smarty Pants, who practiced in a nearby city and was affiliated with a nationally recognized heart program. Dr. Pants agreed to see Mrs. Yoo the next day, at which time he administered a nuclear stress test. The test revealed a significant perfusion defect, and a subsequent cardiac catheterization revealed significant three-vessel disease with a 99% stenosis in the left anterior descending artery. Within three days of seeing Dr. Brilliant, Mrs. Yoo was in the operating room undergoing coronary artery bypass and grafting by nationally renowned cardiovascular surgeon, Dr. Divine. Although the surgery was a success, the heart/lung machine unfortunately was contaminated with another patient's blood. As a result, Mrs. Yoo contracted hepatitis C.

Mrs. Yoo, through her attorneys Larry, Mo, and Curly, filed a lawsuit against the hospital, Dr. Divine, Dr. Pants, and Dr. Brilliant. She also sued Dr. Soused, Dr. Brilliant's partner, who had no contact with the patient except that he said "Hi" to the patient as she walked down the hall for her appointment. Shortly after being named as a defendant, Dr. Soused received a signed letter from Larry, Mo, and Curly saying "If you don't pay up, we'll expose you for the lush that you are!" Fearing his prior drinking problem would be made public if he went to trial, Dr. Soused settled with the patient for $20,000. Due to a mix-up at her attorneys' office, Mrs. Yoo's claim against Dr. Pants was not filed until a day after the statute of limitations expired. As a result the action against Dr. Pants was dismissed on technical grounds. Further, the claim against Dr. Brilliant was dismissed for failure to state a claim, since there was no allegation that she did anything wrong. The case against Dr. Divine and the hospital went to trial. Prior to a verdict in the case, all four physicians filed a countersuit against Mrs. Yoo and her attorneys for malicious prosecution and abuse of process.

ISSUES

Introduction

Physicians sued for frivolous claims have the right to countersue the plaintiff and the attorney who filed the original malpractice suit.[2] However, these suits are often difficult to prove and meeting the legal burden to win is very challenging. Courts generally disfavor physician countersuits, citing the public policy that the courts should be open to all potential litigants without fear of punishment. Only in extreme cases where every legal requirement is met can the physician win. This is one reason why many physicians shy away from pursuing them. The cost in time and money with such a small chance of success is often not worth it to many physicians, who just want to get on with their lives after a distasteful encounter with the legal system. Some, however, are taking on this challenge with the hope that it will deter future frivolous suits.[3]

Physicians may pursue a countersuit under two theories: malicious prosecution and abuse of process.[4] Each theory is described below. Other legal theories, such as defamation, infliction of emotional distress, invasion of privacy, legal malpractice, prima facie tort, violation of attorney's ethical code, willful and wanton institution of a lawsuit, harassment, and civil rights violation, have not been successful and probably will not be in the future.

Malicious Prosecution

Malicious prosecution is the most likely theory under which a physician may prevail on a countersuit. However, even malicious prosecution is difficult to win and the physician must prove each element of the claim. Those elements are as follows:

- The defendant *filed a lawsuit* against the physician;
- The suit was filed or continued *without probable cause*;
- The defendant filed the suit with *malice*;
- A *favorable termination* of the underlying lawsuit; and
- *Injury* to the physician as a result of the suit.

The first element, the defendant filing a lawsuit against the physician, is obvious from the record and is rarely the subject of dispute.

The second element, probable cause, is often difficult to prove. Probable cause means that a person or attorney, based upon the facts known at the time the suit was instituted, reasonably believed they could win the case. Lack of probable cause may occur where the attorney intentionally ignored certain facts or did not reasonably investigate the facts of the case. Probable cause may arise from certain facts such as a thorough investigation of the case by the attorney or utilizing an expert witness. The fact that the attorney does not have an expert witness at the time of filing, however, does not prove a lack of probable cause. Neither does a less than thorough investigation, especially where time is limited. Even if the facts of the case prove to be weak, as long as there was a reasonable belief that the facts merited litigation, there is probable cause. Clearly, the element of lack of probable cause is a major barrier to successfully winning a malicious prosecution claim.

The third element, malice, requires a wrongful purpose or motive. It means pursuing a legal claim for a purpose other than appropriately adjudicating a claim. It does not arise, however, solely from a contingent-fee arrangement. It is often inferred by proving a lack of probable cause.

The fourth element, a favorable termination of the underlying malpractice suit, must somehow reflect the merits of the claim. A favorable termination may occur where the physician wins at trial, wins summary judgment, gains a dismissal in his or her favor on the merits, or where the plaintiff drops the suit because there is no case. A favorable termination cannot occur where the physician loses at trial, settles out of court, or gains a dismissal on technical grounds, since none of these is reflective of the merits of the claim.

The fifth element, injury to the physician, requires that the physician suffer some type of definable injury as a result of the suit. Some jurisdictions require a "special injury" to the physician beyond the injuries normally sustained in any litigation. Injuries that do not qualify as "special" include defamation, mental suffering, loss of income, cost of defending the suit, or increased malpractice premiums or cancellation of the malpractice policy. One court found that a "special injury" occurred when the physician's reputation was "assailed." All in all, special injuries are very difficult to prove.

With respect to the physicians in the above case, Dr. Soused will not be able to win his claim for malicious prosecution. Although the lawsuit was filed against him with malice and there was clearly no probable cause that he in any way contributed to Mrs. Yoo's infection with hepatitis C, he loses because he settled. Settlement is not a favorable termination in the physician's favor, and so fails to prove all of the elements of the claim.

With respect to Dr. Divine, his suit will not prevail and will likely be dismissed before going to trial. Since his suit is still pending, there has not been a favorable termination in his favor. If he wins at trial he may be able to refile his claim. Even then, he will have a difficult time proving there was a lack of probable cause. As the surgeon, he had a duty to explain the risks and benefits of the procedure to the patient and discuss other options. Since it is unclear whether he discussed the possibility of an "off the pump" procedure with the patient, there very well may be probable cause against Dr. Divine.

With respect to Dr. Smarty Pants, he does not have a claim for malicious prosecution either. Although there is no probable cause for the suit, and there is evidence of malice shown from the nature of the suit, there has been no favorable termination of the suit in his favor. Since his suit was dismissed on technical grounds, this dismissal does not reflect on the merits of the case. Therefore, he loses his malicious prosecution countersuit.

Finally, with respect to Dr. Brilliant, she may have a claim, although she will have difficulty proving "special injuries" if her state requires it. The suit was filed against her with a profound lack of probable cause. In fact, she found a very serious medical problem and took appropriate action to investigate and treat it. The nature of the suit and the behavior of the attorneys imply malice. Further, she had a termination of the underlying malpractice suit in her favor since it was dismissed for cause. In a state that does not require "special injuries," she appears to have a strong case. However, in a state that does require "special injuries," she may have trouble. Her injuries involve the cost of the suit, injury to her reputation, and emotional stress associated with being sued. Since none of these injuries rises beyond those normally sustained by a physician in litigation, she will be unable to prove "special injuries" and would not prevail in these jurisdictions.

Abuse of Process

Abuse of process is a second theory under which a physician may counter-sue for a frivolous lawsuit. It is less likely to be successful and courts are also averse to ruling against patients under this theory. To succeed in proving an abuse of process case, a physician must prove all of the following:

- The plaintiff or the attorney made an improper use of the legal process,
- With an ulterior motive,
- And the physician as a result was injured.

To prove the first two elements, the physician must show that the legal process was used to obtain "an end unintended by law ... not regularly or legally obtainable." An ulterior motive alone is not enough. There must be a perversion of the legal system for an improper purpose. One example of such a perversion of the legal process is where someone filed a suit solely to coerce a nuisance settlement from the physician. In this case, there was clear evidence that the physician did nothing wrong. The attorney did not investigate the case, took no depositions, and did not hire an expert. In this case, there is evidence of abuse of process. However, if a plaintiff or attorney simply files a lawsuit with the hope of forcing a settlement, this in itself is not abuse of process since settlement is a recognized goal of the legal system. Even egregious acts by the attorney, such as calling a physician incompetent, a liar, and a scoundrel at trial, although indecorous, would not rise to the level of abuse of process. Evidence of abuse of process would include a willful act of using the legal process to obtain a collateral advantage or coerce another. Some type of overt act is needed to show that the legal process was misused.

In addition to proving an improper use of process and an ulterior motive, the physician must prove that he or she was injured from the suit. There must be an actual injury to the person or property, and injury to a physician's good name or reputation would not qualify as an injury. However, special damages are not required in abuse of process claims.

With respect to each of the physicians in the clinical case, Dr. Divine is unlikely to prevail in the abuse of process case. There is no evidence that the suit was filed for an ulterior purpose or that the legal process was misused. In fact, the case against Dr. Divine appears to be an appropriate use of the legal process to resolve a legitimate claim.

With respect to Dr. Brilliant and Dr. Pants, their countersuits for abuse of process are stronger than Dr. Divine's, but they still are unlikely to prevail. Although the malpractice suits against both of these physicians appear to be nuisance suits, there is no overt evidence of an ulterior motive and perversion of the legal process. The lawyers in both cases could argue they were simply using the legal process to adjudicate potential claims and that this is an appropriate purpose of the legal system. The mere filing of a lawsuit is not in itself an abuse of process. Therefore, both Dr. Pants and Dr. Brilliant are unlikely to prevail on their countersuit.

With respect to Dr. Soused, his claim for abuse of process seems the strongest. Under this theory, favorable termination of the proceedings is not required. The letter from Larry, Mo, and Curly clearly shows their effort to coerce money from Dr. Soused and to threaten him with public embarrassment. Although settlement is an appropriate goal of the legal system, extortion is not. The attorneys in this case clearly perverted the legal system for an ulterior purpose and Dr. Soused was injured as a result. Consequently, he should prevail on countersuit under this theory.

SURVIVAL STRATEGIES

Practice Good Medicine

This goes without saying, but the best defense against malpractice in general is practicing sound medicine and taking good care of your patients. Since winning a malicious prosecution case requires an outcome in your favor and a lack of probable cause, sound medical practice is the first part of winning a countersuit.

Keep Accurate and Complete Records

This applies to medical records as well as all records involving any potential litigation. In the medical record, document your thought process, your recommendations to the patient, and the patient's response to treatment. Document any noncompliance on the patient's part. Further, keep copies and records of all communications related to any actual or potential litigation. These records may help prove any malice or ulterior purpose down the road.

Plan Early for a Countersuit

Discuss with your attorney early any thoughts you might have in bringing a countersuit. During the process of a lawsuit, several pitfalls may arise that can thwart a successful countersuit. It is important to think about a countersuit early in the process to plan for this.

Know What You Want

As stated earlier, physician countersuits are difficult to win and prosecuting one, especially just after you have been sued, can be emotionally challenging. You need to know if you have the energy to pursue this legal option and what you specifically hope to gain from the process.

FURTHER READING

Lee BH, "Countersuits by Health Care Providers." In *Legal Medicine/American College of Legal Medicine*, 7th ed., ed. S. Sandy Sanbar *et al*. Philadelphia: Mosby, 2007.

61 A.L.R. 5th 307. Contributory negligence or comparative negligence based on failure of patient to follow instructions as defense in action against physician.

Brennan TA, Sox CM, Burstin HR, *Relation Between Negligent Adverse Events and the Outcomes of Medical-Malpractice Litigation*. 335 New Engl. J. Med. 1963 (1996).

Rawson J, *Wong v. Tabor: The Latest Word in Physician–Attorney Countersuits*. 17 Valparaiso Law Rev. 153 (1983).

REFERENCES

1. McCammon K, *Fighting Fire with Fire: Physician Countersuits*. Medical Sentinel 7(3):88 (2002).

2. 61 Am. Jur. 2d Physicians, Surgeons, etc. 294.

3. Witlin L, *Countersuits by Medical Malpractice Defendants Against Attorneys*. 9 J. Legal Med. 421 (1988).

4. *Dutt v. Kremp*, 111 Nev. 567, 894 P. 2d 354 (1995), a case involving malicious prosecution and abuse of process claims. See also *Epps v. Vogel*, 454 A. 2d 320 (D.C. Ct. App. 1982), because of loss of income, several doctors sued the lawyer who had represented a group; and *Wong v. Tabor*, 422 N.E. 2d 1279 (Ind. Ct. App. 3d Dist. 1981), involving malicious prosecution.

Tort Reform System: Medical Negligence in New Zealand

James C. Johnston, M.D., J.D., F.C.L.M., F.A.C.L.M.

> It may yet come to pass that the most effective remedy for the ills of our tort reparation system will be disclosed by demonstration, in an attractive, usually tranquil, and very civilized little country half-a-world away.... The developments "down under" thus merit our most careful and continuing observation.[1]

The New Zealand accident compensation scheme is the most comprehensive tort reform system in the common law world. It has successfully operated for over 30 years. The fundamental nature of the scheme is simple: for personal injury, no-fault compensation replaces the common law action for damages. This chapter provides an overview of medical negligence "down under," with particular attention to the relationship between statutory tort reform and the common law.

BACKGROUND

It is difficult for an outsider to understand how a nation can make the sweeping legislative reforms that will be discussed in this chapter. It may be helpful to review three unique features of the country's legal framework. First, New Zealand is a unitary state, allowing Parliament to enact national legislation without a fragmented amalgam of state, province, or territory law. Second, New Zealand, a Westminster-style constitutional monarchy, does not have a written constitution; thus, there are no entrenched provisions or superior law to restrain the government's ability to legislate. Third, Parliament, a unicameral General Assembly, has sovereign power to legislate and courts are absolutely bound to apply the law. These factors, among others, allow a flexible, dynamic approach to legislative reform.

INTRODUCTION

New Zealand provides a comprehensive public health system that is funded by the Ministry of Health and administered by 21 District Health Boards. Each Board is responsible for providing services in a particular geographic region. This public health service coexists with a parallel system of private insurance and private hospitals. Both systems are underpinned by a no-fault accident compensation scheme, which provides coverage for personal injury regardless of fault or cause, and at the same time bars the right to sue for compensatory damages covered by the scheme.

THE CURRENT REGIME

The scheme is administered by the Accident Compensation Corporation (ACC), a Crown-owned entity, which operates under the current regime entitled the Injury Prevention, Rehabilitation, and Compensation Act 2001 (IPRCA). ACC is responsible for preventing injury, determining whether claims for injury are covered, providing entitlements including compensation, buying health services to treat and rehabilitate the injured, and advising the government. The funding for ACC is through Parliament and a series of levies on employers, earners, motor vehicle owners, health professionals, and medical organizations.

The IPRCA covers New Zealand residents and citizens, with limited benefits for temporary visitors. An eligible person is covered for a personal injury provided it falls within one of eleven statutory categories, which include accident, medical misadventure, or a gradual process, disease, or infection that is employment-related, secondary to personal injury or its treatment, or due to medical misadventure. The scope of this cover is to be interpreted in a "generous, unniggardly" fashion.[2] Personal injury is statutorily defined as death, physical injury, mental injury consequent on physical injury, or damage to dentures or prostheses. The term "physical injury" is neither obvious nor precisely defined, but courts consider it to mean any condition involving harm to the human body including sickness or disease.[3] There is no coverage for a willfully self-inflicted injury or suicide.

The benefits of coverage under the scheme include medical treatment, social and vocational rehabilitation, weekly compensation during incapacity, lump-sum compensation for permanent impairment, weekly compensation for the spouse and dependants of a deceased claimant, childcare payments, survivors' grants, and funeral grants.

The IPRCA prohibits independent proceedings, whether under any rule of law or enactment, in any court in New Zealand, for damages arising directly or indirectly out of any covered injury.[4] Thus, a person may not sue for compensatory damages for any personal injury that is covered by the scheme. The purpose of the bar is to prevent compensation twice over, not to prevent recovery of any compensation.[5] This represents "a kind of social charter, largely replacing the common law in a defined field."[6]

HISTORY

A review of the history is paramount to understanding why New Zealand decided to replace the common law with this radical, far-reaching scheme. Prior to inception of the scheme, injured persons could seek relief through either a common law action or, depending on the situation, statutory compensation under the Workers' Compensation Act 1956, Social Security Act 1964, or Criminal Damages Act 1963.[7] In 1966 the Minister of Labour established a Royal Commission of Inquiry charged with investigating the adequacy of workers' compensation benefits. The commission produced a landmark report far exceeding the terms of reference (Woodhouse Report):[8]

> The negligence action is a form of lottery. In the case of industrial accidents it provides inconsistent solutions for less than one victim in every hundred. The Workers' Compensation Act provides meagre compensation for workers, but only if their injury occurred at their work. The Social Security Act will assist with the pressing needs of those who remain, provided they can meet the means test. All others are left to fend for themselves. It is a situation which needs to be changed.

It is worth reviewing the commission's arguments to abolish the common law, which were adopted by the major political parties in New Zealand but largely ignored in the rest of the world:[9]

- The failure of the common law to compensate large numbers of accident victims;
- The waste involved in the system in that much of the money was chewed up in legal and administrative expenses;
- The long delays in delivering benefits to those who secured them;
- That personal blameworthiness was not the real rationale for the law because negligence law required individuals to meet the community average standard;
- "Reprehensible conduct can be followed by feather blows while a moment's inadvertence could call down the heavens," as the Woodhouse Report put it;
- That liability insurance had blunted or removed the deterrent effect of tort law;
- That an assessment of damages in one lump sum involved guesswork and speculation and tended to overcompensate less serious injuries;
- That the process of adjudication was a lottery and impeded the rehabilitation of injured people, and there were strong incentives to maximize misery; and
- Accident prevention was impeded by the system.

The Woodhouse Report proposed a comprehensive scheme of accident prevention, rehabilitation, and compensation based on five guiding principles: community responsibility, comprehensive entitlement, complete rehabilitation, real compensation, and administrative efficiency. There was no question about the goal: "Injury arising from accident demands attack on three fronts. The most important is obviously prevention. Next in importance is the obligation to rehabilitate the injured. Thirdly, there is the duty to compensate them for their losses."[10] The Royal Commission concluded: "If the scheme can be said to have a single purpose it is 24-hour insurance for every member of the workforce, and for the housewives who support them."[11]

Parliament, following the Woodhouse Report, a White Paper, and a Select Committee Report, enacted the Accident Compensation Act 1972, bringing the accident compensation scheme into effect on April 1, 1974. The fundamental nature of the reform was to replace the common law with a no-fault scheme to compensate personal injury by accident. The remainder of this chapter will be limited to a discussion of medical misadventure under the scheme. Lack of space necessitates omitting many laws, ignoring important cases, and oversimplifying the entire picture. Therefore, this overview should not be considered a complete or definitive statement of the law.

MEDICAL MISADVENTURE

The Accident Compensation Act 1972 defined personal injury by accident to include "medical, surgical, dental, or first aid misadventure." A 1982 re-enactment made no changes regarding medical misadventure. The High Court never established a clear definition of medical misadventure, resulting in cost increases as the boundaries of the scheme expanded. This prompted the National Party government to retreat from the original scheme by enacting the Accident Rehabilitation and Compensation Insurance Act 1992, which provided restrictive definitions excluding certain claims and limiting benefits. The new, narrowed definitions for medical misadventure cover were carried over in the Accident Insurance Act 1998 and the subsequent IPRCA, although the latter did restore some of the previously limited benefits such as lump-sum compensation. These restrictive definitions precluded a true no-fault scheme and resulted in a revival of the common law with novel claims circumventing the statutory bar. Parliament responded with the Injury Prevention, Rehabilitation, and Compensation Amendment Act (No. 2) 2005 (Amendment Act), replacing the term "medical misadventure" with the broad concept of "treatment injury," expanding coverage in a move back toward the Woodhouse recommendations. The pre-amendment regime will be reviewed before discussing the latest changes because the evolution of this particular statute provides a unique view of the challenges involved in developing a true no-fault compensation scheme and, from a practical standpoint, the pre-amendment legislation still applies to claims of medical misadventure occurring prior to Royal Assent of the Amendment Act.

Fault Within the Scheme

Medical misadventure is defined as personal injury suffered by a person seeking or receiving treatment given by or at the direction of a registered health professional (hereinafter health professional or physician), and which is caused by medical error or medical mishap. Personal injury may include injury by disease or infection, or by a heart attack or stroke, as well as an existing condition that does not improve or gets worse. It also includes a secondary infection passed by medical misadventure to a spouse, child, or third party.

Medical mishap means an adverse consequence of properly administered treatment that is rare and severe. The definition of severe is death, hospitalization for more than 14 days, or significant disability lasting more that 28 days; rare means that the adverse event occurs in 1% or less of the cases where treatment is given. There is no mishap where an adverse consequence is rare in the ordinary course but is not rare for a particular person, and the person knew the greater risk before treatment.

Medical error means the failure of a health professional to observe a standard of care and skill reasonably to be expected in the circumstances, and can include failure of an organization when error cannot be attributed to a particular professional. The error may arise in the diagnosis of a person's condition, deciding whether or not to give treatment, deciding what treatment to provide, obtaining consent, or actually giving treatment. It is not medical error because desired results are not achieved, subsequent events show that different decisions might have produced better results, or the failure in question consists of a delay or failure attributable to an organization's resource allocation decisions. Thus, medical error requires proof of fault even though the accident compensation scheme operates as a no-fault system.

This anomaly of a negligence-based standard embedded within a no-fault system required the scheme to resolve some of the same problems that occurred under the tort system. It set the stage for a reawakening of the common law and development of various statutory remedies. The necessity of finding fault perpetuated a "blaming culture" that precluded patient safety improvements, generated significant expense investigating medical errors, and caused delays in deciding claims.[12] Additionally, the mishap provisions of severe and rare were considered arbitrary and confusing. A public consultation process supported the need for reform of the medical misadventure provisions.[13]

Revival of the Common Law

The complex social, political, and legal climates surrounding the legislative history of the scheme are beyond the scope of this chapter. The crucial point, for this discussion, is that from 1992 the various Acts restricted coverage and limited benefits, resulting in a less generous scheme. As coverage under the scheme contracted, the scope of actionable negligence expanded, most notably involving claims for nervous shock and exemplary damages.

Nervous Shock

The original Act covered mental consequences of an injury including transient trauma (anger, embarrassment, distress) as well as more severe psychiatric ailments. Since 1992 the schemes have excluded transient emotional trauma by defining "mental injury" as "clinically significant behavioral, cognitive or psychological dysfunction."[14] Moreover, mental injury is now only covered where it amounts to personal injury, and it is due to physical injury or certain crimes. Coverage in these limited circumstances bars a common law action. Conversely, there is no cover for mental injury alone, and thus no bar against an action for damages. Moreover, secondary victims of medical negligence, such as relatives of a patient who died, may bring an action for nervous shock.

Exemplary Damages

The IPRCA does not bar a claim for exemplary damages, because such damages are not considered compensation.[15] These damages are awarded to punish the defendant, not to compensate the plaintiff. Claims were generally confined to cases of intentional conduct, but *McLaren Transport Ltd. v. Sommerville* extended actions to gross negligence.[16] The escalating intrusion of exemplary damages into negligent conduct prompted the Court of Appeal to curtail these actions: "Exemplary damages are awarded to punish a defendant for high-handed disregard of the rights of a plaintiff.... Negligence simpliciter will never suffice."[17] The Court subsequently tightened this restriction in *A. v. Bottrill*, ruling that exemplary damages should only be available where "the defendant is subjectively aware of the risk to which his or her conduct exposes the plaintiff."[18] The Privy Council overturned *Bottrill*, restoring *McLaren*, and reopening the door for exemplary damages in negligence.[19] Their Lordships did caution that "a perceived need for compensation, or further compensation, is not a proper basis for making an award of exemplary damages."[20]

Other Claims

Common law actions are available where the statutory definition of personal injury is not satisfied. For example, negligent surgery may fail to produce the desired results but does not cause physical or mental injury. Similarly, negligent failure to sterilize a patient may give rise to a suit for the financial loss of raising the child. The IPRCA provides that certain proceedings can be maintained, including actions related to property damage, any express term in a contract, or any personal grievance arising out of a contract for service, as well as actions under the relevant provisions of the Health and Disability Commissioner Act 1994 or the Human Rights Act 1993. There may be claims for compensatory damages where statutory definitions are not met, and participation in certain clinical trials may open the door for a negligence action against the manufacturer or investigator.

Development of Statutory Remedies

The common law resurgence occurred contemporaneously with several high-profile Ministerial Inquiries recommending, *inter alia*, a statement of patient rights and appointment of a Health Commissioner to investigate complaints. These Inquiry outcomes, along with a confluence of other factors, including a paucity of common law decisions on professional standards and public desire for increased accountability, precipitated a series of Parliamentary Acts and regulations on patient rights, informed consent, privacy, and a host of related matters. The recently promulgated legislation focuses on consumer (legislative terminology) rights and creates a number of interrelated regulatory bodies and tribunals: evidence from one may be used by another; there are mechanisms for increased reporting among these organizations as well as with the ACC, authorities, and employers; and complaints may be simultaneously addressed in other fora including, for example, Coronial hearings, Inquiries, and Bill of Rights Act and Privacy Act proceedings. The result of this milieu is a quest for accountability and compensation under several relatively new statutory provisions. The following Acts are particularly relevant to the accident compensation scheme because they provide a means for consumers to seek redress for negligence, and are not barred by the scheme.

Health and Disability Commissioner Act 1994 (HDCA)

The HDCA contains the Code of Health and Disability Services Consumers' Rights (Code), which confers ten rights for the protection of consumers (e.g., Right 4 is a right to services of an appropriate standard; Rights 6 and 7 pertain to informed consent; Right 10 is the right to complain to the Commissioner). Consumers may complain directly to the Commissioner, who has the authority, upon determining there is a breach of the Code, to make recommendations to the provider or Ministry of Health, file a complaint with the relevant professional body, or refer the matter to the Director of Proceedings. The Director of Proceedings, an independent statutory office, may call proceedings in the Human Rights Review Tribunal or Health Practitioners Disciplinary Tribunal, or both.

Human Rights Act 1993 (HRA)

This Act established the Human Rights Review Tribunal (HRRT), which can hear proceedings about matters infringing upon the Code, the HRA, the Privacy Act 1993, or the Health Information Privacy Code. Complaints to the Tribunal may arise by referral from the Commissioner to the Director of Proceedings or, in accordance with the Health Practitioners Competence Assurance Act 2003, directly from the consumer. The Tribunal can make a declaration, issue an order restraining the provider, order the provider to redress any loss or damage suffered by the consumer, provide damages up to $200,000 for pecuniary loss, expenses, loss of benefit, humiliation, or action that was in "flagrant disregard" of the consumer's rights, or provide any other relief as the Tribunal thinks fit.[21] This statutory provision provides a wider basis than the common law for a claim of exemplary damages, since "flagrant disregard" requires a lower threshold of proof than the common law "outrageous conduct" test.

Health Practitioners Competence Assurance Act 2003 (HPCAA)

This omnibus Act covers the regulation and discipline of all health professionals. A separate "authority" is established for each profession, responsible for matters related to education, registration, practicing certificates, scope of practice, and competence reviews. A single multidisciplinary Health Practitioners Disciplinary Tribunal chaired by the legal profession conducts all disciplinary hearings.[22] Consumers may complain directly to the disciplinary tribunal, or complaints may originate from the Commissioner or the HRRT. The HPCAA provides direct consumer access to the HRRT. The tribunal has wide disciplinary authority ranging from the imposition of fines to cancellation of practicing certificates.

Parliament Enacts the Amendment Act

The Woodhouse scheme was designed "to supplant the vagaries of actions for damages for negligence at common law."[23] The successive statutory re-enactments retreated from the original scheme by excluding certain claims and limiting benefits, resulting in a renewed resort to common law actions with all the attendant vagaries. This did not go unnoticed. The High Court sent a warning: "The compensation entitlements of the victims of negligence have fallen far short of the much-trumpeted recommendations of the 1967 Woodhouse Commission Report. Such a perception may well lead to the courts providing remedies which are not currently available."[24] There is not yet any apparent trend to create other remedies, and the courts have not developed exemplary damages as a remedy for inadequate ACC compensation. Indeed, later judicial decisions suggest that the perceived limitations of the scheme will be considered "a matter for Parliament."[25]

Parliament responded with the Amendment Act, which adopts a more generous approach to the injured. It replaces the terms "medical mishap" and "medical error" with "treatment injury" effective July 1, 2005. Treatment injury means personal injury suffered by a person seeking or receiving treatment from a health professional that is caused by treatment and not a necessary part or ordinary consequence of the treatment, taking into account all circumstances including the person's underlying health condition and the clinical knowledge at the time of treatment. It does not include personal injury that is wholly or substantially caused by the person's underlying health condition, attributable to a resource allocation decision, or a result of a person unreasonably delaying or withholding consent to treatment. The fact that treatment did not achieve a desired result does not, of itself, constitute treatment injury. Treatment includes diagnosis of a condition, a decision on treatment to be provided, giving a treatment, delay or failure in providing treatment, obtaining or failing to obtain consent, the provision of prophylaxis, failure of any equipment used in treatment, and application of any support systems (including administrative systems) used by the organization responsible for treatment. Thus, claimants must establish causation, but it is unnecessary to prove any degree of fault, severity, or rarity.

THE FUTURE

There will undoubtedly be an increase in compensation claims under the new legislation, especially with the exclusion of any "seriousness" requirement. The changes will enable more patients to receive compensation and rehabilitation, and hopefully create a culture encouraging health professionals to report adverse events for the purpose of improving patient safety. The wider coverage may diminish pressure on the common law to provide for victims of personal injury. Additionally, the fact that consumers may seek remedies including exemplary damages through statutory provisions such as the HRRT may further dampen common law actions. Thus, expanding coverage under the scheme should result in a corresponding decrease of the already limited negligence claims.

There will, with the new law, be a focus of litigation to "prove" an unexpected event separating treatment injury from ordinary treatment of disease or illness. The reason is simple—the scheme continues to cover injury but not sickness, which is relegated to the lesser entitlements of the social security program. Unless New Zealand takes the Woodhouse "next step" and integrates the accident scheme with social security to provide equitable benefits, which appears unlikely at this time, there will be a litigation penumbra surrounding the scheme. The litigation will simply shift from fault issues, no longer relevant under the Amendment Act, to proving causation.

SUMMARY

A person suffering injury due to medical misadventure or treatment injury is entitled to cover under the scheme, and may not sue for compensatory damages. An injury that falls outside the scheme such as nervous shock may give rise to a common law action for compensatory damages. The bar does not prohibit claims for exemplary or punitive damages. Even if a negligence claim is barred, the negligence may breach a statutory right (e.g., Right 4 of the Code mandating a reasonable standard of care), and result in an award of exemplary damages.

CONCLUSION

The New Zealand accident compensation scheme is unquestionably an enduring success. It avoids the economic and social injustices that the common law inflicts upon injured persons. It is not a panacea. There remain policy and administrative challenges concerning an acceptable balance between statutory coverage and the common law, as well as integration of social security. Nevertheless, the scheme is part of the social fabric and it is unlikely that there will ever be a widespread return to the common law. Jurisdictions considering tort reform may benefit from a full understanding of this unprecedented scheme.

REFERENCES

1. Bernstein A, *No-Fault Compensation for Personal Injury in New Zealand*, in U.S. Dept. of Health, Education and Welfare Report of the Secretary's Commission on Medical Malpractice (1973), Supp. Vol. 848.

2. *ACC v. Mitchell* (1992) 2 NZLR 436, 438–9 (CA).

3. *Childs v. Hillock* (1993) NZAR 249, 2 NZLR 65 (CA).

4. §317(1) IPRCA.

5. *Queenstown Lakes District Council v. Palmer* (1999) 1 NZLR 549 (CA).

6. *Brightwell v. ACC* (1985) 1 NZLR 132, 139–40 (CA).

7. McKenzie P, *The Compensation Scheme No One Asked For: The Origins of ACC in New Zealand*, VUWLR 34(2), at 195 (June 2003).

8. Royal Commission of Inquiry, *Compensation for Personal Injury in New Zealand* (Woodhouse Report) (Wellington, 1967) at para. 1.

9. Palmer G, *The Nineteen-Seventies: Summary for Presentation to the Accident Compensation Symposium*, VUWLR 34(2) at 241 (June 2003).

10. *Supra* note 8, para. 2.

11. *Supra* note 8, para. 18.

12. ACC, *Review of ACC Medical Misadventure: Consultation Document* (2003).

13. Accident Compensation Corporation and the Department of Labour, *Summary of ACC Medical Misadventure Consultation* (2003).

14. §27 IPRCA.

15. §319(1) IPRCA. *See Taylor v. Beere* (1982) 1 NZLR 81 (CA) and its progeny.

16. *McLaren Transport Ltd. v. Sommerville* (1996) 3 NZLR 424 (HC).

17. *Ellison v. L.* (1998) 1 NZLR 416, 419.

18. *A. v. Bottrill* (2001) 3 NZLR 622 (CA).

19. *A. v. Bottrill* (2003) 2 NZLR 721 (PC).

20. Id. at para. 66.

21. *Director of Proceedings v. O'Neil* (2001) NZAR 59 (HC). *See also* §57(1)(d) Health and Disability Commissioner Act 1994.

22. §84 HPCAA 2003.

23. *Green v. Matheson* (1989) 3 NZLR 564 (CA).

24. *Residual Health Management Unit v. Downie* (2001) CA 147/01, 3.

25. *Wardle v. ACC*, HC Wellington AP 134/02.

LIABILITY OF SPECIALTIES

Family Practice and Internal Medicine

Katherine A. Hawkins, M.D., J.D., F.A.C.P., F.C.L.M.

GOLDEN RULES

1. Document all tests/referrals made and to whom/where.
2. Communicate with patients about the purpose and importance of tests/referrals.
3. Follow up on tests/referrals—a difficult problem; patients often do not understand the serious nature of the test/referral and the practitioner, not wanting to scare patients, often does not tell patients the worst possible scenario. Realize that it is more likely for patients to follow through on those tests/referrals in which they themselves are interested (such as dermatology or ophthalmology referrals) and less likely for them to pursue tests/referrals that only the practitioner feels are important (such as screening colonoscopies or mammograms).
4. Document receipt of test/referral reports with signatures or clear initials and dates. It may be useful to enter a note on the report indicating that the patient was informed or plans made for follow-up.
5. Communicate with patients about test results—by phone, note, or copy of test results with doctor's comments. In cases where a serious issue is involved, consider sending letter by certified mail, return receipt requested.
6. Document efforts to communicate with all patients, but especially in the case of a noncompliant patient. A pattern of noncompliance with office appointments, referrals, and advice—especially when the practitioner attempts to contact the patient and reinforce the need for follow-up—can help the practitioner defend a malpractice case. Conversely, a patient whose medical record indicates that he or she always followed through with referrals and advice makes a sympathetic and credible witness/plaintiff when it is the practitioner who fails to follow through with notifying the patient or tracking referrals.
7. Primary care to specialist communication is essential for continuity of care.
8. Chart notes, while always important to good practice, may aid the defendant practitioner—especially when easy to read. If the efforts to contact the patient are documented and notes are easy to read, they will be easy for plaintiff's lawyers to read as well and may forestall a lawsuit. Conversely, illegible notes may hurt the defendant practitioner as the plaintiff's attorney may have to bring him or her to a deposition in order to interpret what may actually be an exculpatory note. Not an experience the practitioner wants to go through.

Failure to diagnose cancer is an increasing area of liability exposure for family practitioners and internists. The hectic pace of office practice, the large numbers of patient visits and calls received in an average week, as well as the torrent of paper and reports that comes into an office, makes it a challenge to prevent patients from "falling through the cracks."

CASE PRESENTATION

On January 14, 2003, Ms. Agness is a 40-year-old woman who comes to the office of her family practitioner/internist for an annual examination. During the visit, she tells her doctor, Dr. Bond, that she feels a lump in her left breast. She shows the doctor the location of what she feels is a lump and the doctor examines the area. Dr. Bond is not sure that he feels anything out of the ordinary. Although he elicits a medication history and verifies that Ms. Agness is not taking any hormonal medications, he fails to review her family history. The history would have indicated that Ms. Agness's mother had breast cancer at the age of 45. That history is in fact in the initial intake form Ms. Agness completed in 2000 when she first became a patient of Dr. Bond's, but Dr. Bond does not review this form at the January 2003 visit and doesn't remember this history.

Dr. Bond suggests that Ms. Agness go for a mammogram, although he tells her he does not find anything worrisome. Since her mother had breast cancer, Ms. Agness is eager to have the mammogram and makes the appointment in a timely fashion.

The requisition Dr. Bond gives to Ms. Agness indicates "lump in left breast" in the history section.

Ms. Agness has her mammogram done at Excellent Radiology on January 28, two weeks after her visit to Dr. Bond. The Radiology office intake form and report indicate "lump in left breast" and family history of breast cancer in the history section. The report indicates that there is an indeterminate finding in the left breast at 3 o'clock and that additional views and a sonogram should be done. The radiologist, Dr. Cook, also writes at the end of the report that 10% of cancers are not diagnosable by mammography and that any clinically suspicious mass should be biopsied.

The radiologist calls Dr. Bond's office with the request that Ms. Agness should return for additional studies. Dr. Bond was not in the office at the time the radiologist called; Dr. Cook gives the message to Dr. Bond's secretary who promises to give it to the doctor. The radiologist also faxes a handwritten preliminary report to Dr. Bond's office that reads "Mammogram is indeterminate, additional studies recommended."

The official mammogram report is received in Dr. Bond's office on February 3, 2003. In addition to the report, the radiologist indicates that a preliminary report was faxed to the office on January 28 and that he had called the office on the same day. The physician assistant, Ms. Debra, sees the report but is told by the secretary that the report was already faxed to the office and that she thinks Dr. Bond has already seen it. The PA initials the report and says it can be filed.

Ms. Agness calls Dr. Bond's office on February 4 and is told by the secretary that yes, they did receive the report and that she is sure the mammogram was fine, otherwise the doctor would have called her. The patient asks if she can speak to the doctor but is told he is making hospital rounds and is not in the office. She is asked to call back on the next day when the doctor is in the office. The doctor is not given the message that the radiologist or Ms. Agness called, does not remember that he sent Ms. Agness for a mammogram nor that she complained to him of a breast lump, and does not see the mammogram report, which has been put in the "To Be Filed" folder.

The patient assumes that since the secretary told her the mammogram must have been normal, and that the doctor did not call her, there must be nothing to worry about.

In August 2003, Ms. Agness returns to the office with an upper respiratory infection. She doesn't mention the breast lump; it just slipped her mind. The doctor does not review his last note (the one when the patient came for an annual exam) and the mammogram report is not in the patient's file. Since the patient came for a URI and did not mention anything about a breast lump, Dr. Bond does not perform a breast exam.

In January 2004, Ms. Agness returns to the office for her next annual exam. She says to Dr. Bond, "You know, doctor, that breast lump seems to be still there." Dr. Bond now palpates a lump about the size of a quarter in the patient's left breast. He immediately sends her to Excellent Radiology for another mammogram. A report is faxed to Dr. Bond's office that reads "Abnormal areas of calcifications and mass in the left breast at the 3 o'clock position. Suggest biopsy. Highly suspicious for carcinoma."

The radiologist also calls Dr. Bond and says he believes the mammogram is highly suspicious for cancer. He asks Dr. Bond if the patient ever went for additional views and sono as he had suggested in 2003. Dr. Bond says he never received that report. The radiologist offers to fax the 2003 report to him. When Dr. Bond sees the 2003 report, he realizes that not only had the 2003 report suggested further evaluation, it indicates that Dr. Cook had also called the office and faxed his preliminary report on the day of the 2003 mammogram.

The secretary calls Ms Agness and informs her that Dr. Bond wants her to see a surgeon because of the mammogram, though she tells Ms. Agness that she's sure it's nothing to worry about. Dr. Bond is quite busy and does not talk to Ms. Agness, either to give her the results of the mammogram or to emphasize the urgency of the consultation. No one in Dr. Bond's office calls the surgeon's office to give Ms. Agness's name, her mammogram results, or why she will be calling for an appointment.

Ms. Agness calls surgeon Dr. Engle in February and when she is asked why she's coming, she tells Dr. Engle's secretary it's something about her mammogram. Dr. Engle's secretary says the doctor is going on vacation for three weeks, and asks her if she wants to see his colleague, Dr. Fish. Ms. Agness says she'll wait until Dr. Engle returns, since it was Dr. Engle's name that Dr. Bond had given her and Dr. Bond's office had not given her the impression that the consultation was urgent. The next available appointment with Dr. Engle is in another month after his return.

Ms Agness is scheduled to see Dr. Engle in April, but her son is sick on the day of the scheduled appointment so she cancels. She has a hard time rescheduling as Dr. Engle is away teaching for a week and then is booked up for several more weeks. The patient remains unaware that there is any urgency in seeing Dr. Engle, so she tells the surgeon's secretary she will call back for an appointment.

No one from Dr. Bond's office calls Ms. Agness to see if she followed through with the surgical consultation. No one realizes that they have not received a call or letter from Dr. Engle.

In July, Ms. Agness returns with a urinary tract infection. She tells Dr. Bond's PA that she never got in to see Dr. Engle and asks the PA if she could check the breast area. There is an obvious mass in the left breast, which now measures 5×5 cm, and there is skin dimpling. The PA informs Dr. Bond who immediately sees the patient, examines the breast, and calls Dr. Engle himself. Dr. Engle, now hearing about this patient for the first time, agrees to see Ms. Agness that afternoon. A FNA (fine needle aspiration) is done in Dr Engle's office on the same day and reveals infiltrating duct carcinoma. Dr. Engle shortly thereafter performs an excision of the mass and an axillary dissection. The cancer is 5 cm in diameter and there are four positive axillary lymph nodes. Estrogen and progesterone receptors are negative. She is referred for chemotherapy and radiation therapy.

As soon as Dr. Engle informs Dr. Bond that his patient Ms. Agness has breast cancer, Dr. Bond's secretary searches and finds the original mammogram report misfiled in another patient's chart. Dr. Bond sees that the PA has initialed the 2003 report. Dr. Bond then initials the report himself and writes "Patient informed; referred for additional studies." He then pulls the 2004 mammogram, initials it, and writes "Patient informed, refer to surgeon for biopsy."

ISSUES

Introduction

Failure to diagnose cancer is the most common malpractice claim brought against internists and family practitioners, and failure to diagnose breast cancer is the most common of these claims. Part of the reason may be that the public—both plantiffs and jurors—has been educated about the importance of early detection of breast cancer and suspects that diagnosis at an advanced stage of disease must be due to negligence. Breast cancer may be diagnosed by screening mammography or after the patient or practitioner palpates an abnormality. Delay in diagnosis may be due to failure of practitioners to pursue breast complaints, to follow breast cancer screening guidelines, to track results of mammograms and referrals, and failure to refer patients for evaluation of breast masses in the setting of negative mammogram reports. Since in general breast cancers diagnosed early tend to be smaller and node negative (that is, to be in lower stages), and since the prognosis of breast cancer is related to the stage at diagnosis, the earlier the diagnosis is made, the better the patient's prognosis will be. Conversely, when patients are diagnosed late, and at later stages, a predictably poorer outcome can be expected. For example, the ten-year survival for a premenopausal woman like Ms. Agness is approximately 85% if diagnosed with stage I breast cancer (tumor <2 cm and negative axillary nodes) but falls to 56% for a tumor 5 cm and with four positive axillary nodes, even with adjuvant therapy.

The leading cause of physician delay in the diagnosis of breast cancer is inappropriate reassurance that a mass is benign without biopsy.[1] In failure to diagnose breast cancer cases most plaintiffs are young women and most often the woman herself discovered her own mass. Mammograms miss from 5% to 30% of breast cancers, especially in premenopausal women, whose breast tissue tends to be dense, obscuring details. The failure of practitioners to investigate a breast mass when the mammogram is negative is a major cause of error.

Review of Concepts

The following review of some pertinent legal concepts is described in detail in other chapters in this Handbook.

Preponderance of Evidence

In medical malpractice cases, as in all civil cases, the plaintiff does not have to prove her case beyond a reasonable doubt. Rather the judge will instruct the jury that the plaintiff must prove (with expert opinion) that the practitioner was negligent and that the negligence was responsible for the patient's damages by the preponderance of the evidence, that is, it is "reasonably probable" or "more likely than not" that the practitioner's negligence was a "substantial factor" in bringing about the injury.[2]

Standard of Care

In order to prevail, the plaintiff must first establish the appropriate medical standard of care and then prove that the practitioner departed from or failed to render care that meets that standard. A family practitioner/internist will be held to the standard of a reasonably prudent family practitioner/internist at the time of the incident in question, not to the standard that would be expected of, for example, a surgical oncologist or for changes in standards that occurred after the time of the malpractice. Many jurisdictions currently hold practitioners to a nationwide standard of care in their own fields of practice.

Proximate Cause

In addition to the practitioner's negligence or liability, the plaintiff also has to prove that the practitioner's negligence was causally linked to her injury. Proximate cause requires a showing that the harm suffered would not have occurred but for the action (or inaction) of the practitioner and that the harm was reasonably foreseeable as a natural and probable result of the practitioner's action (or inaction).

Where the practitioner was negligent, for example, by not acting on a mammogram report, but the patient's cancer was diagnosed shortly after the mammogram by some other means (such as the patient who refers herself to a surgeon), proximate cause is not met and the patient will not prevail against the original practitioner.

Loss of Chance

In many jurisdictions, the loss of chance doctrine is utilized; this requires only that the omission of proper care reduced the patient's chances and is employed when the traditional probability standard of causation is not met. Under this theory, the compensable injury is the lost opportunity to achieve a better result, not the physical harm caused by the patient's initial condition.[3] The doctrine is applied where, due to negligence, the diagnosis is not made in time for the patient to have a chance or a better chance of recovery or survival. In states that do recognize this cause of action, generally the patient must show that the lost chance amounted to a substantial possibility of survival or better recovery. This doctrine is most commonly applied to failure to diagnose cancer cases (see, for example, *Gagliardo v. Jamaica Hospital* and *Provos v. Hassam*), where the plaintiff will argue that his or her lost chance is statistically significant or that the lost chance was at least a 50% chance or a substantial chance of cure or survival.[4]

Clearly Dr. Bond was not responsible for Ms. Agness's original condition, that is, breast cancer. Rather, the plaintiff will argue that had she been diagnosed at the time she initially mentioned the breast lump she would have had an excellent prognosis and that through Dr. Bond's conduct her diagnosis and thus treatment was delayed 18 months, allowing her small cancer to grow in size and spread to multiple axillary lymph nodes. As a consequence, she will argue that that her prognosis is now much worse and she lost that chance for an excellent prognosis and cure.

Expert Medical Testimony

Expert medical testimony is virtually always required to draw the connection between the negligence of the defendant physician and the injury, and the medical expert must base his or her opinion as to proximate cause on a reasonable medical probability.[5]

Both the plaintiff and the defendant will present expert testimony at trial and it will be up to the finder of fact (usually a jury but in some cases a judge) to decide which expert is more credible.

Failure to Refer

Failure to refer when the practitioner lacks the expertise to appropriately treat a patient may create malpractice liability. Further, a practitioner who does not give the patient information about the potential consequences associated with not seeing a specialist may also be held liable.[6]

Comparative/Contributory Negligence

This concept involves the responsibility, or fault, of the plaintiff in a tort case. The plaintiff/patient has a duty to exercise the care that a reasonably prudent person would exercise in order to avoid an injury.[7] For example, if the patient negligently fails to follow through with referrals, recommendations, or treatment, she may be found liable in part for her injuries. The defendant has the burden of proving contributory or comparative negligence and must show that the plaintiff's negligence was a proximate, direct, efficient, and contributing cause of his or her own injuries. Contributory negligence that significantly contributes to the injury may bar (prevent) recovery. Most jurisdictions have abandoned a pure contributory negligence standard and instead have adopted some form of comparative negligence. Under this standard, the plaintiff's own negligence in failing to follow instructions may result in assignment of a percentage of fault to the plaintiff and a corresponding decrease in the amount of the award that is the responsibility of the defendant practitioner.[8]

Spoliation of Evidence

Spoliation, which is discussed in detail in Chapter 5, is the destruction of evidence or significant or meaningful alteration of a document or instrument. In medical malpractice cases, spoliation generally means absence or disappearance of medical records, x-rays, or other documents. A spoliation charge permits the judge to instruct the jury that they may find as a matter of law that the missing record contained information relevant to the medical care at issue, that the information was contrary to the position of the defendant at trial, and that the defendant willfully destroyed it. This charge results in a rebuttable presumption on the main issue of medical negligence and causation against the practitioner or even an irrebuttable, conclusive presumption of negligence.[9]

More Detailed Look: Traps for Practitioners

1. Failure to take patient complaints seriously (history should include precise location of lump, how discovered and when, any accompanying nipple discharge, pain, or tenderness, change in size of lump, and whether the lump, varies in size with the menstrual cycle).
2. Failure to verify patient complaint on physical exam (proper technique including examination with the patient in sitting and supine positions, documentation of the number of lesions if multiple, tenderness, density of mass, mobility, borders and diameter, examination of skin and axilla).
3. Failure to obtain family history or history of hormone or other drug therapy.
4. Failure to follow complaints to resolution or refer.
5. Failure to follow each physical exam finding to resolution or refer.
6. Failure to repeat exam at best phase of next menstrual cycle if ovulating.
7. Failure to communicate with patient/consultant.
8. Failure to document referral/results/consultations.
9. Failure to have knowledge of abnormal mammogram results.
10. Misinterpretation of abnormal findings on physical exam as benign.
11. Misinterpretation of breast lump with normal mammogram as benign.
12. Failure to consider sonography, especially in a woman younger than 35.
13. Failure to refer to specialist.
14. Failure to track referrals to radiologist or surgeon.
15. Failure to perform or arrange for biopsy.
16. If intervention is deferred, failure to establish clear follow-up plan.[10]

More Than the Primary Physician Involved

Radiologist Responsibility

The radiologist clearly documented his attempts to contact Dr. Bond's office about Ms. Agness's 2003 mammogram; he made a phone call to the office and left a message and also sent a fax with his preliminary report on the day he reviewed the mammogram. His typed report indicated his official interpretation and documented his contacts with Dr. Bond's office. This was good practice on his part. Unfortunately for Dr. Cook, he failed to notify the patient that her mammogram was not normal and that he recommended additional studies. Radiologists are expected to send to the patient a letter or note that indicates in layman's language the findings of the mammogram. The American College of Radiology (ACR) Practice

Guideline indicates that "the [mammography] facility shall send or give directly to all patients a written summary, in lay terms, of the results of the study no later than 30 days from the date of the mammographic examination."[11] This guideline is taken from the Federal Mammography Quality Standards Act, which requires that "each [mammography] facility shall send each patient a summary of the mammography report written in lay terms within 30 days of the mammographic examination. If assessments are 'Suspicious' or 'Highly suggestive of malignancy,' the facility shall make reasonable attempts to ensure that the results are communicated to the patient as soon as possible."[12] In this case, therefore, it was not sufficient for Dr. Cook to communicate with Dr. Bond's office; he was expected to send Ms. Agness a note indicating that additional studies were indicated. Since this was not done, Dr. Cook may share in the liability for the failure to diagnose Ms. Agness's breast cancer at an earlier stage of the disease.

Patient Responsibility

The defense will likely raise the issue of contributory or comparative negligence on the part of Ms. Agness, pointing to her failure to timely see a surgeon when she had been advised to do so. In all likelihood, Dr. Bond's misconduct will greatly outweigh any negligence on the part of Ms. Agness so that, at most, any negligence on her part would diminish her monetary recovery by a small percentage.

The situation is different, however, when a patient is clearly advised and counseled by the practitioner as to abnormalities or findings of importance about which some further investigation or referral is needed and the consequences of the patient's failing to comply. Such counseling is advisable and must be well documented in the patient's medical record and letters sent to the patient, return receipt requested. Such measures will go a long way toward lessening or even eliminating the practitioner's liability.

Secretary's Responsibility

Will Dr. Bond's secretary be responsible to Ms. Agness for her false reassurance about the results of the 2003 mammogram? And will she be responsible for misfiling Ms. Agness's mammogram?

Unfortunately for Dr. Bond, his secretary is not liable to Ms. Agness for medical malpractice, because she is not a physician. Actually, her inappropriately false reassurances to Ms. Agness and her misfiling of the mammogram will be attributed to Dr. Bond under agency principles. Dr. Bond should have a policy in place that the office staff shall not give results to patients unless directed by the physician. The office/practice must also have a system for tracking referrals and reports and ensuring that reports are not filed until they have been seen and initialed or signed by the physician.

Physician Assistant

Physician assistants are health care professionals licensed to practice medicine with physician supervision. As part of their comprehensive responsibilities, PAs conduct physical exams, diagnose and treat illnesses, order and interpret tests, counsel on preventive health care, assist in surgery, and in virtually all states can write prescriptions. The supervising physician is ultimately responsible for coordinating and managing the care of patients. The physician and PA together should review all delegated patient services on a regular basis as well as the mutually agreed upon guidelines for practice.[13] While in most cases PAs are covered under their employer's malpractice policy, PAs may still be liable for their own negligence and thus may be liable for all or part of a plaintiff's award or settlement. PAs may carry individual malpractice insurance.[14]

Will Dr. Bond's PA be responsible to Ms Agness for initialing the 2003 mammogram report and permitting it to be filed without Dr. Bond seeing it? Since PAs work directly under physician supervision, Dr. Bond will likely be responsible for the PA's negligence. However, if Dr. Bond had a clear policy that the PA must review all reports and patients with him, the PA could be personally responsible if he or she departed from that policy. In addition, PAs often have their own malpractice insurance, and a plaintiff's attorney will likely be able to discover this coverage, making it more likely that the PA will be named. If the plaintiff is successful in her malpractice suit, a percentage of the fault may be assigned to the PA.

Nurse Practitioner

Nurse practitioners are registered nurses with advanced academic and clinical experience, which enables them to diagnose and manage most common and many chronic illnesses, either independently or as part of a health care team.[15] Practice agreements include provisions for referral and consultation and periodic review of patient records by the collaborating physician; practice protocols identify the area of practice to be performed by the NP in collaboration with the physician.

SURVIVAL STRATEGIES
Alteration of Medical Records

This is a most serious issue in the case of Ms. Agness. Dr. Bond should not have written anything on the original mammogram reports to give the impression that he knew about the findings in 2003 and 2004 and had acted upon them.

All entries in patient records must be signed and dated with the date on which they were written. Changes in the medical record should be made with care, and the actual date on which a late entry or correction is made must always be indicated.

Failure to Follow Up on Test Results and Referrals

A system for tracking test results and referrals is necessary. This can be as simple as a notebook or as complex as a computerized system that gives a warning when a report or referral is not received within a certain period of time. Patients can be asked to call the office for test results, but this practice requires motivated patients and does not relieve the physician of his or her obligation to track down results and contact the patient in the case of abnormal results. These are not easy issues in a busy practice. Patients should not assume that if they have not heard from the office, their results are normal, and telling patients this is risky from a malpractice standpoint.

FURTHER READING

Barton MB, Elmore JG, Fletcher SW, *Breast Symptoms Among Women Enrolled in a Health Maintenance Organization: Frequency, Evaluation and Outcome*. Ann. Intern. Med. 130:651–657 (1999).

Dovey SM, Meyers DS, Phillips RL, Green LA, Fryer GE, Galliher JM, Kappus J, *A Preliminary Taxonomy of Medical Errors in Family Practice*. Qual. Saf. Health Care 11:233–238 (2002).

Goodson WH, Moore DH, *Causes of Physician Delay in the Diagnosis of Breast Cancer*. Arch. Intern. Med. 162:1343–1348 (2002).

Kerlikowske K, Smith-Bindman R, Ljung, B-M, Grady D, *Evaluation of Abnormal Mammography Results and Palpable Breast Abnormalities*. Ann. Intern. Med. 139(4):274–284 (2003).

Kuzel AJ, Woolf SH, Gilchrist VJ, Engel JD, LaVeist TA, Vincent C, Frankel RM, *Patient Reports of Preventable Problems and Harms in Primary Care*. Ann. Family Med. 2(4):333–340 (2004).

Levinson W, Roter DL, Mullooly JP, Dull VT, Frankel RM, *Physician-Patient Communication: The Relationship with Malpractice Claims Among Primary Care Physicians and Surgeons*. JAMA 277(7):553–559 (1997).

Osuch JR, Bonham VL, *The Timely Diagnosis of Breast Cancer: Principles of Risk Management for Primary Care Providers and Surgeons*. Cancer 74(1 Suppl): 271–278 (1994).

Poon EG, Gandhi TK, Sequist TD, Murff HJ, Karson AH, Bates DW, *"I Wish I Had Seen This Test Result Earlier!": Dissatisfaction with Test Result Management Systems in Primary Care*. Arch. Intern. Med. 164:2223–2228 (2004).

Richards MA, Westcombe AM, Love SB, Littlejohns P, Ramirez AJ, *Influence of Delay on Survival in Patients with Breast Cancer: A Systematic Review*. The Lancet 353:1119–1126 (1999).

Shandell RE, Smith P, *The Preparation and Trial of Medical Malpractice Cases*. Law Journal Press, 2005.

Tabar L, Duffy SW, Vitak B, Chen H-H, Prevost TC, *The Natural History of Breast Carcinoma: What Have We Learned from Screening?* Cancer 86(3): 449–462 (1999).

Gagliardo v. Jamaica Hospital, 288 A.D. 2d, 179, 732 N.Y.S. 2d 353 (2nd Dept. App. Div. N.Y., 2001).

Provos v. Hassam, 256 A.D. 2d 583, 437 N.Y.S. 2d 820 (3rd Dept. App. Div. N.Y., 1998).

Mammography Quality Standards Act, 42 U.S.C. §263b (1999); see also 21 C.F.R. §§900.1–900.9.

REFERENCES

1. Goodson WH, Moore DH, *Causes of Physician Delay in the Diagnosis of Breast Cancer*. Arch. Intern. Med. 162:1343–1348 (2002).

2. Shandell RE, Smith P, *The Preparation and Trial of Medical Malpractice Cases*. Law Journal Press, 2005, pp. 1-19–1-26.

3. Id., pp. 1-26–1-28.1.

4. Liang BA, *Health Law and Policy: A Survival Guide to Medicolegal Issues for Practitioners*. Butterworth-Heinemann, 2000, p. 20.

5. Shandell, p. 1-28.1.

6. Id., p. 19.

7. Id., p. 1-28.7.

8. Id., pp. 1-11–1-28.18.

9. Id., p. 1-26.

10. Osuch JR, Bonham VL, *The Timely Diagnosis of Breast Cancer: Principles of Risk Management for Primary Care Providers and Surgeons*. Cancer 74(1 Suppl): 271–278 (1994).

11. American College of Radiology, *Practice Guideline for the Performance of Diagnostic Mammography*, revised 2002, effective January 1, 2003.

12. Mammography Quality Standards Act of 1992 amended 2002, 67 F.R. 5446.

13. American Academy of Physician Assistants, http://www.aapa.org/geninfo1.html, accessed November 23, 2005.

14. Id., at http://www.aapa.org/gandp/risky.html, accessed November 23, 2005.

15. American College of Nurse Practitioners web site, http://www.nurse.org/acnp/facts/whatis.shtnl.

Clinical and Forensic Pathology

Cyril H. Wecht, M.D., J.D., F.C.L.M.

CASE PRESENTATIONS

Case 1. In May 1982, the surgeon removed a lump from behind a patient's knee, which was assumed to be a Baker's cyst. During the operation, a frozen section was reported as benign. Several days later, the pathologist returned from an absence and examined the tissue microscopically. He reported in writing that the mass was a benign neurilemoma.

On December 6, 1982, the patient reported to the surgeon that she was experiencing swelling at the operative site. He examined her and told her to return in a month.

In January 1983, the surgeon wrote to the pathologist, asking him to review the slides again. The pathologist personally assured the patient that the tumor was benign.

On February 24, 1983, a surgeon at a second hospital removed two tumors from the patient's knee. They were diagnosed as malignant. Pathologists at this hospital reviewed the previous slides and concluded that the mass removed in May 1982 was a malignant schwannoma. The patient's leg was amputated above the knee.

On February 14, 1985, the patient filed a malpractice action against the first pathologist, the hospital, and others. Because the lawsuit was filed more than two years after the initial surgery on December 6, 1982, the trial court granted summary judgment for the hospital and physicians.

On appeal, the patient contended that the statute of limitations did not begin to run until the termination of the first surgeon's continuous course of treatment, which occurred when he referred her to the surgeon at the second hospital, on February 15, 1983. The court agreed that the continuing course of treatment applied to the surgeon. However, the patient's claim was not against the surgeon.

The appellate court agreed that the surgeon's course of treatment should be imputed to the pathologist. It was the surgeon's adherence to the pathologist's diagnosis that dictated the nature and duration of treatment.

The court said that until the alleged misdiagnosis was corrected or the surgeon ceased to rely on it, the pathologist's constructive involvement in the treatment was sufficient to constitute the required assistance or association to prevent the running of the statute of limitations. Thus, the court found that the patient's claim against the pathologist and her vicarious liability claim against the hospital were not barred by the statute of limitations.[1]

Case 2. A compensatory damages award of $135,000 for emotional suffering was not excessive in the decedent's family's action against a medical examiner who exceeded the scope of his authorization by removing the decedent's heart during the autopsy without permission. Each member of the decedent's family testified about the effect that the discovery of the unauthorized removal had on them, including physical illness, uncontrollable crying, nightmares, and familial tension that culminated in a family member moving out of the family home.[2]

Case 3. Evidence supported a jury's award of $3.5 million in a survival action against a pathology lab whose purported negligent interpretation and reporting of the results of a patient's postpartum Pap smears allegedly resulted in the failure to discover her cancer when she had a 95% chance of survival. The patient spent seven months engaged in a painful battle for her life, which she knew from the beginning she would lose. In addition to the excruciating physical pain she suffered, she endured the mental anguish of spending the last several months of her life unable to care for her two small children. The evidence further demonstrated her consternation over the loss of a normal relationship with her husband.[3]

MISDIAGNOSIS OF SURGICAL SPECIMENS

The misdiagnosis of a surgical specimen by a pathologist does not automatically indicate that malpractice has occurred. The possibility of malpractice should be viewed against the following widely accepted criteria:

1. To render a correct diagnosis, the pathologist must first determine the adequacy of the tissue sample submitted, and ensure that it is representative of the suspected disease process. If specimen adequacy is questionable, this should be discussed with the submitting physician, and further samples should be submitted prior to rendering a diagnosis. A failure to do so may result in a finding of malpractice against the pathologist.
2. In examining the specimen, it is the responsibility of the pathologist to correlate the tissue findings with all other clinical data, laboratory findings, and radiology findings. If inconsistencies are present, they should be resolved prior to issuing a diagnosis. Failure to do so may result in a finding of malpractice against the pathologist.
3. If in the course of routine evaluation a diagnosis of the specimen cannot be reached without the use of special testing techniques and additional studies, these must be employed prior to issuing a final diagnosis. Failure to utilize fully all necessary testing may be grounds for malpractice.
4. The issuance of a final diagnosis should be based on standardized histologic criteria. The failure to employ these criteria may result in malpractice.
5. In the event that some doubt exists about the final diagnosis, it is the responsibility of the pathologist to consult with other pathologists regarding the true nature of the disease process present.

Even though a consensus diagnosis is reached, the final report should include alternative diagnoses expressed as dissenting opinions, along with the reasons given by the dissenters in support of their findings. This will serve to alert the attending physician to the possibility of other diagnoses. A failure to consult and to provide all diagnostic possibilities may result in malpractice.

Misdiagnosis of Frozen Sections

The misdiagnosis of frozen section tissue slides may result in a malpractice action against the pathologist if there are findings that indicate negligence based on items 1 through 4 above. It is not uncommon to be unable to make a diagnosis on frozen section slides, and to have to defer final diagnosis until permanent sections are prepared. This failure to reach a diagnosis on frozen section examination results from the inherent weakness of the frozen section method as compared to the permanent section method.

Benign Versus Malignant Tumors: Classification, Grading, and Staging of Malignant Tumors

The failure to differentiate between benign and malignant tumors may result in a successful malpractice action against the anatomic pathologist if it is found that there was an incorrect diagnosis. If reasonable care has been taken, and none of the special circumstances listed is found to exist, it is unlikely that malpractice will be found.

The correct classification, grade, and stage of a malignant tumor can significantly influence both the degree and extent of surgical intervention and type of postoperative therapy. The failure to provide this information correctly can result in a finding of liability against the anatomic pathologist if it can be proved that the correct information would have resulted in an improved therapeutic outcome.

Failure to Consult Other Pathologists

Where the pathologist cannot adequately establish a diagnosis, there is a clear need to consult with other pathologists. Failure to do so can be malpractice. Additionally, if an incorrect diagnosis was established on a specimen that is not normally within the range of expertise of the pathologist, and it can be shown that there was a clear need for the specimen to be evaluated by a particular specialist, a malpractice action also may be well grounded.

Failure to Recognize an Inadequate Specimen

The failure to recognize the inadequacy of the tissue slide being evaluated can result in negative findings in otherwise malignant tissue. This can cause a delay in treatment and present a risk to the patient. It also could suggest a failure on the part of the pathologist to correlate anatomic findings with clinical impressions.

Failure to Communicate with the Surgeon in a Timely and Proper Manner

On receipt of a surgical specimen for evaluation, the pathologist assumes the responsibility of providing the submitting surgeon with a diagnosis in a timely and proper manner. The failure to do so can result in a delay in starting treatment, and thus subject the patient to an increased risk. If the pathologist is unable to reach a diagnosis, this information should be transmitted to the surgeon, along with any information available about the tissue. In some cases a provisional diagnosis can be rendered pending final results of other studies. In no case should the surgeon be expected to wait for an extended period of time without receiving some communication from the pathologist.

Failure to Resolve Conflicting Diagnoses

In the event two sequentially excised portions of the same lesion present different diagnoses, it is the responsibility of the pathologist to resolve and adequately explain this finding. A failure to do so is a deviation from the standards of good practice, and could result in a successful malpractice action.

Failure to Report Revised Findings

There will be cases in which a revised report must be issued because of supplemental findings. It is the responsibility of the pathologist to ensure that the surgeon is fully informed of any changes in findings and the reasons for such changes. Failure to do so can delay proper treatment and can be grounds for malpractice.

CYTOLOGY STUDIES

Misdiagnosis of a Cytology Preparation

The standards governing the diagnosis of Pap smears or other cytology preparations closely parallel those governing the diagnosis of surgical specimens. Additionally, the pathologist has direct responsibility for the actions of the cytotechnologists in his or her employ, and the cytotechnologists can be held to the same general standards of professional conduct as the pathologist.

In cytology, one is presented with cells that are not only benign and malignant, but cells that are classified "atypical." A failure to distinguish between the three categories of cells can result in malpractice. Incorrect negative findings can delay additional investigative procedures and possibly the diagnosis of cancer or other significant pathologic conditions.

The classification and grading of cytology specimens present a situation similar to that relating to malignant tumors. The failure to make classifications based on standardized histopathologic features can result in a finding of negligence.

In the event that the classification of a cytology smear is in question, the pathologist has a responsibility to consult with other pathologists in an attempt to reach a diagnosis. The same rules that apply to surgical specimens will apply to cytology preparations, and similar findings of negligence can result from the failure to consult.

Since the cytology specimen, for the most part, is obtained noninvasively, specimens that prove inadequate for proper evaluation should be resubmitted for repeat testing. It is the responsibility of the pathologist to inform the attending physician of the inadequacy of the specimen, and the need for a repeat test. This request should be explained in writing.

The failure to provide cytology test results in a timely and proper manner can create the same problems as the failure to provide the same information on surgical specimens.

The pathologist's duty to resolve a quandary in cytology smears is virtually the same as in the case of different diagnoses obtained in sequentially excised portions of a surgical lesion.

The identification of specific infectious microorganisms can be relevant in certain cytology smears (especially the Pap smear), and the failure to properly identify these organisms can result in the delay of treatment. A successful malpractice action can be brought against the pathologist if these organisms are not identified and the pathologic process is allowed to reach advanced stages because of lack of treatment caused by this diagnostic failure.

AUTOPSIES
Misdiagnosis of Disease Processes

Although the cases are far from common, the misdiagnosis of disease processes at autopsy can result in a malpractice action against the pathologist. For example, the pathologist finds at autopsy that a patient has died of pneumonia. Later, a family member of the deceased develops tuberculosis, and it is discovered that what has been diagnosed by the pathologist as pneumonia was actually pneumonia secondary to tuberculosis.

The misdiagnosis of injuries also can lead to a malpractice action against the pathologist. For example, while performing an autopsy on a burn victim, the pathologist finds evidence of skull fractures and brain hemorrhage, in addition to the findings associated with the thermal injuries. The pathologist concludes that the death resulted from the skull fracture, and as a result homicide charges are filed against a suspect. However, testimony presented at trial showed that the skull facture was in reality an artifactual injury caused by the intense heat of the fire.

The above-cited situation could occur in reverse. By mistake, a pathologist could overlook evidence of a homicide, and in theory a legal action could be considered by a family member of the deceased.

Mistaking postmortem artifacts for an antemortem finding also could lead to the failure to diagnose an accident, and result in a malpractice action against the pathologist.

Pathophysiologic Processes

The failure on the part of the pathologist to recognize postmortem artifacts, and instead attribute them to antemortem processes, has led to charges of negligence. For example, an individual was discovered dead in a swimming pool. On autopsy, it was found that the deceased had sustained injuries consistent with strangulation. The pathologist's finding was death by homicide, and a suspect was arrested. During the criminal trial, testimony was introduced that in the process of recovering the deceased's body from the swimming pool, the police dragged it out of the water with a pole and a strap around the neck. The cause of death was changed to accidental, and the accused suspect brought suit against the pathologist.

The failure on the part of the pathologist to identify infectious or communicable diseases and notify interested parties can result in liability.

Failure to diagnose certain genetic central nervous system disorders in deceased newborns can lead the parents of the deceased child into a false sense of security with regard to future pregnancies. Should additional children suffer the same fate, the parents would have grounds for malpractice against the pathologist who performed the initial autopsy.

The pathologist's failure to recognize certain disease processes as having been caused by industrial or environmental exposure could lead to charges of negligence. An example would be a finding at autopsy of mesothelioma, a type of lung malignancy. Failure to recognize that this condition arose as a result of exposure to asbestos (a common cause of this cancer) could result in litigation against the pathologist.

MALPRACTICE: CLINICAL PATHOLOGY

Hematology

The improper collection or preservation of specimens needed for hematologic analysis can result in serious problems. One of the most common errors is a failure to obtain an adequately anticoagulated specimen to be used for a complete blood count (CBC). The failure to properly anticoagulate the specimen will result in the specimen containing many small clots. When this is subjected to analysis, the result may be an incorrect diagnostic impression that may lead to therapeutic measures that would not otherwise be called for.

A failure on the part of the hematology section to recognize specimens that have been improperly preserved can result in misinterpretation of the final results. The problem of specimen preservation is of particular concern to the non-hospital-based laboratory, or the hospital laboratory that accepts specimens from distant sites. In many cases, individuals obtaining the specimens may not be aware of proper preservation techniques. It is the responsibility of the testing laboratory to provide guidelines to collection sites, and to recognize the characteristics of a specimen that may have been improperly preserved. In all cases where specimen quality is questionable, the testing laboratory should make appropriate notations to this effect on the final report.

The incorrect labeling of a specimen collected for any test performed in the hematology laboratory can have serious consequences that could lead to liability for negligence. It is the responsibility of the testing laboratory to provide specific identification procedures and protocols to ensure that proper specimen identification is made. While the specific protocol will vary from laboratory to laboratory, the general principles remain the same. The patient's name should be clearly printed on the specimen, the date and time of specimen collection should be present on the request form that accompanies the specimen, and the initials of the individual collecting the specimen should appear on the request form. In the case of hospitalized patients, the laboratory technician should confirm the patient's identity by checking the information on the request form with the patient's identification band.

Even if all protocols are followed, errors will still occur; these errors, however, should be detectable if proper protocols have been established.

Errors in labeling can result in necessary treatment being withheld and unnecessary treatment being given. In some cases the result can be relatively harmless, as where the specimens of two normal individuals are mislabeled. The more serious the error, the greater the likelihood that it will be detected, since the patient's radical change in condition will not be supported by the results obtained.

The incorrect interpretation of tests in the hematology laboratory can result in inappropriate therapeutic measures being instituted. In some cases, incorrect follow-up testing may be ordered as a result of the initial error. This will result in further delay in recognizing the actual pathologic process that is occurring.

The hematology laboratory has a responsibility in some instances to indicate to a physician that additional or different testing may be required. For example, in the case of an anemic patient who clearly presents a pattern consistent with macrocytic anemia, the laboratory has a responsibility to see that the attending physician orders follow-up testing for both vitamin B_{12} and folic acid deficiencies. If the physician chooses only to test for folic acid deficiency, the laboratory should advise the physician that vitamin B_{12} deficiency can result in a very similar anemia, and that the test for B_{12} is clearly indicated. If the physician declines to test for the B_{12}, the laboratory should document this fact.

Another example might involve a physician who orders a hemoglobin and hematocrit determination on a patient. The testing laboratory, as a matter of policy, would likely perform this test on an instrument that provides several other tests, including a white blood cell (WBC) count. The WBC count is found to be greatly elevated, and appears to be consistent with a severe infection. Even though the only test ordered was the hemoglobin and hematocrit, the laboratory should inform the physician of the coincidental finding because it could significantly alter the treatment of the patient.

Failure to Recognize Special Disease Characteristics

In acting as the testing agent for the attending physician, the hematology laboratory assumes the full responsibility for providing all relevant information that can be obtained from the test that has been ordered; this includes the recognition of unusual disease processes. By way of illustration, consider a patient with an intermittent fever and night sweats. As a part of the routine investigation, a complete blood count and white cell differential are ordered. The laboratory completes the tests and uncovers no unusual findings. The patient undergoes additional diagnostic measures, and only then does it become known that the patient has just returned from an endemic malaria zone. A blood smear for malarial parasites is requested, and proves to be positive. A review of the initially ordered blood film is conducted, and malarial parasites are identified. The testing laboratory can be held liable, even though malaria is not a common disease and is not frequently identified. A missed diagnosis has occurred, and the patient may have suffered as a result.

Venipuncture Trauma

Litigation can arise as a result of obtaining blood from a vein (venipuncture). The most likely problems involve: (1) local infections following venipuncture; (2) thrombophlebitis following venipuncture; and (3) injuries resulting from fainting following venipuncture.

In the case of infection, the most relevant issue is the sterilization technique used prior to and during the process of obtaining the specimen. How was the venipuncture site prepared prior to puncture? Also, was more than one puncture attempted with the same needle? Specific written laboratory policies should be available for inspection.

The complication of thrombophlebitis also involves technique. How many attempts should the laboratory technician make to obtain a suitable specimen before the benefits of obtaining the test are outweighed by the potential harm to the patient? Was the attending physician contacted for an opinion on this issue? Was the patient questioned prior to the collection procedure about unexpected bleeding tendencies that might require special precautions? Is this documented? Was the patient receiving any medication that might result in unexpected bleeding? Was he questioned on this point?

With regard to injuries that result from a patient fainting, one should inquire about the collection site where the venipuncture occurred. What type of seating was provided? Was the patient assisted in getting off the table? Was the patient questioned about the outcome of previous venipuncture experiences? Was this documented?

Failure to Correlate Test Results with Clinical History and Previous Tests

The failure on the part of the hematology laboratory to correlate test results with the patient's clinical history and previous test results invites a malpractice action. Failure in this area often causes other errors to go undiscovered, for example, in specimen collection, labeling, diagnostic misinterpretation, and failure to recognize special disease characteristics.

Additionally, the failure to compare current tests with the patient's earlier tests and clinical history can result in the failure to recognize new disease processes that might be developing, which could have an important bearing upon the therapeutic measures being used.

Failure to Report Test Results in a Timely Manner

It is of little consequence that a test has been properly performed and carefully correlated with the patient's previous test results and clinical history if the current test result does not reach the attending physician in time to institute appropriate treatment. The amount of time that can elapse between the beginning of the testing procedure and the final reporting of the test result will vary greatly depending on the complexity of the test and the urgency of the request. In some instances, up to 48 hours is acceptable, but in other cases 30 minutes may be excessive. It is the responsibility of the testing laboratory to provide all test results in the most timely manner possible, and notification of the physician should occur in a manner that is appropriate to the medical urgency of the result.

Consider two patients who have had the same test requested by the same physician. Both individuals are seen in an outpatient setting, and the physician requests that a CBC be performed on both. The first patient shows a mild anemia, probably iron deficiency, and no other abnormalities. While these constitute abnormal results, it is considered acceptable merely to see that the physician receives the results within 24 hours. The CBC on the second patient reveals that the patient has a markedly reduced platelet count, with no other abnormalities. In the second case, 24 hours is much too long to wait. In this case, an immediate telephone call to the physician is indicated. Failure to do so could subject the testing laboratory to a successful malpractice action.

Each individual test should be evaluated at the laboratory, and a "panic value" should be established. A panic value is a numeric point at which the patient is considered at serious risk of suffering life-threatening injury if their condition does not receive immediate medical attention. Values that fall into this category should be immediately transmitted to the attending physician. The laboratory should document the transmission of this information to the physician with specific notations as to the time of the reporting.

Urinalysis

Improper collection and preservation of specimens obtained for urinalysis can result in the tests being invalid and the attending physician being misled as to the proper treatment for the patient. There are many formed elements in the urine that can deteriorate if improperly preserved. Failure to detect these elements can result in a diagnosis not being established. Similarly, the chemical constituents of the urine can be broken down and not detected, leading to a delay in diagnosis and clinical problems. The general guidelines governing urinalysis are similar to those applicable to the collection and preservation of blood.

The failure to obtain a sterile specimen can result in the misdiagnosis of bacterial infection. This can be a particular problem in the outpatient setting where a catheterized specimen is not obtained. One must rely on the patient to collect the specimen in an acceptable manner, and this is not always done because of the failure of the testing laboratory to adequately instruct the patient. This frequently results in the physician establishing a diagnosis of bacterial infection, when in fact the bacteria seen were merely a contaminant resulting from poor collection procedures.

The labeling and identification of urine specimens should be as stringent as those for blood. The diagnostic significance is no less important than that of the most sophisticated hematology test.

The potential for error in urine testing is much less than in other areas because there are fewer tests, and their interpretation is much less complex. There can still be problems in interpretation, however. One of the constituents in a routine test is the evaluation of protein. The finding of a positive urine protein can result from many pathologic and benign conditions, and yet in many cases the cause of this abnormality is left uninvestigated. This can lead to a delay in the diagnosis of potentially damaging kidney diseases. The same basic principles with respect to a laboratory's general duty to inform and advise the attending physician are applicable here.

The urine testing section of a clinical laboratory has the same responsibility to recognize and identify uncommon or unusual disease conditions as the hematology section. These conditions will most commonly be found during the microscopic examination of the urine sediment in characteristic but unusually formed elements. Examples would include tumor cells that have been shed into the urine from a urinary tract tumor, and amino acid crystals in patients suffering from inborn errors of amino acid metabolism.

A special problem exists regarding proof in these cases. Since the specimen usually is disposed of once testing is completed, there is no practical method of proving that the formed element in question actually existed in the specimen when evaluated.

A failure to correlate current test results with the patient's clinical history and previous urinalysis tests will result in problems similar to those discussed with other pathologic specimens.

Urinalysis test results need to be reported in a timely manner just as blood tests, although numeric trigger values for immediate reporting of abnormal results are not used. A series of general guidelines is used instead. A finding of tumor cells in a urine specimen would most certainly constitute a finding of sufficient importance to warrant an immediate notification of the attending physician, while the finding of formed elements consistent with a mild urinary tract infection would not, and routine communication channels would suffice.

Chemistry Tests

Improper collection or preservation of specimens by the chemistry section of a clinical laboratory present a group of problems not unlike those discussed regarding hematology. However, these problems can be much more serious because of the greater variety of testing done in the chemistry section. Each test should be accompanied by specific guidelines established for proper collection and preservation, and a failure to adhere to these guidelines can result in serious diagnostic errors.

Specific areas of concern include the time of the specimen collection, when the patient last ate, quality of the specimen obtained (non-hemolyzed), medications that could interfere with the test method in use, postcollection handling procedures, and many others.

In investigating a misdiagnosis arising from an erroneous chemistry test, it is essential that the investigation include a review of the collection and preservation policies and procedures of the laboratory. The specificity and highly individualized nature of those tests cannot be overemphasized. What is a perfectly acceptable specimen for a given chemistry test in one laboratory may prove to be totally inappropriate in a second laboratory, even though the test being performed is the same.

The discussion of the consequences of incorrect specimen labeling of blood is equally applicable in chemistry testing. An additional problem is the need to split the specimen to allow multiple tests on the same sample. This increases the chance of mislabeling, and specific criteria must be established and adhered to by laboratory personnel to reduce this risk.

With the current availability of so many possible chemical tests, the opportunity for incorrect selection or misinterpretation of a given test has been greatly increased. It is the responsibility of both the patient's physician and the testing laboratory to select the correct tests and correctly interpret the results. A failure to do so places both parties at risk of being found liable for a resulting therapeutic failure. In addition to the large array of tests now available, new and improved versions of old tests are being introduced. The courts have generally held that once a newer technology gains wide acceptance, it is the responsibility of the physician to use this technology in keeping with acceptable standards of care.

Test interpretation is complex. With any set of basic chemistry tests, the possible number of patterns that can be seen becomes astronomical. Selecting the correct follow-up tests from initial findings also can be difficult, and as a result there is a tendency to overorder tests to ensure that no possible situation is missed. Follow-up testing is more the responsibility of the laboratory, because most physicians will order the correct basic tests. Similarly, the laboratory that fails to inform the clinician of new methodologies runs the risk of liability for resulting misdiagnoses.

The failure of the chemistry section of a clinical laboratory to recognize and diagnose special disease processes results in problems similar to those encountered by the other sections of the laboratory.

Failure to correlate chemistry test results with the patient's clinical history and prior test results carries the same risks of liability faced by other departments of the clinical laboratory, only more so. It is not uncommon for an individual patient to have the same test repeated several times in a 24-hour period. The intent of the repeat testing usually is to monitor the progress of therapeutic measures being taken. It can be difficult to correlate previous results with current results for a patient on therapy. Values can change rapidly and dramatically, and every attempt must be made to consider how this therapy will influence the results being obtained. In these cases, the documentation is extremely important in determining possible negligence.

Failure to report chemistry test results in a timely manner involves problems similar to those in hematology. The so-called "panic values" are employed to indicate the need for immediate notification of the attending physician. The failure to report life-threatening values can be viewed as negligent.

Microbiology

Improper collection and preservation of specimens submitted for testing by the microbiology section of the clinical laboratory can have serious consequences. Since microbiology deals with the recovery and identification of microorganisms, it is essential that the specimens be collected properly. Failure to collect and preserve the specimens properly will result in nonviable organisms reaching the laboratory, with the end result being no growth on culture media and a subsequent failure to isolate and identify infective agents. This failure to isolate and identify causative organisms will result in a delay in instituting the proper antibiotic therapy, and in severe infections can lead to the patient's demise. It is the responsibility of the microbiology section to ensure that proper collection and preservation protocols are established, and that the proper collection equipment is available and correctly used.

Microbiology is unlike other sections of the laboratory in that many of the specimens are collected by other than laboratory personnel. Where the adequacy or appropriateness of a specimen is questionable, this information should be clearly included in the record transmitted to the attending physician.

In addition to the specimen labeling precautions that laboratory personnel should observe generally, the microbiology section must additionally concern itself with proper identification of the site of culture collection. The site of collection directly influences the types of organisms that are sought, and the type of culture techniques that are used. In other words, one does not culture a throat specimen in the same manner one cultures a puncture wound. The puncture wound would be cultured for both aerobic and anaerobic organisms, while the throat specimen would be cultured for aerobic organisms only. The failure to identify a wound correctly could result in not finding a significant pathogenic organism, which could result in serious consequences for the patient.

Errors that can cause a misinterpretation of culture results include failure to identify the pathogenic organism, failure to interpret the results of antibiotic sensitivity testing, failure to identify mixed cultures of multiple pathogenic organisms, and similar occurrences.

Incorrect results also can arise from the use of inappropriate culture techniques and culture media for the site under investigation. Furthermore, failure to evaluate plates at the correct time intervals can result in overgrowth of pathogenic organisms by so-called normal flora, and failure to observe cultures for a sufficiently long period of time might result in slow-growing organisms not being identified.

It is the responsibility of the microbiology section to recognize organisms that are currently considered major infective agents. The ability to recognize these agents must be made available to physicians. An example is best illustrated by the activity that ensued following the deaths of several individuals from what was eventually designated as Legionnaire's disease. When the disease first appeared, no one was aware of the causative agent, and thus no blame for failure to recognize it could be established. However, now that the causative agent has been identified and characterized, and appropriate culture techniques have been developed, a failure to recognize the relatively rare disease could constitute negligence on the part of a microbiology section.

The failure to collect a sterile specimen for the microbiology laboratory can result in the finding of a bacterial infection that in reality does not exist. This can result in the inappropriate, and perhaps harmful, treatment of a patient with antibiotics. While antibiotics are commonly used, their use is not without risk. This is especially true of the newer aminoglycoside antibiotics that carry the risk of renal damage and ototoxicity. Additionally, the failure of a microbiology laboratory to recognize the characteristics of non-sterile specimens can result in delay in obtaining properly collected specimens, and may thus delay the identification of serious pathogenic organisms.

The potential for liability resulting from the microbiology section's failure to correlate test results with the patient's clinical history and previous microbiology tests is similar to that encountered in the other sections of the clinical laboratory.

The problems created by the lack of timely reporting of results obtained in the microbiology section of the laboratory most closely parallel those found in the urinalysis section. There is no numeric data generated, and generally a listing of specific circumstances that require immediate notification is used. In the case of certain organisms, such as tuberculosis bacillus, a great deal of time may be required for growth to occur in the culture. The patient may have long since been discharged from the hospital. It remains the responsibility of the microbiology section to see that the attending physician is notified of positive findings, so that appropriate measures can be instituted. It is not sufficient to assume that the physician will remember to follow up every discharged patient's test to see that the final culture results are negative.

The microbiology section of the clinical laboratory is required to report certain infectious organisms to the public health authorities. These requirements normally are dictated by state law.

Immunology and Serology

Improper collection or preservation of specimens obtained for testing by the immunology and serology sections involves the same risks incurred by other departments of the laboratory.

The incorrect labeling of specimens collected for the immunology and serology sections carries risks similar to those described for other areas of the laboratory.

Testing done in the immunology and serology sections of the laboratory is for antibodies that have a long-term persistence in the body. In most cases, this allows one to prove or disprove errors in interpretation through repeated testing. This is particularly true in syphilis tests, where a positive test result can have serious psychological and social consequences for the individual. (If the test was done incorrectly or misinterpreted, it is a relatively simple matter to prove through repeated testing, because a true positive test for syphilis will remain positive for a long time.)

The failure of the immunology and serology sections to recognize and diagnose special disease processes poses problems similar to those found in the other areas of the laboratory.

The problems that can arise from the failure of the immunology and serology sections to correlate testing with the patient's clinical history and previous test results do not differ from those of other sections of the laboratory.

The failure to report testing done in the immunology and serology sections in a timely manner will have consequences similar to those discussed in other areas of the laboratory, but generally the time element is not as critical. An exception would be in the case of certain infectious diseases that are identified through serologic techniques (e.g., Rocky Mountain spotted fever, psittacosis). Here the need to transmit the results of positive findings to the attending physician can be critical to the patient's survival, because appropriate therapy must begin as soon as possible after the causative agent has been identified. Certain diseases required by law to be reported to the proper authorities will be diagnosed in the immunology and serology sections of the laboratory.

Blood Bank

In the area of blood banking, improper specimen collection or preservation is seldom a problem because of the relatively stable nature of the antigens and antibodies that are studied during compatibility testing. A specimen would have to be subjected to severe and prolonged abuse to become unsuitable.

An incorrect labeling of a specimen collected for blood bank testing can have extremely serious consequences for the recipient of the blood. Complications include renal failure and possibly death in severe cases. The specimen collection procedures for the blood bank are much more stringent than in any other area of the laboratory. Usually, the following information is required:

1. Patient's full first and last names.
2. Hospital identification number.
3. Date of collection.
4. Time of collection.
5. Initials of the technician collecting the specimen.

The above information should be taken directly from the patient's identification band, and written onto the specimen container at the bedside. All information on both the specimen container and the identification band must reconcile fully with the information on the request form sent to the blood bank.

An incorrect test or misinterpretation of a test performed in the blood bank can lead to a patient being transfused with incompatible blood, where the consequences can range from a shortening of the lifespan of the transfused cells to the death of the patient. The result will depend upon the nature of the incompatibility.

The receipt of incompatible blood will become obvious by a rapid deterioration in the patient's condition (hemolytic transfusion reaction). The number of such reactions that result from incorrect testing or misinterpretation of a test is small. The great majority of them are the direct result of clerical errors made during the process of transfusing the blood, i.e., the blood is given to the wrong patient.

It is the responsibility of the blood bank to maintain a record of a patient's previous tests. An individual's blood type (for all practical purposes) never changes, and failure to review available records to confirm this information is negligence.

It also is necessary to review a patient's files for information on any previous identification of unexpected or atypical *alloantibodies*. These are antibodies that individuals can develop (as the result of previous blood transfusions, pregnancy, etc.) to specific antigens that can be present in the donor blood. The recipient with an alloantibody who is transfused with red cells containing the corresponding antigen will suffer a transfusion reaction. The severity of the reaction is highly variable, but death can result.

In an emergency, the failure of the blood bank section of a laboratory to report on a test in a timely manner could result in a delay in a patient receiving a life-saving transfusion. Otherwise, the failure to comply with a request for test results promptly will subject the department to risks similar in scope to those encountered by other laboratory sections.

MALPRACTICE: ADMINISTRATIVE FUNCTIONS BY PATHOLOGISTS

The pathologist, in his or her role as a laboratory director, can be held liable for the negligent actions of those in his or her employ, even though he or she may be innocent of personal fault, under the theory of *respondeat superior*.

Employment of Incompetent or Inadequately Trained Personnel

It is the responsibility of the laboratory director to see that individuals in his or her employ are competent and properly trained to perform the tasks assigned to them. Failure on the part of the director to recognize incompetent or inadequately trained personnel could subject him or her to liability in the event that an employee's error could be proved to result from such failure.

The laboratory director should conduct periodic reviews of the work of all technical staff, and should judge their performance against objective performance-related criteria to ensure that expected levels of competence are being demonstrated. Additionally, the director should ensure that the technical staff are kept abreast of current developments in the field of laboratory medicine, and that technologists are using the most appropriate testing methods available.

If, during the course of performance evaluations of the technical staff, the director discovers suboptimal performance that cannot be corrected through retraining and education, he or she has a responsibility to discharge the individual.

Failure to Monitor Physicians

The director of a hospital laboratory has the responsibility to monitor the actions of staff physicians who use the laboratory in any capacity. If, for instance, the director discovers that the death of a patient was caused by the negligent act of a physician, and fails to inform both the medical director and the hospital administrator of the fact, the director could become involved in any litigation that is brought against the physician. The failure to notify could even be viewed as collusion, and as such the director could be named a co-defendant.

The laboratory director also has a specific responsibility to monitor surgeons for the rate of operative complications, appropriateness of procedures performed, and for the removal of normal tissue in an excessive number of cases. Many of these monitoring functions are carried out through the interaction of the director with the various hospital committees. A failure on the part of the director to carry out this responsibility can result in incompetent surgeons remaining on the staff of the hospital, and their negligence can lead to malpractice claims that might very well involve the director.

HOSPITAL COMMITTEES

The hospital pathologist frequently serves on one or more of the following committees.

The Tumor and Tissue Committee is usually chaired by the pathologist, and is responsible for evaluating the surgical procedures that are being performed. The name of the committee is somewhat misleading, since the members also review cases where no tissue is removed. In such cases, the appropriateness of the procedure performed is evaluated based on both the clinical history and the laboratory data present. In cases where tissue is removed, a review of the preoperative diagnosis versus the tissue diagnosis is conducted, and differences are reconciled. It is through the actions of this committee that most of the incompetent actions of surgeons are discovered.

The function of the Transfusion Review Committee is to evaluate the use of all blood and blood products by the hospital medical staff. Both the surgical and medical staff are included in this review. The committee evaluates utilization, ensuring that blood and blood products are given only when appropriate, and that excessive amounts of blood are not being used by any individual staff member. (The use of excessive amounts of blood utilization on a regular basis by a surgeon might be an indication of incompetent surgical technique.)

The Mortality Committee is responsible for reviewing hospital deaths. The purpose is to ensure that appropriate medical care was rendered, and that the death did not result from a negligent act. An individual physician with an excessive mortality rate might be the subject of further scrutiny to determine that no inappropriate or incompetent care is being provided.

The Infection Control Committee is responsible for evaluation of the rates and types of hospital-based infections. This evaluation includes both medical and surgical infections, and is designed to ensure that proper infection control measures are being utilized by the hospital staff.

The Medical Staff Executive Committee serves as the internal credentialing group for the hospital. It grants staff privileges to individual physicians after reviewing their qualifications. It also is responsible for reviewing any unfavorable reports generated on a physician by any of the committees discussed above. This committee is responsible for the decision to take action against an allegedly incompetent staff member.

The Utilization Review Committee is responsible for evaluating the appropriateness of care provided to a patient during the hospital stay. It evaluates length of stay, procedures performed, outcome of the procedures performed, laboratory tests and radiology procedures ordered and their appropriateness, etc. The committee evaluates the total care given to the patient, and identifies those areas or individuals providing less than optimal care according to the national standards.

The DRG Review Committee came into being with the development of the DRG (Diagnosis Related Group) method of payment by the federal government. This committee seeks to ensure that the care given patients is appropriate for their DRG category, and more importantly, that individuals entering the hospital under the Medicare and Medicaid programs are not given suboptimal care because of the DRG fixed payment method.

MALPRACTICE: THE PATHOLOGIST AS AN EXPERT

Utilization of the pathologist to review hospital and medical records in malpractice cases is often mandatory. There are few individuals better qualified to evaluate the care received by a patient. The pathologist can compare the defendant physician's findings against the findings presented by the records, and determine the appropriateness of both the diagnosis and treatment.

When reviewing the reports and depositions of other medical experts, the pathologist frequently can present valuable alternative opinions. The pathologist can review these depositions and reports for errors of omission—relevant facts that may not have been presented or have been glossed over. The inclusion of a pathologist as a reviewer frequently ensures that all material facts in the case are fully explored, and that all possible explanations are provided.

The pathologist can usually provide information that will correlate the various laboratory test data, and provide insight as to how such data supports or does not support the clinical diagnosis. The pathologist usually can determine the appropriateness of the testing selected and evaluate the results for correctness. Where conflict appears to exist in the clinical diagnosis, he or she often can provide information that will relate the laboratory findings to the actual disease process, and suggest other possible diagnoses that should have been considered.

By the careful examination of microscopic surgical and autopsy tissue slides, a pathologist can make determinations relating to the correctness of tissue diagnosis and, where appropriate, the grading and staging of tumors. The pathologist is most useful when malpractice actions involve a missed diagnosis or misdiagnosis. His or her review may uncover findings that were overlooked during the initial evaluation of tissue studies, or may uncover additional or alternative disease processes that could have contributed to a patient's death.

In a similar manner, cytology slides, peripheral blood smears, bone marrow biopsies, and other special slide preparations can be evaluated for a missed diagnosis or misdiagnosis.

The examination of gross tissue specimens can be helpful in cases of malpractice. When these examinations are performed by the pathologist, tissue specimens are evaluated for the appropriateness and completeness of sampling done. For example: Was the submitted tissue sampled in all relevant areas to ensure that all possible sites of pathologic process were evaluated? In the case of tissue containing tumor, were the edges of the tissue sampled to ensure that the margins were free from tumor? Were contiguous lymph nodes evaluated? These issues of sampling can be relevant in cases of malpractice, and if any questions are to be raised in this area, the tissue should be evaluated by a pathologist.

When questions are raised regarding a missed diagnosis, it may be that appropriate sections of tissue were not cut from the paraffin tissue blocks. The pathologist can obtain the tissue blocks and cut additional and deeper sections to determine if this was the case. And if indicated, the pathologist also can perform special staining procedures that may prove that a diagnosis was missed during the original examination. Special stains may not have been done, and the routine sections may not have provided conclusive evidence of the pathologic process at issue.

POSTMORTEM EXAMINATIONS

Circumstances may arise in a malpractice case where members of the family feel that the care received by the patient contributed to the patient's death. A private pathologist may be asked to perform a postmortem examination to determine the exact cause of death, or perhaps to offer an opinion as to the appropriateness of the care. This examination probably would not be performed by the hospital pathologist where the deceased was a patient because the family would feel that his or her opinion might be biased.

Cases may arise where malpractice litigation is instituted following the burial of the deceased. It may be necessary to retain a pathologist to perform an exhumation autopsy. In these cases the body is removed from the burial site and an autopsy is performed following the standard protocols. In some cases, vital tests will not be available, such as toxicology studies for certain drugs. Also, body fluids would not be available for chemical analyses.

This will make the pathologist's job much more difficult, but nevertheless valuable information often can be obtained.

FORENSIC PATHOLOGY
Coroners and Medical Examiners

Coroners and medical examiners are officials who are charged by law with the investigation of unnatural deaths (sometimes limited only to homicides and suicides), medically unattended deaths, and cases in which no physician is willing to sign the death certificate.

The term "violence" includes all types of extraneous injuries (mechanical, chemical, thermal, electrical, etc.), drowning, rape, criminal abortion, etc. In questionable cases, the medical examiner has the authority to decide if he or she has jurisdiction and whether an autopsy should be performed.

Generally, both coroners and medical examiners are charged with the responsibility of investigating deaths of a suspicious nature, i.e., all cases of death where the cause is not known to be natural. This involves answering the following questions:

1. Who is the victim (sex, race, age, particular characteristics)?
2. When did the death and injuries occur (timing of death and injuries)?
3. What injuries are present (type, distribution, pattern, path, and direction of injuries)?
4. Which injuries are significant and may have caused death (major versus minor injuries, true versus artifactual or postmortem injuries)?
5. Where did the death occur (scene and circumstances)?
6. Why and how were the injuries produced (mechanism and manner of death)?

The determination of cause of death is normally made during the course of an autopsy, and is presented as a portion of the autopsy report. It consists of a factual description of the condition or injuries responsible for the death. Examples would include, "gunshot wound to the head," "pulmonary embolus," "blunt force injuries to the chest," "bacterial meningitis." These determinations are not to be confused with the "manner of death" discussed below.

The determination of the manner of death takes into consideration the cause of death and other available information surrounding the death (i.e., scene investigation, witnesses' accounts, medical history, etc.), and places the death into one of five categories:

1. Natural (death due to natural pathologic processes).
2. Accidental (death resulted from an accident in which no individual or individuals can be held responsible or negligent).
3. Suicide (death resulted from the individual act of taking one's own life).
4. Homicide (death resulted from the act of another individual).
5. Undetermined (the circumstances are not sufficiently clear to arrive at a decision of any of the above).

Sometimes it is extremely difficult, even for an experienced forensic pathologist, to be certain about the manner of death. A thorough and complete review and evaluation of all the investigative data in the case, correlated with the postmortem anatomic and toxicologic findings, must be performed before expressing final and official opinions and rulings in questionable cases.

Relationship of Forensic Pathologist with Attorneys

The relationship of the forensic pathologist to the district attorney or prosecutor should always be on an impartial and professional basis. If an investigation shows that no crime was committed, this should be clearly stated, irrespective of how the prosecuting attorney feels about the criminality of the case.

The forensic pathologist should evaluate each case in which he or she will be called to testify, and review the testimony relevant to the particular case under consideration.

The forensic pathologist can enter into several different relationships with private attorneys. The role will vary depending upon the specific relationship. The forensic expert can serve as an expert witness in both criminal and civil cases, where he or she will be called upon to provide specific details that will help a jury better understand the medical aspects of the case. He or she also is frequently called upon to determine if the attorney's client has grounds to file a civil or criminal action. This is usually done by review of medical records, tissue slides, etc.

The relationship of the forensic pathologist to a family or family member is most often one of medical advisor following the death or injury of a relative. Often, the family will request that the forensic pathologist review details of the case to determine if there are sufficient grounds to pursue legal action.

A forensic pathologist acting as a coroner or medical examiner should develop a working relationship with law enforcement agencies. It is sometimes easy to allow a law enforcement official to influence a pathologist's interpretation of findings. This cannot be allowed. The forensic expert must establish his or her role clearly in an investigation, and not allow the law enforcement official to hurry them into conducting anything less than a thorough investigation.

In the course of his or her investigations, the forensic pathologist may uncover deaths that have been caused by diseases that are of general concern to the population at large. This would be true in the case of highly communicable diseases. In these cases, the forensic expert is responsible for promptly identifying and reporting the disease to public health officials, and he or she should fully cooperate in any investigation they conduct.

Forensic Consultation: Medical Malpractice Cases

Private forensic consulting is limited to a small number of pathologists who are certified in forensic pathology. While the number of these consultants is small, their involvement in cases that involve medical testimony can be critical, since they can provide a high degree of expertise, and are widely recognized for providing impartial testimony on the medical evidence of a case.

These consultants can determine if there is sufficient evidence of professional negligence to warrant the filing of an action in a suspected case of medical malpractice. They can provide expert evaluation by reviewing all aspects of a case, and testify to these findings. They can aid both plaintiff and defense attorneys in establishing lines of questioning to be used during trial, and counsel attorneys as to what aspects of the case are most relevant. They can conduct autopsy investigations in an impartial atmosphere, uninfluenced by the hospital or physician involved in the case.

REFERENCES

1. *Sharsmith v. Hill*, 764 P. 2d 667 (Wyo. Sup. Ct., Nov. 9, 1988).
2. *Coleman v. Sopher*, 1997 WL 725775 (W.Va.).
3. *Hawkins v. Pathology Associates of Greenville, P.A.*, 1998 WL 11711 (S.C. App.).

CHAPTER 30

Genetics

Gary Birnbaum, M.D., J.D., F.C.L.M.

GOLDEN RULES

1. Obtain a third-degree pedigree family health history including siblings, parents, aunts, uncles, cousins, grandparents, and great-grandparents.
2. Inform patients if they are at increased risk for a genetic disorder based on their family history.
3. Order the appropriate testing for the genetic disorder after obtaining the patient's informed consent.
4. Discuss the results with the patient including the chances for false positives and false negatives.
5. Inform the patient of the implications of the test result and consider referring the patient to a genetic counseling specialist.
6. Advise the patient to notify all potentially affected relatives to discuss the matter with their physician to determine if any action is warranted.
7. If the patient is unable or unwilling to notify potentially affected relatives, obtain the patient's permission to do so.
8. If the patient refuses to allow the information to be disclosed to potentially affected relatives, consider seeking legal advice.
9. Women should be counseled before or early in pregnancy to avoid wrongful birth lawsuits.
10. This field is constantly evolving. Internet research may be helpful in getting the most up-to-date information.

This chapter will address two key issues concerning genetics and medical malpractice. First, what is the physician's duty to diagnose genetic disorders in their patients? Second, what is the duty of the physician to warn relatives who may be affected with the same genetic disorder?

Genetics is no longer the "next big thing." It is the big thing. Medicine has come a long way since Mendel discovered in the 19th century that certain traits are hereditary and Watson and Crick described the DNA double helix in 1953. The human genome was defined in 2003. Now there are genetic tests available to clinicians that identify individuals who are carriers (heterozygote) of certain disorders and those who are destined to have the complete expression of the disorder (homozygote). For example, hemochromatosis, a disorder of iron metabolism, used to be referred to as "bronze diabetes" because patients were only diagnosed after they developed a bronze skin hue consequent to iron deposition in the dermis and diabetes as a result of iron deposition in the pancreas. Now physicians can order a blood test, decades before there is "bronze diabetes," and determine whether an individual carries the genetic mutation.

CASE PRESENTATION

Mrs. Jones, 35 years old, visits her new internist. Dr. Smith discovers during the family history that Mrs. Jones' mother died at the age of 32 years of injuries sustained in an accident. Dr. Smith inquires no further and fails to determine that a maternal aunt died of colon cancer at age 41 years.

The following year, Mrs. Jones moves to another city. Her new internist, Dr. Adams, discovers the family history of colon cancer and suggests that Mrs. Jones undergo a colonoscopy with a gastroenterologist, Dr. Daniels. Dr. Daniels discovers a large polyp in the transverse colon that proves to be an adenocarcinoma. Unfortunately, the cancer has spread to the liver and some of the mesenteric lymph nodes are positive. Dr. Daniels does not advise Mrs. Jones to notify her relatives of their increased risk for colon cancer and to check with their individual doctors regarding further evaluation.

A few years later another maternal aunt, Ms. Jesse, the youngest of the sisters, goes to see Dr. David for unexplained weight loss and anorexia. Workup reveals colon adenocarcinoma, metastatic to the liver.

Does Mrs. Jones have a medical malpractice case against Dr. Smith for failing to diagnose her colon cancer? Does Ms. Jesse have a medical malpractice case against Dr. Daniels for failure to warn her of the potential increased risk of colon cancer?

ISSUES

In the foregoing hypothetical case, Mrs. Jones might have a good case against Dr. Smith for medical malpractice and failing to diagnose her colon cancer. The plaintiff's attorney will argue that Dr. Smith had a duty to obtain a reasonable medical history from Mrs. Jones. Moreover, by learning that a sister had colon cancer, Dr. Smith would have a duty to Mrs. Jones to advise her to see a gastroenterologist for a colonoscopy since it is well known that first-degree relatives of an affected individual with colon cancer are at heightened risk. As we shall see later in this chapter, Ms. Jesse might have a strong case against Dr. Daniels. Although Ms. Jesse was not a patient of Dr. Daniels, the current trend in the law imposes a duty on physicians to direct their patients to notify relatives who might be at an increased risk for a serious illness.

Duty to Diagnose Genetic Disorders

The duty to diagnose genetic disorders begins with an appropriate family history. Information obtained in the family history may lead to the identification of a genetic disorder in the patient. Identifying the genetic disorder may then trigger the need for preventive measures or surveillance testing.

For instance, a young patient presenting with a strong family history of cardiovascular disease in relatives under the age of 50 years should be tested for familial lipid disorders and instructed on healthy eating habits. A patient with a relative who develops breast cancer below the age of 40 may be a carrier for one of the two BRCA genes. This necessitates further evaluation for breast and ovarian cancer risk as well as the possibility for colon, prostate, and pancreatic cancer risks.

Physicians need to obtain a complete family history, a three-generation pedigree.[1] First-degree relatives include children, parents, and siblings. These blood relatives share 50% of the patient's genes. Aunts, uncles, grandparents, half siblings, nieces, and nephews are second-degree relatives sharing 25% of the patient's genes. Third-degree relatives are first cousins and great-grandparents. They share 12.5% of the patient's genes. This information may be obtained by the physician, trained staff, or by having the patient complete a form detailing conditions and disorders that have occurred in their relatives. If the patient is adopted and does not know the natural parents, some courts may reveal the health history of the biological parents without revealing their personal identity.

Hereditary Disorders

Once a complete third-degree family history is obtained, the patient may require surveillance for disorders such as cardiovascular disease, diabetes, colon cancer, breast cancer, ovarian cancer, prostate cancer, and abdominal aortic aneurysm. Other examples of conditions that are suggestive of genetic diseases include but are not limited to hemochromatosis, tuberous sclerosis, autosomal-dominant polycystic kidney disease, hereditary hemorrhagic telangiectasia, long QT syndrome (LQTS), hereditary thrombophilias, hereditary bleeding disorders (especially von Willebrands and hemophilia), alpha-1 antitrypsin deficiency, Duchenne muscular dystrophy, hereditary glaucoma, and hereditary pancreatitis.

With the explosive acceleration of new information, it is important to be aware of the many disorders that might trigger heightened scrutiny of the patient in the face of a positive family history for any of the aforementioned disease entities or other disorders. For instance, a recent report suggests that in the LQTS, a genetic disorder predisposing to sudden death in young people, disease severity varies according to the genetic loci.[2] Restless legs syndrome, a common cause of insomnia and leg cramps, may be familial in some patients due to defects on the 12q and 14q chromosomes. Up to 30% of patients with Paget's disease of the bones have other family members with it. Referral to a genetic specialist for counseling or to a consultant specialist may be considered, depending on the circumstances, as new information is constantly appearing in the medical literature.

In considering a patient's risk for a genetic disorder status, information regarding the patient's ancestry may be important because carrier testing is usually available. Gaucher disease is the most common genetic disorder in Jewish people of Eastern European ancestry (Ashkenazi). Tay-Sachs carriers are usually of European Jewish origin, Cajun ethnicity, or members of a small inbred community of French Canada. Sickle-cell anemia is most common in those of African ancestry. Beta-thalassemia is usually linked to those of Mediterranean origin while alpha-thalassemia is more likely to be associated with Asians. Those of Anglo-Saxon descent appear to be at an increased risk for Paget's disease of bone.

Wrongful Birth and Wrongful Life Cases

The pregnant female patient should be under the care of a physician who is familiar with hereditary disorders. There have been successful claims for wrongful birth and even some for wrongful life, although presently the latter is disfavored by the law.

Wrongful birth suits for damages are brought by parents claiming that the physician's failure to uncover the risk or presence of a genetic illness resulted in the parents not being given the opportunity to consider adoption rather than pregnancy, pregnancy termination, or other interventions to protect the health of the fetus.[3]

Wrongful life actions brought by the parents on behalf of the child posit that, but for the defendant tortfeasor's malfeasance, the child would not have been born. These suits are disfavored because courts are often reluctant to award damages on the basis of nonlife being better than life.[4,5] Alternatively, sometimes wrongful birth cases are allowed to go forward.[6]

Women contemplating pregnancy and those who become pregnant may be offered testing to determine risks to the fetus. Relevant disorders include but are not limited to Tay-Sachs, sickle-cell anemia, Down's syndrome, neural tube defects, and cystic fibrosis. Failure to inform pregnant women of the availability of appropriate screening may result in a lawsuit for wrongful birth or wrongful life, as well as intentional and negligent infliction of emotional distress.[7]

Genetic counseling should take place *before* pregnancy when possible. The process of counseling includes an evaluation of the medical records and family history, genetic testing, evaluating the results of the testing, and helping parents understand and reach decisions about which options to consider and act on. Errors leading to malpractice claims may occur at any stage of the counseling process.

Once pregnancy occurs, a variety of tests may be performed including alpha-fetoprotein (AFP) screening, chorionic villus sampling (CVS), ultrasound (US), amniocentesis, and percutaneous umbilical blood sampling (PUBS). Abnormal AFP levels, usually taken during the 15th and 20th weeks, may indicate an open neural tube defect (ONTD), such as spina bifida, anencephaly, Down syndrome, or other chromosomal abnormalities. Prior to testing, patients should be informed that AFP is a screening test and that there may be false positives or false negatives. CVS is usually performed during the 10th and up to the 13th week of pregnancy in women who are at increased risk for chromosomal abnormalities or have a family history of a genetic defect that is testable from placental tissue. This procedure does not detect ONTDs. US may detect fetal abnormalities in the first trimester but is of greater value at the 18th through that 22nd weeks. Amniocentesis recovers cells that may be used for genetic or chromosomal tests. It may be recommended for women over 35 years of age or those with abnormal AFPs, abnormal USs, prior birth or family history of a child with a genetic or chromosomal condition, or parental carrier status for certain genetic conditions. Amniocentesis cannot test for many types of mental retardation, certain heart defects, and cleft lip/palate. PUBS may be considered when the other tests are inconclusive and there is no alternative to achieve a timely diagnosis. The appropriate use of these tests during pregnancy with documentation of informed consent or refusal to allow for possible pregnancy termination or even intrauterine fetal surgery, e.g., myelomenigocele with spina bifida, may prevent a malpractice case.

Genetic State of the Patient

All states require varying degrees of genetic testing at birth. Every state mandates tests for congenital hypothyroidism and phenylketonuria (PKU). New York State has a screening program that tests every newborn for more than 40 disorders.

Diagnosing a patient's genetic state may become important once a condition is suspected or diagnosed. For instance, the evaluation of a patient with deep vein thrombosis, pulmonary embolism, recurrent miscarriages, and other coagulation-related disorders may reveal a factor V Leiden or prothrombin gene 20210 mutation mandating consideration of lifelong anticoagulation.

Hemochromatosis, the most common hereditary disease in persons of northern European ancestry, should be suspected in patients with abnormal liver functions, endocrine dysfunction manifesting as erectile dysfunction, or polyarthralgias. If the diagnosis is suspected, the transferrin saturation should be checked. A level greater than 45% mandates ordering genetic testing to check for the C282Y HFE mutation.

Patients with unexplained emphysema and cirrhosis may have the alpha-1 antitrypsin deficiency disorder. Genetic testing is available if a low level is reported.

Symptoms of cognitive dysfunction may trigger a duty to offer genetic testing for the apolipoprotein E4 allele to evaluate for an increased risk of developing Alzheimer's disease.[8]

Marfan's syndrome typically involves the cardiovascular, skeletal, and ocular systems. Aortic valve regurgitation, mitral prolapse, aortic dissection, scoliosis, pectus excavatum, and dislocation of the ocular lens trigger consideration of this genetic disorder of the FBN1 gene, which results in a deficiency of fibrillin-1. Presently there is no rapid and efficient molecular diagnostic test for this disorder.

Infertility, hypogonadism (small testes), decreased facial hair, and gynecomastia suggest the possibility of Klinefelter syndrome, which is typically caused by an extra X chromosome in males. Early diagnosis may allow for the consideration of androgen therapy when a therapeutic benefit is likely.

Infants and children with sensorineural hearing loss should have the genetic screening test for gap junction beta-2 (GJB2), which is inherited in an autosomal recessive pattern.

A recent report indicates that young patients with unexplained strokes, especially in the vertebrobasilar system, need to be checked for Fabry's disease, which is an X-linked recessive lysosomal storage disease.[9]

Pharmacogenetic testing is an exciting new area that uses genetic information to help in the therapeutic treatment of a disease. For instance, multigene analysis may predict whether or not chemotherapy is necessary for certain cancers. A test for the Her-2 receptor in breast cancer patients can determine who will respond to the drug trastuzumab (Herceptin), and a test for the EGFR receptor in non-small-cell lung cancer patients can predict who will respond to gefitinib (Iressa). Pharmacogenomics studies how an individual's genetic makeup determines the response to a drug. For example, a recent report suggests that individuals with acute coronary syndrome and the ADRB2 genotype groups may not be helped and are potentially harmed by long-term beta-blocker therapy.[10] Also, patients with essential thrombocytosis (elevated platelets) and the V617-F mutation gain particular benefit from hydroxyurea as compared to anagrelide. Although some of these tests may not immediately be considered standard, in the future, failure to appropriately test prior to initiating certain therapies may lead to a malpractice claim.

Duty to Warn Relatives

The second issue concerns the duty to warn relatives when a genetic condition is identified in a patient.[11] The old rule stated that there was no duty to warn relatives, who would be considered as "third party," because the physician's relationship was directly with the patient. A relative of the patient was a third party who had no physician–patient relationship, and hence no duty was owed.

In 1976, the "old rule" was changed by the *Tarasoff v. Regents of the University of California* decision.[12] In this often cited case, a patient confided to his psychiatrist/psychologist his wish to harm his girlfriend. Adhering to the doctrine of patient–physician confidentiality, the doctor did not warn the girlfriend. After the patient killed the girlfriend, her family sued the psychiatrist and the court ruled in favor of the family, even though the psychiatrist/psychologist had no direct legal relationship with the girlfriend. The court held that under the circumstances of this case, the duty to warn outweighed the confidences of the relationship with the patient. Analogous reasoning has been used in cases involving genetic disorders and claims of medical malpractice for failing to warn potentially affected kin.

In *Pate v. Threlkel*,[13] the Supreme Court of Florida held in 1995 that a physician owed a duty of care to the children of a parent to warn the patient of the genetically transferable nature of the condition for which the physician treated the patient. In 1987, the mother was diagnosed and treated for medullary thyroid cancer. A few years later the daughter was diagnosed with the same condition. The daughter sued the physician, claiming that if the mother had been informed of the genetic nature of the disease, the mother would have notified the daughter who would have been diagnosed earlier in the curable stage of the disease. The ruling held that there was a duty to warn the mother of the genetic nature of the illness and that this warning satisfied the duty to other relatives since in most instances the patient would notify potentially affected family members.

A year later in 1996 the Superior Court of New Jersey, Appellate Division, expanded the holding of the *Pate* decision. In *Safer v. Pack*,[14] the court held that a physician had a duty to warn those known to be at risk of avoidable harm from a genetically transmissible condition even if those individuals were not patients of the defendant physician. The court declined to hold, as in *Pate*, that in all circumstances the duty to warn is satisfied by informing the patient. The plaintiff Safer was diagnosed with colon cancer at the age of 36. Her father had died of colon cancer when she was 10. Dr. Pack had determined that the father had multiple colon polyposis and that one of the polyps had become malignant. The court held that Dr. Pack had a duty to take reasonable steps to warn immediate family members at risk for this genetically transmissible condition.

Privacy Issues

Privacy issues focus on a patient's genetic information being disclosed to employers and health insurance companies. Although no federal legislation concerning genetic discrimination in the workplace and in individual insurance companies has been enacted into law, there are some protections in state statutes and other federal laws. Some state laws regulate the disclosure of genetic test results and discrimination against individuals with certain genetic disorders. On the federal level, both the Americans with Disabilities Act of 1990 (ADA) and the Health Insurance Portability and Accountability Act of 1996 (HIPAA) may come into play. ADA does not expressly address genetic information but provides some protections against disability-related genetic discrimination in the workplace. HIPAA contains sections that directly address genetic discrimination, but this privacy law only applies to employer-based and commercially issued group health insurance as contrasted with individuals seeking health insurance in the individual market. Physicians may need to seek legal advice in some cases, before disclosing sensitive genetic information to employers or health insurance plans.

Gene Therapies

Currently gene therapy, the replacement of an abnormal gene with a normal gene, is experimental. In 1999 a patient named Jesse Gelsinger underwent experimental gene therapy for ornithine transcarboxylase deficiency. He died a few days later. In 2003 a patient in France developed a leukemia-like condition after being successfully treated for X-linked severe combined immunodeficiency disease (bubble baby syndrome). When the patient's life is at risk, the physician may be obligated to inform the patient about the availability of gene therapy in certain situations. However, care must be taken to ensure comprehensive informed consent when patients elect experimental therapies.

SUMMARY: AVOIDING GENETIC LIABILITY

The explosion of new genetic information will continue. The best way to avoid a medical genetics medical malpractice case will be to obtain a complete family history. If the family history is suggestive of a genetic disorder, the patient should be informed about the risks and benefits of genetic testing. When a genetic disorder is found, the patient should be encouraged to notify potentially affected family members so that those relatives can review the situation with their physicians.

REFERENCES

1. Wattendorf DJ, Hadley DW, *Family History: The Three-Generation Pedigree*. American Family Physician 72:441–448 (2005).

2. Napolitano C, *et al.*, *Genetic Testing in the Long QT Syndrome*. JAMA 294: 2975–2980 (2005).

3. *Karen Keel and Danny Keel v. Warren Branch, M.D., and Warren Beach, M.D., P.C.*, 624 So. 2d 1022 (Ala. 1993).

4. *Jeffrey Goldberg, a Minor, et al. v. Stephen B. Ruskin et al.*, 499 N.E. 2d 406 (Ill. 1986).

5. *Laureen Doolis et al. v. IVF America (MA), Inc., et al.*, 12 Mass. L. Rep. 482 (Mass. 2000).

6. *Shauna Tamar Curlender, a Minor, etc. v. Bio-Science Laboratories et al.*, 106 Cal. App. 3d 811 (Cal. 1980).

7. *Alexander A. Munro, a Minor, etc., et al. v. The Regents of the University of California et al.*, 215 Cal. App. 3d 977 (Cal. 1989).

8. Kapp MB, *Physicians' Legal Duties Regarding the Use of Genetic Tests to Predict and Diagnose Alzheimer Disease*. Journal of Legal Medicine 21:445–475 (2000).

9. Rolfs A, *et al.*, *Prevalence of Fabry Disease in Patients with Cryptogenic Stroke: A Prospective Study*. Lancet 366:1794–1796 (2005).

10. Lanfear DE, Jones PG, Marsh S, Cresci S, McLeod HL, Spertus JA, *Beta$_2$-Adrenergic Receptor Genotypes and Survival Among Patients Receiving Beta Blocker Therapy After an Acute Coronary Syndrome*. JAMA 294:1526–1533 (2005).

11. Offit K, Groeger E, Turner S, Wadsworth EA, Weiser MA, *The "Duty to Warn" a Patient's Family Members About Hereditary Risks*. JAMA 292:1469–1473 (2004).

12. *Tarasoff v. Regents of the University of California*, 551 P. 2d 334 (Cal. 1976).

13. *Heidi Pate and James Pate v. James B. Threlkel, M.D., et al.*, 661 So. 2d 278 (Fla. 1995).

14. *Donna Safer and Robert Safer v. The Estate of George T. Pack, et al.*, 677 A. 2d 1188 (N.J. Supp. 1996).

CHAPTER 31

Obstetrics and Gynecology

Curtis E. Harris, M.S., M.D., J.D., F.C.L.M.
Victoria L. Green, M.D., M.H.S.A., M.B.A., J.D., F.C.L.M.

GOLDEN RULES

1. Take all complaints seriously.
2. Evaluate every complaint fully to *both* your satisfaction and that of the patient.
3. Encourage open communications, to include open and free communications with you and your professional staff concerning ongoing physical and emotional concerns.
4. Create redundancy (systems) in the reporting of all data obtained in your office or requested by your office, including criteria for screening normal or near-normal information. Encourage your patients to be part of that system by asking them to call you (personally) if they have not received a report by a certain date.
5. Assume the role of advocate for good medical care, helping your patient navigate the complexity of health care delivery. Make certain your patient understands that your role is to help them, and encourage them to communicate any and all problems they encounter, including those that involve you.
6. Keep good records for indefinite periods of time, including conversion to electronic medical records capable of data search as appropriate.

Malpractice liability influences every aspect of the practice of obstetrics and gynecology (OB/Gyn). Nearly 8 out of 10 OB/Gyn practitioners have been sued at least once in their career,[1] and almost half have been sued three or more times. In addition, the threat of malpractice begins early in residency training for many physicians: 1 in 3 residents will be sued during their training, a fact that cannot but affect future practice decisions. Fear of malpractice suits in general can and does cause physicians to order more tests than medically necessary (the so-called practice of "defensive medicine"), and to refer a patient to a specialist who frequently suggests additional procedures, which are often invasive and redundant.[2]

One of the central reasons that OB/Gyn persistently remains a "high-risk" liability speciality is the amount of monetary damages associated with virtually all aspects of the practice. Younger women and their children are sympathetic plaintiff groups: juries simply feel sorry for their loss and want to be able to help them. In addition, the amount of the damages associated with such cases is often high because of the projected longer life span of a child or of a woman of childbearing age, compared with other patient groups. Attorneys recognize both principles and seek such clients when possible.

There are several areas of OB/Gyn practice that have been recognized as high-risk. We will discuss these areas first, and then make suggestions on how to both avoid liability and deal with cases when they come.

CASE PRESENTATION

Sally is now 34 years old. She first saw Dr. Diana Cox as a teenager for birth control advice, and off and on over the years for various gynecology needs, including two abortions and one miscarriage. She had not seen Dr. Cox for more than five years. However, she made an appointment with Dr. Cox because she was worried about a new "lump" she noticed in her left breast. It had been there for over three months. Her mother died of breast cancer when Sally was a child, so she was silently frantic by the day of the appointment. In addition, Sally had recently married, and wanted to have a family. She spent most of her visit with Dr. Cox discussing her plans for a new family, and mentioned the lump in passing toward the end of the interview. Dr. Cox was behind in her schedule, exhausted from an early morning C-section, and elected to have her PA examine Sally further. She did order a mammogram before leaving the room. The PA noted a small 1.0–1.5 cm mobile soft mass in the left breast, and extensive fibrocystic changes in both breasts. In addition, she ordered a pelvic ultrasound for the finding on exam of an enlarged right ovary. She told Sally that the exam was just routine, and "not to worry. I'll call you if anything is wrong." However, before the ultrasound result returned the PA took another job at the local hospital. No one called Sally with the result.

The mammogram returned two days later with an indefinite reading of "dense tissue," and the suggestion of an MRI "if clinically indicated." A nurse called Sally with the result, told her about the MRI recommendation, but added that "insurance will probably not pay for the MRI." Sally elected to do nothing more, and felt reassured in general that the problem had been addressed.

When she returned for her follow-up appointment with Dr. Cox one year later, she told Dr. Cox that "she and her husband have been trying to get pregnant, but have not been successful." It is then that she discovered that her pelvic exam was abnormal. Her cervix showed minor damage from the previous abortions, but the pelvic ultrasound indicated multiple areas of uterine scarring and the possibility of polycystic ovarian disease (PCOD). Two weeks after that appointment, Dr. Cox preformed a salpingogram, with the additional finding of extensive bilateral fallopian tube damage. She is infertile. In tears, Sally asked why all of this had happened, and received the answer of "Maybe it had something to do with the previous abortions. Gonorrhea and trich can do this. I just don't know."

Devastated, she returned home to her husband with the bad news. He knew nothing of the previous abortions, but was very supportive. His only comment was "I thought abortions were no big deal. Do you think Dr. Cox messed up?"

Sally made an appointment with Dr. James Jones, a cross-town competitor of Dr. Cox. He wondered aloud if Dr. Cox had caused the various problems leading to Sally's infertility. Sally then mentioned that a "lump in my breast that Dr. Cox ignored" had gotten bigger. Dr. Jones performed an ultrasound-guided fine needle biopsy later that week, which returned malignant. A subsequent mastectomy showed axillary lymph node involvement.

Sally decided to sue Dr. Cox.

ISSUES

Delayed Diagnosis of Breast Cancer

Breast cancer remains a significant public health issue affecting more than 211,000 women each year. Breast complaints, in general, are an important reason for visits to the obstetrician/gynecologist. Despite the immense experience in this arena, delayed diagnosis of breast cancer remains a major source of malpractice allegations for gynecologists and is the most common error in diagnosis resulting in claims for medical malpractice.[3] It is also a leading reason for malpractice claims against radiologists, general surgeons, family practitioners, and internal medicine physicians, making it the most prevalent condition resulting in malpractice claims with an average cost per case of over $200,000.

The etiology of breast cancer is multifactorial, and although numerous risk factors have been identified, they only explain 21% of the risk of breast cancer in women aged 30–54 years and only 29% of that in women aged 55–84 years. Nearly 75% of women with breast cancer have no identifiable risk factors other than gender and age; thus all women should be considered at risk for breast cancer.

Common reasons for a delayed diagnosis include a disregard of the risk of breast cancer in young women, overreliance on a "normal" mammogram and on a "normal" biopsy, inattention to medical history and examination (including a history of pain or nipple retraction), failure to diagnose recurrent disease, and "systems" failures in reporting and follow-up by both medical and nonmedical personnel.[4,5] Frequent additional diagnostic errors that occur are due to a failure: to perform a breast examination in the presence of an obvious tumor while treating the patient for an unrelated disease; to find an apparent tumor during palpation of the breast; to recommend a referral or biopsy/excision for a mass found on examination; to determine the cause of a nipple discharge; and to distinguish between carcinoma and an infection.[6]

Women who sue for a delayed diagnosis are often young and present with a self-discovered breast mass in the face of a negative mammogram. Even though breast cancer has been documented in 1–3% of women younger than 30 years of age, an abnormal breast examination in a woman less than 35 years old is often dismissed as a fibrocystic condition.

Legally inadequate informed consent is frequently alleged.[7] In general, a physician must discuss the anticipated benefits of a surgery or treatment plan, expected adverse outcomes, and the consequences and/or benefits of doing nothing. The standard of informed consent varies from state to state, but is typically a variation of one of three standards: the professional or locality standard, the objective standard, or the subjective standard. (See the discussion of informed consent in Chapter 14.) Medical malpractice cases based on a delayed diagnosis are sometimes dismissed due to a statute of limitations action. Various state courts have interpreted their state law to create either a broad or a narrow exception to such a dismissal, with a significant difference between and among the states. Ongoing therapy in a context of deception or false reassurances concerning an outcome (including a failure to later inform of a likely more distant complication), latent injuries (injuries not capable of discovery until some later date), erroneous or false assurances that an injury did not occur, or falsification of the medical record have all been reasons used by a court to "toll" or stop a dismissal based on a statute of limitations claim.

Another doctrine that may be asserted in the case of a delayed diagnosis of breast cancer is the "loss of chance" doctrine. In general, an adverse outcome must have been *more likely than not caused by* the negligence actions of the caregiver (that is, more than 50% probability) for a physician to be held liable. The "loss of chance" doctrine has been used where it cannot be proven that the physician was the *major* cause of a patient's death or injury, but rather the patient lost a possible benefit of an intervention by a delay in the diagnosis of the disease. Loss of chance in a case of a delayed diagnosis is typically based on a statistical chance of survival or benefit of less than 50% had the diagnosis been made in a timely manner. The amount of monetary damages given to the patient is a fraction of the amount she would have received in a more standard liability case, with the fraction determined by expert testimony that establishes the percentage of those who would be expected to benefit from timely therapy.[8]

The hereditary risk associated with certain forms of breast cancer is evolving rapidly as a liability issue. Allegations have included a failure to diagnose, including a failure to test for the BRCA1/2 mutation, failure to inquire about the genetic testing of other family members known to have disease, and failure to inform other at-risk family members of an inheritable condition. Litigation surrounding a failure to test for Tay-Sachs disease has been a model for this area of liability law. Since this is a complex and changing area of medicine and law, the single most important piece of advice for the medical practitioner is simple: *when in doubt, refer*. Unless you are trained in medical genetics, or are quite familiar with the question being asked, refer such questions to a medical geneticist or someone who has training. Medical genetics (and genetic testing) is a specialized area of medical practice, not easily amenable to general practice.

Because the delay of diagnosis of breast cancer has created a contentious, high-risk liability situation, one medical authority has advised that "[T]he price of skill in the diagnosis of breast carcinoma is a kind of eternal vigilance based upon an awareness that any indication of disease in the breast may be due to carcinoma."[9]

Gynecologic Surgery

Surgical Sterilization

Gynecologic surgery accounts for nearly 40% of all claims in OB/Gyn care, according to the 2003 ACOG Professional Liability Survey. Delayed diagnosis or a failure to diagnose was the most frequent allegation, followed closely by a claim of direct surgical injury.

Bilateral tubal sterilization and vasectomy are both safe and effective methods of permanent contraception. Worldwide, over 220 million couples use sterilization as their contraceptive method of choice. In a recent survey in the United States, tubal ligation was used by 28% of women of reproductive age and vasectomy by 11% of men of all ages. In comparison, 27% use oral contraceptives, 21% use male condoms, 3% use injectable contraceptives, 2% use diaphragms, and 1% use intrauterine devices (IUDs). Approximately 700,000 tubal sterilizations and 500,000 vasectomies are performed in the United States annually.[10]

Vasectomy failure rates range from zero to 2% in most studies. Failure rates of tubal ligation are roughly comparable with those of the IUD. The risk of sterilization failure persists for years after the procedure and varies by method, with postpartum partial salpingectomy having the lowest and spring clip having the highest. Thickened or dilated tubes, major pelvic adhesions, and an enlarged uterus may increase the complication rate. Other risks of the procedures consist of infection, bleeding, injury to bowel, bladder, or major vessels, cellulites, pelvic abscess (posterior colpotomy), and granuloma formation. Vasectomy complications include epididymitis and "postvasectomy pain syndrome." The most recent randomized, case-control study from New Zealand concluded that vasectomy does not increase the risk of prostate cancer, although earlier data showed a weak but statistically significant increased risk in certain subgroups.[11,12] The rate of impotence was similar in men who had undergone vasectomy compared to those who had not, consistent with the fact that the nerves involved in the male erectile function and ejaculation are not affected by vasectomy.

Effective counseling is a critical aspect of these procedures. Although regret for having had a sterilization procedure is uncommon, thorough and constructive counseling may minimize this risk even more. Determining capacity and competence to consent are important facets of the decision-making process. In general, sterilization is regarded as a voluntary procedure, but is subject to increased legal scrutiny. Reproductive freedom, especially any medical or state action that limits such freedom, has a unique place in the American legal system, in no small measure as a reaction to past abuses, including forced or coerced sterilization of mentally incompetent persons. Therefore, it may be advisable to have a separate consent form for sterilization that incorporates clear statements of procedure and of any specific failure rates and complications. Thorough documentation of the informed consent process is of key importance. Any woman requesting a procedure in the postpartum period should have been given a thorough discussion of all relevant information prior to the stressful period of labor and delivery, and any appearance of an undue third-party influence avoided. Any perceived ambivalence at any stage of the pregnancy or in the postpartum period should be addressed immediately and serious consideration should be given to delaying the procedure until a later date. Inclusion of the partner is often helpful. In addition, federal, state, and local statutes and regulations may control the interval from the time of consent to the actual procedure, the location in which the procedure must be performed, and other requirements, such as additional physician collaboration and signature of the spouse. Finally, a number of hospitals do not allow sterilization procedures (on religious grounds), except in emergency medical situations. Such restrictions must be discussed in advance to avoid unnecessary conflict.

The most common allegations involving sterilization are negligence in performance of the procedure and lack of informed consent.[13] In addition, failed sterilization is the most common basis for the allegation of "wrongful birth," "wrongful life," and "wrongful conception." There is a close relationship between the torts of wrongful birth (which often involves the negligent failure to inform a pregnant woman of the risk of birth defects prior to conception), wrongful life (which often involves the negligent failure to properly advise the parents of birth defects after conception, thereby interfering with their choice to terminate the pregnancy), and wrongful conception (which involves the negligent failure to prevent a child's conception). Additional circumstances that result in a wrongful birth or conception claim include ineffective prescription of contraceptives or counseling on contraception, failure to diagnose pregnancy in time for an elective abortion, and an unsuccessful abortion.

Recovery of medical expenses and for the pain and suffering associated with the delivery of an unwanted child are often allowed, under a claim for wrongful conception or wrongful birth. However, actions seeking recovery of expenses of raising a healthy, normal child, born after an unsuccessful sterilization procedure (a version of a wrongful life suit), are often denied. The concept of "wrongful life" has been the subject of much scholarly debate. Most states have not allowed this cause of action or have specifically rejected such claims as a matter of public policy. Most courts (and state legislatures) have considered the intrinsic and inestimatable value of an individual human life as paramount to any claim that a life should not be or exist, and have refused to assign a damage claim as too speculative. While jurisdictions differ, there is a body of opinion that recovery for wrongful life *should* be allowed. As stated by the Supreme Judicial Court of Massachusetts:

> The judicial declaration that the joy and pride in raising a child always outweigh any economic loss the parents may suffer, thus precluding recovery for the cost of raising the child, simply lacks verisimilitude. The very fact that a person has sought medical intervention to prevent him or her from having a child demonstrates that, for that person, the benefits of parenthood did not outweigh the burdens, economic and otherwise, of having a child.[14]

Further, jurisdictions differ regarding recovery for the wrongful life of a child with congenital defects, where such a birth (but not the congenital defects) was caused by negligent sterilization.[15] In such jurisdictions that allow a wrongful life claim for a child with congenital defects, damages are determined by a comparison of the extraordinary expenses associated with caring for a child with defects verses one without.

Laparoscopy

Laparoscopic surgery is another source of malpractice litigation. Allegations have included an injury due to a failure to obtain consultation (where technical skills are not optimum); failure to follow up in a timely manner; failure to order testing for apparent complications of a procedure; failure of sterilization (discussed earlier); and inadequate clinical examination for the existence of comorbid health conditions that contraindicate laparoscopic surgery. Clinicians must be familiar with relative and absolute contraindications of surgery, including bowel obstruction, ileus, generalized peritonitis, intraperitoneal hemorrhage, diaphragmatic hernia, severe cardiorespiratory disease, extremes of body weight, inflammatory bowel disease, or large abdominal mass. Certain laparoscopic procedures require a high level of expertise and training. Operative and postoperative documentation should include listing adequate visualization of bleeding sites, visualization of organs, elevation of structures prior to cautery or suturing, lack of difficulty in ventilation, and a follow-up plan of action (especially if a complication is noted or the patient is having difficulty).

Obstetrics

Obstetric claims account for the majority of claims against OB/Gyn physicians, with recovery rates in childbirth negligence lawsuits that are nearly 50% greater than the overall rate of all other medical malpractice claims.[16] Jury awards for childbirth injuries are routinely listed among the top jury awards nationwide,[17] a fact that has forced many physicians to change their practice by either reducing high-risk deliveries, reducing the total number of deliveries, or discontinuing obstetric care. High-risk injuries in obstetric care include the following.

Shoulder Dystocia

Shoulder dystocia is an obstetric emergency associated with failure of the shoulders to deliver spontaneously. It is most commonly caused by the impaction of the anterior fetal shoulder behind the maternal pubis symphysis or impaction of the posterior fetal shoulder on the sacral promontory, and may be heralded by the "turtle sign" where the fetal head retracts against the maternal perineum upon delivery. The reported incidence ranges from 0.6% to 1.4% among vaginal deliveries of fetuses in the vertex presentation. Failure of the shoulders to deliver spontaneously places both the pregnant woman and fetus at risk for postpartum hemorrhage, fourth-degree lacerations, brachial plexus injuries, and fractures of the clavicle and humerus. Severe cases of shoulder dystocia may result in significant maternal morbidity (especially with more advanced maneuvers), hypoxic-ischemic encephalopathy, and even death.[18]

Risk factors for shoulder dystocia are helpful but do not predict all cases and are not present in each case. Prior history of shoulder dystocia, postdates pregnancy, gestational diabetes, need for instrumental delivery, insulin-dependent diabetes, obesity, excessive weight gain, cephalopelvic disproportion, prolonged second stage, and macrosomia may be present in patients with shoulder dystocia.

Failure to Perform Timely Cesarean Section

Many recent cases have asserted the issue of a failure to perform a timely cesarean section, often associated with a claim that the failure caused the child to suffer from cerebral palsy. A recent scientific "white paper" by the American College of Obstetrics and Gynecology was designed to counter what the College believes to be illegitimate claims by plaintiff experts concerning the known causes of cerebral palsy.

Abortion

Elective abortion is the most common obstetric surgical procedure in the United States, and although "safe," it is associated with significant complications and liability. As would be predicted, the most serious complications occur in abortions performed in late-term pregnancies. Long-term complications of repeat abortions include increased rates of miscarriage, ectopic pregnancy, and sterility. A number of states have laws requiring the abortionist to inform a woman of the known and suspected complications of abortion. Failure to provide that information has been used as evidence of an inadequate level of informed consent. RU486 (an abortifacient) and Plan B offer medical options to surgical abortion, but are without clear long-term safety data.

Recent Liability Concerns

Genetic Testing and Wrongful Birth/Conception/Life

As noted above, many states are abolishing wrongful birth causes of action because they force a jury to "quantify the unquantifiable and measure the benefits of a disabled child's whole life when the child's potential is unknown." However, genetic testing of multiple disease states and the recognition of the wealth of information obtained from the Human Genome Project are forcing reconsideration of these cases. Failure to provide genetic counseling or testing as part of effective prenatal and pregnancy management represent a growing area of litigation and liability.[19] After an initial period of expanding liability, some courts are now placing limitations on the duty to inform parents of a genetic risk or the failure to offer genetic services. The recognition of several hundred (even several thousand) detectable genetic risks has made it unreasonable to assume that physicians will be able to warn each patient of all the potential risks and the tests available to determine those risks. However, if a patient is in a high-risk category and the test for that trait is sufficiently predictive, liability may attach.

Wrongful Death

Jurisdictions differ regarding recognition of wrongful death as a cause of action in the birth of a stillborn child. Many jurisdictions have allowed the mother to claim her personal damages for both the physical and emotional injuries of the delivery of a stillborn child. More critically, some jurisdictions have allowed the parents to make a wrongful death claim on behalf of the stillborn child, if the child reached viability before it died, or if the child was born before viability but was born alive (that is, had a heart beat and/or drew a breath). As the science of neonatology expands and *in utero* interventions become more common, these cases will take on greater significance.

SURVIVAL STRATEGIES

Dr. Cox made a number of errors in her care of Sally. Avoiding the mistakes she made illustrates how to structure an OB/Gyn practice to survive (even thrive) in a clearly complex area of medicine.

First, Sally will raise the issue of informed consent concerning the long-term complications of her two abortions. It is important to note that most states will allow a liability action to proceed years after the normal statute of limitations would expire when the injury would not be detectable until later, would otherwise be occult, would not develop until later in life, or when the physician was providing ongoing care without informing the patient of a possible risk. A physician is charged with the responsibility of revealing a known risk at the time it is known, which is in reality an ongoing responsibility in the face of advancing medical knowledge. Thus, even if the risk of infertility was not fully appreciated at the time of the original abortions, but was discovered later, Dr. Cox must make a reasonable effort to inform her patients of the subsequent findings. (The model for this area of liability is the litigation surrounding the use of DES in the early 1950s.) Good record keeping, especially when those records are electronic, will help solve this problem. However, as it becomes easier to inform patients of subsequently discovered risks, the standard for what is a "reasonable" effort to inform will become more strict. Here, the failure to notify Sally of the findings on the ultrasound in a timely manner was due to a "systems failure." Good intraoffice organization would have precluded the delayed notification and would have brought the result to the attention of Dr. Cox earlier, even though the PA left for another job. The delay damaged the rapport between Dr. Cox and Sally, as did the unfeeling comments of Dr. Cox after the salpingogram. Several important studies have shown that the risk of suit (especially in OB/Gyn care) is reduced by good patient rapport rather than by the training or technical skill of the physician. By the time Dr. Jones was examining Sally, rapport had been lost, and Sally was questioning the competence and dedication of Dr. Cox. Further, the comments of Dr. Jones fueled Sally's anger, which should remind us all that idle speculation on another physician's level of care should remain unspoken, unless known with certainty. It was not possible for Dr. Jones to know all he needed to know to link any action of Dr. Cox to Sally's problem of infertility.

The self-important temptation to appear more competent than a colleague must be avoided.

Second, Sally will probably sue Dr. Cox for a delayed diagnosis of breast cancer. She may sue under the "lost chance" doctrine, if in fact complications (including the possibility of her eventual death from the cancer) do result as *a* cause (rather than *the* cause) of the delay. However, if expert testimony establishes that a cure was possible *more likely than not*, and she can no longer be cured, then Sally will not need to resort to the "lost chance" doctrine.

The single most important reason for the delay was a lack of follow-up by Dr. Cox in the face of a delegation of responsibility to the PA, parallel to the same reason for a delay in the follow-up of the ultrasound. Dr. Cox was tired and stressed at the time she saw Sally, problems that are normal and recurrent in medical practice. Unless a backup system is in place for dealing with individual caregiver failures, mistakes will be made. It is also possible that Dr. Cox did not take the complaint of Sally seriously, since she was a young woman complaining of a breast lump. Finally, allowing an uninvolved nurse to call Sally and to suggest that insurance would not pay for additional studies, thereby placing an economic barrier to good care in Sally's mind, was a serious error. A physician and her staff should maintain the role of an advocate of quality care rather than that of an insurance agency. In summary, had Dr. Cox and her office staff maintained good, open communications with Sally, encouraging her to be active as a co-participant in her medical care, most if not all of the complications Sally has suffered would not have happened, or could have been ameliorated.

FURTHER READING

MacLennan A, Nelson K, Hankins G, Speer M, *Who Will Deliver Our Grandchildren? Implications of Cerebral Palsy Litigation.* JAMA 294: 1688–1690 (2005)

Green VL, "Liability in Obstetrics and Gynecology." In *Legal Medicine/American College of Legal Medicine*, 7th ed., ed. S. Sandy Sanbar *et al.* Philadelphia: Mosby, 2007.

REFERENCES

1. American College of Obstetrics and Gynecology, *2006 Professional Liability Survey.* American College of Obstetrics and Gynecology, Washington, D.C., 2006.

2. *Vital Signs: Fear of Malpractice Causes Doctors to Order Unnecessary Tests.* OB/GYN News 38(3):1 (2003).

3. Physicians Insurers Association of America, *Data Sharing Reports, Executive Summary (1995, 2001)*. Washington, D.C., 1995, 2001.

4. *Erby v. Columbia Hospital for Women,* U.S.D.D.C. No. CA-82-0799, January 6, 1983.

5. Nichols EE, Raines E, "Breast Disease and Professional Liability." In Hindle WH (Ed.), *Breast Disease for Gynecologists*. Norwalk, Conn.: Appleton & Lange, 1990.

6. Bland. In, Bland KI; Copeland EM III (Eds.), *The Breast: Comprehensive Management of Benign and Malignant Diseases*, 2nd ed. Philadelphia: W.B. Saunders Co., 1998, pp. 19–37.

7. *Dries v. Greger*, 72 A.D. 2d 231; 424 N.Y.S. 2d 561 (1980).

8. *Truan v. Smith*, 578 S.W. 2d 73 at 77 (Tenn. 1979).

9. Hindle, *supra*.

10. Piccinino LJ, Mosher WD, *Trends in Contraceptive Use in the United States: 1982–1995*. Fam. Plan. Perspect. 30:4–10, 46 (1998).

11. Cox B, Sneyd MF, Paul C, *et al.*, *Vasectomy and Risk of Prostate Cancer*. JAMA 287:3110–3115 (2002).

12. Giovannucci E, Asherio A, Rimm EB, *et al.*, *A Prospective Cohort Study of Vasectomy and Prostate Cancer in US Men*. JAMA 269:873–877 (1993).

13. *Custodio v. Bauer*, 59 Cal. Rptr. 463 (Cal. 1967).

14. *Burke v. Rico*, 406 Mass. 764 at 769; 551 N.E. 2d 1 (1990).

15. *Williams v. University of Chicago Hosps.*, 688 N.E. 2d 130 (Ill. 1997).

16. *Vital Signs: Plaintiff Recovery Rate in Childbirth Negligence Lawsuits*. OB/GYN News 39(11):1 (2004).

17. Jury Verdict Research, 2004. An LRP Publications Company, http:/www.juryverdictresearch.com/index.html

18. *Young v. Louisiana Med. Mutual Insurance Co.*, 725 So. 2d 539 (La. Ct. App. 1998).

19. *McAllister v. H.*, 496 S.E. 2d 577 (N.C. 1998).

Neonatology and Pediatrics

Jonathan Fanaroff, M.D., J.D., F.C.L.M.
Robert Turbow, M.D., J.D., F.C.L.M.

GOLDEN RULES

1. Stay current by reading journals and textbooks and by attending CME conferences.
2. Maintain professional ties with a large medical center.
3. If facing a difficult situation, consider consulting with a colleague.
4. Maintain open communication with parents and families.
5. Ensure timely documentation of procedures, communication, complications, who was present.
6. Document telephone advice.
7. If unsure, do not diagnose over the phone.
8. Be aware of state laws that affect your practice.

This chapter will focus on medical malpractice issues in pediatrics and in perinatal/neonatal medicine that can affect the daily professional lives of those who work with infants, children, and adolescents. Note that most of the neonatal issues are common issues and apply to pediatricians who care for newborns and attend deliveries as well as neonatologists. Practicing clinicians must understand their rights, duties, and liabilities as physicians.

CASE PRESENTATION

In their pediatric malpractice lawsuit, Mr. and Mrs. Smith claimed that on July 27, 2005, Mrs. Smith called Dr. Case for advice regarding their 15-month-old daughter Samantha. Samantha had been well until July 25, when she developed a low-grade fever. At that time Mrs. Smith talked to Dr. Case's partner, who recommended acetaminophen. By the next day (July 26), in addition to the fever, Samantha had developed a significant cough. Dr. Case recommended Robitussin and also thought that she may be dehydrated and stated that Pedialyte should be given to see if she would produce a wet diaper by 2:00 P.M., which she did. Mrs. Smith called back to inform Dr. Case of this, and also that Samantha seemed abnormally drowsy and sluggish and still had a fever despite the acetaminophen. Mrs. Smith also allegedly asked whether she should take Samantha to the

Emergency Department, but was told by Dr. Case that this was not necessary and that Samantha could be given ibuprofen and to see if she produced six wet diapers by that evening. Samantha produced five by that evening, so the Smiths thought everything was fine and went to bed.

The next morning on July 27, at about 9:00 A.M., Mrs. Smith had a hard time waking Samantha and called Dr. Case again about taking her to the Emergency Department, but he told her to "give it half an hour" to see if she improves. The Smiths were unsatisfied with this advice and took her to the ED at the Main Street Hospital where they waited half an hour before being seen by the triage nurse. At that time she was immediately taken to a treatment room where a spinal tap was performed and she was diagnosed with bacterial meningitis. Antibiotics were started but by that time she was severely brain-damaged.

When Dr. Case visited the family he told them that antibiotics seemed unnecessary because their baby would be better off dead. He also argued with the family over whether he should have diagnosed the meningitis earlier, stating that "over the phone it sounded like dehydration."

While not admitting to any negligence or responsibility, the suit was settled for $9 million.

ISSUES

Introduction

As the above case illustrates, pediatric malpractice claims can result in very large money damages. Pediatric patients are often treated with enormous sympathy by juries. Also, many of the most common errors in diagnosis, such as meningitis and brain-damaged infants, lead to severe and permanent injuries. Furthermore, children are at the beginning of their lives, so that the lifetime cost of care for a permanently injured child can easily run in the millions of dollars.

Because of the factors mentioned above, the average closed pediatric malpractice claim in 2004 was approximately $468,000 according to the Physician Insurers Association of America (PIAA). This is 43% higher than the overall average for all physician specialties. Indeed, the PIAA ranks pediatrics fourth in highest average indemnity from 1985 to 2004, behind neurology, neurosurgery, and obstetrics/gynecology.

The relatively high malpractice risks are due in part to the tremendous clinical and ethical challenges surrounding pediatric and neonatal medicine. In both fields, there are some unique challenges and issues that differ somewhat from adult medicine. First, parents or guardians have a moral and legal responsibility to care for and protect their children and thus become an additional and essential party in the doctor–patient relationship. Second, infants and young children are unable to create or express their own preferences and thus the physician has their own legal and moral obligation to ensure that the parents are acting in the best interests of the child. Third, as children get older, they generally can communicate their own preferences. Therefore, their assent to treatment becomes increasingly important.

Neonatologists, like pediatricians, face multiple challenges, especially surrounding the care of premature infants at the limits of viability. Does the physician have to honor whatever the parents request? What if the parents do not want resuscitation and the medical team disagrees? What if there is conflict between the parents' wishes and hospital policy or national guidelines? These questions are not just academic. A recently overturned $60 million verdict (*HCA, Inc. v. Miller ex rel. Miller*) accentuates the importance of knowing the multitude of cases and legislation that affect clinical practice. These areas remain contentious and ill-defined in many states. Physicians are often caught in the middle with potential liability for either resuscitating or not resuscitating, although certainly good communication can minimize this risk.

Common Malpractice Suits in Pediatrics

Malpractice suits in pediatrics most commonly arise from:

- Meningitis
- Appendicitis
- Specified nonteratogenic anomalies
- Pneumonia
- Brain-damaged infants
- Telephone triage—failure to treat/delayed treatment.

The most prevalent causes of malpractice suits against pediatricians involve errors in diagnosis. Part of the reason for this lies with the nature of pediatrics; obtaining a history from a child is very different from that of an adult. Does the 8-year-old with abdominal pain have a surgical emergency such as appendicitis, or are they trying to avoid confronting the school bully on the playground? Additionally, the pediatrician is often trying to provide medical care and advice over the telephone, without the advantage of having the patient in front of them.

One theme that arises repeatedly in pediatric malpractice cases, however, is a failure of the physician to heed the concerns of the parent. In general, no one knows their child better than the parents, and their concerns should always be taken seriously. Furthermore, while parents may not be able to explain their exact concern, they are often able to correctly intuit that something is wrong. Much of the advice in this book applies to pediatric patients. In the following paragraphs we will examine some specific issues in pediatrics.

Meningitis

As the case illustrates, pediatric meningitis malpractice cases lead to some of the highest average indemnities paid and also have among the highest payout ratios. Often these cases involve children too young to verbalize their symptoms, with the median age of patients being 2 years old in the PIAA Meningitis Claims Study undertaken in 2000. Many of these cases, almost 25% in the PIAA study, claim a delay in diagnosis, and, as in the case noted above, often the first contact is over the phone. Symptoms are often generalized and can include fever, nausea and vomiting, lethargy, change in mental status, and neck stiffness. Furthermore, it is important to maintain a low threshold to work up (including lumbar puncture) and treat possible meningitis, especially in infants and toddlers. Finally, a prudent physician will note if a parent states that a child is lethargic or not acting normally.

Appendicitis

Abdominal pain is an extremely common presenting complaint for pediatric patients. Approximately 15% of school-aged children are brought to a physician because of abdominal pain, of which the most common serious disorder is appendicitis. Misdiagnosing appendicitis or other causes of abdominal pain, such as constipation, gas pain, or gastroenteritis, can lead to a lawsuit. In the PIAA Data Sharing System Report from 1985 to 2003, failure to diagnose appendicitis was the second most frequent patient condition missed. One important problem in many of these cases was poor documentation. If a child presents with symptoms that may represent a "surgical abdomen," it would seem prudent for the pediatrician to document the presence or absence of pain in each quadrant, distension, guarding, rebound, tenderness, and bowel sounds. It is also important to recognize that the diagnosis of gastroenteritis is generally associated with vomiting and diarrhea. Finally, the parents need to be educated as to their most appropriate course of action should the child's condition worsen. Parents should be instructed that prompt reevaluation may stave off a serious medical/surgical problem, and the physician's instructions to the parents should be documented in the child's chart.

Telephone Triage

Pediatricians regularly offer medical advice over the telephone. Indeed, it has been estimated that up to 30% of all ambulatory pediatric care is delivered via the phone. This care led to almost 100 malpractice claims and over $11 million to plaintiffs during the period 1985–2004. In the case presented at the beginning of the chapter, it is certainly possible that the outcome would have been different had Samantha been seen and examined in the office rather than over the phone. Thorough documentation is important, as is accessibility, when setting up a phone triage system. It is particularly important to recognize that the parent or caregiver who has made the call is not a trained health care professional and cannot be expected to know exactly what to look for and what to tell you. If the telephone triage personnel determine that the parents seem to be overly nervous or the parents are insisting that their child be evaluated in person, then the prudent practitioner will strongly consider accommodating the family or referring the family to an acute care center or emergency department. The American Academy of Pediatrics Section on Telephone Care has developed a comprehensive set of management guidelines. When followed appropriately, these guidelines can mitigate the considerable legal risk associated with telephone care.

Common Malpractice Suits in Neonatology

Malpractice suits in neonatology most commonly arise from:

- Delivery room management/resuscitation
- Poor neurologic outcome—cerebral palsy/hypoxic-ischemic encephalopathy
- Line complications—thrombus and vascular accidents related to central lines
- Delay in diagnosis/treatment—acidosis, hypotension, antibiotics, developmental dysplasia of the hip, congenital heart disease
- Failure to adequately monitor/treat—hypoglycemia, hypoxia, hyperoxia, seizure.

In recent years, considerable advances have been made in the care of sick newborns. New ventilator techniques, surfactant replacement therapy, and antenatal steroids have provided vital tools in the armamentarium of the neonatologist. However, many sick newborns either die in the newborn intensive care unit (NICU) or ultimately emerge from the NICU with significant complications. Often, when a newborn is handicapped, extremely premature, or has suffered from oxygen deprivation, the NICU can be a sad and troubling environment. When these clinical situations arise, it is not uncommon for legal action to be initiated. A small but growing body of law addresses care provided in the delivery room and during the neonatal period.

Delivery Room Management/Resuscitation

Pediatricians and neonatologists are often called to attend deliveries when complications are present or anticipated. First and foremost, the clinician must ensure that the facility is properly equipped to handle "this" delivery. Does this facility have a staff that is trained in newborn resuscitation? Is the resuscitation equipment present and functional? It is virtually a certainty that unanticipated events will arise. However, proper preparation of the resuscitation team and the presence of the appropriate equipment are tantamount to a successful resuscitation.

Whether the resuscitation team is called because of a nonreassuring fetal monitoring strip, concern for placental abruption, extreme prematurity, or other circumstances, the presence of the pediatrician or neonatologist in the delivery room is often an indication of some type of problem. A variety of interventions are often attempted in the delivery room. Depending on the needs of the newborn, the clinician may simply ensure adequate thermal regulation, evaluate the ABCs, and check for anomalies. However, in other cases the delivery room management may require the physician to perform endotracheal intubation, initiate cardiac compressions, secure vascular access, administer cardiac medications, give volume expansion, or a variety of other emergency interventions.

Any time that procedures are being performed in an emergency setting, there is an increased possibility that complications will arise. Further complicating this picture is the fact that the resuscitation team often meets families for the first time in the delivery room setting. While the obstetrician may have known the family throughout the pregnancy (and perhaps through earlier pregnancies), the resuscitation team often does not have the luxury of establishing rapport with the family prior to initiation of care for the infant. This lack of rapport can contribute to malpractice litigation. Without a foundation of trust between the family and the resuscitation team, an untoward outcome may result in a family filing suit.

Poor Neurologic Outcome—Cerebral Palsy/ Hypoxic-Ischemic Encephalopathy

Evaluation of fetal monitoring strips is a common cause of malpractice cases for obstetricians. Under certain circumstances, an infant will be born in a depressed state following a nonreassuring fetal monitoring strip. Because it is often difficult to determine if a specific injury is due to *in utero* complications or immediate postnatal events, plaintiffs will often sue the neonatologist as well.

Perhaps no area of legal medicine is more contentious than the "brain-damaged newborn." In fact, many plaintiff's attorneys advertise that this area of law is one of their specialties. Fetal monitoring has become a staple of labor-delivery management. Despite the almost universal use of this technology, there is a paucity of evidence that fetal monitoring actually improves neonatal outcome. Additionally, there is evidence that neonatal brain injury is frequently present days to weeks prior to labor. Furthermore, data suggests an association between chorioamnionitis and cerebral palsy in the child. While there remains debate over the precise mechanism of cerebral cellular injury during a hypoxic/anoxic event, it is commonly accepted that a variety of events or insults suffered prior to labor, during labor, and following parturition can be associated with long-term neurologic impairment. A great deal has been written on the neurologic effects of fluctuating blood pressure, poor autoregulation of cerebral blood flow, and perfusion–reperfusion injury. These physiologic mechanisms are beyond the scope of this chapter. However, the clinician is advised to be well versed in the various theories of cerebral injury suffered in the antepartum period.

When expert witnesses review these types of malpractice cases, there is often significant importance placed on the interpretation of the fetal monitoring strip and umbilical cord pH. Experts will opine on the significance of severe, repetitive, late decelerations, or "overshoot," or prolonged fetal bradycardia. If a nonreassuring fetal monitoring strip is accompanied by a low cord pH, a plaintiff's attorney will attempt to demonstrate that a child's neurologic impairment is a direct result of delayed intervention on the part of the obstetrician. If the neonatal resuscitation or post-resuscitation stabilization does not go smoothly, the neonatologist may also be named as a defendant in a malpractice action.

As mentioned in the Introduction to this chapter, obstetricians are one of the few specialists who have the unpleasant distinction of being sued more commonly than pediatricians. Many obstetricians have stopped delivering infants, citing medical malpractice insurance premiums as the reason.

Hypoglycemia

Pediatricians and neonatologists are commonly called by staff from the normal nursery and a serum glucose level is reported. There is disagreement among clinical experts as to the exact plasma glucose level that qualifies for a diagnosis of hypoglycemia. While threshold levels of 30 or 40 mg/dl have been debated, it is generally accepted that severe or prolonged hypoglycemia can be associated with brain damage. It is often important to understand the etiology of the hypoglycemia. Is this an infant of a diabetic mother? Is this a premature infant with decreased glycogen stores? Does the infant have metabolic disease? Has the infant been cold-stressed? As in all other areas of medicine, the prudent physician will attempt to understand the etiology of the disease so that the appropriate therapy can be initiated.

Early initiation of feeds may be indicated for some infants, while intravenous boluses of glucose may be more appropriate for another infant. In rarer cases, glucagon or intravenous steroids will be required to treat severe, refractory hypoglycemia. Regardless of the treatment initiated, the prudent physician will follow serum glucose levels until it is clear that the danger of hypoglycemia has passed.

Newborn Sepsis

Accurate diagnosis of neonatal bacteremia often starts with a high index of suspicion. Certain maternal risk factors place an infant at higher risk of sepsis. These factors include maternal Group B Strep cervical culture status, length of time that membranes have been ruptured, and presence of maternal fever. Has the clinician documented whether or not the above factors are present? If an infant is born to a woman whose membranes have been ruptured for more than 18 hours, and the woman had a fever, and she was pretreated with antibiotics, a prudent physician will carefully monitor or screen that newborn. Clinicians should be familiar with current hematologic screening criteria, including immature white blood cell ratios, C-reactive protein values, and other blood tests. By practicing careful medicine and documenting one's thinking, the neonatologist can minimize the chance that there is a delay in diagnosing a bacteremic infant. A delay in making this diagnosis can have profound implications for the infant, including death.

Developmental Dysplasia of the Hip

Part of the physical exam of any newborn includes an evaluation of the hips. Are "hip clicks" present when the hips are abducted and adducted? The hip click is detected if there is an abnormality in the acetabulum or femoral head. If this abnormality is promptly discovered, good orthopedic care can often lead to an excellent clinical outcome. On the other hand, if the femoral head remains outside of the joint for an extended period of time, good function may never be achieved. Because of this, documentation of a proper hip exam is vital to all pediatricians and neonatologists.

Congenital Heart Disease

This clinical situation is somewhat similar to the above section on developmental dysplasia of the hip. A high index of suspicion and prompt referral can often mitigate substantial complications. Many types of congenital heart disease (CHD) do not necessarily present with significant hypoxemia in the immediate neonatal period. Ductal-dependent lesions may or may not be associated with a murmur in the newborn. A thorough cardiac exam of any newborn requires evaluation and documentation of the following: overall appearance of the infant, breath sounds, heart tones, murmurs, hepatomegaly, splenomegaly, femoral pulses, peripheral pulses, and perfusion.

Infants with CHD often present in the first two to six weeks of life. The presentation may include lethargy, poor feeding, failure to thrive, or a variety of other nonspecific findings. It is common for the pediatrician or emergency room physician to confuse an infant with a ductal-dependent lesion with neonatal bacteremia. Because newborn sepsis is so much more common, these infants are often cultured and started on antibiotics. Often, there are long and costly delays in making the correct diagnosis that can lead to the infant's death. The prudent pediatrician or emergency room physician must always maintain a high index of suspicion for congenital heart disease. In the appropriate situations, these clinicians will consider a chest x-ray, EKG, arterial blood gas, echocardiogram, or consultation with the neonatologist or pediatric cardiologist to assist in the diagnosis and management. The prompt initiation of certain therapies, such as PGE1 infusion, can be life-saving. Clearly, every infant with suspected sepsis does not require a pediatric cardiology consultation. However, the ability to promptly recognize and treat a case of congenital heart disease can potentially save a child's life.

Prematurity

Managing premature infants requires comprehensive training and preparation of the health care team. Every decision, including the facility in which delivery will take place, can have lifelong implications for a premature infant. A matter as simple as a malfunctioning radiant warmer can have catastrophic results. Because hypothermia has been associated with intraventricular hemorrhage, proper thermal regulation is an integral part of care for the premature infant.

Premature infants, and especially extremely premature newborns, are often born in critical condition. There is little margin for error in these small, fragile patients. Starting in the delivery room, all preparation must be comprehensive. Will the infant be intubated in the delivery room? Can the staff accomplish this? Will exogenous surfactant be administered? Should the infant be resuscitated with 100% oxygen even if the infant's oxygen saturation is reading 100%?

Are proper ventilators available and are there staff that know how to use them? If a complication such as a pneumothorax arises, will this be promptly recognized and treated? More importantly, could the complication have been prevented?

Retinopathy of Prematurity

Retinopathy of prematurity (ROP), formerly referred to as retrolental fibroplasia, is a common cause of litigation for the neonatologist as well as the pediatric ophthalmologist. While controversy exists concerning ideal oxygen and ventilator management of the sick premature newborn, close follow-up for ROP is absolutely required for these patients. With various interventions, including laser surgery, the effects of ROP can, in some cases, be somewhat mitigated.

Line Complications

Deep venous lines and central or peripheral arterial lines are routinely placed in sick newborns. For a variety of reasons, including small vessels, high hematocrit, and fluctuating blood pressure, line complications are not a rare complication in neonatology.

Malpractice cases have been based on negligence theory related to placement and management of vascular access in sick newborns. The clinician should generally document the indications for the vascular access. Why was central access required or preferred? Was the line heparanized? Was the fluid running through the line at an appropriate rate to ensure line patency? Have the physicians and nurses documented good perfusion to the limb, hand, or other part of the infant's anatomy? Was an Allen's test documented prior to peripheral arterial line insertion? Was proper care offered after the injury was discovered? If a skin graft was ultimately required, was a plastic surgeon promptly consulted?

Neonatal Transport

As mentioned above, it is ideal to deliver an infant at a facility that can provide the care that the infant will require. It is generally preferable to arrange for a maternal transport as opposed to a neonatal transport. If the pregnant woman can tolerate a transport, then the transfer of a sick infant can be avoided. Unfortunately, it is common for an infant to be critically ill without an antecedent history that forewarns the obstetric and pediatric teams that the newborn will be so sick. If a newborn is unstable after birth, then a neonatal transport may be required. The transport relocates the infant to a facility that can deliver a higher level of care.

There are a variety of risks associated with neonatal transport. The equipment, including ventilators, warmers, and infusion pumps, can fail. Ambulances can be involved in collisions. In rare cases, helicopter and airplane transports have ended in tragedy for the infant, the health care team, and the crew. If possible, informed consent should be obtained from the family prior to neonatal transport. If a parent is not available (such as a single mother with post-delivery complications) to give informed consent, then the referring and accepting physicians should both document the emergency nature of the transfer and the reasons for a lack of informed consent.

Avoiding Malpractice Suits in the Delivery Room and NICU

As in other areas of medicine, strong clinical practice, clear documentation, and good communication with the family are strategies to help avoid a malpractice action. Practicing good medicine helps avoid bad outcomes. Is the delivery room staff prepared for a sick newborn? Does the respiratory therapist have experience in the resuscitation of newborns? Does the equipment function? Are there spare batteries for the laryngoscope? Has the infant warmer been turned to the "on" position?

SURVIVAL STRATEGIES

Pediatricians are generally an optimistic group, and most of our patients do well. When there is a bad outcome, pediatricians often feel guilty and to blame and also fear a lawsuit. Furthermore, in addition to the mental anguish that one can experience as a result of being named as a defendant in a malpractice case, these proceedings are often time-consuming and expensive. There are, however, steps that one can take to minimize the chances of being named in a malpractice suit.

Maintaining competency is always crucial, not just to minimize malpractice risk, but also as a moral and ethical duty in and of itself. Pediatricians and neonatologists need to take the necessary steps in order to stay current in their discipline. In addition to conferences, journals, and textbooks, the internet is a relatively new source of continuing education that may assist physicians in their clinical practice. Medical practices change rapidly. For example, dexamethasone was used routinely ten years ago to wean premature babies with chronic lung disease from ventilators. After studies revealed long-term neurologic concerns, however, steroids are now reserved for only the sickest of babies. Failing to keep up with the latest standards and practices could lead a neonatologist to continue administering a medication or offering a form of therapy well after its use has been widely abandoned or curtailed.

Pediatric subspecialty and tertiary care services are generally organized in a regional system, often around free-standing children's hospitals. Through this system, small and large community pediatricians and neonatologists can maintain professional ties with one another and with larger medical centers. These ties allow an exchange of ideas and practices. As the American Board of Pediatrics has recently recognized, clinicians must consider their professional development as a continuous process.

If a clinician is faced with a rare or particularly challenging case, they should not hesitate to call a colleague. Maintaining contact with one's former attendings and mentors from residency and fellowship can provide great benefit for one's patients. Experienced neonatologists who work at other institutions can often assist with difficult cases. Most academic centers with training programs generally make it a point to regularly discuss the most difficult clinical cases at management conferences, morning report, grand rounds, or other venues.

In addition to maintaining good communication with colleagues, it is essential that parents are kept updated and involved. This is a requirement for legal as well as ethical reasons, and it is an essential component of informed consent. Maintaining good communication with parents is not always easy, but the consequences of poor communication may include a malpractice suit. Parents who feel uninformed and out of the loop will often become frustrated and angry. It is hard enough to deal with having a sick child. Feelings of mistrust can quickly lead to conflict. Furthermore, as the case demonstrates, a suboptimal relationship with the family of a sick child can be a harbinger of a pending malpractice suit.

While communication with the family is important, it is also essential to document appropriately. Indeed, of all the closed claims involving a problem with the medical record in 2004, the PIAA found that there was a payout in 62% of them. Chart entries need to be punctual, legible, and accurate. Time and date should be on every note, and "late entries" need to be documented as such. Important events, such as a significant complication with the patient or a comprehensive family conference, should be documented in the chart. Furthermore, a note documenting a family conference should include the content of what was discussed as well as a delineation of who was present during the conference.

As discussed earlier, phone advice can be a source of liability and appropriate documentation is important. This can be accomplished with standard phone log forms, although detailed documentation is required for complex calls. Referring doctors or parents do not always follow a physician's advice. Proper documentation of the phone discussion can provide protection for the physician.

Finally, while many United States Supreme Court cases necessarily generate a significant amount of attention, it is important to realize that most government regulation of medical practice involves state law. These state regulations include issues ranging from basic medical malpractice standards to resuscitation of extremely premature infants to professional licensing. Thus, staying up to date on the state laws and regulations that affect their practice is important for every practicing pediatrician and neonatologist.

FURTHER READING

Turbow R, Fanaroff JM, "Legal Issues in Neonatal-Perinatal Medicine". In Martin RJ, Fanaroff AA, Walsh WC, *Fanaroff and Martin's Neonatal-Perinatal Medicine,* 8th ed. Philadelphia: Mosby, vol. 1, pp. 47–62.

Medical Liability for Pediatricians, 6th ed. AAP Committee on Medical Liability, 2004.

McAbee GN, *Lessons Can Be Learned from Malpractice Cases Involving Meningitis.* AAP News 24(4):180 (2004).

Reynolds SL, *Failure to Diagnose Appendicitis Among Top Medical Misadventures.* AAP News 26(4):13 (2005).

Hertz AR, *Pediatric Telephone Care Malpractice Claims Highlight Need for Risk Management Strategies.* AAP News 26(9):12 (2005).

Pediatric Call Centers and the Practice of Telephone Triage and Advice: Critical Success Factors. AAP Provisional Section on Pediatric Telephone Care and the Committee on Practice and Ambulatory Medicine, November 1998.

Neufeld MD, Frigon C, *et al.*, *Maternal Infection and Risk of Cerebral Palsy in Term and Preterm Infants.* J. Perinatol. 25(2):108–113 (2005).

Williams AF, *Neonatal Hypoglycaemia: Clinical and Legal Aspects.* Semin. Fetal Neonatal Med. 10(4):363–368 (2005).

HCA, Inc. v. Miller ex rel. Miller, 118 S.W. 3d 758 (Tex. 2003).

Marshall v. Hartford Hosp., 783 A. 2d 1085 Conn. App., 2001.

Cardiology

S. Sandy Sanbar, M.D., Ph.D., J.D., F.C.L.M.

The cardiologist, like any other physician, is expected to evaluate a patient in a manner that will make possible the formulation of effective treatment. Although a cardiologist is not expected to ensure the correctness of a diagnosis, a patient is entitled to as thorough and careful cardiac evaluation as the attending circumstances will permit, with the utilization of cardiovascular diagnostic methods approved and implemented by similarly situated cardiologists. In recent years, the cardiovascular diagnostic and therapeutic modalities have vastly expanded, for example, in the areas of preventive and interventional cardiology.

Cardiologists are trained and certified first as internists then venture into their own subspecialty. Hence, the general liability of internal medicine specialists may apply. The reader is encouraged to review Chapter 28 on liability in internal medicine in this Handbook.

This chapter will focus on the legal aspects of acute coronary syndromes: unstable angina and myocardial infarction, and implantable cardiac devices.

UNSTABLE ANGINA

CASE PRESENTATION

On July 26, a 67-year-old white male, 5 ft 10 in. tall, weighing 210 pounds, ate a taco salad with hot sauce for supper. Two hours later, he developed chest pain and indigestion. Rolaids relieved his indigestion but not the chest pain. One month earlier he had indigestion after eating Fritos and spicy bean dip. Two years previously he had experienced a 10–15-minute episode of chest pain. Fifteen years previously, the patient developed mild hypertension that was controlled with chlorthiazide. Prior levels of serum cholesterol were 250 mg% to 284 mg%, and triglycerides ranged from normal to 484 mg%. He stopped smoking cigarettes at age 57. His father died at age 75 years of heart disease and his mother had hypertension and died of old age.

On July 27, about seven hours after the onset of chest pain, the patient drove himself to the emergency room of a community hospital. His condition upon arrival was nonurgent, pulse and respirations were normal, and the BP was 182/112 mm Hg. His chest pain was substernal, without radiation, sharp, and constant. He had nausea, but no vomiting or diaphoresis. He had bilateral inspiratory rales in the lung bases. His heart rate was regular and rhythmic with no murmurs and no third or fourth heart sounds audible. The rest of the physical exam proved to be negative.

The initial electrocardiogram revealed no acute changes with sinus bradycardia, rate 52 bpm. The chest x-ray, total CPK, CPK-MB fraction, troponins, and arterial blood gases were all normal.

The patient was treated at the emergency room with oxygen; nitroglycerin, three sublingual and one-inch transdermal; nifedipine, 10 mg by mouth; and morphine sulfate, 2 mg intravenously; after which he was admitted to the intensive care unit with the diagnosis of "rule out acute myocardial infarction."

His chest pain persisted and was not relieved after two more tablets of sublingual nitroglycerin, as well as two IV injections of Demerol.

Thrombolytic Therapy. About 9½ hours after the onset of chest pain, the patient prophylactically received cortisone and lidocaine IV; followed by a bolus of heparin, 5000 units IV; and then streptokinase, 1,500,000 units infused over a 40-minute period. Immediately after streptokinase administration, heparin was infused at a rate of 1000 units IV per hour. Despite the administration of streptokinase, the patient's chest pain increased, and he became slightly restless; he then received Demerol. There were no reperfusion arrhythmias.

Three hours after the administration of streptokinase, the patient ate a meal, after which he complained of nausea, mid-sternum chest pain, and vomited his food; he received compazine, nitroglycerin, Riopan Plus, and Zantac. Repeat electrocardiogram and cardiac enzymes were normal.

Six hours after streptokinase, the patient's pulse increased to 116 and respiration to 36 per minute. His temperature rose to 99.2°F. His eyes were deviated to the left, and he had right hemiplegia. Heparin was discontinued, and 10 mg of Decadron were given intravenously. One hour later he became aphasic, then he vomited approximately 200 ml of "golden" liquid. The CAT brain scan revealed a massive, left intracerebral hemorrhage.

About nine hours after streptokinase, he became unresponsive, his BP was 200/96, pulse 64, and his respirations were "snorting" at a rate of 60 per minute. His pupils were pinpoint and nonreactive. One hour later he became cyanotic, and had complex ventricular cardiac arrhythmias, with poor response to lidocaine. He was in moderate respiratory distress. Pupils were mid-range and nonreactive to light. Corneal and doll's eyes reflexes were absent. He had papilledema, flaccid paralysis, and no response to painful stimuli. He was intubated, hyperventilated, then placed on a respirator. Bretylol was given for the cardiac dysrhythmia.

Approximately six hours after heparin was discontinued and 12 hours after streptokinase, the partial thromboplastin time was 69 seconds, and the prothrombin time was 17 seconds. White blood count was 12,500, hemoglobin 15.2 g/dl, hematocrit 47.7%, and platelet count 290,000. Serum electrolytes, BUN, and creatinine were normal. EKG revealed sinus tachycardia with a rate of 161 bpm, and the cardiac monitor showed multifocal ventricular premature beats, with couplets and volleys of ventricular tachycardia. The patient was then declared "brain-dead," and permission was granted by his wife and son to disconnect the respirator, which was done.

Postmortem Findings. Autopsy was performed on July 28. The brain had a large, intracerebral hemorrhage of the left hemisphere. The hemorrhage began with the occipital lobe and extended forward approximately 7 cm. It involved the basal ganglia. The hemorrhagic cavity reached a maximum of 5 cm. There were scattered areas of subarachnoid hemorrhage noted over the left cerebral hemisphere and over the left portion of the cerebellum. The cerebral vessels showed scattered foci of minimal, nonocclusive atherosclerosis. No intracranial aneurysms were found.

The heart weighed 520 g. There was left ventricular hypertrophy. The pericardium and heart valves were normal. The coronary arteries were normal in distribution. There was a significantly stenotic lesion, approximately 75% luminal narrowing, of the left anterior descending branch of the left coronary artery. No fissuring, thrombosis, subintimal hemorrhage, or eccentricity was noted. The circumflex and the right coronary arteries were normal. The aorta had numerous, slightly raised, ulcerated and nonulcerated atherosclerotic plaques.

The gallbladder contained about 30 ml of viscous bile. It revealed chronic cholecystitis with cholelithiasis. There were approximately ten calculi, each of which measured 5 mm in diameter.

The gastrointestinal tract, liver, and spleen were normal. The lungs had moderate, bilateral atelectasis. The left kidney had a benign cortical cyst. The prostate was slightly enlarged and nodular.

(This is an actual case that did not get to trial; it was settled shortly after depositions were completed for a six-figure settlement.)

ISSUES

Failure to Prevent Coronary Artery Disease (CAD)

The patient was a hypertensive, hyperlipidemic, obese male in his 60s, whose father had heart disease. The hypertension was treated with medications, but not his lipids and obesity. From the preventive cardiology standpoint, treating all the cardiac risk factors would in all likelihood have resulted in a more favorable outcome, vis-à-vis the coronary artery disease. A jury might find that it is more likely than not that the failure to treat cardiac risk factors (in hopes of preventing the development of an acute coronary syndrome) was negligent; the issue of causation may pose a difficult hurdle for the plaintiff to cross. Nevertheless, care should be exercised when treating all cardiac factors in accordance with guidelines by the American College of Cardiology/American Heart Association,[1] and other national guidelines for the treatment of hypertension, hyperlipidemia, diabetes, and obesity.

Failure to Detect or Diagnose CAD

The treating physician knew or should have known that the patient had a high risk of developing CAD. In addition to not preventing CAD, the physician had never performed an exercise tolerance test (ETT) on the patient prior to the event of July 27, despite the fact that the patient had prior episodes of chest pain. Because the left anterior descending coronary artery had a significant stenosis of 75%, in all likelihood an ETT might have been positive in the months preceding the terminal event. The jury may conclude that the failure to detect or diagnose the CAD was negligent. Failure to diagnose is one of the most common allegations made by plaintiffs in malpractice lawsuits.

Failure to Properly Conduct a Differential Diagnosis

Because the patient had a normal EKG and normal cardiac enzymes, the treating physician was under a duty to search for and rule out other causes of chest pain, including gastrointestinal and gallbladder disease, prior to the administration of thrombolytic therapy.

The patient's chest pain could have been due to unstable angina, diffuse esophageal spasm, gastroesophageal reflux, chronic cholecystitis and cholelithiasis, and less likely musculoskeletal chest wall pain, pneumonia, pneumothorax, peptic ulcer disease, myocardial infarction, cardiac trauma, pericarditis, cardiomyopathy, mitral valve prolapse, aortic dissection, pulmonary hypertension, or pulmonary embolism.

An ultrasound test of the gallbladder in the case above would have revealed the evidence of cholelithiasis and cholecystitis, but would not have negated the concomitant presence of CAD; the treating physician was convinced that the patient had unstable angina, with proof of significant CAD at autopsy. The jury may conclude that the failure to conduct a proper differential diagnosis of the chest pain was negligent.

Failure to Follow Hospital Protocol

Should thrombolytic therapy be administered to a patient who has clinically unstable angina; with no prior history of known coronary disease; who presents with new chest pain at rest of over nine hours duration; who has no cardiac abnormalities on physical exam; and who has no objective, diagnostic, abnormalities in the initial electrocardiogram or cardiac enzymes and isoenzymes?

With the help of the cardiology department, the hospital where the above case was treated had developed specific criteria for the use of thrombolytic therapy within 6–8 hours of onset of chest pain and in the presence of EKG evidence of ST elevation. In the case above, thrombolytic therapy was begun 9½ hours after the onset of chest pain and there was no ST elevation on the EKG.

It behooves the treating physician to review the hospital policy and procedure regarding the proposed treatment. If the cardiologist elects to choose a course of treatment that is different from the hospital procedure, then the patient's informed consent should be obtained for that deviation, and the cardiologist should note the reasons for electing the chosen treatment.

In addition, the hospital nurse in charge of the patient may refuse to comply with the treatment that is against hospital policy. The hospital becomes liable when its own employees fail to follow hospital policy and procedure with resultant detriment to the patient.

Failure to Perform Myocardial Perfusion Studies and Coronary Arteriography

Should the cardiologist have performed myocardial perfusion studies, nuclear or echocardiographic, or coronary arteriogram prior to the administration of thrombolytic therapy?

Unstable angina, as compared to *stable angina*, denotes a more serious stage of angina pectoris, and it is managed differently.[2] The pain lasts over 15 minutes and is not relieved by rest. There is a change or acceleration of the coronary arterial disease process. It is a stage before heart muscle damage or myocardial infarction. Unstable angina is a syndrome and does not represent one disorder. It depicts the myocardial ischemic chest pain syndrome of patients with differing pathologic findings in the coronary arterial system, which vary from pure coronary spasm without thrombotic or atherosclerotic disease to stenotic lesions that may be fixed, smooth, or ulcerated, with or without thrombi, fissuring, eccentricity of plaque, or subintimal hemorrhage. It is no wonder that the prognosis of patients with unstable angina is variable and depends on the type, extent, and severity of the underlying coronary disease process.

During the pain of unstable angina, patients may demonstrate paroxysmal hypertension and sinus tachycardia and/or ischemic ST segment depression on electrocardiogram, and coronary artery arteriography demonstrate 50% or greater narrowing of one or more of the major coronary arteries. Patients with unstable angina pectoris of recent onset may not develop myocardial infarction or die unexpectedly of a cardiac arrhythmia.

The degree of coronary stenosis is critical. Resistance to flow is normally maximal at the level of the coronary arterioles. It requires more than a 75% reduction of the lumina in the conduit major arterial trunks to affect the volume flow through the arterioles. This important hemodynamic fact must be kept in mind when interpreting the functional significance of atherosclerotic narrowing of lesser severity.

In the case above, the left anterior descending coronary artery had 75% stenosis, which is significant and may have been a contributing cause of the chest pain. Myocardial perfusion studies and coronary arteriography would have justified angioplasty with stent placement in the left anterior descending coronary artery, which would have been a prudent course of treatment prior to cholecystectomy for cholecystitis and cholelithiasis. Neither the specific lesion of CAD nor the gallbladder disease was diagnosed prior to death.

Proper diagnosis is the foundation for rational therapy. Both noninvasive and invasive procedures should be utilized in the evaluation of coronary artery disease. The legal standards are set both by the medical profession and by the courts, for the diagnosis and treatment of coronary artery disease. In the case above, the failure on the part of the treating physician to obtain appropriate tests represented a departure from the national standard of accepted medical practice by internists and/or cardiologists under similar circumstances.

Treatment of Unstable Angina

Aspirin, antiplatelet agents, intravenous nitroglycerin, beta- and calcium-blockers, and heparin have been shown to have significant beneficial effects in patients with unstable angina.

Intravenous nitroglycerin has been sanctioned by the Food and Drug Administration for use in unstable angina. Oral nitrates, beta-blockers, calcium-blockers, and heparin have all been shown effective in the treatment of unstable angina, in combination with rest, sedation, and oxygen. Some patients with unstable angina syndromes may benefit from intra-aortic balloon counterpulsation, coronary angioplasty, and bypass surgery.

Thrombolytic therapy is a well-recognized modality for the treatment of patients with acute myocardial infarction. To be most successful, thrombolytic therapy should be administered during the first four hours after the onset of the infarction. A number of thrombolytic (or fibrinolytic) agents, so-called "clot busters," are currently approved by the Food and Drug Administration for acute myocardial infarction, including streptokinase, urokinase, tissue-type plasminogen activator, and others.

Thrombolytic therapy in unstable angina involving intravenous and intracoronary thrombolysis has in some instances shown clinical benefit but generally no angiographic improvement. There may also be an advantage in giving aspirin and thrombolytic therapy simultaneously.

Complications of Thrombolytic Therapy

Thrombolytic therapy may result in severe internal bleeding involving gastrointestinal, genitourinary, retroperitoneal, or intracerebral sites. Fatalities due to cerebral and other internal hemorrhage have occurred during intravenous thrombolytic therapy. Other complications of streptokinase include fever, allergic reactions, occasional nausea and vomiting, and headache. In addition, drug-induced, life-threatening "reperfusion arrhythmias" may develop in a significant number of patients in whom the occluded coronary artery is reopened with thrombolytics.

Most bleeding complications from thrombolytic therapy can be avoided with proper patient selection, minimizing invasive procedures, limiting the duration of therapy, and using judicious anticoagulation methods.

Negligence Standard Set by the Judge

Ordinarily, in medical malpractice cases, the standards set by the medical profession are generally accepted by the courts as being the standards imposed by law. But under certain circumstances the judge and not the physician determines the professional standard of care as a matter of law, and this may differ from common medical practice.

In the famous case of *T. J. Hooper*,[3] the court held that: "In most cases reasonable prudence is in fact common prudence; but strictly it is never its measure. . . . Courts must in the end say what is required; there are precautions so imperative that even their universal disregard will not excuse their omission." Relying on *T. J. Hooper*, the Washington State Supreme Court rejected in *Helling v. Carey*[4] the standard set by common medical practice. In *Helling*, the physician did not test the patient for glaucoma; she became blind. The court held that the physician was negligent as a matter of law for not testing the patient for glaucoma. In 1979, the same court held that the doctrine of *Helling* requiring a higher standard of care than the prevailing standard of care applied in *Gates v. Jensen*,[5] and it could not be abrogated by enacted legislation. In *Keogan v. Holy Family Hospital*,[6] the Washington Supreme Court again held both the physician and the hospital negligent as a matter of law for not utilizing a simple and safe diagnostic tool, the EKG, in a patient presenting with chest pain due to myocardial infarction. The *Keogan* court also relied on *Hicks v. United States*[7] and *Steeves v. United States* in reaching its decision; these cases are cited in *Keogan*.

The case presented above did not have an ultrasound of the gallbladder. Had the latter been done, thrombolytic therapy and the patient's death from intracerebral hemorrhage probably might have been avoided. The physician's conduct in this case could conceivably be construed by some courts as negligence as a matter of law.

When considering treatment, the physician should first utilize safer drugs in the treatment of unstable angina—that is, aspirin and nitroglycerin IV, among others—before utilizing FDA-approved thrombolytics for unapproved uses. Unapproved uses of drugs should be in accordance with the manufacturer's recommendations; otherwise, the physician's deviation from the latter is *prima facie* evidence of negligence. Such was the holding of the Minnesota Supreme Court in *Mulder v. Parke Davis & Co.*[8]

Survival Stategy

"First, do no harm."

Second, "The burning candle of life is such a precious light in anyone's existence that no one has a right to extinguish it before it flickers out into perpetual darkness and oblivion" (*Valdez v. Lyman-Roberts Hospital, Inc.*).[9]

MYOCARDIAL INFARCTION

CASE PRESENTATION

The Reverend Allan David McKellips[10] was brought to the emergency room of St. Francis Hospital in Tulsa, Oklahoma, at 2:30 P.M., complaining of chest pain. The physician diagnosed his condition as gastritis and released him at about 4:15 P.M. A few hours later, he suffered cardiac arrest and was returned to the hospital. He died at 9:30 P.M.

The survivors of Mr. McKellips brought a wrongful death action against (1) St. Francis Hospital, (2) the company under contract with the hospital to provide physicians for the emergency room, and (3) the physician who had been on duty in the emergency room when Mr. McKellips was seen.

The plaintiffs' expert witness, a board-certified emergency physician, testified at the trial that the defendants had been negligent in failing to diagnose the patient's heart attack and in releasing him from the hospital.

The expert said that admitting Mr. McKellips to the hospital would not have prevented his attack. As to ultimate chances of survival if admission had taken place, he testified: "I think unquestionably his chances would have been significantly improved. As to whether or not it would have, in fact, changed the outcome, I think this is a statistical probability statement that is difficult to answer. But as far as improving his chances, there's no question that that's true."

Questions on Appeal

The case was appealed and two questions were certified for consideration by the Oklahoma Supreme Court:

1. In a medical malpractice action under Oklahoma law, absent evidence that the patient more likely than not would have survived with proper treatment, may a plaintiff establish causation under the loss of chance doctrine by presenting evidence that the alleged negligence lessened the chance of survival?
2. If the loss of chance doctrine is recognized in Oklahoma, is expert testimony that "unquestionably [the patient's] chances would have been significantly improved" sufficient under the doctrine to create a question for the jury, even though the expert cannot quantify the increased chance of survival?

The Oklahoma Supreme Court answered "yes" to both questions.

The Court's Reasoning

The court reasoned that the general principles of proof of causation in medical malpractice cases were the same as in ordinary negligence cases. It recognized, however, a developing trend to relax the traditional standard for sufficiency of proof of causation necessary for a jury to consider causation in lost chance of survival cases. The court reasoned that, in the typical loss of chance case, the plaintiff patient maintains that negligence has helped increase the risk of harm by either hastening or aggravating the effect of a preexisting medical ailment, condition, or risk—as, for example, in negligent failure to diagnose cancer or myocardial infarction in a timely manner.

In adopting the loss of chance doctrine, the court limited its application to medical malpractice cases in which the duty breached was one imposed to prevent the type of harm that occurred. The court considered the Restatement 2nd of Torts, §343, as the most rational approach to follow: Health care providers should not be given the benefit of the uncertainty created by their own negligent conduct. To hold otherwise would in effect allow care providers to evade liability for their negligent actions or inactions in situations in which patients would not necessarily have survived or recovered, but still would have significant chance of survival or recovery.

The court also noted that, although the plaintiff's burden of production has been lowered, it only allows the plaintiff to establish more easily a jury question on the issues of causation, thereby giving the jury a greater role in the decision-making process. When the case does reach the jury, however, the plaintiff still has the burden of persuading the jury by a preponderance of the evidence.

Apportionment of Damages

When applying the loss of chance doctrine in medical malpractice cases, courts commonly limit damages to those proximately caused by the defendant's breach of duty owed. A total recovery of all damages would be unfair to the negligent party. A simple formula is therefore used, based on statistical evidence of the plaintiff's reduced chance of recovery or survival. Damages equal the percentage of chance lost multiplied by the total amount of damages that would have been allowed in a wrongful death action.

The jury selects the original percentage of chance and the percentage of diminished chance from the defendant's negligence. Then the trial court multiplies the total amount of damages by the net reduced figure to determine the final damages. If, for example, the jury determines from statistical findings combined with specific relevant facts that the patient originally had a 40% chance of cure and that the physician's negligence reduced that chance to 25%, then the patient's loss of chance was 15%. Thus, if the total amount of damages proved by the evidence is $500,000, the damages caused by the defendant are 15% of $500,000, which is $75,000.

The loss of chance doctrine allows compensating an injured patient for being deprived of a chance to recover or survive. The doctrine also recognizes that the chances of survival may be less than even to begin with. It reflects the growing trend to hold health care providers liable if they increase the seriousness of a patient's existing illness or injury by their acts or omissions. If liability is predicated on the lost chance for cure or survival, it is imposed when the health care provider has been a concurrent or intervening cause of the loss.

The Difference an Hour Makes in Myocardial Infarction

Where there is no contraindication, the intravenous administration of thrombolytic therapy during the first two or three hours following the development of acute, anterior, transmural, myocardial infarction is life-saving. Therefore, with the passing of every hour there is a gradual, albeit significant, loss of the chance to survive or recover from the complications of complete occlusion of the left anterior descending branch of the left coronary artery. The same may not be true, however, in cases of acute inferior myocardial infarction, since here there is no consensus as to mortality reduction.

From a medicolegal perspective, if a patient develops an acute anterior myocardial infarction and seeks medical attention in time to benefit from the administration of thrombolytic therapy, failure to administer such therapy may form a basis of liability.

Loss of Chance in Unstable Angina

If the traditional burdens of proof of negligence cannot be met by a preponderance of the evidence, failure to diagnose and hospitalize patients with unstable angina for treatment may be the basis for liability on grounds of loss of chance of survival or recovery.

A trend has been emerging nationally in recent years to relax the traditional burdens of proof in medical malpractice cases. The traditional view required an injury to have been the "probable" result of a negligent act or omission, with greater than 50% likelihood. In contrast, the "loss of chance" doctrine is related to a loss of the plaintiff's chance of recovery and may allow compensation for an injury that resulted even when the chance of recovery may have been less than 50% to begin with.

This doctrine does not depend on the patient's ultimate injury. Instead, it focuses on the loss of an opportunity for recovery or survival. Compensation may be given as long as the proximate cause of the loss of chance is proven. For the plaintiff to prevail, the medical expert does not necessarily have to state that the injury was the probable result of negligence.

When considering the loss of chance doctrine, the courts have basically taken three different approaches:

1. Several jurisdictions still hold to the traditional "all or nothing" view, in which the plaintiff must go forward with the burden of proof and show that it is probable or more likely than not that the unstable angina patient would have recovered or survived with appropriate care. Courts that have held to the all-or-nothing approach state three concerns about adopting the loss of chance doctrine. First, the courts feel that jurors would have to speculate as to the lost chance of survival. Second, defendants in medical malpractice cases would be subject to a far lesser standard of proximate cause than other malpractice defendants. Third, a loss of chance recovery eliminates the requirement of proximate cause.

2. The second theory is the "substantial possibility" of survival doctrine based on the opinion that if there was any substantial possibility of survival and the defendant has destroyed it, he or she is answerable. Courts have applied the "substantial possibility" inconsistently, and consequently this lack of uniformity has resulted in some confusion.

3. The third theory pertaining to the loss of chance of survival follows the Restatement 2nd of Torts, §323 (1965). This section pertains to those who provide a service necessary for protection of others. In medical malpractice cases, the application of §323(a) would relax the degree of evidence required of the plaintiff. It would also allow the jury to determine loss of chance on a showing of increased risk of harm to the patient. The task of balancing probabilities is left to the jury. Liability is imposed if the defendant proximately caused the harm. In medical malpractice cases, uncertain evidence may often be the only available evidence.

Courts have held that a caregiver could be liable for negligence if the patient's death is accelerated by even an hour, minutes, or seconds. One Texas court eloquently stated the reasoning involved in the loss of chance doctrine as follows: "The burning candle of life is such a precious light in anyone's existence that no one has a right to extinguish it before it flickers out into perpetual darkness and oblivion" (*Valdez*). This may indeed describe a patient in acute, evolving myocardial infarction, where time matters. Whether or not this can be translated into a legal remedy, however, will depend on the jurisdiction.

IMPLANTABLE CARDIOVASCULAR DEVICES

The reader is advised to read Chapter 19 in this Handbook on medical products liability. Some of the most astounding advances in implantable devices involve artificial cardiovascular implants, including artificial hearts, artificial valves, pacemakers, defibrillators, prosthetic vessels, and vascular stents. In 1960, Chardack and his colleagues implanted the first successful internally powered pacemaker in a human.[11] There have been rapid strides since then, with continuous growth in the number of patients with pacemakers, attributable to improvements in our knowledge of cardiac arrhythmias, more accurate diagnosis, and the availability of better pacing systems.

More recently, the automatic implantable defibrillator has been utilized successfully to terminate ventricular fibrillation and ventricular tachycardias, and its improved performance capabilities allow for biventricular cardiac pacing, cardioversion, monitoring and storage of information, and extensive noninvasive interrogation.

Permanent Pacemaker Implantation

The indications for permanent artificial cardiac pacing are continually being revised for both symptomatic and asymptomatic patients, but there are some clear indications and national guidelines.[12] Cardiologists involved in the implantation of permanent pacemakers must be thoroughly familiar with the accepted indications for their use. Bradyarrhythmias are among the most commonly found indications. In contrast, pacemaker implantation may be considered inappropriate under certain clinical circumstances. For example, the so-called "overdrive suppression" of ventricular arrhythmias often has been unsuccessful and the use of implantable pacemakers for this purpose also may be considered inappropriate.

Implantable Defibrillators

Implantable defibrillators, which may combine pacemaker functions, deal primarily with ventricular tachycardias and fibrillation. Initially, criteria for defibrillator implantation were very strict. Recently, however, the criteria have been relaxed to require only a single episode of ventricular fibrillation or hemodynamically unstable ventricular tachycardia.[13]

Liability Issues of Implantable Devices

A physician will be liable for negligent failure to implant a pacemaker, defibrillator, or other cardiac device when such a device is indicated, as well as for negligently implanting such a device that is not medically indicated. Undue delay in implantation of the cardiac device may also constitute negligence.

The soaring health care cost has become a significant factor in the physician's judgment as to the need for pacemakers, defibrillators, and other implants, and in determining whether the implant is justified. The benefit versus risk rule is particularly critical in the decision to recommend an implantable cardiac device.

Physicians are becoming sensitized to cost-containment. There has been greater scrutiny of implantable devices due to concerns of patients, government, and health care insurers over the cost of such devices. And it is conceivable that an "affordable" type of care may become a determinant of the legal "standard of medical care" for implantable devices, thereby redefining the traditional standard of care set by the medical profession.

Informed Decisions

The patient should be fully informed of and involved in each phase of the diagnosis and treatment of cardiac arrhythmias, heart failure, and the need for implantable cardiovascular devices. This legal duty of informed decision making is being imposed by all courts in all aspects of medical care. If a patient's differential diagnosis includes cardiac arrhythmia, and the physician decides not to confirm the diagnosis by further testing, the patient must be fully advised of this decision and its implications. Also, if the patient refuses additional testing or implantation of a pacemaker, defibrillator, or other device, the patient must be advised of all the material risks of his or her decision, i.e., an informed refusal by the patient.. Permanent pacemakers, for example, are generally not indicated unless the patient has a potentially life-threatening arrhythmia. Failure to inform the patient as to this decision carries potentially serious legal liability, at least for the failure to obtain informed consent.

A patient who undergoes implantation of a permanent device must give a fully informed consent to the procedure. Otherwise, the attending or consulting physician may be subjected to allegations of "technical battery" on grounds of lack of informed consent. This is particularly likely to happen if complications occur and the plaintiff proves that proper warning of the material risks involved in the procedure was not provided by the physician.

A physician may also be found negligent for failing to properly advise the patient of the signs of device malfunction. Patients should be warned about the possibility of pacemaker malfunction due to microwave ovens, magnetometers, or radar systems. Patients should be taught how to monitor their own heart rates at home and should know what their own rate should be. They should be advised about which changes in heart rate may signal malfunction. Generator malfunction can lead to sudden death. Every physician clearly has a duty to fully inform and educate patients on how to recognize possible warning signs.

Economic Considerations

Cardiologists should consider nonmedical determinants among the indications for the use of implantable cardiac devices. The third-party reimbursements, cost-effectiveness, government intervention, case law legislation, as well as individual and public considerations, all help to determine the standard of care for the use of cardiac devices in patients.

Legal Implications

What are the legal implications of implantable cardiac pacemakers, defibrillators, and other cardiac devices? As the number of patients with cardiac implants has increased, there has been a concomitant increase in the number of malpractice lawsuits. These actions have been based on the tort of negligence, breach of expressed or implied warranty, and strict product liability. They have been brought against the manufacturer, the hospital, the cardiologist, the attending physician, and the cardiovascular surgeon.

The implantation of a pacemaker, defibrillator, or other cardiac device is burdened with the usual legal problems inherent in any other medical or surgical procedure. In addition, several areas of unique liability can be identified.

Tort Action

A patient who is injured during the implantation procedure may bring a medical malpractice action in tort against the attending and consulting physicians, the hospital, and the device manufacturer. The plaintiff may allege any of the following: negligent failure to reach a decision on whether to implant a device when such is clearly indicated medically; negligent failure to warn the patient of potential material risks, side effects, and complications; improper selection of the appropriate type of pacing system needed; negligent postimplantation care; and improper design and manufacture of the device.

Cardiovascular Product Liability

A tort action may be brought against the manufacturer of a device for defective design or manufacture of the cardiovascular product. Manufacturers of defective implantable devices may be held liable under several legal theories. Recovery may be based on negligent failure to conform to the appropriate standard requiring due care in design, manufacture, assembly, packaging, inspection, or testing. However, an action in negligence poses difficulty in proving each of the necessary elements.

These difficulties have led to the development of the doctrine of strict product liability. Under this doctrine, the manufacturer can be held liable for a defect despite the exercise of all possible due care in design and manufacture of the product. No proof of negligence is necessary. Liability is based on the theory that the manufacturer owes a duty of care to the ultimate consumer to protect that consumer from defects. No contractual relationship or privity between the consumer and the manufacturer need exist. The trend has been toward "increased and widespread" application of this doctrine.

Difficulty in applying §402(a) of the Second Restatement of Torts arises when the defendant is not the manufacturer. The section applies to the "one who sells" the product and is "engaged in the business of selling" the product.

Most courts have held that neither physicians nor hospitals fall within the scope of §402(a). However, hospitals and physicians may incur liability for failure to inspect the device for discoverable defects.

Failing to warn of dangers may result in a manufacturer's liability regardless of whether a defect exists. The manufacturer may not be subject to strict product liability if adequate warnings of all potential hazards are given to the physician/purchaser. In such cases, the physician's failure to heed and disclose the dangers to the patient is deemed a superseding cause that relieves the manufacturer from liability. However, if the dangers and warnings are minimized or downplayed, the manufacturer may be found negligent. If the physician's acts were reasonably foreseeable in light of the warnings, a manufacturer will not be exonerated from liability.

Generally, the manufacturer will be held to a "reasonable man" standard in determinations of whether the warning is inadequate. Five relevant standards concerning the adequacy of warnings have been identified:

1. The warning must adequately indicate the scope of the danger.
2. The warning must reasonably communicate the extent or seriousness of the harm that could result from misuse.
3. The physical aspects of the warning must be adequate to alert a reasonably prudent person to the danger.
4. A simple directive warning may be considered inadequate when it fails to state the consequences that might result from failure to follow it.
5. The means of conveying the warning must be adequate and the drug manufacturer must bring the warning home to the doctor.

Breach of Contract

As in any doctor–patient relationship, the cardiologist may be liable for breach of contract if the physician guarantees a specific result or cure. Physicians should avoid making any statements that could be misunderstood as an implied or expressed guarantee of a specific outcome. Generally, the "reasonable man" standard is used to determine whether a contract was made. Would a "reasonable man" in the patient's situation understand the physician's words as a guarantee? If so, legal liability may result for failure to obtain the promised results.

Breach of Warranty

Most suits against manufacturers are based on an expressed or implied warranty. Generally, pacemakers and other devices carry an expressed, albeit limited, warranty for replacement in the event of a defect. Rarely, however, does the patient see this warranty. This, coupled with the fact that the physician selects the brand of implant to be used, makes it very difficult for the patient to prove reliance on an expressed warranty. To succeed in an action for breach of expressed warranty, the plaintiff must prove the existence of the expressed warranty, the scope of coverage of the warranty, and reliance on the warranty.

In some situations, the implantation of a particular pacemaker generator without appropriate prior electrophysiologic studies may constitute negligence on the part of the cardiologist or surgeon.

The types of negligence discussed above all involve failure of the physician, hospital, or both, to adhere to the appropriate standard of care in treatment of the patient. These types of claims deal with the service aspect of implantation as distinguished from the product aspect. None of the actions discussed so far would include allegations of a defective product.

Implied Warranties

Implied warranties under the Uniform Commercial Code include fitness for purpose or use and merchantability. To recover under a theory of implied warranty, the plaintiff must prove that the cardiovascular product was defective when it was sold, that because of the defect the device did not conform to the implied warranty, and that the defect was the proximate cause of injury.

Expert medical testimony would be necessary for a plaintiff in an implantation case to succeed on a breach of warranty cause of action. In a New York case, the plaintiff brought an action against Medtronic[14] for breach of the expressed and implied warranty. At trial, evidence showed that there were at least three possible reasons why the pacemaker electrode in question broke, causing the plaintiff injury. The court held that a finding by the jury as to the cause of the break would be highly speculative and presumptuous without the aid of medical testimony. Without such testimony, the jury would have no grounds upon which to base a finding of breach of warranty.

Literature supplied with a cardiovascular device is not an expressed warranty as a matter of law. In one case, the literature dealt with the "life-expectancy" of the power pack. Although there may have been an expressed warranty as to the power pack, there was none with respect to the electrode. Since there was no allegation that the battery failed, the expressed warranty was found to be irrelevant. In general, a breach of warranty cause of action for a defective device cannot be sustained against a physician or hospital. The courts generally have held that the sale of the device by the health care provider is incidental to the services provided by the hospital and physician and, therefore, that they are not subject to a warranty cause of action.

Class Actions

A plaintiff who desires to bring a class action suit based on a defective cardiovascular implantable product may have difficulty. The court may consider medical device cases as ill-suited for prosecution as a class action and may refuse to allow their trial as such because:

1. The defendants' liability could vary from claim to claim;
2. The extent of damages could range from essentially nonexistent to wrongful death;
3. The pleadings might not suggest a preponderance of common questions of law; and

4. Issues related to statute of limitations, contributory negligence, and assumptions of risk could vary from state to state and would require diverse rulings by the court.

The plaintiff also may have a potential problem in obtaining personal jurisdiction over the defendant. The plaintiff must establish that the manufacturer has sufficient "minimum contacts," i.e., business dealings, to allow the court to exercise jurisdiction. Merely placing the implant device into the stream of commerce with no knowledge about where the patient who ultimately receives it will reside, may not be adequate to allow jurisdiction over the defendant in the plaintiff's home state.

Well-documented records are essential. The patient's record must include pertinent data such as manufacturer, model, and serial number, and measure physiologic data. Equally important is documentation regarding the patient's under standing of the device and compliance with recommended follow-up procedures. Failure or refusal to keep appointments, take medications, or participate in telephonic monitoring should all be noted. Contributory negligence or assumption of the risk may prevent a plaintiff patient's recovery on a negligence cause of action. The physician should attempt to inform the patient who refuses follow-up of the possible consequences of refusal.

FURTHER READING

Lehv M, "Medical Product Liability." In *Legal Medicine/American College of Legal Medicine*, 7th ed., ed. S. Sandy Sanbar *et al*. Philadelphia: Mosby, 2007.

REFERENCES

1. *AHA/ACC Guidelines for Preventing Heart Attack and Death in Patients with Atherosclerotic Cardiovascular Disease: 2001 Update*. Circulation 104:1577 (2001).

2. Braunwald EW, *et al*., Management of Patients with Unstable Angina and Non-ST-Segment Elevation Myocardial Infarction Update, http://www.acc.org/clinical/guidelines/unstable/incorporated/index.htm (ACC/AHA 2002 Guideline Update for the Management of Patients with Unstable Angina and Non-ST-Segment Elevation Myocardial Infarction).

3. *T. J. Hooper*, 60 F. 2d 737 (1932).

4. *Helling v. Carey*, 83 Wn. 2d 514, 519 P. 2d 981, 67 A.L.R. 3d 175 (1974).

5. *Gates v. Jensen*, 92 Wn. 2d 246, 595 P. 2d 919 (1979).

6. *Keogan v. Holy Family Hospital*, 95 Wn. 2d 306 (1980).

7. *Hicks v. United States*, 368 F. 2d 626 (4th Cir. 1966).

8. *Mulder v. Parke Davis & Co.*, 288 Minn. 332, 181 N.W. 2d 882, 887 (1970).

9. *Valdez v. Lyman-Roberts Hosp., Inc.*, 638 S.W. 2d 111 (1982).

10. *McKellips v. St. Francis Hosp., Inc.*, 1987 Okla. 69, 741 P. 2d 467, 58 O.B.J. 2229.

11. Greatbatch W, http://www.greatachievements.org/?id=3839

12. *ACC/AHA Guidelines for Implantation of Cardiac Pacemakers and Antiarrhythmia Devices: Executive Summary.* Circulation 97:1325–1335 (1998).

13. *ACC/AHA/NASPE 2002 Guideline Update for Implantation of Cardiac Pacemakers and Antiarrhythmia Devices: Summary Article.* Circulation 106:2145 (2002)

14. *Medtronic Inc. v. Lohr,* 518 U.S. 470 (1996).

Emergency Medicine

James R. Hubler, M.D., J.D., F.A.C.E.P., F.A.A.E.M., F.C.L.M.
James T. Brown, M.D., F.A.C.E.P.

GOLDEN RULES

1. Detailed history and physical examination will prevent allegations of substandard care.
2. Nurse–physician discrepancies must be addressed in the medical record.
3. Risk factor analysis may help the physician in diagnosing the underlying medical illness.
4. Repeating of patient's abnormal vital signs is critical to avoid medical errors and to support the high-quality level of care provided.
5. Detailed documentation regarding the patient's emergency department course, differential diagnosis, and treatment plan is essential in preventing medical malpractice.
6. Discharge documentation must be specific and detailed.
7. Communication—making a good impression with the patient and his family is the key to avoid disgruntled patients and prevent medical malpractice.
8. Maintain a team atmosphere in the emergency department.
9. Honesty regarding medical mistakes or errors has been shown to decrease medical malpractice claims.
10. Beware of the dangers of shift change.

The practice of emergency medicine is riddled with medical legal risk to the emergency department (ED) practitioner. It is considered a high-risk specialty; in fact, emergency physicians are named in 53% of all lawsuits. By its nature, the specialty requires decisions that allow only for a narrow margin of error. Those judgments are subject to hindsight analysis. Unlike other specialties, emergency physicians cannot limit their practice. They must care for "all comers" walking through the emergency department doors. Decisions must be made immediately and information is frequently limited. The loss of subspecialty care, particularly neurosurgery, oral surgery, and plastic surgery, has increased the risk for the emergency physician. Patients remain in the emergency department longer, while waiting transfer to facilities that offer a higher level of care. These delays in definitive treatment increase the risk for both the emergency physician and the patient. Emergency departments have been forced to address overcrowding and long wait times. In the past ten years, hundreds of emergency departments have closed despite a 20% increase in ED visits, thereby compounding the overcrowding problem.

Emergency physicians come in contact with numerous acutely ill patients. Some may be admitted; others may be discharged and evaluated by other physicians at a later date. Unfortunately, once the emergency physician's name is on the chart, he or she runs the risk of becoming a party to a lawsuit. Plaintiff's attorneys often name all the physicians who have come in contact with the patient. This is done to avoid physicians "pointing" the finger at an unnamed physician; this also prevents potential claims of legal malpractice against the plaintiff's attorney for failing to name the correct party.

Malpractice litigation may simply be the result of an unexpected bad outcome, rather than the result of substandard care. When the patient returns to the emergency department having deteriorated since discharge, there is a suspicion of medical negligence. Unfortunately, these cases are unpredictable, and therefore, detailed documentation on every patient is required. Physicians should document actual physical exam findings. Documentation such as "within normal limits" or "normal" will not reflect the high-quality medical care provided to the patient. There will always be an expert willing to point out the emergency physician's deficiencies. However, performing detailed history and physical examinations and thorough documentation will create a strong medical record. This documentation may help protect the physician in future legal proceedings.

Medical malpractice does occur. For example, 4% of myocardial infarctions are sent home and over one-half of these had obvious EKG abnormalities that were misinterpreted by the emergency physician.[1] Using the following case as an illustration, this chapter will discuss the risks of practicing emergency medicine, medical errors that lead to medical malpractice litigation, and a risk-sensitive approach aimed at preventing potential litigation.

CASE PRESENTATION

Janice Jones was a 43-year-old white female who presented at the emergency department with complaints of fever and body aches. She had a one-day history of nonspecific symptoms including myalgias, malaise, fever, and chills. On her initial presentation she had no other complaints. The emergency physician recorded a detailed review of her symptoms, including a lack of chest pain, shortness of breath, nausea, vomiting, diarrhea, urinary symptoms, or rash. The patient had a significant past medical history for diabetes and pneumonia.

On her physical examination she was found to be mildly dehydrated, tachycardic with a heart rate of 138, a blood pressure of 92/60, a temperature of 101.3°F, a respiratory rate of 23, and oxygen saturation of 98%. She was alert, but slow to respond to questions. Her lung, abdomen, and chest examinations were noted to be "normal." During her stay in the emergency department, she received 2 liters of normal saline. She had a normal urinalysis and an Accu-Check that read 212. She reported feeling better to the nurse and was subsequently discharged with the diagnosis of a viral illness. The discharge instructions given encouraged her to return for abdominal pain, high fever, or poor urine output. If she had not improved in two to three days, she was told to follow up with her doctor.

Mrs. Jones returned to the emergency department approximately 12 hours later and was evaluated by a second emergency physician. Her blood pressure was 60/0. She had an altered level of consciousness and decreased gag response. The emergency physician immediately prepared for rapid sequence intubation and subsequently intubated the patient successfully. She had a normal chest x-ray. Her CBC demonstrated a white blood cell count of 27,000 with 27% bands. Her urinalysis was normal and her electrolytes showed mild acidosis with a CO_2 of 9. Her glucose was 180. She was immediately started on antibiotics and steroids and admitted to the intensive care unit. Unfortunately, despite aggressive IV fluid resuscitation, dopamine use, and mechanical ventilation, her sepsis progressed and she died. The patient's mother and children brought suit against the hospital, the nursing staff, and the emergency physician for their alleged negligence in the failure to diagnose and treat Mrs. Jones' sepsis on her initial presentation.

ISSUES

In many cases of failure to diagnose sepsis, there is a recurring theme. Patients present with either an altered mental status or subtle findings on physical exam that are not identified by the treating physician. For example, in this case the patient's tachycardia and low blood pressure did not represent dehydration, but, rather, septic shock. The key in diagnosing early sepsis is the recognition of subtle vital sign abnormalities or other physical examination findings that are inconsistent with the proposed diagnosis. Sepsis litigation frequently includes another common theme, delay in antibiotic therapy. When sepsis is in the differential diagnosis, physicians should consider initiating antibiotic therapy at the earliest possible time. Every hour's delay in antibiotic therapy increases mortality by 7%; therefore, emergency physicians should not wait for lab results or other diagnostic testing to begin antibiotic therapy. ED practitioners should not rely on another physician to call in antibiotics or to begin antibiotics on the floor.[2] The ED practitioner should take the initiative to start antibiotics in patients with suspected sepsis.

The chaotic state of the emergency department is of minimal significance in a medical malpractice case. There may be times when the diagnosis of sepsis cannot be made in the emergency department. In spite of this, if sepsis is in the differential diagnosis and is considered to be the likely etiology of the patient's symptoms, antibiotics should be administered rapidly.

Medical malpractice cases involving emergency physicians are generally premised upon a theory of negligence. *In order to prove negligence, the patient or plaintiff must prove that the physician had a duty to the patient; that they breached that duty; that there was causation—or that the breach of the standard of care actually caused the injury; and that there were damages.* Since 1986, the Emergency Medicine Treatment and Active Labor Act (EMTALA) has provided federal protection for patients.[3] The Act mandates that all patients receive a medical screening exam sufficient to rule out an emergency medical condition. If an emergency medical condition is found, the patient shall receive stabilizing treatment and/or transfer to a facility capable of addressing the emergency medical needs. Crafty plaintiff's attorneys have been attaching EMTALA claims to their negligence claims against emergency physicians.

The allegation of negligence in failing to make the diagnosis of sepsis is the first issue in the care provided to Mrs. Jones. A variety of factors may play a part in a missed diagnosis. Most frequently, physicians fail to take and/or document a detailed history and physical of the patient. Less commonly, the physician may have a knowledge deficit regarding life-threatening or infrequently occurring conditions. In this case, the patient actually had a history of pneumonia, but her medical records reflect that she actually had a history of pneumonia with sepsis. The physician did not review her medical records or obtain a history of sepsis from the patient or her family. The plaintiff's experts alleged that this was a breach in the standard of care. It was their position that the physician's failure to inquire about sepsis delayed the diagnosis, thereby causing her death. With respect to an inadequate history, often the emergency physician obtains an adequate history; however, the information is inadequately documented. It is critical that the physician document the key elements of the history of present illness, including the characteristics of the disease, the onset, location, and radiation of any pain, and exacerbating and relieving factors. *Risk factors* for coronary artery disease, pulmonary embolus, or even sepsis may help in making a diagnosis in difficult cases. Far too often, risk factor analysis is absent from the documentation. Incorporation of risk factor analysis into the emergency physician's routine history may help make the appropriate diagnosis.

In regard to allegations of failure to perform an adequate physical examination, again, the critical elements of the physical exam were not documented, thereby creating a presumption that aspects of the exam were not performed. This puts the burden on the defense to prove that a detailed exam was performed. The purpose of the medical record is to communicate with other health care providers the care that has been provided. The medical record should accurately reflect the patient's presenting illness and complaints, the diagnosis, treatment, and disposition. Although detailed documentation will support CMS's billing requirements, it is only a secondary reason for detailed documentation. It is imperative that addenda made to the medical record are timed and dated. A physician should not alter a chart. Rather, if a physician is of the opinion that an addendum is needed after the outcome of the treatment of a patient is known, he or she should discuss the decision to add an addendum with legal counsel prior to taking any action.

At the time the patient is treated, discrepancies between the physician's notes and nurse's notes should be reconciled. *Physician–nursing discrepancies* provide plaintiff's attorneys with potential evidence of substandard care. It is imperative that ED physicians read the prehospital records, the triage notes, and the primary ED nursing notes. Any significant discrepancy should be addressed prior to discharging or admitting the patient. Furthermore, any abusive behavior or language by the patient should be documented. Be sure that any aggressive or threatening behavior is documented and security called as needed. Disgruntled patients should be brought to the attention of the risk manager or medical director. If the patient or family threatens to sue, this should be documented in the patient's chart. Make sure that the documentation is factual, specific, and nonjudgmental.

Another allegation that frequently accompanies claims against emergency physicians is *failure to order or interpret diagnostic studies.* The plaintiff's expert will have the benefit of hindsight at the time he reviews the records. This is not to suggest that a physician should just "shotgun" or order labs just for the sake of defensive medicine. While this allegation frequently accompanies a claim for medical negligence, the test may or may not have had an effect on the outcome. There is significant literature to support the application of evidence-based theories for the ordering of diagnostic studies. For example, the assumption that the white blood cell count would have been elevated during the previous encounter is one that is frequently made; however, it is unknown whether or not this would be true. As far as misinterpretation of tests is concerned, it is critically important that the overreads by radiologists or cardiologists of x-rays or ECGs be performed promptly. Any misinterpretation of these studies should be relayed back immediately to the emergency physician or someone caring for the patient who can address the misinterpretation. Additionally, if a physician orders a test, and it is abnormal, he or she should document the abnormality.

As in the case of Mrs. Jones, the *failure to diagnose* is the most common allegation. When she re-presented 12 hours later with altered mental status and a high white blood cell count, retrospect allowed for the diagnosis of sepsis. The standard of care should not be judged based on the subsequent diagnosis or examination, but, rather, the standard of care should be evaluated based upon the known facts on the first visit. Careful analysis of the first visit may actually suggest sepsis. The patient had hypotension and tachycardia without a known source. This certainly could have been sepsis. The lack of vital sign rechecks and documentation of Mrs. Jones' observation while in the emergency department makes the case more difficult to defend.

A study done by the Sullivan Group, a risk management group that performs an audit of emergency physicians' performance, analyzed how frequently very abnormal vitals were repeated. In their audit, the Sullivan Group evaluated 89,895 patients. Of those, 9838 (11%) had very abnormal vital signs. Of these, 8276 had a repeat of the very abnormal vital signs. This left 1562 or 15.9% of patients with very abnormal vital signs with no repeat documentation of this information during their emergency department visit. As in the case of Mrs. Jones, this is a quality of care issue that suggests substandard care. This data was taken from 10% of the U.S. emergency departments and reveals that significant medical errors are occurring and represent a significant risk to patients' safety and a potential breach in the standard of emergency medical care for both the physician and the nurse.[4]

Finally, in Mrs. Jones' case, the plaintiff's attorney alleged a *failure to treat* the sepsis. These claims generally go along with the failure to diagnose. However, it is obviously impossible to treat a diagnosis of which a physician is unaware. The failure to treat claim assumes that had Mrs. Jones been treated in a timely manner, her outcome would have been different.

Oftentimes plaintiff's experts will allege a *failure to consult* a subspecialist and *failure to admit* the patient on the initial visit. Again, these allegations are made retrospectively, after the diagnosis is known. As in the case of Mrs. Jones, there may have been a failure to identify the abnormal vital signs; however, there was no indication that subspecialty consultation was required.

When a patient is discharged to home, *detailed discharge instructions* must be supplied. As in this case, the follow-up instructions lacked critical elements. Mrs. Jones' instructions simply told her to return for abdominal pain, high fever, or poor urine output. She was also informed to follow up with her doctor in two to three days if she had not improved. Although the plaintiff's expert alleged that the discharge instructions did not meet the standard of care, it is unlikely that the discharge instructions would have made any difference. It is of critical importance that the discharge instructions explicitly state signs and symptoms to watch for, when to follow up, and reasons to return to the emergency department. When patients call the emergency department with complaints of worsening symptoms, staff should advise them to return for a reevaluation. Finally, close follow-up recommendations may prevent subsequent medical catastrophes.

The second major issue in this case is the claim of violation of the Emergency Medical Treatment and Active Labor Act (EMTALA). Frequently plaintiff's attorneys may attach an EMTALA claim to their medical negligence claim in an attempt to avoid state caps on medical malpractice, although this has been largely unsuccessful. In these claims, there is an allegation that the patient did not receive an adequate medical screening examination. As in the case of Mrs. Jones, a medical screening examination was performed in detail sufficient to satisfy EMTALA. She had vitals taken by the nursing staff; she had a documented past medical history, allergies and medications, and a history and physical examination performed by the nurses and doctor. This would constitute "an appropriate medical screening examination" required under the EMTALA statute.

The medical screening exam required under EMTALA is not a national standard of care, but rather a standard that the hospital must apply uniform treatment to patients. As long as the hospital performs a "reasonable" medical screening examination to determine if there is an emergency medical condition, EMTALA has been satisfied. In addition, it is important that the medical screening examination "process" be followed similarly and applied equally to all patients, regardless of their ability to pay. When evaluating a claim of a potential EMTALA violation, it must be determined whether the hospital and staff deviated from their *own* processes.

In cases such as Mrs. Jones', the plaintiffs will provide expert reports, based on retrospective information, as to what testing or evaluations should have been performed; however, this is done in hindsight. Mrs. Jones was believed to be suffering from a viral infection that was treated according to that diagnosis. She received IV fluids, acetaminophen, and ibuprofen. Similarly, a misdiagnosis of myocardial infarction or appendicitis may not meet the standard of care; however, this does not necessarily equate to an EMTALA violation, so long as the hospital followed its own procedures and applied them uniformly to its patients.

A physician obviously cannot stabilize an emergency medical condition of which they are unaware. EMTALA requires that the physician have knowledge of an underlying emergency medical condition if they are presumed to have failed to stabilize such medical condition. Under the circumstances, Mrs. Jones' perceived emergency medical condition was stabilized with IV fluids. Mrs. Jones' claim was not that she received nonuniform treatment, but that she received an incorrect diagnosis. Therefore, her claim is one of ordinary negligence, not an EMTALA violation. Under these circumstances, it is essential that the hospital's policies, procedures, and clinical practice guidelines are followed. If they are not followed, then the physician should document their reasoning and judgment for deviating from these policies. This is a critical defensive strategy, as the plaintiff's expert will take one part of a protocol and allege a violation through an EMTALA claim.

For those physicians being sued, ACEP has compiled a list of physicians who are willing and available to provide support to their peers. Contact ACEP or go to www.ACEP.org for further information. Since the majority of emergency physicians now have claims made insurance policies, it is imperative that a physician contact their insurance carrier immediately upon notification of a claim or even a potential claim. Remember, the defense lawyer is an expert at defending medical malpractice; he is not an expert at emergency medicine. Any help or resources that an emergency physician may be able to provide your lawyer and risk manager will help in the defense of the case.

SURVIVAL STRATEGIES

First, it is essential that detailed history and physical examination be performed. "Intelligent" medical records may prompt or remind physicians to question patients regarding risk factors and associated symptoms, as well as to identify abnormal vital signs. These "intelligent" medical records, whether paper or electronic, contain prompts that help to remind physicians to inquire about details that have been determined to be of high clinical value during patient encounters. The "intelligent" medical records also prompt physicians and nurses to document that they have reviewed discharge vitals. An internal chart audit, with individual provider feedback regarding poor charting habits, may help decrease the number of potential lawsuits.

Regarding abnormal vital signs, emergency departments should set up a monitor in the department and determine how frequently "very abnormal vital signs" are evaluated. This may be a system issue that is easily fixed and may prevent significant injury to patients and deflate the plaintiff's case. Electronic medical records should have the ability to warn either the nurse or the physician that a patient is being discharged with an abnormal vital sign. Those facilities without electronic systems should use a prompted or intelligent medical record to remind them to check for abnormal vital signs. Remember, a note or a documentation that a physician has evaluated the last set of vitals before discharge may help or reduce the amount of vital sign recognition medical errors that are occurring. Finally, education of the entire staff, including technicians and nurses, will help facilitate abnormal vital sign recognition.

Computerized discharge instructions that neatly summarize the symptoms for which the patient should return are far superior to any handwriting the physician or nurse may make on the patient's discharge instructions. Always welcome the patient to return if there is confusion or worsening symptoms. Be sure that the medical staff discusses the discharge instructions with the patient to avoid confusion. This level of communication will enhance patient satisfaction and understanding of their diagnosis and when to return to the emergency department.

Families have repeatedly stated that money is not the primary motive for litigation. They just want access to the medical records and information; however, the doctor would not provide them with any medical information. Honesty regarding medical errors and saying "I am sorry" have been shown to decrease medical malpractice litigation. Therefore, in order to reduce the chances of being named in a lawsuit, sit down with the patient and answer their questions. If patients are treated with the same level of respect that any reasonable person would want, they are less likely to pursue litigation.

Research has shown that improved communications decrease medical malpractice litigation.[5] Efforts to enhance patient satisfaction and better communications should include several easy steps. A detailed and thorough patient assessment will provide the patient with the impression that a competent exam has been performed. Although a patient may have multiple concerns, each should be addressed. Developing a good rapport with the patient and their family may be as easy as providing updates regarding laboratory tests, radiographic evaluations, and waiting times. Simple strategies, such as adding televisions to the patient rooms, and placing patients immediately into a room and performing bedside registration, have both decreased the perception of wait times and increased patient satisfaction in the emergency department.

Once a diagnosis is made, be sure that the physician, as well as the nurse, takes time to answer questions regarding the diagnosis and treatment of the patient and the reasons for admission or discharge. These simple steps may increase the patient's satisfaction, enhance communication, and decrease the potential for subsequent litigation by disgruntled patients or their families.

There are several high-risk medical conditions in which physicians must take extraordinary care. These include cardiac conditions (such as unstable angina and acute MI), thoracic aortic dissection, pulmonary embolus, febrile children (particularly the failure to diagnose meningitis and sepsis), missed appendicitis, and missed foreign bodies in wounds.

There are inherent dangers to patients when health care providers become fatigued from long hours and swing shifts. These situations should be avoided as much as possible. Special attention during shift change and changeover of patients should be paid by both the outgoing and oncoming physicians and nurses. This is a time for very accurate communication and plan development. All too commonly, it is also a time for miscommunication. It is recommended that the oncoming physician evaluate the patient independently. This second evaluation may provide the opportunity to make a diagnosis where one would otherwise have been missed.

Physicians should chart throughout one's shift to ensure more accurate memorialization. Do not wait until the end of the shift to chart for the entire day. This is a medical legal nightmare for physicians and is a bad practice from a risk management perspective.

Emergency physicians may contact several physicians and consultants throughout the course of their shift regarding patient care. It is important that these telephone contacts between physicians and members of the medical staff are documented in the patient chart. It is helpful if the times of test interpretations and consultations are documented, as delays may be unforeseeable and unrecognized by the emergency physician.

Unfortunately, medicine is a 24-hour, seven days a week specialty. Emergency physicians are aware of the higher risk to patients who present on weekends and holidays due to the delay in obtaining necessary diagnostic tests or procedures.[6] For example, there is an inherent danger in having second- and third-year radiology residents read diagnostic tests after 5:00 P.M. until 7:00 A.M. in the morning without the supervision of an attending physician. Yet this is an accepted practice nationally. Other interventions, such as exercise stress testing, must wait until Monday morning and are not permitted to be performed on the weekend at many hospitals.

Finally, maintaining a team atmosphere in the emergency department with EMTs, nurses, technicians, and other departments will facilitate patient care. All members of the team should feel as though the information they provide is relevant and important and that every effort should be made to provide the highest level of quality care for the patient.

REFERENCES

1. Christenson J, et al., Safety and Efficiency of Emergency Department Assessment of Chest Discomfort. Can. Med. Assoc. J. 170(12):1803 (2004).

2. Houck PM, et al., Timing of Antibiotic Administration and Outcomes for Medicare Patients Hospitalized with Community-Acquired Pneumonia. Arch. Intern. Med. 164:637 (2004).

3. 42 C.F.R. §489.20 (see also 68 Fed. Reg. 53262 (Sept. 9, 2003), amending 42 C.F.R. §§489.20 and 489.24; see also CMS State Operations Manual (SOM), Appendix V, found in the internet-only manuals at www.cms.hhs.gov/manuals).

4. www.thesullivangroup. See on-line education CME course, Medical Error and Risk Reduction: Sepsis.

5. Moore PJ, et al., Medical Malpractice: The Effect of Doctor–Patient Relations on Medical Patient Perceptions and Malpractice Intentions. West. J. Med. 173:244 (2000).

6. Frumkin K, The Next Big Thing? Ann. Emerg. Med. 46(1):24–27 (2005).

Anesthesiology

Terrence J. Webber, M.D., J.D., F.C.L.M.

GOLDEN RULES

1. Emphasize patient safety first.
2. Stay familiar with published standards, guidelines, and practice parameters.
3. Standard of care is what is reasonable under the circumstances.
4. Individualize preoperative workup.
5. Evaluate and document preoperative airway assessment and plan.
6. Know the Difficult Airway Algorithm.
7. Keep the alarms on.
8. The anesthetic record is your legacy.
9. Always document CO_2 after intubation.
10. View the consent process as an opportunity.

Anesthesia incidents are relatively rare, but can be catastrophic when they do occur. "Anesthesia" is performed in a variety of places by persons with a wide disparity of training and skills. In 1996 there were about 31.5 million ambulatory procedures performed in the United States. In 2001 there were roughly 40 million in-hospital procedures performed in the United States. Even though overall complication rates for anesthesia are low (some would say very low or rare), small increases in morbidity and mortality, when superimposed upon the large population or denominator of tens of millions of anesthetic procedures, are potentially significant. Furthermore, the cost of implementing further safeguards or tests should be considered when projected over the same large number of procedures.

The primary focus of a discussion of anesthesia (or any type of medical) malpractice survival, malpractice litigation, liability reform, etc., should be patient safety and the prevention of malpractice events, rather than simply the prevention of medical malpractice lawsuits or limitation of damage award payments.

Whenever the issue has been systematically examined, medical mistakes have been found to be numerous. The 1999 Institute of Medicine report, which applauded the anesthesia community for improvements in safety, has also documented the large number of medical mistakes and resulting deaths. Furthermore, while most clinicians agree that anesthesia safety has dramatically improved with the introduction of improved monitoring devices, hard data to support this proposition is lacking.[1]

CASE PRESENTATIONS

Case 1. A 40-year-old woman underwent a laparoscopic cholecystectomy under general anesthesia. The anesthesiologist stopped the ventilator for an intraoperative cholangiogram. The anesthesiologist assisted the x-ray technician in removing the film from beneath the operating table, but found it difficult because the gears on the table had jammed. Finally, the x-ray was removed, and the surgical procedure recommenced. Sometime thereafter the anesthesiologist noticed that the EKG showed severe bradycardia, and then realized that he had never restarted the ventilator. The patient expired sometime later.

Lesson: The disconnect, pulse oximeter, and CO_2 alarms are essential and should not be ignored, neglected, or disabled.

Case 2. A 50-year-old man underwent an open reduction of an ankle fracture under spinal. The patient was spontaneously breathing, but snoring loudly. Toward the end of the case the patient was agitated, and the spinal appeared to be wearing off. The anesthetist gave additional fentanyl and midazolam and silenced the pulse oximeter alarm because the patient kept moving, knocking off the probe and triggering the alarm. He then went to the foot of the bed to observe the closure, and became engaged in a discussion with the surgeon. At the end of the case when the drapes were removed, the patient was noted to be profoundly cyanotic with an agonal rhythm on EKG. This patient was resuscitated, but he sustained profound brain damage.

Lesson: Leaving the head of the bed with the monitor alarms off (particularly the pulse oximeter alarm) is a dangerous combination. If you think cases like these could never happen to you, please think again.

Case 3. A 20-year-old healthy male presented for a laparoscopic bilateral inguinal hernia repair. The anesthesia course was uneventful, and the patient was maintained on isoflurane and paralyzed with rocuronium. The anesthesiologist left the head of the bed so that he could watch the procedure on the video monitors, and talk with the surgical team during closure. When the anesthesiologist returned to the head of the bed he found that the patient was in cardiopulmonary arrest. There had been an undetected breathing circuit disconnection and all the anesthesia machine alarms were flashing, but had apparently been silenced. The patient sustained severe permanent brain damage.

Lesson: Esophageal and precordial stethoscopes have fallen into disuse, and anesthesia providers are therefore dependent upon the anesthesia machine and monitors. Silenced alarms eliminate an essential patient safety feature of modern anesthesia practice. Without constant direct observation of the monitors the patient is essentially unmonitored. Alarms intentionally silenced at the end of cases to prevent false-alarming between cases must be activated prior to beginning the next case.

Case 4. A 62-year-old male was undergoing lumbar laminectomy and three-level fusion with instrumentation in the prone position.

Patient's history was significant for longstanding mild treated hypertension and left branch retinal artery occlusion in the distant past. The surgery proceeded and lasted eight hours. Blood pressure was maintained at between 80 and 90 mmHg systolic throughout the procedure using a variable concentration of approximately one MAC of isoflurane. The estimated blood loss was 2000 cm³. The patient was given 5800 cm³ of crystalloid and two units of 5% albumin and two units of PRBC. Preoperative hematocrit was 38. Hematocrit drawn approximately midway through the procedure was 30. Urine output was between 0.5 and 1.0 cm³/kg/hour during the procedure. Hematocrit immediately after surgery was also 30. Patient awoke the evening of surgery and reported bilateral blindness that persisted and was permanent. Patient was diagnosed with posterior ischemic optic neuropathy (PION). Review of mean arterial pressures (MAP) during the procedure indicated that MAP had been between 50 and 60 mmHg during approximately 3–4 hours of the procedure, and between 50 and 55 mmHg for a significant portion of that time.

Case 5. A 43-year-old male, 5 ft/11 in. tall, weighing 320 pounds, was admitted for a rotator cuff repair under general anesthesia. The intraoperative course was uneventful. He was admitted to hospital overnight for pain control. Five hours after surgery, he received an injection of meperidine 100 mg/phenergan 25 mg IM. This was repeated three hours later when severe pain prevented him from sleeping. Two hours later he was noted to be in cardiac arrest during a routine postoperative check, but could not be resuscitated. He had been noted to have sleep apnea on the internist's preoperative history and physical examination.

Case 6. A 29-year-old male presented for an ORIF of a right radial fracture under general anesthesia. He was discharged to the ward on a fentanyl PCA (patient-controlled analgesia) with a 25 µg bolus, 12-minute delay, and 25 µg hourly rate. The nurses noted that the evening after surgery he was snoring loudly. He was found in respiratory arrest one hour after his last normal vital signs and was successfully resuscitated, but with residual signs of anoxic brain damage. Review of patient's history with his wife revealed that the patient had a history of heavy snoring and nocturnal apnea consistent with a diagnosis of sleep apnea.

ISSUES

Basis for Anesthesia Liability

Anesthesia liability, as with all medical malpractice litigation, most often takes the form of tort or negligence law. In order to prove an anesthesia malpractice claim for negligence, the patient plaintiff must prove four elements regarding the conduct of the defendant physician:

1. *Duty*—that the anesthesiologist had an obligation to care for the plaintiff;

2. *Breach*—that the anesthesiologist failed to meet the obligation to care for the plaintiff, usually described as the standard of care for an anesthesiologist;
3. *Causation*—that the anesthesiologist's breach of duty, or standard of care, was the cause of the damage or harm to the plaintiff; and
4. *Damages*—that the plaintiff indeed sustained actual harm or damage.

Health care providers in many states are protected by some of the most stringent requirements for bringing medical malpractice lawsuits: certificates of review, medical malpractice review panels, damage caps, and other requirements prior to filing a medical malpractice claim. Prefiling evaluation of standard of care, causation, and the extent of economic damages is critical to a medical malpractice action.

The average cost to prosecute a medical malpractice case from investigation through trial is usually $50,000–$100,000. The average cost to defend a medical malpractice lawsuit that goes to trial is also in the same range. The practicality and economic viability of potential medical malpractice claims with damages less than $1 million, except perhaps in the most clear-cut cases of negligence, are questionable. Therefore, the medical malpractice cases that go to trial are those expected to result in million-dollar awards. However, the majority of trial court cases end up with verdicts in favor of the physician defendant.

Resources and Sources of Standards

There are numerous resources for the discussion of standards, guidelines, practice parameters, etc. in anesthesia care, a few of which are listed below.

1. *The American Society of Anesthesiologists (ASA)*, www.asahq.org. This is an educational and political organization of over 40,000 anesthesiologists. The website contains a plethora of information including standards, guidelines, the *ASA Newsletter*, and other publications. The *ASA Newsletter* is a great source for information regarding current topics, activities, and controversies in anesthesiology. The ASA is responsible for the journal *Anesthesiology*.

2. *The American Association of Nurse Anesthetists (AANA)*, www.aana.com. This is an educational and political organization for more than 30,000 member Certified Registered Nurse Anesthetists (CRNAs). The AANA promulgates education and practice standards and guidelines, and provides consultation regarding issues of importance to nurse anesthetists. It also publishes educational resources and materials including, but not limited to, the following: *AANA Journal, AANA News Bulletin,* and *Legal Briefs.*

3. *The American Society of Regional Anesthesia and Pain Medicine (ASRA)*, www.asra.com. This society "addresses the clinical and professional educational needs of physicians and scientists; assures excellence in patient care utilizing regional anesthesia and pain medicine; and investigates the scientific basis of the specialty." The organization has promulgated

guidelines and recommendations for the administration of regional anesthesia under a variety of circumstances including perioperative anticoagulation therapy, and recently sponsored a conference regarding neurologic complications of regional anesthesia.

4. *The American Society of PeriAnesthesia Nurses (ASPAN)*, www.aspan.org. ASPAN publishes nursing standards and provides resources regarding all phases of inpatient and ambulatory surgery, and preanesthesia and postanesthesia nursing care.

5. *The Anesthesia Patient Safety Foundation (APSF)*, www.apsf.org. Founded in 1984, the APSF was formed: to foster investigation into the understanding of preventable anesthetic injuries; to encourage programs and research leading to the reduction of anesthetic injuries; and to promote national and international communications and ideas regarding the causes and prevention of anesthetic morbidity and mortality.

Since that time the APSF has been instrumental in the discussion and advancement of many of the safety initiatives in the field of anesthesia including, for example, and without limitation: establishment of minimum essential monitoring; use of pulse oximetry and capnography; preanesthesia checklists; disconnect alarms; audible alarms; ventilator safety; office-based anesthesia standards; conscious sedation guidelines; anesthesia simulation; and many others.

6. *The International Anesthesia Research Society (IARS)*, www.iars.org. The IARS is a nonpolitical, not-for-profit international medical society founded in 1922 to "foster progress and research in all phases of anesthesia" including perioperative medicine, critical care, pain management, etc. The IARS is the owner and publisher of the journal *Anesthesia and Analgesia*, which addresses a broad range of anesthesia-related topics from an international perspective.

7. *ASA Closed Claims Project*, www.asaclosedclaims.org. Since 1985 the American Society of Anesthesiologists Committee on Professional Liability has conducted the Closed Claims Project, a database of structured analysis of over 6800 closed medical malpractice claims. The database contains standardized and detailed information from closed insurance claims files, mostly from 1980 through the late 1990s, from 35 medical liability insurance carriers covering approximately one-half (14,500) of the practicing anesthesiologists in the United States. Analysis of the data from these closed claims has revealed types and pattern of injuries, which has in turn been used to assist establishment of standards, guidelines, and monitoring to help prevent injuries.

Standard of Care in Anesthesia

The standard of care (SOC) in an anesthesia negligence or malpractice case is the same as that for an ordinary negligence case, namely, the reasonably prudent person standard. In anesthesia cases, the standard is whether a reasonably prudent anesthesia provider would have acted, or refrained from acting, in the same or similar manner under the same or similar circumstances.

In the vast majority of instances by case law and often by statute the SOC is required to be established by expert testimony with reference to accepted and published standards.

However, strictly speaking, the SOC remains one of reasonably prudent conduct under the circumstances.[2] Justice Holmes stated in *Texas & P. Ry. v. Behymer,* "[w]hat usually is done may be evidence of what ought to be done, but what ought to be done is fixed by a standard of reasonable prudence, whether it is usually complied with or not."[3] In *T. J. Hooper,*[4] Judge Learned Hand said:

> In most cases reasonable prudence is in fact common prudence; but strictly it is never its measure; a whole calling may have unduly lagged in the adoption of new and available devices. It never may set its own tests, however persuasive be its usages. Courts must in the end say what is required; there are precautions so imperative that even their universal disregard will not excuse their omission.

Preoperative Evaluation

The value of proper preoperative examination, evaluation, planning, and documentation with regard to proper patient care and protection from medical malpractice suits cannot be overemphasized. Modern emphasis on production pressure and operating room throughput has placed increasing importance on the practicing anesthesiologist as the "perioperative physician" with the specialized knowledge and skills to provide a wide range of patient care and services beyond the operating room. The expanding role for anesthesiologists will likely lead to new areas of anesthesia liability, such as liability for inadequate workup, inadequate pain relief, failure to refer to other specialists, premature discharge, etc.

Preoperative assessment and evaluation for anesthesia is recommended and required for proper anesthesia practice, but what that entails is left, for the most part, undefined. Generally, routine preoperative tests are not required in healthy asymptomatic individuals. This is a considerable change during the last 25 years, when previously a battery of blood tests, along with EKG and chest x-rays, were required prior to surgery.

The report by the American Society of Anesthesiologist Task Force on Preanesthesia Evaluation in some 40 pages citing 198 references of a noninclusive bibliography of the literature considered, along with the disclaimer that advisories are not intended as guidelines, standards, or absolute requirements, concluded:

> The current literature is not sufficiently rigorous to permit an unambiguous assessment of the clinical benefits or harms of routine preoperative tests.
>
> The Task Force agrees with the consultants and ASA members that preoperative tests should not be ordered routinely. The Task Force agrees that preoperative tests may be ordered, required or performed *on a selective basis* for purposes of guiding or optimizing perioperative management.

Content of preanesthetic evaluation includes but is not limited to

1) readily accessible medical records,
2) patient interview,
3) a directed preanesthesia examination,
4) preoperative tests when indicated, and
5) other consultations when appropriate.

At a minimum, a directed preanesthetic physical examination should include assessment of the airway, lungs and heart.[5]

Airway Assessment and Management

Assessment of the airway should include evaluation of potential ability to ventilate and intubate, as well as the formulation of an alternative plan(s) should the initial procedure fail. If there is any question as to whether the airway can be managed while the patient is anesthetized, an awake intubation should be considered. The anesthesiologist or nurse anesthetist should be, first and foremost, the "master of the airway." It is vitally important that the anesthesia provider be familiar with the ASA Difficult Airway Algorithm.[6] The algorithm and airway management begin with a thorough examination and evaluation of the patient's airway preoperatively in order to anticipate airway management and ventilation difficulties, as well as to develop alternative plans in the event that intubation or ventilation is difficult or fail on the initial attempts. The algorithm emphasizes the limitation on the number of repeated direct laryngoscopy attempts, early call for help, and the use of alternative methods of intubation besides repeated laryngoscopy. The algorithm also emphasizes the use of the laryngeal mask airway (LMA) for critical points in the management of patients with a difficult airway or who are difficult to ventilate. Extensive and detailed questions regarding patient management and the Difficult Airway Algorithm should be anticipated in any case involving airway management or complications.

Perioperative Monitoring

No single factor regarding anesthesia care has been heralded as important in improving anesthesia patient safety as the ASA Standards for Perioperative Monitoring. These include mandatory EKG, blood pressure, pulse oximetry, and capnography.

Turn the Alarms On and Keep Them On

ASA Standards for Basic Anesthetic Monitoring do not address audible tones and alarms except for one: disconnection of the breathing circuit. There have been recent recommendations that a new standard be required for using the audible tone and one other audible physiologic alarm.

Incidents of patients sustaining brain damage or death continue despite the institution of monitoring standards. Review of these anesthesia disasters reveals that the ignored or deactivated alarms on standard pulse oximeter or end-tidal monitor alarms lead to delayed or lack of response by the anesthesia providers.

Documentation

The anesthesia record is the main document of the intraoperative course of anesthesia administration. The chart is your legacy and the record of what happened many years after the occurrence of an incident. It can be your best ally or your worst enemy. A sloppily completed anesthesia record bespeaks a sloppy anesthesia provider, even if that is not true in reality. Needless to say, the record will be carefully scrutinized in the evaluation of a potential medical malpractice claim. It is likely that some or all of the anesthesia record will be blown up or projected for viewing in the courtroom. Omissions of important or relevant data, write-overs, and inaccuracies may be damaging to your case, even if only as an implication of carelessness.

Cases of patient awareness during surgery have been noted in which the anesthesiologist never documented that the patient was receiving an inhalation anesthetic at the time of the alleged awareness.

The presence or absence of paresthesia during performance of a block should be documented.

Monitoring of end-tidal CO_2 is an ASA Standard of Basic Intraoperative Monitoring for verification of proper endotracheal tube placement, and the presence of CO_2 at the time of endotracheal tube placement should be documented. CO_2 should be monitored for at least six breaths after tube placement to ensure that the CO_2 initially being measured is from the lungs and is not coming from the stomach from previously aspirated exhaled air. End-tidal CO_2 may decrease to very low levels, or even to zero, if there is no cardiac output and blood is not being moved through the lungs. If there is a question of endotracheal tube placement or dislodgement during CPR, direct laryngoscopy should be performed to confirm correct endotracheal tube placement.

Verification of endotracheal tube placement with CO_2 is standard practice in the operating room and should apply to the PACU and other locations as well. Inexpensive, portable, colorimetric CO_2 detectors are readily available and should be utilized, if capnography is not available.

Informed Consent for Anesthesia

Isolated anesthesia informed consent cases are rarely, if ever, successful or even attempted. However, informed consent claims may be brought in along with negligence claims in order to attempt to add an element of indignation to an ordinary negligence claim. Informed consent is both ethically and legally required for all medical procedures including anesthesia. The ethical requirement is based on the principle of patient autonomy and an individual's right to self-determination.

Obtaining a proper informed consent is required to avoid a claim of battery or nonconsensual touching of a patient. However, even a proper informed consent is not a defense against a claim of negligence, and not a release from liability for complications that arise from negligence, even if those complications are described in the consent form.

The presence or absence of a separate consent form for anesthesia does not change the basic requirements. Many anesthesiologists take the position that a separate consent form is not required, since the surgical consent form includes consent for anesthesia and a patient who consents for surgery impliedly consents for anesthesia. However, this position ignores the requirement of a discussion of specific anesthesia options or procedures that may be planned (i.e., additional lines, regional anesthesia, specific risks, etc.), and misses an important opportunity to discuss specific anesthesia-related aspects of the planned procedure, not to mention an opportunity to build rapport with the patient.

Postoperative Anesthesia Complications

By some estimates as many as 24% of men and 9% of women have obstructive sleep apnea (OSA), and 4% of middle-aged men and 2% of women have clinically significant OSA. Obesity is an important predictor/risk factor/causative agent for OSA. As many as 90% of obese adult patients with OSA are undiagnosed, placing them at increased risk for a variety of perioperative complications including failed intubation, respiratory obstruction post extubation, or respiratory arrest with narcotic and sedative medications. Admission to hospital with continuous visual and electronic respiratory monitoring has been recommended for obese OSA patients to detect and prevent postoperative obstruction and respiratory arrest. Others have advocated the routine use of regional anesthesia (e.g., interscalene block for shoulder surgery) in order to decrease the amount of narcotic and sedative pain medicine required.

Cardiac Arrest/Resuscitation/ACLS

It is important to be familiar with Basic Life Support (BLS) and the Advanced Cardiac Life Support (ACLS) Algorithms, as well as other applicable specialized methods such as Pediatric Advanced Life Support (PALS) and the Neonatal Resuscitation Program (NRP). Documentation and timing of the steps taken, procedures performed, and drugs administered may be critical to the evaluation of such cases. Was a board placed under the patient for cardiac compressions? How was the airway secured? Was the presence of CO_2 confirmed? Many of the significant areas of liability for anesthesia providers are likely to involve issues regarding proper management of cardiac arrest and resuscitation.

Postoperative Vision Loss

Medical malpractice insurance carriers have noted an increase in claims involving postoperative blindness or severe visual impairment, mostly ischemic optic neuropathy (ION), following spine surgeries. There are different types of blindness following spine surgery with potentially different causes: unilateral or bilateral, central retinal artery occlusion (CRAO), and ischemic optic neuropathy (ION). The problem of ION is also known to occur in cardiac bypass cases and head and neck surgeries. Although researchers are quick to point out that "causality" cannot be established, there is an association of ION with prolonged surgical times, prone position, large blood loss, large fluid replacement, hypotension, anemia, and vaso-occlusive disease.

Blindness after massive blood loss and hypotension is not a new or mysterious problem. Articles describing this problem have been published more than ten years ago in the anesthesia literature[7,8] and even longer in the neuro-ophthalmology literature.

The ASA recently published a Practice Advisory regarding Perioperative Vision Loss that was approved by the House of Delegates on October 25, 2005.[9]

REFERENCES

1. Lagasse RS, *Anesthesia Safety: Model or Myth? A Review of Published Literature and Analysis of Current Original Data.* Anesthesiology 97:1609–1617 (2002).

2. *Helling v. Carey*, 83 Wash. 2d 514, 519 P. 2d (Wash. 1974).

3. 189 U.S. 468, 470, 47 L. Ed. 905, 23 S. Ct. 622 (1903).

4. 60 F. 2d 737 (2d. Cir. 1932) at 740.

5. *Practice Advisory for Preanesthesia Evaluation*, approved by the ASA House of Delegates on October 17, 2001, and last amended October 15, 2003.

6. *Practice Guidelines for Management of the Difficult Airway: An Updated Report by the American Society of Anesthesiologists Task Force on Management of the Difficult Airway.* Anesthesiology 98(5):1269–1277 (2003).

7. Williams EL, Hart WM, Tempelhoff R, *Postoperative Ischemic Optic Neuropathy.* Anesthesia and Analgesia 80:1018–1029 (1995).

8. Brown RH, Shauble JF, Miller NR, *Anemia and Hypotension as Contributors to Perioperative Loss of Vision.* Anesthesiology 80:222–226 (1994).

9. *Practice Advisory for Perioperative Vision Loss Associated with Spine Surgery*, approved by the ASA House of Delegates on October 25, 2005.

Surgery

S. Sandy Sanbar, M.D., Ph.D., J.D., F.C.L.M.

GOLDEN RULES

1. When time, opportunity, and adequate medical facilities are available, the law requires the surgeon to employ those fact-finding modalities in common usage to arrive at a diagnosis.
2. A decision as to when to perform surgery lies within the realm of judgment. No surgical procedure should be delayed for the surgeon's convenience. Primary concern must be for the welfare of the patient.
3. Even with all the updated, state-of-the-art machinery, patients do die. All probabilities must be explained to patients or their surrogates prior to commencing any complex diagnostic or operative procedure.
4. Improper communication between surgeons and patients can be interpreted legally as misinformation. If surgeons are considerate and listen to patients, they will be respected as persons and honored for professionalism. Patients will be reticent to think of the lawsuit.
5. Performing unnecessary surgery nips at the conscience, which inevitably becomes defensibly disturbed.
6. Surgeons not well trained in their field of endeavor invites legal problems. Surgeons must pay attention to their own personal identity, respect their patients, and practice in the surgical terrain they know. Otherwise, the surgeon wastes energy in defensive mechanisms under the shadow of malpractice allegations.

Surgeons, regardless of their specialty or subspecialty, have generally pursued specific and traditional guidelines that give them courage and simultaneously bolster the stature of surgery. Surgeons master their profession by being familiar with the foundations and generalizations of medicine. An admirable surgeon is perceived as being moderately bold, not prone to unwarranted disputations, and who only operates upon patients after much premeditated study. Prior to every surgical procedure, the surgeon sees to it that he or she is provided with every asset necessary for successful surgery. In some ways, the surgeon seems to have burdens over and above colleagues in other medical specialties.

The signs of a good surgeon include a temperate, moderating disposition, coupled with a cautious utterance of prognoses. Such a surgeon is logical, and knows his or her spoken language so as to be able to communicate and understand their patients in both speech and written words. Their surgical opinions are supported by proper reasoning when needed. In addition, good surgeons have ingenious creativity with the ability to adapt to either unforeseen situations or complications. They are stern, yet fearful of unanticipated situations, and are constantly aware of the reality that the operation itself is but one incident, no doubt the most dramatic, in the constellation of events between the illness and expected recovery. This chapter deals with some of the unanticipated situations, complications, and surgical errors that confront surgeons.

Sterling qualities of surgeons are their mental, mechanical, and moral attributes. The first is founded on knowledge acquired by education, prescribed training, examinations, licensure, personal studiousness, and intellectual inquisitiveness. The second deals with manual dexterity leading to individualized technical skill, which is learned, perfected, and embellished during surgery residency training. Third and foremost is the moral attribute, which equates with judgment that is gained in the vineyard of professional life. Of this trinity, the greatest is the last. From it arises the ethical conduct, moral behavior, individualized judgment, and the need to avoid legal pitfalls. Without the moral sense, there is no security, sanity, safety, or salvation in the surgical practice. It is the basis upon which valued decisions are made. Additionally, it is legally protected against the onslaught of unfavorable allegations of negligence.

CASE PRESENTATIONS

Case 1. The Arizona case of *Murphy v. Board of Medical Examiners*[1] involves an insurance company Medical Director who made a "medical decision" that overruled the surgeon's recommendation to perform a cholecystectomy, thereby denying precertification for treatment. On December 29, 1992, Dr. M contradicted the advice of the patient's surgeon and her referring physician by refusing to precertify a patient's laparoscopic cholecystectomy; he stated that the surgery was "not medically necessary."

Despite the refusal to precertify, the surgery was performed by the patient's surgeon. Following the cholecystectomy, the surgeon registered a complaint against Dr. M with the Board of Medical Examiners. In February 1993, the Board sent Dr. M a copy of the surgeon's complaint and requested a response. Dr. M responded by questioning whether the Board of Medical Examiners could review his action because he was "not involved in patient care and not involved in the practice of medicine." Dr. M provided the requested information "as a courtesy" and to avoid "a claim of unprofessional conduct." In October 1993, the Board ordered an investigation and subpoenaed the insurance company documents concerning 20 cases in which the company's Medical Director, Dr. M, denied precertification. The insurance company objected to the subpoena and said that the Board lacked jurisdiction because Dr. M worked for an insurance company and he was not practicing medicine. The case was appealed.

The Appellate Court ruled that although Dr. M was not engaged in the traditional practice of medicine, to the extent that he rendered medical decisions his conduct was reviewable by the Board of Medical Examiners. The Appellate Court found that Dr. M substituted his medical judgment for that of the patient's surgeon and determined that the surgery was "not medically necessary." The court ruled that such decisions were not insurance decisions but, rather, medical (surgical) decisions because they required Dr. M to determine whether the procedure was "appropriate for the symptoms and diagnosis of the condition," whether it was to be "provided for the diagnosis, care or treatment," and whether it was "in accordance with standards of good medical practice in Arizona."

Case 2. The Louisiana case of *Fusilier v. Dauterive*[2] involved a laparoscopic cholecystectomy. In 1989, plaintiff F was diagnosed by an abdominal ultrasound test to have a gallstone in her gallbladder. She elected not to have a cholecystectomy at that time. On May 8, 1990, plaintiff F visited for the first time Dr. D, a general surgeon, complaining of nausea, indigestion, epigastric discomfort, and fatty food intolerance. Repeat abdominal ultrasound confirmed the diagnosis of cholelithiasis. Dr. D initially treated the patient conservatively, by observation and symptomatic treatment. However, the plaintiff's symptoms became more severe, and Dr. D discussed treatment alternatives and recommended surgery. Meantime, plaintiff F's surgery was delayed because she developed congestive heart failure, which was treated by her family physician and improved.

On November 9, 1990, she was admitted to the IG Hospital to undergo a laparoscopic cholecystectomy. Dr. D performed the cholecystectomy, during which time he was *observed* by Dr. R, a gynecologist, who was familiar with the use of the trocar, needle, and other instruments used in laparoscopy. Dr. F did not participate in the actual performance of the surgery. The gallbladder was successfully removed.

Following the completion of the laparoscopic cholecystectomy, the anesthesiologist noticed blood coming from the patient's mouth. Laparotomy revealed perforations of the duodenum, mesentery, and aorta. While attempting to repair the perforations, the surgeon punctured the plaintiff's intestine and her splenic capsule, which necessitated a colostomy.

The plaintiff incurred a tremendous blood loss, causing severe hypotension on several occasions during the operation. To stabilize the plaintiff's condition, the medical staff administered 38 units of blood, 9 units of plasma, and 8 liters of Plasmalite. Eventually the bleeding was controlled, but the patient was still hypotensive. Her abdomen was then closed, and she was taken first to the recovery room in critical condition, then to the Intensive Care Unit.

The postoperative course was complicated with recurrence of congestive heart failure; the development of adult respiratory distress syndrome, which required extended ventilatory support; continued blood loss over the first weeks of her recovery, requiring intermittent blood transfusions; the performance of a tracheostomy after several failed attempts to wean the plaintiff from the ventilator; and insertion of a PEG feeding tube to facilitate nutritional intake.

On December 24, 1990, plaintiff F was discharged from the hospital. Five days later she was readmitted to the hospital with sepsis, internal herniation with infarction of the ileum, and significant adhesions in her abdomen. She underwent an abdominal exploration, relief of the abdominal adhesions, a small bowel resection, a right hemicolectomy, and an excision of her colostomy.

On January 18, 1991, she was admitted to a skilled nursing facility, where she remained until February 14, 1991.

Medical Review Panel. Following surgery, the plaintiff F discovered that the surgeon had never performed a laparoscopic cholecystectomy on a human prior to the one he performed on her, and that the only training Dr. D had received concerning the procedure was during a two-day course entitled "Surgical Laser in Laparoscopic Cholecystectomy" in May 1990. The course consisted of one day of lectures and one day of participation in handling the instruments to remove the gallbladder of a pig.

The plaintiff filed a claim with the Medical Review Panel on October 25, 1991. On August 6, 1992, the panel concluded that the plaintiff had not proven that Doctors D and F and the IG Hospital deviated from the standard of care that is required of physicians, health care providers, their staff and/or employees of the same specialty. The panel specifically concluded that:

1. Dr. F, who acted as an assistant, both preoperatively and postoperatively, was never assigned to treat the plaintiff.
2. The equipment at IG Hospital was adequate and appropriate; the credentialing for laparoscopic cholecystectomies was appropriate as to requiring the physician to attend a "hands-on" course; there is no "standard" accrediting method for all hospitals—each hospital is different, yet most have similar criteria.
3. Dr. D obtained adequate and appropriate consent; he demonstrated appropriate skill as a general surgeon; the complication experienced by the plaintiff is a known complication which, once discovered, was treated and handled appropriately.

On November 6, 1992, the plaintiff filed a petition in District Court for damages, naming Dr. D, Dr. F, and IG Hospital as defendants. The petition alleged *inter alia* that the defendants deviated from the accepted standards of medical practice for health care providers and caused injuries and damages to the named plaintiff. The plaintiff specifically asserted that the defendants:

1. Failed to comply with the appropriate standard of care.
2. Failed to have the proper training and experience to take those actions necessary so as to avoid an accident of the type that occurred to the plaintiff.
3. Utilized inadequate equipment and personnel.
4. Failed to secure informed consent.
5. Failed to warn of, recognize, or properly treat medical risks and emergencies.

The jury verdict, which was in favor of the defendant surgeons and hospital, was affirmed by the court of appeal. However, the Supreme Court of Louisiana granted a writ of certiorari (i.e., accepted to review the case) to determine whether the jury's determination that the defendant surgeon was not negligent in performing the surgery and that his negligence was not a cause of plaintiff's injuries was erroneous. The Louisiana Supreme Court held that the jury's determination was *manifestly erroneous* in finding that the defendant did not fail to inform the plaintiff of material risks to the surgery. And after reviewing all of the evidence and testimony, the court held that the jury was *manifestly erroneous* in concluding that Dr. D was not negligent. Accordingly, the Louisiana Supreme Court reversed the court of appeal's decision to affirm the jury's verdict and remanded this matter to the court of appeal to assess damages. In essence, the Supreme Court in a nice way informed the trial judge that he or she should have ruled as a matter of law that Dr. D was negligent, and that the jury's role should have been to assess damages only.

ISSUES

The first case presented above points out a number of important issues that pertain to a physician who is employed by an insurance company as a medical director for the purpose of precertifying patients without ever having seen the patient. Denial of precertification, i.e., substituting judgment for the treating physician by the medical director, is considered "practicing medicine," and is thereby subject to review by the State Board of Medical Examiners. Secondly, the patient's surgeon is in charge and is fully responsible for the safety and welfare of the patient. The surgeon acted appropriately in a timely fashion and then reported the matter to the authorities by filing the complaint.

Surgical Judgment

Surgical judgment is a priceless treasure. As a privilege, it is not acquired easily. It is sown in the field of honesty, grows in the soil of knowledge, and is watered by the perspiration of hard work. Being tempered in the heat of failure, it is nurtured into maturity by the wisdom born through the painful labor of sad experiences. Proper judgment breeds legal protection and ethical propriety, because good, rational judgment upholds proper norms that are morally correct and legally defensible.

Surgeon–Patient Relationship

There are hazards in surgery that demand an alertness against them. One hazard relates to the surgeon–patient relationship. The surgeon should always maintain the human element in professional relationships with patients, their relatives, and other inquiring friends. Because most patients are not well educated on the subject of the surgery, the surgeon should explain the nature of the disorder and the surgery contemplated in layperson's terms, while being respectful and courteous. This implies allowing sufficient time to the patient, answering questions, and explaining anticipated diagnostic procedures, as well as programmed therapy, with their merits and demerits.

Mechanical Aids and Devices

The surgeon should convey the impression that he or she is not dependent entirely upon mechanical equipment to arrive at a diagnosis. This eliminates the notion that surgeons are relegated to a secondary role, and refutes their being labeled as mechanical technicians. Misimpression of mechanical technical surgeons leads to the concept of absent compassion, which further lends credence to the dehumanization of surgical care. When a sympathetic understanding exists between the patient and the surgeon, legal intransigences rarely occur. What is of equal importance is the rise in confidence as the patient passes from the diagnostic phase to the active treatment.

Surgeons know that mechanical ancillary diagnostic and/or treatment facilities are not infallible. Failure in diagnosis occurs even with sophisticated, complicated equipment. Furthermore, sufficient training in the use of new equipment, such as the laparoscope, is mandated prior to use by the surgeon. Insufficient training and experience with a surgical technique can lead to disastrous surgical errors and complications, as occurred in the second case presented above. Caution should be exercised when using newer equipment and techniques. The rising popularity of laparoscopic cholecystectomy, lithotripsy, adhesiolysis, and laparoscopic laser appendectomy may give rise to a false sense of security that may tempt surgeons into a state of legal lethargy. Every surgical encounter utilizing instrumentation poses a risk to the patient, even in the hands of an expert. The surgeon must be candid with the patient and must disclose their experience, knowledge, and complication rate.

When instruments are used, the hands that hold them are the control. The instruments must be used for the purpose for which they are manufactured and in the manner recommended. Limitations of use as instructed are to be followed. If proper procedure and maintenance are proven when misadventures occur, then the manufacturer may be culpable under the law of products liability.

However, an instrument is not to be blamed for human error. Iatrogenic errors, misadventures, or accidents are mishaps that may happen to individual patients during medical/surgical diagnosis and/or treatment. Such an unfortunate occurrence is independent of the natural course of the illness for which the patient sought relief. The iatrogenic episodes are random events. They are unpredictable, unanticipated, and similar to those accidents occurring in nonmedical life. These experiences are not the result of discernible errors in conception, design, or implementation of a medical/surgical practice.

Instruments that have been used for ten years are considered to be old. This is a reasonable estimation that is acceptable both medically and legally.

Monitors, laboratory equipment, and all other mechanical supplementary modalities must be tested periodically for accuracy.

Surgical Consultation

A surgical consultant can become involved legally in a malpractice action, even when there was no active participation by him or her in patient treatment. This occurs when the treating physician follows the advice given by the surgical consultant. The greatest protection for the surgeon is the written consultation report, disagreeing with the therapeutic procedure performed, when liability is claimed. The surgical consultant's report should remain attached to the hospital records, and a copy must be retained in the consultant's private office files.

A request for a surgical consultation should be answered only when one is properly qualified to render an honest responsible opinion on the subject at issue. Surgical consultants can be sued for mishandling a consultation request. It is legally dangerous to participate in opinion rendering in a specialty beyond the surgical consultant's expertise. Likewise, surgeons can incur legal involvement by failing to answer a consultation, even as they can be involved by answering it.

Before each surgical procedure, the anesthesiologist is an automatic consultant whose findings are to be considered seriously. As a specialist, the anesthesiologist's opinion should be respected. Acknowledgment of the patient as a total human person is the preamble to safe physiologic conduction through intravenous, gaseous, or spinal anesthesia. Preanesthesia evaluation is an advisory respite examination that can warn against complications, or even death. Anesthesiologists assess the physical as well as the psychological status of the preoperative patient. The anesthesiologist should be regarded not only as a specialist in his or her field, but also as a risk evaluator, a respiratory physiologist, and a pharmacologist.

Diagnostic Problems

One source of surgical malpractice is likely when an exploratory operation is performed and no disease is found. Before surgery is undertaken, the surgeon should perform all necessary tests and biopsies in an effort to increase the diagnostic accuracy preoperatively. However, a biopsy should never be performed if that procedure would compromise future care.

Common errors that contribute significantly to professional liability losses are errors in diagnosis, failure to provide continuous, acceptable, high-quality medical care, and attempts at procedures or treatments beyond the training, experience, and skill of the surgeon.

Medical Care Before Surgery

When an elective surgical procedure is being contemplated, the indication for the surgical procedure requires close scrutiny and evaluation. When possible, remediable medical intervention should be tendered before deciding that surgery is the best or only way. Examples include correction of hypokalemia, control of diabetes, control of severe hypertension, stabilization of vital signs and hemodynamic status, and consideration of side effects of medications that the patient may be taking. Evidence of right heart strain or significant pulmonary hypertension interposes an objective contraindication to pulmonary resection. Infectious problems should be cleared, or at least controlled, before elective surgery is undertaken.

Timeliness of surgical treatment is paramount. A surgeon must not delay surgery because of a personal or professional problem. Problems generally occur during so-called off-duty hours. However, they require the same diligence, if not more, since support personnel are frequently less experienced, whether it involves x-ray or laboratory personnel, house staff, or nurses. Additional partners or shared coverage may be needed, if the surgeon's practice demands are overburdening. Competent alternative coverage is important in times of such need.

Wrong Side Surgery

Operating on the wrong side is simple human negligence that is inexcusable. The surgeon should always verify the x-rays of the patient, the position of the patient on the table in the surgical suite, and carefully review the medical records prior to starting the operation.

Operating on the wrong side is the result of moments of inadvertence. One method of avoiding surgery on the wrong side is to insert a needle into the suspected area and inject a radiographic material to not only determine the right site but also the exact location. The needle can be left in situ, and methylene blue or a radio-opaque substance can be injected to help in continued identification of the operative site. By so doing, the patient will be spared an unwanted and unneeded surgical procedure.

Vascular Injuries and Wound Problems

Vascular injuries are rarely due to negligence, but vascular compromise due to delayed correction is inexcusable. This can only be decreased by a high degree of constant suspicion. When it is considered, a prompt arteriogram is indicated and early intervention mandated. In cardiopulmonary bypass surgery, for example, central nervous system anoxia or toxic injury can occur from underperfusion or embolization of the aortic or mitral valves by a calcium plaque or a left atrial/left ventricular clot. The subclavian artery and vein are a not uncommon source of injury. Such injuries are readily recognized, and these vessels must be restored to normal function before completing the operation.

Wound infections occur with the best of efforts to prevent them, even in clean cases. When they do occur, the standard of care requires taking bacterial smears and cultures. This should be followed by a prescription for an appropriate antibiotic. These measures should be routine when early resolution does not occur with simple local procedures.

Foreign Bodies Left Behind

As a complication of surgery, foreign bodies usually involve broken instruments with retained pieces, needles, and sponges. In order to avoid this type of adverse incident when a major cavity is opened, instrument, needle, and sponge counts should be demanded before closing. A second count should be taken when the skin is closed. If there is an error, there is still time to remove the foreign body before the anesthetic has worn off. If such a scenario occurs postoperatively, an x-ray should be taken as soon as it is convenient after the patient is stable. The patient and/or family should be informed promptly, followed by appropriate documentation.

Other Surgical Complications

Esophageal procedures are fraught with problems and potential liability losses. It is well known that perforation during an esophagoscopy may be unavoidable, particularly where there is an impacted foreign body that is sharp, which may have already penetrated the wall of the esophagus. The surgeon should remember that unrelieved, violent vomiting leads to spontaneous rupture. Esophageal anastomotic leaks are common following an esophagectomy. They are also common with colon interposition. Through and through permanent sutures are said to facilitate a leak. Thus, many surgeons advise at least two-layer anastomosis. Some surgeons use absorbable sutures internally and permanent sutures in the serosa.

Recurrent laryngeal nerve injury may be unavoidable in a mediastenoscopy, an aggressive pulmonary resection for a pulmonary malignancy, or when the nerve is incorporated in an aneurysm of the aorta. If the lesion is unilateral, the opposite cord often migrates across the midline, resulting in a functional speech voice. Other corrective procedures are successful if the diagnosis is made and the procedure implemented promptly.

Carotid endarterectomies maybe performed without the use of shunts, in some elective cases or in managing traumatic aneurysms. However, juries are not sympathetic to end results that are unsuccessful, even when they are beyond the control of the surgeon. The rationale for not using shunts either in elective or traumatic carotid surgery should be well documented and fortified with concurring data.

Tracheal incubation can result in death when the endotracheal tube is wrongly placed, either into the esophagus or too far down the respiratory tract, ending up usually on the right side of the bronchus and obstructing the left-sided flow. Portable x-rays should not be needed to make the diagnosis. Auscultation of the chest should afford immediate diagnosis if there is reason to suspect a catastrophe during an emergency.

Tracheostomy is a relatively simple procedure, but dire consequences causing injury to the carotid vessels or loss of control of the trachea may occur, unless the procedure is performed with precision by knowledgeable physicians.

Subclavian lines should be inserted with the patient's head down, if possible, to reduce the risk of air embolization. Venous cannulas should be sutured and anchored to the skin to avoid embolization.

Stab wounds can be the source of liability suits for the physician serving in the emergency room, particularly when death occurs. Consultation should be secured early in emergencies to avoid complications, particularly when lack of proper care can lead to extensive, permanent, adverse results.

Continuity of Care

One of the causes of malpractice action involves who is in charge. The surgeon is in charge of the surgical case, and timely decisions should be made by the surgeon, taking into consideration the recommendations of consultants, such as the radiologist, the intensivist, the pulmonologist, the infectious disease specialist, or the cardiologist. From the prehospital phase through rehabilitation, the surgeon must direct the care of the patient who has undergone surgery. The surgeon should be involved in the total continuum of care. Emergency physicians, intensivists, and other consultants should not be primarily responsible for triage, decision making, or specific treatment recommendations of known surgical patients. However, although the surgeon must directly manage the primary care of the surgical patient, consultants invariably are necessary for proper total care. Consultants must not impose their orders, but rather cite their opinions in the progress note.

Guidelines/Statements by the American College of Surgeons

The American College of Surgeons[3] provides numerous statements or guidelines for management of surgical patients, e.g., Guidelines for Standards in Cardiac Surgery, which were first published in 1991 and updated by the Advisory Council for Cardiothoracic Surgery and approved by the College's Board of Regents in October 1996. Additionally, the American College of Surgeons has several publications that consider surgical liability, including:

- *Professional Liability Information Kit.* This contains information for surgeons involved in a medical malpractice lawsuit, including claims management, the expert medical witness, the psychological trauma of the medical malpractice lawsuit by Dr. Sarah C. Charles, and about the deposition.
- *Disclosing Surgical Error: Vignettes for Discussion.* This provides teaching tools to stimulate dialogue regarding strategies for communicating effectively about surgical errors and adverse outcomes with patients and their families.
- *Surgical Patient Safety: Essential Information for Surgeons in Today's Environment.* This provides guidance and leadership in evolving areas of patient safety as well as strategies for preventing crime-side surgery, use of blood and blood components for their safe implementation, and patient safety in trauma care.
- *Professional Liability/Risk Management: A Manual for Surgeons,* 2nd edition, 1997.

SURVIVAL STRATEGIES

The following represent sundry survival safeguards against allegations of surgical negligence:

- Every injury to the face, head, or neck demands a complete neurologic examination to eliminate the presence of intracranial and/or spinal cord injury. In emergency departments, many facial, cranial, ear, and nose lacerations are repaired without written notation that a neurologic injury has been eliminated.
- In neck surgery, injury to the internal jugular vein is a common vascular accident, especially in cancer removal. Hemorrhage and air embolism may occur. Suture needle injury to the carotid artery is not a rarity.
- Pathologic disturbances within the abdominal cavity remain a challenge to surgical diagnosticians. Appendicitis continues to be a frequent cause for acute abdominal signs and symptoms. It is still a difficult diagnosis in many cases. Women can have equivocal findings more frequently than men. The presence of cystitis can be confusing, but the dilemma can generally be resolved by a urinalysis. Right-sided ovulation pain is not so easily differentiated. Pelvic inflammatory disease can be confusing, particularly in somewhat older females, but pain on uterine manipulation should alert the diagnostician to its presence. Ureteral calculi can be confusing and should be strongly suspected if red blood cells are found on urinalysis, particularly in males.
- Blunt trauma to the abdomen can produce perforations in the intestinal tract, as well as to solid organs such as the spleen and the liver.
- In the management of patients with severe trauma, especially to the abdomen and spinal column, diagnostic thought must be given to kidney injuries with or without retroperitoneal hemorrhage and hematomyelia.
- The diagnostic importance of vaginal and anorectal examinations has been proven repeatedly.
- Lymphadenopathy is generally not due to acute primary injuries.
- Every traumatic derangement of bone has associated soft tissue damage of varying degrees. Often, the tendon, ligament, muscle, and skin disruptions may be more extensive than the bone damage warrants. Soft tissue injury may cause post-traumatic complications, including nerve impairment.
- Pelvic fractures frequently are associated with injury to the urinary bladder or pelvic organs with accompanying bleeding.
- Following accidental injuries to the lower extremities, a nonhealing, ulcerating wound may be due to cancer.
- Vascular injuries are known to accompany injuries to bones, ligaments, and tendons, which should be identified and treated with other injuries.
- In automobile accidents, the line of force striking the body does not have to be severe to produce serious injuries.

- Narcotic addicts can have symptoms suggesting gastrointestinal diseases.
- Neck node biopsies and excisions should be planned considering the possibility of future radical neck dissection. The facial nerve needs identification when preauricular and parotid biopsies are performed.
- With appropriate advice as to examination, mammography and biopsy of breast lumps are critical. All deserve careful physician follow-up. Mammograms are not infallible and should be repeated, along with a repeat physical examination of any breast lump, a possible biopsy, and even second opinions. Breast surgery is emotionally traumatizing to all women. The fear of recurrent cancer is as distressing as the woman's concern about disfigurement.
- Statistics indicate that biliary surgical injuries occur in reverse frequency to the experience of the surgeon. A young surgeon should do as many cases as possible with an experienced surgeon, before assuming primary responsibility, particularly with less experienced assistance. There is no substitute for complete knowledge of the anatomy of the biliary tract and surrounding organs, particularly since there are frequent abnormalities.
- Rectal surgery is fraught with medicolegal hazards, often resulting in substantial awards when there is a bad result that can be traced to negligence, since the defects are so dehumanizing. At best, hemorrhoidectomy patients face their first bout of evacuation with anxiety over anticipated pain. Frequently, patients will avoid a bulk laxative, which could assist in needed dilation during the healing stage. The surgeon should place sufficient columns of the uninterrupted mucocutaneous junction to reduce the likelihood of circumferential stricture. Severance of the anal sphincter is extremely demoralizing to the incontinent patient, and causes many practical and social problems. If it occurs, it should be repaired.
- Patients undergoing hernia repairs have been known to end up with an atrophic testicle, resulting from torsion of the testicle, injury to its blood supply, or nerve entrapment.
- Excised pigmented skin lesions should always be followed by microscopic evaluation.
- Cosmetic surgery should be left to board-certified specialists.

CONCLUSION

To be a surgeon is a vocational gift bestowed upon a selected few when compared to the nation's population. It is a unique distinction that benefits other people, while sustaining an inner realization of accomplishment. Many social restraints affect the work and behavior of surgeons due to controls originating within professional ranks, from external government agencies, state board regulations, legislative statutes, and common law derived from court decisions. While it is undoubtedly correct that medical/surgical malpractice allegations will not disappear, nonetheless medicosurgical progress far outweighs the legal threat of negligence. Prophylaxis against surgical malpractice is the goal to achieve rather than attempt to cure malpractice or go to court to defeat the accusation.

Acknowledgment

The author gratefully acknowledges the permission granted by Dr. Cyril H. Wecht, editor of the *Medicolegal Primer*, published by the American College of Legal Medicine Foundation (1990), to utilize, revise, and update materials from the *Primer* for this chapter.

FURTHER READING

Shelton PA, "Liability of Ophthalmologists." In *Legal Medicine/American College of Legal Medicine*, 7th ed., ed. S. Sandy Sanbar *et al.* Philadelphia: Mosby, 2007.

King RC, "Liability of Otolaryngologists." In *Legal Medicine/American College of Legal Medicine*, 7th ed., ed. S. Sandy Sanbar *et al.* Philadelphia: Mosby, 2007.

Green VL, "Liability in Obstetrics and Gynecology." In *Legal Medicine/American College of Legal Medicine*, 7th ed., ed. S. Sandy Sanbar *et al.* Philadelphia: Mosby, 2007.

Lehv MS, "Liability of Plastic Surgeons." In *Legal Medicine/American College of Legal Medicine*, 7th ed., ed. S. Sandy Sanbar *et al.* Philadelphia: Mosby, 2007.

REFERENCES

1. *Murphy v Board of Med. Examiners*, 949 P. 2d 530 (Ariz. Ct. App. 1997).
2. *Fusilier v. Dauterive*, 764 So. 2d 74 (La. 2000).
3. http://www.facs.org/fellows_info/guidelines/cardiac.html.

Urology

Scott D. Cohen, M.D., J.D., F.C.L.M.

1. Obtain, read, and frequently refer to all of the American Urological Association's published guidelines.
2. When obtaining informed consent, discuss all alternatives, including those interventions that you do not perform. Discuss not only the possible complications, but also the likelihood of each complication and the necessary interventions to treat each complication.
3. Appropriately screen all male patients for prostate cancer.
4. Use ureteral stents and surgical drains judiciously, but when in doubt, know that you are less likely to get sued for placing a drain or a stent than not placing a drain or a stent. Make sure that all stents that you put in are eventually removed.
5. Inquire about and document a patient's sexual function prior to any intervention.
6. Do not criticize another urologist or a referring physician. What comes around goes around.
7. Personally review all films that you are relying upon when making a diagnosis or intervening surgically.
8. Know all of the commonly prescribed medications that contain nitrates and nitrites.
9. Intervene immediately when a patient presents with a kidney or ureteral stone and fever.
10. Inform the vasectomy patient that his sterility cannot be assured until he has a negative semen analysis. Noncompliant patients should receive a certified letter notifying them of the consequences of noncompliance.

A urologist can expect to be sued for medical malpractice twice during his or her professional career. In a recent analysis by the Physician Insurers Association of America (PIAA), a trade association of over 50 medical malpractice insurance companies, urology claims ranked 12th out of the 28 specialty groups in their database between 1985 and 2004. This ranking was the same for both total number of claims and total indemnity paid. In 2004, the average indemnity paid on behalf of urologists was $269,405.[1]

When analyzing the urologist's medical malpractice exposure in terms of procedures performed, the most prevalent claims were the bladder (26%), the prostate (22%), the kidney (14%), the penis (10%), the ureter (9%), and male sterilization (8%). In terms of clinical illnesses, the most prevalent claims were disorders of the male genitalia (21%), calculus disease (18%), voiding dysfunction (17%), prostate cancer (13%), and hyperplasia of the prostate (9%).

Like its companion medical and surgical specialty chapters, this chapter begins with a case presentation. To more broadly reflect some of the clinical scenarios faced by a urologist, a hypothetical case is presented. Using an anatomic and physiologic categorization, some of the more common medical liability issues faced by the urologist are then discussed. Some "Golden Rules" for the practicing urologist are offered at the head of this chapter.

CASE PRESENTATION

A 50-year-old policeman presents to the emergency department with a two-day history of severe left flank pain. The patient has nausea and vomiting but no fever. A CT scan reveals an 8 mm stone in his distal left ureter causing moderate obstruction. He is observed for two hours, given a prescription for Percocet, and instructed to follow up with a urologist. The following day, the patient consults his insurance directory and sees a participating urologist. The patient undergoes endoscopic surgery to remove the stone. His remaining recovery is uneventful, and then he sees the urologist one week later for a final office visit. No follow-up is recommended.

Two years later, the same patient participates in a free prostate cancer screening program at his community hospital. As part of the screening program, he has a digital rectal exam (DRE) and a PSA test. His DRE was normal, but his PSA was 7.0 ng/ml (normal 0–4.0). The nurse practitioner overseeing the cancer screening program advises the patient to see a urologist. Because his insurance has changed, the patient sees a different urologist. A repeat PSA confirms the abnormal value, so he undergoes a transrectal ultrasound-guided prostate biopsy. The biopsy is positive for Gleason 7 adenocarcinoma of the prostate. This urologist recommends either brachytherapy (radioactive "seeds") or surgery.

The patient decides to have a radical prostatectomy. He has an uneventful surgery, but the surgical margins are positive, i.e., the cancer is not confined to the prostate. In the postoperative period, the patient experiences urinary incontinence, which slowly improves after three months, and erectile dysfunction, which, with the aid of Viagra, improves after six months.

The patient's PSA six weeks after the prostatectomy is 0.3 ng/ml, a value that represents persistent cancer (after a radical prostatectomy, the value that represents cure is ≤0.1 ng/ml). Six months later his PSA is 0.6 ng/ml, a value that represents a significant doubling time for this persistent cancer. A bone scan is negative for metastatic disease, and a ProstaScint scan shows activity at the bladder neck, an indication of recurrent cancer. The patient is subsequently treated with salvage radiotherapy.

Shortly after completing his radiation treatments, the patient develops significant and permanent urinary incontinence. He loses his ability to have an erection, despite the use of Viagra. Six months later his PSA rises to 2.0 ng/ml. His urologist then prescribes hormonal ablation. An LRH agonist is administered every three months. After being on the LRH agonist for six months, his PSA is 0.2 ng/ml, a value that represents good control of the prostate cancer. However, the urologist explains to the patient that the effectiveness of the LRH agonist will likely last only three to five years.

To control his urinary incontinence, the patient has to wear a condom catheter, which frequently leaks. He can no longer obtain an erection. As a direct and known result of the LRH agonist, he has no libido and suffers frequent hot flashes. The patient has been pressured by his employer to take early retirement and is clinically depressed. The patient has now hired an attorney to pursue a malpractice claim against the first urologist for not diagnosing his prostate cancer while under his care for the kidney stone.

Although this is a hypothetical case, there have been many successful cases against urologists involving the missed diagnosis of prostate cancer. From a clinical perspective, the above case may seem extreme, but it is not too unusual for an experienced urologist. Furthermore, this hypothetical case illustrates aspects of medical malpractice liability uniquely found in the field of urology.

ISSUES

Urology is a surgical specialty dealing with diseases of the male and female urinary tract and diseases of the male reproductive organs. The urinary system includes the kidneys, ureters, and bladder. The reproductive organs of the male include the penis, prostate, seminal vesicles, testes, epididymis, and vas deferens. Whether analyzing urology malpractice claims in terms of procedures or clinical presentations, a common denominator is the anatomy and physiology unique to urology.

An in-depth review of medical malpractice issues encompassing the entire diagnostic and therapeutic realm of urology is beyond the scope of this chapter. However, by discussing the urologist's malpractice exposure in terms of anatomy and physiology, some meaningful generalizations can be made and prophylactic strategies recommended. Referenced cases are offered as examples and should not be construed as dispositive. Although negligence claims against urologists that involve circumcision may involve substantial awards,[2] the majority of reported circumcision claims involve newborn infants. Since newborn circumcisions are usually performed by obstetricians or pediatricians and not by urologists, circumcision will not be discussed in this chapter.

The Prostate: Cancer

Several juries have determined that it is the standard of care for a urologist to screen for prostate cancer. One study analyzed 48 such prostate cancer malpractice cases. Of these 48 cases, 22 resulted in awards to plaintiffs totaling over $8.4 million. Of that amount, approximately $7.5 million could have been avoided if PSA screening and diagnostic guidelines had been followed.

The hypothetical case at the beginning of this chapter illustrates why there is a malpractice dilemma. If this case is brought to trial, the jury must determine the standard of care for the defendant urologist (the urologist that treated the kidney stone). Does the standard of care require a urologist to screen all of his male patients for prostate cancer? This is not an easy question for the jury, for there are widespread differences among urologists and medical organizations regarding the benefits of prostate cancer screening and the utility of the PSA test.

The American Urological Association and American Cancer Society recommend offering a PSA test and a digital rectal exam to men over the age of 50, African-American men over the age of 40, and all men over the age of 40 who have a family history of prostate cancer. However, the National Cancer Institute, the American Academy of Family Practitioners, and the United States Preventive Services Task Force currently offer no recommendation (previously, the latter two organizations had recommended *against* screening). These latter two organizations concluded that there is no clear evidence as to the benefits of screening for prostate cancer. The American College of Physicians recommends patient counseling, rather than across-the-board screening. Finally, the Canadian Task Force for Preventive Health Care continues to recommend against prostate cancer screening.[3]

Why is screening for prostate cancer controversial? In the United States, prostate cancer is the second most common cause of cancer death in men. Approximately 30,000 men will die of prostate cancer each year. The PSA, a blood test introduced in the late 1990s, and a digital rectal exam can detect prostate cancer at an early stage and thus improve the chances for cure. However, because a significant number of men with prostate cancer die of other causes, screening can result in overdiagnosis and overtreatment.

Whether prostate cancer screening actually saves lives is the paramount question, and this question has yet to be determined. Because preliminary studies suggest that prostate cancer screening lowers prostate cancer mortality rates, the American Urological Association recommends prostate cancer screening. Other organizations are awaiting the final results of long-term studies.[4]

Returning to the hypothetical case, the patient might succeed with a claim of medical malpractice against the first urologist (the urologist that treated the stone) if the patient shows that the standard of care requires a urologist to offer prostate cancer screening to *all* of his male patients, regardless of the patient's presentation.

The first urologist's defense is that he was treating the patient for a specific problem (the kidney stone). Once that acute urologic problem had been treated, the defendant can argue that it is then the responsibility of the patient's primary care physician to screen for prostate cancer and other health maintenance issues. If the patient lacked a primary care physician, then it is the patient's responsibility to find a primary care physician. The jury is left to decide the standard of care. Given the discrepancies between the recommendations of prominent medical organizations, the jury may simply decide this issue on bias and emotion rather than scientific principles.

For further discussion, let us change the facts of the hypothetical case. Assume that the first urologist performed a history and physical exam on the patient before he proceeded with surgery (arguably, the standard of care for a surgeon *is* to perform such a history and physical exam before operating on a patient). Let us further assume that in taking the medical history, the urologist learned that the patient's father died of prostate cancer at the age of 60 and that the patient never had a PSA test performed. Given this medical history and that a positive family history places a man at higher risk for prostate cancer, the plaintiff now has a more compelling argument that the standard of care requires the urologist to screen for prostate cancer before the urologist releases the patient from his care.

What if we change the facts so that the patient first saw his family physician and was indeed referred to the urologist? The urologist can argue that the primary care physician had the responsibility to address health care maintenance issues, such as prostate cancer screening. But given the strong family history of prostate cancer, should the standard of care at least require the urologist to inquire about the patient's prostate cancer screening status? The primary care physician may not have screened for prostate cancer because the American Academy of Family Practitioners has no recommendation, yet the American Urological Association clearly recommends a PSA test and a digital rectal exam in this clinical situation. Even though a clinical guideline is not *prima facie* evidence of the standard of care, it is very difficult to convince a jury that the recommendations of the American Urological Society (the premier urology specialty organization with over 14,500 urologist members) do not constitute the standard of care for the urologist.

Prostate Cancer Strategies

A PSA test is relatively inexpensive. Most laboratories charge less than $100 for the test, and Medicare and most private health plans cover the cost of the test. The American Urological Association's PSA guidelines offer the best prophylaxis to avoid a malpractice claim of a missed diagnosis of prostate cancer. The guidelines recommend the early detection of prostate cancer by offering prostate cancer screening to every patient (1) with a life expectancy of over 10 years and over the age of 50 and (2) every male over the age of 40 with a life expectancy of over 10 years who is African-American or who has a first-degree relative diagnosed with prostate cancer. The urologist should follow this guideline for all of his or her patients, *regardless of the reason for the visit to the urologist*.

A significant number of patients are not aware of their prostate cancer screening status. If the patient states that his primary care physician performs an annual DRE and orders an annual PSA, the urologist should verify this by requesting a copy from that physician's office. If a recent PSA result cannot be verified or if the patient's most recent PSA was performed more than a year prior, then the urologist should notify the patient of this fact and offer the patient prostate cancer screening. If the patient declines, it should be clearly documented in the patient's chart.

The Prostate: Benign Prostatic Hyperplasia (BPH)

Benign prostatic hyperplasia is noncancerous enlargement of the prostate. It is associated with bothersome urinary symptoms, such as daytime and night-time frequency, sudden strong urges to void (which may lead to incontinence), and incomplete emptying. BPH is one of the most common diseases of the aging man, with perhaps half of men over the age of 60 experiencing BPH symptoms of varying degree and bother. The treating urologist may perform diagnostic studies, prescribe medication, or recommend surgical treatments. Approximately 350,000 surgical procedures for BPH are performed each year. Minimally invasive surgical treatments have evolved over the past decade such that a significant number of patients now have their BPH treated surgically in the urologist's office.[5]

In contrast to prostate cancer, BPH is rarely fatal. BPH is characterized by its effect on quality of life, so most procedures to alleviate the symptoms of BPH are elective. As such, the urologist's goal is to alleviate the bothersome symptoms of a patient rather than cure the patient of a life-threatening illness. Surgical treatment of BPH is technically challenging, expectations are high, and imperfect outcomes are often scrutinized. Medical malpractice cases involving technical errors are often jury-dependent and have varying success.

In *Longhini v. Michigan Medical,* the plaintiff underwent a transurethral resection of the prostate (TURP) to alleviate his symptoms of frequency, urgency, and terminal dribbling. The plaintiff's symptoms continued, so he had a repeat TURP six months later. After the second procedure, he developed urinary incontinence. The patient then went to the Mayo Clinic and was told that his incontinence was the result of "inappropriate cutting" of his urinary sphincter by the defendant urologist. The defendant urologist argued that the damage to the sphincter was caused not by a technically "inappropriate cutting" but by heat from the operative instrument. The jury found for the defendant and the verdict was upheld on appeal.[6] A contrary result, however, was reached in *Cleveland v. Wong.* In that case, the plaintiff also experienced urinary incontinence after a TURP. The plaintiff had been advised of this complication and had signed a consent that specifically included this possibility. A subsequent treating urologist concluded that the plaintiff's incontinence was due to sphincter damage as a direct result of the TURP. The plaintiff sued the urologist that performed the TURP. The jury found for the plaintiff and awarded damages of $698,506.26 to the plaintiff and $325,000 to the wife for loss of consortium. The judgment was affirmed on appeal.[7]

In *Cleveland,* informed consent was not enough to shield the defendant urologist from a claim of negligence as a result of a known complication. The importance of informed consent, however, was demonstrated in *Hager v. Shanmugham.* In that case, the plaintiff underwent a TURP to alleviate his obstructive urinary symptoms. Following the surgery, the plaintiff developed persistent incontinence. A subsequent urologist had determined that the plaintiff's incontinence was the result of damage to the urinary sphincter. In his medical negligence claim, the plaintiff alleged that damaging the urinary sphincter was *res ipsa loquitur* medical negligence. The defendant urologist admitted to damaging the urinary sphincter. However, the urologist claimed that urinary incontinence was a known and recognized complication, and the plaintiff's injury was the result of patient variation in anatomy. The defendant introduced expert testimony that even when performing prostate surgery to the most precise standards, inadvertent injury can still occur. The jury found for the defendant, and the verdict was upheld on appeal. Much of the testimony focused on the fact that the plaintiff was clearly informed about the possibility of urinary incontinence. The defendant urologist documented such a conversation with the plaintiff, and a second urologist, who was not a party to the suit, also informed the patient of this possibility.[8]

BHP Strategies

As the above referenced cases demonstrate, medical negligence claims relating to surgery for BPH have varying outcomes. What is considered substandard care in one instance may be considered a known complication in another. To limit one's medical malpractice exposure, the urologist must not lose sight of patient expectations. Informed consent, as shown in the *Cleveland* case, does not provide an absolute shield. However, in the process of obtaining informed consent, the urologist has the opportunity to educate the patient. Numerous patient education materials are available. The American Urological Society's BPH Guidelines and its companion Patient's Guide are good examples.[9] Limitations of the proposed procedure need to be outlined, alternative therapies discussed, and an honest assessment of the urologist's own personal results and experiences provided. The possibility of failure to cure the patient's presenting symptoms as well as the possibility of worsening preexisting symptoms need to be discussed. In addition to incontinence, retrograde ejaculation is another known (and more likely) complication of prostate surgery. If not properly informed about this complication, a patient may be quite surprised and disappointed. The urologist should not assume that an older male patient is not sexually potent, especially in the age of Viagra.

The Bladder: Micturition

The urinary system is perhaps the most conscious bodily function of the human body. During most of the day, the human mind is usually not conscious of the lungs breathing or the heart beating. However, after a cup of coffee or a long car trip, the human mind often turns its attention to the bladder. If the body's bladder is not functioning properly, that person will be continually reminded of this malfunction throughout the day and probably the night as well.

In terms of a urologist's malpractice exposure, if a bladder ailment occurs after an adverse surgical outcome, that patient has a constant reminder of his or her predicament. Depending on how the urologist manages this complication, that patient may become a potential malpractice plaintiff.

The hypothetical case at the beginning of this chapter demonstrates this point. The patient has incurable prostate cancer, has lost his sexual function, and suffers from urinary incontinence. Of these three conditions, his urinary incontinence is arguably the most bothersome for the patient. Because the patient's prostate cancer is currently in remission, he may not always dwell on his diagnosis of advanced prostate cancer. Because he has lost his libido secondary to the LRH injections, he may not dwell on his inability to obtain an erection. However, because the patient has to wear a condom catheter to control his incontinence, he is reminded on a daily, if not hourly, basis of this complication. Indeed, health-related quality-of-life studies have consistently shown that urinary incontinence is an independent predictor for global quality of life following treatment for prostate cancer.

As mentioned in the introduction to this chapter, the PIAA analysis of urology malpractice claims found that voiding dysfunction is the third most prevalent condition for which a medical negligence claim was filed. Of the 428 total claims between 1985 and 2004, 150 (35%) involved female stress incontinence. Technological advancements in the treatment of female stress urinary incontinence have made this condition one of the most rapidly growing areas in urology. The number of procedures to correct female stress urinary incontinence, by conservative estimate, has nearly doubled in the last decade.[10] Success rates of the newer procedures, such as tension-free slings, approach 90%.[11] Overall complication rates vary, but major complications are generally less than 10%.[12] The major area of dissatisfaction for these sling procedures, whether or not categorized as a complication, is new onset urge symptoms.

Yoe v. Cleveland Clinic Foundation is a representative medical negligence case. In that case, the plaintiff underwent a vaginal sling procedure. Following the procedure, the patient developed urinary retention, which required a urethrolysis to loosen the sling. After this second procedure, the plaintiff suffered from total urinary incontinence. The plaintiff alleged that the urologist negligently tied the sutures too tight. The jury returned a verdict for the defendant, and the judgment was affirmed on appeal.[13]

Micturition Strategies

As with surgery for BPH, surgical misadventures in urinary incontinence involve quality-of-life issues rather than serious injury or loss of life. Strategies to avoid medical malpractice need to focus on patient education. Before undergoing treatment, whether medical or surgical, the incontinent patient needs to understand the rationale behind treatment, treatment options, treatment success rates, surgical complications (type of complication and likelihood), and diagnostic and therapeutic steps to address those complications. The patient should understand the differences between urgency, urge incontinence, and stress incontinence. The patient should understand that urge incontinence is primarily treated with medical therapy (anticholinergic and antispasmodic agents) and that stress incontinence is primarily treated with surgical intervention. Urgency (a sudden and strong desire to void), urge incontinence, and stress urinary incontinence may often coexist, and treatment of one type of incontinence may unmask symptoms of the other type of incontinence. The uninformed patient may expect a complete cure and be surprised and disappointed by anything less.

The principles of informed consent, discussed elsewhere in this Handbook, will not shield the urologist from liability if the urologist is found to have negligently performed the consented procedure. However, the informed consent process does create an educational atmosphere where the urologist may speak frankly to his or her patient about the success rates and complications of the proposed procedure. The urologist should not proceed until the patient demonstrates an understanding of the goals and limitations of the procedure.

Personal experience and idiosyncrasies dictate a physician's approach as to how he or she educates their patients. Numerous visual aids and educational materials are at the urologist's disposal. One valuable tool, although becoming dated, is the American Urological Association's *The Surgical Management of Female Stress Urinary Incontinence: A Doctor's Guide for Patients.*[14] This readily available handout uses straightforward illustrations and laymen's terminology to discuss the anatomy and physiology of urinary incontinence. Diagnostic methods, etiologies, and concomitant conditions (such as urge incontinence) are discussed. The urologist treating urinary incontinence is encouraged to review, update, and incorporate the principles outlined in this Patient Guide when obtaining informed consent from the incontinent patient. If a postoperative patient develops a complication, the urologist must be cognizant of its impact on the patient's quality of life and promptly treat the complication with empathy and humility. Personal capabilities and experience should dictate the threshold for referring a surgical complication to a tertiary center.

The Bladder: Cancer

The most common presenting symptom of bladder cancer is painless hematuria, either gross or microscopic. It is generally agreed upon by urologists that gross hematuria warrants a diagnostic workup. Microscopic hematuria, however, is often intermittent, so the absence of hematuria on a urine specimen does not rule out the presence of bladder cancer. Population data vary, but a Mayo Clinic study reported that approximately 1% of patients with asymptomatic microscopic hematuria have an underlying urologic malignancy.[15]

A significant portion of a urologist's practice involves the diagnostic workup of hematuria. The American Urological Association's Best Practice Policy Recommendations provides strong evidence as to the standard of care.[16] The urologist must first determine if the microscopic hematuria is significant. The recommended definition of significant microscopic hematuria is three or more red blood cells per high-power field on two of three properly collected specimens. However, a lesser amount of hematuria in patients with recognized risk factors for significant disease may also, on an individualized basis, be considered significant.

The complete urologic evaluation includes a history and physical examination, laboratory analysis of renal function, cytologic examination of the urine, imaging of the upper urinary tracts, and cystoscopy. After a negative evaluation, the

American Urological Association recommends close follow-up. At 6, 12, 24 and 36 months, a urinalysis, voided urine cytology, and blood pressure determination are recommended. This follow-up can be quite cumbersome and expensive for the patient. Patient compliance with such a follow-up schedule is often poor.

Bladder Cancer Strategies

The AUA's Best Practice Guidelines may not encompass every clinical presentation, but they represent a good framework. The practicing urologist should certainly be cognizant of these guidelines and consider documenting the rationale for deviation. The urologist should incorporate subsequent medical advancements, such as fluorescence *in situ* hybridization (FISH) and multislice CT imaging, into his or her own treatment algorithm. Patients presenting with gross hematuria or irritative voiding symptoms usually warrant a full evaluation. When stratifying a patient's risk, obtain and review all available medical records and review previous imaging studies.

To help ensure patient compliance, educate the patient about the rationale for follow-up recommendations and the consequences of noncompliance. When a patient does not keep a scheduled follow-up appointment, the patient should be notified in writing, and a copy of such communication should be placed in the patient's record.

The Kidney and Ureter

Similarly to bladder cancer, kidney and ureter malignancies also present with hematuria, so the above discussion on bladder cancer, as well as the AUA Best Practice Guidelines, are equally applicable. As outlined in the PIAA analysis, benign conditions of the kidney and ureter account for a significant number of medical malpractice claims filed against urologists. Another study analyzed 259 malpractice claims against urologists insured by the St. Paul Companies from 1994 to 1999. That study found that endourologic procedures had the greatest incidence of claims when compared to other surgical procedures. Like surgical procedures to treat BPH, endourologic procedures to treat ureteral and kidney stones are technically challenging, and medical negligence cases are usually the result of surgical complications.

In *Verbance v. Altman*, the defendant urologist injured the bladder during a failed attempt to remove the plaintiff's symptomatic ureteral stone. The plaintiff successfully claimed that as a direct result of the injury to the bladder and subsequent extravasation of urine around the genitofemoral nerve, he suffered severe and incapacitating pain. The jury agreed with the plaintiff's claim that the defendant urologist did not meet the standard of care and awarded him $511,836.78. The case was upheld on appeal.[17]

Delay in diagnosis is another important medical negligence issue for the urologist. Infection associated with obstructing kidney or ureteral stones can be a potentially life-threatening urologic emergency. Patients are typically febrile and may present with hypotension or septic shock. Urgent drainage of the obstructed kidney is essential. In *Townsend v. Puckett*, the plaintiff was diagnosed in the emergency room with a urinary tract infection after she presented with fever and back pain. Her condition deteriorated, and she expired less than 24 hours later. An autopsy found that she had a kidney stone, which caused her infection and ultimately septic shock and death. The jury awarded $850,000 to the plaintiff's estate.[18]

Kidney and Ureter Strategies

The urologist needs to be familiar with the American Urological Association's published clinical guidelines regarding the management of ureteral stones.[19] Similarly to the previous discussions regarding stress urinary incontinence and BPH, the urologist needs to inform his patient about treatment options, the types and likelihood of complications, and the diagnostic and treatment algorithm for such complications. Acute presentations of sepsis must not be ignored.

The Penis: Surgical Treatment for Erectile Dysfunction

The human male is often fixated on his genitalia and will usually value his penis over other organs or appendages of the body. Would a man rather lose a limb, an eye, or his penis? Any surgery on the penis thus involves significant malpractice exposure for the urologist.

Before the introduction of Viagra in 1998, surgical implantation of a penile prosthesis was a more common treatment for erectile dysfunction. Surgical prostheses have given rise to a significant number of medical negligence claims. Many of these cases have focused not only on medical negligence but also informed consent. As discussed elsewhere in this Handbook, the doctrine of informed consent is dependent upon the jurisdiction where the case arises. In jurisdictions following a professional standard, the physician must disclose as much information as an average practitioner would disclose under similar circumstances. For those jurisdictions under the objective standard, the physician must disclose information that the average patient would consider necessary and important in order to make a decision. Genital injuries and resulting erectile function tend to be an emotional issue for the male patient. Similar to urinary incontinence quality-of-life issues discussed earlier, health-related quality-of-life studies also show that erectile dysfunction is an independent predictor for global quality of life.

Consider the following representative hypothetical case. A 55-year-old diabetic man presents to his urologist with a two-year history of worsening erectile dysfunction. He is able to achieve an erection with the aid of Viagra, but has significant side effects of headache and heartburn. The urologist offers the patient surgery to implant an inflatable penile prosthesis. Like most competent surgeons, the urologist counsels the patient that his diabetes puts him at a higher risk of infection. Following the surgery, the patient is extremely satisfied, but six months later the prosthesis becomes infected and requires removal. The patient has to wait six months for his penis to heal before a replacement prosthesis can be implanted. As a result of scar tissue from the original infection, the patient experiences significant pain with the use of his new prosthesis. His penis has an "SST" deformity (downward-dropping head of the penis secondary to loss of rigidity), and his penis is one inch shorter.

Depending on other facts of this hypothetical case, the patient may have a negligence claim. Did the urologist properly evaluate and treat the patient for any contributing co-morbid illnesses? For example, did the urologist ensure that the patient's diabetes was under control? Were the urologist's surgical technique and postoperative care appropriate? Did the urologist, for example, appropriately size the prosthesis? Did the urologist administer appropriate antibiotics during and after the procedure? Prior to recommending surgery, did the urologist maximize medical treatment by prescribing a higher dose of Viagra or alternative medications such as Cialis or Levitra? Did the urologist discuss alternatives such as a vacuum constriction device or intra-cavernosal injections?

The 1996 American Urological Association's Erectile Dysfunction Clinical Guidelines Panel published its evidence-based recommendations for the treatment of erectile dysfunction.[20] In accordance with the 1992 NIH Consensus Statement, the Panel recommended that a patient presenting with a new diagnosis of erectile dysfunction should undergo a diagnostic assessment that includes a general medical history, a detailed sexual history, psychological evaluation, a physical examination, and basic laboratory studies. These "basic laboratory studies" included a complete blood count, urinalysis, creatinine, lipid profile, and fasting blood sugar or glycosylated hemoglobin. After addressing any identified co-morbid conditions, the Panel then recommended that treatment be individualized and based on patient choice and informed consent. The three recommended and evidence-based treatment options were vacuum constriction device therapy, intracavernosal vasoactive drug injection therapy, and penile prosthesis implantation.

Erectile Dysfunction Surgical Strategies

Most medical negligence claims arising from the treatment of erectile dysfunction involve complications from penile prosthesis surgery. In *Hopkins v. Silber*, the plaintiff had an inflatable penile prosthesis implanted by one of the defendant urologists. Seven weeks later, the plaintiff experienced significant pain at the head of his penis. Unhappy with the first defendant urologist, the plaintiff sought the services of the second defendant urologist. The second urologist told the plaintiff that, due to incorrect sizing, the prosthesis was causing tissue ischemia. Two months later, the second urologist recommended and subsequently removed the inflatable prosthesis and replaced it with a malleable prosthesis. The malleable prosthesis subsequently eroded, and was removed by a third urologist. A fourth urologist was then consulted about the possibility of another replacement prosthesis. The fourth urologist told the plaintiff that although the risk of failure was higher for repeat surgery, the likelihood for success was "actually quite good." The patient declined a repeat procedure. The plaintiff filed a negligence claim against the first and second urologists. The plaintiff claimed that both surgeries were negligently performed and that the second urologist was further negligent in not promptly removing the first prosthesis. A jury found both urologists negligent, and the judgment was affirmed on appeal.[21]

When considering strategies to avoid medical malpractice, the *Hopkins* case illustrates the importance of the medical record and surgical technique.

Typically, many urologists have treated the plaintiff in a negligence case involving a penile prosthesis. The disillusioned patient often seeks several opinions and undergoes several revisions, so the patient's medical record is further developed with each subsequent treating urologist. Furthermore, each subsequent treating urologist will often scrutinize the first urologist's treatment algorithm and surgical technique.

The 1996 Guidelines specifically discuss surgical technique. The urologist should be familiar with both the 1996 and 2005 Guidelines. Although not *prima facie* evidence of the standard of care, the AUA Guidelines certainly provide strong evidence for the plaintiff, so the rationale for any deviation should be explained and documented in the patient's record. Finally, informed consent, as outlined in the Guidelines, remains crucial. To avoid a claim of negligence, the urologist must ensure that his patient understands the rates and consequences of the known complications of penile prosthesis surgery and that his patient has reasonable expectations.

The Penis: Medical Treatment for Erectile Dysfunction

In 1998, Pfizer revolutionized the treatment of erectile dysfunction with the introduction of the PDE5 inhibitor, Viagra (sildenafil). Some 350,000 prescriptions were filled during the first month of its release. Two similar competing drugs, Levitra (vardenafil) and Cialis (tadalafil), were introduced in 2003 and have steadily gained market share. Recognizing that oral medications have quickly become first-line treatment options for erectile dysfunction, the American Urological Association appointed an Erectile Dysfunction Clinical Guidelines Update Panel in 2000 to review the new literature and update the 1996 recommendations. The Panel concluded that informed patient decision making remains paramount, that the recommendations for diagnostic evaluation in the 1996 Guidelines required no changes, and that psychological and endocrine disorders are an important consideration in the etiology of erectile dysfunction. Furthermore, the Panel specifically recommended that oral PDE5 inhibitors (i.e., Viagra, Cialis, or Levitra), when not contraindicated, should be offered as first-line treatment.

The Update Panel also adopted the Princeton Consensus Panel's recommendations when prescribing PDE5 inhibitors to patients with cardiovascular disease. High-risk patients, including those with unstable angina, uncontrolled hypertension, CHF class II, certain arrhythmias, recent MI, cardiomyopathies, or mild to moderate valvular disease, should not receive treatment. A cardiologist should further evaluate patients at intermediate risk, and patients at low risk may receive treatment with PDE5 inhibitors.

PDE5 inhibitors potentiate the hypotensive effects of nitrate- and nitrite-containing medications, so all PDE5 inhibitors are clearly contraindicated in patients who take nitrates, either on a scheduled or p.r.n. basis. A large percentage of men with erectile dysfunction also have BPH. Alpha-blockers, such as Flomax, Hytrin, and Cardura, are commonly used to treat the symptoms of BPH. PDE5 inhibitors have the potential to adversely lower blood pressure in these men, so PDE5 inhibitors should be administered in this setting with caution and patients warned of this potential adverse side effect.

Pharmaceutical companies have recently marketed their treatments for erectile dysfunction to primary care physicians. Television and print advertisements encourage men to discuss erectile dysfunction with their "doctor," and not necessarily their urologist. Accordingly, the urologist now sees more patients with erectile dysfunction who have already been prescribed, and failed, a PDE5 inhibitor by his primary care physician. Should the urologist assume that the primary care physician has performed the basic recommended diagnostic workup? Does this scenario change the standard of care for the urologist?

Erectile Dysfunction Medical Strategies

The urologist should request and review any records from the primary care physician to confirm that co-morbid diseases, such as diabetes and cardiovascular disease, have been screened or stabilized and that health prevention measures, such as smoking cessation and lifestyle changes, have been addressed. It is essential for the prescribing urologist to know all the medications that a patient takes on a scheduled and p.r.n. basis. Furthermore, the urologist must recognize both the generic and trade names of the commonly used nitrates and nitrites. Table 2 in the 2005 Updated Guidelines is an excellent resource. The prescribing urologist should be cognizant of all prescribing updates.

Any urologist that prescribes intraurethral suppositories or intracavernosal injections should counsel his patient about the risk of priapism. If, after treatment with these medications, the patient sustains an erection lasting more than four hours, the patient must understand that this is a urologic emergency. The patient should be instructed to either call the urologist (not a friend!) or go immediately to the nearest emergency room. The prescribing urologist should be proficient in the treatments for priapism and have the appropriate antidotes available in his office.

The Vas Deferens: Male Sterilization

It is estimated in the United States that over 500,000 vasectomies are performed each year. Based on numbers alone, it is understandable why negligence claims involving vasectomies were the sixth most common claim against urologists in the PIAA analysis. The average indemnity was $44,444. Complications following a vasectomy, often the source of medical negligence claims, include chronic pain, swelling, and failure to achieve sterilization.

In *Gerver v. Benavides*, the plaintiff experienced severe pain following his vasectomy. During a two-month period after the procedure, the plaintiff sought medical attention on 21 occasions. In his claim for medical negligence, the plaintiff argued that the defendant urologist negligently placed a suture through a nerve. The jury agreed with the plaintiff and awarded $2,168,433.11 in damages. The trial court set aside the verdict after the defendant submitted video surveillance at a post-trial hearing that contradicted the plaintiff's disability testimony. On appeal, the appellate court reinstated the jury verdict.[22] In *Walker v. Elliot*, the plaintiff experienced pain shortly after his vasectomy. A few months later, he underwent surgery to remove an atrophied testicle. In his medical negligence claim, the plaintiff argued that the artery to the testicle was negligently injured. The jury found in favor of the defendant, and the verdict was upheld on appeal.[23]

A wrongful life claim and a spousal derivative claim were the focus in *Dean v. Edgecomb*.[24] In that case, the defendant was the primary care physician that referred the plaintiff to a urologist for a vasectomy. The urologist expressly warned that the procedure may not be effective and that, to assure sterility, the plaintiff should continue to use contraception until three negative semen analyses were obtained six months later. The plaintiff ignored this advice. When the plaintiff later asked his primary care physician about the necessity of this semen analysis, the defendant told the plaintiff "not to worry about it." The plaintiff and his wife subsequently conceived a child. The jury found that the primary care physician's statements were indeed negligent, but on contributory negligence grounds, the jury returned a verdict in favor of the defendant. In upholding the verdict, the appellate court recognized that, although no doctor–patient relationship existed between the wife and the defendant physician, the spouse might have a derivative claim of wrongful life under Maryland law. However, such a claim was foreclosed by the husband's contributory negligence.

Sterilization Strategies

Similar to the cases involving the surgical treatment of benign prostatic hyperplasia, the *Gerver* and *Walker* cases represent similar fact patterns that resulted in different jury verdicts. In the *Dean* case, one may surmise that the urologist was not a defendant because he expressly informed the patient about the risk of failure and the steps necessary to assure sterility. To limit malpractice liability in vasectomy cases, the urologist must clearly document informed consent. A signed consent form that includes a detailed listing of the known complications of a vasectomy, including but not limited to chronic pain, swelling, infection, and failure to achieve sterility, should be in the patient's record. The urologist should provide clear instructions about the need to continue contraceptive measures until a negative semen analysis is obtained. The urologist should also provide clear instructions about when and where to get such a post-vasectomy semen analysis. The urologist should monitor his vasectomy patients for compliance. Those patients that do not comply with these instructions should receive a certified letter reminding them of the consequences of noncompliance.

CONCLUSION

In a negligence claim, the plaintiff must establish a duty, breach of that duty, causation, and damages. In a medical negligence claim, the physician has a duty to meet the standard of care. Although not absolute, guidelines established by professional associations provide a jury with strong evidence as to the standard of care. Informed consent cannot shield the physician from a negligence claim, but an informed patient, having been told about the potential risks of a given procedure, may be less inclined to initiate a medical negligence action.

This chapter has introduced some of the clinical scenarios that are most likely to result in a medical malpractice claim against a urologist and has offered certain strategies to avoid litigation. Although a urologist may treat certain unique anatomic and physiologic conditions, the urologist shares many of the same malpractice issues with the other surgical specialists discussed in this Handbook.

FURTHER READING

White C, Rosoff AJ, Leblang TR, "Informed Consent to Medical and Surgical Treatment." In *Legal Medicine/American College of Legal Medicine*, 7th ed., ed. S. Sandy Sanbar *et al.* Philadelphia: Mosby, 2007.

REFERENCES

1. Physician Insurers Association of America, *Risk Management Review—Urologic Surgery*, 2004.

2. See Kahan SE, *et al.*, *Urological Medical Malpractice*. Journal of Urology 165(5):1638–1642 (2001). An analysis of claims filed against the St. Paul Companies between 1995 and 1999 showed that claims involving circumcision had the second highest amount paid per claim ($153,343).

3. Smith RA, *et al.*, *American Cancer Society Guidelines for the Early Detection of Cancer*. CA: Cancer Journal for Clinicians 53:27–43 (2003). See also Vassey PA, *ESMO/ASCO Joint Symposium: Screening for Prostate Cancer, Chemoprevention of Breast Cancer*, Proceedings of the 25th Congress of the European Society for Medical Oncology, Hamburg, Germany (2000).

4. See *Prostate-Specific Antigen (PSA) Best Practice Policy of the American Urological Association*, Oncology 14(2):267–280 (2000).

5. See "Benign Prostatic Hyperplasia," in *Campbell's Urology*, 8th ed., ed. P Walsh. Philadelphia: Saunders, 2002, Section 6.

6. *Longhini v. Michigan Medical, P.C.*, Mich. Court of Appeals, No. 243124, April 2004. See also *Lopez v. Steven Jense*, Mich. Court of Appeals, No. 245243, March 2004. In that case, the plaintiff failed to show that incontinence following a TURP was cause in fact that the plaintiff's sphincter was damaged. The trial court's granting of summary judgment was affirmed.

7. *Cleveland v. Wong*, 237 Kan. 410, 701 P. 2d 1301 (1985).

8. *Hager v. Shanmugham*, 190 W. Va. 703 (1993).

9. *Guideline for the Management of Benign Prostatic Hyperplasia*, American Urological Association, Baltimore, 2003.

10. Waetjen LE, *et al.*, *Stress Urinary Incontinence Surgery in the United States*. Obstetrics and Gynecology 101:671–676 (2003). See also Boyles SH, *et al.*, *Procedures for Urinary Incontinence in the United States, 1979–1997*. American Journal of Obstetrics and Gynecology 189(1):70–75 (2003).

11. Morgan TO, *et al.*, *Pubovaginal Sling: 4-Year Outcome Analysis and Quality of Life Assessment*. Journal of Urology 163(6):1845-1848 (2000).

12. Taub DA, *et al.*, *Complications Following Surgical Intervention for Stress Urinary Incontinence: A National Perspective.* Neurourology and Urodynamics 24(7):659–665 (2005).

13. *Yoe v. Cleveland Clinic Foundation,* 2003 Ohio 875 (2003).

14. *The Surgical Management of Female Stress Urinary Incontinence: A Doctor's Guide for Patients,* American Urological Association Health Policy Department, Baltimore, 1997.

15. Mohr DN, *et al.*, *Asymptomatic Microhematuria and Urologic Disease: A Population-Based Study.* JAMA 256:224 (1986).

16. Grossfield GD, *et al.*, *Asymptomatic Microscopic Hematuria in Adults: Summary of the AUA's Best Practice Policy Recommendations.* American Family Physician 63(6):1145–1154 (2001).

17. *Verbance v. Altman,* Appellate Court of Illinois, 2nd District, No. 2-00-1275 (August 2001).

18. *Townsend v. Puckett,* Appellate Court of Illinois, 1st District, No. 1-00-1301 (December 2000). On appeal, the jury's verdict was vacated because the plaintiff did not provide evidence from either a urologist or an interventional radiologist as to proximate cause.

19. *Ureteral Stones Clinical Guidelines Panel Report on the Management of Ureteral Calculi,* American Urological Association, Baltimore, 1997.

20. *Erectile Dysfunction Clinical Guidelines Panel Report on the Treatment of Organic Erectile Dysfunction,* American Urological Association, Baltimore, 1996.

21. *Hopkins v. Silber,* Maryland Court of Special Appeals, No. 1159, September 2000. The awarded damages of $35,000 were significantly reduced by the defendant's claim of contributory negligence. The plaintiff disregarded instructions to refrain from sex for five weeks. His wife testified that he had attempted sex six times within four weeks of the initial sugery.

22. *Gerver v. Benavides,* W. Va. Court of Appeals, No. 26355, September 1999.

23. *Walker v. Elliot,* Tn. Court of Appeals, No. 03A01-9903-00085, December 1999.

24. *Dean v. Edgecomb,* Md. Court of Appeals, No. 1536, September 2002. A discussion of wrongful life is beyond the scope of this chapter. For a thorough discussion of a wrongful life claim, see Hensell W, *The Disabling Impact of Wrongful Birth and Wrongful Life Actions.* Harvard Civil Right–Civil Liberties Law Review 40(1):141–196 (2005).

Neurology and Neurosurgery

James C. Johnston, M.D., J.D., F.C.L.M., F.A.C.L.M.

GOLDEN RULES

1. A careful history and complete examination remain the cornerstone of good medical practice, thereby reducing the risk of a malpractice suit.
2. Most claims against the neurologic practitioner stem from spine disorders, headache (HA), brain tumor, subarachnoid hemorrhage, stroke, and epilepsy.
3. HA key points:
   (a) HA evaluation requires a systematic approach to exclude secondary HAs, diagnose the primary HA disorder, and develop an individualized treatment plan.
   (b) Many patients have more than one type of HA, and each must be addressed separately.
   (c) "Red flags" such as thunderclap HA mandate immediate and thorough evaluation.
   (d) Consider imaging every patient with primary HA and normal neurologic examination.
4. Stroke key points:
   (a) Anticoagulation is the standard of care for stroke prevention in select high-risk patients, and requires accurate monitoring.
   (b) Follow the tissue plasminogen activator (tPA) protocol inclusion and exclusion criteria for treatment of acute ischemic stroke.
   (c) Carotid endarterectomy is the standard of care for select patients with high-grade carotid stenosis, and must be performed in a timely fashion.
5. Epilepsy key points:
   (a) Epileptics who drive expose the neurologist to extraordinary liability, which must be addressed through meticulous documentation.
   (b) There are a multitude of issues to consider in women taking antiepileptic drugs (AEDs) during reproductive years.
6. Informed consent is a process (not a form), and relevant guidelines should be closely followed.
7. Documentation must be clear, accurate, legible, complete, and timely without alteration or spoliation.
8. Most malpractice claims are triggered by a breakdown of the physician–patient relationship due to poor communication.

The scope of neurologic malpractice liability precludes a compendium of potential claims. Moreover, any such listing would be outdated before publication, as emerging diagnostic and therapeutic options open the door for new claims. It is, however, instructive to consider the most prevalent patient conditions generating suits against the neurologic practitioner (in decreasing order of frequency): back disorders; cerebrovascular accident; displacement of intervertebral disk; convulsions; headache (HA); epilepsy; migraine; malignant neoplasm of the brain; subarachnoid hemorrhage (SAH); and musculoskeletal disorders affecting the neck region.[1]

Intervertebral disk displacement and spine disorders are not discussed because these claims are predominantly simple diagnostic errors, few result in an indemnity payment, and the total indemnity is a small fraction of the total paid for all claims.

This chapter outlines several management strategies for the remaining conditions, arbitrarily grouped together as stroke, epilepsy, and HA, the latter subsuming migraine, brain tumor, and SAH. Lack of space precludes a discussion of the myriad disparate claims involving these conditions. Therefore, several particular topics were selected because they are frequently seen by neurologists and neurosurgeons alike, affect a large segment of the population, generate recurring claims, and have the potential for devastating outcomes with exceptionally high indemnity payments or judgments.

CASE PRESENTATION

A 42-year-old female presented to the neurologist with a three-month history of headaches and vague dizziness. The exam was reported as normal, and sumatriptan was prescribed for "common migraines." Over the next three years, the patient returned to the neurologist sixteen times with complaints of a generalized daily headache, dull with occasional throbbing and typically worse later in the day. The neurologist reported a normal neurologic exam at each visit, never ordered any diagnostic testing except for an in-office EEG (reported as normal), and unsuccessfully treated the patient with a host of anti-inflammatory, analgesic, and prophylactic migraine medications.

On the seventeenth visit, the patient described a more severe, nearly constant headache with "stabbing" pains in the occipital region and blurred vision. The neurologist referred her to a neurosurgeon who performed cervical spine radiographs (interpreted as showing minimal osteophytic changes at C4–5 and C5–6), and prescribed Elavil for "atypical mixed headaches with cervical spine disease" and "mild depression." She returned to the treating neurologist with complaints of progressive visual impairment. The neurologist described a "normal neuro exam," changed the Elavil to Paxil, and concluded "The neurosurgeon and I agree that the patient is depressed, which is contributing to her headaches, and the visual complaints are probably due to Elavil side effects." The patient consulted another neurologist nine days later. Examination revealed papilledema, partial cranial nerve VII, VIII, and XII palsies, and ataxia. Imaging revealed a large acoustic neuroma.

There were permanent deficits postoperatively. The patient sued the treating neurologist and consulting neurosurgeon for failure to diagnose a brain tumor, and the case settled for over $5 million.

Comment: This case illustrates the need to consider secondary causes of headache, especially with a history of progressive symptoms and multiple "red flags" (atypical headache, dizziness, unresponsive to treatment, visual impairment). There was no indication for an EEG. Imaging would have been appropriate after the initial consultation, leading to an earlier diagnosis and avoiding some of the permanent deficits. The neurologist failed to recognize that the patient complained of visual blurring before starting Elavil, even though the nurse documented this symptom in the follow-up note. If the neurologist actually examined the patient, instead of simply writing "normal neuro exam" in the chart, some of the focal deficits pointing to an intracranial lesion would have been evident.

ISSUES

The Common Ground

The most prevalent neurology misadventure is diagnostic error, and the most frequent incorrectly diagnosed conditions are brain tumor, followed by abscess, SAH, and other causes of HA.[2] Neurosurgeons are most *frequently* sued for technical procedural errors and postoperative complications, although diagnostic and nonoperative treatment errors appear to underpin many *successful* claims. Technical surgical errors are usually straightforward, promptly recognized, and unpredictable. The mere occurrence of a technical error is not malpractice without additional evidence of substandard skill. Claims alleging such errors are generally not successful and, for the competent surgeon, there are few risk management protocols that would minimize these isolated events. Therefore, technical error claims will not be discussed. Postoperative complications include known risks stemming from each particular procedure, and claims frequently allege lack of informed consent. Informed consent guidelines are well documented in the literature, and they are discussed elsewhere in this Handbook.

The confluence of several unrelated trends portends an increase in neurosurgical claims alleging diagnostic or treatment error:

- First, neurosurgeons are often the initial point of contact for nonsurgical conditions traditionally referred to neurologists.
- Second, the unprecedented growth of sophisticated neurodiagnostic testing raises the standard of care and hence the likelihood of suit.
- Third, the surgical specialists, perhaps due to reimbursement issues, seem increasingly likely to assume nonoperative patient care such as conservative spine management, pharmacologic treatment of postoperative or post-traumatic epilepsy, and evaluation of HA and facial pain.
- Fourth, medical and surgical treatments are often inextricably intertwined, leaving each specialist vulnerable to any claim against the other.

Thus, the management strategies discussed in this chapter are equally applicable to the medical and surgical neurologist, focusing on the common ground of diagnostic and treatment error (hereinafter the term "neurologist" refers to both the medical and surgical specialist unless otherwise specified).

STRATEGIES FOR HEADACHE
General Considerations

HAs are ubiquitous, arguably the most common disorder encountered by the practicing physician, and the most common presenting symptom in malpractice claims against medical neurologists.[3] HA may be of little clinical significance or, paradoxically, herald a catastrophic illness, such as brain tumor, SAH, or meningitis. A complete and accurate diagnosis of the HA patient requires a detailed history coupled with a full neurologic and general medical examination, as well as diagnostic testing and neuroimaging in selected cases.

The single most important step in the evaluation is to classify the type of HA and, *pari passu*, ascertain whether it is acute, longstanding, or with recent change. This practical approach will allow the neurologist to determine the need for any diagnostic testing and initiate a proper treatment plan, all with the appropriate degree of urgency. Too often, the inexperienced, poorly trained, or hurried neurologist distorts a patient's history or fails to perform an adequate examination, resulting in the wrong diagnosis. Most malpractice suits stem from the failure to establish a rapport and elicit an accurate history. The art of history taking cannot be taught in this or any other book, and includes an innate ability to instill confidence and trust. The author suggests the following methodology for taking a history, and recommends that physicians formulate their own techniques, which will evolve with time, experience, and continuing education:

- Allow ample time for the consultation. Introduce yourself and invite the patient to sit for the interview before changing into a gown. Advise the patient that you have read the referring doctor's letter, but never accept either the patient's or referring physician's diagnosis.
- Ask the patient, "Tell me about your HAs." Allow the patient to speak uninterruptedly before asking questions. Then begin taking a history with open-ended questions to determine the quality, severity, location, duration, and time course of the pain, as well as precipitating, exacerbating, and relieving factors. It is often helpful to ask the patient to describe a typical attack. Be certain to determine whether the patient has more than one type of HA. It is essential to separately evaluate each type of HA, which may not be possible during the initial consultation due to time constraints.
- Communication skills are critical. Knowing which clues to follow and when to interrupt the patient are fundamental to an accurate history. Failure to understand the patient's terminology often leads to a misdiagnosis. For example, the word "throbbing" may be incorrectly translated into a migraine. It is not uncommon for a HA specialist to distort the history until it fits a preconceived diagnostic category.
- The scope of the history must be sufficiently broad to address systemic diseases that may be relevant to the HA. Past, family, and social

histories provide valuable information about the patient's condition. Before concluding the history, always ask the patient's opinion about the cause of the HA. This is often the most enlightening part of the interview.

Specific Approach

HAs are classified as primary or secondary disorders. A primary HA disorder means that there is no specific cause and the HA itself is the problem, while in a secondary disorder the HA is symptomatic of an underlying disease. Evaluating a patient with HA requires a systematic approach to distinguish the benign (primary) HA from more serious conditions causing secondary HAs. The following discussion is limited to nontraumatic HAs in the adult population, with particular attention to the more common causes of malpractice suits. Lack of space necessitates omitting many conditions, truncating differential diagnoses, and ignoring various diagnostic and therapeutic options. Therefore, this overview should not be considered a definitive or complete guide for HA management.

Exclude Secondary HAs

The first step is to exclude serious conditions causing secondary HAs. The neurologist performing a history and examination should direct particular attention to the following warning signs or "red flags" suggesting a secondary HA, and proceed with appropriate diagnostic and therapeutic intervention.

Sudden Onset (Thunderclap) HA. The sudden onset of a severe HA mandates an immediate and thorough evaluation. Potential etiologies include SAH, intracerebral hemorrhage, venous or sinus thrombosis, aneurysmal expansion, intracranial or extracranial arterial dissection, pituitary apoplexy, and less common conditions such as intermittent hydrocephalus (e.g., due to colloid cyst of the third ventricle).

SAH warrants further discussion. More than half of patients presenting to the emergency room with a sentinel HA and SAH are misdiagnosed. The failure to diagnose this condition results in the highest average and highest total indemnity for all claims involving diagnostic error.[4] The *sine qua non* of SAH is a sudden HA classically described as the "first" or "worst HA of my life," and often associated with nausea or vomiting. The HA is usually followed by pain radiating into the cervical or occipital region, followed by meningismus as blood enters the spinal subarachnoid space. There may be focal neurologic deficits, cognitive impairment, or a history of premonitory symptoms suggestive of a sentinel bleed or expansion of an aneurysm. A thorough history of the HA is essential—even known migraineurs may suffer a SAH. The patient with a thunderclap HA must have immediate computerized tomography (CT) of the brain, and, if the CT is negative, a lumbar puncture (LP) to include measurement of opening pressure and testing for xanthrochromia. Some conditions such as venous or sinus thrombosis may not be evident on CT. It may be reasonable, based on the clinical history, sequence of events, and time of presentation, as well as CT and LP results, to proceed with MRA or angiography.

Escalating or Worsening HA. The HA pattern must be interpreted in light of the patient's overall history. Recent onset HAs with progression may indicate a tumor, abscess, subdural hematoma, or other mass lesion, and focal deficits may be present. However, a slow-growing mass may not be associated with any neurologic signs. Chronic primary HAs with progression may represent the development of a new, superimposed HA disorder (primary or secondary), or transformation of the primary disorder. It may be difficult or impossible to clinically distinguish the transformed migraine, often precipitated by medication overuse, from a new HA disorder. Thus, the presentation of an escalating HA, whether acute or chronic, warrants investigation.

HA with Focal Signs. In general, a HA associated with focal deficits other than a typical aura requires further evaluation. Transient focal signs may represent seizure phenomena, transient ischemic attacks, collagen vascular disease, or a host of other disorders. Permanent deficits may occur with mass lesions of any etiology, cerebrovascular infarction, or autoimmune diseases.

HA Triggered by Cough or Exertion. A sudden severe HA triggered by coughing or exertion may be due to SAH, increased intracranial pressure, or posterior fossa structural abnormalities such as tonsillar ectopia or Chiari malformation. Orgasmic or postcoital HAs are also "red flags" due to the possibility of SAH or mass lesions. Neurodiagnostic evaluation is necessary to provide a definitive diagnosis.

HA with Systemic Disease. There are a plethora of systemic diseases presenting with acute headache including, *inter alia*, intracranial (meningitis and encephalitis, sphenoid sinusitis) and generalized (Lyme disease) infections, neoplasm (including paraneoplastic disease and leptomeningeal metastasis), vascular conditions, autoimmune disorders, metabolic diseases, and toxic exposure. The diagnosis requires proficient examination with attention to systemic signs such as fever, stiff neck, rash, arthralgias, fatigue, and related findings. The clinical picture guides specific diagnostic intervention. For example, the older patient with HA and visual loss may need a temporal artery biopsy for giant cell arteritis. Patients with cancer and HA require neuroimaging and an LP for metastases including leptomeningeal disease. Opportunistic infections (toxoplasmosis, cryptococcal meningitis) causing HA may occur in patients with immune disorders or taking immune suppressing drugs. HA secondary to exercise may be an anginal equivalent warranting cardiology consultation.

HA During Pregnancy or Postpartum. The new onset of HAs or progression of a known primary HA during pregnancy or postpartum raises the concern of sinus thrombosis, cerebral infarction, carotid dissection, pituitary apoplexy, and preeclampsia. These disorders most commonly occur during the third trimester or early postpartum, present with HA, and may be associated with focal signs or seizures. Neurodiagnostic evaluation may require MRI or MRA.

Diagnose the Primary HA

After excluding a secondary HA, the primary HA disorder must be diagnosed in accordance with International Headache Society (IHS) criteria.[5] It is beyond the scope of this chapter to review the various HA syndromes; however, the importance of correctly diagnosing the patient cannot be overstated.

It is commonplace for the neurologist to label a patient with a particular HA type during the initial consultation and, despite a poor response to treatment, never consider revisiting the diagnosis. These patients are branded with the wrong diagnosis, and resultant therapy is ineffective. It creates a breeding ground for malpractice claims. The more common primary HAs that are misdiagnosed include cluster HA, hemicrania continua, hypnic HA, cervicogenic HA, and various facial pain syndromes.

Treat the Primary HA

The primary HA must be treated with a comprehensive multi-modality approach incorporating pharmacologic intervention predicated on evidence-based guidelines.[6] This approach is frequently ignored by the neurologist content with simply prescribing a medication. The following general management principles should be considered, keeping in mind that the goal of therapy is to improve the patient's quality of life by reducing HA frequency, severity, and disability.

Confirm the Diagnosis Before Initiating Treatment. If it is difficult to classify the HA, or the symptoms are atypical, then it is crucial to reconsider the possibility of a secondary HA.

Educate the Patient. The diagnosis, pathophysiology, and treatment options should be reviewed in a discussion commensurate with the patient's level of education and comprehension. The patient should be instructed to keep a HA diary, and the neurologist should review this material during follow-up visits. Avoidance of trigger factors must be emphasized. Dietary instructions should be provided if indicated, and the patient should be encouraged to maintain a diet record. It is important to consider the impact of HAs on the patient's occupational, social, and recreational activities, which can be measured with disability assessment and specific quality-of-life tools. Lifestyle and behavioral adjustments may be necessary. Careful, detailed instructions regarding medication are paramount. The patient's partner or other significant family members and employers must be educated on HA management.

Pharmacologic Treatment. Pharmacologic treatment is generally empiric, using medications with the highest benefit to risk ratio, and considering coexistent diseases. The potential benefits, side effects, and contraindications of each drug should be explained to the patient in detail and documented in the records. A surprising number of suits allege medication error. Acute HA therapy for moderate to severe migraines or those nonresponsive to routine medications (nonsteroidal anti-inflammatory agents, aspirin, etc.) requires a migraine-specific drug with the fewest side effects. The medication should be provided in a nonoral form if the HAs are associated with nausea and vomiting. Guard against rebound phenomena from medication overuse, which is the most common cause of treatment failure and a frequent malpractice claim. In general, acute therapy should be limited to two HA days per week. If HAs are more frequent, or especially disabling, then prophylactic therapy is warranted. Another indication for prophylactic treatment is the presence of complicated HAs such as basilar or hemiplegic migraine, migraine with prolonged aura, or migrainous infarction. The choice of medication should be determined by appropriate guidelines. It is imperative to adopt a systematic approach: initiate treatment with the lowest effective dose; slowly titrate until maximum benefits are achieved or adverse effects intervene; give each drug an adequate trial of several months; consider long-acting formulations to improve compliance; and monitor efficacy with the patient's HA diary. If the HAs are well controlled for 6 months or more, then it is reasonable to consider tapering the medication.

Nonpharmacologic Treatment. The patient may benefit from nonpharmacologic modalities including but not limited to behavioral training, biofeedback, and physical therapy.

Consider Coexisting Disorders. It is vital to identify coexisting conditions such as stroke, epilepsy, hypertension, asthma, and Raynaud's phenomena, as well as associated psychiatric disorders including depression, anxiety, and panic attacks. Select the drug that will treat both the HA and the coexisting disorder, or at least medications that are not contraindicated for the associated condition. For example, beta-blockers would be a first consideration for migraine prevention in patients with hypertension, but contraindicated with underlying asthma or Raynaud's phenomena. Valproic acid is an excellent choice for the patient with migraine and epilepsy, but should not be used in the presence of liver disease. Note that women who are pregnant or of reproductive age require special attention since many of the prophylactic agents are teratogenic.

Individualized Treatment Plan. There is no "standard" therapy for HAs. The treatment plan must be tailored to the individual patient, and thoroughly documented in the medical records. It is crucial for the patient to have realistic expectations, understanding that the HA cannot be "cured." The goal of treatment is to reduce HA frequency to a level that does not significantly interfere with occupational, recreational, and social activities, while using abortive medications to treat acute attacks as efficaciously as possible.

The Unresponsive Patient

The majority of patients with refractory HA have simply been misdiagnosed or improperly treated. Consider the following common errors:

1. *Incomplete or incorrect diagnosis:* The primary HA disorder may be misdiagnosed or there may be an undiagnosed secondary HA. The patient may have two or more HAs, or the number may not be clear.
2. *Imaging studies failed to target pathology:* Imaging studies interpreted as normal may have failed to target the site of neuropathology, such as the sphenoid sinus, sella turcica, or posterior fossa.
3. *Exacerbating factors or triggers overlooked:* Physicians and patients alike frequently overlook dietary, hormonal, and lifestyle triggers as well as exacerbating factors including occupational, environmental, and psychosocial issues.
4. *Rebound phenomena:* Medication overuse can lead to persistent rebound HAs that are quite difficult to treat, and may require

hospitalization in a tertiary center. Many patients will not report use of over-the-counter drugs unless specifically asked.

5. *Improper pharmacotherapeutics:* Refractory HAs may be due to incorrect dosing strategies such as an excessive initial dose, subtherapeutic final dose, or inadequate length of treatment. Poor absorption or drug interactions must be considered. The chosen drug may simply be ineffective or combination therapy may be necessary. The patient may be noncompliant.

Lastly, if the patient still fails to respond, consider an LP to exclude the possibility of chronic meningitis (including granulomatous, vasculitic, and inflammatory meningitides).

Role of Neuroimaging in the Patient with HA

Where the neurologic examination is normal, the role of imaging in the patient with HA remains a controversial area. The American Academy of Neurology (AAN) Practice Guidelines state "neuroimaging is not usually warranted in patients with migraine and a normal neurological examination," but should be considered in patients with an abnormal examination or "patients with atypical headache features or headaches that do not fulfill the strict definition of migraine or other primary headache disorder."[7] These parameters presuppose an accurate diagnosis of the patient's HA, which is frequently not the case. The case presentation provides a classic example where the neurologist diagnoses a patient's HA in the absence of neuroimaging, and finds that subsequent evaluation uncovers a brain tumor. Arguments that earlier diagnosis would not have materially affected the outcome are generally unsuccessful. There may be absolutely no relationship between the HA and the brain tumor, but the trier of fact, the jury or the judge, will likely find otherwise if the neurologist failed to order a timely imaging study. Thus, the decision to forgo imaging in a patient with HA requires a great deal of experience and clinical acumen. For many neurologists, it would simply be prudent to perform an imaging study on every HA patient early in the evaluation. Of course, there is no point in repeating a test if it was already performed, assuming that there is no change in the patient's condition and treatment is successful. There are no evidence-based recommendations in the United States for the relative sensitivity of MRI as compared with CT in the evaluation of HA disorders.[8] However, MRI is probably a superior choice in most circumstances given its sensitivity and ability to visualize the posterior fossa. Unfortunately, concerns over deselection and negative capitation may deter the neurologist from ordering these studies, and the failure to diagnose brain tumor will probably remain one of the most common malpractice claims.

STRATEGIES FOR STROKE

Thrombolysis

Tissue plasminogen activator (tPA) thrombolysis represents the neurological standard of care for acute ischemic stroke. The administration of tPA within 3 hours of ischemic stroke onset significantly improves functional outcome in selected patients.[9] The therapeutic window is narrow and strict adherence to the approved protocol inclusion and exclusion criteria is imperative. The hospital, emergency department, and neurology consultant should establish a dedicated stroke team capable of responding to every acute ischemic stroke patient in a timely fashion and, if indicated, administering tPA. Alternatively, tPA-eligible patients must be promptly transferred to another institution for definitive treatment. Failure of the hospital to provide appropriate facilities and personnel may create liability for all parties.

The failure to recommend or administer tPA to an eligible patient may constitute negligence, unless it can be proven that tPA would not have made a material difference in the patient's outcome. The neurologist deciding not to use tPA in an acute ischemic stroke should clearly document the reasons for that decision in the medical records. It is equally important for the neurologist to resist pressure from the emergency physician or family to use tPA unless the patient meets all inclusion and exclusion criteria. Modification of the criteria, especially the 3-hour time constraint, decreases the benefit of tPA and increases the risk of intracerebral hemorrhage. Thus it is crucial to determine the time of stroke onset. A common error is to consider the onset time as the time when symptoms were first observed rather than the last time the patient was known to be well. For example, if the patient awakens with deficits, then the onset time must be considered to be the last time the patient was known to be well (usually the night before), not when the symptoms were first noticed upon wakening. The same is true if the patient is unable to communicate the onset time. Additionally, neurologists must be attentive to patients with stroke-related neglect syndromes who cannot reliably observe the time of onset. Another frequent error is the administration of anticoagulants or antiplatelet agents during the first 24 hours after tPA administration, which greatly increases the risk of intracerebral hemorrhage. Again, it is imperative to follow the protocol guidelines. There are cases, however, where the neurologist may consider all of the risks and benefits, and decide that it is in the patient's best interest to deviate from the protocol. This decision should be discussed with the patient or legal representative and family, and thoroughly documented in the records.

The failure to obtain valid consent may precipitate a malpractice action separate from negligence. Informed consent mandates a frank discussion regarding the benefits and risks of tPA, including the potential for hemorrhage, coma, and death. The acute stroke patient may not be able to fully participate in the process due to communication deficits or cognitive impairment. Options should then be discussed with a close family member and documented, but only a legal representative (guardian or person with written power of attorney) can give consent. If the patient is unable to give consent and no legal representative is available, the neurologist may proceed with tPA when it is the most reasonable option. Courts will recognize an implied consent based on the assumption that a competent individual would have agreed to the procedure.

Anticoagulation

The use of heparin to prevent an impending stroke remains controversial, although evidence supports immediate anticoagulation for fluctuating basilar artery thrombosis and impending carotid artery occlusion, as well as in certain cases of cardioembolic cerebral infarction. Warfarin may be beneficial in the first few months after an ischemic event, but there is no definitive evidence that the benefits of long-term anticoagulation for thrombosis or embolism outweigh the potential risks except in patients with nonvalvular atrial fibrillation (AF), prosthetic heart valves, and acute myocardial infarction. AF increases the risk of stroke 4- to 6-fold across all age groups. The 5% annual rate of ischemic stroke in untreated AF patients increases with high risk factors such as hypertension, left ventricular dysfunction, transient ischemic attack (TIA), or prior stroke. Anticoagulation with warfarin significantly reduces this risk of stroke, and represents the standard of care for stroke prevention in these patients.[10] If warfarin is contraindicated, or the patient is at low risk of stroke, then antiplatelet therapy is the appropriate treatment.

Neurologists may be reluctant to use warfarin because of the amount of monitoring and follow-up required or they may inappropriately minimize the medication dosage out of undue concern about bleeding. This is a frequent subject of litigation, with the claim that a major stroke would have been prevented if the patient was properly anticoagulated. It is imperative, therefore, to identify patients at risk for stroke in accordance with established clinical guidelines. Accurate diagnosis is essential and neuroimaging to rule out intracranial hemorrhage must be performed before initiating therapy. The reasons for or against anticoagulating a patient at risk should be documented in the medical records. For example, if the increased risk of bleeding due to gait instability outweighs the potential benefits of anticoagulation, then careful documentation may protect against litigation if the patient suffers a massive embolus. Patient and family education concerning the management of anticoagulation is crucial, and should be clearly documented. Certain medication increasing the risk of bleeding should be avoided or used with extreme caution (i.e., aspirin, barbiturates, cephalosporins, sulfa drugs, high-dose penicillin). Establish and follow written procedures for monitoring patients on warfarin, or enlist one of the anticoagulant management services.

Carotid Endarterectomy

Over one-quarter of recently symptomatic patients with a high-grade carotid stenosis (70% to 99% diameter reduction) will suffer an ipsilateral stroke within two years, despite appropriate management of risk factors and antiplatelet therapy. Carotid endarterectomy (CEA) significantly reduces the incidence of cerebral infarction in these patients, and represents the standard of care.[11] There must be careful patient selection (i.e., exclusion of patients with a high-grade tandem lesion in the ipsilateral intracranial arteries or asymptomatic patients with severe contralateral carotid artery stenosis or occlusion), and skill of the surgical team is paramount. The most common malpractice claim is the failure to diagnose TIA or minor stroke, or failure to perform a workup for carotid stenosis, allowing the patient to suffer a recurrent or massive stroke. Every patient with a TIA or stroke should have a carotid doppler or magnetic resonance angiography (MRA) unless surgery is plainly contraindicated. Patients with symptomatic carotid artery stenosis greater than 70% should be offered CEA. Delay in referring a TIA patient with high-grade stenosis for definitive treatment may also constitute negligence, since a high percentage of strokes occur within 48 hours of the TIA. Surgery should be offered as soon as possible after a TIA or nondisabling stroke, preferably within two weeks of the last symptomatic event. Premature surgical intervention following a moderate to severe stroke creates a liability risk for extension or hemorrhagic conversion of the infarction; however, there is insufficient evidence to support or refute delaying CEA for 4–6 weeks. Informed consent issues are critical, and all decisions should be thoroughly documented in the records.

STRATEGIES FOR EPILEPSY
Driving

Every state restricts issuance of a driver's license to individuals who have suffered a loss of consciousness. The laws differ among the states, but generally require that an individual be seizure-free for a period of time before obtaining a driver's license. The seizure-free interval is variable within individual state jurisdictions, ranging from no fixed duration to one year. A physician's evaluation must be submitted to the state before a license will be issued. Neurologists are rightfully concerned about their potential liability when certifying to the state that a patient with epilepsy is capable of driving. Some states grant immunity to the physician, although the level of immunity varies among the jurisdictions, ranging from "good faith" immunity to immunity from suit. In other states, physicians are not granted statutory immunity from liability for the information they provide to the state or for damages arising out of a seizure-related accident. In states without physician immunity laws, courts may still refuse to impose liability on the neurologist who exercised reasonable care in reporting to the state.

Six states—California, Delaware, Nevada, New Jersey, Oregon, and Pennsylvania—have express mandatory reporting statutes requiring physicians to report patients with epilepsy (or other disorders associated with a loss of consciousness or impaired ability to drive) to the state. All other states have voluntary reporting statutes. The neurologic standard of care for the epileptic patient varies according to the laws and regulations of each state. It is incumbent upon neurologists to know the relevant statutes of their jurisdiction, and have an understanding of the common law trends for any ambiguous issues. The neurologist has a duty to advise patients of the legislation in their particular state, and emphasize the importance of complying with the law. If the state has an explicit self-reporting requirement, patients should be advised in writing to comply, with a copy of the letter kept in the medical records. The discussion of driving restrictions as well as restriction on other activities, the effect of discontinuing or reducing dosage of a drug, and possible side effects of medications in relation to driving should be clearly documented in the records. These issues should be reiterated and documented upon any change in medication, due to the increased risk of breakthrough seizures.

If an epileptic continues driving because the neurologist either failed to report where reporting is mandatory or failed to instruct the patient in a voluntary reporting state, then a seizure-related accident may trigger a malpractice suit by the patient or patient's estate. Therefore it is imperative that the neurologist clearly document patient instructions in the medical records, and keep a copy of any notification sent to the state. It is also advisable to record any factors that may mitigate liability for not filing a report. The patient who drives against medical advice is a special concern for every neurologist, especially in voluntary reporting states. In this situation the neurologist should inform the patient in writing about the potential consequences of driving, and consider filing a voluntary report with the appropriate state agency. There may be statutory protection for a voluntary report that is made in good faith and consistent with the prevailing standard of care. However, the level of protection varies among jurisdictions, and it is advisable to consult legal counsel.

Neurologists may be liable to third parties for failing to report a patient or certifying a patient to drive. This is an emerging area of liability, and most decisions turn on whether the neurologist owes a duty to the third party. Courts have ruled in both directions and the issue is far from settled. Neurologists should adapt practice patterns to comport with the relevant legal trends in their jurisdiction, but even third-party liability is minimized by effective patient discussions, proper reporting, and thorough documentation as outlined above.

Teratogenesis

There are over 1 million women with epilepsy of childbearing age in the United States; 3–5 births per thousand are to epileptic mothers. Epilepsy is the most common neurologic disorder in pregnant women and it raises a number of legal and medical issues. However, the most serious concern is the potential for congenital malformations in the offspring of mothers taking antiepileptic drugs (AEDs). These mothers have an up to 7% risk of bearing a child with congenital malformations, threefold higher than nonepileptic mothers. Although this higher risk is probably multifactorial with genetic and social components, AEDs are clearly implicated as human teratogens. All conventional AEDs—phenytoin, phenobarbital, carbamazepine, and sodium valproate—share an increased risk of congenital malformations, which commonly include orofacial clefts, congenital heart disease, neural tube defects, skeletal abnormalities, and urogenital malformations. There are a number of ongoing pregnancy registries collecting data on AED-associated fetal abnormalities, and neurologists must stay current with the results. For example, emerging data demonstrates that valproic acid harbors a much greater risk of major fetal malformations than other antiepileptics, and should be avoided in women who may become pregnant.[12] The teratogenic potential of the newer AEDs remains unknown, and these drugs should be avoided in pregnancy.

Malpractice suits for AED-induced fetal malformations have the potential for extraordinarily large settlements or judgments, and tolling of the statute of limitations is commonplace. The neurologist must address a variety of complex issues in epileptic women who take AEDs during their reproductive years in order to minimize liability for these claims.[13] Detailed counseling early in the reproductive years should include a discussion of the increased risk of seizures during pregnancy, importance of medication compliance, necessity of regular follow-up with AED levels, risk of malformations, folic acid and vitamin K supplementation, and the importance of avoiding co-teratogens. Prior to pregnancy, it is important to determine whether AEDs are necessary; for example, if the patient is receiving an anticonvulsant for migraine, depression, or some other disorder, it may be possible to discontinue the drug. Additionally, if the patient with a single type of seizure has been in remission for 2–5 years, and has a normal neurologic examination with no EEG abnormalities, then it may be reasonable to gradually withdraw the drug. The withdrawal must be performed slowly over months, and completed 6 months before conception, since recurrence of seizures is most likely during this time. If treatment is indicated, every effort should be made to place the patient on monotherapy with the lowest effective dose of the most suitable AED. Frequent daily dosing will avoid high peak levels, possibly decreasing the potential for teratogenesis. The administration of folic acid in the earliest stages of pregnancy reduces the incidence of neural tube defects and should be given to all women of childbearing potential. Optimal dosage for epileptics is controversial, and data must be extrapolated from studies of nonepileptic women; the author recommends 4.0 mg/day combined with vitamin B_{12}.

It is not uncommon for women with epilepsy to present to the neurologist after becoming pregnant. In general, the risk of uncontrolled epilepsy is greater than the risk of AED-induced teratogenesis, and drug treatment must be continued throughout pregnancy. It is a serious albeit common error to change medications for the sole purpose of reducing teratogenic risk: there is a risk of precipitating seizures that may reduce placental blood flow and impair fetal oxygenation; exposing the fetus to a second agent during the crossover period increases the teratogenic risk; and discontinuing an AED does not lower the risk of congenital malformations since the critical phase of organogenesis has usually passed. Thus, if an epileptic woman presents after conception on effective monotherapy, the AED should generally not be changed.

The free (non-protein-bound) AED levels should be monitored at least pre-conception, at the beginning of each trimester, in the last month of pregnancy, and 2 months postpartum. Pregnancy screening should include serum alpha-fetoprotein at 16–18 weeks and a level II ultrasound at 18–20 weeks. If indicated, amniocentesis may be offered at 18–20 weeks. The patient should be properly counseled if there is a serious malformation, and provided with the option to terminate the pregnancy.

CONCLUSION

This chapter emphasizes clinical strategies to reduce the risk of several common malpractice claims. However, providing care that meets or exceeds the prevailing standard may not shield the neurologist from a lawsuit. A solid physician–patient relationship, valid consent, and proper medical record documentation are essential for successful risk management and malpractice defense. Although the root of a malpractice claim is injury or perceived injury, most suits are actually triggered by a breakdown in the physician–patient relationship due to poor communication. A thorough understanding of the relationship is essential, since meeting patient expectations through effective communication significantly reduces the risk of suit. Informed consent issues are a frequent source of malpractice suits, wholly unrelated to negligence claims. The legal theories of informed consent are applicable to all specialties and therefore not reviewed in this chapter. Poor documentation is the leading factor in the forced settlement of most malpractice suits. The literature is replete with recommendations for ensuring that records are clear, accurate, legible, complete, and timely without alterations or other evidence of spoliation. It is unnecessary to reiterate good record-keeping principles in this chapter, but one legal maxim cannot be overemphasized: *If it is not in the record, it never happened.*

REFERENCES

1. Physician Insurers Association of America, *Risk Management Review (Neurology)* (2004).

2. *Id.* at v (Exhibit 5). Other prevalent misadventures include (in decreasing order of frequency): improperly performed procedure; failure to supervise or monitor case; medication errors; failure to recognize a complication of treatment; procedure performed when not indicated or contraindicated; procedure not performed; delay in performance; and failure to instruct patient.

3. *Id.*

4. *Id.*

5. Headache Classification Subcommittee of the International Headache Society, *The International Classification of Headache Disorders*, 2nd ed. Cephalalgia 24(Suppl 1):1–160 (2004).

6. American Academy of Neurology, *Report of the Quality Standards Subcommittee: Practice Parameter: Evidence-Based Guidelines for Migraine Headache* (2000).

7. *Id.*

8. A European Task Force recently recommended MRI in these circumstances. Sandrini G, *et al.*, *Neurophysiological Tests and Neuroimaging Procedures in Nonacute Headache: Guidelines and Recommendations.* Eur. J. Neurol. 11(4): 217–224 (2004).

9. American Academy of Neurology, *Report of the Quality Standards Subcommittee: Practice Advisory: Thrombolytic Therapy for Acute Ischemic Stroke* (2003).

10. American Academy of Neurology, *Report of the Quality Standards Subcommittee: Practice Parameter: Stroke Prevention in Patients with Nonvalvular Atrial Fibrillation* (1998).

11. American Academy of Neurology Clinical Practice Guidelines, *Assessment: Carotid Endarterectomy—An Evidence-Based Review: Report of the TTA Subcommittee of the AAN.* Neurology 65(6):794–801 (2005).

12. Wyszynski DF, *et al.*, *Increased Rate of Major Malformations in Offspring Exposed to Valproate During Pregnancy.* Neurology 64:961–965 (2005).

13. American Academy of Neurology, *Report of the Quality Standards Subcommittee: Practice Parameter: Management Issues for Women with Epilepsy (Summary Statement)* (1998).

Ophthalmology

Philip A. Shelton, M.D., J.D., F.C.L.M.

GOLDEN RULES

1. If you are going to co-manage preoperative screening:
   (a) pick your co-manager carefully;
   (b) know everything about how your co-manager gets the information that is passed on to you.
2. Review your current screening regimen to ensure that it aims to uncover all presently recognized LASIK risks.
3. Stay current on the stream of literature about patient risks in LASIK and modify your screening regimen accordingly.
4. Give thought and time in order to discuss patient-specific risks.

The practice of ophthalmology concerns far more than LASIK (and other refractive surgeries; for convenience, we will refer here just to LASIK), but litigation *about* ophthalmology probably concerns LASIK more than any other area of the practice.[1] That fact virtually compels framing this discussion about ophthalmologic medical malpractice issues and survival strategies within a LASIK-based case study. Before we begin, however, it is worth pointing out that LASIK lawsuits present one significant difference from almost any other that an ophthalmologist is likely to face—or any other doctor, for that matter, *other than* a plastic surgeon or dermatologist. You can probably guess now what we mean: LASIK patients generally do not need the surgery to improve their health. They just want it (enough to spend their own money on it), and this fact carries both legal and nonlegal consequences.

The nonlegal consequence concerns the emotional reasons that are bound up with self-image and that impel people to elect LASIK in hopes of forgoing the use of spectacles or the inconveniences of contact lenses. Any disappointment of those hopes may provide the flashpoint for litigation. The legal consequence, which is related to and reinforces the first consequence, is that the patient's disappointment may (with hindsight, after an adverse surgical outcome) be uncompensated by a perception that the risk was worth running in the first place. This is the issue of informed consent. A reasonable glaucoma patient, for example, would certainly consent to surgery in certain circumstances even if the surgeon properly described the risks. To consent would be the objectively correct decision and, in that case, there could be no claim for lack of informed consent. But there is no obvious measure by which to determine whether a myope would, in certain circumstances, act reasonably or unreasonably in choosing to undergo LASIK. That decision is subjective. In this respect, what we will say below concerning the standard for informed consent for refractive surgery is generally not the same as it is for nonelective ophthalmologic surgeries. For discussion of informed consent in that setting, see Chapter 14 in this Handbook.

CASE PRESENTATION

Mr. CPA, an accountant in his early 20s, had recently moved and visited a new optometrist for an annual eye exam. He expected that the refraction would indicate the need for a new contact lens prescription because he had been having headaches and this, in his experience, usually signaled that need. In the waiting room he saw a flyer concerning LASIK, so when the examination began he asked the optometrist some questions about it. The optometrist said that no, he did not himself perform LASIK but worked with an ophthalmologist who did. (The optometrist and ophthalmologist had a co-management arrangement for preoperative and certain postoperative care.) If Mr. CPA wanted, the optometrist said that he could ask some questions to help determine Mr. CPA's suitability and, if he was suitable, then he would refer Mr. CPA to the ophthalmologist for additional workup and possible surgery. He made clear to Mr. CPA that his own suitability screening was preliminary and any final decision to proceed with surgery was to be entirely between Mr. CPA and the ophthalmologist.

The optometrist performed the refraction (without dilation) and noted that Mr. CPA's myopia had worsened since his last prescription, but just slightly—by about 0.5 D down to −4 D. Then he took out a form—one that had been supplied by the ophthalmologist—and began asking questions about general medical history. He also entered Mr. CPA's refractive error in the space calling for that information. After determining that there was no contraindication in the patient's general medical history, the optometrist scheduled Mr. CPA for a follow-up visit in three weeks' time for corneal topography. He advised Mr. CPA not to wear his contact lenses for two weeks before the appointment, but Mr. CPA wore them anyway until the day before the test. The result of the test was within normal ranges for LASIK candidates. In particular, there was no evidence of keratoconus. The optometrist referred Mr. CPA to the ophthalmologist.

The ophthalmologist received the optometrist's record on Mr. CPA. He reviewed the general medical history, the refractive error, and the corneal topography. His office staff measured Mr. CPA's pupil size under low-light conditions, and then the ophthalmologist performed a visual examination of Mr. CPA's eyes. He said that Mr. CPA was a suitable candidate for LASIK and that his nurse would provide Mr. CPA information about the risks of LASIK so that he could make a final decision on whether he wanted to proceed. The information given to Mr. CPA provided statistical information on the incidence of adverse outcomes from LASIK, listing a number of possibilities from legal blindness in both eyes (Mr. CPA was planning bilateral same-day surgery) to night-time halos and starbursts to the need for follow-up surgery in the event of under- or overcorrection. The document did not suggest that Mr. CPA faced any heightened risk

The surgery was performed without incident and Mr. CPA was seen on routine follow-up visits by the ophthalmologist and then by the optometrist. There were no infections or other postoperative complications. But Mr. CPA noticed that he seemed to have gone from being nearsighted to being farsighted—before surgery, he could read spreadsheets even if he was not wearing his contacts, but now such documents were definitely blurry. The optometrist performed a refraction and determined that Mr. CPA was, indeed, hyperopic, and sent him back to the ophthalmologist to discuss retreatment. At the ophthalmologist's office, a new corneal topography was performed. This test detected early-stage keratoconus, which the first topography (performed by the optometrist) had not found. The ophthalmologist informed Mr. CPA that he was not a candidate for retreatment and that the combination of developing keratoconus and ablation of his corneas during the first LASIK put him at risk for significant corneal problems later in life. Mr. CPA would have to go back to wearing contact lenses or spectacles, only now to correct hyperopia.

Mr. CPA sued the ophthalmologist and the optometrist. In discovery, he learned that the ophthalmologist had not specified that refractions must be cycloplegic (his wasn't), and that lens accommodation during noncycloplegic refractions can lead—as in his case—to overcorrection resulting in hyperopia. He also learned why it was important not to wear his contact lenses for at least two weeks before the corneal topography, but recalled that the optometrist did not explain the importance nor ask him before the topography whether he had complied with the no-contact order. As a result, lens warpage masked the early-stage keratoconus.[2]

ISSUES

This hypothetical raises three key, overarching issues that appear to be typical of LASIK litigation. The first concerns the broad topic of patient screening. This has proven to be a somewhat tricky topic for ophthalmologists as manufacturers continue to release, and the FDA continues to approve, laser devices that measure better, cut better, etc. But what also continues to happen is the release of studies showing that LASIK is not for everyone. The contraindications are many and there is a steady stream of new literature on the topic. One cannot safely practice LASIK without staying abreast of the developments in medical research. This ever-growing body of peer-reviewed material establishes the standard of care.

In this case, for example, the ophthalmologist provided the optometrist a preoperative screening form with a blank for inserting the patient's refraction, but with no specification that the refraction be performed under cycloplegic conditions. Either the ophthalmologist assumed that a cycloplegic refraction was performed or was not concerned with whether the refraction was cycloplegic. Either way, the ophthalmologist's conduct deviated from the standard of care since the medical literature strongly supports the value of obtaining a cycloplegic refraction to avoid the possibility of overcorrection as a result of lens accommodation. That is precisely the damage that Mr. CPA suffered, and it would certainly be possible for his expert witness to connect the deviation from the standard of care (i.e., operating on someone without a cycloplegic refraction) with the damage.

The literature also advises avoiding surgery on patients whose refractive error has changed 0.5 D or more within the past year: better results have been noted when the patient's refraction error has been stable preoperatively. Here, Mr. CPA's error changed −0.5 D and the hypothetical suggests that the change occurred within the past year (this was an annual eye exam). Mr. CPA was a questionable candidate for LASIK.

The second overarching issue is informed consent. One of the subissues here was the appropriateness of providing risk information to Mr. CPA in the form of a laundry list of LASIK complications and their overall statistical incidence, without any customization or tailoring to Mr. CPA's personal circumstances. As we have noted earlier, informed consent to elective surgery is a subjective decision. We do not mean that in some sort of abstract, inconsequential sense. Courts have *recognized* the subjective nature of such a decision and have made clear that a plaintiff suing over a bad result due to lack of informed consent does not need a medical expert to testify that the properly explained risks outweighed the potential benefits. There are no benefits to LASIK (in an objective medical sense), so all the patient has to do is convince the court that the risks were not properly explained and, as a result, the election of surgery was uninformed. (Remember, the plaintiff also does not have to prove any degree of medical negligence when alleging injury due to lack of informed consent.) Therefore, a better way to present risk information is to customize or tailor it to each patient, making sure that the patient fully understands the *relevant* risks.

A second subissue is how, in any particular case, to accomplish this admittedly difficult task. The contraindications to LASIK are not categorical—there is even some research now suggesting that individuals with autoimmune or other connective tissue diseases can safely undergo LASIK when the condition is well controlled.[3] Contraindications for the most part (except at the extreme margins, which are changing anyway) indicate degrees of unsuitability. Moreover, how one contraindication may aggravate another contraindication—i.e., whether the risk from two or more contraindications is more than the sum of their separate risks—is not very clear. But in this hypothetical, this much *is* clear: Mr. CPA's refractive instability put him at increased risk of an adverse result even in the event of a surgery that was competently performed in every respect. Whenever any patient presents a contraindication, the informed consent documents and the doctor–patient discussion must be tailored to recognize that risk. Further, surgeons should be cognizant of their patients' professions and avocations. For example, any patient whose job *requires* good vision (some people in law enforcement, airline and military pilots, etc.) should receive special counseling on the risks of LASIK.

The third overarching issue involves the ophthalmologist's decision to farm out to the optometrist some of the preoperative screening without adequate controls. The ophthalmologist failed to specify a screening regimen that included a cycloplegic refraction. Concerning the corneal topography, its validity depended on the patient's compliance with the optometrist's instruction not to wear contact lenses for two weeks before the measurements were taken. When a patient does not comply with instructions, an adverse outcome is generally not the physician's fault. But on such an important issue, an oral instruction without explanation of its medical basis might be deemed by a fact-finder to be inadequate. Such instructions with explanation should also be in writing, and the patient should be questioned about compliance on the day of the screening (with a chart note documenting the answer).

The fact that the optometrist performed the refraction and the corneal topography does not necessarily relieve the ophthalmologist of medical negligence for the ultimate outcome. The decision to perform surgery was the ophthalmologist's in consultation with Mr. CPA, and the ophthalmologist had a duty to collect accurate, verifiable information relevant to that decision.

In addition to being vulnerable to a claim of medical negligence for making treatment decisions based on defective screening information, the ophthalmologist's reliance also brings us back to the issue of informed consent. Previously we have noted the importance of an informed consent discussion that covers risks particular to the patient, and the absence of such a discussion here on Mr. CPA's refractive instability. The ophthalmologist could undoubtedly have discovered the instability from reviewing the optometrist's patient chart on Mr. CPA and included it as part of the informed consent discussion.

The ophthalmologist did *not* know that Mr. CPA had early-stage keratoconus, and so that element was also missing from the informed consent discussion. But if the ophthalmologist was negligent in relying on the optometrist's corneal topography, then the ophthalmologist should have diagnosed the keratoconus and discussed it with Mr. CPA. Further, it should be fairly easy for Mr. CPA to prevail against the ophthalmologist for performing surgery after inadequately explaining—because the ophthalmologist had inadequately explored—the risks to Mr. CPA.

SURVIVAL STRATEGIES

Because so many physical conditions present at least a measure of contraindication against LASIK, preoperative co-management is a risky proposition. Any ophthalmologist choosing this arrangement should be able to justify a high degree of confidence in the co-manager's thoroughness and competence, *and* in the co-manager's ability to communicate patient information between their offices. The ophthalmologist must completely understand the procedures provided by each office and how each professional contributes to the totality of patient screening.

Screening should include:

1. Consideration of the patient's general medical history. Here, the ophthalmologist must determine in particular whether the patient has rheumatoid arthritis or any other autoimmune or connective tissue disease; diabetes mellitus; or herpes simplex or zoster keratitis.
2. An ophthalmologic examination that covers scotopic pupil size; cycloplegic refraction; degree and type of refractive error; periocular

anatomy; ocular motility; ophthalmic pathologies, including Fuchs corneal endothelial dystrophy, corneal epithelial basement membrane dystrophic changes, significant blepharitis, and retinal tears; dry eyes complaints; corneal topography; corneal pachymetry; recurrent corneal erosions; refractive stability; and whether the patient has previously been treated with refractive surgery.

After the patient information has been compiled, the ophthalmologist must decide whether LASIK could be safe and effective and, if not, refuse to perform surgery. If the patient is suitable, then the informed consent process must begin. We have already discussed why the information presented to the patient should be customized as much as possible to the patient's profile, but want to reemphasize that it is impossible for you to customize the consent correctly if you have wrong information from the patient screening. Screening and informed consent go hand in hand. You must perform or have access to the results of a competent screening in order to counsel a patient about risks. Otherwise, no matter how perfect your surgical technique, bad results will follow and patients will sue. The largest verdict to date in a LASIK case—$7.25 million by a New York City jury in 2005, with an undisclosed postverdict settlement—involved just such a combined failure in screening and informed consent: the ophthalmologist failed to diagnose keratoconus and told the patient that he was a suitable candidate for LASIK when he wasn't. It was that simple, and it cost the defendant a large sum of money and reputation.

FURTHER READING

Pop M, Payette Y, *Risk Factors for Night Vision Complaints after LASIK for Myopia.* 111 Ophthalmology 3 (2004).

Shelton PA, "Liability of Ophthalmologists." In *Legal Medicine/American College of Legal Medicine*, 7th ed., ed. S. Sandy Sanbar *et al.* Philadelphia: Mosby, 2007.

Sugar A, *et al.*, *Laser In Situ Keratomileusis for Myopia and Astigmatism: Safety and Efficacy.* 109 Ophthalmology 175 (2002).

Thompson KP, *et al.*, *Using InterWave Aberrometry to Measure and Improve the Quality of Vision in LASIK Surgery.* 111 Ophthalmology 1368 (2004).

Varley GA, *et al.*, *LASIK for Hyperopia, Hyperopic Astigmatism, and Mixed Astigmatism.* 111 Ophthalmology 1604 (2004).

REFERENCES

1. Abbott RL, *et al.*, *Medical Malpractice Predictors and Risk Factors for Ophthalmologists Performing LASIK and Photorefractive Keratectomy Surgery.* 110 Ophthalmology 2137 (2003).

2. *Schiffer v. Speaker*, No. 0101191/2003 (N.Y. Sup. Ct. Dec. 16, 2004) (order denying motions for summary judgment). The case went to trial; for a report of the

$7.25 million verdict, *see* Lawyers Weekly USA, Aug. 15, 2005, at 1 (N.Y. Sup. Ct. July 27, 2005). The case settled for an undisclosed sum during the post-trial phase. *Schiffer v. Speaker,* No. 0101193/2003 (N.Y. Sup. Ct. Oct. 5, 2005) (order permitting withdrawal of post-trial motion based on settlement).

3. Watson SL, *et al., Improved Safety in Contemporary LASIK.* 112 Ophthalmology 1375 (2005).

CHAPTER 40

Otorhinolaryngology

Matthew L. Howard, M.D., J.D., F.A.C.S., F.C.L.M.

GOLDEN RULES

1. Perform a complete examination.
2. Write complete notes that reflect a complete examination.
3. When obtaining informed consent, list all the known risks, side effects, and complications, no matter how rare.
4. If asked your qualifications, don't embellish.
5. When called about a problem, put the patient's needs first.
6. Do unto others as you would have them do unto you.

This chapter focuses on liability issues involving otolaryngologists. Many medical mistakes never become "malpractice" issues because they either self-correct or lead to no harm. The following is an example of an error with no resulting liability.

CASE PRESENTATION

Case 1. An 80-year-old man with dysphagia and odynophagia presented with no loss of weight, no voice change, and no symptoms of aspiration. The examination, which was normal, included direct fiberoptic laryngoscopy; there were no mass lesions, and no pooling. The examining otolaryngologist ordered an esophogram, which showed coordinated, unobstructed, swallowing of the barium, and a smooth mass impinging on the cervical esophagus. The otolaryngologist interpreted the esophogram report as evidence of an osteophyte, without having personally reviewed the films. The otolaryngologist informed the patient that the esophogram showed no evidence of cancer, that there was no evidence of any medical problems that required immediate treatment, and advised the patient to discuss further workup with his primary care doctor.

A week later the patient presented to the Emergency Department with a complaint of rapidly increasing dysphagia and odynophagia. A CT scan was performed, which showed a smooth, circumscribed lesion in the wall of the esophagus, which was interpreted as a malignancy. An attempt to dilate and biopsy the lesion was unsuccessful. Two days later, the patient aspirated and expired. No autopsy was performed. The family was told that the underlying diagnosis was *cancer* of the esophagus.

ISSUES IN CASE 1

The examining otolaryngologist failed to appreciate the significance of the esophogram findings. Additionally, the patient's family was told that the lesion represented "cancer of the esophagus," when in fact there is no histologic proof of the diagnosis; the smooth surface of the lesion suggests an intramural leiomyoma rather than a carcinoma.

However, the missed diagnosis did not alter the patient's course. If the examining otolaryngologist had ordered a CT after reviewing the esophogram report, the same findings would have resulted, with no earlier discovery. The same attempt at biopsy would have resulted. The same end result would have occurred. Further, if it was malignant, the known cure rate of cancer of the cervical esophagus in an 80-year-old man is not good. If it was not malignant, and biopsy proved that it was not, immediate surgery would not have been performed. The patient was not aspirating, and he had no evidence of weight loss. A period of observation would almost surely have been proposed before a major operation. Hence, whether the diagnosis ultimately was of a malignancy or a benign lesion, no harm resulted from the failure to order the CT scan earlier. Hence, there is no liability.

Liability for otolaryngologists/head and neck surgeons will exist under the same circumstances as for other physicians. However, certain areas are more likely to cause problems than others.

CASE PRESENTATION

Case 2. The following describes the related cases of *Humble v. Bumble, M.D.* and *Humble v. Rotten, M.D.*, which is a composite of three actual malpractice cases.

Harry Humble, a 55-year-old man, was referred to otolaryngologist Dr. Bumble by his primary care physician. Humble smoked for a year when he was 16 years old, and had consumed two glasses of wine daily, with occasional cocktails on social occasions, for 30 years. Humble presented with several complaints, including a sore throat, pain when swallowing sometimes radiating to his ear, and a lump near his right ear.

According to Humble, the lump had been present for several years. He had never bothered to bring it to his doctor's attention until consulting her about the throat problem. The sore throat had been present, especially when swallowing, for two months and the radiation to the ear for about three weeks. He denied voice change, reflux symptoms, hearing loss, or weight loss.

Dr. Bumble examined Humble's ears with an otoscope, his nasal passages with a speculum, using a head mirror to illuminate the nose, and similarly examined the mouth, tongue, and oropharynx. He performed indirect laryngoscopy. He palpated Humble's temporomandibular joints and his neck.

Dr. Bumble listed as his working diagnoses, gastroesophageal reflux-induced laryngitis and neck mass consistent with benign pleomorphic adenoma.

Dr. Bumble recommended to Humble that he undergo needle biopsy of the neck mass, and carefully outlined the proper management of GERD. Dr. Bumble's notes of the encounter read, in their entirety, as follows:

S: neck mass, throat pain with radiation to the ear.
O: EAC clean, TMs benign. Nose, mouth, tongue unremarkable. Larynx wnl except trace erythema arytenoids. Neck mass 1 cm discrete nontender (R) infraauricular. TMJ wnl.
A: GERD with laryngitis, benign mixed tumor v. node.
P: anti-gerd instructions, ranitidine, FNA.

The fine needle biopsy (FNA) was accomplished without difficulty. A pleomorphic adenoma was found. Superficial parotid lobectomy was recommended. The surgical consent noted risks of the surgery, which included facial paralysis, bleeding, infection, and cosmetic deformity. Dr. Bumble's admitting note concluded with the statement, "All risks, benefits and alternatives were discussed, and an informed consent given."

Following the surgery, which confirmed the benign adenoma, Humble had complete facial paralysis, numbness of the ear, gustatory sweating, and required tarsorrhaphy to protect his cornea because the usual less intrusive treatments such as contact lenses, artificial tears, and patching were not successful. The patient complained bitterly about the tarsorrhaphy; he was upset both by the additional cosmetic deformity and the reduced field of vision resulting.

Two months after the parotid surgery, a left jugulodigastric area mass appeared in the neck. Humble was seen by another otolaryngologist, Dr. Rotten. FNA revealed well-differentiated squamous cell carcinoma. Direct laryngoscopy revealed a lesion of the base of the epiglottis, on the laryngeal surface, which on biopsy proved to be squamous cell carcinoma. During the course of discussion regarding the best management of this cancer, Humble asked Dr. Rotten about his qualifications. Dr. Rotten stated, truthfully, that he had completed a one-year fellowship in Head and Neck Surgery after his residency, and considered himself a subspecialist in head and neck cancer. In response to a question from Mrs. Humble whether her husband would be better off seeking treatment at the City of Hope, Dr. Rotten told both Mr. and Mrs. Humble that he had personally treated 80 patients with similar cancers and that his cure rate was significantly better than the average. In fact, Dr. Rotten had treated 30 patients with supraglottic tumors, half during his residency and fellowship, and half in his subsequent practice, and had kept no statistics by which one could compare his results to published statistics.

Supraglottic laryngectomy with neck dissection was performed, followed by radiation therapy and adjunctive chemotherapy. Humble succumbed two years later due to complications. The terminal event was carotid hemorrhage after necrosis and ulceration in his neck. During the two years before death, a tumor recurrence was suspected; however, biopsies were negative. Humble was treated with hyperbaric oxygen. Surgery to close the defect with a pectoralis major myocutaneous flap was scheduled for a date six weeks after the last biopsy, with the intention of covering the defect if it failed to respond to the pressure chamber treatments. The bleeding began in the center of the small area of ulceration the morning of Saturday, October 9.

Mrs. Humble called Dr. Rotten's office number and received a return call. When she explained the problem, Dr. Rotten said he would see them at the hospital Emergency Department at 4 P.M. Brief bleeds occurred thereafter, and Mrs. Humble called again at 10:00 A.M., 11:00 A.M., 1:00 P.M. and 2:00 P.M., each time reporting that terry cloth hand towels were soaked with blood. On each occasion, Dr. Rotten reiterated that he would see them at 4:00 P.M. At 3:00 P.M., Humble exsanguinated at home and expired. No autopsy was performed.

During pretrial discovery, Dr. Rotten explained his whereabouts on October 9. He was attending his alma mater's homecoming football game and activities, and scheduled the appointment time to coincide with the expected end of the game. He explained his lack of concern by saying that the biopsies were negative so he was confident that the bleeding was not important.

Before his death, Humble sued Dr. Bumble alleging negligent delay in diagnosis of the laryngeal carcinoma, failure to obtain informed consent prior to the parotidectomy, and negligent performance of the surgery resulting in the facial paralysis. He particularly alleged that he had never been warned of the risks of gustatory sweating, the numbness of his ear, or the risk to his vision. After his death, his wife was substituted as the party in interest and the court granted her motion to add additional causes of action against Dr. Bumble for wrongful death and loss of consortium.

Mrs. Bumble also filed separately a malpractice lawsuit against Dr. Rotten alleging fraudulent inducement to enter into a contract, medical negligence because fraudulent inducement invalidated the consent, abandonment, and loss of consortium.

ISSUES IN CASE 2

Humble alleged that Dr. Bumble (a) failed to diagnose the cancer at an early time when the chance of cure would have been greater, (b) failed to obtain an informed consent for the parotid surgery, and (c) negligently performed the parotid surgery, thus resulting in the facial paralysis. His wife was allowed to add specifications including (d) wrongful death (an extension of the delayed diagnosis claim arising as a result of his allegedly premature death) and (e) loss of consortium. Dr. Rotten was also sued alleging (f) fraudulent inducement to enter into a contract, (g) abandonment, and also loss of consortium.

Delayed Diagnosis

Humble had a history of alcohol intake, but not of smoking. Moderate alcohol intake may have an effect on the incidence of oropharyngeal cancer.[1] Further, Humble had pain in the throat, which was caused by or worsened by swallowing, and the pain radiated to the ear. These symptoms would prompt an otolaryngologist to consider and rule out the diagnosis of a laryngeal or hypopharyngeal malignancy. It is the responsibility of the otolaryngologist to prove that cancer does not exist in these circumstances.[2]

A thorough physical examination was required. Dr. Bumble asserted that he did perform a thorough examination, and offered as proof his notes showing "larynx wnl" as evidence that he examined the laryngeal surface of the epiglottis. Yet, as has been taught to generations of otolaryngology residents, "Death lurks under the overhanging epiglottis," and mirror examination must be carefully and successfully completed to evaluate the laryngeal surface.[3] Practicing otolaryngologists are well aware of the frequency with which the undersurface of the epiglottis and the anterior commissure are obscured when attempting indirect examinations, and many direct examinations are performed solely because that one area cannot be seen by indirect examination.

Dr. Bumble testified that his cryptic note, "larynx wnl," meant just what it said—namely, that the larynx was normal. Humble's experts testified that Humble's symptoms when he was examined were the expected symptoms of a carcinoma, and that if Dr. Bumble had truly examined the laryngeal surface he would have found the tumor. The absence of a direct examination, and the absence of a specific note, was proof that the laryngeal surface of the epiglottis was never examined.

The legal result hinged on the jury's opinion of Dr. Bumble's credibility. Possible findings by the jury include finding that Dr. Bumble did not perform a thorough examination, that he did perform the examination but missed the disease through carelessness or incompetence, or that he performed the examination but is not liable for missing the diagnosis because it was not evident at the time of the examination. Although it would not be correct to analyze this as purely a statistical issue, it is nevertheless true that two of the three possible findings by the jury would lead to liability for Dr. Bumble.

But, assuming Dr. Bumble did indeed perform a thorough examination that had no positive findings, he could have avoided the issue by writing a complete note. He held in his own hands the ability to create a situation where the chance of a finding holding him liable was reduced to a minimum. Instead of "larynx wnl," his note would have been more useful, and more protective, if it had read, "The laryngeal and lingual surfaces of the epiglottis, aryepiglottic folds, true and false cords, arytenoids, interarytenoid space, valleculae and pyriform sinuses, and all mucosal surfaces connecting the named structures, were inspected. No erythema, edema, ulceration or mass was identified. True cords were smooth, approximated in the midline and moved well." The reader may object that such a note is too time-consuming in comparison to the note Dr. Bumble actually used, and that they mean the same thing. The time issue can be dealt with by check-off forms incorporating all the specific points, or by dictating, or by using "smart phrases" or "expanders" in computerized systems like EPIC. That the two notations mean the same thing, ultimately, is not open to question, yet they mean very different things in court where one note shows a conscientious attention to detail that supports the image of a physician who actually performed the examination as described, while the other portrays a slapdash practitioner who may well have taken short cuts in his examination, thus explaining the missed tumor.

Lack of Informed Consent

"Laundry Lists" v. Blanket Statements

Many experts advise physicians to avoid laundry lists of side effects and complications, but to use instead a blanket statement such as the one described above in which the physician asserts that all risks were discussed. The rationale is that if one does fail to include a risk when explaining the surgery to the patient, the jury, which tends to believe physicians in such circumstances, will believe the physician who says, "Yes, we talked about gustatory sweating and risk to the eyes," even when the physician knows that he did not mention it. One underlying assumption of such a recommendation is the morally repugnant assumption that this method makes it easier to avoid the consequences of error. On the other hand, goes this argument, a list of complications that omits the single problem that arose is proof that informed consent was never given. Here, Humble is upset because his ear is numb, his face perspires when he eats, and he needed eye surgery to protect his cornea, which has the side effect of reducing his field of vision. He alleges that none of these risks was explained to him beforehand. Some readers may complain that Humble's suit is "frivolous" because all three of these unfortunate results are known side effects or complications of the surgery, and can occur even when it is performed properly. However, the American rule, that patient autonomy requires that the balance between risks and benefits is a value that the patient must determine, demands that the physician provide the patient with all the information needed to make an informed choice.[4] The suit is not frivolous to Humble, who was not warned ahead of time. The suit illustrates the adage that information provided beforehand is patient education, while the same information after the fact is perceived as self-serving excuse making. For this reason, the author advocates the longest "laundry list" possible, trying to cover all known risks, no matter how rare. Then, Dr. Bumble would not be facing the jury asking them to take his word that the blanket statement did indeed cover the problems that arose. Instead it would be evident in black and white that he had provided the warnings.

The law does not require that all risks be disclosed. The rule is that serious risks, such as death or disfigurement, even though they are rare, must be disclosed as well as less serious risks that occur often enough that a reasonable person would consider them when making the decision whether to accept the recommendation for surgery. But, in the rare instance of a problem arising not covered by the laundry list, the extent and completeness of the risks that *were* disclosed will reinforce the image of a conscientious physician who did indeed disclose every risk that was reasonable to disclose, which is what the law requires.

Invalidation by Fraud

In the second suit, Mrs. B has sued on the grounds that Dr. Rotten misled her husband when asked about his qualifications. The courts take for granted that a person facing surgery agrees to the surgery only when they trust the competence of the surgeon. A surgeon who is licensed to practice medicine is assumed to be competent. However, it is common knowledge that a more experienced surgeon is often better prepared to perform a particular operation than one less experienced.* This is a new issue for the legal system, and there are few cases involving misrepresentation of credentials. However, those cases that have been litigated have not gone well for the physician who has chosen to inflate his résumé. Where a neurosurgeon inflated his credentials, and the patient came to harm, expert witnesses testified that surgeons available at the nearby university medical center were more than likely able to perform the same operation without the complication resulting.[5] The surgeon was found liable. In Pennsylvania, a decision holding that a surgeon could not be held liable in medical negligence for inflating his credentials[6] was overruled by the state legislature, which added honest disclosure of credentials to the requirements of an informed consent, nullifying the consent if the "physician knowingly misrepresents to the patient his or her professional credentials, training or experience" (MCARE Act).[7] The court had found that the suit should have proceeded as a fraudulent inducement to enter into a contract case. On the other hand, in a very similar case, a New Jersey court ruled that the suit should proceed on a lack of informed consent theory rather than fraud.[8] Rather than risk putting the matter before a jury, a California bariatric surgeon settled a similar case based on a complication and the surgeon's exaggeration of his experience. Both courts here, and courts in other cases, have ruled that physicians have no duty to discuss their experience or lack of it, but must answer truthfully if questioned.

Negligently Performed Surgery

The allegation of negligently performed surgery arose because Dr. Bumble did not use a facial nerve monitor during surgery. There is a division between two schools of thought. One school, which I choose to call the anatomy-dependent school of thought, says that thorough understanding of the anatomy by the surgeon renders artificial aids like the facial nerve monitor unnecessary.[9] The other school, which follows the T. J. Hooper rule,[10] demands the use of any useful technology. Under that rule, Dr. Bumble cannot rely on customary physician practice to exonerate him if the evidence supports a finding that readily available and affordable technology could have prevented the complication. In the T. J. Hooper case, the court wrote:

Indeed in most cases reasonable prudence is in fact common prudence; but strictly it is never its measure; a whole calling may have unduly lagged in the adoption of new and available devices. It may never set its own tests, however persuasive be its usages. Courts must in the end say what is required; there are precautions so imperative that even their universal disregard will not excuse their omission.

This concept of court determination when technology should be adopted has rarely been applied to medical malpractice cases, which is little comfort to those physicians where it was applied. The best-known such case involved an ophthalmologist in Washington State who failed to test a woman in her thirties for glaucoma, and was found liable for her blindness despite expert testimony that the standard of care had been met.[11] The *T. J. Hooper* rule is always lurking in the wings, and should influence decisions to purchase such advances as image localizing systems for endoscopic sinus surgery, as well as the use of facial nerve monitors in parotid and mastoid surgery. When something goes wrong, there is a real risk of the issue being raised in circumstances of absence of up-to-date technology. For example, except in a life-threatening situation, would it be appropriate to bronchoscope a 2-year-old for a peanut foreign body if telescopes, optical forceps, and bronchoscopes capable of ventilation were not available, or should such a child be referred to a center with the equipment?

Wrongful Death

Wrongful death is a death that would not have occurred except for the error of the person being sued. Malpractice leading to a death that would have occurred anyway would not be a wrongful death. This leads to suits based on the "last chance" theory. Extensive calculations come into play balancing the chances of cure, the relationship of the chance of cure to the time of diagnosis, etc.

Loss of Consortium

Technically, "loss of consortium" means loss of a lawful partner for sexual intercourse. While this is certainly the heart of a loss of consortium claim, the term also refers to care, companionship, and affection between the injured party and spouse, whether or not there is a decrease or change in sexual activity. However, because of the original and still technically correct meaning of the term, most lawyers will advise leaving such a claim out of the case if there is any question about the sexual component. In other words, the claim would not be made at all, despite the loss of companionship and affection, if Humble had been impotent, and certainly avoided if the couple were separated or actually in divorce proceedings. On the other hand, when defensible, as it usually is, such an allegation increases jury sympathy for the aggrieved spouse and hurts the physician's chances.

Fraudulent Inducement to Enter into a Contract

This has already been discussed above under the heading of informed consent. This author predicts that it will become an increasingly popular cause of action because the statute of limitations for fraud complaints is typically as long as six years, whereas many states have limited malpractice actions to a year or two. A physician sued for, among other things, representing himself as a plastic surgeon was found not liable where he held himself out to be "certified as an otolaryngologist, facial surgeon, and cosmetic surgeon," and was not asked whether he was a board-certified plastic surgeon. The court found that he had no affirmative duty to disclose but had a duty to respond truthfully.[12]

Abandonment

Abandonment refers to the requirement that, once a physician has established a duty to his patient, he must be available when the patient requires physician services. This is a reasonable and prudent standard. Nothing prevents physicians from signing out for coverage, if the covering physician is competent to deal with the problems that arise. Dr. Rotten, however, was available and responded by telephone to the first notice of a problem. In this case, expert witnesses will testify that the physician knew, or should have known, that a patient with local recurrence in his neck is at risk for carotid bleeding, and should have responded to the second call, if not the first. The hypothetical situation described is taken from the real case of *Aengst v. BMQA*,[13] where Dr. Aengst declined to respond when called about post-tonsillectomy bleeding at 8 and 11 P.M., each time instructing the patient's mother that he would see the child at 10 A.M. the following morning. By morning, the child had expired. A similar case occurred where a physician declined to leave his golf game unfinished, resulting in the death of a child after tonsillectomy.

SURVIVAL STRATEGIES

There are two themes to the above discussion. The first is the need to behave toward patients the way we ourselves would like to be treated. If we are the patient, we want a thorough examination, full explanation of the risks, benefits, and side effects of any treatment proposed, and a conscientious doctor who puts our needs first. Patients deserve no less. This leads naturally to the second theme, which is to be thorough and complete, truthful, and to practice within the scope of our training and experience. Examinations need to be thorough. We all know that indirect mirror examination of the larynx is fully satisfactory only in a segment of the patient population. We need therefore to use the fiberoptic laryngoscope or whatever other modality is needed to obtain a complete examination in patients whose symptoms are in the relevant area. And then we need to document it so that others may see what was done. Lack of time to write detailed notes is not an adequate reason for not keeping detailed notes. We can dictate, use computerized systems that facilitate entries of long notes through the use of templates, or use various forms of check-off systems.

REFERENCES

1. Muscat JE, Wynder EL, Cancer 69(9):2244–2251 (1992). (Alcohol is a causative factor for laryngeal cancer, even in the absence of smoking; tobacco, alcohol, asbestos, and other occupational risk factors for laryngeal cancer.)

2. Ares Camerino A, Escolar Pujolar A, Sainz VB, Rev. Clin. Esp. 195(12): 825–829 (1995). (Delay in the diagnosis of malignant tumors [breast, larynx, bladder]; delay in diagnosis is the responsibility of the physician.)

3. *Scott-Brown's Diseases of the Ear, Nose and Throat*, 3rd ed., vol. 4, ed. J. Ballantyne and J. Groves. Lippincott, 1971, p. 403.

4. *Cobbs v. Grant* (1972) 8 Cal. 3d 229, 243 [104 Cal. Rptr. 505, 502 P. 2d 1], where it was held that a physician has a duty to his patient "of reasonable disclosure of the available choices with respect to proposed therapy and of the dangers inherently and potentially involved in each." A breach of this duty that causes injury to the patient may justify an action pleaded in negligence (*Cobbs v. Grant, supra*, 8 Cal. 3d at pp. 241, 245).

5. *Johnson v. Kokemoor*, 545 N.W. 2d 495 (Wis. 1996).

6. *Duttry v. Patterson*, 565 Pa. 130, 771 A. 2d 1255 (2001).

7. MCARE Act, 40 Pa. Stat. §1303.504(d)(2) (2001).

8. *Howard v. Univ. of Med. & Dentistry*, 800 A. 2d 73 (N.J. 2002).

9. Witt RL, *Facial Nerve Monitoring in Parotid Surgery: The Standard of Care?* Otolaryngol. Head Neck Surg. 119(5):468–470 (1998).

10. *In re T. J. Hooper*, 60 F. 2d 737 (2d Cir. 1932), cert. denied, 287 U.S. 662.

11. *Helling v. Carey*, 519 P. 2d 981 (S. Ct. Wash. 1974).

12. *Ditto v. McCurdy*, 947 P. 2d 952 (Haw. 1997).

13. *Aengst v. BMQA*, 110 Cal. App. 3d 275 (1980). Dr. Aengst was again subjected to discipline for gross negligence in treatment of a patient with a nasal deformity. He performed six rhinoplasty procedures on the same patient, with each result worse than the preceding.

Psychiatric Malpractice

Marvin H. Firestone, M.D., J.D., F.C.L.M.
S. Sandy Sanbar, M.D., Ph.D., J.D., F.C.L.M.

GOLDEN RULES

1. Diagnose psychiatric patients only after doing a competent assessment.
2. Obtain and thoroughly document informed consent, especially before utilizing physical therapies, such as electroconvulsive therapy and psychotropic medication.
3. Avoid even the appearance of sexual exploitation of a patient.
4. Control or supervise a dangerous patient with great care and document such care.
5. Warn and protect third parties from potentially dangerous patients.
6. Use the least intrusive alternative to commit or restrain a psychiatric patient.

The development and emergence of malpractice lawsuits against psychiatrists has been very gradual and seemingly of recent occurrence. Malpractice actions against psychiatrists have steadily increased since the early 1970s. In 1970, Slawson noted that defendant psychiatrists try to avoid publicity, and many cases escape notice. A survey of psychiatric malpractice claims in southern California between 1958 and 1967 showed no increase in claims rate and an average of 1.5 claims per 100 psychiatrists per year. Most claims were settled for a modest fee before trial.[1] In 1993, the low-frequency risks of psychiatric malpractice were reported again, based on the American Psychiatric Association professional liability insurance program that had insured an average of 10,000 psychiatrists each year since 1984. Two thousand malpractice insurance cases had been entered into a purpose-configured relational database to permit analysis of clinical, demographic, and economic variables. The results indicated low-frequency risks of psychiatric malpractice.[2]

CASE PRESENTATIONS

Case 1. In 1976, *Tarasoff v. Regents of the University of California*[3] was the first case to find that a mental health professional may have a duty to protect others from possible harm by their patients. In *Tarasoff*, a lawsuit was filed against, among others, psychotherapists employed by the

Regents of the University of California to recover for the death of the plaintiffs' daughter, Tatiana Tarasoff, who was killed by a psychiatric outpatient. Two months prior to the killing, the patient had expressly informed his therapist that he was going to kill an unnamed girl (who was readily identifiable as the plaintiffs' daughter) when she returned home from spending the summer in Brazil.

The therapist, with the concurrence of two colleagues, decided to commit the patient for observation. The campus police detained the patient at the oral and written request of the therapist, but released him after satisfying themselves that he was rational and exacting his promise to stay away from Ms. Tarasoff. The therapist's superior directed that no further action be taken to confine or otherwise restrain the patient. No one warned either Ms. Tarasoff or her parents of the patient's dangerousness.

Upon her return from Brazil, Ms. Tarasoff was killed by the patient. After the patient murdered Ms. Tarasoff, her parents filed suit alleging, among other things, that the therapists involved had failed either to warn them of the threat to their daughter or to confine the patient. The California Supreme Court, while recognizing the general rule that a person owes no duty to control the conduct of another, determined that there is an exception to this general rule where the defendant stands in a special relationship to either the person whose conduct needs to be controlled or in a relationship to the foreseeable victim of that conduct. The court made an analogy to cases that have imposed a duty upon physicians to diagnose and warn about a patient's contagious disease and concluded that, by entering into a doctor–patient relationship, the therapist becomes sufficiently involved to assume some responsibility for the safety, not only of the patient, but also for any third person whom the doctor knows to be threatened by the patient.

The court also considered various public policy interests determining that the public interest in safety from violent assault outweighed countervailing interests of the confidentiality of patient–therapist communications and the difficulty in predicting dangerousness. The California Supreme Court held: When a therapist determines, or pursuant to the standards of his profession should determine, that his patient presents a serious danger of violence to another, he incurs an obligation to use reasonable care to protect the intended victim against such danger.

Case 2. On June 27, 1991, at 9:25 A.M., Gad Joseph telephoned his mental health counselor to tell him that he was going to kill his ex-girlfriend, Teresa Hausler. The counselor immediately had him come in for therapy, which began at 11:00 A.M. and ended at noon, that same day. Gad promised his counselor that he would not hurt Teresa. Fifteen minutes later, Teresa telephoned the counselor to tell him that she was going to Gad's apartment to pick up her clothing. The counselor advised her not to go to the apartment but to return to her new home in Reading. Teresa ignored the counselor's advice and continued onto Gad's apartment. At 12:30 P.M. Gad arrived and, in a fit of rage, fatally shot Teresa six times in the head and abdomen.

Subsequently, Teresa Hausler's family filed a lawsuit against the mental health counselor and his employer, Albert Einstein Medical Center in

Philadelphia, alleging failure to warn Teresa.[4] At that time, the law in
Pennsylvania was unclear regarding what duty a medical professional
owed to a third party who is not the patient. The plaintiff cited *Tarasoff v.
Regents of the University of California*. The facts of *Tarasoff* were eerily
similar to the facts in the Teresa Hausler case. In 1998, because of the
actions of Gad and Teresa, the Supreme Court of Pennsylvania expressly
adopted *Tarasoff* as law.

ISSUES

Along with the incidence of malpractice actions, the variety of claims
against psychiatrists has also increased. Some causes of action reflect acts of
negligence or substandard care for which any physician may be found
liable. These malpractice areas include negligent diagnosis, abandonment
from treatment, various intentional and quasi-intentional torts (assault and
battery, fraud, defamation, invasion of privacy), failure to obtain informed
consent, and breach of contract. Areas of liability specific to psychiatry
include harm caused by organic therapies (electroconvulsive therapy
[ECT], psychotropic medication), breach of confidentiality, sexual exploitation of patients, failure to control or supervise a dangerous patient or negligent release, failure to protect third parties from potentially dangerous
patients, false imprisonment, and negligent infliction of mental distress.
These claims represent the major causes of action that may be brought
against a psychiatrist.

Malpractice actions based on a psychiatrist's use of psychotropic drugs
have been fairly infrequent considering the widespread use of this form of
treatment during the past 20 years. With managed care, more frequent utilization of the psychiatrist as the prescriber of medication with the psychotherapy, and primary care parceled out to psychologists and other
nonmedical therapists, more actions based on medication can be expected.

Negligence is more likely to be found in high-risk situations in which
either the psychiatrist's choice of intervention or manner of supervision was
unreasonable under the circumstances. The *Clites v. Iowa* case is one of the
first decisions specifically dealing with tardive dyskinesia (TD) and aptly illustrates some of the liability considerations.[5] The court ruled that the defendants were negligent because they deviated from the standards of the
"industry." Specifically, the court cited a failure to administer regular physical
examinations and tests; failure to intervene at the first sign of TD; the inappropriate use of drugs in combinations, in light of the patient's particular condition and the drugs used; the use of drugs for the convenience of controlling
behavior rather than therapy; and the failure to obtain informed consent.

Breach of Confidentiality

The duty to safeguard the confidentiality of any communication in the course
of psychiatric treatment is the cornerstone of the profession. This obligation
of confidentiality is fundamental, but no one is more keenly sensitive to its

importance than mental health professionals. This point is aptly reflected in the ethical codes of the various mental health organizations.

Confidentiality in a psychiatric perspective embodies two fundamental rationales. First, a patient has a right to privacy that should not be violated except in certain legally prescribed circumstances. Second, physicians have historically been enjoined (on an ethical basis) to maintain the confidences of their patients. In doing so, patients should feel more comfortable revealing information, which would enhance their treatment.

Psychiatrists have always been susceptible to ethical sanctions if they breach patient confidentiality, but liability for monetary damages is a relatively recent development. Several legal theories allow a patient plaintiff recovery for breach of confidentiality. Besides statutory bases, some courts have upheld a cause of action based on breach of confidentiality on a contract theory. Accordingly, a psychiatrist is considered to have implicitly agreed to keep any information received from a patient confidential, and when he or she has failed to do so, there is a breach of that implied contract term by the psychiatrist. In cases based on this theory, damages typically have been restricted to economic losses flowing directly from the breach, but compensation based on any residual harm (e.g., emotional distress, marital discord, loss of employment) is precluded.

Theories based on invasion of privacy have supported recovery involving breach of confidentiality. The law defines invasion of privacy as an "unwarranted publication of a person's private affairs with which the public has no legitimate concern, such as to cause outrage, mental suffering, shame, or humiliation to a person of ordinary sensibilities."[6]

In many states the legal duty to maintain patient confidentiality is governed by mental health confidentiality statutes. These statutes outline the legal requirements covering confidentiality.

Failure to Warn or Protect

Confidentiality was considered sacrosanct by the psychiatric profession until the Supreme Court of California heard the case *Tarasoff v. Regents of the University of California* in 1976 (Case 1 presented above). The response by the courts following the 1976 California decision has been inconsistent and at times confusing. Several courts have followed the holding of *Tarasoff*, concluding that a therapist was liable for not warning an identifiable victim. A slightly broader but analogous limitation has been fashioned by decisions where the courts have recognized a duty to warn only when the victim is "foreseeable." Cases to date involving some form of the duty-to-warn theory can be viewed as falling somewhere on a continuum based on two common factors: (1) a threat (or potential for harm) and (2) a potential victim. At one end is the "specific threat specific victim" rule,[7] and at the other end is where "foreseeable violence" created a duty to protect "others," regardless of whether the victim was identified or specified.[8] At present, most courts have held that in the absence of a foreseeable victim, no duty to warn or protect will be found. Reviewing the cases, a few facts stand out. Most notable is the relative absence of litigation that most commentators thought would occur after the *Tarasoff* decision.[9]

The liability considerations that underlie the treatment and care of the dangerous patient generally differ according to the amount of control a psychiatrist, therapist, or institution has over the patient. As a general rule, psychiatrists who treat dangerous or potentially dangerous patients have a duty of care, which includes controlling that individual from harming other persons inside and outside the facility as well as himself or herself. On the other hand, the outpatient who presents a possible risk of danger to others creates a duty of care, which may include warning or somehow protecting potential third-party victims.

Whatever the extent of the duty imposed by the *Tarasoff* decision and its progeny, a psychiatrist or therapist cannot be held liable for a patient's violent acts unless it is found that (1) the psychiatrist determined (or by professional standards reasonably should have determined) that the patient posed a danger to a third party (identified or unidentified) and (2) that the psychiatrist failed to take reasonable steps to prevent the violence.

Sexual Exploitation

From a legal standpoint, the courts have consistently held that a physician or therapist who engages in sexual activity with a patient is subject to civil liability and in some cases to criminal sanctions. The reason for this overwhelming condemnation rests in the exploitative and often deceptive practice that sex between a health care professional (e.g., psychiatrist, physician, therapist) and patient represents. The fundamental basis of the psychiatrist–patient relationship is the unconditional trust and confidence patients have in the therapist. This trust permits patients to share their most intimate secrets, thoughts, and feelings.

Abandonment

Once an agreement (explicit or implicit) to provide medical services has been established, the physician is legally and ethically bound to render those services until the relationship has been appropriately terminated. If a physician terminates treatment prematurely and the patient is harmed by the termination, a cause of action based on "abandonment of treatment" may be brought. Generally, in the absence of an emergency or crisis situation, treatment can be concluded safely if a patient is provided reasonable notice of the termination and is assisted in transferring the care to a new physician. Proper transfer of care typically implies that the original psychiatrist prepares and makes available the patient's records as needed by the new psychiatrist. It is also prudent for the original care provider to give the patient written and verbal notice to avoid any possible questions regarding the nature, timing, or extent of the announcement of termination.

The issue of abandonment frequently arises when either no notice of termination has been given or the extent of this notice has been insufficient in some way. Although there are no rules or guidelines *per se* regarding sufficiency of the notice, a therapist who decides to terminate treatment is expected to act reasonably.

Patient Control and Supervision

The treatment of patients who pose a risk of danger to themselves or others presents a unique clinical and legal challenge to the mental health profession. A lawsuit for patient suicide or attempted suicide is often brought by a patient's family or relatives claiming that the attending psychiatrist, therapist, or facility was negligent in some aspect of the treatment process. Specifically, there are three broad categories of claims that encompass actions stemming from patient suicide. The first is when an outpatient commits suicide or is injured in a suicide attempt. Plaintiffs in this situation claim that the psychiatrist or therapist was negligent in failing to diagnose the patient's suicidal condition and provide adequate treatment, which is typically hospitalization. The second situation is when an inpatient is given inadequate treatment and commits or attempts suicide. Typically, the essence of a negligence claim involving inadequate treatment is that the patient was suicidal and the psychiatrist failed to provide adequate supervision. The last general situation is when a patient is discharged from the hospital and shortly thereafter attempts or commits suicide. Family members, or the injured patient, frequently claim that the decision to release the patient was negligent.

The treatment of suicidal or potentially suicidal patients inherently requires a psychiatrist or other practitioner to make predictions regarding future behavior. The mental health profession has frequently disclaimed ability to predict future behavior with any degree of accuracy. As a result, the law has tempered its expectation of clinicians in identifying future dangerous behavior. Instead of a strict standard requiring 100% accuracy, the law requires professionals to exercise reasonable care in their diagnosis and treatment of patients at risk.[10]Accordingly, a court will not hold a practitioner liable for a patient's death or injury resulting from suicide if the treatment or discharge decision was reasonably based on the information available.

As in cases involving suicide, a treating psychiatrist or other practitioner cannot be held liable for harms committed after a patient's discharge (e.g., negligent release) unless the court determines (1) that the psychiatrist knew or should have known that the patient was likely to commit a dangerous or violent act and (2) that in light of this knowledge, the psychiatrist failed to take adequate steps to evaluate the patient when considering discharge. Similarly, in cases involving third parties injured by a dangerous patient who has escaped, the court evaluates (1) whether the psychiatrist knew or should have known that the patient presented a risk of elopement and (2) in light of that knowledge, whether the psychiatrist took reasonable steps to supervise or control the patient. The actions of a psychiatrist in a negligent discharge or negligent control or supervision claim are scrutinized based on the reasonableness of the actions and the standards of the profession.

SURVIVAL STRATEGIES

    1. All psychiatric patients should be medically evaluated, in addition to the psychiatric evaluation. Medical conditions, such as subdural

hematoma, encephalitis, and AIDS, sometimes present primarily psychiatric symptoms. Psychiatric patients may have associated medical problems, including diabetes and other metabolic disorders, hormonal imbalance, and abuse or failure to conform to their medications.

2. Appropriate psychiatric, neurologic, neuropsychological, laboratory, and radiologic testing should be performed and documented genetic testing may be indicated in some patients.

3. Psychiatrists must conform to good psychiatric (medical) community standards and act like "reasonable individuals" under like circumstances.

4. Careful and scrupulous documentation is indicated in the care of all psychiatric patients, but the psychiatric record should include only clinical data, and never legal opinions or derogatory comments. Good record keeping is a must because it is the strongest defense against a lawsuit, or in support of a contention.

5. Psychiatric patients share the same substantive constitutional rights as other patients. Compulsory medication may be regarded by the courts as an intrusion on the patient's liberty interest, a deprivation of the freedom of thought, and cruel and unusual punishment.

6. A psychiatric patient may not be confined involuntarily if he or she is not dangerous to anyone and can live safely in freedom.

7. It is permissible for a psychiatrist to confine a patient involuntarily after a proper evaluation determines that a mental disorder exists, without being liable for malpractice, under the following circumstances:
   (a) when the patient actually injures himself or others;
   (b) when the patient can be expected in the near future to injure himself or others;
   (c) when the patient has engaged in recent overt acts or made significant recent threats that substantially support those expectations; and
   (d) when the patient is unable to attend to his or her basic needs (gravely disabled).
   Mere acts of destruction of property by the mentally ill patient are usually insufficient to justify involuntary commitment.

8. Psychiatrists should respect the rights of hospitalized patients to refuse medication unless there is evidence that the individual is determined to be incompetent after a hearing before an independent trier of fact who provides consent on behalf of the patient. This applies equally to the voluntarily and the involuntarily hospitalized individuals. The psychiatrist often has to decide whether the patient is truly competent to refuse the medication offered. If the refusal is based on a delusional system of the patient's illness, he or she may not be competent to refuse treatment. If the situation becomes an emergency, and medication is required, the physician may administer a temporary dose of medication to handle the emergency, and then reassess the patient's condition and the situation. A physician should not give long-acting psychotropic medication in an emergency situation.

9. Psychiatric patients who are placed in seclusion and/or restraint should be observed regularly. Failure to do so could lead to a malpractice lawsuit. In addition to regulations regarding seclusion and restraint, hospitals should have specific policies and procedures regarding observation of suicidal patients and elopement precautions.

10. Psychiatric patients should be treated in the least restrictive environment necessary for the clinical needs of the patient. For example, it would be improper to place a homicidal or suicidal patient in a situation where he or she may act out the destructive behavior.

11. Psychiatric patients most commonly become the source of malpractice actions if they injure themselves or others. Psychiatrists may be found liable for damages if psychiatric patients injure themselves, commit suicide, injure others, elope, prove false imprisonment, or prove sexual abuse. Psychiatrists should take appropriate steps to avoid such allegations. At all times, they should use good clinical judgment, and adequately document the risks and benefits of treatment.

12. In psychiatry, the most common reasons for malpractice include improper diagnosis and treatment, suicide, violence to others, mishandling the transference (sexual exploitation of the patient), and violation of the patient's rights.

CONCLUSION

The issue of reasonableness, whether involving the diagnosis, supervision, or treatment of a patient, is usually measured in terms of the accepted standards of the profession. Expert testimony is needed to establish or disprove that the defendant psychiatrist failed to exercise the reasonable care that other psychiatrists would have used in those or similar circumstances. The risk of liability is greatly enhanced when it can be demonstrated that a practitioner or institution failed to follow its own usual practices and procedures for treating a patient

FURTHER READING

Firestone MH, "Psychiatric Patients and Forensic Psychiatry." In *Legal Medicine/American College of Legal Medicine*, 7th ed., ed. S. Sandy Sanbar *et al.* Philadelphia: Mosby, 2007.

Reed DB, *Therapist's Duty to Protect Third Parties: Balancing Public Safety and Patient Confidentiality*. Community Mental Health Report 1(5):72 (2001). http://www.northshorelij.com/workfiles/lawandpsych/cmhr_1_5_p_72.pdf

REFERENCES

1. Slawson PF, *Psychiatric Malpractice: A Regional Incidence Study*. Am. J. Psychiatry 126:1302–1305 (1970).

2. Slawson PF, *Psychiatric Malpractice: The Low Frequency Risks.* Med. Law 12(6–8):673–680 (1993).

3. *Tarasoff v. Regents of the University of California*, 17 Cal. 3d 425, 529 P. 2d 334, 131 Cal. Rptr. 14, 551 P. 2d 334 (1976).

4. *Ronald B. Emerich, Administrator of the Estate of Teresa M. Hausler v. Philadelphia Center for Human Development, Inc., Albert Einstein Healthcare Foundation, Albert Einstein Medical Center, et al.* (J-253-96, in the Supreme Court of Pennsylvania, Eastern District, decided Nov. 25, 1998).

5. *Clites v. Iowa*, 322 N.W. 2d 917 (Iowa Ct. App. 1981).

6. *Doe v. Roe*, 93 Misc. 2d 201, 400 N.Y. S.Z. 668 (1977); *Clayman v. Bernstein*, 38 Pa. D&C 543 (1940); *Spring v. Geriatric Authority*, 394 Mass. 274, 475 N.E. 2d 727 (1985).

7. *Brady v. Hopper*, 570 F. Supp. 1333 (D. Colo. 1983).

8. *Lipari v. Sears, Roebuck and Co.*, 497 F. Supp. 185 (D. Neb. 1980).

9. Buckner F, Firestone MH, *Where the Public Peril Begins: 25 Years after Tarasoff.* J. Legal Med. (Sept. 2000).

10. *Brown v. Kowlizakis*, 331 S.E. 2d 440 (Va. 1985).

Radiology

Michael M. Raskin, M.D., J.D., M.S., M.P.H., M.A., F.C.L.M.

GOLDEN RULES

1. Three-quarters of radiology lawsuits allege failure to diagnose or failure to communicate in a timely manner.
2. Carefully check the credentials of those you hire or you may be charged with negligent hiring.
3. Mistakes are inevitable in the practice of medicine and will occur with even the best-trained radiologist.
4. If you sign a colleague's report, do so with the full understanding that you will most likely be held responsible for the contents of the report.
5. Failure to communicate is a causal factor in 80% of all lawsuits, although not the primary factor.
6. The communication of a diagnosis, if it is to be beneficial, is sometimes as important as the diagnosis itself.
7. Routine communication is the formal written report. Nonroutine communication should be handled in a manner that gets the information to the physician.
8. It is essential to document all nonroutine communication. This is the one area in medical malpractice litigation where you can play the most important role in reducing your risk and liability.

This chapter discusses liability issues confronting radiologists. The case presented is fictional, but it is based on an actual case. The italicized text was taken verbatim from the interpretive report.

CASE PRESENTATION

Dr. Oldtimer, a semiretired, non-board-certified radiologist, was on his first day of working as a weekend locum for Dr. Exploiter at Hogwarts Community Hospital, an 80-bed facility in rural Hogsmeade. Hogwarts had no MRI or angiography suite, but did have an old single slice CT scanner. On Dr. Oldtimer's first night, Mrs. Dumbledore, a 43-year-old woman, was brought to Hogwarts' small Emergency Room by her husband, Professor Dumbledore, complaining of severe frontal headaches. A nonenhanced CT was ordered by Dr. Snape, the Emergency Room physician. After a few hours, the on-call CT technologist came in and performed a CT scan of her brain. Dr. Oldtimer, who was staying at Dr. Exploiter's home while he was away, viewed the CT scan by teleradiography (Figure 42-1) and then called Dr. Snape, and told him that it was completely normal. The next morning, after a good night's sleep, Dr. Oldtimer saw something on the scan that he didn't see the night before. He dictated in his final written report that there was a *"minute region of high density just anterior to the corpus callosum which is felt to more likely represent some normal blood within the inferior sagittal sinus than bleeding in the corpus callosum."* His conclusion was that the nonenhanced CT scan of the brain was *"within normal limits."* Dr. Oldtimer went down to the Emergency Room to see Dr. Snape since he was concerned that he had previously told Dr. Snape the night before that the CT scan was "completely normal." However, Dr. Snape was off duty and Dr. Oldtimer left the Emergency Room mumbling, to no one in particular, that they would get the written report shortly. The final written report was

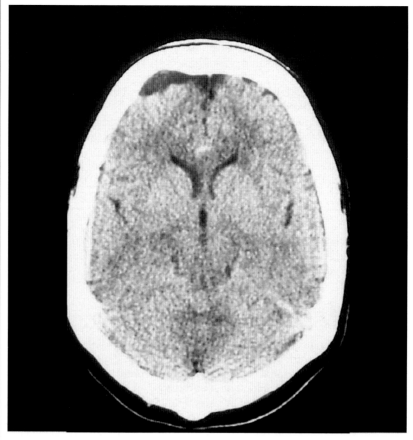

Figure 42–1. Nonenhanced CT scan of the brain of a 43-year-old woman complaining of severe frontal headaches.

printed on Monday and signed by Dr. Exploiter; Dr. Oldtimer, who had only covered for the weekend, had already left.

The problem was that the CT scan of the brain was not "completely normal" or even "within normal limits." The "minute region of high density" was actually hemorrhage into the cistern of the lamina terminalis from a leaking aneurysm (Figure 42-2). Mrs. Dumbledore was sent home the evening before by Dr. Snape since he was told by Dr. Oldtimer that the CT scan was "completely normal." Ten days later, Professor Dumbledore called 911 for an ambulance to take her from home to the Emergency Room as she was unresponsive. A nonenhanced CT scan of the brain was again performed (Figure 42-3).

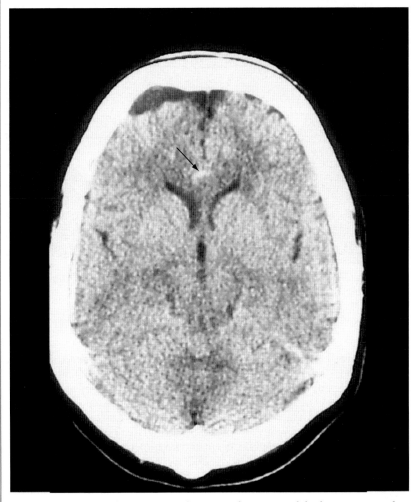

Figure 42–2. Arrow points to hemorrhage into the cistern of the lamina terminalis from leaking aneurysm.

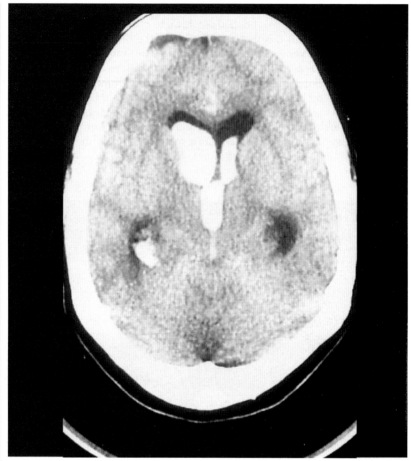

Figure 42–3. Nonenhanced CT scan of the brain ten days later shows massive hemorrhage into the third and lateral ventricles.

Mrs. Dumbledore was then transferred to St. Elsewhere Hospital, a major medical facility, where an aneurysm of the anterior communicating artery was identified by angiography. Fortunately, she stabilized and the aneurysm was later clipped. However, she was left with significant residual disability and initiated a lawsuit against Dr. Oldtimer, Dr. Exploiter, Dr. Snape, and Hogwarts Community Hospital. She alleged that both Dr. Oldtimer and Dr. Exploiter provided negligent and improper medical care by failing to timely and adequately diagnose and/or communicate the abnormality. She further alleged that Dr. Snape, the Emergency Room physician, also provided negligent and improper medical care for failing to timely and adequately diagnose the abnormality. She also sued Dr. Exploiter for negligent hiring and negligent supervision, and Hogwarts Community Hospital for negligent credentialing, negligent supervision, and apparent agency.

Dr. Oldtimer claimed that, although his impression was "within normal limits," the body of the report should have suggested to Dr. Snape that there was some abnormality and that Mrs. Dumbledore should have then been referred to a neurologist or neurosurgeon. He also claimed that he should not be held to the same standard as a neuroradiologist since he was only a general radiologist and had completed his radiology training before CT was a clinical modality, and never had any formal training in CT interpretation. He further claimed that he should not be responsible for knowing that the hospital required the radiologist to call all abnormal reports or that radiologists needed to be board certified, since he was only covering for Dr. Exploiter for the weekend. Dr. Exploiter claimed that he signed the report by Dr. Oldtimer merely to expedite delivery of the report, although he did not read the report or review the CT scan. Dr. Snape claimed that he is not a radiologist and that he relied on the oral report by Dr. Oldtimer that the CT scan of the brain was normal.

ISSUES

Failure in Perception

Dr. Oldtimer fell below the standard of care by failing to perceive the abnormality by teleradiography on the night of the CT scan. An error in perception, often called a "miss" or "missed diagnosis," is the most common reason why a radiologist is sued. These cases are usually settled, because radiologists lose most of the time if this goes to a jury verdict. There is a nationwide standard for radiology: if you interpret a CT scan of the brain, you are held to the same standard as a neuroradiologist. It does not matter whether or not you had any formal training.

It is extremely difficult to convince jurors that it was not malpractice for you to miss something that they can obviously see in court. Jurors think, "If I can see it, why couldn't he?" However, a Wisconsin Court of Appeals in 1997 held that errors in perception by radiologists viewing x-rays may occur in the absence of negligence. While this decision may be useful if you are practicing in Wisconsin, it will probably not be helpful if you practice anywhere else, especially in rural Hogsmeade.

Failure in Interpretation

Dr. Oldtimer fell below the standard of care by failing to correctly interpret the finding on the CT scan that he formally dictated the next morning. Upon reviewing the actual images the next morning, he perceived the abnormality but considered it to be a normal structure. Interpretation errors are cognitive errors in which the abnormality is perceived but is incorrectly identified. The radiologist wins most of these lawsuits that only allege interpretation errors. An appropriate differential diagnosis may help.

Failure to Suggest the Next Appropriate Procedure

Dr. Oldtimer fell below the standard of care by failing to suggest the next appropriate procedure, which, in this case, should have been an angiogram or MRA of the brain. The suggested procedure must be appropriate and should add meaningful information to clarify, confirm, or rule out the initial impression.

Failure to Correct Discrepancy

Dr. Oldtimer needed to directly communicate to Dr. Snape, or other Emergency Room personnel, the discrepancy between his preliminary oral report and the final written report. Under some circumstances, practice constraints may dictate the necessity of a preliminary report before the final report is prepared. A significant change between the preliminary and final interpretation should be reported to the referring physician by nonroutine communication and you should document that communication. Nonroutine communication can be accomplished in person, or by telephone, fax, email, PDA, etc. Routine communication is the preliminary or final written report.

Failure in Communication

Dr. Oldtimer needed to communicate the findings on the CT scan in a timely manner. Failure to communicate the results in a timely manner is one of the greatest problems facing radiologists today. It is a causal factor in 80% of all lawsuits, although not the primary factor. This is the one area in medical malpractice litigation where you can play the most important role in reducing your risk and liability.

Many courts have repeatedly held that the communication of a diagnosis, if it is to be beneficial, is sometimes as important as the diagnosis itself. The communication must be timely and appropriate, and should be documented. Failure to document a communication is one of the major reasons why radiologists will lose a lawsuit when failure to communicate is alleged. Radiologists who argue that their liability ends when they have correctly dictated a report will quickly find out that the jurors will not agree. While a correctly written report may have sufficed in the past, nonroutine communication may be necessary when the findings suggest a need for immediate treatment or urgent intervention. This communication needs to be accomplished in a manner that will most likely reach the treating or referring physician, and you should document that communication. Even if the communication is in person or by telephone, you need to document your communication. The communication needs to be to the referring physician, or other health care provider, or even an appropriate representative. If that individual cannot be reached, there are times when communication may be directly to the patient or responsible guardian. You should always document all communications as to date, time, person spoken to, and what was said.

Substituted Signature

Since Dr. Oldtimer was not available to sign his interpretative report, Dr. Exploiter signed the report, substituting his signature for Dr. Oldtimer's signature. Dr Exploiter was sued under the same cause of action as Dr. Oldtimer since he signed the final written report.

Failure to Refer

As the Emergency Room physician, Dr. Snape needed to refer Dumbledore to a neurologist or neurosurgeon based on the radiograph findings and the clinical presentation. The common law tort duty to refer is well established, especially when the situation may be beyond one's expertise.

Negligent Hiring

Since Dr. Exploiter hired Dr. Oldtimer, who was neither board certified nor board eligible, a requirement of Hogwarts Community Hospital, Dr. Exploiter may be guilty of negligent hiring and failure to use reasonable care in the employment selection process. Dr. Exploiter had a contract with the hospital in which he agreed to assign radiology responsibilities only to board-certified or board-eligible radiologists. Furthermore, his contract with the hospital required that he notify administration prior to radiology coverage, which he did, but he did not tell administration that Dr. Oldtimer was not board eligible or board certified. Unlike *respondeat superior*, negligent hiring includes potential liability for the acts of independent contractors. In order to succeed in a negligent hiring claim, Dumbledore would need to show that a prudent employer would have made an appropriate investigation, that Dr. Exploiter failed to do so, and that a reasonable investigation by Dr. Exploiter would have revealed that Dr. Oldtimer did not have the proper credentials. Furthermore, Dumbledore would need to allege that it was unreasonable for Dr. Exploiter to hire Dr. Oldtimer in light of the information that he knew or should have known, and that Dr. Oldtimer's negligence caused Dumbledore's injuries. Although there is no gross negligence or recklessness in the selection of Dr. Oldtimer, if there were, Dr. Exploiter could be exposed to punitive damages.

Apparent Agency

Hogwarts Community Hospital may be vicariously liable under the doctrine of apparent authority or agency, which would allow Dumbledore to sue Hogwarts Community Hospital for negligence of its independent contractor positions. Patients naturally assume that Emergency Room physicians are hospital employees unless put on notice otherwise.

SURVIVAL STRATEGIES

Mistakes are inevitable in the practice of medicine and will occur with even the best-trained radiologists. The radiology literature reports a 30% error rate in radiology. However, it does not help your case to claim that 30% of other radiologists would have missed what you missed. The general public has come to expect perfect results from physicians and the facilities in which they practice. Claiming that errors or mistakes are part of the practice of medicine, and that you should not be held accountable for them, makes you sound cold, uncaring, and callous before a jury.

The real question is, then, does the mistake equate to malpractice? The definition of medical malpractice is a legal one and is defined as what a reasonable and prudent physician would do under the same or similar circumstances. Knowledge on the part of the radiologist only has to be ordinary and average, but it must be reasonable. This is a difficult concept for jurors to understand since they do not accept mistakes and expect perfection from doctors. Seventy percent of errors are perceptual while 30% are cognitive. However, you can also be sued for failure to communicate even a correct interpretation in a timely manner. A poorly worded or incorrect report is rarely the cause for medical malpractice action by itself, but poor imaging reports may leave you vulnerable in court, as sloppy work will indicate a sloppy attitude to jurors.

In the United States, the tort system accounts for approximately $100 billion per year in the field of medicine alone. The average indemnification has doubled in the last fifteen years for all physicians; however, it has tripled for radiology. Also, one-third of lawsuits are lost by the radiologist. This is especially true if it is alleged that there was a missed diagnosis.

An analysis of radiology claims from 1990 through 2000 showed that radiologists have a 1 in 3 chance of being sued for medical malpractice. The odds of being sued are the highest in Pennsylvania and Oregon, where more than half of the radiologists practicing there have been sued. States where 41% to 50% of radiologists have been sued at least once are Idaho, Illinois, New York, Michigan, New Jersey, Louisiana, and Mississippi. Florida, while infamous for the size of monetary settlements of medical malpractice, ranks near the national average. Only 30% to 40% of Florida radiologists have been involved in a malpractice claim.

Although risk cannot be eliminated, it can be minimized and managed. Reducing your risk will reduce your exposure to medical malpractice lawsuits. Reducing risk is also better for patient care and patient safety. There are positive steps that can be taken to reduce the risk of being sued and/or losing lawsuits. That is why we need to study risk management in radiology as the first step involves identification of the highest areas for risk.

Failure to diagnose has been determined to be the number one reason why radiologists get sued. Three-quarters of radiology lawsuits allege failure to diagnose or failure to communicate in a timely manner. Approximately one-third of these lawsuits are lost by the radiologist. Mammograms and chest radiographs expose you to the greatest risk.

Once the risk has been identified, it needs to be analyzed. We need to determine if there is a trend or even a need for change. After the risk is analyzed, we need a method to evaluate and monitor the results. Otherwise, if any change is made, you will not be able to adequately assess the results of that change.

Improve Perception

Some perception errors can be minimized by paying proper attention to clinical information when it is available, or by obtaining clinical information when it is not. The accuracy of perception may be improved with clinical information. Look at the imaging studies before reading prior reports. If a colleague missed an abnormality, you probably will too, if you read the report before looking at the imaging studies. Understand that errors will occur even with the best-trained radiologist. It does little to impress a jury that a panel of ten other board-certified radiologists missed the same lesion that you did. The public has come to expect perfect results.

Radiologists need to be aware of alternative presentations of pathology and that certain anatomic sites may warrant special attention because of the difficulty in analyzing them. This is especially true in the mediastinum and retrocardiac region, where even large lesions can be missed.

Improve Interpretation

Errors can be minimized through continuing education. The old saying that "you don't know what you don't know" certainly applies here. If you have never heard of pneumoocystis carinii pneumonia, you will probably never make the diagnosis. Your chances of losing in a lawsuit are less if the actual diagnosis is included in your differential. As with perception, interpretation can be improved with clinical information. However, be aware that more things are missed because they are not thought of, rather than because they were not known or understood.

Suggest the Next Appropriate Procedure

A radiologist should be familiar with the *ACR Appropriateness Criteria*. This is especially true if the procedure you suggest is not as appropriate as a proce-dure that you failed to suggest. If you do suggest a procedure that is not listed in the *ACR Appropriateness Criteria*, or that is listed but further down the list in appropriateness, make sure that you justify your reasons for doing so in the report. Understand that the next appropriate procedure may not be a radio-logic procedure. Be aware of all modalities, even if not offered at your institu-tion. Sometimes, a follow-up study may be the most appropriate procedure.

In reality, radiologists are rarely sued for failing to perform or suggest an additional imaging procedure. Failure to perform an additional imaging test was relevant in only 21 of 3000 claims filed against radiologists between 1990 and 2000. That is less than 1%, so there is not much to worry about unless you were one of those 21 radiologists.

Better Communication

Unexpected findings are those that may seriously affect the patient's health but do not require immediate or urgent intervention. These should be handled as nonroutine communication. This is the one area where radiologists have the most problems. Prior to 2002, it had to be by direct communication, either in person or by telephone. The courts have held that the radiologist cannot escape the duty to immediately communicate with the referring physician when urgent or life-threatening conditions are found. However, it is unclear what the radiologist needs to do when the finding is unexpected but not life-threatening.

The final written report has always been considered to be the definitive means of communicating the results of an imaging study or procedure to the referring physician. However, when a preliminary report, sometimes called a "wet read," is issued by the radiologist prior to the preparation of the final report, any significant change between the preliminary report and the final report should be reported directly to the referring physician by nonroutine communication and documented in the final report. Any written preliminary report or wet read should be maintained as part of the radiology record or medical chart, and not thrown away.

If the author of an interpretive report is not available to sign the report, a colleague will often sign the report, substituting their signature for the author's signature. There is a danger to signing a colleague's interpretive report because, if he or she is sued for malpractice, you will almost certainly be sued as well. If you are signing a colleague's report, you should review the images and make corrections to the report, if necessary, with the full understanding that you will most likely be held responsible for the contents of the report.

Since failure to communicate is one of the greatest problems facing radiologists today, directly communicate when immediate treatment or surgical intervention is needed. Nonroutine communication should be handled in a manner that gets the information to the physician. If in doubt, use nonroutine communication, and document it. Radiologists should become familiar with the *ACR Practice Guideline for Communication*. Communicating the results in a timely manner is the one area where you can make a significant change to reduce your risk and liability.

Substituted Signature

There is a real danger to signing a colleague's interpretive report because, if he or she is sued for malpractice, you will almost certainly be sued as well. Jurors believe the commonsense argument that anyone should read a document before they sign it. Any disclaimer for lack of responsibility for the contents of the report or the findings on the scan will be insufficient to avoid being sued. If you are signing a colleague's report, you should review the images and make corrections to the report, if necessary, with the full understanding that you will most likely be held responsible for the contents of the report.

FURTHER READING

American College of Radiology, *ACR Appropriateness Criteria*, pp. i–ii. Reston, Va.: American College of Radiology, 2001.

American College of Radiology, *ACR Guideline for Communication: Diagnostic Radiology*, in Standards, pp. 5–9. Reston, Va.: American College of Radiology, 2005.

Berlin L, "Radiology and Malpractice," in *Radiology*, ed. J. Tavernas and J. Ferrucci, vol. II, chap. 100, pp. 1–25. Philadelphia: Lippincott Williams & Wilkins, 2002.

Raskin MM, *Why Radiologists Get Sued*. 30 Appl. Radiol. 9–13 (2001).

Dentistry

Daniel L. Orr II, D.D.S., Ph.D., J.D., M.D., F.C.L.M.

GOLDEN RULES

1. Document treatment options, including no treatment, in the record as the treatment options are developed.
2. Document informed consent for the treatment options.
3. Be very wary of collegial criticism without at least consulting your colleague.
4. Document any extraordinary front office arrangements, such as financial planning, special after-hours appointments, etc., and always have at least one staff member present during any doctor–patient interview or treatment.
5. Request that your staff advise you of any patient–staff controversy.
6. Follow the ADA's Code of Professional Conduct recommendations regarding emergency or after-hours care.
7. Consider maintaining hospital staff privileges and when possible direct one's patient to one's own staff hospital.
8. Always be the primary decision maker with regards to dental-legal issues, such as requests for records.
9. Be knowledgeable regarding the requirements for effective coverage from your liability carrier.
10. Be cautious about turning patients over to a collection agency. Consider personally approving all such dispositions.

Liability claims for alleged dental malpractice have been somewhat "under the radar" compared to medicine. However, dentists are held to the same set of rules as physicians and other health professionals with regard to the tort of malpractice, the most common legal theory used by plaintiff patients to secure remuneration for alleged wrongs.[1]

One of the most common bases for claims for damages in dentistry is for removal of the "wrong" tooth, a somewhat limited scope of damage. However, often the damage associated with alleged dental malpractice can be more severe, e.g., the N2 paste endodontic sequelae of the 1980s.[2,3] Ultimately dental treatment can result in any complication seen with medical treatment, including death. Several reviews of the actual statistics related to alleged dental malpractice are available, although differing findings are seen. For instance, Seidberg reports that 15–25% of claims from various insurance sources include endodontics, simple extractions, and crown/bridge work.[4]

Sanbar reports that private practitioners are those most often sued and that claims usually involve faulty management/performance of treatment, unsatisfactory technical/esthetic quality, and wrong diagnosis/indication.[5] Governmental reports from the U.S. National Practitioner Data Bank, the U.S. Department of Health and Human Services, and the U.S. Department of Justice are seen in Table 43-1.

The following case history will serve to illustrate several important legal considerations for office-based private dental practitioners to remember when faced with potential legal liability.

CASE PRESENTATION

A 34-year-old married father in relatively good health presented for an initial screening examination. The patient's chief complaint was of a chronic toothache associated with tooth number 20. Historically, the patient related that he had seen another dentist for the complaint and had been told that the best option was to remove the tooth because that was the "least expensive way to go." The patient currently insisted that he preferred to save the tooth. Clinically, no. 20 was moderately broken down, but restorable. Radiographically, a 2–3 mm periapical radiolucency was evident. There were no signs of inflammation or evidence of an acute infection during this examination.

The practitioner opined that indeed the previous dentist was in error and that no. 20 could likely be salvaged via endodontic therapy and a full-coverage restoration.

When the patient was presented with the proposed treatment plan and associated fees, he shared that he couldn't afford the treatment at that time but would soon be in touch. The patient, also an artist, offered to exchange services. The screening appointment ended with an admonition to address the pathology in a timely manner. The patient paid one-half the examination fee and committed to submit the balance within two weeks.

The patient did not follow up with an appointment for treatment or by remitting the balance of the examination fee and was subsequently turned over to a collection service by front office staff three months after the office examination. Six months after the screening appointment, the dentist's staff received a request from the patient's spouse for the patient's records. The front office staff promptly forwarded the patient's records without advising the defendant dentist of the request. At nine months after the screening appointment, the dentist was served with legal papers alleging dental malpractice including misdiagnosis, improper treatment planning, improper treatment, and abandonment, all resulting in significant morbidity.

At this point in time the dentist notified his carrier about the claim.

ISSUES

Patient's Deposition

During discovery, the dentist was apprised of additional allegations that he had previously been unaware of. At the patient's deposition, the patient sat

Table 43–1 Dentistry malpractice statistics

Medical malpractice lawsuit payment statistics for dentist malpractice in the U.S.A:
- Roughly 5% of medical malpractice trials related to dentists in the 75 largest counties in the U.S. 2001 (Bureau of Justice Statistics, U.S. Department of Justice)
- 12.1% of medical malpractice payment reports were against dentists in the U.S. 2002 (2002 Annual Report, National Practitioner Data Bank, U.S. DHHS)
- Roughly 38.9% of medical malpractice trials against dentists were won by the plaintiff in the 75 largest counties in the U.S. 2001 (Bureau of Justice Statistics, U.S. Department of Justice)

Medical malpractice lawsuit payment report statistics for dentist malpractice in the U.S.A.
- 17,469 malpractice payment reports were made against dentists in the U.S. 1990–96 (The National Practitioner Data Bank Public Use File)
- 15% of malpractice payment reports were made against dentists in the U.S. 1990–96 (The National Practitioner Data Bank Public Use File)

Medical malpractice lawsuit statistics for dental malpractice in the U.S.A.:
- 8 medical malpractice reports were made to the National Practitioner Data Bank regarding dental assistants in the U.S. 1990–2004 (NPDB Summary Report, National Practitioner Data Bank, U.S. DHHS)
- 17 medical malpractice reports were made to the National Practitioner Data Bank regarding dental hygienists in the U.S. 1990–2004 (NPDB Summary Report, National Practitioner Data Bank, U.S. DHHS)
- 137 medical malpractice reports were made to the National Practitioner Data Bank regarding dental residents in the U.S. 1990–2004 (NPDB Summary Report, National Practitioner Data Bank, U.S. DHHS)
- 34,691 medical malpractice reports were made to the National Practitioner Data Bank regarding dentists in the U.S. 1990–2004 (NPDB Summary Report, National Practitioner Data Bank, U.S. DHHS)
- 19 medical malpractice reports were made to the National Practitioner Data Bank regarding denturists in the U.S. 1990–2004 (NPDB Summary Report, National Practitioner Data Bank, U.S. DHHS)

Medical malpractice statistics for the U.S.A. 2003:
- 27,793 (13.5%) dentists had a malpractice report made against them in the U.S. 1990–2003 (2003 Annual Report, National Practitioner Data Bank, U.S. DHHS)
- 45,166 (13.1%) malpractice reports were made against dentists in the U.S. 1990–2003 (2003 Annual Report, National Practitioner Data Bank, U.S. DHHS)
- Dentists had an average of 1.63 malpractice reports made against each of them in the U.S. 1990–2003 (2003 Annual Report, National Practitioner Data Bank, U.S. DHHS)

Medical malpractice statistics for the U.S.A. 2003:
- 24 (0.01%) dental assistants, technicians, and hygienists had a malpractice report made against them in the U.S. 1990–2003 (2003 Annual Report, National Practitioner Data Bank, U.S. DHHS)
- 25 (0.01%) malpractice reports were made against dental assistants, technicians, and hygienists in the U.S. 1990–2003 (2003 Annual Report, National Practitioner Data Bank, U.S. DHHS)

(continued)

Table 43–1 (cont'd.)

- Dental assistants, technicians and hygienists had an average of 1.2 malpractice reports made against each of them in the U.S. 1990–2003 (2003 Annual Report, National Practitioner Data Bank, U.S. DHHS)

Medical malpractice statistics for the U.S.A. 2003:

- 10 (0.005%) denturists had a malpractice report made against them in the U.S. 1990–2003 (2003 Annual Report, National Practitioner Data Bank, U.S. DHHS)
- 10 (0.003%) malpractice reports were made against denturists in the U.S. 1990–2003 (2003 Annual Report, National Practitioner Data Bank, U.S. DHHS)
- Denturists had an average of 1.0 malpractice reports made against each of them in the U.S. 1990–2003 (2003 Annual Report, National Practitioner Data Bank, U.S. DHHS)

Medical malpractice statistics for the U.S.A. 2003:

- 4 (0.03%) dental assistants, technicians, and hygienists had a malpractice report made against them in the U.S. 2003 (2003 Annual Report, National Practitioner Data Bank, U.S. DHHS)
- 3 (0.01%) malpractice reports were made against dental assistants, technicians, and hygienists in the U.S. 2003 (2003 Annual Report, National Practitioner Data Bank, U.S. DHHS)

Medical malpractice statistics for the U.S.A. 2003:

- 1418 (10.6%) dentists had a malpractice report made against them in the U.S. 2003 (2003 Annual Report, National Practitioner Data Bank, U.S. DHHS)
- 2540 (9.6%) malpractice reports were made against dentists in the U.S. 2003 (2003 Annual Report, National Practitioner Data Bank, U.S. DHHS

---

in a wheelchair, was blind in the left eye, and had compromise of other motor and sensory nerves of the left face. During the deposition, the patient was unable to control salivary secretions and constantly used a towel in an attempt to control his drooling. The patient testified that at the screening appointment he asked the defendant dentist what he should do about his chronic toothache in no. 20. The patient stated that he had previously determined to remove the tooth based on another dentist's advice but that the defendant had talked him into trying to save no. 20. The defendant's root canal and crown treatment plan would have cost about ten times more than the extraction of no. 20. The patient also testified that he told the defendant he could not afford to pay cash for the treatment but offered to trade artwork for the therapy.

The patient then stated that he had called the office a week later to schedule an appointment and that the receptionist refused to schedule him as he did not have the cash balance for initial examination, let alone the planned root canal. Approximately a month later, the patient noted acute swelling near no. 20 one evening. He called the defendant's office for help and was told by an answering service that the defendant was on vacation and to call back in a week. When the patient expressed his concern that he had a serious emergency, the answering service instructed him to "call 911 or go to a hospital."

The patient did go to a local emergency room and was admitted by a physician general practitioner. Within several hours the patient began to deteriorate neurologically and was admitted to the ICU where multiple diagnostic procedures were initiated on an emergency basis. The diagnosis reached was that of an intracranial central nervous system abscess. Additional consults from Infectious Disease, Neurosurgery, and other specialties were obtained. The dental service, including Oral and Maxillofacial Surgery, was not consulted.

The patient underwent a neurosurgical procedure in which a copious quantity of pus was drained. After the general anesthetic agents had been metabolized, the patient remained unconscious and comatose for several weeks until he slowly began to recover.

When the patient was finally discharged to a long-term care facility, the admitting general practitioner opined in the discharge note that no one had definitively identified the etiology of the infection but that it was probably "dental." In his deposition, the patient stated that he had never been informed that a toothache could cause a brain abscess.

While in rehabilitation, the patient had applied for financial assistance for ongoing medical bills already totaling well into six figures. During this time frame, the family received notice that they had been turned over to collections by the defendant dentist's office for not paying half of his screening examination fee.

Dentist's Deposition

During the defendant dentist's deposition, the office records were produced to reconstruct the interaction between the plaintiff and the dentist. The records supported the plaintiff's statements that the defendant had opined that the first dentist was wrong and that the tooth could be saved with endodontic therapy. There was notation in the records about a "follow-up as needed" appointment. No writing about informed consent regarding the proposed treatment or alternative treatments, financial arrangements, or subsequent calls by the plaintiff were seen. The answering service did have a record of the after-hours emergency call placed by the plaintiff.

Expert and Legal Counsel Evaluation

The defendant's liability company retained an oral and maxillofacial surgeon as an expert witness to analyze the case. Part of the defense focused on plaintiff questions such as the lack of an antibiotic prescription at the initial appointment and the discharge note relating the central nervous system abscess to the dentition. However, the expert and defense counsel also agreed that several areas of legal, as opposed to dental, concern regarding the defendant's conduct existed:

1. A lack of documentation that although endodontic therapy was recommended, extraction was a viable option and observation was not recommended.
2. A lack of any documentation regarding informed consent about recommended treatment or alternative treatments, including no treatment, other than the "follow up prn" note.

3. The charted negative statement about the first dentist's treatment planning.
4. The lack of records regarding special financial arrangements.
5. The lack of office records memorializing any controversial contact with the front office and the fact that the defendant was not advised about any such contact.
6. The lack of more optimal coverage for the defendant's practice while he was unavailable and the fact that the defendant had not been advised about the plaintiff's call to his answering service.
7. The finding that although the defendant had hospital privileges, the patient had elected to go to a hospital where the defendant did not have privileges.
8. The fact that the defendant's front office staff had forwarded the plaintiff's records without advising the dentist of the request for records.
9. The concern that there was a significant delay in contacting the defendant's liability insurance carrier from the time that records were initially requested.
10. The fact that the doctor's billing office had turned the patient over to collections without the dentist's approval.

In addressing the legal conduct concerns, the following opinions were formed relating to 1–10 above:

1. Optimally the records will reflect a considered evaluation and resulting opinion regarding the therapeutic options open to a patient. There is generally no single perfect treatment plan, but several viable treatment options, ultimately depending on the totality of the presenting signs, symptoms, patient history, and patient and doctor preferences. Records can be the most effective resource for the defense in a liability issue if carefully written. Careful writing would most likely include some evidence of the thought process including differential diagnosis, differing treatment options, and practitioner and patient preferences for treatment.
2. Part and parcel of the differential diagnosis and treatment options presented is the provision of informed consent. Informed consent entails advising the patient of the reasonable treatment options and the risks and benefits of each of those treatment options, including no treatment at all.[6] A lack of documented informed consent may be interpreted by a jury as evidence that such a discussion was never held. (A copy of the author's general written informed consent follows.)

ORAL AND MAXILLOFACIAL SURGERY CONSENT

The procedures to be performed have been explained to me and I understand what is to be done. This is my consent to the procedures discussed and to any other procedures found to be necessary or advisable in addition to the preoperative treatment plan. I agree to the use of local, sedation, or general anesthesia depending on the judgment of Dr. _____.

I have been informed and understand that occasionally there are complications of the surgery, drugs, and anesthesia. The more common complications are pain, infection, swelling, bleeding, bruising, and temporary or permanent numbness and/or tingling of the lip, tongue, chin, gums, cheeks or teeth. I understand that pain, numbness, swelling, and inflammation of veins or other structures may occur from injections. I understand death from office procedures has been estimated at 1/400,000. I understand the possibility of injury to the neck and facial muscles, and changes in the bite or jaw joint. I understand the possibility of injury to the adjacent teeth, restorations, and tissues, referred pain to other areas of the head and neck, bone fractures or infections, and delayed healing. I understand the combination of anesthesia and surgery may lead to nausea, vomiting, allergic reactions, and other physical or psychological reactions. I understand sinus complictions may include an opening into the sinus from the mouth after the removal of teeth. I understand injury may occur when instruments fail. I understand that many other complications not listed may occur.

I understand medications, drugs, anesthetics, and prescriptions may cause drowsiness and a lack of coordination which could be increased by the use of alcohol or other drugs; I have been advised to not operate any vehicle or potentially hazardous devices, or work, while taking medications and/or drugs or until fully recovered from their effects.

I acknowledge the receipt of and understand the postoperative instructions. I understand that there is no guarantee related to treatment. I undderstand that most complications can be rectified with proper follow-up care. I agree to follow up as needed or advised for any concerns or complications. I understand I can receive a review of these and other possible risks by asking.

Signature

Signature

Date

3. Practitioners would be well advised to be very circumspect with regard to offering any criticism of a colleague, particularly without personally communicating with that colleague. A patient's subjective history and recollection of prior health professional interactions are notoriously inaccurate.

4. Financial arrangements that are out of the ordinary for one's practice should be documented in the financial records. In today's world,

barter for health services is usually not the norm. Aggressive plaintiff attorneys presented with an alleged barter have been known to even subpoena tax records to see if the value of such transactions was reported to the IRS.

5. Trusted office staff should be sensitive enough to know when the doctor needs to be advised about any confrontational or less than satisfactory patient/office staff interaction. Patient comments insisting that the doctor said or agreed to something out of the norm regarding finances or otherwise should not be summarily rejected by staff. Strong consideration should be give to advising the doctor about all such conversations.

6. The ADA Code of Professional Conduct mandates that dentists are responsible to provide "reasonable arrangements for emergency or after-hours care"[7] for their practices when they are unavailable. "Call 911" or "go to the ER" instructions generally do not require any effort or special arrangements on the part of the practitioner who may be unavailable. In the author's opinion, it is unlikely that such instructions would satisfy the ADA's CPC recommendation. One needs to be cognizant of the potential attendant legal ramifications that follow such cavalier call arrangements. Additionally, part of the responsibility for reasonable arrangements likely includes mutual communication and follow-up between the individuals or other agents covering one another.

7. Hospital privileges certainly are not mandatory for many typical dental practices. However, if one does have hospital privileges, it seems reasonable that any practice patient hospitalized for a practice or other dental-related condition would be referred to a hospital that the practitioner has access to. Advantages to notifying staff, other covering dentists, answering services, and patients of the hospital of choice are obvious. Especially important is the fact that the dentist has convenient continued access to the hospitalized patient and is not "on the outside looking in" as his patient is evaluated and treated by others.

8. Prudent office policy might include direction to one's staff that *any* patient communications that are not uniformly positive should be reported to the dentist daily. Not only might patients be "right," but occasionally dependable staff members may have bad communication days, something an insightful doctor cannot allow to occur without his knowledge. Almost any staff member can deal successfully with happy patients, but only the doctor should be responsible for rectifying unresolved nonoptimal interactions between staff and patients.

9. The injudicious unconsidered release of records is an occurrence related to a lack of communication for what is generally an unusual request, i.e., for records. Most often, requests for records should be passed on to the doctor for his approval prior to the records' release. In addition, some liability policies allow insurers to defer or deny coverage for less than timely notification of possible incidents. A request for records may be indicative of a situation that one's liability carrier should be advised of.

10. Similar to other adverse interactions, turning a patient over to a collection agency should probably only be done after careful consideration by the doctor, not by a potentially disgruntled, frustrated, or less informed staff member.

The ten iterated legal concerns above had to be addressed during the course of discovery prior to trial in addition to the plaintiff's alleged treatment deficiencies. Fortunately, the defendant's insurer elected to provide coverage for the case in spite of the less than timely notification about the request for records. The defense expert's opinions about the dentist's actual treatment and about the causation and management of the CNS abscess truncated an in-depth plaintiff analysis of the legal concerns noted.

Defense Expert's Deposition

During the defendant expert's deposition, a strong opinion was proffered that it was not the standard of care to prescribe antibiotics for chronic odontalgia alone. In fact, he opined that it would be below the standard of care to do so whether a periapical radiolucency was present or not.

The potentially problematic issue of a lack of informed consent was also addressed. The defense expert explained that reasonable informed consent for the endodontic therapy and extraction options available for chronic odontalgia in a broken-down tooth would include, optimally, the retention of a functional tooth versus, at worst, the loss of the tooth. He opined that it is not ordinary or reasonable to routinely advise chronic odontalgia patients that they could be exposed to a toothache-related brain abscess or near death. No objective literature that definitively related CNS abscess to chronic odontalgia was identified, confirming the rarity of the relationship if it occurs at all.

Finally, the plaintiff treating physician/expert's opinion that the CNS infection was of odontogenic etiology needed to be addressed. The defendant OMS expert pointed out several non-sequiturs relative to this case. Included was the fact that in spite of the plethora of medical experts consulted and battery upon battery of diagnostic tests performed during the prolonged hospitalization, periapical or panoramic radiographic studies were never obtained. A dentist or oral and maxillofacial surgeon was never consulted during the patient's admission. No objective attempt was ever made to correlate the bacteria from the CNS abscess with any bacteria present in no. 20, which was also asymptomatic during the hospital stay. The OMS expert mentioned that many more commonplace things than chronic odontalgia, such as toothbrushing, can cause transient bacteremia. [8]

Finally, the defense expert pointed out that the plaintiff expert/treating physician who opined that the abscess was likely secondary to pathology in no. 20 never addressed the treatment of this CNS and life-threatening tooth during hospitalization. Not only was no. 20 never treated in the hospital, the physician's discharge orders never mentioned the need to follow up with a dentist for the still retained life-threatening no. 20.

Case Resolution

The case was settled for a nominal four-figure amount within a week after the defense expert's deposition. In spite of the efficient disposition of this particular case, dentists would be well advised to avoid repetition of the questionable dental-legal related conduct seen in this defendant's office.

REFERENCES

1. Malamed SF, Orr DL, *Handbook of Local Anesthesia*, 5th ed., "Legal Considerations" chapter. St. Louis: Mosby, 2004, pp. 333–348.

2. Orr DL, *Paresthesia of the Trigeminal Nerve Secondary to Endodontic Manipulation with N2*. Headache 25(6):334–336 (1985).

3. Orr DL, *Paresthesia of the Second Division of the Trigeminal Nerve Secondary to Endodontic Manipulation with N2*. Headache 27(1):21–22 (1987).

4. Seidberg BH, *Legal Medicine*, 6th ed. (chapter 48, "Dental Litigation: Triad of Concerns"). Philadelphia: Mosby, 2004, p. 490.

5. Sanbar SS, personal communication, 2005.

6. Orr DL, Curtis WJ, *Obtaining Written Informed Consent for the Administration of Local Anesthetics in Dentistry*. JADA 136:1568–1571 (2005).

7. ADA Code Principles of Ethics and Code of Professional Conduct, Sec. 4B.

8. Orr DL, *Controlling Bacteremia*. JADA 109(6):876 (1984).

GLOSSARY OF MALPRACTICE TERMS

abandonment Termination of a physician–patient relationship by the physician without the patient's consent at a time when the patient requires medical attention, without making adequate arrangements for continued care.

abuse of process Use of legal mechanisms in a manner or for a purpose not supported by law. For example, pursuit of litigation based on little or no legal grounds, intended to harass and cause expense to the defendant. Damages may be recovered for expenses or loss incurred by a defendant as a result of abuse of process.

action Legal action, lawsuit.

affidavit Sworn statement for use in legal process.

affirmative defense An answer to a lawsuit that does not deny the alleged conduct or failure but asserts a legal basis to excuse or foreclose liability. Good Samaritan immunity or a statute of limitations defense are examples.

agent A person authorized by another, the principal, to act for or represent the principal. Agency relationships may include authority to exercise personal judgment.

allegation Asserted fact or circumstance that is expected to be proved by legal process.

appeal A claim to a superior court of error in process or law by a lower court, asking the higher court to correct or reverse a judgment or decision. An appellate (appeals) court has the power to review decisions made in the trial court or a lower appellate court. An appellate court does not make a new determination of facts but examines the law and legal process as applied in the case.

battery Intentional and unauthorized physical contact with a person, without consent. For example, a surgical procedure performed without express or implied consent constitutes battery. Victims of medical battery may obtain compensation for the touching, even if no negligence occurred. A crime of battery may be defined differently.

borrowed servant Agent temporarily under the supervision, direction, and control of another. For example, an operating room nurse technically employed by a hospital may be borrowed by a surgeon in the operating room to perform certain tasks.

breach of contract Failure to perform a legal agreement. If a legally enforceable contract is established, performance of agreed promises may

Adapted from S. Fiscina, Glossary, *Legal Medicine/American College of Legal Medicine,* 7th ed., ed. S. Sandy Sanbar *et al.* Philadelphia: Mosby, 2007.

be compelled or adequate compensation for failure to perform may be required.

burden of proof Responsibility of proving certain facts required to support a lawsuit. If the burden of proof is not met, the opposing side prevails on that point, even without a defense or response.

captain of the ship doctrine A special agency relationship establishing liability for an employee's or agent's acts. This agency relationship imposes what is called *vicarious liability* on the one employing the agent. Initially used as an analogy in malpractice cases, it asserts that the surgeon in the operating room has total authority and full responsibility for the performance of the operating crew and the welfare of the patient. By this doctrine, the surgeon may be vicariously liable for the negligent act of any member of the surgical team. The doctrine is not accepted in every jurisdiction.

case law Legal principles applied to specific factual situations. Case law is drawn from judicial decisions in similar cases in a jurisdiction. Case law is used to make decisions that are based on precedent, the judicial principle that requires that similar cases be treated alike. Assembled case law principles are also called the *common law*.

cause Proximate cause. A reasonable connection between an act or failure alleged as negligence and an injury suffered by the plaintiff. In a suit for negligence, the issue of causation usually requires proof that the negligence of the defendant directly resulted in or was a substantial factor in the plaintiff's harm or injury.

cause of action Facts or circumstances that support a legal right to seek corrective action or compensation.

civil action Legal proceeding by a party asking for correction or compensation, distinguished from a criminal action, which is brought by the state to punish offenses against public order.

civil liability Legal responsibility to compensate for losses or injuries caused by acts or failures to act. Compensation is awarded as monetary damages paid by the defendant to the injured party. In contrast, criminal liability is the legal responsibility imposed by the state for violation of criminal laws. Consequences of criminal acts may include death, imprisonment, fines, and loss of property or privileges. Civil liability is limited to monetary damages; however, a single act may be both a criminal act and a civil wrong, also called a *tort*.

class action A legal action instituted by one or more persons on behalf of others in a similar situation. Class actions are used if many plaintiffs must prove the same allegations against the same defendant. An example would be litigation over responsibility for a plane crash with hundreds of victims.

clear and convincing evidence A level of persuasion required to support certain noncriminal legal actions. For example, involuntary civil commitment to mental treatment may require clear and convincing evidence of danger to self or others.

common law See *case law*.

complaint Initial document filed by a plaintiff, also called a *pleading*, which begins a civil lawsuit. The complaint is intended to give the defendant notice of facts alleged in the cause of action on which the plaintiff bases a demand for corrective action or compensation.

confidential communication Medical information given to health care providers in the course of diagnosis and treatment of an illness or injury. Providers are entrusted with the duty to keep the information from disclosure to third parties, subject to existing requirements of statute and case law.

consent Agreement to accept the consequences of an action, such as to allow another person to do something or to take part in some activity. Express consent may be oral or written. Implied consent is agreement shown by signs or actions. An example of conduct showing that consent has been given for an injection or blood test is to roll up a sleeve and extend an arm for vein puncture. Taking part indicates consent to the risks of a game, such as hockey. Where no actual consent or refusal is possible (e.g., in the case of an unconscious person in an emergency situation), consent to others' actions to save life or limb is presumed. Consequences of actions taken without consent remain the burden of the individual acting without consent.

consortium Element of damages generally recoverable by one spouse for loss of company, services, and conjugal relations caused by the spouse's injury. Company, participation, counsel, and affection are consortium losses recoverable by other close family members in some jurisdictions.

contract Agreement by two or more parties to exchange obligations. A contract depends on a similar mutual understanding of the terms of the contract and performance promised. A legally enforceable contract means that compensation for promises not kept can be compelled.

contributory negligence Affirmative defense in which a defendant contends that the plaintiff's negligence wholly or substantially caused the injury complained of by the defendant. The effect of plaintiff's negligence on liability or compensation varies among the states, depending on the timing and circumstances of the plaintiff's and the defendant's acts or failures to act.

counterclaim Defendant's complaint against a plaintiff alleging obligation, failure, and damages for which compensation is demanded. For the counterclaim issues, the defendant is seen as having the burden of a plaintiff.

covenant Specific agreement or promise to act or refrain from acting in exchange for similar promises or payments. For example, a covenant not to sue one defendant may exchange relinquishment of that claim for a payment or a promise not to counterclaim. However, a specific covenant would not release all persons alleged to have a role in causing the injury and does not accept the payment as full satisfaction for the injury. A covenant with one defendant therefore does not bar actions against others.

criminal liability Legal consequence imposed by the government for violation of an offense against the public interest in safety and liberty, and is not directed toward compensating the losses of victims. Consequences of criminal acts may include death, imprisonment, fines, and loss of property or privileges.

damages Money receivable through judicial order by a person sustaining harm, impairment, or loss to person or property as the result of the intentional or negligent act of another. Damages may be compensatory, to reimburse a person for economic losses such as lost income and medical expenses. Other damages recoverable include noneconomic losses, such as pain and suffering or mental anguish, or hedonic damages awarded for the loss of life's enjoyment and aesthetic and other pleasures, such as music, athletics, sunsets, or children. Sometimes, token damages are awarded to demonstrate that a legally recognized error has been committed. So-called nominal damages can be awarded even if no actual economic or noneconomic losses are suffered. Punitive damages are those awarded to inflict economic punishment on defendants who have been found to act maliciously or in reckless disregard of others' rights.

decedent A person who has died and whose interests are involved in a legal proceeding.

defamation Intentional communication of false personal or business information that injures the reputation or prospects of another. Spoken defamation is slander; written defamation is libel. Truth is a defense to claims of defamation. Publication of true information may nevertheless violate duties of confidentiality or may be invasion of privacy.

deposition Part of pretrial discovery process in which a sworn out-of-court statement is taken. In a deposition, a witness is asked questions and cross-examined. The statement may be admitted into evidence if it is impossible for a witness to attend in person. Deposition testimony also can be used to cross-question a witness at trial.

diagnosis-related group (DRG) Classification system that groups patients according to diagnosis, age, presence of comorbidity or complications, and other relevant data.

disclaimer Statement before or after disputed events that announces one party's stance and commitment regarding legal aspects of facts and circumstances in question (e.g., a statement that no warranties were intended or offered as part of contract terms or that risks of activities were not assumed by a party). Ordinarily a disclaimer of responsibility for future negligent conduct is not recognized by the law and would be ineffective as a defense.

discovery Pretrial activities in the litigation process to determine the essential questions and issues in dispute and what evidence each side will present at trial. Discovery is intended to narrow trial questions to allow fair presentation of opposing evidence without surprise during trial. Discovery communications and disclosures may facilitate out-of-court settlement.

due care Level of reasonable and ordinary observation and awareness owed by one person to another in specific relationship or circumstances, such as a physician's duty of due care in attendance of patients. It anticipates and appropriately manages known, expected, or foreseeable events, especially complications of the patient's disease or treatment.

due process Level of fair method required by the U.S. Constitution in execution of governmental activities. Due process in legal proceedings must reflect both fair substance—the activity is appropriate and constitutional—and fair means—method of proceeding that provides parties involved the opportunity to present appropriate advocacy and evidence in any dispute or legal process.

evidence beyond reasonable doubt A level of persuasion required to support a judgment of criminal responsibility.

expert witness Person invited to testify at a hearing or trial to bring special training, knowledge, skill, or experience to the proceeding where matters in legal dispute are beyond the average person's knowledge. Unlike a fact witness, who is compelled to testify because of involvement in the facts and circumstances of the dispute, an expert witness may be asked for an opinion about specific issues in the case. Fact witnesses are percipient witnesses who testify to what they experienced through their senses. Experts educate the court about the scientific, medical, technical, or other specialized circumstances involved in the dispute.

fiduciary A person in a position of confidence or trust who undertakes a solemn duty to act for the benefit of another who must trust the good intention and performance of the fiduciary. In a fiduciary relationship, virtually all the power reposes in the trusted fiduciary, and vulnerability lies with the beneficiary of the relationship. This disparity of knowledge and power imposes major duties on the fiduciary. Examples of fiduciary relationships are guardian and ward, parent and child, attorney and client, physician and patient, estate trustee and beneficiary, and other financial relationships. This type of relationship requires that the fiduciary never act to the detriment of the trusting party, certainly not for personal gain or profit.

finder of fact In a trial, the jury, or in trials without juries, the judge. Findings of fact generally are not appealable. Appeals courts review findings of law, admissions of evidence, and application or interpretation of appropriate legal principles and laws.

fraud Intentional misdirection, misinformation, or misrepresentation to another person that causes legal injury or loss to that person. Fraud is an intentional wrong, to be contrasted with negligent conduct causing loss. Examples of fraud in medical practice could be to mislead a patient about indicated procedures or therapies; to misstate diagnoses or treatment codes to falsely maximize reimbursement; or to conspire with patients to misstate injuries to obtain undeserved benefits.

good faith Honest intent to avoid taking unconscionable advantage of another, even if technicalities of law might permit it.

Good Samaritan statute Law enacted by state legislatures to encourage physicians and others to stop and assist emergency victims. Good Samaritan laws grant immunity from liability for negligence to a person who responds and administers care to a person in an emergency situation. Statutes vary among the states regarding persons covered, the scene and type of emergency, and nature of conduct for which immunity is granted.

guardian Person appointed by a court to manage the affairs and to protect the interests of a person who is declared incompetent to manage personal affairs. Incompetence may be due to physical or mental status;

guardians may be appointed to manage economic or personal matters, including medical treatment choices.

holding A specific conclusion made by a court in a case, which is used to support the court's final judgment, and may be used to persuade later courts on the same point in similar cases.

immunity Protection of individuals or entities that shields them from liability for certain acts by establishing as an affirmative defense disallowing prosecution or trial of the dispute. Examples include nonprofit hospitals granted charitable immunity, government agencies' complete or limited sovereign or governmental immunity, or immunity for peer review comment and activities.

in loco parentis A Latin phrase for the status of one assigned by law to stand in the place of parents and exercise their legal rights, duties, and responsibilities toward a minor.

incompetence Legal status of dependence on a natural or appointed guardian to make decisions and manage personal and business affairs. Incompetent persons cannot bind themselves by contract, consent to or refuse medical treatment, or be held to assume consequences of choices made. Parents are the natural guardians of children, who are legally incompetent until the age of majority or until emancipated. Legally recognized incompetent adults have appointed guardians. Medical incompetence is the inability of a person to understand and manage personal affairs or to take responsibility for personal choices. Once this status is legally recognized, a guardian is appointed to act in the person's place.

informed consent A patient's consent to undergo a proposed procedure based on the patient's knowledge of facts needed to choose whether or not to submit it after risks, benefits, alternatives, and consequences have been discussed and weighed.

interrogatories Written questions submitted to an opposing party to be answered before and in preparation for trial, the answers to which are signed and affirmed as true by the party in the suit.

invasion of privacy Violation of person's right to be free from unwarranted publicity and intrusions or the unauthorized dissemination of private information about the person, including the disclosure of a medical condition without legal justification or release, which could represent such a violation. It is a tort, for which civil liability damages are awarded to compensate for mental suffering and anguish suffered by the person whose privacy was violated.

joint and several liability Responsibility shared by a number of persons who are found to have contributed to a plaintiff's injury in which each or any one of those liable can be made to satisfy the whole loss to the plaintiff and must then sue the other liable parties for contribution to the payment.

judgment Official decision of a court about the respective rights and claims of the parties to an action or suit litigated and submitted for determination.

libel Written defamation by any type of communication or publication, including pictures.

malice The performance of a wrongful act without excuse, with apparent intent to inflict an injury. Under some circumstances of conduct, the law will infer malicious intent from the evidence of the defendant's actions.

malicious prosecution Lawsuit or countersuit seeking damages that have been caused to a defendant by a civil suit filed by a plaintiff in bad faith and without probable cause. Ordinarily the countersuit may not be brought until the initial suit has been found meritless.

malpractice Professional misconduct or failure to properly discharge professional duties by failing to meet the standard of care required of a professional.

material Influential and necessary. Material facts or issues concern the substance of the matter in dispute as distinguished from form.

minor A person who has not yet reached the age determined by law for transactional capacity, that is, a legally incompetent person. Minors generally cannot be held responsible for their contracts or other civil actions; thus minors ordinarily cannot consent to their own medical treatment. An exception exists for emancipated minors, defined as persons substantially independent from their parents, supporting themselves, married, or otherwise on their own, or mature minors, defined as persons who have demonstrated the capacity to make decisions that an adult would be expected to make. A statute also may provide exceptions to legal incapacity to allow minors authority to consent to treatment for drug abuse, venereal disease, birth control, or pregnancy.

misrepresentation Words or conduct amounting to an assertion not in accordance with the existing facts or circumstances. A person who has reasonable grounds for believing that the representation is true makes an "innocent misrepresentation." A "negligent misrepresentation" is made when a person has no reasonable grounds for believing that the representation is true, even if the speaker believes it to be true. A "fraudulent misrepresentation" is made by a person who is aware of the falsity of the representation that causes the other party to enter an arrangement or an agreement or to rely to a detriment on the false representation.

motion Request to a judge for an order or a ruling.

negligence Failure to exercise the degree of diligence and care that a reasonably prudent person would be expected to exercise under the same or similar circumstances. Failure that proximately causes an injury is recognized as a basis for compensation owed to the injured party.

opinion of the court An appellate court's outline of a case, which states the factual findings and the law applied to the case. It also details the legal reasoning supporting the decision and any issues appealed as error while finally affirming, reversing, or remanding the case appealed.

parens patriae Description of the role of the state as the sovereign guardian of persons under the state's protection. It is the legal basis for the state's power to act to protect the health and welfare of persons who suffer from legal disabilities, such as minority or mental incapacity.

party A more general term than a legal person because it may refer to organizations, groups, and legal entities, such as corporations and partnerships.

perjury Willful false testimony under oath and punishable as a crime.

preponderance of evidence A level of persuasion required to award judgment in civil actions for damages. Usually a standard of better-than-equal evidence.

presumption An initial rational position of law, which can be challenged unless irrefutable by evidence presented in legal proceedings. An example is the presumption of transactional competence in adult persons.

prima facie case A complaint with supporting evidence that apparently supports all the necessary legal elements for a recognized cause of action if it is sufficient to produce a verdict or judgment for the plaintiff until overcome by evidence in defense of the case.

privilege Exemption or immunity connected to a specific legal situation. For example, the physician–patient privilege is a rule of evidence by which communications made to a physician by a patient in the course of treatment may not be used as evidence in court. It is the patient's privilege to keep such information from disclosure; it is the physician's duty to resist attempts to compel disclosure. This privilege is conditional and usually subject to certain exceptions.

probable cause Evidence that would lead a reasonable person of ordinary intelligence to conclude that a cause of action is supportable in a civil lawsuit.

reasonable person Hypothetical person used as an objective standard against which a litigant's conduct can be judged. The reasonable person is the figurative standard of care. For example, a standard of care in medical practice could be established by the answer to the question, "What would a reasonably knowledgeable and skilled physician be expected to have done under the circumstances described?"

release An agreement to relinquish a right or claim against another person or persons, usually exchanged for a payment or a promise, called *consideration*. A signed release agreement indicates that a claimed injury has been compensated. A release is distinguished from a covenant not to sue by the element of satisfaction of the claim.

res ipsa loquitur (Latin, "the thing speaks for itself.") A legal doctrine sometimes applied in a negligence action when the plaintiff has no direct evidence of negligence but the nature of the injury under the particular circumstances indicates to reasonable persons that such injuries do not occur in the absence of negligence. The doctrine is applicable to cases in which the defendant had exclusive control of what caused the harm to the plaintiff and the plaintiff could not have contributed to the injury. Use of the doctrine does not assure the plaintiff a judgment. After proof of the elements of *res ipsa loquitur*, the doctrine shifts to the defendant the burden to prove that conduct was reasonable and appropriate or that other mechanisms caused the plaintiff's injury.

respondeat superior (Latin, "let the master answer.") A legal doctrine that imposes vicarious liability on the employer for breaches of duties by employees. The duty is the employer's and is imposed if the employer engages others to perform tasks on the employer's behalf, which is work within the scope of employment. For example, a hospital is liable for the negligent acts of a nurse it employs if the acts occurred while the nurse was performing tasks within a nursing job description.

slander Spoken defamation about one person in the presence of another person that harms the slandered person's income, reputation, or character.

standard of care The measure of assessment applied to a defendant's conduct for liability determination, comparing what occurred with what an ordinary, reasonable, and prudent person would have done or not done under similar circumstances.

stare decisis (Latin, "let the decision stand.") The principle of case law that requires courts to apply the approach and rationale of previously decided cases to subsequent cases involving similar facts and legal questions. When a point of law has been settled by decision, it forms a precedent that is binding. Later decisions may distinguish their facts or circumstances to come to different results but otherwise must adhere to the rule of precedent. On rare occasion, precedent is rejected, and a new ruling case decision is adopted. Such a case is called a *landmark case.*

statute A written law enacted by the legislature to achieve a specified legislative objective. Statutes apply legislative prescriptions to some of the same factual situations dealt with by case law and administrative law. Generally, former case law governing the situation is no longer operative in situations in which a subsequent statute is applicable.

statute of limitations Laws that specify the permissible time interval between an occurrence giving rise to a civil cause of action and the filing of the lawsuit. Failure to file suit within the prescribed time is an affirmative defense. These time limits for filing suit vary among the states, even for similar legal actions. Most statutes of limitation have exceptions that stop the time from elapsing. Stopping the time is called *tolling the statute.* In malpractice actions the time allowed for bringing suit may not begin to run until the party claiming injury first discovers or should reasonably have discovered the injury. Fraudulent concealment of an injury by the defendant tolls the statute.

strict liability Liability without the need to prove a negligent act or failure, one form of which is enterprise liability. The proof of damages sustained by the plaintiff in connection with the situation and the involvement of the defendant support the finding of strict liability. Examples could be management by the defendant of inherently dangerous activities, placing a defective and dangerous product into commerce, or assembling hazardous substances.

subpoena A court order requiring a person to appear in court to give testimony or be punished for not appearing.

subpoena duces tecum Subpoena that requires a person to personally present to the court a specified document or property possessed or under the person's control.

tort Civil wrong in which a person has breached a legal duty with harm caused to another. To establish liability for a tort, an injured party must establish that a legal duty was owed to the plaintiff by the defendant, that the defendant breached that duty, and that the plaintiff suffered damage caused by the breach. Torts can be negligent or intentional.

vicarious liability Derivative responsibility for an agent's or employee's failures based on the defendant's employer–employee or principal–agent relationship. The responsibility is imposed because the ability to supervise, direct, and control hazardous conduct of employees lies with the employer or principal.

wanton act Grossly negligent, malicious, or reckless conduct that implies a disregard for the consequences or for the rights or safety of others.

warranty Express or implied commitment or promise undertaken as part of a contract but aside from the central contract purpose. It is to be distinguished from a representation. A warranty is given contemporaneously with the contract agreement as part of the contract. A representation precedes and may be seen as an inducement to enter the contract. For example, a representation would be the disclosed indication for surgery; a warranty would be a promise of a specific result from the procedure.

INDEX

Risk 19, 161, 162, 165, 169, 190, 212
  assumption of 7, 8, 264–265, 380
  of death 161, 162–163, 170
  explanation of 454, 455, 456, 464, 467
  factors 386, 389, 425, 426, 476
  in LASIK cases 454, 455, 456
  management 18–20, 59, 137–138, 171,
      193, 448–449, 486
  reducing 486
  unreasonable 168
Royal Commission of Inquiry into personal
      injury 288–289
Rules of locality 248

S

Safe havens 168
Safety officers 20
St. Jude's Silzone heart valve 205
St. Paul Fire and Marine Insurance
      Company 243
Satisfaction 265–266, 390
Screening
  cancer 419–422
  of employees 186, 190, 193–194,
      196–197, 200, 202
  medical 388
  preoperative 453, 454–456
  pretrial 242
Secretary's Commission on Medical
      Malpractice 243
Sepsis 385, 386, 387, 427
Septic shock 385, 426–427
Serology 323–324
Settlement 24, 225–226, 233,
      266–267, 276
  clauses 80–81
  compulsory 70
  consent to 73
  consequences of 26–27, 84
  and countersuits 282
  demands 82–85
  of dental cases 498
  duty not to settle 85
  as goal 283, 284
  of medical device cases 214, 217
  multiple 63
  and personal attorneys 82–83
  reporting 74
Sexual exploitation 175, 473
Sexual history 428
Shell corporations 216–217

Shift changes 390
Shoulder dystocia 347–348
Side effects 130, 370, 371, 429, 441
Signatures 154, 159, 162–163, 170–171,
      231, 346, 431, 484, 488
Slander 130, 177, 502, 507
Slot coverage 65
Special damages 123, 273
Special injury 282
Special stains 328
Specialty
  of expert medical witnesses 254
  high-risk liability 341–342, 383
  and levels of damages 354,
      355, 417, 420
  policy restrictions on 65, 72
  See also named specialties
Specific exclusions 72
Specimens 312–314
  collection and preservation of 316,
      319–321, 322, 323, 324
  and culture techniques 322–323
  evaluation of 328
  inadequate 313, 315, 322
Spoliation 25, 45–53, 75–76, 116, 253,
      273, 305–306, 449
  case presentations 46–47
  as criminal offence 50
  definition of 47
  detection of 48–49
  inference 49–50, 51
  intentional 48, 308
  negligent 48
  remedies 49–50
Stab wounds 412
Staff
  educating 20
  nonphysician 19
  operating room personnel 187–188
  See also Employees
Standard exclusions 71–72
Standard of care 507
  in anesthesia 397–398
  based on literature 453–454
  breach of 264, 269
  carotid endarterectomy 445
  in clinical trials research 97–108
  compliance with 259–260
  and consulting physicians 139
  in contract cases 127, 138
  and criminal negligence 114, 115
  in dentistry 497
  determining 254
  in emergency medicine 384, 387